EARLY MORMON DOCUMENTS

VOLUME III

COMPILED AND EDITED BY

DAN VOGEL

SIGNATURE BOOKS
SALT LAKE CITY

JACKET DESIGN BY SCOTT KNUDSEN

∞ *Early Mormon Documents*, Volume III, was printed on acid-free paper
and was composed, printed, and bound in the United States.

13 12 11 10 09 7 6 5 4 3 2

Library of Congress Cataloging-in-Publication Data
Early Mormon documents / compiled and edited by Dan Vogel
p. cm.
Includes bibliographical references and index.
ISBN 1-56085-133-3 (v. 3)
1. Mormon Church—History—Sources. 2. Church of Jesus Christ of
Latter-day Saints— History—Sources. 3. Smith, Joseph, 1805-1844—
Family—History—Sources. I. Vogel, Dan
BX8611.E19 2000
289.3'09—dc20 94-40565
CIP

http://www.signaturebooks.com

CONTENTS

PART III. (*Continued*)

K. MISCELLANEOUS NON-RESIDENT SOURCES

L. MISCELLANEOUS DOCUMENTS

Illustrations

INTRODUCTION

This third volume of *Early Mormon Documents* follows volume two in gathering published and unpublished sources relating to Mormon origins in Palmyra and Manchester, New York. The previous volume included the major document collections of Philastus Hurlbut, William H. and Edmund L. Kelley, Chester C. Thorne, and Arthur B. Deming, as well as excerpts from Palmyra newspapers and interviews and statements of local residents Martin Harris, Oliver Cowdery, and John H. Gilbert. This volume contains an assortment of documents arranged under the following headings: "Miscellaneous Early Sources" (pre-1844); "Miscellaneous Late Sources" (post-1844); "Miscellaneous Non-resident Sources"; and "Miscellaneous Documents."

This collection groups together early sources that are not well known, even to Mormon historians. An excerpt from Eli Bruce's diary, dated 5 November 1830, documents his interview with Joseph Smith, Sr., while both were incarcerated in Canandaigua's jail (see III.I.1, ELI BRUCE DIARY, 5 NOV 1830). Although published in 1861, this important diary entry has frequently been overlooked. The same is true of the 12 March 1831 letter from ten unnamed residents of Palmyra to Ohio publisher E. D. Howe, which includes a description of Joseph Smith's treasure seeking and mentions "Walters the Magician" (see III.I.3, PALMYRA RESIDENTS TO *PAINESVILLE* (OH) *TELEGRAPH*, 12 MAR 1831). Published for the first time in its entirety is a letter from six leading citizens of Canandaigua, dated January 1832, which contains information about Martin Harris and Joseph Smith that is found in no other source (see III.I.4, NATHANIEL W. HOWELL AND OTHERS TO ANCIL BEACH, JAN 1832).

The late sources include the accounts of well-known non-Mormons Orsamus Turner and Pomeroy Tucker (see III.J.2, ORSAMUS TURNER ACCOUNT, 1851; and III.J.8, POMEROY TUCKER ACCOUNT, 1867), as well as the lesser known statement of Daniel Hendrix (see III.J.26, DANIEL HENDRIX REMINISCENCE, 1893). Hendrix's document, although known to historians, is preceded by new information about Hendrix. While some of these documents have been previously published, many have resisted notice. Among the more important of these are: Robert Richards [pseud.], *The Californian Crusoe* (see III.J.3, DR. WILLIAMS ACCOUNT, 1854); Pomeroy Tucker, "Mormonism and Joe Smith" (see III.J.5, POMEROY TUCKER REMINISCENCE, 1858); Jared S. Nasmith, "Joseph Smith and Mormonism Which Started 100 Years Ago. Some Incidents Related About Smith By Professor Philetus B. Spear, D.D., a Man Born in Palmyra in 1811" (see III.J.9, PHILETUS B. SPEAR ACCOUNT, CIRCA 1873); and William Hyde Interview, in "Birth of Mormonism" (see III.J.23, WILLIAM HYDE INTERVIEWS, 1888). Previously unpublished documents composed after 1844 are the letters from E. E. Baldwin to W. O. Norrell, dated 3 August 1887, and from Philana A. Foster to E. W. Taylor, dated 16 July 1895 (see III.J.21, E. E. BALDWIN TO W. O. NORRELL, 3 AUG 1887; and III.J.27, PHILANA A. FOSTER TO E. W. TAYLOR, 16 JUL 1895); the statements of Carlos Osgood and Wallace Miner in M. Wilford Poulson's "Notebook containing statements made by residents of Palmyra, N.Y., Manchester, N.Y., and other areas ..." (see III.J.38. CARLOS OSGOOD STATEMENT, 1932; and III.J.37, WALLACE MINER REMINISCENCE, 1932); and the document entitled "Concerning Joseph Smith" (see III.J.41, PALMYRA RESIDENT REMINISCENCE, NO DATE).

This third volume also includes testimony from non-residents, meaning those who either lived in New York outside Wayne and Ontario counties or were visitors from other states. The earliest accounts here are usually excerpted from newspapers: *Rochester Gem, Geauga* (OH) *Gazette, Wayne County* (PA) *Inquirer, Illinois Patriot, Broome County* (NY) *Courier,* and *Lockport* (NY) *Balance* (see III.K.1; III.K.2; III.K.3; III.K.4; III.K.7; III.K.8; III.K.9). Accounts of Mormon converts, such as Parley P. Pratt and Thomas B. Marsh (see III.K.16, PARLEY P. PRATT AUTOBIOGRAPHY, CIRCA 1854; III.K.21, PARLEY P. PRATT REMINISCENCE, 1856; III.K.22, THOMAS B. MARSH AUTOBIOGRAPHY, 1857), have received some attention previously, while those of non-Mormons have been largely ignored. Among the most interesting in this latter group are David S. Burnett's 1831 account (III.K.5); James Gordon Bennett's 1831 account (III.K.6); John Barber and Henry Howe's 1841 account (III.K.14); Thurlow Weed's reminiscences of 1854, 1858, 1880, and 1884 (III.K.17); and Thomas Davies Burrall's 1867 reminiscence (III.K.27). Even some well-known Mormon sources have received little scholarly attention, perhaps because they deal with Joseph Smith's treasure seeking. See, for example, James Colin Brewster's 1843 account (III.K.15); Brigham Young's 1855, 1857, and 1877 accounts (III.K.19 and III.K.30); and Elizabeth Kane's 1872-73 interview with Brigham Young, Artemisia (Beaman) Snow, and Orrin Rockwell (III.K.37). Documents published here for the first time in their entirety include: William E. McLellin's letter to Samuel McLellin, dated 4 August 1832 (III.K.10); Emer Harris's 1856 account (III.K.20); Henry O'Reilly's

1879 reminiscence (III.K.31); and Sara Melissa Ingersoll's 1899 reminiscence (III.K.34).

The concluding section contains civil records (for example, road lists, a highway survey, census records, land deeds, tax rolls, merchant documents, and court records) dealing only incidentally with Smith family history, as well as records directly treating the topic of Mormon origins (such as the copyright to the Book of Mormon, the testimony of the Eight Witnesses, the preface to the Book of Mormon, the 1831 agreement between Joseph Smith, Sr., and Martin Harris, and the Missionaries Covenant).

I.
Miscellaneous Early Sources

1.
ELI BRUCE DIARY, 5 NOVEMBER 1830

Robert Morris, *The Masonic Martyr: The Biography of Eli Bruce, Sheriff of Niagara County, New York* (Louisville, Kentucky: Morris and Monsarrat, 1861), 266-67.

EDITORIAL NOTE

Eli Bruce (1793-1852) was born at Templeton, Massachusetts. Prior to his removal to western New York, Bruce taught at the Academy in Lancaster, Massachusetts. In November 1825 he was elected High Sheriff of Niagara County, New York. Following the disappearance of William Morgan, a disaffected Mason suspected of being murdered by members of the fraternity in 1826, Bruce, a Mason since 1824 or 1825, was tried and found guilty of conspiracy in Morgan's abduction, then confined in the Canandaigua jail for twenty-eight months (from 23 May 1829 to 23 September 1831). While incarcerated, Bruce studied medicine and soon after his release went into practice (Morris 1883, 203-248).

While in jail, Bruce learned about Mormonism from Joseph Smith, Sr., who had been incarcerated for thirty days in the Canandaigua jail because of an unpaid debt of four dollars. On 5 November 1830 Bruce made the following entry in his journal about his conversation with the senior Smith. Also, from prison, Bruce wrote a letter, dated 21 March 1831, to his brother, Dr. Silas Bruce of Boston, Massachusetts, in which he made reference to the Mormons: "There is a stir here in the religious world. I allude to a set of persons styled Mormons, who claim to be the peculiar favorites of Heaven by immediate revelation" (Morris 1883, 244). Bruce evidently was not convinced by Smith's recital.

Lucy Smith may have alluded to Bruce when she reported that her son Samuel had found his father "confined in the same dungeon with a man committed for murder" (I.B.5, LUCY SMITH HISTORY, 1845, 1853:164). Since it was commonly assumed Morgan had been murdered by Masonic conspirators, Lucy may have been led to describe Bruce as a murderer. Also, since convicted murderers were usually sent to the state prison in Auburn, the suggestion that Lucy refers to Bruce seems even more probable.

According to Lucy Smith, Joseph Sr. was arrested on a Thursday, the day following Hyrum's move to Colesville, which may have occurred on either Wednesday, 29 September 1830, or Wednesday, 6 October 1830 (Porter 1971, 109). Since Joseph Sr. spent thirty days in the Canandaigua jail, according to Lucy Smith, and was still there on 5 November 1830 when Bruce made the present entry in his diary, it follows that he was arrested on 7 October 1830. However, this reconstruction is not without its difficulties, for Lucy also says her husband did not rejoin his family at Fayette until mid-December (I.B.5, LUCY SMITH HISTORY, 1845, MS:Frag. 10 [back]; 1853:170), leaving Joseph Sr.'s whereabouts for about a month unaccounted for. Perhaps Joseph Sr.'s jail term was sixty-days, or, more likely, he was incarcerated at a later date than Lucy remembered, possibly the same day of Bruce's entry or shortly before.

In 1855 or 1856 Robert Morris met the widow of Eli Bruce and other family members in Centralia, Illinois, who soon after loaned him Bruce's three volumes of manuscript diaries which covered the period of Bruce's incarceration in the Canandaigua jail. According to Morris, these now lost diaries spanned from 30 May 1829 to 7 January 1831 (Morris 1883, 203-4). In 1861 Morris published a biography of Bruce which included the text of his journals. The following transcription has been taken from that publication.

November 5th—Not so much pain in my head as yesterday. Had a long talk with the father of *the Smith,* (Joseph Smith,) who, according to the old man's account, is the particular favorite of Heaven! [p. 266] To him Heaven has vouchsafed to reveal its mysteries; he is the herald of the latter-day glory. The old man avers that he is commissioned by God to baptize and preach this new doctrine. He says that our Bible is much abridged and deficient; that soon the Divine will is to be made known to all, as written in the *new Bible,* or *Book of Mormon.*

2.
WILLIAM W. PHELPS TO E. D. HOWE, 15 JANUARY 1831

William W. Phelps to E. D. Howe, 15 January 1831, E. D. Howe, *Mormonism Unvailed: or, A Faithful Account of That Singular Imposition and Delusion, from Its Rise to the Present Time* (Painesville, Ohio: E. D. Howe, 1834), 273-74.

EDITORIAL NOTE

Eber D. Howe,[1] publisher of the *Painesville* (Ohio) *Telegraph,* wrote to William W. Phelps[2] in Canandaigua, New York, on 11 January 1831, requesting information about Mormonism, which had recently gained numerous converts in nearby Mentor, Ohio. Howe, an anti-Mason, probably sought Phelps out because he was familiar with Phelps's *Ontario Phoenix,* an anti-Masonic paper he began editing in 1828. But Howe was probably unaware that Phelps had already started investigating Mormonism and was a serious candidate for membership (subsequently being baptized on 16 June 1831). Phelps had received a copy of the Book of Mormon on 9 April 1830, and had met Joseph Smith on 24 December 1830 (see *Deseret News,* 11 April 1860). Howe was undoubtedly surprised by Phelps's response, since in Howe's mind anti-Masons would naturally reject a book published on a pro-Jackson press (see Vogel 1989). Howe's disappointment is apparent in the short biography of Phelps he appended to the letter:

> Before the rise of Mormonism, he [Phelps] was an avowed infidel; having a remarkable propensity for fame and eminence, he was supercilious, haughty and egotistical. His great ambition was to embark in some speculation where he could shine pre-eminent. He took an active part for several years in the political contests of New York, and made no little display as an editor of a partizan newspaper, and after being foiled in his desires to become a candidate for Lt. Governor of that state, his attention was suddenly diverted by the prospects which were held out to him in the Gold Bible speculation. ... It will be [proved] by the foregoing letter, that he had already made up his mind to em-

---

1. On E. D. Howe (1798-?), see "Introduction to Philastus Hurlbut Collection."

2. On William W. Phelps (1792-1872), see introduction to III.G.6, OLIVER COWDERY TO W. W. PHELPS, 7 SEP 1834.

brace Mormonism, but still wished to conceal his intentions. It was not till about six months after that he had made definite arrangements to join them (Howe 1834, 274-75).

Howe also states that he is publishing Phelps's letter in order to "show what was taught him [Phelps] while a pupil under [Joseph] Smith and [Sidney] Rigdon, and that the story about Mr. [Charles] Anthon's declarations, was one upon which they placed great reliance" (Howe 1834, 273). Phelps's letter contains important insight into early Mormonism from the point of view of an investigator.

Canandaigua, Jan. 15, 1831.

Dear Sir—Yours of the 11th, is before me, but to give you a satisfactory answer, is out of my power. To be sure, I am acquainted with a number of the persons concerned in the publication, called the "*Book of Mormon.*"—Joseph Smith is a person of very limited abilities in common learning—but his knowledge of *divine things,* since the appearance of his book, has astonished many. Mr. Harris,[3] whose name is in the book, is a wealthy farmer, but of small literary acquirements; he is honest, and sincerely declares upon his soul's salvation that the book is true, and was interpreted by Joseph Smith, through a pair of silver spectacles, found with the plates. The places where they dug for the plates, in Manchester, are to be seen.[4] When the plates were said to have been found, a copy of one or two lines of the characters,[5] were taken by Mr. Harris to Utica, Albany and New York; at New York, they were shown to Dr. Mitchell,[6] and he referred to professor Anthon [7] who

3. On Martin Harris (1783-1875), see "Introduction to Martin Harris Collection."

4. Phelps's use of the plural "they" and "places" may refer to the digging of Joseph Smith and company at several locations, including Miner's Hill and the excavation on the east side of the Hill Cumorah mentioned by Lorenzo Saunders and others (see III.J.20, LORENZO SAUNDERS TO THOMAS GREGG, 28 JAN 1885; III.J.8, POMEROY TUCKER ACCOUNT, 1867, 34; and III.K.32, EDWARD STEVENSON REMINISCENCE, 1893, 12-13).

5. See V.E.2, BOOK OF MORMON CHARACTERS, DEC 1827-FEB 1828.

6. On Samuel L. Mitchell (1764-1831), see I.A.15, JOSEPH SMITH HISTORY, 1839, n. 45.

7. On Charles Anthon (1797-1867), see introduction to V.D.2, CHARLES ANTHON TO E.D. HOWE, 17 FEB 1834.

translated and declared them to be the ancient shorthand Egyptian.[8] So much is true. The family of Smiths is poor, and generally ignorant in common learning.

I have read the book, and many others have, but we have nothing by which we can positively detect it as an imposi[p. 273]tion, nor have we any thing more than what I have stated and the book itself, to show its genuineness. We doubt—supposing, if it is false, it will fall, and if of God, God will sustain it.

I had ten hours discourse with a man from your state, named Sidney Rigdon,[9] a convert to its doctrines, and he declared it was true, and he knew it by the power of the Holy Ghost, which was again given to man in preparation for the millennium: he appeared to be a man of talents, and sincere in his profession. Should any new light be shed on the subject, I will apprise you.

Respectfully,
W. W. PHELPS.

E. D. HOWE, ESQ.

---

8. Regarding Harris's visit to Anthon, see discussion in "Introduction to Martin Harris Collection."

9. Phelps probably spoke with Rigdon at the same time he met Joseph Smith on 24 December 1830 (III.I.9, W. W. PHELPS TO OLIVER COWDERY, 21 FEB 1835; see also VI.F.5, SIDNEY RIGDON REMINISCENCE, 1844, 522). On Sidney Rigdon (1793-1876), see introduction to I.A.13, SIDNEY RIGDON ACCOUNT, CIRCA 1836.

3.
PALMYRA RESIDENTS TO *PAINESVILLE* (OH) *TELEGRAPH*, 12 MARCH 1831

Unidentified Palmyra Residents to Editor, 12 March 1831, *Painesville* (Ohio) *Telegraph* 2 (22 March 1831): 2.

EDITORIAL NOTE

On 22 March 1831, E. D. Howe published a letter, dated 12 March 1831, from unidentified persons in Palmyra, New York. Concerning this letter, Howe reports: "We have received the following letter from Palmyra, N.Y. on the subject of Bible imposture. It is signed by ten individuals of the first respectibility." The letter was probably written by Abner Cole, and signed by nine others, since it mentions Luman Walters and reaffirms that "the facts published in the 'Reflector,' are true as far as has come to our knowledge." Cole had made reference to the *Painesville Telegraph* in early February (see *Palmyra Reflector,* 1 February 1831, 93), and Howe had previously published extracts from Cole's paper (e.g., *Painesville Telegraph,* 8 March 1831). The letter may have been prompted by a letter from Howe requesting verification of some statements he saw printed in the *Reflector.*

Palmyra, March 12, 1831.

The "gold bible" question excites but little interest in this section of country, its followers being few and generally of the dregs of community, and the most unlettered people that can be found any where, and besides there is much reason to doubt the sincerity of many of them.

The first idea of a "Book," was doubtless suggested to the Smiths by one Walters,[1] a juggling fortune-teller, who made the ignorant believe that an old book in his possession, in the Latin language, contained an account of the ante-deluvians, &c. and the word was given out that the book Smith was about to find, was a history of hidden treasures.[2]

---

1. On Luman Walters (c. 1788-1860), see III.E.3, *PALMYRA REFLECTOR,* 1829-1831, n. 21.

2. See III.E.3, *PALMYRA REFLECTOR,* 1829-1831, under 12 June 1830 and 28 February 1831.

Smith and his father belonged to a gang of money-diggers, who had followed that business for many years, Jo pretending he could see the gold and silver by the aid of what they called a "*peep stone.*"

The book is chiefly garbled from the Old and New Testaments, the Apocraphy having contributed its share: names and phrases have been altered, and in many instances copied upwards—A quarto Bible now in this village, was borrowed and nearly worn out and defaced by their dirty handling.[3] Some seven or eight of them spent many months in copying, Cowdery[4] being principal scribe. Some of these people will probably go to your state, but few of them are able to live without assistance. Their numbers may be 20 in this vicinity, and but two or three of them own any property to our knowledge. Near Waterloo there is said to be about 40, three or four being men of propty. Chamberlain and Burrows, two of the principal ones, it is said have refused to sell, or obey Jo any longer.[5] The truth of it is, Jo overdid his business at the commencement and *bore on too hard.*

The whole gang of these deluded mortals, except a few hypocrites, are profound believers in witchcraft, ghosts, goblins, &c. From the best information we can obtain, the work has entirely stopped in this country, and some who have been the most ardent are beginning to have misgivings on the subject. Martin Harris,[6] the head man here as it respects property, left here a few days ago on a sojourn to your country, having received a special command thither forthwith.[7] Cowdrey has been heard of far up the Missouri, pretending to have great success in his mission[8]; but as ignorant as too many

---

3. See III.E.3, *PALMYRA REFLECTOR,* 1829-1831, under 28 February 1831.

4. On Oliver Cowdery (1806-50), see "Introduction to Oliver Cowdery Collection."

5. On Orrin Chamberlain and Philip Burroughs, see III.E.3, *PALMYRA REFLECTOR,* 1829-1831, under 9 March 1831, n. 53.

6. On Martin Harris (1783-1875), see "Introduction to Martin Harris Collection."

7. On 22 February 1831 Joseph Smith wrote to Harris requesting him to "bring or cause to <be> brought all the books [of Mormon]" (LDS Church archives, Salt Lake City, Utah). Harris arrived at Painesville, Ohio, on 12 March 1831 (*Painesville Telegraph,* 15 March 1831, 3), but returned to Palmyra to sell his farm to Thomas Lakey on 1 April 1831 (see III.L.14, MARTIN HARRIS MORTGAGE, 25 AUG 1829). Later, during the third week of May, Harris again left Palmyra, leading a small group of Mormons to Ohio (see III.E.1, *WAYNE SENTINEL,* 1824-1836, under 27 May 1831).

8. See III.E.3, *PALMYRA REFLECTOR,* 1829-1831, under 9 March 1831.

of the people are, it is hardly possible that so clumsy an imposition can spread to any considerable extent. We have only to add that the facts published in the "Reflector," are true as far as has come to our knowledge.

Yours, &c.

[*names withheld*]

4.
Nathaniel W. Howell and Others to Ancil Beach, January 1832

Nathaniel W. Howell, Walter Hubbell, Ansel D. Eddy, Henry Chapin, Jared Willson, and Lewis Jenkins to Ancil Beach, January 1832, Walter Hubbell Collection, 1831-1833 Correspondence, Princeton University Library, Princeton, New Jersey.

EDITORIAL NOTE

The present letter, dated January 1832, was written by six leading citizens of Canandaigua, New York, and contains an account of early Mormonism. The letter was apparently written in response to a letter of inquiry sent to the post master of Canandaigua, Lewis Jenkins, by the Reverend Ancil Beach, at the time a Methodist minister serving in eastern Indiana's New Castle circuit. According to Methodist historian Allen Wiley, Beach "was a man of some year's standing as a member of the church, but young in the ministry, who had just been received on trial. He was zealous, and so remains to this day [5 August 1846]; for he is yet in the work, being a member of the North Indiana conference. He is a man of only medium preaching talents, but his diligence and zeal have made him successful beyond many others. His travels in Indiana have been extensive" (Wiley 1927, 406, 411-12). In 1830 Beach replaced Amos Sparks in the Connersville circuit. Beach (in his thirties), together with his wife and two sons, is listed in the 1830 Manchester, Dearborn County, Indiana, census. The following year the Connersville circuit was divided, and Beach was assigned to the newly formed New Castle circuit (Wiley 1927, 419, 424). While making his new circuit, Beach may have become aware of the branch of Mormons in Winchester, Randolph County, Indiana, which had been established during June-September 1831 by Levi Hancock and Zebedee Coltrin. From 29 November to 7 December 1831, several conferences were held in Winchester at which Oliver Cowdery presided (Cannon and Cook 1983, 33-38, 34, n. 1). Beach's letter of inquiry therefore may have resulted from his concern over the movement of the Mormons into his area and their increased activity.

Besides postmaster Lewis Jenkins, the men who responded to Beach's inquiry were the pillars of the community. Walter Hubbell (1795-1848),

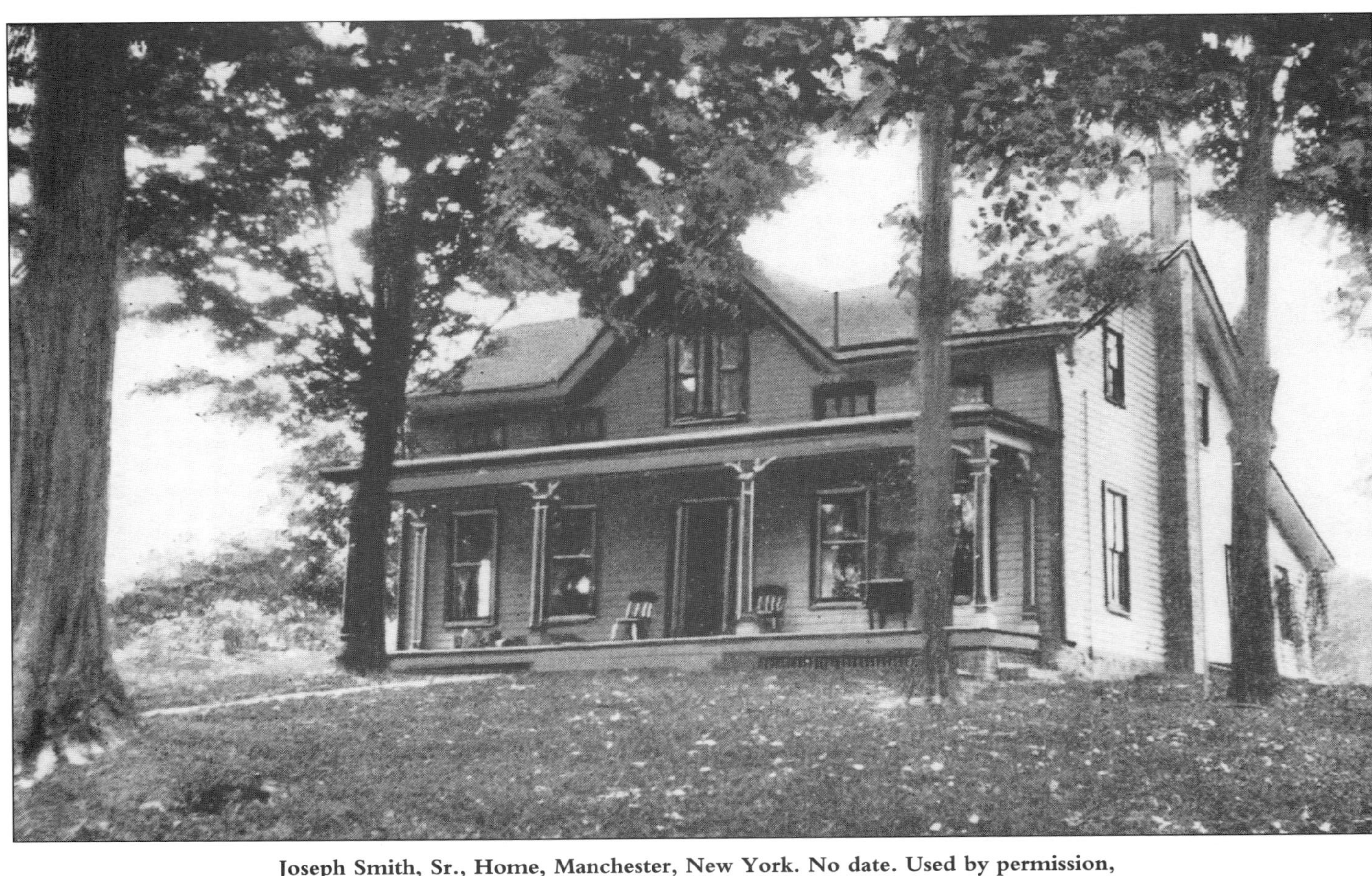

Joseph Smith, Sr., Home, Manchester, New York. No date. Used by permission,

who settled in Canandaigua in 1814, was a prominent lawyer and member of the Ontario County bar. He was elected to the state assembly in 1829. Under Ansel D. Eddy's pastorship, Hubbell served as a deacon in the Congregational Church from 1824 until his death in 1848 (McIntosh 1876, 32, 38, 39, 41, 52, 58, 112; *Wayne Sentinel,* 29 February 1828).

Jared Willson (1786-1851) settled in Canandaigua in 1813, where he became a noted lawyer and very active in the economic and political concerns of the community. At the writing of the Beach letter, he was apparently acting as court surrogate in Canandaigua (McIntosh 1876, 37, 38, 39, 52, 58, 108; see also *Wayne Sentinel,* 25 July 1828). Willson apparently served under Henry Chapin, commissioner of the judiciary, who also signed the letter to Beach. Chapin may have also been the Henry Chapin who was a trustee of a school district in 1839 mentioned in the *History of Ontario County* (McIntosh 1876, 110).

Probably the most distinguished name on the document is that of Nathaniel W. Howell (1770-1850). Beginning his law practice in Canandaigua in 1795, Howell became a distinguished public servant, serving as assistant attorney-general in 1797, as a representative in the Thirteenth Congress from 1813 to 1815, and as first judge of Ontario County from 1819 to 1833. In 1830 Howell helped found the successful Ontario Savings Bank, which included among its incorporators Jared Willson and Walter Hubbell. Howell's other business dealings included the establishment in 1824 of the Western Fire Insurance Company, of which he was president. His estate included in 1814 one "negro man-slave," whose ownership was certified by Walter Hubbell (McIntosh 1876, 37, 38, 52, 53-54, 58; G. Conover 1888, 464-65).

Also well-known is Ansel D. Eddy, who became the pastor of the Congregational Church at Canandaigua in 1824 and served until 1835. During Eddy's pastorate, "several very extensive revivals of religion were enjoyed, as the result of which large accessions were made to the church, and the standard of morals in the community considerably elevated" (Hotchkin 1848, 399-400; see also McIntosh 1876, 112). In 1826 Eddy published a pamphlet, titled *A Discourse Delivered in Canandaigua by Rev. A. D. Eddy, New York, July 4, 1826* (Canandaigua: Bemis, Morse & Ward, 1826), in which he argued that national prosperity was dependent upon "keeping our religious principles pure" (p. 20). In 1832 Eddy was praised by Edward D. Griffin, president of Williams College, for not indulging in extreme revivalistic practices (Griffin 1832). In 1848 James H. Hotchkin reported that Eddy was then living in Newark, New Jersey (Hotchkin 1848, 400).

Beach evidently requested information regarding Joseph Smith and the individuals whose names were appended to the Book of Mormon as special witnesses to the divinity of its origin. As members of the legal profession, the Canandaigua correspondents were careful to state the limitations of their personal observations. They admitted, for example, that of the eleven witnesses, they had personal knowledge only of Martin Harris, the Book of Mormon's financier. Indeed, previous to publication of the Book of Mormon, Harris was the most publicly visible of the Mormon witnesses. The eccentric Harris owned a sizable farm and was well-known for his participation in community activities, occasionally taking a leading role (see R. W. Walker 1986; R. L. Anderson 1981, 95-105). As early as 1823, Jared Willson, acting as surrogate of Ontario County, officiated over the sale of land held jointly by Martin Harris and Reuben Hewitt (*Wayne Sentinel,* 1 October 1823). Given the professions and social interests of the letter's signers, it is entirely possible that some of them were either professionally acquainted with Harris or had otherwise heard of his social activities.

The letter was discovered by Wesley P. Walters in November 1986 while searching through the Walter Hubbell Collection at Princeton University at my urging. It is not the original letter sent to Ancil Beach, but a copy Hubbell kept for his files. Comparison of the handwriting with other letters in the collection indicates that the Beach letter was copied by someone other than Hubbell (or Howell). According to librarians, the Hubbell collection was donated by a family member in 1957. On the outside of the letter when folded, Hubbell wrote the following: "copy of a letter / to / Rev[eren]d Ancil Beach / Jan[uar]y—1832."

Sr.

Your communication addressed to the post master in this place requesting information in relation to the Character of the individuals who have published the Book of Mormon and who call themselves Mormonites was duly received[.] And as it may serve the cause of truth and guard against imposition we cheerfully afford you the information in our possession. The town of Manchester in this county is the next town north East of this and the individuals whose names are published as the actors in getting up the Book of Mormon were not heard of <by us>, except the name of Martin Harris[1] before this farce was brought to light. The neighbours of Smith and the others give the following account of them—Joseph Smith has <lived>

1. On Martin Harris (1783-1875), see "Introduction to Martin Harris Collection."

in and about Man=chester for several years an idle worthless fellow; previous to the Mormon project he had been engaged for some time in company with several others of the same Character ~~Employed~~ in digging for money[.][2] They were poor as well as worthless and for a time were supported by a ~~man~~ Mr Fish[3] an illiterate man of some property who was duped by them, and when [p. 1] he found that his money diggers were like to consume what he had gathered by his industry he turned them off—Joseph Smith then pretended to have found a box, in digging in the woods, containing some gold plates with Characters upon them which none but himself could decypher[4]—Cowdry[5] who certifies to the Book of Mormon was a school master in the town of Manchester and went away with Smith to the State of Pennsylvania and was employed by Smith to write <down> for him what he interpreted from the mystic characters upon the plates—They then induced Martin Harris a

---

2. For recent discussions of the Smiths' treasure-seeking activities, see Quinn 1987; R. L. Anderson 1984; R. W. Walker 1984; and Taylor 1986.

3. The Canandaigua correspondents neglect to give the first name of Mr. Fish, but they probably refer to Abraham Fish (c. 1773-1845) of Manchester, New York, a business acquaintance of both Joseph Smith, Sr., and Joseph Smith, Jr. On 19 January 1830, Lemuel Durfee, Jr., sued Joseph Sr. and Abraham Fish for "damages" amounting to $39.92, which they paid plus interest on 13 September 1830 (see III.L.19, NATHAN PIERCE DOCKET BOOK, 1830). Under the date 10 March 1827, six months prior to Smith's reception of the plates, Joseph Smith's financial records include the following note: "rec[ieve]d Joseph Smith, Jr. four dollars which is accredited to the account of A. Fish" (see III.L.11, JOSEPH SMITH RECEIPT TO ABRAHAM FISH ACCOUNT, 10 MAR 1827). Pomeroy Tucker included the names of David and Abram Fish in his list of "pioneer Mormon disciples" who first "made a profession of belief either in the money-digging or golden bible finding" (III.J.8, POMEROY TUCKER ACCOUNT, 1867, 39), but apparently only Abraham had financial ties with the Smiths. In Justice Nathan Pierce's docket book, Fish wrote an "X" near the words "Abraham Fish his mark," supporting the letter's characterization that "Mr Fish" was "an illiterate man." The *Wayne Sentinel* for 23 July 1845 reports that Fish had recently been hit in the head by a hired hand and soon after died at age seventy-two. See also III.L.5, GAIN C. AND GAINS C. ROBINSON ACCOUNT BOOKS, 1820-1830, #9.

4. Regarding the claim that only Smith could interpret the characters on the plates, see discussion in "Introduction to Martin Harris Collection." See also V.E.2, BOOK OF MORMON CHARACTERS, DEC 1827-FEB 1828.

5. On Oliver Cowdery (1806-50), see "Introduction to Oliver Cowdery Collection."

farmer of respectable property to become responsible for an edition of 5000 copies of the Book which was accor=dingly published in Palmyra in the County of Wayne about fourteen miles from this place—Harris became very boisterous on the subject of the book and preached about the country in endeavoring to make sale of it—Harris is by some considered a deluded man partially insane,[6] and by others as a cunning speculator in publishing this book for the sake of gain[7]—

The Book and the whole movement connected with the character of those engaged in it has been considered too ridiculous to attract any serious attention, and [p. 2] in this part of the country they have been joined by very few and those who did fall in with them were such as were glad to be provided with bread to eat by whatever means obtained & perhaps a few honest and ignorant men who were deluded by the falsehoods published by the authors of the plan—We are informed that <the> Mormonites as they are called generally removed to the State of Ohio from which we learn they have removed still farther west—Martin Harris lately testified on a trial[8] which related to the work of printing and publishing the Book that he had sent 2300 copies of it to the west—In this State the movers in this project can do no harm and we should hope that their imposition, so gross, would not succeed in any part of our land—

signed by N. W. Howell[,] First Judge &c
W. Hubbell[,] Master in Ch[anceller]y
A. D. Eddy[,] Pastor &c
Henry Chapin[,] Comm[issione]r of Jud[iciar]y.
Jared Willson[,] Surrogate
Lewis Jenkins[,] Post Master

Rev[eren]d Ancil Beach

---

6. A judgement probably resulting from Harris's eccentric character and propensity for visionary experiences (see discussion in "Introduction to Martin Harris Collection").

7. On the claim that Harris was motivated by monetary gain, see III.A.7, LUCY HARRIS STATEMENT, 29 NOV 1833; and III.A.6, ABIGAIL HARRIS STATEMENT, 28 NOV 1833.

8. This possibly relates to Joseph Smith's request for Harris to send copies of the Book of Mormon to Kirtland, Ohio. In a letter dated 22 February 1831, Smith wrote Harris to "bring or cause to <be> brought all the books [of Mormon], as the work is here breaking forth on the east[,] west[,] north and south" (Joseph Smith to Martin Harris, 22 February 1831, LDS Church archives, Salt Lake City, Utah).

5.
William W. Phelps Account, 1833

[William W. Phelps], "Rise and Progress of the Church of Christ," *The Evening and The Morning Star* 1 (April 1833): [84].

EDITORIAL NOTE

On 6 April 1833, Bishop Edward Partridge and about eighty officials and other members met at a special conference of the church in Jackson County, Missouri. Joseph Smith's History states that it was "three years since the Church had come out of the wilderness, preparatory for the last dispensation. ... This was the first attempt made by the Church to celebrate the anniversary of her birthday, and those who professed not our faith talked about it as a strange thing" (J. Smith 1948, 1:337). It is in this spirit that the following editorial, believed to have been written by editor W. W. Phelps (and possibly aided by Oliver Cowdery, who did not leave Missouri until July 1833), outlined the organization and progress of the Church of Christ.

Having promised in our last number,[1] something on the rise and progress of the church of Christ, we commence with the intention of giving a relation of a few facts, as they have occurred since the church was organized in eighteen hundred and thirty. We shall be brief in this article, as we design to give from time to time the progress of this church, for the benefit of inquirers as well as the satisfaction of those who believe.

Soon after the book of Mormon came forth, containing the fulness of the gospel of Jesus Christ, the church was organized on the sixth of April, in Manchester[2]; soon after, a branch was established in Fayette,[3] and the June

---

1. In an article in the previous issue, "Prospects of the Church," it was stated: "As it is our intention, in a future number to give the particulars of the rise and progress of the church, we omit some things of interest. ..." (*The Evening and The Morning Star* 1 [March 1833]: [76]).

2. In the previous issue of the *Star,* it was also stated: "It will be three years the sixth of April next, since the church of Christ was organized, in Manchester, New York, with six members" (*The Evening and The Morning Star* 1 [March 1833]: [76]). On the location of the church's organization, see discussion in I.A.15, JOSEPH SMITH HISTORY, 1839, n. 82.

3. Baptismal meetings were held in Fayette, New York, on 11 and 18 April 1830 (I.A.15, JOSEPH SMITH HISTORY, 1839, 39), as well as the

following, another in Colesville, New York.[4]

We shall not give, at this time, the particulars attending the organization of these branches of the church; neither shall we publish in this, the account of the persecution of those who were then called and authorized to preach the everlasting gospel. Twenty more were added to the church in Manchester and Fayette, in the month of April[5]; and on the 28th of June, thirteen were baptized in Colesville[6]: and of these we can say as Paul said of the five hundred who saw the Savior after he had risen from the dead: The greater part remain unto this present, but some are fallen asleep [1 Cor. 15:6]. In October, (1830) the number of disciples had increased to between seventy and eighty,[7] when four of the elders started for the west, and founded a branch of the church at Kirtland, Ohio, around which many have since arisen.

---

first church conference on 9 June 1830 (VI.G.2, FAR WEST RECORD, 9 JUN 1830, 26 SEP 1830 & 2 JAN 1831).

4. A baptismal meeting was held at the Joseph Knight residence in Colesville, New York, on 28 June 1830 (I.A.15, JOSEPH SMITH HISTORY, 1839, 43).

5. "Twenty more" apparently indicates twenty baptisms besides those performed prior to the organization of the church. At least two were baptized on 6 April 1830: Martin Harris and Joseph Smith, Sr.; with the baptisms of Lucy Smith and Sarah Witt Rockwell apparently following a day or two later (I.A.15, JOSEPH SMITH HISTORY, 1839, 38, DRAFT:9-10). Six, possibly seven, were baptized in Fayette on 11 April 1830: Hiram Page, Catherine Whitmer Page, Mary Page, Christian Whitmer, Anne (Schott) Whitmer, Jacob Whitmer, and Elizabeth (Schott) Whitmer (compare I.A.15, JOSEPH SMITH HISTORY, 1839, DRAFT:11; and ibid., 1839, 39 [minus Mary Page]). Seven more were baptized in Fayette on 18 April 1830: Peter Whitmer, Sr., Mary (Musselman) Whitmer, William Jolly, Elizabeth Jolly, Vincent Jolly, Richard B. Peterson (or Ziba Peterson), and Elizabeth Ann Whitmer (ibid., 39). Solomon Chamberlain and wife Hope (Haskins) Chamberlain may have also been baptized about this time (see Porter 1971, 260).

6. Smith's History names thirteen persons baptized at Colesville, New York, on 28 June 1830: Emma Smith, Hezekiah Peck, Martha (Long) Peck, Joseph Knight, Sr., Polly (Peck) Knight, William Stringham, Esther (Knight) Stringham, Joseph Knight, Jr., Aaron Culver, Esther (Peck) Culver, Levi Hall, Polly Knight, and Julia Stringham (I.A.15, JOSEPH SMITH HISTORY, 1839, 43). Sally (Colburn) Knight was probably baptized at the same time, although one source has 29 June 1830 (see IV.E.3, SALLY KNIGHT OBITUARY, 1834; see also Porter 1971, 201-202).

7. Church records indicate that on 26 September 1830, at the second church conference, there were sixty-two members (see VI.G.2, FAR WEST RECORD, 9 JUN 1830, 26 SEP 1830 & 2 JAN 1831).

These first four, having added one to their number, proceeded to the west, after having baptized one hundred and thirty disciples in less than four weeks and ordained four of them elders, and finally stopped in the western bounds of the state of Missouri, having been preserved by the hand of the Lord, and directed by his Spirit.

In the winter, (1831) the church in the state of New York, after a commandment had been received from the Lord [D&C 38], began to prepare to remove to the state of Ohio. The following is a part of the revelation referred to above: And that ye might escape the power of the enemy, and be gathered unto me a righteous people without spot and blameless: wherefore for this cause I gave unto you the commandment that ye should go to the Ohio; and there I will give unto you my law, and there you shall be endowed with power from on high, and from thence, whomsoever I will shall go forth unto all nations, and it shall be told them what they shall do, for I have a great work laid up in store: for Israel shall be saved, and I will lead them withersoever I will, and no power shall stay my hand [D&C 38:31-33].

In the spring the greater part of the disciples who were in New York, removed to the Ohio. ...

6.
JESSE TOWNSEND TO PHINEAS STILES, 24 DECEMBER 1833

Jesse Townsend to Phineas Stiles, 24 December 1833, Pomeroy Tucker, *Origin, Rise, and Progress of Mormonism* (New York: D. Appleton and Co., 1867), 288-91.

EDITORIAL NOTE

Jesse Townsend (1766-1838), a graduate of Yale University, was ordained in 1792. He was installed as pastor of Palmyra's Western Presbyterian Church on 29 August 1817. After serving three years, he moved to Illinois and later to Missouri. Returning to Palmyra in 1826, he served as pastor in neighboring Sodus from 1827 to 1831. After several years of illness, Townsend died at Palmyra (McIntosh 1877, 147; T. Cook 1930, 261; Walters 1969a, 67-68; Backman 1980, 69).

Townsend's letter, dated 24 December 1833 (but not published until 1867), is contemporaneous with his signing of Philastus Hurlbut's group statement of Palmyra residents earlier the same month (see III.A.11, PALMYRA RESIDENTS GROUP STATEMENT, 4 DEC 1833). The letters of those writing to the Palmyra postmaster asking about the Mormons may have sometimes been forwarded to Townsend for response. This letter, and a similarly worded letter written less than a year later to Elisha Camp of Sackets' Harbor, New York, suggest that Townsend may have sent out a sort of "form letter" to various persons asking about Mormon origins in the Palmyra/Manchester area (see III.I.7, JESSE TOWNSEND TO ELISHA CAMP, 16 AUG 1834). Regarding the origin of Townsend's 1833 letter to Phineas Stiles, Pomeroy Tucker informs:

> For the following sketch of the origin of the Mormon imposture, and of its leader "Joe Smith" and his early associates and dupes, the author of this work is indebted to the kindness of Mrs. PERRINE, daughter of the writer, the late Rev. JESSE TOWNSEND. It is the original manuscript of the letter written at its date, by Mr. Townsend, in answer to inquiries for information addressed to him by Mr. Phineas Stiles, of Wendell, Franklin County, Massachusetts, in November, 1833, who set forth that two men from Ohio were actively engaged in his town and vicinity, and with an alarming degree of success, in efforts to disseminate among the people and in the churches, "a

new revelation and a new religion, which they call the Mormon religion," and that they "pretend to be inspired and empowered by God to teach" the same.[1] This statement of Mr. Townsend, made soon after the Mormon advent, now first published, may be regarded as a further important authentication of the foregoing pioneer history[2] of the sect of people now become so prosperous and powerful in Utah Territory (Tucker 1867, 287).

PALMYRA, WAYNE COUNTY, N.Y., *December* 24, 1833.

MR. PHINEAS STILES:[3]

DEAR SIR,—Your letter of 29th ultimo, requesting information concerning the class of people called Mormonites, has been received, and the following is a sketch of their history:

This new sect was commenced by Joseph Smith, Jr., in the vicinity of this village some four years ago, and the statement I give you is the *truth,* incredible as it may appear to you, and shows the folly and weakness of the people who have listened to and heeded the impositions and falsehoods propagated by Smith and his associates in iniquity.

I begin with the leader, "Joe," as he is and always has been called here. For the ten years I have known any thing of him, he has been a person of questionable character, of intemperate habits,[4] and latterly a noted *money-digger.* He lived in a sequestered neighborhood, where, with his dupes, his impostures and low cunning gave him a reputation for being "smart." He has had a stone, into which, when placed in a hat, he pretended to look and see chests of money buried in the earth. He was also a *fortune-teller,* and he claimed to know where stolen goods went—probably too well.

Smith flattered a few of his peculiar fraternity to engage with him in digging for money. After a while, many of these got out of patience with his false pretensions and repeated failures; and, finally, to avoid the sneers of those who had been deceived by him, he pretended that he had found, in digging alone, a wonderful curiosity, which he [p. 288] kept closely secreted. After telling dif-

---

1. The words in quotations were evidently taken from Phineas Stiles's original letter to Tucker.

2. Referring to his own history of Mormon origins (see III.J.8, POMEROY TUCKER ACCOUNT, 1867).

3. Perhaps the same Phineas Stiles (between sixteen and twenty-six years of age) listed in the 1820 Middletown, Essex County, Massachusetts, census (1820:582).

4. On Joseph Smith's drinking, see III.A.2, BARTON STAFFORD STATEMENT, 3 NOV 1833, n. 4.

ferent stories about it, and applying to it different names, he at length called it *the golden plates of the Book of Mormon*. As he was questioned on the subject from time to time, his story assumed a more uniform statement, the term finally given to the marvellous treasure being the "Golden Bible."

In the mean time, Joe visited a visionary fanatic by the name of Martin Harris,[5] and told him he had received some golden plates of ancient records from the Lord, with a "revelation" to call on him for fifty dollars to enable him to go to Pennsylvania and translate the contents of the plates; at the same time telling Harris that the Lord had revealed to him that they (Smith and Harris) were the only honest men in the world. This at once took with the dupe, who had specially prided himself on his honesty; and the wily deceiver understood this fact; he knew this was the assailable point in his victim's visionary mind. The delicious bait was greedily swallowed; and the fifty dollars was soon put into the hands of Smith, who cleared for Pennsylvania or elsewhere.[6]

At that time Martin Harris was worth five or six thousand dollars, while the Smiths were not worth a cent. The latter used Martin's money freely; and some other men, having a great dislike to labor, joined Joe in his deceptions, among whom was a sort of schoolmaster named Cowdery,[7] who assisted him in writing or transcribing the "Book of Mormon," as a pretended translation of the golden plates which he affirmed he had been directed by the Spirit of the Lord to dig from the earth. This was all done in the most secret manner. At the same time it was assumed to the un[p. 289]initiated that it would be "immediate death" for any except the translators to see the plates. Poor Martin's faith was apparently strengthened by this pretension, but afterward the "command" was modified, and he claimed to have seen the plates with "spiritual eyes."[8]

This Harris, who is or has been second in authority among the Mormonites,[9] was an industrious farmer, living near this village, who had

---

5. On Martin Harris (1783-1875), see "Introduction to Martin Harris Collection."

6. Compare I.A.5, JOSEPH SMITH HISTORY, 1839, 9; I.B.5, LUCY SMITH HISTORY, 1845, MS:73; and III.A.14, WILLARD CHASE STATEMENT, CIRCA 11 DEC 1833, 246.

7. On Oliver Cowdery (1806-50), see "Introduction to Oliver Cowdery Collection."

8. Regarding Harris's claim to have seen the plates with "spiritual eyes," see discussion in "Introduction to Martin Harris Collection."

9. Harris was undoubtedly prominent in the Mormon community, but Oliver Cowdery was the "second elder" and later assistant president in the church.

been unfortunate in the choice of a wife, or she had been in that of a husband. Like his leader, he gives to their preachers the power to preach and put their proselytes under water by authority of the new "revelation." He has whipped his wife and beaten her so cruelly and frequently, that she was obliged to seek refuge in separation.[10] ....[11] He is considered here, to this day, a brute in his domestic relations, a fool and dupe to Smith in religion, and an unlearned, conceited hypocrite, generally. He paid for printing the Book of Mormon, which exhausted all his money and most of his property.[12] Since he went to Ohio he has attempted to get another wife, though it is believed he was frustrated in this design by the discovery of his having a living wife here.

All the Mormonites have left this part of our State, and so palpable is their imposture that nothing is here said or thought of the subject, except when inquiries from abroad are occasionally made concerning them. I know of no one now living in this section of country that ever gave them credence. Joe Smith dare not come to Palmyra, from fear [p. 290] of his creditors; for he ran away to avoid their just demands.[13]

You, sir, may think we treat this matter lightly; but I give you a correct statement. You have asked for the facts, and I give them. We consider the founders and propagators of the Mormon "religion" simply as base impostors, whose sectarian assertions are false and absurd.

Respectfully yours, etc.,
JESSE TOWNSEND.

---

10. See III.A.7, LUCY HARRIS STATEMENT, 29 NOV 1833.

11. Ellipses are Tucker's.

12. See III.L.14, MARTIN HARRIS MORTGAGE, 25 AUG 1829.

13. See III.A.1, MANCHESTER RESIDENTS GROUP STATEMENT, 3 NOV 1833, n. 3.

7.
JESSE TOWNSEND TO ELISHA CAMP, 16 AUGUST 1834

Jesse Townsend to Elisha Camp, 16 August 1834, Camp Family Papers, John M. Olin Library, Cornell University, Ithaca, New York. Published in *Sackets' Harbor Courier* (Watertown, New York), date unknown; reprinted in the *Salem* (Massachusetts) *Landmark,* 3 December 1834; unidentified and undated newspaper clipping in Jonathan B. Turner Papers, Illinois Historical Society Library, Springfield, Illinois.

EDITORIAL NOTE

Elisha Camp, a lawyer with an extensive practice, came to Sackets Harbor, Jefferson County, New York, in 1804. Later he helped to settle nearby Hounsfield. About 1820 Camp and others bought out the local paper *Sackets' Harbor Gazette and Advertiser* (1817-20), renaming it the *Jefferson Republican* (1820-23). He was also closely associated with the Watertown Presbytery (Emerson 1898, 185, 242, 319, 640, 650, 653, 654). Camp, in his forties, along with his wife and many children, are listed in the 1830 census of Hounsfield, Jefferson County, New York (1830:174).

It was perhaps the early success of Mormon missionaries in Jefferson County that prompted Camp's 5 August 1834 letter to the Reverend Jesse Townsend (see Perciaccante 1993), but the editor of the *Sackets' Harbor Courier* gave another reason.

> A lazy fellow who was formerly a country pauper, has lately attempted to raise recruits for "Joe Smith," on Pillar Point, near this place. He pretended that he had a withered arm miraculously cured. From a knowledge of this bold attempt at imposition, and with a view of getting correct information on this subject of Mormonism, a person in this village addressed a letter to a gentleman of the first respectability in Palmyra, and received the following answer.[1]

Townsend responded on 16 August 1834 with a brief letter relating information about Joseph Smith and Mormon origins. Soon after, Camp had

---

1. *Sackets' Harbor Courier,* reprinted in unidentified and undated newspaper clipping, Jonathan B. Turner Papers, Illinois Historical Society Library, Springfield, Illinois.

the letter printed in the *Sackets' Harbor Courier,* published by James Howe at Watertown. The original issue of the *Courier* cannot be found, but the Jonathan B. Turner Papers at the Illinois Historical Society Library, Springfield, Illinois, include an undated clipping from an unknown newspaper that reprinted the item directly from the *Courier.* The present letter, located in the Camp Family Papers at Cornell University, follows very closely the wording of Townsend's previous letter of 24 December 1833 to Phineas Stiles (compare III.I.6, JESSE TOWNSEND TO PHINEAS STILES, 24 DEC 1833, which also includes fuller documentation).

Palmyra, County of Wayne, State of New York. August 16th, 1834.

Dear Sir. Your letter, of the 5th ult, requesting information concerning the people called Mormonites, & concerning their origin & leaders, has been received.

This imposition was begun by Joseph Smith in the vicinity of this village.

However incredible it may appear, the following statement is correct & shows the great folly & weakness of the people who have credited the impositions & falsehoods which Joseph Smith & his associates in iniquity have propagated.

I begin with the leader "Joe," as he is & has been called here for 20 years past.—For 10 years he has been a man of questionable character, of intemperate habits & a noted Money Digger. He lived in a sequestered neighborhood, where his loquacity gave him a reputation, with some, for being smart; these he flattered to assist him in digging for money. These soon saw his deception & got out of patience with him. To avoid their sneers, Joe pretended that he had, at length, found, by digging, a wonderful curiosity, which he kept closely concealed.

After Joe had told different stories & had called the pretended curiosity by different names, he, at length, called it, The Golden Plates of the Book of Mormon.

As Smith was, from time to time, questioned, his story assumed a more uniform statement.

In the mean time, Joe visited a visionary fanatic, by the name of Harris[2] & told him he had received some Golden Plates from the Lord with directions to call on Martin Harris for fifty dollars to enable him to go to Pennsylvania

---

2. On Martin Harris (1783-1875), see "Introduction to Martin Harris Collection."

& there translate the contents of those Plates. At the same time he affirmed to Harris that the Lord had told him that he & Martin Harris were the only honest men in the world. Joe had doubtless heard Martin frequently say this of himself. This he knew was the assailable point in his visionary mind. The delicious bait was greedily swallowed. The fifty dollars were soon put into the hands of Joe & he cleared for Pennsylvania.

Martin Harris was then worth five or six thousand dollars & the whole brotherhood of the Smiths were in very low worldly circumstances.

The Smiths used Martin's money freely—some other men, who had a great dislike to honest labor, about that time, joined Joe in his acts of deception. In that reinforcement was a ready writer by name Cowdry[3] and a Whitney[4] who declared he had once been in heaven, who assisted Joe in writing the Book [p. 1] of Mormon, as a pretended translation of the Golden Plates which Smith affirmed he had been directed by the Spirit of the Lord to dig from the earth. The whole was done in the most secret manner. At the same time, Smith affirmed that it would be immediate death for any one to see those plates besides himself & the writers of the Book of Mormon. Poor Martin, through his lack of faith & his having, at a certain time, refused to hand over to Joe more money, was excluded from a view of the Plates.[5]

Previous to that base course of imposition & deception Martin Harris was an industrious farmer, but unfortunate in his choice of a wife; or rather she was unfortunate in her choice of a husband. It is a truth <of public notoriety> that Martin Harris, who is the second in authority among the Mormonites, who gives to their preachers licence to preach & authority to put their prosylites under water, has laid violent hands on his wife, & so cruelly & frequently whipped & beaten her, that she has had to seek refuge from his abuse & cruelty, among her relatives. To this day he is considered, in this section of country, in domestic matters, a base scoundrel; in religion, a dupe to the Smiths; in all things, an un=learned, conceited hypocrite. He paid for printing five thousand copies of the Book of Mormon, which

---

3. On Oliver Cowdery (1806-50), see "Introduction to Oliver Cowdery Collection."

4. This person is not mentioned in Townsend's earlier letter and remains unidentified (compare III.I.6, JESSE TOWNSEND TO PHINEAS STILES, 24 DEC 1833).

5. This sentence reads differently in Townsend's previous letter: "Poor Martin's faith was apparently strengthened by this pretension, but afterward the 'command' was modified, and he claimed to have seen the plates with 'spiritual eyes'" (III.I.6, JESSE TOWNSEND TO PHINEAS STILES, 24 DEC 1833). The earlier reading is more accurate.

exhausted all his funds. In Ohio he has attempted to get another wife—Some one wrote from Ohio & ascertained that his long & greatly abused wife is still alive in the vicinity of Palmyra & thus defeated him in his iniquity.

All the Mormonites have left this part of our state. I know of no one in, this section of country, who ever gave them credence. Joe Smith dare not come into this region from a fear of his creditors from whom he absconded to avoid paying their just demands. He has had a stone, into which, when it is placed in a hat, he pretends to look, & to see chests of money buried in the earth. He is a fortune teller, & says he can tell where stolen goods go, probably too well.

Harris prophesied that this village was to have been destroyed by lightning more than two years ago. Some other things, he in like manner said were then to have happened. As his predictions have all failed, he is now seldom seen in this region. He knows that he is considered to be a false prophet & imposter. [p. 2]

The founders & propagators of the Mormon imposition are here considered as not uttering the truth in any of their sectarian assertions, & as wholly unworthy of public & individual confidence. The truth always loves the light, & does not refuse to come to the light.

Thus, Dear Sir, you have a general, <but> true delineation of the Mormonites in their origin & the character of their prominent characters Smith & Harris. Make what use of this communica=tion you please—such use as you may judge the cause of true religion requires; such as may prevent the propagation of error & delusion.

Yours respectfully,

[s] Jesse Townsend

/[6] The above Letter can be seen at this office, & the Writer can be vouched for by persons who know him here, as one in whose statements the fullest reliance can be placed—

Palmyra Augt. 16. 1834—

Mr Elisha Camp

6. The following note is written in a different hand, evidently that of James Howe, editor of the *Sackets' Harbor Courier.* These words followed the publication of Townsend's letter in the *Courier.*

8.
W. W. PHELPS TO OLIVER COWDERY, 25 DECEMBER 1834

W. W. Phelps to Oliver Cowdery, 25 December 1834, "Letter No. 4," *Latter Day Saints' Messenger and Advocate* 1 (February 1835): 65-67.

EDITORIAL NOTE

In a letter to William W. Phelps,[1] dated 7 September 1834, Oliver Cowdery outlined some early Mormon history, including the angelic ordination of Joseph Smith and himself to the priesthood in May 1829. When it appeared in the *Messenger and Advocate* in October 1834, it became the first published announcement of the event—the general membership apparently being unaware of the angelic source of the priesthood they had been exercising for the previous four years (see III.G.6, OLIVER COWDERY TO W. W. PHELPS, 7 SEP 1834). In the present letter, dated 25 December 1834, Phelps responds to Cowdery's previous letter and asks for information about the angel's appearance to Joseph Smith in 1823. Phelps also requests Cowdery to be more specific in his description of the angel who had appeared in May 1829, which Cowdery failed to do. Instead, Cowdery describes the angel who appeared to Smith in 1823. For Cowdery's response to the present letter, see III.G.8, OLIVER COWDERY TO W. W. PHELPS, FEB 1835.

Liberty, Mo. Christmas, 1834.

DEAR BROTHER:—

Your letter from Norton (O.) dated Sept. 7, 1834, came to me by mail, last week, through the medium of the Messenger and Advocate. I am glad you "have thought that a full history of the rise of the church of Latter Day Saints, and the most interesting part of its progress, to the present time, would be worthy the perusal of the saints." The history of the saints, according to sacred writ, is the only record which has stood the test and ravages of time from the beginning; and a true account of the revival of the Lord's church, so near the great Sabbath of creation, must be a source and subject of holy

1. On W. W. Phelps (1792-1872), see introduction to III.G.6, OLIVER COWDERY TO W. W. PHELPS, 7 SEP 1834.

joy to the pure in heart; and an interesting preface of things to come, that might arrest the attention of the world, before the Lord shows his naked arm to the nations, if the children of men would read and understand.

I pray our heavenly Father to assist you, so that you may be enabled to spread the truth before the eyes of this generation, ere destruction comes as a whirl-wind upon the ungodly. Strive, with your might, to be simple, plain, easy and unaffected in your style, showing the shining world, that though many may continue to run after one that is able to give *gold* to his friends, and *lead* to his enemies, you, with the Israel of God, will rejoice in having light enough to follow HIM who has power to give eternal life to *his* friends, and will overcome *his* enemies.

There are some items in your letter which are great, and revive old thoughts that, long since, were left to float down the gulf of departed things, into the maze of forgetfulness. The first one is where you sat day after day and wrote the history of the second race that inhabited this continent, as the words were repeated to you by the Lord's prophet, through the aid of the "Urim and Thumim," "Nephite Interpreters," or Divine Spectacles. I mean when you wrote the book of Mormon, containing the fulness of the gospel to the world, and the covenant to gather Israel, for the last time, as well as the history of the Indians, who, till then, had neither origin among men, nor records amid the light and knowledge of the great 19th century.

Fresh comes a story into my mind, that, in 1823, before the book of Mormon was known among us, a sacred record, or, as I had it, another bible, written or engraved upon thin gold leaves, containing more plainness than the one we had, but agreeing with it, had been found near Canandaigua, N.Y. The characters in which it was written, were of a language once used upon the eastern continent, but obsolete and unknown then. I was somewhat surprised at the remarkable discovery, or news, though I never knew to this day, how I came by it. Like Paul, who did not know whether he was in the body, or out of it, at a certain time, I cannot tell whether I dreamed; or whether some person told me; or whether an angel whispered such *strange tidings*. I mentioned it a few times, but was rather laughed at, and so I said no more about it, till after I had removed to Canandaigua, when the book of Mormon was published.

At that day, or, in fact, I always believed the scriptures, and believed that there was such a sacred thing as *pure religion*; but I never believed that any of the sects of the day, *had it,* and so I was ever ready to argue up, or down, any church; and that, too, by evidence from the good old book, an intimacy with which I had formed in infancy and cherished in age. When the story related above, first found a resting place in my tabernacle, I rejoiced that there was something coming *to point the right way to heaven.* So it was, and, thank God, so it is.

In the history you are writing,[2] you cannot be too plain and minute in particulars. ... [p. 65] ...

While I think of it, let me ask you to explain, or state what the angel said when he informed brother J[oseph]. S[mith]. jr. that a *treasure* was about to come forth to this generation.

The next item I shall notice, is, (a glorious one,) when the angel conferred the "priesthood upon you, his fellow servants." That was an august meeting of men and angels, and brought again, upon earth, the keys of the mysteries of the kingdom of God. I am aware that our language lacks terms, and we fail in power to set forth the sublimity of such a holy scene, but we can remember the glory and tell the appearance in such words as we have, and let God add the majesty and omnipotence to the sacred interview. Our ancient brethren were careful to notice angel's visits, and note what they said, and how careful ought we to be? ... [p. 66] ...[3]

W. W. PHELPS.

---

2. This refers to Cowdery's ongoing correspondence with Phelps and their publication in the *Messenger and Advocate* (see "Oliver Cowdery Collection").

3. Phelps relates a dream/vision that he experienced on the night of 16 November 1834, then states: "From this I judge, that a scene of heavenly things, seen with the naked eye, is so perfectly retained, that you can give every particular" (66).

9. W. W. PHELPS TO OLIVER COWDERY, 21 FEBRUARY 1835

W. W. Phelps to Oliver Cowdery, 21 February 1835, "Letter No. 6," *Latter Day Saints' Messenger and Advocate* 1 (April 1835): 97.

EDITORIAL NOTE

On 21 February 1835, William W. Phelps[1] responded to Oliver Cowdery's letter published in the *Messenger and Advocate* in December 1834 (see III.G.7, OLIVER COWDERY TO W. W. PHELPS, DEC 1834). In the present letter, Phelps describes his early investigation of Mormonism in New York.

Liberty, Mo. Feb. 21, 1835.

Dear Bro. in the Lord:—I take little time to answer your 3rd letter, addressed to me in the December number of the Messenger and Advocate. Passing your apology, I come at once to the great point in question, that this church has suffered persecution from its commencement; and that, too, in most cases, without the least provocation. Here suffer me to say, as you and I are fellow members, and have been co-servants nearly from the beginning, that we have known by example, what thousands are preaching in precept, that "they that will live Godly in Christ Jesus, must suffer persecution."

Now, notwithstanding my body was not baptized into this church till Thursday the 16th of June, 1831, yet my heart was there from the time I became acquainted with the book of Mormon; and my hope, steadfast like an anchor, and my faith increased like the grass after a refreshing shower, when I for the first time, held a conversation with our beloved brother Joseph, (December 24th, 1830,) who I was willing to acknowledge as a prophet of the Lord, and to whom, and to whose godly account of himself and the work he was engaged in, I owe my first determination to quit the folly of my way, and the fancy and fame of this world, and seek the Lord and his righteousness, in order to enter a better world, where the duration, and glory, and honor, and power, and space, are equal and endless. ...

1. On W. W. Phelps (1792-1872), see introduction to III.G.6, OLIVER COWDERY TO W. W. PHELPS, 7 SEP 1834.

Well may you say that it is known unto me, "that this church has suffered reproach and persecution from a majority of mankind who have heard but a rumor, since its first organization,["] &c.—So it is. On the 30th of April, 1830, I was thrown into prison at Lyons,[2] N.Y. by a couple of Presbyterian traders, for a small debt, for the purpose, as I was informed, of "keeping me from joining the Mormons."[3] How many hair-breadth escapes you and brother Joseph passed, for writing and publishing the truth in the book of Mormon, as the constitution and law allowed, I know not, but I heard church members and others declare in language similar to the following: that every believer in the 'Golden Bible,' (as the book of Mormon was called by many) ought to be sued and sent or driven out of society. The Rochester Observer, one of the principal Presbyterian organs of the day, introduced the book of Mormon to the world with a flashy article headed *Blasphemy*![4] and to cap the climax of gullibility, against which the 'men of the meeting houses' showed an ardent zeal to guard their flocks, it was carefully circulated, that 'a Jesuit' had employed a young man by the name of Cowdery, to write, and through the aid of one Smith, was bringing forth a book to break down all religions. ...

But I will not pursue this subject further at present, leaving it for your addition of facts. Instead of standing in the way, and asking for the old paths, they have *stood in the way,* and put darkness for light, and light for darkness, till not only 'large *check* of their opinions, and *attested* volumes of our lives and characters,' have '*inundated* our land with scurrilous reports,' but the

2. Footnote in original reads: "My family sick at my residence in Canandaigua." Phelps's dating of his imprisonment is one year off as indicated by a letter he wrote from the Lyons jail dated 30 April 1831, a portion of which reads: "While I was at Palmyra, comparing the 'Book of Mormon' with the Bible, to find out the truth, and investigating the matter for public good, —— —— — ——, members of the church and *pretended* anti-masons, sent their foolish clerk from Canandaigua, and took me with a warrant, and obtained a judgment against me, on a balance of their account. This was done after I had engaged a passage home, having learned that my family were sick. An execution was sworn out on the spot, and I was hurried to jail in the course of the night, where I shall stay thirty days ..." (*Wayne Sentinel* 8 [13 May 1831]: [3], reprinting from *Geneva Gazette, and Mercantile Advertiser* 22 [11 May 1831]: [2]).

3. Concerning this incident, Sidney Rigdon said: "I recollect elder Phelps being put in jail for reading the Book of Mormon. He came to see us, and expressed great astonishment, and left us apparently pondering in his heart" (VI.F.5, SIDNEY RIGDON REMINISCENCE, 1844).

4. Compare III.K.1, *ROCHESTER* (NY) *GEM,* 15 MAY 1830.

blood of the saints has curdled upon the sacred soil of freedom. ...

As ever,

W. W. PHELPS.

10.
J. N. T. TUCKER STATEMENT, 1842

J. N. T. Tucker to the Editor, 23 May 1842, "Mormonism—Some Curious Facts," *Signs of the Times, and Expositor of Prophecy* (Boston) 3 (8 June 1842): 79-80. Reprinted in John C. Bennett, *The History of the Saints; or, An Exposé of Joe Smith and Mormonism* (Boston: Leland and Whiting, 1842), 122-23.

Editorial Note

According to John H. Gilbert, J. N. T. Tucker was a cousin of Pomeroy Tucker[1] and, after a short stay in Palmyra, "went to Groton, Ct., got married, became a preacher—Baptist I believe—committed some crime,—was tried and accquitted on the plea of insanity—he was a 'bad egg.'" Gilbert also refuted Tucker's published statement: "J. N. T. Tucker ... did not work in the office at the time the Mormon Bible was printed, but did subsequently a short time, if my memory serves me. ... His statement in regard to a page of the manuscript being spirited away by some of the typos in the office, is totally untrue" (see III.H.3, JOHN H. GILBERT TO JAMES T. COBB, 16 MAR 1879, 1).

MESSRS. EDITORS,—Having noticed in a late number of the Signs of the Times, a notice of a work entitled "Mormon Delusions and Monstrosities"[2]—it occurred to me that it might perhaps be of service to the cause of truth, to state one circumstance in relation to the authenticity of the "Book of Mormon" which occurred during its publication, at which time I was a practical printer, and engaged in the office where it was printed, and became familiar with the men and their principles, through whose agency it was "got up."

The circumstance alluded to was as follows:—We had heard much said by Martin Harris,[3] the man who paid for the printing, (and the only one in

---

1. On Pomeroy Tucker (1802-70), see introduction to III.J.5, POMEROY TUCKER REMINISCENCE, 1858.

2. Joshua Vaughan Himes, *Mormon Delusions and Monstrosities. A Review of the Book of Mormon and an Illustration of Mormon Principles and Practices* (Boston: Joshua V. Himes, 1842).

3. On Martin Harris (1783-1875), see "Introduction to Martin Harris Collection."

the concern worth any property) about the wonderful wisdom of the translators of the mysterious plates, and resolved to test their wisdom. Accordingly, after putting one sheet in type, we laid it aside, and told Harris it was lost, and there would be a serious defection in the book in consequence, unless another sheet like the original could be produced. The announcement threw the old gentleman into quite an excitement. But after a few moment's reflection, he said he would try to obtain another. After two or three weeks another sheet was produced, but no more like the original than any other sheet of paper would have been, written over by a common schoolboy, after having read, as they did, the manuscripts preceding and succeeding the lost sheet.[4]

As might be expected, the disclosure of the plan greatly annoyed the authors, and caused no little merriment among those who were acquainted with the circumstance. As we were none of us Christians, and only labored for the "gold that perisheth," we did not care for the delusion, only so far as to be careful to avoid it ourselves and enjoy the hoax. *Not one* of the hands in the office where the wonderful book was printed ever became a convert to the system, although the writer of this was often assured by Harris if he did not, he would be destroyed in 1832.[5]

I am well acquainted with the two gentlemen whose names appear on page[s] 50, 51, in the work referred to at the head of this article, and know the certificate above their names to be [p. 79] true. I have known several instances of the grossest impostures by them in their pretensions of working miracles, &c. &c., and am greatly surprised that such a man as Nickerson[6] of

4. With Gilbert's denial and the existence of two manuscript copies of the Book of Mormon, one is tempted to dismiss Tucker's story as a complete fabrication, perhaps inspired by Martin Harris's loss of the manuscript in 1828 and Smith's preface to the 1830 edition. However, apparently typesetting had exceeded preparation of the printer's manuscript, so rather than having the press work stop, the original dictated manuscript was used by the typesetter for the portion from Helaman 13 through Mormon (Skousen 1992, 23-24). Thus Tucker's story is not as easily discredited as one might assume.

5. Concerning Harris's prediction, see III.H.10, JOHN H. GILBERT MEMORANDUM, 8 SEP 1892, 4.

6. Freeman Nickerson (1778-1847) was born in South Dennis, Massachusetts. He married Huldah Chapman in 1801, and together they parented nine children. He was baptized by Zerubbabel Snow in April 1833, and soon after moved to Kirtland, Ohio. He served several missions in the United States and Canada, including one to Boston. He died at Chariton River, Iowa (Jenson 1971, 4:690-91). In 1842 Nickerson published in the local newspaper a warning to the inhabitants of Boston: "I request the citizens and

your city, can induce any rational person to follow in his pernicious ways.

Mrs. Harris, the wife of Martin Harris, was so familiar with the monstrous wickedness and folly of her husband, and the trio who were engaged with him, that she would not follow him nor live with him.[7] His conduct was not such as a man of God would have been. After he had been absent about two years, and frequent reports of his having power to heal the sick, &c. had reached his neighborhood, he returned and assured his wife that he could cure her of deafness with which she was afflicted. But as a condition of so doing, he required her to put into his hands about $1,500 of money which she had managed to secure out of the avails of his property, which he sold on joining the "latter day saints" colony. She assured him he should have every dollar as soon as her hearing was restored. But he very wisely replied, he could "have no evidence of her faith until she put the cash down"—so of course she remained deaf, and Martin went back to the "promised land" with pockets as light as when he came.

This is no doubt one of the great deceptions which should come upon the people on the eve of the second coming of the Son of Man. Let the saints of God beware of them. Let no persecution or violence be opposed to them, but simply an avoidance, and we shall soon find them without faith.

Yours in the gospel of Christ,

J. N. T. TUCKER.

Groton, May 23, 1842.

---

authorities of the city of Boston, to open a house for the servant of the people, that the Lord hath sent to this city to warn the people of the destruction which will take place in this generation, that is now on earth, and teach them how they may escape, and come through and abide the day of the second coming of Christ" (from the *Dollar Weekly Bostonian,* as reprinted in the *Times and Seasons* 3 [16 May 1842]: 798).

7. See III.A.7, LUCY HARRIS STATEMENT, 29 NOV 1833.

J.
Miscellaneous Late Sources

1.
Solomon Chamberlain Accounts, 1845 & Circa 1858

1. John Taylor, Journal (January 1845-September 1845), 50-54, entry of April 1845, in possession of Brent Ashworth, Provo, Utah.

2. Solomon Chamberlain, "A Short Sketch of the Life of Solomon Chamberlin," circa 1858, 4-12, LDS Church Archives, Salt Lake City, Utah.

EDITORIAL NOTE

Solomon Chamberlain (1788-1862) was born in Old Canaan, Connecticut. By 1829 he was living in Lyons, Wayne County, New York. He visited the Smiths in Palmyra about August-September 1829, while the Book of Mormon was at press. Taking sixty-four uncut pages from Grandin's press, Chamberlain became one of the first missionaries of the church as he traveled through western New York and as far as Canada preaching the Book of Mormon. He may have been the first to contact Brigham and Phineas Young (see III.K.23, PHINEAS HOWE YOUNG AUTOBIOGRAPHY, 1863). He was also responsible for the conversions of Mayhew, Sarah, and Silas Hillman of Spafford, Onondaga County, New York (see III.K.25, SILAS HILLMAN REMINISCENCE, 1866). Shortly after the church's organization on 6 April 1830, Chamberlain was baptized by Joseph Smith in Fayette, New York, and was ordained a priest by Hyrum Smith. Chamberlain was also one of the first in the church to settle in Jackson County, Missouri, in the early 1830s, and was a member of the first company of Mormons to arrive in the Salt Lake Valley in 1847. Chamberlain, age sixty-two, is listed in the 1850 census of Salt Lake City, Utah, as a "Cooper" (1850:25). He died in Washington County, Utah (Jenson 1971, 2:605-606, 4:696; Cannon and Cook 1983, 253).

Chamberlain's early experience with Mormonism is preserved in two sources. The earliest was recorded by John Taylor in his journal in April 1845. Taylor's journal is presently in the possession of collector Brent Ashworth of Provo, Utah, but was published by Dean C. Jessee in 1983, from which the present transcription was taken (see Jessee 1983, 44-46; see also *Ensign,* December 1983, 48-49). The second version, written by

Chamberlain himself, was probably composed in 1858. Chamberlain states near the end of his autobiography that his youngest daughter at the time of writing was eight years old; this evidently refers to Chamberlain's daughter, Louisa, who was born about 1850 (see U.S. Census, Salt Lake City, Utah, 1850:25). Included with Chamberlain's autobiography is a cover letter to Albert Carrington, dated 11 July 1858, giving the latter permission to publish "a short sketch of my life" in the *Deseret News,* although apparently it was never published in that periodical. According to Larry C. Porter, as of 1972 the holograph of Chamberlain's autobiography was in the possession of Mrs. Albert D. Swensen (Jennie Romney), a great-granddaughter of Chamberlain living in Provo, Utah (see Porter 1971, 360-63; and Porter 1972, 315-18), and was subsequently donated to the LDS Church Archives, Salt Lake City, Utah, in 1977 (Porter 1977-78, 124, n. 1). While Taylor's account varies from Chamberlain's autobiography in a number of places, the nearly identical language and order may indicate that Taylor took his information from an early draft of Chamberlain's autobiography.

[*1. John Taylor Journal, April 1845*][1]

Speaking a few days since with a man of the name of Solomon Chamberlin, he related some particulars that I thought interesting concerning the manner that he was brought to obey the truth; and concerning the early rise of the Church as he was one of the first members. I will relate it in his own words: [p. 50]

"I joined the Methodists when I was 19 years of age. I then commenced reading and studying the bible, and found they (the Methodists) were wrong in many things. About the year 1814 or 1815 the reformed Methodists came off from the Episcopal; and I was in hopes they were right. I joined them, and remained a member until some time after 1816. At this time the heads of the Church and some families myself with the rest, purchased a farm that cost $25,000, and moved on to it, thinking that the day of gathering had come; and we came into common stock, striving to come on to the Apostle's ground. We believed in revelation and the healing of the sick through faith and prayer; but we were wrong in many things, we had no prophet nor priesthood. This year (1816) we found we were mistaken in many things. At this time I felt very anxious to know whether there were any people on the earth whose principles were right in all things; for I was tired of all orders

---

1. On John Taylor (1808-87), see introduction to I.A.27, JOHN TAYLOR ACCOUNT, 1850.

unless they had the true principles of God: I believed we might receive revelation for ourselves: I believed if we lacked wisdom and humbled ourselves before God in mighty prayer, and asked in sincerity he would give us; I did so with all my heart, and he answered my prayer. The Lord revealed to me in a vision of the night an angel, I thought if I could ask him, he could tell me all I wanted to know. I accordingly asked him if we were right. He said not one of us were right, and that there were no people on earth that were right; but that the Lord would in his own due time raise up a church, different from all others, and he would give power and authority as in the days of Christ; and he would carry it through, and it should never be confounded; and that I should live to see the day, and know the work when it came forth; and that great persecution should follow, and much more after this he told me. I proclaimed it to the world and all people what I had seen and heard; [p. 51] and that all denominations on earth were as John said constituted the great whore of all the earth.

Somewhere about the time that Joseph Smith found the record of the Book of Mormon, I began to feel as though the time was nearly come, that had been made known to me by the angel. I made some inquiries through the country if there was any strange work of God, such as had not been on the earth since the days of Christ. I was then living on the Erie Canal forty miles below Rochester[2]; I had occasion to go on a visit to Canada. I took [a] boat for Lockport; when the boat came to Palmyra, I felt as if some genii or good spirit told me to leave the boat, and go or travel a south course; I did so for about three miles. (I had not yet heard of the gold bible so called at that time, nor any of the Smith family, I was an entire stranger in that part of the country.) Here my guide told me I must put up for the night; and I heard of the Smiths and the gold bible for the first time. I was now within half a mile of Joseph Smith's father's house where my guide had brought me.—In the morning the woman asked me if I had heard of the gold bible. I told her I had not; and there was something began on the top of my head and went to my toes like electricity: I said to myself I shall soon find why I have been led to this place in this singular manner. It only being about half a mile from there across lots to Father Smith's. I soon arrived at the house, and found Hyrum[3] walking the floor; as I entered the room, I said peace be to this house; he looked at me and said "I hope it will be peace." I then said

2. At this time, Chamberlain apparently lived at Lyons, Wayne County, New York.

3. On Hyrum Smith (1800-44), see I.A.15, JOSEPH SMITH HISTORY, 1839, n. 12.

is there any one here that believes in visions and revelations. He said yes, we are a visionary house. I then said I will give you one of my pamphlets,[4] (which was visionary and of my own composition) and if you are a visionary house, I wish you would make [p. 52] known some of your discoveries, I think I can bear them. They then began to make known to me, that they had obtained a gold record, and had just finished translating it. Here I staid, and they instructed me in the manuscripts of the Book of Mormon; after I had been there two days, I went with Hyrum and some others to [the] Palmyra printing office, where they began to print the Book of Mormon; and as soon as they had printed sixty-four pages I took them and started for Canada[5]; and I preached to all that I saw, high and low, rich and poor, and all that I knew concerning the work. I had but few to oppose, they had not made up their minds, and they knew not what to think of it. I did not see any one in travelling six or seven hundred miles, that had ever heard of the gold bible so called. When I returned from Canada, I went to Massachusetts, and preached the work to all both great and small; and told them to prepare for the great work of God, that was now coming forth, that would never be confounded nor be brought down; but would stand for ever and be like unto the apostolic church. As soon as the books were printed, I took eight or ten of them, and started off to sell and to preach; for you could not sell one without a great deal of preaching. I labored hard for eight days and sold one book on which I made twenty-five cents, and bore my own expenses. I carried them to the reform Methodist Conference, there I found Phineas[6] and Brigham Young[7] with whom I had been acquainted before. I thought I

4. In 1989 Rick Grunder located and sold to Brigham Young University: [Solomon Chamberlain], *A Sketch of the experience of Solomon Chamberlin, to Which Is Added a Remarkable Revelation or Trance, of His Father-in-Law, Philip Haskins: How His Soul Actually Left His Body and Was Guided by a Holy Angel to Eternal Day* (Lyons, New York: [Published by the Author?], 1829), 12pp. (recently published in Porter 1997-98, 131-40).

5. Chamberlain evidently was not the only person to carry away proof sheets of the Book of Mormon. Oliver Cowdery also gave proof sheets to his brother Warren A. Cowdery of Freedom, Cattaraugus County, New York, who then showed them to Heman Hyde of the same town. Hyde was later converted to Mormonism (see "The Private Journal of William Hyde," 6, typescript, Special Collections, Harold B. Lee Library, Brigham Young University, Provo, Utah; cf. Jenson 1971, 1:759).

6. On Phineas H. Young (1799-1879), see introduction to III.K.23, PHINEAS HOWE YOUNG AUTOBIOGRAPHY, 1863.

7. On Brigham Young (1801-77), see introduction to III.K.19, BRIGHAM YOUNG ACCOUNTS, 1855 & 1857.

could soon convince the whole conference of the truth of the Book of Mormon, but I soon found my mistake, for after laboring with them for two days, they rejected me. Phineas and Brigham Young used me well. I returned home and on the way preached it to the Free Will Baptist Church, and they received it, and soon after the Church was established a number of them were baptized. Soon after this I was bap[p. 53]tized by Joseph Smith in the waters of Seneca Lake,[8] and emigrated to Ohio. ...

[*2. Solomon Chamberlain Autobiography, Circa 1858*]

... About the year 1814, or 15, the reformed Methodist[s] broke off from the Episcopal Methodists. I found them to be more right than the Episcopal, and joined them about this time the Lord shewed me in a vision, that there was no people on the earth that was right, and that faith was gone from the earth, excepting a few and that all Churches were corrupt. I further saw in the vision, that he would soon raise up a Church, that would be after the Apostolic Order, that there would be in it the same [p. 4] powers, and gifts that were in the days of Christ, and that I should live to see the day, and that there would a book come forth, like unto the Bible and the people would be guided by it, as well as the Bible. This was in the year of 1816. I then believed in gifts and miracles as the Latter day Saints do, for which I was much persecuted and called deluded. This vision I received from an Angel or Spirit from the Eternal World that told me these things.

About the time that Joseph Smith found the gold record, I began to feel that the time was drawing near, that the Lord would in some shape or other, bring forth his Church. [p. 5] I made some inquiry thro the country where I traveled if there was any strange work of God, such as had not been on the earth since the days of Christ. I could hear of none, I was living about 20 miles east of where the gold record was found, on the Erie Canal. I had occasion to go on a visit into upper Canada. I took [a] boat for Lockport, when the boat came to Palmyra, I felt as if some genii or good Spirit told me to leave the boat, this was a few miles from where the record was found. After leaving the boat, the spirit manifested to me, to travel a South course, I did so for about 3 miles, I had not as yet heard of the gold bible (so called) nor any of the Smith family. I was a stranger in that part of the [p. 6] Country, a Town where I never before had set my foot, and knew no one in the

8. The exact date of Chamberlain's baptism is unknown. In his autobiography, Chamberlain says that he was baptized "a few days after" the church's organization on 6 April 1830 (see below).

Town. It was about sun down, and my guide directed me to put up for the night, which I did to a Farm house, in the morning the people of the house asked me if I had heard of the Gold Bible, when they said Gold Bible there was a power like electricity went from the top of my head to the end of my toes, This was the first time I ever heard of the gold Bible. I was now within half a mile of the Smith family where Joseph lived. from the time I left the boat until now, I was wholly led by the Spirit or my Genii. The women spoke considerable of the gold bible that Joseph Smith had found. When she mentioned gold Bible, I felt a shock of the power of God go from head to foot, [p. 7] I said to myself, I shall soon find why I have been led in this singular manner. I soon made my way across lots, to Father Smith's and found Hyrum walking the floor, As I entered the door, I said, peace be to this house. He looked at me as one astonished, and said, I hope it will be peace, I then said, Is there any one here that believes in visions or revelations he said Yes, we are a visionary house. I said, Then I will give you one of my pamphlets, which was visionary, and of my own experience. They then called the people together, which consisted of 5 or 6 men who were out at the door. Father Smith[9] was one & some of the Whitmer's. They then sat down and read my pamphlet. Hyrum read first, but was so affected he could not read it. He then gave it to a man, which I learned was [p. 8] Christian Whitmer, [10] he finished reading it. I then opened my mouth and began to preach to them, in the words that the angel had made known to me in the vision, that all Churches and Denominations on the earth had become corrupt, and no Church of God on the Earth but that he would shortly rise up a Church, that would never be confounded nor brought down and be like unto the Apostolic Church. They wondered greatly who had been telling me these things, for said they we have the same things wrote down in our house, taken from the Gold record, that you are preaching to us. I said, the Lord told me these things a number of years ago, I then said, If you are a visionary house, I wish you would make known some of your discoveries, [p. 9] for I think I can bear them. They then made known to me that they had obtained a gold record, and just finished translating it here. <Now the Lord revealed to me by the gift & power of the Holy Ghost that this was the work I had been looking for.>[11] Here I staid 2 days and they instructed me, in the manuscripts of the Book of Mormon. After I had been

9. On Joseph Smith, Sr. (1771-1840), see "Introduction to Joseph Smith, Sr., Collection."

10. On Christian Whitmer (1798-1835), see I.A.15, JOSEPH SMITH HISTORY, 1839, n. 96.

11. This insertion is in different ink.

there 2 days, I went with Hyrum and some others to [the] Palmyra printing office where they began to print the Book of Mormon, and as soon as they had printed 64 pages, I took them with their leave and pursued my journey to Canada, and I preached all that I knew concerning Mormonism, to all both high and low, rich and poor, and thus you see this was the first that ever printed Mormonism was preached to this generation. I did not see any one in traveling for 800 miles, that had ever heard of the [p. 10] Gold Bible (so called). I exhorted all people to prepare for the great work of God that was now about to come forth, and it would never be brought down nor confounded. As soon as the Book was printed, I took 8 or 10 of them & traveled for 8 days, and sold one in that time. About this time I thot if I could see the reformed Methodists I could convince them of the truth of the Book of Mormon. I accordingly went to one of their conferences, where I met about 40 of their preachers and labored with them for 2 days to convince them of the truth of the Book of Mormon, and they utterly rejected me, and the Book of Mormon. One of their greatest preachers so called, by the name of [p. 11] Buckly,[12] (if I mistake not) abused me very bad, and ordered me off from their premises. He was soon, taken crazy, and died a miserable death. at this conference was Brigham and his brother Phinehas Young, they did not oppose me but used me well. On my way home I stopped at their Camp meeting, where I found one of their greatest preachers, whom I contended with concerning the Book of Mormon, by the name of W[illia]m Lake,[13] who utterly condemned it and rejected it, who spurned at me and the Book and said, if it was of God, Do you think He would send such a little upstart as you are round with it. but he soon after died a poor drunken sot. While on my way home I stopped at a free will Baptist Church, and preached to a large congregation, and they received the [p. 12] work, but there was no one to baptize them, the Church was not yet organized, but was soon after [on] April 6th 1830. a few days after I was baptized in the waters of Seneca Lake by Joseph Smith,[14] and emmigrated [the] same spring[15] to Kirtland[,] Ohio ...

---

12. This person, also named by Phineas Young, remains unidentified (see III.K.23, PHINEAS HOWE YOUNG AUTOBIOGRAPHY, 1863, 375).

13. This person remains unidentified.

14. Later in his autobiography, Chamberlain also states that "[i]n the spring of 1830 I was ordained a Priest, under the hands of Hyrum Smith."

15. This is apparently an error since Chamberlain immigrated to Kirtland, Ohio, in the spring of 1831.

2.
Orsamus Turner Account, 1851

O[rsamus]. Turner, *History of the Pioneer Settlement of Phelps and Gorham's Purchase* (Rochester, New York: William Alling, 1851), 212-17. Published in *Littell's Living Age* 30 (July-September 1851), reprinting from *Rochester American.*

EDITORIAL NOTE

Orsamus Turner (1801-55) was born in western New York. A printer by trade, he served his "apprenti[ce]ship in a newspaper office at Palmyra" in 1818 and 1819 (Turner 1851, 400). He evidently worked under Timothy S. Strong, who began publishing the *Palmyra Register* in October 1818. Turner also served an apprenticeship under James Bemis at Canandaigua, perhaps in 1821 and 1822 (Turner 1851, 459, 499; R. L. Anderson 1969a, 377). About August 1822 Turner moved to Lockport, New York, where he purchased the new *Lockport Observatory* (1822-27) (Turner 1850, 655; R. L. Anderson 1969a, 378). Turner also published at Lockport the *Sentinel and Observatory* (1827) and the *Lockport Balance* (1831).

The gap (from 1827 to 1831) in Turner's publishing carrier was perhaps the result of his difficulties with the Masons. In 1827 Turner was "arrested and charged to appear" in the trial of William Morgan's kidnappers at Canandaigua, New York (see *Rochester Observer,* 1 September 1827, and 11 September 1827). Turner was freed on a $1,000 bail, necessitating the liquidation of his interest in the *Niagara Sentinel* (see *Rochester Album,* 23 October 1827). The widely publicized trial took place in Canandaigua in August 1828. Turner was cited for contempt for refusing to testify, but was eventually acquitted for lack of evidence (see *Ontario Phoenix,* 21 July 1830, and 4 August 1830).

In later years Turner became a regional historian, writing and publishing *Pioneer History of the Holland Purchase of Western New York* (Buffalo, New York: H. Derby and Co., 1850), and *History of the Pioneer Settlement of Phelps and Gorham's Purchase* (Rochester, New York: William Alling, 1851). In preparing an article, titled "Gold Bible—Mormonism," for his last named book, Turner wrote a letter, dated 22 September 1851, to Thomas Gregg of Warsaw, Illinois, seeking information about the Mormons in that state. In this letter Turner explained: "I am preparing for the press a History of Mormonism. I start with them from Palmyra, in this state, where I am fa=miliar with their history and trace them to Salt Lake and Beaver Island" (Mormon Collection, Chicago Historical Society, Chicago, Illinois).

Richard L. Anderson has argued that "Turner's personal recollections of Joseph Smith of necessity refer to the period prior to the late summer of 1822 and are probably no later than 1820, the latest date of Palmyra memoirs in his writings" (R. L. Anderson 1969a, 378). While Turner includes the reminiscences of "several citizens of Palmyra," it is also possible for Turner to have occasionally returned to the Palmyra/Manchester area either on business or to visit friends. Indeed, his participation in the Morgan trial brought him into the area for an extended time in 1828 (see Walters 1969b, 99). Yet much of what Turner writes, particularly about events subsequent to his departure from the area, is from the standpoint of a distant observer.

As we are now at the home of the Smith family—in sight of "Mormon Hill"—a brief pioneer history will be looked for, of the strange, and singularly successful religious sect—the Mormons; and *brief* it must be, merely starting it in its career, and leaving to their especial historian to trace them to Kirtland, Nauvoo, Beaver Island, and Utah, or the Salt Lake.

Joseph Smith,[1] the father of the prophet Joseph Smith, Jr., was from the Merrimack river, N.H.[2] He first settled in or near Palmyra village,[3] but as [p. 212] early as 1819 was the occupant of some new land on "Stafford street" in the town of Manchester, near the line of Palmyra.[4] "Mormon Hill" is near the plank road about half way between the villages of Palmyra and

1. On Joseph Smith, Sr. (1771-1840), see "Introduction to Joseph Smith, Sr., Collection."

2. Joseph Smith, Sr., was born in Topsfield, Massachusetts, south of the Merrimack River, in 1771. In 1772 his parents moved to Windham, New Hampshire, northeast of the river, then on the west side to Dunbarton in 1774. In 1778 Joseph Sr.'s father, Asael Smith, purchased a 100-acre farm on the Merrimack River at Derryfield. It was here that Joseph Sr. grew up. Smith was about twenty when he moved with his family to Tunbridge, Vermont (see R. L. Anderson 1971b, 89-115).

3. The Smiths originally lived in Palmyra Village at the west end of Main Street, from about 1816 to 1819 (see III.J.8, POMEROY TUCKER ACCOUNT, 1867, 12; and III.L.1, PALMYRA [NY] ROAD LISTS, 1817-1822).

4. Footnote in the original reads: "Here the author remembers to have first seen the family, in the winter of '[18]19, '[18]20, in a rude log house, with but a small spot underbrushed around it." This was probably the Jennings cabin just north of the Palmyra/Manchester township line (see III.L.2, PALMYRA [NY] HIGHWAY SURVEY, 13 JUN 1820).

Manchester. The elder Smith had been a Universalist,[5] and subsequently a Methodist; was a good deal of a smatterer in Scriptural knowledge: but the seed of revelation was sown on weak ground; he was a great babbler, credulous, not especially industrious, a money digger, prone to the marvellous; and withal, a little given to difficulties with neighbors, and petty law-suits.[6] Not a very propitious account of the father of a Prophet,—the founder of a state; but there was a "woman in the case." However present, in matters of good or evil!—In the garden of Eden, in the siege of Troy, on the field of Orleans [France], in the dawning of the Reformation, in the Palace of St. Petersburgh, and Kremlin of Moscow, in England's history, and Spain's proudest era; and here upon this continent, in the persons of Ann Lee, Jemima Wilkinson, and as we are about to add, Mrs. Joseph Smith! A mother's influences; in the world's history, in the history of men, how distinct is the impress!—In heroes, in statesmen, in poets, in all of good or bad aspirations, or distinctions, that single men out from the mass, and give them notoriety; how often, almost invariably, are we led back to the influences of a mother, to find the germ that has sprouted in the offspring.

The reader will excuse this interruption of narrative, and be told that Mrs. Smith[7] was a woman of strong uncultivated intellect; artful and cunning; imbued with an illy regulated religious enthusiasm. The incipient hints, the first givings out that a Prophet was to spring from her humble household, came from her[8]; and when matters were maturing for denouement, she gave out that such and such ones—always fixing upon those who had both money and credulity—were to be instruments in some great work of new revelation. The old man was rather her faithful co-worker, or executive exponent. Their son, Alvah [Alvin], was originally intended, or designated, by fireside consultations, and solemn and mysterious out door hints, as the forth coming Prophet. The mother and the father said he was the chosen one; but Alvah, however spiritual he may have been, had a carnal appetite; ate too many green turnips, sickened and died.[9] Thus the world lost a Prophet, and

5. On Joseph Smith Sr.'s Universalism, see II.B.2, TUNBRIDGE (VT) UNIVERSALIST SOCIETY, 6 DEC 1797; and I.D.2, WILLIAM SMITH NOTES, CIRCA 1875, 28-29.

6. See, for example, III.L.19, NATHAN PIERCE DOCKET BOOK, 1830.

7. On Lucy Smith (1775-1856), see "Introduction to Lucy Smith Collection."

8. Compare III.J.37, WALLACE MINER REMINISCENCE, 1932.

9. Because Alvin's death occurred on 19 November 1823 after Turner's departure from the area, Turner must have learned this detail from subsequent visits to the area. Note that Turner neglects to mention Alvin's

Mormonism a leader; the designs impiously and wickedly attributed to Providence, defeated; and all in consequence of a surfeit of raw turnips. Who will talk of the cackling geese of Rome, or any other small and innocent causes of mighty events, after this? The mantle of the Prophet which Mrs. and Mr. Joseph Smith and one Oliver Cowdery,[10] had wove of themselves—every thread of it—fell upon their next eldest son, Joseph Smith, Jr.[11]

And a most unpromising recipient of such a trust, was this same Joseph Smith, Jr., afterwards, "Jo. Smith." He was lounging, idle; (not to say vicious,) and possessed of less than ordinary intellect. The author's own recollections of him are distinct ones. He used to come into the village of Palmyra with little jags of wood, from his backwoods home; sometimes patronizing a village grocery too freely; sometimes find an odd job to do about [p. 213] the store of Seymour Scovell[12]; and once a week he would stroll into the office of the old Palmyra Register, for his father's paper. How impious, in us young "dare *Devils*"[13] to once and a while blacken the face of the then meddling inquisitive lounger—but afterwards Prophet, with the old fashioned balls, when he used to put himself in the way of the working of the old fashioned Ramage press! The editor of the Cultivator, at Albany—esteemed as he may justly consider himself, for his subsequent enterprize and usefulness, may think of it, with contrition and repentance; that he once helped, thus to disfigure the face of a Prophet, and remotely, the founder of a State.

But Joseph had a little ambition; and some very laudable aspirations; the mother's intellect occasionally shone out in him feebly, especially when he used to help us solve some portentous questions of moral or political ethics, in our juvenile debating club, which we moved down to the old red

---

taking a lethal dose of calomel.

10. On Oliver Cowdery (1806-50), see "Introduction to Oliver Cowdery Collection."

11. This statement contains two errors. First, Oliver Cowdery had nothing to do with Joseph Jr.'s prophetic mantle since the latter had received revelations before the former's arrival. Second, Hyrum Smith was the next oldest son of the Smiths, and Joseph Jr. the third.

12. Seymour Scoville was a Palmyra merchant described as "a prominent and influential man" (see McIntosh 1877, 141; T. Cook 1930, 73; original Land Indenture, dated 25 April 1816, for Palmyra Lots 12 and 26, Palmyra King's Daughters Free Library, Palmyra, New York).

13. Footnote in original reads: "To soften the use of such an expression, the reader should be reminded that apprentices in printing offices have since the days of Faust and Gottenberg, been thus called, and sometimes it was not inappropriate."

school house on Durfee street, to get rid of the annoyance of critics that used to drop in upon us in the village[14]; and subsequently, after catching a spark of Methodism in the camp meeting, away down in the woods, on the Vienna road, he was a very passable exhorter in evening meetings.[15]

Legends of hidden treasure, had long designated Mormon Hill as the depository. Old Joseph had dug there, and young Joseph had not only heard his father and mother relate the marvelous tales of buried wealth, but had accompanied his father in the midnight delvings, and incantations of the spirits that guarded it.

If a buried revelation was to be exhumed, how natural was it that the Smith family, with their credulity, and their assumed presentiment that a Prophet was to come from their household, should be connected with it; and that Mormon Hill was the place where it would be found.

It is believed by those who were best acquainted with the Smith family, and most conversant with all the Gold Bible movements, that there is no foundation for the statement that their original manuscript was written by a Mr. Spaulding, of Ohio.[16] A supplement to the Gold Bible, "The Book of Commandments" in all probability, was written by [Sidney] Rigdon,[17] and he may have been aided by Spaulding's manuscripts; but the book itself is

---

14. Turner's reference to the "juvenile debating club" is confirmed by periodic newspaper notices to "the young people of the village of Palmyra and its vicinity" inviting attendance at "a debating school at the school house near Mr. [Benjamin] Billings'" (see *Western Farmer,* 23 January 1822; *Palmyra Herald,* 26 February 1823; see also R. L. Anderson 1969a, 379). But when the debating club began or was moved to the school house cannot be determined. Turner's use of "us" indicates that Smith was likely involved with the debating club before the former's departure from the area in 1822.

15. "Camp meeting" is "a technical term from that period, meaning extended preaching in a rural setting, ordinarily by several ministers of various ranks" (R. L. Anderson 1969a, 379). "Vienna road" refers to the road running between the villages of Palmyra and Vienna (now Phelps). The Methodists did not acquire their property in the woods on the Vienna Road until July 1821 (see Walters 1969a, 99). A Methodist "exhorter" followed the minister's sermon, reemphasizing its message and *exhorting* the people to follow its teaching. Joseph Smith could not have been a licensed exhorter since membership was a prerequisite. Turner likely refers to Smith's involvement with the Methodists during the 1824-25 revival in Palmyra. Regarding Smith's early interest in Methodism, see I.A.15, JOSEPH SMITH HISTORY, 1839, 2; and III.J.8, POMEROY TUCKER ACCOUNT, 1867, 18.

16. On the Spaulding theory, see Bush 1977.

17. On Sidney Rigdon (1793-1876), see introduction to I.A.13, SIDNEY RIGDON ACCOUNT, CIRCA 1836.

without doubt, a production of the Smith family, aided by Oliver Cowdery, who was a school teacher on Stafford street, an intimate of the Smith family, and identified with the whole matter. The production as all will conclude, who have read it, or even given it a cursory review, is not that of an educated man or woman. The bungling attempt to counterfeit the style of the Scriptures; the intermixture of modern phraseology; the ignorance of chronology and geography; its utter crudeness and baldness, as a whole, stamp its character, and clearly exhibits its vulgar origin. It is a strange medley of scriptures, romance, and bad composition.

The primitive designs of Mrs. Smith, her husband, Jo and Cowdery, was money-making; blended with which perhaps, was a desire for notoriety, to be obtained by a cheat and a fraud. The idea of being the founders of a new sect, was an after thought, in which they were aided by others. [p. 214]

The projectors of the humbug, being destitute of means for carrying out their plans, a victim was selected to obviate that difficulty. Martin Harris,[18] was a farmer of Palmyra, the owner of a good farm, and an honest worthy citizen; but especially given to religious enthusiasm, new creeds, the more extravagant the better; a monomaniac, in fact. Joseph Smith upon whom the mantle of prophecy had fallen after the sad fate of Alva [Alvin], began to make demonstrations. He informed Harris of the great discovery, and that it had been revealed to him, that he (Harris,) was a chosen instrument to aid in the great work of surprising the world with a new revelation. They had hit upon the right man. He mortgaged his fine farm to pay for printing the book,[19] assumed a grave, mysterious, and unearthly deportment, and made here and there among his acquaintances solemn annunciations of the great event that was transpiring. His version of the discovery, as communicated to him by the Prophet Joseph himself, is well remembered by several respectable citizens of Palmyra, to whom he made early disclosures. It was in substance, as follows:

The Prophet Joseph, was directed by an angel where to find, by excavation, at the place afterwards called Mormon Hill, the gold plates; and was compelled by the angel, much against his will, to be the interpreter of the sacred record they contained, and publish it to the world. That the plates contained a record of the ancient inhabitants of this country, "engraved by Mormon, the son of Nephi." That on the top of the box containing the

18. On Martin Harris (1783-1875), see "Introduction to Martin Harris Collection."

19. See III.L.14, MARTIN HARRIS MORTGAGE, 25 AUG 1829.

plates, "a pair of large spectacles were found, the stones or glass set in which were opaque to all but the Prophet," that "these belonged to Mormon, the engraver of the plates, and without them, the plates could not be read." Harris assumed, that himself and Cowdery were the chosen amanuenses, and that the Prophet Joseph, curtained from the world and them, with his spectacles, read from the gold plates what they committed to paper. Harris exhibited to an informant of the author, the manuscript title page. On it were drawn, rudely and bunglingly, concentric circles, between above and below which were characters, with little resemblance to letters; apparently a miserable imitation of hieroglpyphics, the writer may have somewhere seen.[20] To guard against profane curiosity, the Prophet had given out that no one but himself, not even his chosen co-operators, must be permitted to see them, on pain of instant death. Harris had never seen the plates, but the growing account of their massive richness excited other than spiritual hopes, and he upon one occasion, got a village silver-smith to help him estimate their value; taking as a basis, the Prophet's account of their dimensions. It was a blending of the spiritual and utilitarian, that threw a shadow of doubt upon Martin's sincerity. This, and some anticipations he indulged in, as to the profits that would arise from the sale of the Gold Bible, made it then, as it is now, a mooted question, whether he was altogether a dupe.

The wife of Harris was a rank infidel and heretic, touching the whole thing, and decidedly opposed to her husband's participation in it. With sacriligious hands, she seized over an hundred of the manuscript pages of the new revelation, and burned or secreted them.[21] It was agreed by the Smith family, Cowdery and Harris, not to transcribe these again, but to let so much of the new revelation drop out, as the "evil spirit would get up a story that the second translation did not agree with the first." A very ingenious method, surely, of guarding against the possibility that Mrs. Harris had preserved the [p. 215] manuscript with which they might be confronted, should they attempt an imitation of their own miserable patchwork.

The Prophet did not get his lesson well upon the start, or the household of impostors were in the fault. After he had told his story, in his absence, the rest of the family made a new version of it to one of their neighbors. They

---

20. Compare the description of Book of Mormon characters in V.D.2, CHARLES ANTHON TO E. D. HOWE, 17 FEB 1834; and V.D.3, CHARLES ANTHON TO THOMAS WINTHROP COIT, 3 APR 1841; see also V.E.2, BOOK OF MORMON CHARACTERS, DEC 1827-FEB 1828.

21. See discussion in introduction to III.L.16, BOOK OF MORMON PREFACE, 1829.

shewed him such a pebble as may any day be picked up on the shore of Lake Ontario—the common horn blend—carefully wrapped in cotton, and kept in a mysterious box. They said it was by looking at this stone, in a hat, the light excluded, that Joseph discovered the plates. This it will be observed, differs materially from Joseph's story of the angel. It was the same stone the Smiths' had used in money digging, and in some pretended discoveries of stolen property.

Long before the Gold Bible demonstration, the Smith family had with some sinister object in view, whispered another fraud in the ears of the credulous. They pretended that in digging for money, at Mormon Hill, they came across "a chest, three by two feet in size, covered with a dark colored stone. In the centre of the stone was a white spot about the size of a sixpence. Enlarging, the spot increased to the size of a twenty four pound shot and then exploded with a terrible noise. The chest vanished and all was utter darkness."

It may be safely presumed that in no other instance have Prophets and the chosen and designated of angels, been quite as calculating and worldly as were those of Stafford street, Mormon Hill, and Palmyra. The only business contract—veritable instrument in writing, that was ever executed by spiritual agents, has been preserved, and should be among the archives of the new state of Utah. It is signed by the Prophet Joseph himself, and witnessed by Oliver Cowdery, and secures to Martin Harris one half of the proceeds of the sale of the Gold Bible until he was fully reimbursed in the sum of $2,500, the cost of printing.[22]

The after thought that has been alluded to; the enlarging of original intentions; was at the suggestion of Sidney Rigdon, of Ohio, who made his appearance, and blended himself with the poorly devised scheme of imposture about the time the book was issued from the press. He unworthily bore the title of a Baptist elder, but had by some previous freak, if the author is rightly informed, forfeited his standing with that respectable religious denomination. Designing, ambitious, and dishonest, under the semblance of sanctity and assumed spirituality, he was just the man for the uses of the Smith household and their half dupe and half designing abettors; and they were just the fit instruments he desired. ... [p. 216] ...

Under the auspices of Rigdon, a new sect, the Mormons, was projected, prophecies fell thick and fast from the lips of Joseph; old Mrs. Smith assumed all the airs of the mother of a Prophet; that particular family of Smiths

---

22. See III.L.17, JOSEPH SMITH, SR., AND MARTIN HARRIS AGREEMENT, 16 JAN 1830.

were singled out and became exalted above all their legion of namesakes. The bald, clumsy cheat, found here and there an enthusiast, a monomaniac or a knave, in and around its primitive locality, to help it upon its start; and soon, like another scheme of imposture, (that had a little of dignity and plausibility in it,) it had its Hegira, or flight, to Kirtland; then to Nauvo[o]; then to a short resting place in Missouri—and then on over the Rocky Mountains to Utah, or the Salt Lake. ...

3.
Dr. Williams Account, 1854

Robert Richards [pseud.], *The Californian Crusoe; or, The Lost Treasure Found. A Tale of Mormonism* (London: John Henry Parker, 1854), 121-25.

EDITORIAL NOTE

Published under the pseudonym Robert Richards, *The Californian Crusoe* is a satirical account of the Mormons in Utah from the point of view of someone not well informed. The present excerpt is an interview between the author and a Dr. Williams, who was passing through Salt Lake City and claimed to have been a physician at Palmyra, New York, while the Smiths were there. Although there were several Williams families in Palmyra, Dr. Williams has yet to be identified. Concerning the circumstances of his interview with Williams, the author states:

> ... A party of travellers from the east, on their way to California, arrived among us in the middle of the summer, half-dead with fatigue and misery attendant on an overland journey from St. Louis of more than twelve hundred miles. They were evidently persons of education, and many of the Mormons did their best to shew them kindness and hospitality. One of their number, a Dr. Williams, became my guest, and remained with me for more than a month. When he was able to look around him, I shewed him something of the neighborhood. I took him to the new temple, then surrounded with scaffolding; I pointed out to him the situation of our most productive land; I gave him a bath in our hot sulphur springs; I led him down to the Salt Lake and its heavy waters glittering in the sun with saline crystals. By the help of a map lately executed by a Mormon surveyor, I indicated to him the situation of our settlements, already extending through above a hundred miles. I explained our political arrangements, and, in reply to his enquiries, made a few statements relative to our religion.
>
> The Doctor looked grave, and after a short silence proceeded to tell me that if I would not take it amiss, he had it in his power to give me some particulars as to the early origin of Mormonism, with which perhaps, as an Englishman, I was not altogether acquainted. I expressed an eager desire to hear him, and he proceeded as follows. ...

I am a native of Vermont, but more recently I [p. 121] have lived in the town of Palmyra, in the western part of New York, where, in fact, I commenced my practice as a physician. Here I accidentally became acquainted with Joseph Smith, your late prophet, and learned various particulars respecting his family; not because I was particularly interested in them, but from the accidental circumstance of their having emigrated, about the year 1815, from my own former neighbourhood in Vermont. At the time when I first met with them near Palmyra, they were living in wretched poverty, and, in fact, were hardly superior to common vagrants. The father, old Joseph Smith,[1] was an irreligious and drunken fellow, and the mother was little better than her husband. There were seven children; and when I first met with your prophet, in 1825, he was about twenty years of age, and notorious, like others of his family, as a *money-digger,* and withal as a drunken, lying, and dissipated young profligate. His father used to say that Joseph had power to look into the depths of the earth, and to discover where money was concealed, by means of a curious stone which had accidentally come into his possession. Many credulous persons hired him to make excavations, but I never heard that anything really valuable was ever discovered by him. Joseph, or Joe, as he was commonly called, managed very early to become a proficient in the art of imposing on simplicity, and cheating became to him, by practice, a kind of second nature. ... [p. 122]

...[2] In 1830, one [Egbert B.] Grandin,[3] a printer at Palmyra, with whom I was well acquainted, published the first edition of the Book of Mormon, purporting to be "By Joseph Smith, junior, Author and Proprietor." Five thousand copies were executed by Grandin, as he himself told me, for the sum of three thousand dollars. This money was supplied by one Martin Harris,[4] a [p. 123] farmer, who had acted as Smiths amanuensis, and on whose credulity as well as avarice the prophet had operated with effect.

In order to make the book sell, Joseph told a story similar to what you have doubtless heard him tell at Nauvoo, and which he concocted while preparing his manuscript for the press. He declared that an angel had directed him to dig in a hill, from which he disinterred a book of golden plates with inscriptions, which he was supernaturally enabled to translate into English.

1. On Joseph Smith, Sr. (1771-1840), see "Introduction to Joseph Smith, Sr., Collection."

2. Williams's rehearsal of the Spaulding theory has been deleted (see Bush 1977).

3. On Egbert B. Grandin (1806-45), see I.A.15, JOSEPH SMITH HISTORY, 1839, n. 77.

4. On Martin Harris (1783-1875), see "Introduction to Martin Harris Collection."

Two other persons, [Oliver] Cowdery[5] and [David] Whitmer,[6] were afterwards engaged in the scheme, who, together with Harris, actually signed a certificate, appended, as you know, to the Book of Mormon, in which they declared that an angel of God had descended from heaven, and laid before their eyes the golden plates with the mystic engravings.[7] Although Smith had originally declared that it was revealed to him, that only the above three persons were to behold the precious book, the certificates of eight others, to the same effect, were afterwards annexed. These supplementary eight were the prophet's unprincipled father, two of his brothers, Hyrum and Samuel, and four brothers of the Whitmer who signed the original certificate.[8] All of the eleven were deeply interested in the success of the imposture, and expected to make their fortune by it. Five of them, as you are probably aware, including Hyrum[9] and Samuel Smith,[10] have died in the profession of Mormonism; but all the rest, including even Martin [p. 124] Harris himself, have abandoned the sect, and become its avowed enemies.

On the 6th of April, 1830, the first Mormon congregation was founded at Manchester, not far from Palmyra.[11] It consisted at first of only six persons, viz. the prophet, his father, and his two brothers named above, Oliver Cowdery, and Joseph Knight.[12] These men began to propagate their religion, in the first instance, as a means of selling their book, making truth entirely subordinate to the love of gain. In Manchester and Palmyra, where their characters were only too well known, they found it impossible to gather any number of converts. But, by adopting a system of itinerancy, they had sold several hundred books, and made about eighty dupes, before the following

---

5. On Oliver Cowdery (1806-50), see "Introduction to Oliver Cowdery Collection."

6. On David Whitmer (1805-88), see "Introduction to David Whitmer Collection."

7. See VI.G.1, TESTIMONY OF THREE WITNESSES, JUN 1829.

8. See III.L.13, TESTIMONY OF EIGHT WITNESSES, JUN 1829.

9. On Hyrum Smith (1800-44), see I.A.15, JOSEPH SMITH HISTORY, 1839, n. 12.

10. On Samuel Harrison Smith (1808-44), see I.A.15, JOSEPH SMITH HISTORY, 1839, n. 13.

11. On the location of the church's organization, see I.A.15, JOSEPH SMITH HISTORY, 1839, n. 82.

12. This list is inaccurate (see discussion in introduction to IV.A.4, JOSEPH KNIGHT, JR., STATEMENT, 11 AUG 1862). On Joseph Knight, Sr. (1772-1847), who did not become a member until 28 June 1830, see introduction to IV.A.1, JOSEPH KNIGHT, SR., REMINISCENCE, CIRCA 1835-1847.

October. Smith's ideas expanded in proportion to his success, and he now appeared, not merely as a book-pedlar and a translator of a revelation, but as an inspired prophet himself. In your "Book of Doctrine and Covenants" you will find, that among his first revelations were those which command his disciples to build him a house, and "to provide him with food and raiment, and whatsoever he needeth [D&C 43:13]."

In the autumn of 1830, four of Smith's emissaries began to preach at Kirtland, in Ohio,[13] where they were openly joined by Elder [Sidney] Rigdon[14] and many of his flock, whom he had collected while a Baptist preacher. Rigdon was a much abler man than Joseph, and Mormonism, as you knew it in Nauvoo, began to take a definite shape. In January 1831, [p. 125] Smith and his family, with a number of proselytes, removed to Kirtland, which for some time was the centre of Mormon operations. ...

13. See III.L.22, MISSIONARIES COVENANT, 17 OCT 1830.

14. On Sidney Rigdon (1793-1876), see introduction to I.A.13, SIDNEY RIGDON ACCOUNT, CIRCA 1836.

4.
Manchester Resident Reminiscence, 8 August 1856

"Mormonism in Its Infancy," *Newark* (New Jersey) *Daily Advertiser,* Circa August 1856, Charles Woodward Scrapbook, New York Public Library, New York, New York (Woodward 1880, 1:125).

EDITORIAL NOTE

This newspaper clipping features an anonymously written letter from Manchester, New York. The letter, signed "Ashes," is dated 8 August, with the year "1856" written on the clipping. The writer, who obviously had before him Orsamus Turner's 1851 account (compare III.J.2, ORSAMUS TURNER ACCOUNT, 1851), claimed that the information had been "related to me by an old gentleman who was cognizant of the whole affair, being a neighbor to them." While Turner had died in 1855, one might speculate that the writer had previously spoken with Turner about Mormonism but referred to his book to reconstruct their conversation. Otherwise it is a fictional account.

MANCHESTER, ONTARIO CO., N.Y.,
AUG. 8. [1856?]

It is not generally known that this country was the birth-place of Mormonism, and the starting point of those God forsaken doctrines, which have since spread themselves over Christendom, carrying desolation to thousands of happy families, destroying the pleasure of social circles, and putting out the light on many a hearthstone: for what reason this beautiful section of Western New York was cursed with this foul stigma, its inhabitants are totally unaware; and to their credit be it said, that the prophet had no honor in his own country, but was compelled, with very few exceptions, to go from home to find his followers. Having been quite interested in the history of the SMITH FAMILY, and the finding of the Gold Bible, as related to me by an old gentleman who was cognizant of the whole affair, being a neighbor to them. I have written out a few of the principal points.

Joseph Smith, father of the Prophet, came from Merrimac River, N.H., and first settled in Palmyra, but in 1819 removed to this place. He was a Methodist; but had formerly been a Universalist, and was quite an adept at

Scriptural arguments. Credulity seems to have been a pretty large ingredient in his composition, as he was a great digger, always seeing "sights;" but never realizing his expectations, he was noted for his indolence, and for generally being in some difficulty with his neighbors. Joe's mother was a far different person from his father: she is described as a woman of strong uncultivated intellect, artful and cunning, and strongly imbued with an illy regulated religious enthusiasm, and much given to vague visions of riches and greatness. As is usually the case, she had much more to do with forming the character of the son than his father, though he had more of the atrocities of the latter, so far as his habits were concerned. Mrs. Smith seems to have been the head and front of the movement; she it was who first gave vague hints that a prophet was to arise from her humble household, and as arrangements progressed towards a consummation, she named those who had been fixed upon as instruments to assist them in getting out the new revelations—always selecting men who were noted for their credulity. In these affairs her husband assisted, and was her executive officer.

ALVAH [Alvin], the eldest son, was originally intended for the prophet, but alas for all human designs, "the spirit was willing, but the flesh was weak;" and one day, ALVAH being rather hungry, he indulged too freely in raw turnips, sickened and died; so the incipient prophet was lost to the world and to Mormonism. Joe Smith thereby became a great man, for it was immediately given out that the mantle of Alvah [Alvin] had fallen upon him, unworthy though he was—for rumor says he was as lazy as his father, rather intemperate in his habits, and possessed of less than ordinary intellect. He had previously professed religion at a camp meeting, and was quite an exhorter at evening meetings; but this did not last long. "Mormon Hill" had been long designated "as the place in which countless treasures were buried;" Joseph, the elder, had "spaded" up many a foot of the hill side to find them, and Joseph Jr., had on more than one occasion accompanied him. Taking all these circumstances together, how perfectly natural was it for the Smith family to be selected as the means of finding, and Mormon Hill as the repository of the long buried revelation, known as the "*Gold Bible.*"

It has been generally believed that this celebrated book was written by Mr. Spaulding, of Ohio, but for this belief there is no foundation; the original production undoubtedly emanated jointly from the Smith family, and a schoolmaster of this village by the name of OLIVER COWDERY, who was intimately connected with the Smiths in all their movements. Any one by observation can be convinced that the author must have been uneducated, and totally ignorant of Geography and Chronology. An imitation of the style of the Scripture is attempted, but the expression, "and it came to pass," is about the only approach to it. Modern sayings are curiously interspersed with ancient language, and taking it altogether, no one can doubt its vulgar origin.

The original design of the movers was undoubtedly to make money and to gain a certain notoriety, of which, as we have said, Mrs. Smith had often had visions, and they had no idea at this time of founding a sect. Joe Smith has himself said as much. As soon as the Bible had been discovered Joe commenced to prophesy and to name individuals who were, as he said, called of God, as chosen instruments to assist him in the translating, &c., of the revelation. The most noted of their assistants was MARTIN HARRIS, a respectable and honest farmer residing at Palmyra—much given to new creeds, and a monomaniac upon the subject of "spiritual manifestations." He mortgaged his farm to pay for the printing of the Gold Bible, but a contract signed by JOSEPH, and witnessed by COWDERY, secure to Harris and his heirs one half the proceeds of the sale of the Gold Bible, until he was reimbursed in the sum of $2500—the cost of printing. This, together with the fact that Harris had procured the services of a village jeweler to help him estimate the value of the plates, taking as a basis Joe Smith's description, leaves us in doubt as to whether he was altogether a dupe.

The Prophet's account of finding these plates was—that an angel appeared, and directed him where to dig; he was then compelled, against his will, to interpret them, and promulgate their contents to the world; that on the plates were the names of the ancient residents in this country, "engraved by Mormon the son of Nephi;" that in the box containing them was "a large pair of spectacles, the stone or glass set in them being opaque to all but the prophet;" that "these belonged to Mormon the engraver, and that the plates could not be read without them." Harris was the principal amanuensis, and having nearly a hundred pages of the manuscript translation in his house, his wife, who was an unbeliever, seized them, and either burned or secreted them—it was supposed the former—but for fear that she should confront them with the lost documents at some future day, the Smiths, Cowdery and Harris, agreed not to translate these again, but to let so much of the new revelation drop out, lest "the evil spirit should get up a story that the second translation did not agree with the first." ...

Yours,

ASHES.

5.
Pomeroy Tucker Reminiscence, 1858

1. "Mormonism and Joe Smith. The Book of Mormon or Golden Bible," *Wayne Democratic Press* (Lyons, New York) 3 (26 May 1858). Reprinted in *Troy Times,* 27 May 1858; *Albany Evening Journal,* 29 May 1858; *Palmyra Courier,* 11 June 1858; and *New York Herald,* 2 July 1858 (see also clipping in Woodward 1880, 1:265).

2. "The Mormon Imposture—The Mormon Aborigines," *Wayne Democratic Press* (Lyons, New York) 3 (2 June 1858): 2.

EDITORIAL NOTE

Pomeroy Tucker (1802-70) was born at Palmyra, New York. He began his printing apprenticeship under Timothy C. Strong of the *Palmyra Register* about 1820 (Turner 1851, 499). In the fall of 1823, Tucker and Egbert B. Grandin purchased Strong's press and began publishing the *Wayne Sentinel.* For the next thirty years, Tucker helped publish this paper. During the printing of the Book of Mormon, Tucker often read proofs of the text. He served in various civic positions, including one term in the state legislature and as post master of Palmyra (1839-41). He was an early member of Palmyra's Mount Moriah Masonic Lodge (see III.L.9, PALMYRA [NY] MASONIC RECORDS, 1827-1828). In 1867 Tucker published a book-length history of Mormonism, which included some reminiscences of his own about Mormon origins (see III.J.8, POMEROY TUCKER ACCOUNT, 1867). Tucker died at Palmyra (Pattengill 1870, 4-9; McIntosh 1877, 43; T. Cook 1930, 283, 306).

Both the *Palmyra Courier* and *Troy Times* identify the author of the first article reprinted below as Pomeroy Tucker. The occasion of Tucker's writing is explained by the *Courier:* "A question having arose between the Albany Journal and Troy Times, as regards the place where the Mormon Bible was printed, Mr. POMEROY TUCKER, of this village, furnished the Wayne Democratic Press, with the following facts. ..." In his response, Tucker joined the *Troy Times* in correcting Thurlow Weed, editor of the *Albany Evening Journal,* who claimed that Elihu F. Marshall of Rochester, New York, had published the Book of Mormon (cf. III.K.17, THURLOW WEED REMINISCENCES, 1854, 1858, 1880 & 1884).

"Hill Cumorah," a view of its northern summit, 1920. Used by permission, Utah State Historical Society, all rights reserved.

Tucker's second article continues the subject of Mormon origins in the Palmyra/Manchester area. This article was evidently expanded and incorporated in Tucker's 1867 book (cf. III.J.8, POMEROY TUCKER ACCOUNT, 1867). Both articles first appeared in the *Wayne Democratic Press,* which was edited by William Van Camp at Lyons, New York.

[*1. 26 May 1858*]

The story of the printing of the first edition of the "Book of Mormon" is truthfully as follows: Joe Smith, the pretended Prophet and finder of the original "metallic records"—Oliver Cowdery,[1] amanuensis of Smith—and Martin Harris,[2] the "chosen" dupe for the payment of expenses—constituting, as they claimed, the "inspired" nucleus of the dawning "Church of Latter Day Saints"—applied about the month of June, 1829,[3] to Mr. Egbert B. Grandin,[4] the then publisher of the Wayne Sentinel newspaper and a job printer at Palmyra, for the printing of the book referred to, commonly called the "Golden Bible." Harris, who was a forehanded farmer at that town—an honest and respected citizen, but noted for his superstitious and fanatical peculiarities in religious matters—was the only man of the party whose pecuniary responsibility was worth a dollar; and he offered to give security by a mortgage upon his unincumbered farm for the cost of the printing and binding of the book. Grandin at once advised them against the supposed folly of the enterprise, and with the aid of other neighbors and friends of Harris sought to influence the latter to desist and withdraw his countenance from the imposture. All importunity of this kind, however, was resisted with determination by Harris, (who no doubt firmly believed in the genuineness of Smith's pretensions,) and resented with assumed pious indignation by Smith. Cowdery took but little part in the conversations. After repeated interviews and much parleying on the subject, Grandin was understood to refuse to give it further consideration. Harris, it was thought, became for a time somewhat staggered in his confidence, but Joe could do nothing in the

1. On Oliver Cowdery (1806-50), see "Introduction to Oliver Cowdery Collection."

2. On Martin Harris (1783-1875), see "Introduction to Martin Harris Collection."

3. Compare III.H.10, JOHN H. GILBERT MEMORANDUM, 8 SEP 1892, 1; see also I.A.15, JOSEPH SMITH HISTORY, 1839, 34; and I.B.5, LUCY SMITH HISTORY, 1845, MS:102-4.

4. On Egbert B. Grandin (1806-45), see I.A.15, JOSEPH SMITH HISTORY, 1839, n. 77.

matter of printing without his aid, and so he persevered in his seductive arts, as will be seen with ultimate success.

About this time, in the fore part of the year 1829, (as recollected,) the same party, or a portion of them applied to Mr. [Thurlow] Weed,[5] of the Anti-Masonic Inquirer at Rochester, (who by the way, seems in his reminiscence to have confused Mormonism with Anti-Masonry,) and there met a similar repulse, as stated by the Journal. Mr. [Elihu F.] Marshall,[6] of Spelling Book notoriety, who was also engaged in the printing and publishing business at Rochester, gave his terms to Smith and his associates for the execution of their work, and his proffered acceptance of the proposed mode of security.

The "Saints" then returned and renewed their request to Mr. Grandin, assuring him that the printing was to be done at any rate, and explaining that they would be saved much inconvenience and cost of travel, (as the manuscripts were to be delivered and the proof sheets examined daily at the printing office,) by having their work done at Palmyra, where they resided. It was upon this state of facts and view of the case, that Mr. Grandin, after some further hesitation, reconsidered his policy of refusal, and finally entered into a contract for the desired printing and binding of 5,000 copies of the book, for the price of $3,000, to be secured by mortgage as proposed[7]; which contract was faithfully performed on his part, completing the work in the summer of 1830, and as faithfully fulfilled in the payment by Harris. Major Gilbert,[8] as stated by the Troy Times, took the foremanship of the printing, and did most of the press and composition work of the job. He still retains an original copy of the book in sheets as he laid them off in a file from the

5. On Thurlow Weed (1797-1882), see introduction to III.K.17, THURLOW WEED REMINISCENCES, 1854, 1858, 1880 & 1884.

6. Elihu F. Marshall, in his forties, is listed in the 1840 census of Rochester, Monroe County, New York (1840:312). He married Mary May in Rochester on 1 September 1827 (*Wayne Sentinel,* 14 September 1827). He was a Quaker and evidently associated with Peter Harris, Martin Harris's brother-in-law (W. F. Peck 1884, 261). Marshall was a bookseller and publisher of the *Rochester Album* (see *Rochester City Directory,* 1827). He was also well-known for his spelling book, which he first published in Bellows Falls, New York, in 1819, and subsequently in Rochester. Joseph Smith and Martin Harris may have been familiar with Marshall's 1829 edition: *Marshall's Spelling Book of the English Language; or, The Teacher's Assistant* (1st rev. ed.; Rochester, New York: Marshall, Dean & Co., 1829), which was advertised in the *Wayne Sentinel* (15 May 1829).

7. See III.L.14, MARTIN HARRIS MORTGAGE, 25 AUG 1829.

8. On John H. Gilbert (1802-95), see "Introduction to John H. Gilbert Collection."

press in working. The manuscripts, in Cowdery's handwriting, were carried to the printing office in daily instalments, generally by Joe or his trusty brother Hiram, and were regularly withdrawn for security and preservation at evening.[9] The pretension was that they were written out by the amanuensis Cowdery from translations verbally given by the Prophet Joe, who alone was enabled to read the hieroglyphics of the sacred plates by means of a wonderful stone and magic spectacles that were found in the earth with the "records." In the performance of this task the "chosen" decypherer was always concealed in a dark room, and by special revelation neither Cowdery or other persons than the said "chosen" was permitted to see the plates on penalty of instant death. Such was the pretension. The hand press which did the printing (Smith's patent) has been in continual use [*in the* Sentinel *office*][10] since that important era in the rise of Mormonism, and in the course of changes of ownership and partizan apostacy, it has finally in its degeneracy (quite appropriately) now come to be used for the printing of a *Know Nothing* newspaper!

A word in regard to the origin of Mormonism, whose advent has furnished so marked an illustration of the susceptibilities of human credulity even at the present age of boasted enlightenment, may not be without interest in this connection, now after the lapse of some thirty years. As early as 1820, Joe Smith, at the age of about 19 years, began to assume the gift of supernatural endowments, and became the leader of a small party of shiftless men and boys like himself who engaged in nocturnal money-digging operations upon the hills in and about Palmyra.[11] These labors were always performed in the night, and during their continuance, many marvellous accounts and rumors in regard to them were put afloat in the neighborhood. Joe professed from time to time to have "almost" secured the hidden treasure, which, however, just at the instant of attempting to grasp it, would vanish by the breaking of the spell of his magic power.—Numbers of men and women, as was understood, were found credulous enough to believe "there might be something in it," who were induced by their confidence and cupidity to contribute privately towards the cost, of carrying on the impos-

9. See III.H.10, JOHN H. GILBERT MEMORANDUM, 8 SEP 1892, 2.

10. Bracketed material in original.

11. Smith was fourteen in 1820, not nineteen (compare III.J.8, POMEROY TUCKER ACCOUNT, 1867, 19, 21-22, 26). Other testimony indicates that the Smiths were involved in treasure seeking in 1820, but not necessarily as leaders (see, e.g., III.A.14, WILLARD CHASE STATEMENT, CIRCA 11 DEC 1833, 240).

ture, under the promise of sharing in the expected gains; and in this way the loaferly but cunning Smith, who was too lazy to work for his living, (his deluded followers did all the digging,) was enabled to obtain a scanty subsistence for himself without pursuing any useful employment.

The silly imposture was persevered in by Smith, and the digging performances occasionally continued by his gang without success, for some eight or ten years, when in 1828 or '29 the climax was reached in the discovery of the wonderful golden record in hieroglyphics, of great antiquity, "written by the hand of Mormon upon plates taken from the plates of Nephi," the translation ndd [and] publication of which are the foundation of Brigham Young's polygamous empire at Salt Lake, were, according to the published testimony of Joe Smith, "found in the township of Manchester, Ontario county, New York." ...[12]

[*2. 2 June 1858*]

It is believed there has never been published a particular and connected biography or description of the chief founders of the "Church of Latter-Day Saints," or as they may be fitly denominated, the Aborigenes of Mormonism. ... It is presumed, therefore, that as a supplement to the reminiscential sketch given in last week's "Press," the following additional recollections on the subject may possess a compensating interest in meeting public curiosity.

JOSEPH SMITH senior,[13] with a family consisting of a wife and eight children, including *Joe the Prophet* (as foreordained to be,) settled upon a lot of mostly uncultivated land located on the northern border of the town of Manchester, about two miles south of Palmyra village, (on what is called Stafford Street,) in the year 1817 or '18.[14] They removed there from the suburbs of said village, where they had resided since 1815, having then emigrated to that place from Vermont. The title of the lot was in non-resident minor heirs, uncared for by any local attorney or agent, and Smith took possession of it only as a "squatter sovereign;" though subsequently he purchased it by contract, paying little or nothing

12. Tucker's brief discussion of the Spaulding theory, wherein he argues that the "pretended translations of Smith were no doubt transcripts from the Spaulding romance as altered for the occasion by Rigdon," is here deleted (see Bush 1977).

13. On Joseph Smith, Sr. (1771-1840), see "Introduction to Joseph Smith, Sr., Collection."

14. In his 1867 version, Tucker settled on the year 1818 (see III.J.8, POMEROY TUCKER ACCOUNT, 1867, 12).

thereon.[15] The same premises are now embraced in the well cultivated farm owned and occupied by Morgan Robinson.[16] Smith's children, in the order of their ages, were Hyrum, (so spelled by his father,) Alvin, Samuel H., Sophronia, *Joseph junior,* William, Catharine and Carlos. They lived there for a number of years, in a small, smoky log hut, of their own construction, which was divided into two rooms, with a garret. The age of the junior Joe at that time was about 17 or 18, though he did not know his own age, nor did any of the family remember it precisely. From the oldest to the youngest, they were an illiterate, shiftless, indolent tribe, without any visible means of a respectable livelihood, nor was it apparent that they *earned* an honest living—young Joe being the laziest of the crew. It was for this reason, in part perhaps, and also because of divers petty thefts from time to time occurring in the neighborhood, that they were so far under suspicion, (may be undeservedly,) as to suggest to the inhabitants the observance of especial vigilance in the care of their sheep yards, smoke houses, pork barrels, &c. The senior Smith and his elder boys (Joe genererally [generally] excepted) did some work upon the land which they occupied, in a slovenly, half-way manner, producing small crops or corn, "taters and garding sass," which, added to limited operations in raising pigs and poultry, with the making of maple sugar in the spring season, contributed towards their necessary subsistence. Old Joe also gathered and sold "rutes and yarbs"—occasionally exchanged a load of wood in the village for tobacco, whiskey, or other notions of trade—and on training and anniversary days, pocketed a few shillings from the peddling of gingerbread, boiled eggs, and root bear. The boys, who were frequently seen lounging about the stores and shops in the village, were distinguished only for their vagabondish appearance and loaferly habits. The female portion of the household were pretty much ditto. The money digging humbug, soon afterwards introduced, of which the junior Joe was the reputed inventor, was participated in more or less by all the male members of the family.

Such were the character and circumstances of the Smith generation, when young Joe's money-digging experiment commenced, which after a few years' continuance grew to the magnitude of his miraculously discovered

15. Compare III.J.8, POMEROY TUCKER ACCOUNT, 1867, 13.

16. In his 1867 version, Tucker updated this statement to read: "the well-organized farm of Mr. Seth T. Chapman" (see III.J.8, POMEROY TUCKER ACCOUNT, 1867, 13). Morgan Robinson purchased the land on 30 March 1855 and sold it to Absalom Weeks on 2 May 1859, who sold it to Seth T. Chapman on 2 April 1860 (see Porter 1971, 357-58).

golden "plates of Nephi" hidden in the earth by the hand of Mormon the Israelite, resulting in the wonderful revelation and publication of the Mormon Bible. ...

JOE SMITH junior, who became the world-renowned translator of the recovered Israelitish records or scriptures—the publisher of the new revelation, in the Book of Mormon or Golden Bible, and founder of the politico-religious institution of Mormonism—was, at the period referred to, a dull-eyed, flaxen-haired, ragged boy. He was of taciturn habits—seldom speaking unless first spoken to while out among folks—but apparently a thinking, calculating, mischief-brewing genius, whose whole secretive mind seemed devoted to some mysterious scheme or marvellous invention. In his mental composition, the organ of "conscientiousness" might have been marked by phrenologists as *not there.* His word, by reason of his propensity for exaggeration, was never received with confidence by any body who knew him, (excepting of course his bigotted dupes.) He was proverbially considered by his neighbor co[n]temporaries "the meanest boy" of the family. Subsequent developments and results, however, have demonstrated that he knew "some things as well as others," and that the hopping capacity of a toad cannot be estimated by the length of its tail.

A single instance of the many anecdotes remembered, in connection with Joe's magic pretensions and undertakings, will sufficiently illustrate his unprincipled cunning, and the strange infatuation of his dupes.—Assuming his accustomed air of mystery, on one occasion, he pretended to know exactly where the sought-for iron chest of gold was deposited in the earth; and in order to secure the glittering prize, means must be contributed to pay for digging, and a black sheep would also be required for a sacrifice before engaging in the labors of the necromantic enterprise. Joe knew that his neighbor S[tafford].,[17] one of his interested listeners—a respectable farmer in good circumstances, now living—had a fine fat black wether, and that meat was scarce at home. So it was agreed that the farmer should give the noble wether as his share of the contribution; while others were to contribute their labor, with a small sum of money. At the approach of the appointed hour at night, the digging gang having been rallied and the black sheep provided, Joe led his party with a lanthern [lantern] to the enchanted spot upon a hill near his residence, where he described [inscribed?] a circle upon the ground,

17. Tucker later specifically identified William Stafford as the person who provided the black sheep (see III.J.8, POMEROY TUCKER ACCOUNT, 1867, 24-25; cf. III.A.13, WILLIAM STAFFORD STATEMENT, 8 DEC 1833, 239).

within which the sacrifice was to be performed, and the prize exhumed. Not a word was to be spoken during the entire performance. Such was the programme. All things being ready, the throat of the animal was cut as previously arranged, (the carcass withdrawn and reduced to mutton by the Smiths,) and the excavation entered upon in good earnest by the expectant diggers. For some three hours the work was continued in utter silence—when, "tempted by the devil," one of the party *spoke!* The spell was broken—and the precious treasure, which was just within reach, vanished!

OLIVER COWDERY, the scribe or amanuensis employed by the *Prophet* in the translation of the "sacred records," was an unpretending young man, of supposed fair character, who had done some service as a country schoolmaster. He could write a legible hand, such as might be read by the printers, by carefully dotting his i's and crossing his t's—an accomplishment not possessed by any of the Smiths; but such spelling, punctuation, capitalizing and paragraphizing as his manuscripts exhibited, awfully multiplied the perplexities of the type-setters. He is believed to have been a native of Palmyra, as his father's family resided there as early as 1810.[18] His present whereabouts or destiny (unknown to the writer hereof) may not involve a question of any moment, as his Mormon career was never distinguished beyond his first connection with the speculation as already explained.

SIDNEY RIGDON[19] who furnished the literary contributions, and MARTIN HARRIS who supplied the fiscal means for carrying forward the imposture, were indispensable spokes in the great driving wheel of the Mormon car. The former had been a clergyman of the Baptist persuasion in Pennsylvania—had fallen from grace and been deposed from his clerical estate—and he "understood the ropes" to be used in the infamous scheme of deception. He was the first "messenger appointed of God," (as he styled himself,) to proclaim the Mormon revelation, and preached his first sermon as such to a general public audience, in the room of the Palmyra Young Men's Association, in the third story of "Exchange Row," in that village. This was in the winter of 1830-'31, soon after the Mormon book was printed. The several churches had been applied to for the desecration of their pulpits,

18. This statement is inaccurate. Oliver Cowdery's father, William, moved to Williamson, Ontario County, New York, in 1810 (see II.A.2, BARNES FRISBIE ACCOUNT, 1867, n. 8). However, the whereabouts of Oliver Cowdery between the years 1810 and 1828, when he began teaching school in Manchester, New York, is uncertain (see "Introduction to Oliver Cowdery Collection").

19. On Sidney Rigdon (1793-1876), see introduction to I.A.13, SIDNEY RIGDON ACCOUNT, CIRCA 1836.

but were very properly refused. It was especially by the importunity of Harris, whose sincerity was unquestioned, that the use of the Association's room was granted. Holding the Book of Mormon in his right hand, and the Holy Bible in his left, the hardened impostor solemnly declared that both were equally true as the word of God—that they were inseparably necessary to complete the everlasting gospel—and that he himself was the called minister of Heaven to proclaim the new revelation for the salvation of sinful man! The discourse was a disgustingly blasphemous tirade, though evincing some talent and ingenuity in the speaker, and was received with such manifestations of disfavor that a repetition of the performance was never attempted there.[20]

Up to this time, Rigdon had played his part behind the curtain. The policy seems to have been to keep him in concealment until all things were ready for the blowing of the Mormon trumpet. An unexpected birth occurring in the Smith family, where Rigdon had been a frequent *incog[nito].* visitor for a year or so, was said to have been accounted for only as a miracle![21]

MARTIN HARRIS was the son of Nathan Harris,[22] now deceased, an early settler in Palmyra, and was universally esteemed as an honest man. He was a prosperous farmer, possessing a benevolent disposition, and good judgment in ordinary business affairs. His mind was overbalanced by "marvellousness," and was very much exercised on the subject of religion; and his betrayal of vague superstitions, with a belief in "special providences," and in the terrest[r]ial visits of angels, ghosts, &c., brought upon him the imputation of being "crazy." He was possessed of a sort of Bible monomania, and could probably repeat from memory every line of the scriptures, quoting chapter and verse in each instance. His family consisted of a wife, (from whom he was separated by mutual arrangement on account of her persistent unbelief in Mormonism,) and one son and two daughters. The farm mort-

---

20. Regarding Rigdon's December 1830 sermon in Palmyra, see also III.J.8, POMEROY TUCKER ACCOUNT, 1867, 75-76; III.B.12, LORENZO SAUNDERS INTERVIEW, 17 SEP 1884, 9; and III.B.14, LORENZO SAUNDERS INTERVIEW, 20 SEP 1884, 5.

21. This alludes to the claim that Katharine Smith was pregnant by Rigdon at the time the Smith family moved from New York to Ohio in the spring of 1831 (compare III.J.5, POMEROY TUCKER REMINISCENCE, 1858; see also III.B.12, LORENZO SAUNDERS INTERVIEW, 17 SEP 1884, 1; III.B.15, LORENZO SAUNDERS INTERVIEW, 12 NOV 1884, 21; and III.D.3, CHRISTOPHER M. STAFFORD STATEMENT, 23 MAR 1885).

22. On Nathan Harris (1758-1835), see I.A.15, JOSEPH SMITH HISTORY, 1839, n. 50.

gaged and sacrificed by him in the printing speculation is the same now owned and occupied by William Chapman,[23] about a mile and a half north of Palmyra village.—He long since abandoned Joe Smith and the Mormons, though he bigotedly adheres to *Mormonism,* and obstinately refuses to acknowledge his deception in the Bogus Bible. His present residence is in some part of Ohio, and his condition that of extreme poverty.

Old Joe Smith, with his family, including the Prophet Joe (under whose spiritual direction the profanity was perpetrated,) were baptized by Rigdon, in the immersion form, into the Mormon "Church of Latter Day Saints," about the date last mentioned. And so also were Harris, Cowdery, the Whitmers, and a number of other fanatical followers.[24]—By "special revelation," the senior Joe was ordained the first Patriarch and President of the Church[25]; and by like authority he was appointed to sell the Mormon Bible at a fixed price, and appropriate a certain percentage of the proceeds to his own use. This was a changed revelation, for in the first instance the "command from above" was that Harris alone should be permitted to sell and receive money for the book until he should be reimbursed the cost of printing.[26]

The exodus of the Smith family, first to some part of Pennsylvania—preparatory to taking possession of the "Promise[d] Land" at Kirtland, Ohio—occurred in 1831 or '32.[27]—The Prophet went first, with Cowdery and a few other followers, and married a wife in Pennsylvania—Rigdon having been instrumental in the match-making of this affair, and was the officiating "clergyman" at its celebration.[28] ...

---

23. William Chapman, a native of England, became owner of Martin Harris's farm in the 1840s (T. Cook 1930, 195, 207). Chapman, age fifty-five, is listed in the 1860 census of Palmyra, Wayne County, New York (1860:858).

24. These assertions are of course incorrect, Rigdon having come to New York after the organization of the church.

25. This did not occur until after the church had been established in Ohio (see "Introduction to Joseph Smith, Sr., Collection").

26. See III.L.17, JOSEPH SMITH, SR., AND MARTIN HARRIS AGREEMENT, 17 JAN 1830.

27. Joseph Smith left Fayette, New York, for Kirtland, Ohio, in late January 1831.

28. For Emma Smith's denial that Rigdon had officiated at her and Joseph's 18 January 1827 wedding, see I.F.3, EMMA SMITH BIDAMON INTERVIEW WITH JOSEPH SMITH III, FEB 1879.

6.
Ezra Thayre Reminiscence, 1862

"Testimony of Brother E[zra]. Thayre," *Saints' Herald* 3 (October 1862): 79-80, 82-84.

EDITORIAL NOTE

Ezra Thayre (or Thayer) (1791-18??) was born in Randolph, Vermont. In 1810 he married Polly Wales. By 1820 Thayre located about three and a half miles outside of Canandaigua, New York, where he earned a living by building bridges, dams, and mills. He was baptized by Parley P. Pratt, perhaps on 10 October 1830 (see note 7 below), ordained an elder by June 1831, and ordained a high priest on 3 June 1831. He did not gather with the Mormons to Utah, but was baptized by William W. Blair into the Reorganized Church of Jesus Christ of Latter Day Saints in Galien, Michigan, on 29 August 1860 (Cannon and Cook 1983, 292; L. Cook 1981, 47-48; Jessee 1989, 518-19; William W. Blair, Journal, 29 August 1860, RLDS Church Library-Archives, Independence, Missouri). Concerning Thayre's baptism into the RLDS church, William W. Blair noted in his Memoirs:

> He had been wandering for many years without church associations, but upon attending our meetings he at once recognized the voice of the good Shepherd and readily united with the church. From him we learned much in regard to Joseph the Seer, his early life and his father's family. Brother Thayre had been a bridge, dam, and mill builder in that section of country where Joseph and his father's family resided in his boyhood, and Father Smith and his sons, including Joseph, had been in Brother Thayre's employ. He told me that, though in humble circumstances in life, the Smith family was an upright and worthy one.
>
> He further said that when Joseph, after translating the Book of Mormon, returned into his region of country with Father Smith, Hyrum Smith, and Oliver Cowdery, he (Brother Thayre) was persuaded by his brother residing in Auburn, New York, to go and hear them set forth their religious views in a meeting near his residence on a Sunday. He said that on reaching the double log house where the meeting was held, he pressed his way through the congregation and took his seat immediately in front of these new preachers, listened to broken remarks by the three others, and then Joseph, taking the Book of Mormon in his hand, proceeded, in his un-

learned manner, to tell the history of its coming forth, and explained how he received the golden plates at the hands of the angel, how he translated the book by the gift of God, with other marvelous matters connected with its coming forth; and he said that immediately upon Joseph's beginning these statements, a new and heavenly power fell upon him, filling his entire being with unspeakable assurance of the truth of the statements, melting him to tears. When Joseph concluded his recital, he said he eagerly stretched forth his hand and said, "Let me have that book." It was handed to him and Brother Thayre kept it, esteeming it a heavenly treasure indeed. He said that afterward he aided them at different times, when he could, in spreading the knowledge of the work to others, but that his family became prejudiced, and they opposed him bitterly (Blair 1908, 39-40; cf. *Saints' Herald* 37 [12 July 1890]: 461).

Perhaps at Blair's instigation, Thayre prepared an account of his early experiences, which was published in the *Saints' Herald* in October 1862. Differing slightly from Blair's remembered account, Thayre's 1862 reminiscence is of course the authoritative version.

... I did not hear much about the Book of Mormon until Joseph Smith was getting it printed, and then my men which were at work on my building brought false stories to me, and I was filled with wrath about it. I said I would let a pair of horses go to take him to prison. I said it is blasphemy. I took a hoe and went into the field. As soon as I commenced I was struck as with a rushing wind, which almost frightened me to death. When I was a little recovered, I started for the house. I got to talking with these men and became more wrathy than ever. I went back again, and was frightened double what I was before. When I recovered I started again for the house and ran.

When they commenced preaching, a messenger came to tell me that my mother was dying. I had a half brother living with me and a nephew, and they took my horses and went to meeting, to hear Hyrum [Smith][1] preach while I was gone. When I came back they told me that they had been to hear him preach on the Golden Bible. I did not like it, and I told them that they must not take my horses again to hear those blasphemous wretches preach. My half brother said that Hyrum said that Joseph had seen an angel. My nephew [p. 79] said that there was something in it, and that I had better go and hear him. About that time I had another brother about 40 miles off. He

1. On Hyrum Smith (1800-1844), see I.A.15, JOSEPH SMITH HISTORY, 1839, n. 12.

came down and wanted me to go for he wanted to go himself.—The next Sunday[2] I went and there was a large concourse of people around his [Hyrum's] father's house, so that they extended to the road, filling up the large lot. I rushed in and got close to the stand, so as to be particular to hear what was said.

When Hyrum began to speak, every word touched me to the inmost soul. I thought every word was pointed to me. God punished me and riveted me to the spot. I could not help myself. The tears rolled down my cheeks, I was very proud and stubborn. There were many there who knew me, I dare not look up. I sat until I recovered myself before I dare look up. They sung some hymns and that filled me with the Spirit. When Hyrum got through, he picked up a book and said, "here is the Book of Mormon." I said, let me see it. I then opened the book, and I received a shock with such exquisite joy that no pen can write and no tongue can express. I shut the book and said, what is the price of it? "Fourteen shillings" was the reply. I said, I'll take the book. I opened it again, and I felt a double portion of the Spirit, that I did not know whether I was in the world or not. I felt as though I was truly in heaven.

Martin Harris[3] rushed to me to tell me that the book was true. I told him that he need not tell me that, for I knew that it is true as well as he. I hunted up my brother and I said, let us go home.—He said, "what do you think of the book?" I said, it is true as sure as God sits upon his throne. I asked him what he thought of it. He said that he believed it, and had an evidence of its truth.—When God shows a man such a thing by the power of the Holy Ghost he knows it is true. He cannot doubt it.

When we started on our way home, there came a bird of the color of a robin, but a little larger. It flew around the horses heads nearly down to my hands as I held the lines, and followed us about 1 1/2 miles chirping all the way. My brother kept saying, what does that mean? I never saw a bird act so in my life. When I got to some woods it flew off, making another singular noise. I came up to the door and my nephew said, Uncle Ezra has bought one of those books, I knew he would. My wife came out and wanted to know what I had got. I said, I have bought a book and it overpowers me to read it, but I am going to lay it alongside of the Bible and see whether they agree. I could not read it for one or two months without being filled with the Spirit of the Lord. When I laid it down by the Bible, I could find

2. Perhaps 3 October 1830 (see note 7 below).

3. On Martin Harris (1783-1875), see "Introduction to Martin Harris Collection."

any passages that I wanted without turning the leaves over, opening to any passage in the Bible which I wanted to find, and I had been very little acquainted with the Bible.

When it got noised around, my house was filled with the neighbors who wanted to see and hear it read. I read it myself because I was filled with the Spirit. Men that swore would say with an oath that it read well. They filled my house all day, and men made my wife be[p. 80]lieve that I was crazy and would lose my friends and all my property. There was a Methodist woman in my house, and her husband came over for her after all the company was gone, and he was a Methodist. He wanted to know what I supposed that book was for. I told him that it was to fulfil the covenants which God made with Abraham, concerning his seed. He wanted to know how I could prove that? I told him by the Bible. He said there was no such thing in the Bible, and they were all cursed people, and they would go to hell at last. I turned instantly to the place where it says, "I will bring my sons from afar, and my daughters from the utmost parts of the earth, and they shall be my people and I will be their God." When I said that, he said "come wife, let's go home, I don't want such a God to rule over me." When they were gone my wife began to cry, and said that I was crazy, and it would ruin me, and she would leave me. I withdrew from the company, and sat down in the sitting room. Suddenly a change came over me. I was sitting down to meditate upon it, and suddenly an angel stood before me. He was a tall, black-eyed man, and he was the handsomest person that I ever saw, and so bright and white that he shined like the sun. he had on the handsomest robe that I ever saw. He had a child in his arms as white as he was, with the most brilliant appearance. He said, "you have come at the eleventh hour." He said, "you must become as this little child, or you can in no wise enter into the kingdom of God." He then said, "behold it is a male child." He said, "take care, the devil is after the child," and I saw a huge black form in the shape of a man at the door, and I had a large dog laying in the room, and he rose up and went to the door and growled three times, and came back and laid down again. The angel disappeared as he spoke, and the devil withdrew. Then a double portion of the Spirit came on me, and I went into the room to my wife, and said hallelujah to God and the Lamb! Hosannah to Jesus on high! I have seen an angel of God, who has been into my room and visited me to-night. The first sermon that ever I preached was to my wife.

They wanted me to bring the book [of Mormon] to Cananda[i]gua, and I did so, and they perused it, first one, then another. Then one spoke and said that he had a boy at home and if he could not make a better book than that he would flog him. Then they all made their comments. Some said one thing and some another, and none believed it. A lawyer (Dudley Martin)[4] was sitting by reading a newspaper. He said, "have you all made your comments on the book?" They said yes. He said let me see it. He looked in it a few minutes and said, well gentlemen, you have all made your comments on the book, and if you wish to bet 500 dollars. I will bet that you cannot make such a book. He said again, I know as much as any of you, and as much as all of you, and I will bet you 500 dollars that you cannot do it. Next day I had occasion to to go to a grist mill, and the most of these men were there. They com[p. 81]menced immediately, enquiring whether I believed it still. I could not say that I believed it, I knew it. Then an editor of a paper asked me if I had a liberal education. I said no. Then he said that he could tell me that I knew nothing concerning God if I had not had a liberal education. He said that there was no God only the God of nature, that we all came by chance. I asked him how all things came, the sun, moon and planets, and who made them and this world teeming with all its live animals. I pointed to the fields with their ripening grain and all the flowers with the green leaves and trees. He said the grain was caused by the labor of men's hands. He said the cattle were all made by nature and came by chance, and likewise the trees and the flowers. There was a Quaker there who said that if the book had come through any of their preachers he would have believed it. I asked him what kind of a man Martin Harris was. He said Martin lived neighbor to him, and was an honest man, and if he should meet him in the woods and he wanted 500 or 1000 dollars, he would let him have it, because he was a punctual man.

Then I rose and testified by the Spirit that there was a God, who made all things—heaven and earth, and things therein. I was in the Spirit all the time. I told them that the books was to gather the house of Israel. After I had borne testimony by the Spirit, I started for home, and when I got home I put up my horse and went into the same room were I saw the angel, and sat down alone. As I did so, while pondering on the things which had transpired that day, there was a rainbow came down on each side of the room, which was the most beautiful that I ever saw. I looked up and said, O Jesus, my God, and then there was a voice said, you have done well, and applauded me very highly. He said, yes, I am God that made heaven and earth, and there is none other God beside me. Then I was so filled with the Spirit that I thought I was in heaven. The rainbow disappeared gradually and all was gone. Then I was in the Spirit again, and a man came and brought me a roll of paper and presented it to me, and also a trumpet and told me to blow it. I told him that I never blowed any in my life. He said you can blow

4. This person remains unidentified.

it, try it. I put it in my mouth and blowed on it, and it made the most beautiful sound that I ever heard. The roll of paper was the revelation on me and Northrop Sweet.[5] Oliver [Cowdery][6] was the man that brought the roll and trumpet. When he brought the revelation on me and Northrop Sweet, he said, here is a revelation from God for you, now blow your trumpet, and I said, I never blowed a trumpet. He said, you can. When that vision passed away I saw in vision that I was driving on a road that I never drove before.

Joseph was then in Harmony, Pa., and the next Sunday[7] he came to his father's house, and we assembled to see him. I had not conversed with him before concerning the book. Then I told him what had happened and how I knew the book was true. He then asked me what hindered me from going into the water, as Oliver Cowdery's [p. 82] mother[8] was going to be baptized. I said, I am ready and willing at any time. Then we started to the water, which was four or five miles off. When I got on the way I saw the same horses and the same persons, (6 of them) that I saw in the before

5. D&C 33. Northrop Sweet (1802-?) was born in New York. Before 1828, he married Elathan Harris (b. 1805), daughter of Emer Harris. He was baptized by Parley P. Pratt on the same day in October 1830 as Ezra Thayre. Soon after moving to Ohio in 1831, he apostatized. About 1845 he moved to Michigan. The details of his death remain unknown, but he was evidently living with his son Hezekiah in Bethel, Branch County, Michigan, in 1880 (L. Cook 1981, 48).

6. On Oliver Cowdery (1806-50), see "Introduction to Oliver Cowdery Collection."

7. Because Joseph Smith had returned to Fayette, New York, by 21 October (at which time he dictated Moses 5:43b-51), there are only three Sundays in October 1830 for Thayre's baptism: 3, 10, or 17. The first Sunday in October seems ruled out by Thayre's hearing Hyrum preach on the Sunday previous to his baptism: the previous Sunday, 26 September, Hyrum was likely in Fayette attending the church's three-day conference. Since Hyrum had moved to Colesville in early October (see I.B.5, LUCY SMITH HISTORY, 1845, 1853:159, and n. 266; IV.A.2, NEWEL KNIGHT JOURNAL, CIRCA 1846, 23) and was not present in Manchester to preach on 10 October, Sunday, 17 October, for Thayre's baptism is also excluded. Thus 10 October is the most likely Sunday in October for the baptisms of Thayre, Sweet, and Keziah Cowdery.

8. Keziah Pearce (Austin) Cowdery (1773-1861), Oliver's stepmother, grew up in Poultney, Vermont. She married William Cowdery about 1810. Their first child, Rebecca Maria, was born in December 1810 at Williamson, Ontario County, New York. Keziah died at Ellery, New York (Mehling 1911, 95-96; tombstone, Bemus Point Cemetery, Ellery, New York).

mentioned vision, and the houses all along were the same as had been shown me. When I came to the grist mill, I saw that I had seen it in the vision, but I had never been there before. We were baptized just below the mill.[9] There was a green meadow which I had seen before. Parley P. Pratt[10] baptized us, and I had seen him in the vision. I saw him pull two fish out of the water and another which was a small fish.—I saw that I and Oliver's mother were the two persons referred to in the vision. The small fish meant Northrop Sweet. He was baptized at the same time, but soon left the church.

About this time my brother came and told me that he dreamt that my mother died and flew away into a swamp, and she was spotted. I felt concerned, fearing that she was lost. She was a Methodist. I prayed to God that I might know whether she was saved.—I prayed in faith, and I never asked for anything about that time but he gave it to me. I saw my mother suddenly standing before me. She had on the same looking dress as I saw the angel have. I said, O my mother! my mother! She said that I had sinned in some things but I must be faithful.

I and Northrop Sweet were both confirmed by Joseph, and Northrop had the Spirit, but I did not. Joseph said to me, you will not receive the Spirit now, but you will soon. The next morning[11] I was going a journey, and I got on the box of the stage. I rode so until 9 o'clock, P.M., then a young man got on, and he swore. I reproved him for it. He said that his parents were Baptists and taught him better, and he was going to quit and go home. Then the Lord poured out his Spirit upon me in the most extraordinary manner.—Then we stopped at a hotel. When I went to bed, as I laid my coat off, I received a greater outpouring. Then I said, I know that Joseph is a prophet, and I have never doubted since.

I invited Joseph to come to my barn and I said that I would go to Cananda[i]gua and get a large congregation. The barn was about 50 feet long by 18 wide. It was filled and some could not get in. Joseph, Hyrum, Oliver Cowdery, D[avid].,[12] J[ohn].[13] and P[eter]. Whitmer,[14] P[arley]. P.

---

9. Concerning the location of these baptisms, see III.J.35, THOMAS L. COOK HISTORY, 1930.

10. On Parley P. Pratt (1807-57), see introduction to III.K.16, PARLEY P. PRATT AUTOBIOGRAPHY, CIRCA 1854 (PART I).

11. Perhaps Monday, 11 October 1830 (see note 7 above).

12. On David Whitmer (1805-88), see "Introduction to David Whitmer Collection."

13. On John Whitmer (1802-78), see "Introduction to John Whitmer Collection."

14. On Peter Whitmer (1809-36), see I.A.15, JOSEPH SMITH HISTORY, 1839, n. 63.

Pratt and Ziba Peterson[15] preached with great power.[16] Then the people invited us to Canand[i]gua. I went down to engage a place for them to preach in. They had promised that we should meet in the Methodist Meeting house, but the Trustees would not agree, so I engaged the Court House. The elders met at my house that night.—We went down and Sydney [Rigdon][17] commenced preaching. I attended the door. The meeting commenced about dark. About 7 or 8 o'clock, I saw a light spring up in the east. I pointed it out to some that were standing out, and they all looked at it, and they said that it was the Montezuma marsh on fire. The marsh was only in the east. I said look in the south as another great light sprung up in that direction, [p. 83] then another in the west, and I said look in the west; then another in the north, and I said look in the north. It became about as light as noon day, and rolled over in the sky

15. On Ziba Peterson (?-1849), see I.A.15, JOSEPH SMITH HISTORY, 1839, n. 103.

16. This event took place in October 1830, before Oliver Cowdery, Parley P. Pratt, Peter Whitmer, Jr., and Ziba Peterson left Manchester, New York, for Ohio and Missouri (see III.L.22, MISSIONARIES COVENANT, 17 OCT 1830). However, the presence of Hyrum is problematic since Hyrum, according to Lucy, left for Colesville the day after Joseph Smith's arrival in Manchester (see I.B.5, LUCY SMITH HISTORY, 1845, 1853:159, and n. 266).

17. The presence of Sidney Rigdon necessarily dates these Canandaigua meetings to December 1830 or January 1831, probably the former. Thayre perhaps conflates two separate meetings: October 1830, when Joseph Smith preached in his barn, and the following December, when Smith perhaps again preached in his barn and Rigdon in the courthouse. Edwin Holden of Avon, Livingston County, New York, may have been at the December 1830 meeting, although he gives a different location and date. He states: "The first time I saw Joseph Smith was in [January?] 1831, in Genesee [County? Geneseo Village, Livingston County?], New York State, about twenty-five miles from the famous hill, Cumorah. On hearing that two men were there calling themselves 'Mormons,' I determined to see them. I rode on horseback fifteen miles from the place I was living to see them—Joseph Smith and Sidney Rigdon. When I got to the place, I learned that they were going to hold a meeting in a barn. It was so crowded that it was with much difficulty I got inside; and by a great effort climbed up on one of the beams of the roof. There I could see and hear them distinctly" (*Juvenile Instructor* 27 [1 March 1892]: 153). Perhaps Holden describes a separate but similar instance of Smith and Rigdon preaching in a barn for which there is no other record. Regardless, this would have been in December 1830 since Smith and Rigdon were not in the area together thereafter.

like a great blaze of fire, extending and met at the zenith. It was seen by about 40 or 50 persons outside. I locked the door and would not let them go in to disturb the congregation, therefore the congregation knew nothing about it. It continued about one hour and a half. It passed away before the meeting broke up.

After the meeting, I got all the brethren into my wagon to go to my house. After we had started we saw a light as large as a hogshead, which followed us all the way, (3 1/2 miles) above the wagon probably 150 feet, and it lighted us so that we could see the horses tracks in the road. Joseph said that it was one of the signs of the coming of the Son of man. When we got to the house, I told the brethren to go in, and I would unharness. The light went no further than we went. I could see to unharness and feed my horses as well as in the day time. There was no moon visible. When I was done, the light flashed and disappeared instantly. ...

I say in the presence of God and all his holy angels, and before all that seraphic host, that this is the truth. If there are any errors, I do not know it.

EZRA THAYRE.

7.
STEPHEN S. HARDING TO POMEROY TUCKER, 1 JUNE 1867

Pomeroy Tucker, *Origin, Rise, and Progress of Mormonism* (New York: D. Appleton and Co., 1867), 280-81, 284-87.

EDITORIAL NOTE

Stephen S. Harding (1808-?), a cousin of Pomeroy Tucker, spent his early childhood in Palmyra, New York. In 1820 he left Palmyra with his parents and relocated in Ripley County, Indiana. In 1828 Harding was admitted to the Indiana bar, and in 1862 was appointed by President Abraham Lincoln as Utah's territorial governor. However, Harding resigned in the fall of 1863 following sharp conflict with Mormon president Brigham Young. After serving as chief justice in the territory of Colorado for about a year, he returned to Indiana and practiced law until becoming blind in 1881. He died at Milan, Indiana (*Indiana Magazine of History* 26 [June 1930]: 157-59).

Shortly after becoming a lawyer, Harding visited relatives in Palmyra during August and September 1829. He was present in E. B. Grandin's shop when printing began on the Book of Mormon, and was introduced to Martin Harris, Oliver Cowdery, Joseph Smith, and others. In a letter to Tucker, dated 1 June 1867, Harding described events relating to Mormon origins he witnessed during his 1829 visit to Palmyra. For another Harding letter on the same subject, see III.J.15, STEPHEN S. HARDING TO THOMAS GREGG, FEB 1882.

MILAN, INDIANA, *June* 1, 1867.

POMEROY TUCKER, ESQ.:

MY DEAR SIR,—Your letter of 22d was received on my coming home from court last night. I entirely approve your plan of Mormon history, beginning as you do with its origin in the illusory tricks of Joe Smith, which he had practised upon his superstitious followers for years anterior to his Golden Bible "vision," and before he had dreamed of becoming a "prophet."

I knew Smith, and also Martin Harris[1] and Oliver Cowdery,[2] with some of their fanatical associates at and around Palmyra, and heard much of their early delusions, and can appreciate the importance to the civilized world of your forthcoming narrative. It has long been needed to complete the history of Latter-Day Saintism, and it has been a matter of wonder to me that such a disclosure of the great pretension, showing the nothingness of its groundwork, was not written up years ago. With your facilities for performing this service—your personal knowl[p. 280]edge of the whole imposture and its authors—you cannot fail in producing a work of general interest and popular favor. I will proceed at once to answer your inquiries so far as I can. ... [p. 281] ...[3]

PIONEER MORMONS—SACRED RELIC.

When I was in Palmyra in 1829,[4] I went with Joe Smith, at his special request, to his father's house, in company with Martin Harris and Oliver Cowdery, for the purpose of hearing read his wonderful "translations" from the sacred plates. This was before these revelations had been given to the world in the printed "Book of Mormon." Subsequently,[5] after the printing contract had been concluded between Grandin[6] and Harris, I was in the printing-office with yourself, and also the three pioneer Mormons named, when the proof-sheet of the first form of the book, including the title-page, was revised by you. A corrected impression of it was passed around to the young prophet and his attendant disciples, all of whom appeared to be delighted with the dawn[p. 284]ing of the new gospel dispensation, and it was accepted by Smith as "according to revelation." By consent of the brotherhood, you finally gave this "revise sheet" to me as a curiosity, and I retained it until some two years after Smith's murder, and before the

1. On Martin Harris (1783-1875), see "Introduction to Martin Harris Collection."

2. On Oliver Cowdery (1806-50), see "Introduction to Oliver Cowdery Collection."

3. Harding's discussion about Mormonism in Utah (pp. 281-84) is here deleted.

4. Harding probably arrived in Palmyra in late August 1829, when the Book of Mormon was first being printed (compare III.J.15, STEPHEN S. HARDING TO THOMAS GREGG, FEB 1882, 35), and left in September 1829 (ibid., 49-50).

5. The event described, according to III.J.15, STEPHEN S. HARDING TO THOMAS GREGG, FEB 1882, 52, occurred in August 1829.

6. On Egbert B. Grandin (1806-45), see I.A.15, JOSEPH SMITH HISTORY, 1839, n. 77.

Mormons had gone to Utah, when it was bestowed by me upon a grateful wandering "saint" of the name of Robert Campbell,[7] who had been cared for over night at my present residence. This "sacred relic" is now among the archives in the "Historian's Office" at Salt Lake City.[8]

COMMAND TO PREACH THE MORMON GOSPEL.

You ask me to write my recollections of the "call" to preach the Mormon gospel, as "revealed" to Calvin Stoddard in 1829.[9] I can do so with as distinct a remembrance as if that unjustifiable act of a "wild and fast young man" had occurred yesterday. I can never forget it, for I was almost as badly scared, before I had got done with the mischief, as poor Calvin was; and I have never to this day been quite satisfied with my conduct. I was especially led to play the trick by the strange credulity which Martin Harris had manifested the same day, as we walked together

---

7. Robert L. Campbell (1825-74) was born in Scotland. He was baptized in 1842, and immigrated to Nauvoo, Illinois, in April 1845. He worked extensively as a clerk for the church, including for Joseph Smith's Manuscript History. He died at Salt Lake City, Utah (Jenson 1971, 3:613-14; Jessee 1971, 460).

8. The title page and first uncut sheet of the Book of Mormon that Harding gave to Robert Campbell is presently in the LDS Church Archives, Salt Lake City, Utah. At the bottom of this page, Harding wrote: "Presented to the Church of Latter day Saints by Stephen S. Harding August 8th 1847." In the right margin, Harding wrote sideways on the sheet: "This is the first impression thrown off from the form, on which was printed the Book of Mormon; and handed to me by the Pressman, in the Village of Palmyra New York. S[tephen]. S. Harding" (see photograph of original in *Church History in the Fulness of Times,* 1989, 64).

9. Compare III.J.8, POMEROY TUCKER ACCOUNT, 1867, 80-81; and III.J.15, STEPHEN S. HARDING TO THOMAS GREGG, FEB 1882, 48-49. Calvin Stoddard (1801-36), a resident of Macedon, New York, was baptized in the Baptist church on 3 April 1825, during the Palmyra revival of 1824-25. He married Sophronia Smith on 30 December 1827. Stoddard began having difficulties with the Baptists over the principle of open communion, and on 16 August 1828 the committee appointed to visit Stoddard reported that he had said of the Baptists "that many of them were Devils" (Minutes of the Palmyra Baptist Church, entries of 5 March 1825, 3 April 1825, 19 July 1828, 16 August 1828, Samuel Colgate Baptist Historical Collection, American Baptist Historical Society, Rochester, New York). Stoddard joined the Mormon church but later was cited for disbelief. He evidently died at Palmyra, New York (Jessee 1984, 658, n. 122; Jessee 1989, 517; Cannon and Cook 1983, 291).

to hear Lorenzo Dow[10] preach in Palmyra. Added to this inducement, Calvin had previously told me of the wonderful things he had seen in the sky, and of his serious impressions about his duty to preach the new gospel. My purpose was to try an experiment in delusion, upon Joe Smith's principle, merely for my own amusement and instruction. The main story is the same as you have related it in the extract [p. 285] of your manuscript sent me, and it need not be repeated in this letter. ...[11] I remained at the door only for a moment, long enough to hear the startled Mormon saint in his fright cry out to his Maker in supplication for mercy and promise of obedience; when, taking to my heels, no young scapegrace ever did *taller running,* in proportion to locomotive capacity, then I did that dark night. I was stopping for a few days as a guest with my relative, Mr. Hill, in the vicinity, and gained access to my room about eleven o'clock without discovery. ...[12] Pale and haggard in appearance, from lack of sleep or perhaps from repentance for his former disobedience, Stoddard was early the next morning in the fulfilment of the "command" among his neighbors, relating in the most earnest manner the marvellous particulars of the miracle of which he was the "chosen" subject. He repeated the words of the "celestial messenger" as addressed to him, with entire accuracy, and said they were communicated amid the roaring thunders of heaven and the musical sounds of angels' wings. For aught I have ever heard since, he held out to the end faithful to his ministerial calling in the Mormon cause. Sincerely regretting my mischievous experiment—for I really began to feel conscientious qualms about it—I sought to relieve my fanatic friend of his delusion, by the suggestion that probably some unprincipled person had imposed upon him, advising him to give no heed to the trick; but I found that no such theory could be made available for my well-intended purpose, for he had "spiritual" evidences on the subject that were above any human testimony! ...[13] Poor Stoddard has gone to his final account. Peace to his ashes! if that thoughtless [p. 286] act of my boyhood, thirty-eight years

10. Lorenzo Dow (1777-1834), known as "Crazy Dow" for his erratic and eccentric manners, was born in Coventry, Connecticut. After becoming a Methodist minister in 1798, he promoted camp meetings in New England, New York, New Jersey, Louisiana, and England. His style of preaching inspired the Primitive Methodist movement. He died at Georgetown, D.C. (Wilson and Fiske 1887, 2:218).

11. Ellipses in original. See III. J, 8. POMEROY TUCKER ACCOUNT, 1867, 80-81.

12. Ellipses in original.

13. Ellipses in original.

ago, caused him one hour's unhappiness, or contributed in any degree to a single conversion to Mormonism, may He who "tempers the wind to the shorn lamb" look upon my offence not in anger, but in mercy, for I know that I did not intend to do a premeditated wrong to any one.

Truly yours,

STEPHEN S. HARDING.

8.
Pomeroy Tucker Account, 1867

Pomeroy Tucker, *Origin, Rise, and Progress of Mormonism* (New York: D. Appleton and Co., 1867), 11-83, 117-19, 129-130.

EDITORIAL NOTE

A significant source for Mormon origins, Tucker's 1867 book has its weaknesses. As Richard L. Anderson has observed: "From the point of view of history, ... [it] is a disappointing performance. With access to the generation that remembered the establishment of the Prophet's work, the experienced editor is content to quote the Hurlbut-Howe affidavits, to repeat common gossip, to quote extensive portions of the Book of Mormon and articles about Brigham Young for the bulk of the book" (R. L. Anderson 1969a, 382). Indeed, one resident of Palmyra reported that "[Willard] Chase said Tucker never called on him at all to find out what he knew" (III.B.9, HIRAM JACKWAY INTERVIEW, 1881). Lorenzo Saunders also states: "Tucker never called on William [Willard] Chase for evidence. He had the paralisis and was not competent to give testimony" (III.B.12, LORENZO SAUNDERS INTERVIEW, 17 SEP 1884, n. 38). In his preface Tucker named Willard Chase for possible corroboration, but in his book he seems to rely on Chase's 1833 statement to Hurlbut (III.J.8, POMEROY TUCKER ACCOUNT, 1867, 19, 26, 31).

Yet there is much to commend in Tucker's account of early Mormonism. As Anderson continues: "Tucker does relate much valuable information concerning the period of the publication of the Book of Mormon. He also claims knowledge of the Smiths 'since their removal to Palmyra from Vermont in 1816, and during their continuance there and in the adjoining town of Manchester' [Tucker 1867, 4]. ... Most of Tucker's unattributed particulars of the Smiths' early Palmyra life are probably based on his observation" (R. L. Anderson 1969a, 382). In his preface Tucker claims that he "was equally acquainted with Martin Harris and Oliver Cowdery, and with most of the earlier followers of Smith, either as money-diggers or Mormons," and that during the printing of the Book of Mormon he "had frequent and familiar interviews with the pioneer Mormons, Smith, Cowdery, and Harris" (Tucker 1867, 4, 5).

For the following reproduction from Tucker's book, chapter headings and synopses (chapters I-VII, IX, and X) have been omitted. For biographical information on Tucker (1802-70), see introduction to III.J.5, POMEROY TUCKER REMINISCENCE, 1858.

JOSEPH SMITH, Jr., who in the subsequent pages appears in the character of the first Mormon prophet, and the putative founder of Mormonism and the Church of Latter Day Saints, was born in Sharon, Windsor County, Vt., December 13, 1805.[1] He was the son of Joseph Smith, Sr.,[2] who, with his wife Lucy[3] and their family, removed from Royalton, Vt.,[4] to Palmyra, N.Y., in the summer of 1816.[5] The family embraced nine children, Joseph, Jr., being the fourth in the order of their ages, viz.: Alvin,[6] Hyrum[7] (so spelled by his father), Sophronia,[8] JOSEPH, Samuel H.,[9] William,[10] Catherine,[11] Carlos,[12] and Lucy.[13] These constituted the chief earthly possessions and respon[p. 11]sibilities of Mr. and Mrs. Smith at the time of their emigration to Western New York.

At Palmyra, Mr. Smith, Sr., opened a "cake and beer shop,"[14] as

---

1. Joseph Smith was born on 23 December 1805.

2. On Joseph Smith, Sr. (1771-1840), see "Introduction to Joseph Smith, Sr., Collection."

3. On Lucy Smith (1775-1856), see "Introduction to Lucy Smith Collection."

4. The Smiths moved to Palmyra, New York, from Norwich, Vermont.

5. Lucy Smith says Joseph Sr. left Norwich after their third crop failure, evidently in the summer or fall of 1816 (see I.B.5, LUCY SMITH HISTORY, 1845, MS:33). However, Lucy and her children arrived in the winter of 1816-17 (see I.A.15, JOSEPH SMITH HISTORY, 1839, Note A).

6. On Alvin Smith (1798-1823), see I.A.15, JOSEPH SMITH HISTORY, 1839, n. 10.

7. On Hyrum Smith (1800-44), see I.A.15, JOSEPH SMITH HISTORY, 1839, n. 12.

8. On Sophronia Smith (1803-76), see I.A.15, JOSEPH SMITH HISTORY, 1839, n. 16.

9. On Samuel Harrison Smith (1808-44), see I.A.15, JOSEPH SMITH HISTORY, 1839, n. 13.

10. On William Smith (1811-93), see "Introduction to William Smith Collection."

11. On Katharine Smith (1813-1900), see "Introduction to Katharine Smith Collection."

12. On Don Carlos Smith (1816-41), see I.A.15, JOSEPH SMITH HISTORY, 1839, n. 15.

13. On Lucy Smith (1821-82), who was born in Palmyra, New York, see I.A.15, JOSEPH SMITH HISTORY, 1839, n. 18.

14. The reporter for the *New York Herald* said that those who knew the Smiths claimed they sold "cake and ale" as well as "beer, hard cider and

described by his signboard, doing business on a small scale, by the profits of which, added to the earnings of an occasional day's work on hire by himself and his elder sons, for the village and farming people, he was understood to secure a scanty but honest living for himself and family. These hired day's works were divided among the various common labor jobs that offered from time to time, such as gardening, harvesting, well-digging, etc.

Mr. Smith's shop merchandise, consisting of gingerbread, pies, boiled eggs, root-beer, and other like notions of traffic, soon became popular with the juvenile people of the town and country, commanding brisk sales, especially on Fourth of July anniversaries, and on military training days, as these prevailed at that period. Peddling was done in the streets on those occasions by the facility of a rude handcart of the proprietor's own construction.

Mr. Smith and his household continued their residence in Palmyra village, living in the manner described, for some two and a half years.[15] In 1818 they settled upon a nearly wild or unimproved piece of land, mostly covered with standing timber, situate[d] about two miles south of Palmyra, being on the north border of the town of Manchester, Ontario County.[16] [p. 12] The title of this landed property was vested in non-resident minor

boiled eggs" (25 June 1893). James Gordon Bennett reported in 1831 that the Smiths had also sold "gingerbread" (III.K.6, JAMES GORDON BENNETT ACCOUNT, 1831).

15. In a sermon given on 26 November 1857 at Palmyra's Presbyterian church, the Reverend Horace Eaton related: "In 1816 Joseph Smith, Sr., moved here from Vermont with his wife and nine children. For two years he kept a cake and beer shop on lower Main street" (H. Eaton 1858, 28-29). Contrary to the tradition recorded by Willard W. Bean that the Smiths originally "rented a small frame building on the eastern outskirts of the village near where Johnson Street takes off Vienna" (Bean 1938, 12), the Smith family apparently lived in Palmyra Village near the west end of Main Street (see discussion in introduction to III.L.1, PALMYRA [NY] ROAD LISTS, 1817-1822).

16. Tucker's claim that the Smiths moved to their Manchester land in 1818 is an error. The shift of Joseph Smith Sr.'s name to the end of the Palmyra road list in 1820 suggests a move to Stafford Road after April 1819 (III.L.1, PALMYRA [NY] ROAD LISTS, 1817-1822). However, this move was to the Jennings cabin north of the Palmyra/Manchester township line (III.L.2, PALMYRA [NY] HIGHWAY SURVEY, 13 JUN 1820). The Smiths evidently contracted for their Manchester land soon after July 1820 (see III.L.4, SMITH MANCHESTER [NY] LAND RECORDS, 1820-1830).

heirs[17]; and the premises being uncared for by any local agent or attorney,[18] the Smiths took possession of it by the rights of "squatter sovereignty."[19] They thus remained unmolested in its possession for some twelve years, occupying as their dwelling-place, in the first instance, a small, one-story, smoky log-house, which they had built prior to removing there. This house was divided into two rooms, on the ground-floor, and had a low garret, in two apartments. A bedroom wing, built of sawed slabs, was afterward added.

Subsequently this property was purchased by Mr. Smith on contract, a small payment thereon being made by him to bind the bargain[20]; and in this way his occupancy of the premises was prolonged until after the blooming of the Mormon scheme in 1829.

But little improvement was made upon this land by the Smith family in the way of clearing, fencing, or tillage. Their farm-work was done in a slovenly, half-way, profitless manner.[21] Shortly before quitting the premises they erected a small frame-house thereon, partly enclosed, and never finished by them,[22] in which they lived for the remainder of their time there, using

---

17. Elizabeth Evertson, wife of Nicholas Evertson (who died in 1807), David B. Ogden, and others (see III.L.4, SMITH MANCHESTER [NY] LAND RECORDS, 1820-1830).

18. On 21 June 1820 the executors of Nicholas Evertson's estate conveyed to Casper W. Eddy, a physician in New York City, power of attorney to sell Evertson's land holdings. On 14 July 1820 Eddy transferred his power of attorney for Evertson's lands to Zachariah Seymour of Canandaigua, New York. Prior to Seymour's appointment, Evertson's Manchester, New York, land was "uncared for by any local agent or attorney" (see III.L.4, SMITH MANCHESTER [NY] LAND RECORDS, 1820-1830).

19. The accuracy of this statement is uncertain since it is not known to what extent the Smiths may have exploited the neighboring land before contracting for it themselves.

20. The Smiths contracted for their Manchester land some time between July 1820 and July 1821, according to Manchester land assessment records (see III.L.6, MANCHESTER [NY] LAND ASSESSMENT RECORDS, 1821-1823 & 1830; and III.L.4, SMITH MANCHESTER [NY] LAND RECORDS, 1820-1830).

21. Both Lucy and William Smith claimed the family had cleared about thirty or sixty acres of wooded land in the first years of their occupancy (I.B.5, LUCY SMITH HISTORY, 1845, MS:37; and I.D.4, WILLIAM SMITH, *ON MORMONISM,* 1883, 12-13). But Tucker's description might apply to the years following the Smiths' loss of their land in December 1825, when as "renters" their interest in its improvement would have naturally subsided.

22. Lucy Smith said that Josiah Stowell came to their home in October 1825, "a short time before the house was completed" (I.B.5, LUCY

their original log hut for a barn.[23] This property, finally vacated by the Smiths in 1831,[24] is now included in the well-organized farm of Mr. Seth T. Chapman,[25] on Stafford Street, running south from Palmyra. [p. 13]

The chief application of the useful industry of the Smiths during their residence upon this farm-lot, was in the chopping and retailing of cord-wood, the raising and bartering of small crops of agricultural products and garden vegetables, the manufacture and sale of black-ash baskets and birch brooms, the making of maple sugar and molasses in the season for that work,[26] and in the continued business of peddling cake and beer in

---

SMITH HISTORY, 1845, 1853:91). While occupied by the Smiths, certain features of the house remained unfinished. According to Martin Harris, when Joseph Smith hid the plates under the hearth in late September 1827, "the wall [of the house] being partly down, it was feared that certain ones, who were trying to get possession of the plates, would get under the house and dig them out" (III.F.10, MARTIN HARRIS INTERVIEW WITH JOEL TIFFANY, 1859, 166-67).

23. Tucker was apparently unaware that the Manchester cabin was occupied by Hyrum and his wife after their marriage on 2 November 1826, and that in April 1829 some of the Smith family moved back into the cabin with Hyrum's family. Hence the use of the cabin as a barn must date to after the Smiths' occupancy. Or perhaps Tucker refers to the Jennings cabin occupied by the Smiths prior to building their own cabin (see Berge 1985, 25). Tucker fails to mention that the Smiths had also built a cooper's shop, which had a wooden floor and loft, and it is possible that this structure doubled as a barn for the Smiths.

24. Actually the Smiths were forced to vacate their home in April 1829, at which time they crowded into Hyrum's cabin (I.B.5, LUCY SMITH HISTORY, 1845, MS:92-93; and I.D.4, WILLIAM SMITH, *ON MORMONISM,* 1883, 14). In 1830 Hyrum paid taxes on fifteen acres on Manchester Lot 1, presumably a portion of the Smiths' former land (see III.L.6, SMITH MANCHESTER [NY] LAND ASSESSMENT RECORDS, 1821-1823 & 1830). In early October 1830 Hyrum moved his family to Colesville, New York, with the remainder of the Smiths moving to Waterloo soon after (I.B.5, LUCY SMITH HISTORY, 1845, 1853:158-69).

25. Seth T. Chapman purchased the property from Absalom and Ruth Weeks for $5,750 on 2 April 1860 (Porter 1971, 358). On 28 January 1867 Chapman sold the property to Charles W. Bennett for $7,500, and on the same day Bennett sold it to Clarissa Chapman, Seth Chapman's wife, for the same amount. Chapman, age forty-eight, is listed in the 1860 census of Manchester, Ontario County, New York, with his wife, Clarissa, and four children (1860:469).

26. On the Smiths' sugar industry, see III.B.12, LORENZO SAUNDERS INTERVIEW, 17 SEP 1884, 7; III.B.13, BENJAMIN SAUNDERS

the village on days of public doings. It was as a clerk in this last-mentioned line of trade that the rising Joseph (the prophet to be) learned his first lessons in commercial and monetary science. And in this connection it may not be out of place to state, in the way of illustration in respect to the beginning of human greatness on his part—though the mention of the fact is by no means creditable to the memory of the mischievous parties implicated—that the boys of those by-gone times used to delight in obtaining the valuable goods intrusted to Joseph's clerkship, in exchange for worthless pewter imitation two-shilling pieces.

The larger proportion of the time of the Smiths, however, was spent in hunting and fishing, trapping muskrats ("mushrats" was the word they used), digging out woodchucks from their holes, and idly lounging around the stores and shops in the village. Joseph generally took the leading direction of the rural enterprises mentioned, instead of going to [p. 14] school like other boys—though he was seldom known personally to participate in the practical *work* involved in these or any other pursuits. Existing as they did from year to year in this thriftless manner, with seemingly inadequate visible means or habits of profitable industry for their respectable livelihood, it is not at all to be wondered at that the suspicions of some good people in the community were apt to be turned toward them, especially in view of the frequently occurring nocturnal depredations and thefts in the neighborhood. On these accounts the inhabitants came to observe more than their former vigilance in the care of their sheepfolds, hencoops, smoke-houses, pork-barrels, and the like domestic interests; though it is but common fairness to accompany this fact by the statement, that it is not within the remembrance of the writer, who in this designedly impartial narrative would "nothing extenuate nor aught set down in malice," if the popular inferences in this matter were ever sustained by judicial investigation.[27]

It is appropriate to remark, however, that the truth of history, no less than proper deference to the recollections of many living witnesses in

---

INTERVIEW, CIRCA SEP 1884, 25; I.D.7, WILLIAM SMITH INTERVIEW WITH E. C. BRIGGS, 1893; and I.B.5, LUCY SMITH HISTORY, 1845, 39.

27. No legal record against the Smiths for theft is known to exist, although the record is incomplete. However, the Smiths' former neighbors did accuse them of stealing livestock (see III.A.12, DAVID STAFFORD STATEMENT, 5 DEC 1833; and III.D.2, SYLVIA WALKER STATEMENT, 20 MAR 1885). S. F. Anderick claimed the neighbors "often sent officers to search the premises of the Smiths for stolen property" (III.D.8, S. F. ANDERICK STATEMENT, 21 DEC 1887).

Palmyra and its vicinity, demand that these reminiscences should be given, intimately blended as they are with the purpose in hand, to present before the public a candid and authentic account of the origin, rise, and progress of Mormonism, from its first foundation. [p. 15]

At this period in the life and career of Joseph Smith, Jr., or "Joe Smith," as he was universally named, and the Smith family, they were popularly regarded as an illiterate, whiskey-drinking, shiftless, irreligious race of people—the first named, the chief subject of this biography, being unanimously voted the laziest and most worthless of the generation. From the age of twelve to twenty years he is distinctly remembered as a dull-eyed, flaxen-haired, prevaricating boy—noted only for his indolent and vagabondish character, and his habits of exaggeration and untruthfulness. Taciturnity was among his characteristic idiosyncrasies, and he seldom spoke to any one outside of his intimate associates, except when first addressed by another; and then, by reason of his extravagancies of statement, his word was received with the least confidence by those who knew him best. He could utter the most palpable exaggeration or marvellous absurdity with the utmost apparent gravity. He nevertheless evidenced the rapid development of a thinking, plodding, evil-brewing mental composition—largely given to inventions of low cunning, schemes of mischief and deception, and false and mysterious pretensions. In his moral phrenology the professor might have marked the organ of secretiveness as very large, and that of conscientiousness "omitted." He was, however, proverbially good-natured, very rarely if ever indulging in any combative spirit toward any [p. 16] one, whatever might be the provocation, and yet was never known to laugh. Albeit, he seemed to be the pride of his indulgent father, who has been heard to boast of him as the "*genus* of the family," quoting his own expression.

Joseph, moreover, as he grew in years, had learned to read comprehensively, in which qualification he was far in advance of his elder brother, and even of his father; and this talent was assiduously devoted, as he quitted or modified his idle habits, to the perusal of works of fiction and records of criminality, such for instance as would be classed with the "dime novels" of the present day.[28] The stories of Stephen Burroughs[29] and Captain

---

28. Concerning Joseph Jr.'s reading habits, Lucy Smith said that her seventeen-year-old son "had never read the Bible throu=gh by course in his life for Joseph was less inclined to the study of books than any child we had but much more given to reflection and deep study" (I.B.5, LUCY SMITH HISTORY, 1845, MS:43).

29. Stephen Burroughs (1765-1840) was born in Hanover, New Hampshire. In his popular *Memoirs of My Own Life* published in 1811 in Al-

Kidd,[30] and the like, presented the highest charms for his expanding mental perceptions. As he further advanced in reading and knowledge, he assumed a spiritual or religious turn of mind, and frequently perused the Bible, becoming quite familiar with portions thereof, both of the Old and New Testaments; selected texts from which he quoted and discussed with great assurance when in the presence of his superstitious acquaintances. The Prophecies and Revelations were his special forte. His interpretations of scriptural passages were always original and unique, and his deductions and conclusions often disgustingly blasphemous, according to the common apprehensions of Christian people.

Protracted revival meetings were customary in [p. 17] some of the churches, and Smith frequented those of different denominations, sometimes professing to participate in their devotional exercises. At one time he joined the probationary class of the Methodist church in Palmyra, and made some active demonstrations of engagedness, though his assumed convictions were insufficiently grounded or abiding to carry him along to the saving point of conversion, and he soon withdrew from the class.[31] The final conclusion announced by him was, that all sectarianism was fallacious, all the churches on a false foundation, and the Bible a fable.

In unbelief, theory and practice, the Smith family, all as one, so far as they held any definable position upon the subject of religion—basing this

---

bany, New York, Burroughs recounts his many exploits, including his counterfeiting money, capture, conviction, and imprisonment at Northhampton, Massachusetts. Later he converted to Roman Catholicism and spent the remainder of his life as a respected teacher (Wilson and Fiske 1887, 1:470).

30. William Kidd (1645-1701) was born in Scotland. He was a ship owner and sea captain, who was commissioned by New York governor Richard Coote as a privateer against pirates in the Red Sea and Indian Ocean. When he returned to New York City in 1690 to clear himself of charges of piracy and murder, he was arrested and sent to London to stand trial. He was convicted and hanged in London on 23 May 1701 (*Who Was Who in America,* 1967, 1:293).

31. Joseph Smith himself said that he "became somewhat partial to the Methodist sect, and I felt some desire to be united with them," but eventually decided against it (I.A.15, JOSEPH SMITH HISTORY, 1839, 2). Since Smith described these feelings in the context of the 1824-25 Palmyra revival (the occasion of his mother's conversion to Presbyterianism), it is possible that the event Tucker describes occurred about that time (see also III.J.2, ORSAMUS TURNER ACCOUNT, 1851, 214; and III.K.35, LOCKWOOD R. DOTY HISTORY, 1925, 56, which follows Tucker but assigns the date 1824-25).

conclusion upon all the early avowals and other evidences remembered, as well as upon the subsequent developments extant—were unqualified atheists. Can their mockeries of Christianity, their persistent blasphemies, be accounted for upon any other hypothesis? [p. 18]

In September, 1819,[32] a curious stone was found in the digging of a well upon the premises of Mr. Clark Chase,[33] near Palmyra. This stone attracted particular notice on account of its peculiar shape, resembling that of a child's foot. It was of a whitish, glassy appearance, though opaque, resembling quartz. Joseph Smith, Sr., and his elder sons Alvin and Hyrum, did the chief labor of this well-digging, and Joseph, Jr., who had been a frequenter in the progress of the work, as an idle looker-on and lounger, manifested a special fancy for this geological curiosity; and he carried it home with him, though this act of plunder was against the strenuous protestations of Mr. Chase's children, who claimed to be its rightful owners.

Joseph kept this stone, and ever afterward refused its restoration to the claimants.[34] Very soon the pretension transpired that he could see wonderful [p. 19] things by its aid. This idea was rapidly enlarged upon from day to day, and in a short time his spiritual endowment was so developed that he asserted the gift and power (with the stone at his eyes) of revealing both

32. Quinn follows Tucker's dating of September 1819 for Smith's acquiring his first stone, suggesting that Tucker's informants were really describing Smith's procurement of his "white stone" rather than the discovery of the dark-brown stone (shaped like a baby's foot), which Willard Chase said was found in the well in 1822 (see Quinn 1987, 38-41; III.A.14, WILLARD CHASE STATEMENT, CIRCA 11 DEC 1833, 240). Despite the fact that all other details are incorrect, Quinn insists that Tucker's date is correct (Quinn 1998, 33, 43-53). The only dateable account of Smith's possession of a stone other than the Chase stone is the transcript of the March 1826 court hearing, which mentions his use of a "white stone" in the Bainbridge area (see IV.F.1, BAINBRIDGE [NY] COURT RECORD, 20 MAR 1826). Moreover, the court record itself limits Smith's stone gazing to the previous three years (c. 1823). If Smith owned a white stone previous to the 1822 discovery of the Chase stone, it was not long before. Because Tucker fails to mention his sources and is inaccurate about the major elements of his account, it is perhaps a mistake to place too much confidence in his dating.

33. The well was situated on land jointly held by Clark Chase and his sons Willard and Mason (see III.J.35, THOMAS L. COOK HISTORY, 1930, 238; see also Quinn 1987, 41, n. 7). Clark Chase, over forty-five years of age, is listed in the 1820 census of Farmington, Ontario County, New York (1820:315).

34. See III.A.14, WILLARD CHASE STATEMENT, CIRCA 11 DEC 1833, 240-41, 247.

things existing and things to come.

For a length of time this clairvoyant manifestation was sought to be turned to selfish advantage, in the way of fortune-telling, and in the pretended discovery by the medium of the seer-stone of lost or stolen property. But the realizations from these sources were insufficient to encourage a long continuance of the experiments, though some small amounts were obtained by them; and a very worthy citizen now living in Palmyra actually paid seventy-five cents in money for being sent some three miles on a fool's errand in pursuit of a stolen roll of cloth. It is presumed to be needless to add, that no genuine discoveries of stolen property were made in this manner, and that the entire proceeds derived from the speculation went into Joe's pocket.

The most glittering sights revealed to the mortal vision of the young impostor in the manner stated, were hidden treasures of great value, including enormous deposits of gold and silver sealed in earthen pots or iron chests, and buried in the earth in the immediate vicinity of the place where he stood. These discoveries finally became too dazzling for his eyes in daylight, and he had to shade his vision by looking [p. 20] at the stone in his hat! Of course but few persons were sufficiently stolid to listen to these silly pretensions, for they were only of a piece with Joe's habitual extravagances of assertion. Yet he may have had believers.

Persisting in this claim to the gift of spiritual discernment, Smith very soon succeeded in his experiment upon the credulity of a selected audience of ignorant and superstitious persons, to an extent which it is presumed he could not himself have anticipated at the outset of the trial. He followed up this advantage, and by its means, in the spring of 1820,[35] raised some small contributions from the people in the vicinity, to defray the expense of digging for the buried money, the precise hiding-place of which he had discovered by the aid of the stone in his hat. At an appointed time, being at a dead hour of night, his dupes and employed laborers repaired with lanterns to the revealed locality of the treasure, which was upon the then forest hill, a short distance from his father's house[36]; and after some preparatory mystic ceremonies, the work of digging began at his signal. Silence, as the condition of

35. Compare III.J.5, POMEROY TUCKER REMINISCENCE, 1858. Although neighbors such as Willard Chase said the Smiths began money digging in 1820 (III.A.14, WILLARD CHASE STATEMENT, CIRCA 11 DEC 1833, 240), the use of a stone by Joseph Jr. dates the event described by Tucker to after 1822, perhaps the spring of 1823 (see n. 32 above).

36. This might be the hill on Manchester Lot 1 immediately east of the Smiths' house.

success, had been enjoined upon the chosen few present, who were to be shares in the expected prize. The excavating process was continued for some two hours, without a word being spoken—the magician meanwhile indicating, by some sort of a wand in his hand,[37] the exact [p. 21] spot where the spade was to be crowded into the earth—when, just at the moment the money-box was within the seer's grasp, one of the party, being "tempted by the devil," *spoke!* The enchantment was broken, and the treasure vanished! Such was Joe's explanation, and, ridiculous as was the idea, it was apparently satisfactory to his dupes.

This was the inauguration of the impostor's money-digging performances; and the description given of this first trial and of its results is as near exactitude as can at this time be recollected from his own accounts. Several of the individuals participating in this and subsequent diggings, and many others well remembering the stories of the time, are yet living witnesses of these follies, and can make suitable corrections if the particulars as stated are not substantially according to the facts.

The imposture was renewed and repeated at frequent intervals from 1820 to 1827, various localities being the scenes of these delusive searches for money, as pointed out by the revelations of the magic stone. And these tricks of young Smith were not too absurd for the credence of his fanatical followers. He was sufficiently artful and persevering to preserve his spell-holding power over their minds, and keep up his deceptions for the length of time before stated. It certainly evidences extraordinary talent or subtlety, that for so long a period he could maintain the po[p. 22]tency of his art over numbers of beings in the form of manhood, acknowledging their faith in his supernatural powers. He continued to use this advantage in the progress of his experiments to raise from them and others contributions in money and various articles of value, amounting to a considerable aggregate sum, being enough to pay the digging expenses (whiskey and labor), and also in this way securing a handsome surplus, which went in part toward necessary domestic supplies for the Smith family.

In some instances individuals were impelled, in their donations in this business, by the motive of ridding themselves of Smith's importunities, while others advanced the idea that there "might be something in it," as they explained in reply to the unfavorable suggestions of reflecting friends. One respectable and forehanded citizen, now living in Manchester, confesses to having patronized Smith's perseverance on this idea, and says he once handed

37. Apparently a reference to Joseph Smith's use of a divining rod (see Quinn 1987, 36).

him a silver dollar, partly in that view and partly to "get rid of the fellow." Smith's father and elder brothers generally participated in the manual labors of these diggings, and their example seemed to revive confidence in the sometimes wavering victims of the imposture, and also to bring others to their aid.

The subsequent operations on this head were conducted substantially in the mode and manner of the first performance, as described, with slight variations [p. 23] in the incantations, and always with the same result—Smith "almost" getting hold of the money-chest, but finally losing it by the coincident breaking of the "spell" through some unforeseen satanic interposition. By this cause the money would *vanish* just at the instant of its coming within the necromancer's mortal grasp!

A single instance of Smith's style of conducting these money-diggings will suffice for the whole series, and also serve to illustrate his low cunning, and show the strange infatuation of the persons who yielded to his unprincipled designs. Assuming his accustomed air of mystery on one of the occasions, and pretending to see by his miraculous stone exactly where the sought-for chest of money had lodged in its subterranean transits, Smith gave out the revelation that a "black sheep" would be required as a sacrificial offering upon the enchanted ground before entering upon the work of exhumation. He knew that his kind-hearted neighbor, William Stafford,[38] who was a listener to his plausible story—a respectable farmer in comfortable worldly circumstances—possessed a fine, fat, black wether, intended for division between his family use and the village market, and Smith knew, moreover, that fresh meat was a rarity at his father's home [p. 24] where he lived. The scheme succeeded completely. It was arranged that Mr. Stafford should invest the wether as his stock in the speculation, the avails of which were to be equitably shared among the company engaging in it. At the approach of the appointed hour at night, the digging fraternity, with lanterns, and the fattened sheep for the sacrifice, were conducted by Smith to the place where the treasure was to be obtained. There Smith described a circle upon the ground around the buried chest, where the blood of the animal was to be shed as the necessary condition of his power to secure the glittering gold. As usual, not a word was to be spoken during the ceremony, nor until after

38. Footnote in original reads: "Mr. [William] Stafford, beginning in early life, had been for many years a sailor, and was largely prone to the vagaries and superstitions peculiar to his class. He was thus an easy victim." On William Stafford, see introduction to III.A.13, WILLIAM STAFFORD STATEMENT, 8 DEC 1833.

the prize was brought forth. All things being thus in readiness, the throat of the sheep was cut by one of the party according to previous instructions, the poor animal made to pour its own blood around the circle, and the excavation entered upon in a vigorous and solemn manner. In this case the digging was continued for about three hours, when the "devil" again frustrated the plan exactly in the same way as on the repeated trials before! In the mean time, the elder Smith, aided by one of the junior sons, had withdrawn the sacrificial carcass and reduced its flesh to mutton for his family use.[39]

Such is a true account, so far as it goes, of the long-continued and astonishingly successful career of vice and deception led by Joseph Smith, Jr., which is [p. 25] believed to be ample in detail for the object of this publication. These delusions, persevered in and improved upon from time to time, culminated in 1827 by the great imposture of the pretended finding of the "ancient metallic plates resembling gold," afterward translated into the "Golden Bible" or Book of Mormon, as will be explained in subsequent pages.

Numerous traces of the excavations left by Smith are yet remaining as evidences of his impostures and the folly of his dupes, though most of them have become obliterated by the clearing off and tilling of the lands where they were made.

It is an interesting illustrative fact to be noticed in the history of Mormonism, as will hereafter be seen, that the origin of that extraordinary politico-religious institution is traceable to the insignificant little stone found in the digging of Mr. Chase's well in 1819.[40] Such was the acorn of the Mormon oak. [p. 26]

The fame of Smith's money-digging performances had been sounded far and near. The newspapers had heralded and ridiculed them.[41] The

---

39. Concerning the sacrifice of William Stafford's sheep, see III.A.13, WILLIAM STAFFORD STATEMENT, 8 DEC 1833, 239; III.J.36, WALLACE MINER REMINISCENCE, 1930; III.J.37, WALLACE MINER REMINISCENCE, 1932; III.J.15, STEPHEN S. HARDING TO THOMAS GREGG, FEB 1882, 56; III.D.4, CORNELIUS R. STAFFORD STATEMENT, [23] MAR 1885. While Tucker dates this event between 1820 and 1827, Thomas L. Cook believed it occurred in 1820 (see III.J.35, THOMAS L. COOK HISTORY, 1930, 221, 238).

40. According to Willard Chase, the stone was found in 1822 (III.A.14, WILLARD CHASE STATEMENT, CIRCA 11 DEC 1833, 240).

41. Tucker's paper, the *Wayne Sentinel,* published items from other papers that ridiculed stone gazing and the notion of enchanted treasures, but never Joseph Smith specifically (see 16 February 1825, and 27 December 1825).

pit-hole memorials of his treasure explorations were numerous in the surrounding fields and woodlands, attracting the inspection of the curious, and the wonder of the superstitious. The outgivings of "spiritual demonstrations," in various forms and in different parts of the country, had perhaps contributed in preparing the fanatical mind for some extraordinary revelation. Notwithstanding the failure of seven or eight years' continued efforts for the attainment of the promised wealth from its hidden earthy deposit, yet "the fools were not all dead," and the time might have seemed opportune for the prediction of some marvellous discovery, and for the great "religious" event that was to follow in the career of Joe Smith! [p. 27]

This review comes down to the summer of 1827. A mysterious stranger now appears at Smith's residence, and holds private interviews with the far-famed money-digger. For a considerable length of time no intimation of the name or purpose of this personage transpired to the public, nor even to Smith's nearest neighbors. It was observed by some of them that his visits were frequently repeated. The sequel of these private interviews between the stranger and the money-digger will sufficiently appear hereafter.[42]

About this time Smith had a remarkable vision. He pretended that, while engaged in secret prayer, alone in the wilderness, an "angel of the

---

42. Tucker later identifies the stranger as Sidney Rigdon (pp. 75-76), claiming that the Ohio preacher visited the Smiths in the "summer of 1827," about the time Joseph Jr. took the plates from the hill, and again in July 1828 in connection with the loss of the manuscript (p. 48). Tucker does not reveal his sources, but says of the stranger's first appearance that "no intimation of the name or purpose of this personage transpired to the public, nor even to Smith's nearest neighbors" (p. 28). Of the second visit, he similarly states: "The reappearance of the mysterious stranger at Smith's was again the subject of inquiry and conjecture by observers, from whom was withheld all explanation of his identity of purpose" (p. 46). Thus at the time Tucker formulated his thesis, no one could positively identify the stranger seen at the Smith residence. Yet late statements by Smith neighbors, including Lorenzo Saunders, who claimed to have helped Tucker prepare his book, claimed the Smiths had freely identified the stranger as Sidney Rigdon (see III.B.12, LORENZO SAUNDERS INTERVIEW, 17 SEP 1884, 3-4; III.B.15, LORENZO SAUNDERS INTERVIEW, 12 NOV 1884, 7; III.J.12, ABEL D. CHASE STATEMENT, 2 MAY 1879; III.J.14, ANNA RUTH EATON STATEMENT, 1881, 2). Saunders, however, had made his statements after a great deal of hesitation and prodding by John H. Gilbert (see III.H.4, JOHN H. GILBERT TO JAMES T. COBB, 14 OCT 1879). It should be observed that the Smiths were about this time visited by Josiah Stowell, Joseph Knight, Sr., and Alvah Beaman.

Lord" appeared to him, with the glad tidings that "all his sins had been forgiven," and proclaiming further that "all the religious denominations were believing in false doctrines, and consequently that none of them were accepted of God as of His Church and Kingdom;" also that he had received a "promise that the true doctrine and the fulness of the gospel should at some future time be revealed to him.["] Following this, soon came another angel, (or possibly the same one,) revealing to him that he was himself to be "the favored instrument of the new revelation;" "that the American Indians were a remnant of the Israelites, who, after coming to this country, had their prophets and inspired writings; that such of their writings as had not been destroyed were safely deposited in a cer[p. 28]tain place made known to him, and to him only; that they contained revelations in regard to the last days, and that, if he remained faithful, he would be the chosen prophet to translate them to the world."[43]

In the fall of the same year Smith had yet a more miraculous and astonishing vision than any preceding one. He now arrogated to himself, by authority of "the spirit of revelation," and in accordance with the previous "promises" made to him, a far higher sphere in the scale of human existence, assuming to possess the gift and power of "prophet, seer, and revelator [cf. D&C 21:1]." On this assumption he announced to his family friends and the bigoted persons who had adhered to his supernaturalism, that he was "commanded," upon a secretly fixed day and hour, to go alone to a certain spot revealed to him by the angel, and there take out of the earth a metallic book of great antiquity in its origin, and of immortal importance in its consequences to the world, which was a record, in mystic letters or characters, of the long-lost tribes of Israel before spoken of, who had primarily inhabited this continent, and which no human being besides himself could see and live; and the power to translate which to the nations of the earth was also given to him only, as the chosen servant of God! This was substantially, if not literally, the pretension of Smith, as related by himself, and repeatedly quoted by his credulous friends at the time. [p. 29]

Much pains were taken by the Smith family and the prophet's money-digging disciples to give wide circulation to the wonderful revelation, and in great gravity to predict its marvellous fulfilment. It is unknown, however, if the momentous announcement produced any sensation in the community, though it is fair to presume that the victims of Smith's former deceptive practices regarded it with some seriousness.

Accordingly, when the appointed hour came, the prophet, assuming his

43. See I.A.17, ORSON PRATT ACCOUNT, 1840, 7.

practiced air of mystery, took in hand his money-digging spade and a large napkin, and went off in silence and alone in the solitude of the forest, and after an absence of some three hours, returned, apparently with his sacred charge concealed within the folds of the napkin. Reminding the family of the original "command" as revealed to him, strict injunction of non-intervention and non-inspection was given to them, under the same terrible penalty as before denounced for its violation. Conflicting stories were afterward told in regard to the manner of keeping the book in concealment and safety, which are not worth repeating, further than to mention that the first place of secretion was said to be under a heavy hearthstone in the Smith family mansion.[44]

Smith told a frightful story of the display of celestial pyrotechnics on the exposure to his view of the sacred book[45]—the angel who had led him to the discovery again appearing as his guide and protector, [p. 30] and confronting ten thousand devils gathered there, with their menacing sulphureous flame and smoke, to deter him from his purpose![46] This story was repeated and magnified by the believers, and no doubt aided the experiment upon superstitious minds which eventuated so successfully.

Mr. Willard Chase,[47] a carpenter and joiner, was called upon by Smith and requested to make a strong chest in which to keep the golden book under lock and key, in order to prevent the awful calamity that would follow against the person other than himself who should behold it with his natural eyes. He could not pay a shilling for the work, and therefore proposed to make Mr. Chase a sharer in the profits ultimately anticipated in some manner not definitely stated; but the proposition was rejected—the work was refused on the terms offered.[48] It was understood, however, that the custodian of the precious treasure afterward in some way procured a chest for his purpose, which, with its sacred deposit, was kept in a dark garret of his father's house, where the translations were subsequently made, as will be explained. An anecdote touching this subject used to be related by William T. Hussey[49] and Azel

44. See, for example, I.B.5, LUCY SMITH HISTORY, 1845, MS:67-68; IV.A.1, JOSEPH KNIGHT, SR., REMINISCENCE, CIRCA 1835-1847, 3.

45. See III.K.24, HEBER C. KIMBALL AUTOBIOGRAPHY, 1864.

46. See III.J.24, ORSON SAUNDERS REMINISCENCE, 1893.

47. On Willard Chase (1798-1871), see introduction to III.A.14, WILLARD CHASE STATEMENT, CIRCA 11 DEC 1833.

48. See III.A.14, WILLARD CHASE STATEMENT, CIRCA 11 DEC 1833, 245.

49. On William T. Hussy, see I.B.5, LUCY SMITH HISTORY, 1845, n. 222.

Vandruver.[50] They were notorious wags, and were intimately acquainted with Smith. They called as his friends at his residence, and strongly importuned him for an inspection of the "golden book," offering to take upon themselves [p. 31] the risk of the death-penalty denounced. Of course, the request could not be complied with; but they were permitted to go to the chest with its owner, and see *where* the thing was, and observe its shape and size, concealed under a piece of thick canvas. Smith, with his accustomed solemnity of demeanor, positively persisting in his refusal to uncover it, Hussey became impetuous, and (suiting his action to his word) ejaculated, "Egad! I'll see the critter, live or die!" And stripping off the cover, a large tile-brick was exhibited. But Smith's fertile imagination was equal to the emergency. He claimed that his friends had been sold by a trick of his; and "treating" with the customary whiskey hospitalities, the affair ended in good-nature.

With the book was also found, or so pretended, a huge pair of spectacles in a perfect state of preservation, or the *Urim* and *Thummim,* as afterward in[p. 32]terpreted, whereby the mystic record was to be translated and the wonderful dealings of God revealed to man, by the superhuman power of Joe Smith. This spectacle pretension, however, is believed to have been purely an after-thought, for it was not heard of outside of the Smith family for a considerable period subsequent to the first story. So in regard to Smith's after-averment, that he had received a revelation of the existence of the records in 1823, but was not permitted to touch or mention them until "the fulness of time" should come for the great event, this idea was also a secondary invention.

The marvellous metallic book and its accompaniment soon became a common topic of conversation, far and near; but the sacred treasure was not seen by mortal eyes, save those of the one annointed, until after the lapse of a year or longer time, when it was found expedient to have a new revelation, as Smith's bare word had utterly failed to gain a convert beyond his original circle of believers. By this amended revelation, the veritable existence of the book was certified to by eleven witnesses of Smith's selection. It was then heralded as the Golden Bible, or Book of Mormon, and as the beginning of a new gospel dispensation. Wonderful stories and predictions fol[p. 33]lowed in regard to the future "light" and destiny of the world, but these were for a time very crude and very conflicting, and therefore scarcely definable or

50. Azel Vandruver is listed among the members of Palmyra's Mount Moriah Lodge of Freemasons (see introduction to III.L.9, PALMYRA [NY] MASONIC RECORDS, 1827-1828).

worth repeating; and they had little attraction for public notice or curiosity. The reader will be content with the narration of these things as they ultimately took shape and system.

The spot from which the book is alleged to have been taken, is the yet partially visible pit where the money speculators had previously dug for another kind of treasure,[51] which is upon the summit of what has ever since been known as "Mormon Hill," now owned by Mr. Anson Robinson, in the town of Manchester, New York.[52]

This book of sacred records, after the dispersion of the first vague reports concerning it, was finally described by Smith and his echoes as consisting of metallic leaves or plates resembling gold, bound together in a volume by three rings running through one edge of them, the leaves opening like an ordinary paper book. The leaves were about the thickness of common tin. Each leaf or plate was filled on both sides with engravings of finely-drawn characters, which resembled Egyptian or other hieroglyphics. The Urim and Thummim, found with the records, were two transparent crystals set in the rims of a bow, in the form of spectacles of enormous size. This constituted the seer's instrument whereby the records were to be [p. 34] translated and the mysteries of hidden things revealed, and it was to supersede the further use of the magic stone. The entire sacred acquisition was delivered into the hands of the prophet by the heavenly messenger attending him, amid the awful surroundings already stated, after the former had thrown up a few spadefuls of earth in pursuance of the Lord's command. Such was Smith's ingenious story at the time, the characterization of which is left for the reader.

Translations and interpretations were now entered upon by the prophet, and manuscript specimens of these, with some of the literally transcribed characters, were shown to people, including ministers and other gentlemen of learning and influence. These translations purported to relate to the history of scattered tribes of the earth, chiefly "Nephites" and "Lamanites," who, after the confusion of tongues at the Tower of Babel, had been directed by the Lord across the sea to this then wilderness-land, where they mostly perished by wars among themselves, and by pestilence and famine, and from whose remnants sprang our North American Indians. They

---

51. Lorenzo Saunders also mentioned seeing the excavation on the northeast side of the hill (see III.J.20, LORENZO SAUNDERS TO THOMAS GREGG, 28 JAN 1885).

52. Anson Robinson, who inherited the property at the death of his father Randall Robinson, sold it to William T. Sampson in the 1870s (T. Cook 1930, 246).

were an attempted imitation of the Scripture style of composition, containing some plagiarisms from the Bible, both the Old and New Testaments, drawing largely upon Isaiah and Jeremiah, and taking from Matthew nearly the whole of Christ's Sermon on the Mount, with [p. 35] some alterations. The manuscripts were in the handwriting of one Oliver Cowdery,[53] which had been written down by him, as he and Smith declared, from the translations, word for word, as made by the latter with the aid of the mammoth spectacles or Urim and Thummim, and verbally announced by him from behind a blanket-screen drawn across a dark corner of a room at his residence[54]—for at this time the original revelation, limiting to the prophet the right of seeing the sacred plates, had not yet been changed, and the view with the instrument used was even too brilliant for his own spiritualized eyes in the light! This was the story of the first series of translations, which was always persisted in by the few persons connected with the business at this early period of its progress. The single significance of this theory will doubtless be manifest, when the facts are stated in explanation, that Smith could not write in a legible hand, and hence an amanuensis or scribe was necessary. Cowdery had been a schoolmaster, and was the only man in the band who could make a copy for the printer.

The manifest purpose of exhibiting these manuscripts in the manner adopted, was to test the popular credulity in regard to their assumed divine character; and also to determine, by the responses that should be elicited, as to the practicability of carrying out a concocted design of printing the "new Bible." Among [p. 36] others, Mr. George Crane,[55] of the adjoining town of Macedon, a Quaker of intelligence, property, and high respectability (now deceased), was called upon by Smith with several foolscap quires of these so-called translations, for his perusal and opinion, and also for his pecuniary aid to get the work through the press. The impious story, in all its extravagance and garniture, was related to him, to which he quietly listened to the end. And then came the answer of the honest old Quaker, which was such as would have been withering to the sensibility of an ordinary impostor—though Smith was unmoved by it, for his spirit of determination was never

53. On Oliver Cowdery (1806-50), see "Introduction to Oliver Cowdery Collection."

54. According to Joseph Smith, the translation did not begin until after his removal to Harmony, Pennsylvania (I.A.15, JOSEPH SMITH HISTORY, 1839, 8-9).

55. George Crane, in his seventies, is listed in the 1830 census of Macedon, Wayne County, New York (1830:101). See also III.K.14, JOHN BARBER AND HENRY HOWE ACCOUNT, 1841.

known to yield consentingly to any adverse human influence. Sternly rebuking Smith's pretensions, and denouncing them as in a high degree blasphemous and wicked, Mr. Crane kindly but earnestly admonished him, for his own good, to desist from his criminal pursuit, warning him that persistence therein would be certain to end in his death upon the gallows, or in some equally ignominious manner.[56] How far this friendly warning was made prophetic, by the murderous catastrophe occurring fifteen years afterward, in Illinois, is a question respectfully submitted to the reader. [p. 37]

Undaunted by any rebuffs, Prophet Smith persisted in his grand design, and, by the power of his expanding genius, secured a few devoted followers in this incipiency of his new revelation—proving that, in his case, "the prophet" was not wholly "without honor" even in his "own country." Here may be recognized the first budding of the Mormon organization, or "Church of Latter-Day Saints."

These pioneer Mormon disciples, so far as their names can now be recollected, were as follows, viz.: Oliver Cowdery, Samuel Lawrence,[57] Martin Harris,[58] Preserved Harris,[59] Peter Ingersoll,[60] Charles Ford,[61] George Proper[62] and his wife Dolly,[63] of Palmyra; Ziba Peterson,[64] and Calvin

56. See III.J.15, STEPHEN S. HARDING TO THOMAS GREGG, FEB 1882, 40; III.K.14, JOHN BARBER AND HENRY HOWE ACCOUNT, 1841; and III.D.7, JOSEPH ROGERS STATEMENT, 16 MAY 1887.

57. On Samuel F. Lawrence, see I.B.5, LUCY SMITH HISTORY, 1845, n. 147.

58. On Martin Harris (1783-1875), see "Introduction to Martin Harris Collection."

59. On Preserved Harris (1785-1867), see I.A.15, JOSEPH SMITH HISTORY, 1839, n. 48.

60. On Peter Ingersoll, see introduction to III.A.9, PETER INGERSOLL STATEMENT, 2 DEC 1833.

61. Charles Ford, over forty-five years of age, is listed in the 1820 census of Palmyra, Ontario County, New York (1820:336). Apparently he was the son of Calvin Ford (McIntosh 1877, 208c).

62. On George Proper, see III.B.12, LORENZO SAUNDERS INTERVIEW, 17 SEP 1884, n. 14.

63. Lorenzo Saunders mentioned seeing Oliver Cowdery baptize Dolly Proper (III.B.12, LORENZO SAUNDERS INTERVIEW, 17 SEP 1884, n. 38).

64. On Ziba Peterson (?-1849), see I.A.15, JOSEPH SMITH HISTORY, 1839, n. 105.

Stoddard[65] and his wife Sophronia,[66] of Macedon; Ezra Thayer,[67] of Brighton; Luman Walters,[68] of Pultneyville; Hiram Page,[69] of [p. 38] Fayette; David Whitmer,[70] Jacob Whitmer,[71] Christian Whitmer,[72] John Whitmer,[73] and Peter Whitmer, Jr.,[74] of Phelps[75]; Simeon Nichols,[76] of Farmington; William Stafford,[77] Joshua Stafford,[78] Gad Stafford,[79] David Fish,[80] Abram

---

65. On Calvin Stoddard (1801-36), see III.J.7, STEPHEN S. HARDING TO POMEROY TUCKER, 1 JUN 1867, n. 9.

66. On Sophronia Smith (1803-67), see I.A.15, JOSEPH SMITH HISTORY, 1839, n. 16.

67. On Ezra Thayre (1791-?), see introduction to III.J.6, EZRA THAYRE REMINISCENCE, 1862. Thayre lived near Canandaigua, Ontario County, New York, not in Brighton, Monroe County, New York, as Tucker states.

68. On Luman Walters (c. 1788-1860), see III.E.3, *PALMYRA REFLECTOR,* 1829-1831, n. 21.

69. On Hiram Page (1800-52), see introduction to VI.C.1, HIRAM PAGE TO WILLIAM MCLELLIN, 30 MAY 1847.

70. On David Whitmer (1805-88), see "Introduction to David Whitmer Collection."

71. On Jacob Whitmer (1800-56), see I.A.15, JOSEPH SMITH HISTORY, 1839, n. 98.

72. On Christian Whitmer (1798-1835), see I.A.15, JOSEPH SMITH HISTORY, 1839, n. 96.

73. On John Whitmer (1802-78), see "Introduction to John Whitmer Collection."

74. On Peter Whitmer, Jr. (1809-36), see I.A.15, JOSEPH SMITH HISTORY, 1839, n. 63.

75. The Whitmers were from Fayette, New York, not Phelps.

76. There are two Simeon Nichols listed in the 1820 census of Farmington, Ontario County, both between twenty-six and forty-five years of age (1820:309, 317).

77. On William Stafford, see introduction to III.A.13, WILLIAM STAFFORD STATEMENT, 8 DEC 1833.

78. On Joshua Stafford (1798-1876), see introduction to III.A.4, JOSHUA STAFFORD STATEMENT, 15 NOV 1833.

79. This person remains unidentified.

80. David Fish, over forty-five years of age, is listed in the 1820 census of Phelps, Ontario County, New York (1820:300).

Fish,[81] Robert Orr,[82] King H. Quance,[83] John Morgan,[84] Orrin Rockwell and his wife Caroline,[85] Widow Sally Risley,[86] and all the remainder of the Smith family, of Manchester.

It is believed that this list embraces all the persons residing at or near the prime seat of the Mormon advent, who from first to last made a profession of belief either in the money-digging or golden bible finding pretensions of Joseph Smith, Jr.; and probably, indeed, not more than one-half of these can be said to have been genuine converts under the one head or the other. It is to be added in this connection, however, that a man of the name of Parley P. Pratt,[87] of Lorain County, Ohio, who, on hearing of the new religion, after the Mormon book was printed (as he said in explanation of his movement), stopped off a canal-boat at Palmyra, and at Smith's residence embraced the Mormon faith, and joined the organization which had then been imperfectly inaugurated. He was a member of an association of anti-sectarians, mostly dissenters from different religious denominations, whose place of worship was at Mentor, Ohio.

---

81. On Abraham Fish (c. 1773-1845), see III.I.4, NATHANIEL W. HOWELL AND OTHERS TO ANCIL BEACH, JAN 1832, n. 3.

82. Robert Orr, in his fifties, is listed in the 1830 census of Seneca, Ontario County, New York (1830:66). He was the stepfather of Christopher and Cornelius Stafford (see III.D.3, CHRISTOPHER M. STAFFORD STATEMENT, 23 MAR 1885).

83. King H. Quance, in his fifties, is listed in the 1840 census of Macedon, Wayne County, New York (1840:169).

84. Perhaps John Morgan, over forty-five years of age, listed in the 1820 census of Lima, Ontario County, New York (1820:366).

85. Evidently a confused reference to Orrin Porter Rockwell and his sister Caroline, both of whom were baptized on 9 June 1830. Their parents were Orin and Sarah (Witt) Rockwell (Sarah was baptized on or about 6 April 1830, but Orin delayed his baptism until after the family had moved to Ohio in 1831). On Orrin Porter Rockwell (1813-78), see I.A.15, JOSEPH SMITH HISTORY, 1839, n. 119; on Caroline Rockwell (1812-87), see introduction to III.D.5, CAROLINE ROCKWELL SMITH STATEMENT, 25 MAR 1885.

86. Possibly the same "Mrs. Risley, of Manchester, a cripple," mentioned by Christopher M. Stafford, whom the "Prophet Jo told ... he could heal her and she joined the Mormons. Jo failed to heal her and she never walked" (see III.D.3, CHRISTOPHER M. STAFFORD STATEMENT, 23 MAR 1885).

87. Parley P. Pratt (1807-57), see introduction to III.K.16, PARLEY P. PRATT AUTOBIOGRAPHY (PART I), CIRCA 1854.

"Rev. Sidney Rigdon"[88] was the regular minister of this congregation; though Pratt himself had done something [p. 39] in the way of preaching there and elsewhere, and was aspiring to still higher position in the clerical vocation. The latter, with his spiritual guide Rigdon, afterward went with the first emigrants to Kirtland, and, continuing his association with the new sect, immediately became a prominent and efficient co-worker in its priesthood, and was subsequently an important spoke in the Mormon hierarchy at Salt Lake.[89]

How many of the preceding list of pioneer "Latter-Day Saints" at Palmyra and vicinity remained faithful, or took more than the first degree in the new institution, is now unknown to the writer. It is recollected that at least a portion, perhaps the majority of them, became backsliders after a very brief experience.

The proposition to publish the new revelation was as yet an adjourned question. Martin Harris enthusiastically favored it, and he was the man calculated on for the means of payment for the printing. He was one of the earliest, if not, in truth, the only real believer. He was a religious monomaniac, reading the Scriptures intently, and could probably repeat from memory nearly every text of the Bible from beginning to end, giving the chapter and verse in each case. His superstition and cupidity were both ap[p. 40]pealed to in this matter. Though he unreservedly gave in his adhesion to the book as of divine appointment, he was by no means so prompt in his willingness to bear the whole cost of printing it, for he was proverbially a covetous, money-loving man, but an honest and benevolent one. His habit had been to look out for the best chances in a bargain, and it was natural that he should desire further opportunity for examination and consideration, and also for trying his influence in proselyting—the latter object being with a view to judging of the question of reimbursement, should he advance the money required—and he was accordingly permitted to take the manuscript translations into his possession. Reading a portion of them to his wife, a Quakeress of positive qualities, she denounced the whole performance as silly and impious. His neighbors and friends, whom he importuned and bored on the

---

88. On Sidney Rigdon (1793-1876), see introduction to I.A.13, SIDNEY RIGDON ACCOUNT, CIRCA 1836.

89. Footnote in original reads: "The reader, as he pursues this history, will discover the bearing of the coincidence here referred to, upon the questions of the literary origin and prime invention of the 'Golden Bible.'" Tucker refers here to his discussion of the Spaulding theory of the Book of Mormon's origin (pp. 111-28), which has been deleted from this reproduction.

subject, uniformly expressed the same sentiment and belief, and cautioned him against being imposed upon and defrauded.

But this opposition served only to strengthen Harris's profession of faith and increase his inclination to make the printing investment. Yet he evidenced some method in his madness, for, before doing so, he sought out the "wisdom of learned men," as he said, relative to the genuineness of the revelation and discovery. He accordingly procured from Smith some resemblances of antique characters or hieroglyphics [p. 41] purporting to be exact copies from the plates; which, together with the translations in his possession, he carried to New York City, where he sought for them the interpretation and bibliological scrutiny of such scholars as Hon. Luther Bradish,[90] Dr. Mitchell,[91] Professor Anthon,[92] and others. All the gentlemen applied to were understood to have scouted the whole pretence as too depraved for serious attention, while commiserating the applicant as the victim of fanaticism or insanity.

Harris, nevertheless, stood firm in his position, regarding these untoward results merely as "proving the lack of wisdom" on the part of the rejecters, and also as illustrating the truth of his favorite quotation, that "God hath chosen the foolish things of the world to confound the wise." This was always his self-convincing argument in reply to similar adversity in his fanatical pursuit.

The following is Professor Anthon's account of Harris's interview with him, as given and published a few years afterward. It was addressed in a letter to a friend in reply to inquiries. ...[93]

Harris appears not to have presented the "translations" with the hieroglyphics to Professor Anthon, or if so, the immaterial fact had left too slight an impression for his recollection at the time of writing the above statement.

The pursuer after knowledge returned home, confirmed rather than shaken in his belief; for he had taken the sensible conclusions of the "learned men" he had seen by the rule of contraries, declaring in a boastful spirit that

---

90. On Luther Bradish (1783-1863), see III.H.10, JOHN H. GILBERT MEMORANDUM, 8 SEP 1892, n. 19.

91. On Samuel L. Mitchell (1764-1831), see 1.A.15, JOSEPH SMITH HISTORY, 1839, n. 45.

92. On Charles Anthon (1797-1867), see introduction to V.D.2, CHARLES ANTHON TO E. D. HOWE, 17 FEB 1834.

93. Tucker's reprint of Anthon's letter to E. D. Howe (pp. 42-45) is here deleted (see V.D.2, CHARLES ANTHON TO E. D. HOWE, 17 FEB 1834).

God had enabled him, an unlearned man as he was, to "confound worldly wisdom." He had apparently become seized with the Golden Bible mania beyond redemption. It was his constant theme wherever he appeared, rendering him, by his readings and commentaries, an object both of sympathy and dread to his friends and all whom he met.

As might have been anticipated, Harris's wife became exceedingly annoyed and disgusted with what she called her husband's "craziness." She foresaw, as she thought, that if he incurred the printing liability, as he had avowed to her his purpose of doing, the event would be the ruin of himself and family. [p. 45] Thus exercised, she contrived, in her husband's sleep, to steal from him the particular source of her disturbance, and burned the manuscript to ashes. For years she kept this incendiarism a profound secret to herself, even until after the book was published. Smith and Harris held her accountable for the theft, but supposed she had handed the manuscript to some "evil-designing persons" to be used somehow in injuring their cause. A feud was thus produced between husband and wife, which was never reconciled.[94]

Great consternation now pervaded the Mormon circles. The reappearance of the mysterious stranger at Smith's was again the subject of inquiry and conjecture by observers, from whom was withheld all explanation of his identity or purpose.[95] It was not at first an easy task to convince the prophet of the entire innocency of his trusted friend Harris in the matter of this calamitous event, though mutual confidence and friendship were ultimately restored. The great trouble was, the lost translations could not be replaced, or at least such apparently was the difficulty. It might be supposed that, with his golden plates and spectacles before him, and with the benefit of the divine aid as he claimed, the prophet could easily have supplied a duplicate; and so he doubtless would have done had he really been the translator or original author of the composition. To explain his inability to reproduce the missing pages, he said he had received [p. 46] a revelation of the Lord's displeasure for his imprudence in placing them in Harris's hands, and on this account forbidding his rewriting the same [D&C 10]; and another reason for this interdiction was, that his enemies had obtained possession of the manuscripts, and altered them with a view of "confounding him" and embarrassing his great work of enlightenment and salvation! He and Harris were undoubtedly led to suppose that the lost manuscripts remained in existence, and might somehow be used for the object assigned. [p. 47]

94. See III.L.16, BOOK OF MORMON PREFACE, 1829.
95. See n. 42 above.

The loss of the first translations checked for a time the progress of Mormon events. But Smith, Harris, and their abiding associates were seemingly undismayed. Some six months passed when the announcement was given out that a new and complete translation of the Book of Mormon had been made by the prophet, which was ready for the press. In the interim the stranger before spoken of had again been seen at Smith's; and the prophet had been away from home, may-be to repay the former's visits. The bearing of these circumstances upon any important question can only be left to reasonable conjecture in reference to the subsequent developments. The second manuscripts, like the first, were in Cowdery's handwriting.

The work of translation this time had been done in the recess of a dark artificial cave, which Smith had caused to be dug in the east side of the forest-hill [p. 48] near his residence, now owned by Mr. Amos Miner. At least such was one account given out by the Mormon fraternity; though another version was, that the prophet continued to pursue his former mode of translating behind the curtain at his house, and only went into the cave to pay his spiritual devotions and seek the continued favor of Divine Wisdom. His stays in the cave varied from fifteen minutes to an hour or over—the entrance meanwhile being guarded by one or more of his disciples. This ceremony scarcely attracted the curiosity of outsiders, though it was occasionally witnessed by men and boys living near the scene.[96]

This excavation was at the time said to be one hundred and sixty feet in extent, though that is probably an exaggeration. It had a substantial door of two-inch plank, secured by a corresponding lock. From the lapse of time and natural causes the cave has been closed for years, very little mark of its former existence remaining to be seen.

Encouraged by the continued favoring hallucination of Harris, an active canvass was now commenced by the Mormons for the printing. Harris was the only man of property or credit known in all Mormondom; and, as will appear, he happened to be exactly the appropriate subject for the prophet's designs; for without his timely aid and pecuniary sacrifice the Golden Bible would probably have remained forever an un[p. 49]published romance. And, as has already been intimated, he alone was depended upon for the means to pay for its printing, for no other man of the whole Mormon tribe could have raised a dollar of his own money for that or any other object. He was a prosperous, independent farmer, strictly upright in his business dealings, and,

---

96. See III.B.12, LORENZO SAUNDERS INTERVIEW, 17 SEP 1884, 8; III.B.15, LORENZO SAUNDERS INTERVIEW, 12 NOV 1884, 8.

although evidencing good qualifications in the affairs of his industrial calling, yet he was the slave of the peculiar religious fanaticism controlling his mental organization. "Marvellousness" being his predominating phrenological development, he was noted for the betrayal of vague superstitions—a belief in dreams, ghosts, hobgoblins, "special providences," terrestrial visits of angels, the interposition of "devils" to afflict sinful men, etc. He was the son of Nathan Harris, an early settler in Palmyra, and aged about forty-three years. His family consisted of a wife, one son, and two daughters.[97]

This was the position of Martin Harris in the community at this important turning-period in his life and career. In June, 1829,[98] Smith the prophet, his brother Hyrum, Cowdery the scribe, and Harris the believer, applied to Mr. Egbert B. Grandin,[99] then publisher of the *Wayne Sentinel* at Palmyra (now deceased), for his price to do the work of one edition of three thousand copies. Harris offered to pay or secure payment if a bargain should be made. Only a few sheets of [p. 50] the manuscript, as a specimen, with the title-page, were exhibited at this time, though the whole number of folios was stated, whereby could be made a calculation of the cost. Mr. Grandin at once expressed his disinclination to entertain the proposal to print at any price, believing the whole affair to be a wicked imposture and a scheme to defraud Mr. Harris, who was his friend, and whom he advised accordingly. This admonition was kindly but firmly resisted by Harris, and resented with assumed pious indignation by the Smiths, Cowdery taking little or no part in the conversation. Some further parleying followed, Harris resolutely persisting in his deafness to the friendly expressions of regard from Mr. Grandin, and also from several other well-disposed neighbors happening to be present at the interview, who vainly united in the effort to dissuade him from his purpose. Afterward, however, it was thought Harris became for a time in some degree staggered in his confidence; but nothing could be done in the way of printing without his aid, and so the prophet persevered in his spell-binding influence and seductive arts, as will be seen, with ultimate success. Further interviews followed, Grandin being earnestly importuned to reconsider his opinion and determination. He was assured by Harris, that

97. The children of Martin and Lucy Harris were Doty L. (1812-15), George W. (c. 1814-64), and Lucy (c.1816-c. 1841) (*Utah Genealogical and Historical Magazine* 26 [July 1935]: 108).

98. On the date of Smith's application to Grandin, see I.A.15, JOSEPH SMITH HISTORY, 1839, 26, 34; and III.H.10, JOHN H. GILBERT MEMORANDUM, 8 SEP 1892.

99. On Egbert B. Grandin (1806-45), see I.A.15, JOSEPH SMITH HISTORY, 1839, n. 77.

if he refused to do the work, it would be procured elsewhere. And the subject was temporarily dropped, except that Grandin complied with Harris's [p. 51] request for an approximate estimate of the cost of the proposed edition.

Immediately thereafter, the same Mormon party, or a portion of them, applied to Mr. Thurlow Weed, of the *Anti-Masonic Inquirer* at Rochester, from whom they met a similar repulse. Mr. Weed's own words in regard to the manuscript and the printing proposal are: "After reading a few chapters, it seemed such a jumble of unintelligible absurdities, that we refused the work, advising Harris not to mortgage his farm and beggar his family." Mr. Elihu F. Marshall, a book publisher, also at Rochester, was then applied to, and he gave his terms for the printing and binding of the book, with his acceptance of the proffered mode of security for the payment.[100]

Whereupon, the "saints" returned to Palmyra, and renewed their request to Mr. Grandin, reassuring him that the work was to be done at any rate, and pleading that they would be saved much inconvenience and cost of travel to have the printing done at Palmyra, where they lived, especially as the manuscripts were to be delivered and the proof-sheets examined daily by them at the printing-office.

It was upon this statement of the facts, and in this view of the case, that Mr. Grandin, on taking the advice of several discreet, fair-minded neighbors, finally reconsidered his course of policy, and entered into contract for the printing and binding of five thousand [p. 52] copies of the Book of Mormon at the price of $3,000, taking Harris's bond and mortgage as offered in security for payment.[101] The contract was faithfully and satisfactorily fulfilled by both parties, and the book in its entire edition as bargained for was completed and delivered early in the summer of 1830.[102]

In the beginning of the printing the Mormons professed to hold their manuscripts as "sacred," and insisted upon maintaining constant vigilance for their safety during the progress of the work,[103] each morning carrying to the printing-office the instalment required for the day, and withdrawing the same

100. Compare III.J.5, POMEROY TUCKER REMINISCENCE, 1858; see also III.K.17, THURLOW WEED REMINISCENCES, 1854, 1858, 1880 & 1884.

101. See III.L.14, MARTIN HARRIS MORTGAGE, 25 AUG 1829.

102. While the Book of Mormon was ready for sale in March 1830, evidently the entire run of the first edition was not completed until the early summer of 1830.

103. According to John H. Gilbert, twenty-four pages were brought to Grandin's office each day (e.g., III.F.2, JOHN H. GILBERT TO JAMES T. COBB, 10 FEB 1879).

at evening. No alteration from copy in any manner was to be made. These things were "strictly commanded," as they said. Mr. John H. Gilbert, as printer, had the chief operative trust of the type-setting and press-work of the job. After the first day's trial he found the manuscripts in so very imperfect a condition, especially in regard to grammar, that he became unwilling further to obey the "command," and so announced to Smith and his party; when, finally, upon much friendly expostulation, he was given a limited discretion in correcting, which was exercised in the particulars of syntax, orthography, punctuation, capitalizing, paragraphing, etc. Many errors under these heads, nevertheless, escaped correction, as appear in the first edition of the printed book. Very soon, too—after some ten days—the constant vigilance by the [p. 53] Mormons over the manuscripts was relaxed by reason of the confidence they came to repose in the printers. Mr. Gilbert has now in his possession a complete copy of the book in the original sheets, as laid off by him from the press in working.[104]

It may be due to the memory of Mr. Grandin, in relation to this Golden Bible printing contract, to mention the fact that Mrs. Harris, who had so strenuously objected to her husband's fanatical course, fully conceded the propriety of Mr. Grandin's action under the circumstances as they existed.

Meanwhile, Harris and his wife had separated by mutual arrangement, on account of her persistent unbelief in Mormonism and refusal to be a party to the mortgage. The family estate was divided, Harris giving her about eighty acres of the farm, with a comfortable house and other property as her share of the assets; and she occupied this property until the time of her death.[105] The main farm and homestead, about one hundred and fifty acres of land, was retained by himself, the mortgage covering only this portion; but Mormonism, more than farming or other business, ever afterward engaged his attention, and this was the beginning of adversity which ultimately reduced him to poverty.

The farm mortgaged was sold by Harris in 1831 at private sale, not by foreclosure, and a sufficiency of the avails went to pay Grandin—though it is pre[p. 54]sumed Harris might have paid the $3,000 without the sale of the

---

104. See III.H.10, JOHN H. GILBERT MEMORANDUM, 8 SEP 1892.

105. On 29 November 1825, Martin Harris deeded eighty acres of land to his brother-in-law, Peter Harris, who in turn deeded the land to Lucy Harris on the same day. Tucker is therefore incorrect in connecting the Harrises' division of property with their separation over Mormonism (see Gunnell 1955, 95-96; James 1983, 124 n. 99; see also introduction to III.L.14, MARTIN HARRIS MORTGAGE, 25 AUG 1829).

farm.[106] This was among the best properties of the kind in the town. Most of it, including the homestead portion, is the same now owned by Mr. Thomas Chapman, a mile and a half north of the village of Palmyra.

As will be seen, Harris was led to believe that the book would be a profitable speculation for him, and very likely in this may be traced his leading motive for taking the venture. He was vouchsafed the security of a "special revelation" commanding that the new Bible should in no instance be sold at a less price than "ten shillings," and that he himself should have the exclusive right of sale, with all the avails—the only purpose of the Mormon saints being the unselfish one to "get the great light before the world for the salvation of mankind!" Indeed, he figured up the profits with all the certainty of their realization, that the most enthusiastic calculator would feel in "counting his chickens before they are hatched." Like thousands of fortunes made on paper, this process by Harris was an easy matter, thus: 5,000 books at $1.25 per book, $6,250. First cost, $3,000. Showing a clear speculation of over one hundred per cent upon the investment!

In October following (1829), the printing was considerably advanced, and the ultimate issue of the Book of Mormon had become a fixed fact. The print[p. 55]ing was done upon a hand-press, and the type of one form had to be distributed before another could be set up; and of course this will account for the tardiness of the work. But the first and second books of "Nephi," and some other portions of the forthcoming revelation, were printed in sheets;—and armed with a copy of these, Smith commenced other preparations for a mission to Pennsylvania, where he had some relatives residing, and where the before-mentioned "Rev. Sidney Rigdon" was then residing or temporarily sojourning.[107] His wardrobe needed replenishing, and Harris, who was abundantly able to do as he did, and withal counting on his prospective profits in the bible speculation, procured for him a new black suit, remarking to the merchant of whom he bought the cloth, that as the prophet was going on a mission to preach the new gospel, it was necessary that he should "appear comely before men;" and consequently ordered the best pattern in the store. Mr. David S. Aldrich,[108] now prominent dry-goods

106. Harris sold about 150 acres of his land to Thomas Lakey for $3,000 on 7 April 1831 (see III.L.14, MARTIN HARRIS MORTGAGE, 25 AUG 1829).

107. Rigdon was in Perry, Ohio, in October 1829 (see E. L. Kelley in RLDS *Journal of History,* 3:16-20).

108. David S. Aldrich came to Palmyra in the 1820s. He was a clerk for "Lovett & Havens" and for "Sexton & Butterfield." Thomas L. Cook states that "while a clerk in the post office, then situated in a dry goods store,

merchant in Palmyra, sold the cloth as a clerk at that time. The result was, that in November, Smith went to Northern Pennsylvania, as previously appointed, where he married the daughter of Isaac Hale,[109] and was baptized after the Mormon ritual[110]—Rigdon being the "match-maker" and the officiating "clergyman" in these celebrations.[111] Mr. Hale, the father-in-law, never became a Mormon. [p. 56]

Smith soon returned to Palmyra, to complete his grand design, having made on this occasion, so far as known, no sensation as a preacher, nor any progress in his proselyting mission beyond his nuptial capture. [p. 57]

The newly revealed gospel having been opened to the world in a printed book, Prophet Smith and his disciples proceeded to a more perfect organization of their church for its practice and dissemination. This ceremony, conducted with apparent seriousness by the prophet, supported on the right and left by Cowdery and Harris—of which it is now too late to give the full particulars from memory—took place in the dwelling-house of Joseph Smith, Sr., in the month of June, 1830.[112] There was no praying, singing, or preaching attempted, but Joseph gave various readings and interpretations of the new bible. The senior Smith was installed "Patriarch and President of the Church of Latter-Day Saints;"[113] while Cowdery and Harris were nominated vicegerents [viceregents] to the prophet, or dignitaries of equivalent import, and a limited commission of priesthood and prophecy was conferred [p. 58] upon them by the prophet, accompanied by the "laying on of hands" and other ceremonious observances, adding great "promises" of future spiritual endowment, to depend in an essential manner

---

he [Aldrich] sold to the Mormon Prophet, Joseph Smith, his first decent suit of cloths." About 1850 Aldrich himself opened a dry goods business. He died in 1882 at Palmyra (T. Cook 1930, 77, 125).

109. Joseph Knight also has Smith coming to live with him in Colesville in November 1826 (IV.A.1, JOSEPH KNIGHT, SR., REMINISCENCE, CIRCA 1835-1847, 2), but Smith did not marry Emma Hale until 18 January 1827.

110. Joseph Smith was baptized by Oliver Cowdery at Harmony, Pennsylvania, on 15 May 1829.

111. Compare III.J.5, POMEROY TUCKER REMINISCENCE, 1858. Emma Smith specifically denied this accusation (see I.F.3, EMMA SMITH BIDAMON INTERVIEW WITH JOSEPH SMITH III, FEB 1879, 289).

112. Probably a reference to the church organization on 6 April 1830.

113. Joseph Smith, Sr., was ordained Patriarch of the Church on 18 December 1833 (L. Cook 1981, 11). However, the church was not known as the "Church of the Latter Day Saints" until 1834.

on their fidelity and efficiency in the trust already reposed in them.

The participants generally in this incipient church inauguration were the individuals named as the pioneer saints in a preceding chapter, with perhaps few changes *pro* and *con.* The rite of baptism by immersion was administered by the prophet to Cowdery and Harris at their particular request—a pool for that purpose having been created by constructing a dam across the brook near the place of meeting[114]; and then the other baptisms on this occasion were conducted by Cowdery, including in these benefits both the aged parents of the revelator, Page, Mrs. Rockwell, Dolly Proper, and several of the Whitmer brothers.[115] So far as can be recollected of the proceedings, as verbally reported at the time, no others were then baptized; but afterward this baptismal service was extended to all the saints who had not already been the favored subjects of that ritual, Cowdery continuing to officiate in these solemnities.

The prophet himself was not baptized in this instance, the explanation of the omission being, as stated by some of the faithful, that he was elevated far above "worldly baptism" by reason of his "spiritual sphere;" but another account—doubtless the ac[p. 59]cepted one—assigned as the reason in the case that he had previously received the ordinance in Pennsylvania by the ministration of "Brother Rigdon,"[116] and was the first Mormon baptized since the times of the primitive Nephites.

A few days after this preliminary launching of the Mormon ship

114. On the location of the 6 April 1830 baptisms of Joseph Smith, Sr., and Martin Harris, see III.J.35, THOMAS L. COOK HISTORY, 1930, 220. However, Cowdery had been baptized by Joseph Smith, Jr., on 15 May 1829 (see III.G.6, OLIVER COWDERY TO W. W. PHELPS, 7 SEP 1834, 15-16; I.A.15, JOSEPH SMITH HISTORY, 1839, 17-18; I.B.5, LUCY SMITH HISTORY, 1845, MS:94).

115. Of this list, those baptized by Oliver Cowdery at Manchester were Martin Harris and Joseph Smith, Sr., on 6 April 1830; Lucy Smith and Sarah Rockwell, on 8 or 9 April; and Dolly Proper, several months later (see I.A.15, JOSEPH SMITH HISTORY, 1839, 38; DRAFT:9-10; III.B.13, BENJAMIN SAUNDERS INTERVIEW, CIRCA SEP 1884, 27; III.B.12, LORENZO SAUNDERS INTERVIEW, 17 SEP 1884, 12 [back]; III.B.15, LORENZO SAUNDERS INTERVIEW, 12 NOV 1884, 7). Page and the Whitmers were baptized in Fayette (see I.A.15, JOSEPH SMITH HISTORY, 1839, 23, 39).

116. Smith had been baptized by Oliver Cowdery on 15 May 1829 (see III.G.6, OLIVER COWDERY TO W. W. PHELPS, 7 SEP 1834, 15-16; I.A.15, JOSEPH SMITH HISTORY, 1839, 17-18; I.B.5, LUCY SMITH HISTORY, 1845, MS:94).

Zion—this primeval foundation of the Mormon theocracy—some ten or twelve of the saints went to Fayette, in an adjoining county, where similar observances were had in the formation of a church. There were about thirty persons in attendance on this occasion, believers and spectators, and a number of new converts were reported, Cowdery again performing the baptismal service. But, finally, it was found that the prophet's own country was an unfavorable locality for success in this wonderful religious speculation; the new gospel was held in light repute by the "Gentile" people; conversions did not come up to the anticipations of the leaders; and in the course of the same year these pioneer Mormons emigrated to Ohio.

Now, let the reader's attention be carried back to the commencement of the Golden Bible publication. The book, as a money-making enterprise, fell dead before the public. As a religious demonstration, it was received by the community as "stale, flat, and fulsome." It was repulsive to the popular common-sense, and, beyond the minds of its preëxistent devotees, simply awakened contempt and ridicule. It [p. 60] found no buyers, or but very few. So that the glittering visions of Harris and others, who might have thought as he had done, seemed to turn out as illusory as had been those of Smith's money-digging dupes. Hence another "command" became necessary in regard to the sale of the book, after a few weeks' faithful but unsuccessful trial of the market by Harris as a monopolist salesman.[117] This was easily called down by Smith in favor of his patriarch father. Time passed, and yet the disappointment was unalleviated. The patriarch having been permitted by this changed revelation, with the consent of Harris, to appropriate a portion of the avails of sales toward his family necessities, he effected some sales, chiefly in barter trades, on accommodating terms for the purchasers of the books, always nominally maintaining the revealed price of ten shillings, to avoid the awful penalty of "instant death" for any departure from it.[118]

117. Tucker's footnote reads: "Harris was proverbially a peaceful as well as an honest man. He was slow to retaliate an offence. The following anecdote will show what manner of man he was. Urging the sale of the book with pertinacious confidence in the genuineness of the Smith revelation, he fell into debate about its character with a neighbor of an irascible temperament. His opponent became angry, and struck him a severe blow upon the right side of his face. Instantly turning toward the assailant the other check, he quoted the Christian maxim, reading it from the book in his hand, page 481 (as it also appears in Matthew [5:39]): 'Whosoever shall smite thee on the right cheek, turn to him the other also [3 Nephi 12:39].'"

118. The terms of the agreement were reversed from what Tucker describes. Rather than Harris agreeing to share his profits with Joseph Sr., it is Smith who agrees to give Harris "an equal privilege with me & my friends."

Pedes[p. 61]trian peddling jaunts were made in the neighboring villages and surrounding country, and books peddled off by him in exchange for various articles of farmers' produce and shop merchandise, such as "wouldn't come amiss for family use in hard times." In this way considerable improvement was made in the old "saint's" exchequer. Harris, meanwhile, seemed to stand firm in his adhesion to the book's divinity, and always had at his tongue's end an amplitude of scriptural and Mormonic quotations of "promises," giving satisfactory assurance of his ultimate pecuniary and spiritual salvation.

Many appropriate incidents might be related from the memory of individuals yet living at the original scene of this blooming of the Mormon Church, illustrative of the shallowness of the great imposture; but which, given in detail, would surfeit the reader's curiosity. A single anecdote will suffice to show the degree of sincerity attached to the pretended "commandment price" of the book.

The Patriarch and President of the Mormon Church [Joseph Smith, Sr.] was now preparing to remove with his family to Ohio, where the Prophet Joseph and his brother Hyrum, with others of the faith, had already preceded them,[119] and it was necessary to procure some articles of outfit. In pursuance of this object, he took a basket of "bibles" in his hand and walked to Palmyra village, where he had usually done his small [p. 62] traffic, and where sundry unadjusted little scores were ready to confront him, which his overplus book avails and other resources had been insufficient to liquidate. By the then prevailing legal system for the collection of debts (residing, as he did, over the county line from Palmyra), he made himself liable to suit by warrant and also detention in imprisonment for non-payment. But necessity being his master, he had taken the incautious venture, and soon found himself in the constable's custody at the suit of a creditor for a small book account. The parties appeared before A. R. Tiffany, Esq.,[120] a justice of the peace for Wayne County, by whom the warrant had been issued. After some preliminary parleying by the debtor, he invited and enjoyed a private

---

Moreover, the date of the agreement is 16 January 1830, two months before the Book of Mormon was released for sale (see III.L.17, JOSEPH SMITH, SR., AND MARTIN HARRIS AGREEMENT, 16 JAN 1830).

119. Hyrum accompanied his father to Ohio in the spring of 1831.

120. Alexander R. Tiffany, in his thirties, is listed in the 1830 census of Palmyra, Wayne County, New York (1830:41). A practicing attorney (e.g., *Wayne Sentinel,* 30 August 1825), Tiffany was justice of the peace for Wayne County in 1823 and 1826 (McIntosh 1877, 140, 143). Thus far, there is no contemporary evidence for the case involving Joseph Smith, Sr., as described by Tucker.

interview with the creditor in an adjoining room. The debt and costs had now reached the aggregate of $5.63. The embarrassments in the case, after some brief discussion, were found to be of a difficult nature. At last, laying the good-natured claimant under strict confidential injunction, and referring with solemn air to the "command" by which he was empowered to sell his Mormon work only at the price of $1.25 per copy, the crafty "patriarch" proposed, nevertheless, on the express condition that his perfidy should not be exposed, the offer of seven books in full for the demand, being a fraction more than eighty cents apiece. The joke was relished as too [p. 63] good to go unpatronized, and though the books were not regarded as possessing any value, the claimant, more in a spirit of mischief than otherwise, accepted the compromise accordingly. The *finale* was, that the Mormon saint was permitted to slip home from a side door, to avoid like importunities from other creditors, and it is believed this was his last appearance in Palmyra by daylight.

Such was the advent, and such the popular reception of the Book of Mormon, and the Church of the Latter-Day Saints founded thereon as its corner-stone, at the place of their professed origin. The book has since gone through many editions in the different languages of the civilized world. ...[121]

Smith's first "command" limiting to his eye alone the mortal sight of the metallic records, except on the penalty of "instant death" denounced against the daring of any other human being, failed in its apparent purpose. It was treated as "Joe's nonsense" outside of the immediate circle of his small band of followers, as were all his stories of visions and of the "golden" book. Hence a modification of the revelation seemingly became necessary to secure the public acceptance of this miraculous spiritual dispensation. Exactly when this change was reached, did not generally transpire, or at least it is not within remembrance, though for months antecedent to the publication of the book, the conclusive "testimony of witnesses" to the actual sight and veritable existence of "the plates which contained the record," was verbally [p. 68] proclaimed by Smith and others in corroboration of the prophetic pretension. This circumstance explains the otherwise apparent inconsistency of the following allegations of eleven witnesses, which are appended to the printed volume: ...[122]

---

121. Tucker's reproduction of the Book of Mormon's title page and preface (pp. 64-67) have been deleted (see III.L.12, BOOK OF MORMON COPYRIGHT, 11 JUN 1829; and III.L.16, BOOK OF MORMON PREFACE, 1829).

122. Tucker's reproductions of the testimony of three and eight witnesses (pp. 69-71) have been deleted (see VI.G.1, TESTIMONY OF THREE WITNESSES, JUN 1829; and III.L.13, TESTIMONY OF EIGHT

How to reconcile the act of Harris in signing his name to such a statement, in view of the character of honesty which had always been conceded to him, could never be easily explained. In reply to uncharitable suggestions of his neighbors, he used to practise a good deal of his characteristic jargon about "seeing with the spiritual eye," and the like.[123] As regards the other witnesses associated with Harris, their averments in this or any other matter could excite no more surprise than did those of Smith himself. ... [p. 71] ...

Mormonism and its bible being thus candidates for acceptance or rejection before the public judgment, an early popular decision was sought by their supporters. Up to this time, Sidney Rigdon had played his part in the background, and his occasional visits at Smith's residence had been noticed by uninitiated observers as those of the mysterious stranger. It had been his policy to remain in concealment until [p. 75] all things should be in readiness for blowing the trumpet of the new gospel. He was a backsliding clergyman of the Baptist persuasion, and at the period referred to was the principal preacher of a sort of religious society calling themselves "Reformers" or "Disciples," at Mentor, Ohio, near Kirtland. ...

This man Rigdon now appeared as the first regular Mormon preacher in Palmyra. Martin Harris was his forerunner, and relieved him of his incognito position. Harris had in vain sought the use of the churches respectively for his appointed clerical service. But the hall of the Palmyra Young Men's Association, in the third story of Exchange Row, was yielded for the object, upon the earnest entreaty of Harris, whose sincerity and good intentions were unquestioned. At the designated hour, a respectable audience had assembled[124]; but it was a small one, for be it remembered that the church of the order of Latter-Day Saints was just emerging from its chrysalis state.

Rigdon introduced himself as "the Messenger of [p. 76] God," declar-

---

WITNESSES, JUN 1829).

123. See discussion in "Introduction to Martin Harris Collection."

124. Regarding Rigdon's 1830 sermon in Palmyra, Tucker subsequently informs the reader of his personal knowledge of the matter. In a letter to Rigdon, dated 19 April 1867, Tucker states: "I am emboldened to address you, without the benefit of a personal acquaintance that you will recognize, from having received a personal introduction to you here in 1830. I heard your sermon at the hall of our Palmyra Young Men's Association in that year, in reference to the then new Mormon revelation according to Joseph Smith, Jr." (Tucker 1867, 126). See also III.B.12, LORENZO SAUNDERS INTERVIEW, 17 SEP 1884, 9; III.B.14, LORENZO SAUNDERS INTERVIEW, 20 SEP 1884, 5; III.B.15, LORENZO SAUNDERS INTERVIEW, 12 NOV 1884, 6; and III.D.9, LORENZO SAUNDERS STATEMENT, 21 JUL 1887.

ing that he was commanded from above to proclaim the Mormon revelation. He then went through the ceremonious form of prayer, in which he expressed his grateful sense of the blessings of the glorious gospel dispensation now opening to the world, and the miraculous light from Heaven to be displayed through the instrumentality of the "chosen revelator," Joseph Smith, Jr. Bespeaking the favor of the Most High in return for the kindness of the Association in granting the use of their hall, he concluded his prayer by commanding all believers to the divine care and protection against the sneers and persecutions of their adversaries.

The discourse was based upon the following text read by the preacher from the recently published Book of Mormon, which the searcher may find in "First Book of Nephi," chapter iv. (page 32, original edition [1 Nephi 13:40]):—

"And the angel spake unto me, saying: These last records which thou hast seen among the Gentiles, shall establish the truth of the first, which is of the Twelve Apostles of the lamb, and shall make known the plain and precious things which have been taken away from them; and shall make known to all kindreds, tongues, and people, that the Lamb of God is the Eternal Father and Saviour of the world; and that all men must come unto Him, or they cannot be saved." [p. 77]

The preacher assumed to establish the theory that the Book of Mormon and the old Bible were one in inspiration and importance, and that the "precious things" now revealed had for wise purposes been withheld from the book first promulgated to the world, and were necessary to establish its truth. In the course of his argument he applied various quotations from the two books to prove his position. Holding the Book of Mormon in his right hand, and the Bible in his left hand, he brought them together in a manner corresponding to the emphatic declaration made by him, that they were both equally the Word of God; that neither was perfect without the other; and that they were inseparably necessary to complete the everlasting gospel of the Saviour Jesus Christ. The "latter-day" theory was dwelt upon at some length, with apparent seriousness. Reiterating the declaration made in his introduction, that he was "commanded" to proclaim these truths for the salvation of fallen man, he wound up his discourse by a warning appeal to the confidence and faith of his hearers; adding a benediction.

This is by no means offered as a literal report of the "sermon" beyond a few points, but is believed to state truthfully and fairly its essential features, as quite distinctly remembered after the lapse of nearly thirty-seven years. Altogether, though evidencing some talent and ingenuity in its matter and manner, [p. 78] and delivered with startling boldness and seeming sincerity, the performance was in the main an unintelligible jumble of quotations, assertions, and obscurities, which was received by the audience as shockingly blasphemous, as it was painful to hear. The manifestations of disfavor were so unequivocal that Harris hesitatingly assented to the suggestion of his "Gentile" friends to withhold all further request for the use of the hall for a repetition of the exhibition. And "regular preaching" upon the Mormon plan was never again attempted by Rigdon or any other man in Palmyra, according to the best knowledge and belief of the writer.

Rigdon, however, remained at Smith's for some days, preaching in the neighborhood, and baptizing several converts. Smith himself, with Harris, Cowdery, and Stoddard, also made some advances toward preaching in an irregular, miscellaneous way, in barns and in the streets; but all these failed to find "orderly-behaved" hearers in sufficient numbers to encourage their persistence in the clerical vocation. They "lacked the gift of public speaking" to communicate the revelation, as was explained by themselves. Cowdery excelled in the baptismal service, but that seemed to be the extent of his ministerial talent.

An anecdote, well remembered by numerous people now living near the scene of the performance, will [p. 79] serve as an illustration of the facility with which Smith gained converts and co-laborers.

[Calvin] Stoddard[125] was an early believer in Mormonism, and was quite as eccentric a character as Harris. He was slightly impressed that he had a call to preach the new gospel, but his mind was beclouded with perplexing doubts upon the question. One dark night, about ten o'clock, Stephen S. Harding,[126] then a stalwart, fun-loving, dare-devil genius of eighteen years, late Territorial Governor of Utah (not a Mormon), who well knew Stoddard's peculiarities, and being bent on making a sensation, repaired with his genial friend, Abner Tucker,[127] to the residence of the enthusiast; and awakening him from sleep by three signals upon the door with a huge stone, deliberately proclaimed, in a loud, sonorous voice, with solemn intonations—"C-a-l-v-i-n S-t-o-d-d-a-r-d! t-h-e a-n-g-e-l o-f t-h-e

---

125. On Calvin Stoddard (1801-36), who married Sophronia Smith in 1828, see III.J.7, STEPHEN S. HARDING TO POMEROY TUCKER, 1 JUN 1867, n. 9.

126. For Harding's own account of the following event, see III.J.7, STEPHEN S. HARDING TO POMEROY TUCKER, 1 JUN 1867, 285-86; and III.J.15, STEPHEN S. HARDING TO THOMAS GREGG, FEB 1882, 48-49.

127. Perhaps Abner Tucker, age thirty-seven, listed in the 1850 census of Macedon, Ontario County, New York, as a "Shoemaker" (1850:71).

L-o-r-d c-o-m-m-a-n-d-s t-h-a-t b-e-f-o-r-e a-n-o-t-h-e-r g-o-i-n-g d-o-w-n o-f t-h-e s-u-n, t-h-o-u s-h-a-l-t g-o f-o-r-t-h a-m-o-n-g t-h-e p-e-o-p-l-e a-n-d p-r-e-a-c-h t-h-e g-o-s-p-e-l o-f N-e-p-h-i, o-r t-h-y w-i-f-e s-h-a-l-l b-e a w-i-d-o-w, t-h-y c-h-i-l-d-r-e-n o-r-p-h-a-n-s, a-n-d t-h-y a-s-h-e-s s-c-a-t-t-e-r-e-d t-o t-h-e f-o-u-r w-i-n-d-s o-f h-e-a-v-e-n!"

The experiment was a complete success. Stoddard's former convictions were now confirmed. Such a convincing "revelation" was final, and not to be disregarded. Early the next morning the subject of this [p. 80] "special call" was seen upon his rounds among his neighbors, as a Mormon missionary, earnestly telling them of the "command" he had received to preach. Luminous arguments and evidences were adduced by him to sustain the foundation of his belief in this his revealed sphere of duty![128]

In further illustration of the strange superstitions characterizing these pioneer disciples of Mormonism, and to complete the chain of facts going to make up this truthful history, it is proper to add one other important incident, which has never appeared in any accepted record of the saints. Enthusiastic members of the brotherhood—perhaps it should be said the more visionary of the believers—had plied the "spirit of prophecy" in foretelling the event of a miraculous birth in association with an unmarried daughter of Joseph Smith, Sr.[129] This predicted event was to astonish the gentile world as a second advent of triune humanity. Harris was exceedingly happy in the belief of a forthcoming prophet or Messiah under the Mormon dispensation, and spoke unreservedly of an "immaculate conception in our day and generation." The ample shrewdness of the prophet had probably been called in requisition to allay some unfavorable surmises on the part of his observing disciple, who was a frequenter at the family mansion; and it is apparent that the theory invented was readily adopted by Harris. Rigdon had been an occasional sojourner [p. 81] at Smith's for a year or more, though the reader may fail to perceive what this circumstance had to do with the case. The upshot of the story is, that soon after the family had started for Ohio, the miracle eventuated somewhere on the route, in the birth of a lifeless female child! The *accident* was readily set down to the account of divine interposition to avenge some act of Mormon disobedience, and Harris was

128. Stoddard's "loud call" was reported in the *Palmyra Reflector* (see III.E.3, PALMYRA REFLECTOR, 1829-31, 14, under 23 September 1829).

129. Later statements name Katharine Smith (see III.B.12, LORENZO SAUNDERS INTERVIEW, 17 SEP 1884, 1; III.B.15, LORENZO SAUNDERS INTERVIEW, 12 NOV 1884, 21; and III.D.3, CHRISTOPHER M. STAFFORD STATEMENT, 23 MAR 1885).

thus easily reconciled.

In the summer of 1830,[130] the founders of the Mormon Church then remaining at the scene of its birthplace, who had talked much of going on a mission into the Western country to convert the Lamanites (meaning Indians), started on their western expedition with their unsold Golden Bibles, and went to Mentor, Ohio, the residence of Rigdon, and Parley P. Pratt, his friend and co-worker. Near this place is Kirtland, where there were a few families belonging to Rigdon's congregation, who had become extremely fanatical under his preparatory preaching and prophecies, and were daily looking for the occurrence of some wonderful event. Seventeen of these people, men and women, readily espoused the new revelation, and were immersed by Cowdery in one night, in attestation of their Mormon faith. By the continued ministration of Rigdon, aided by Pratt, Smith, Cowdery, and their auxiliaries, conversions rapidly followed; a powerful impetus was given to the cause; and over one [p. 82] hundred persons were added to the fold in a short time. Kirtland from about this period became the headquarters of the Mormons, where their Church and colony were thoroughly organized and temporarily established. [p. 83] ...[131] ...

The legend proceeds with descriptions of the metallic volume, a part of which was sealed and not to be seen, even by Smith himself, until further revelation, and also of the Urim and Thummim or large spectacles to be used in translating, which are substantially the same as given elsewhere.

According to similar "latter-day" accounts, the wonderful event was followed by great popular commotion; though these things were not perceived or heard of at the time and locality of the original story. The following exciting description has been published by the Mormons:

"Soon the news of these discoveries by Joseph Smith, Jr., spread abroad throughout all those parts. False reports, misrepresentations, and base slanders, flew as if upon the wings of the wind, in every direction. His house was frequently beset by mobs and evil-designing persons. Several times he was shot at, and very narrowly escaped. Every device was used to get the plates away from him. And being continually in danger of his life from a gang of abandoned wretches, he at length concluded to leave the place and go to Pennsylvania; and, accordingly, packed up his goods, putting the plates into a barrel [p. 117] of beans, and proceeded upon his journey. He had not gone far, before he was overtaken by an officer with a search-warrant, who

130. Actually the latter part of October 1830.

131. Tucker's description of the Book of Mormon's contents as well as his discussion of the Spaulding theory (pp. 84-117) have been deleted.

flattered himself with the idea that he should surely obtain the plates; but after searching very diligently, he was sadly disappointed at not finding them. Mr. Smith then drove on, but before he got to his journey's end he was again overtaken by the officer on the same business, and after ransacking the wagon very carefully, he went his way as much chagrined as in the first instance, at not being able to discover the object of his search. Without any further molestation, he pursued his journey until he came into the northern part of Pennsylvania, near the Susquehanna River. Here, by the power of God, and with the aid of two crystals set in a bow (the Urim and Thummim), he translated the unsealed portion of the records into the English tongue, in obedience to the divine command."[132]

The latter portion of this Mormon second-thought—the alleged procurement of the "translations" in Pennsylvania—is probably a little nearer the truth than the pretensions first put forth by Smith, Cowdery, Harris, and their prime associates; for their story then was, that the translations were made in the manner before stated, at Smith's residence in Manchester. Whereas, no doubt, the exact truth is, that a *copy* of their production was made from a manuscript then held by an accomplice in Pennsylvania. [p. 118]

The whole idea of an attempt to harm Smith in any way, or to rob him of his "golden bible," is purely a Mormon invention, based upon no other circumstance in truth, than that an individual creditor in vain sent a constable after him in the hope of securing the payment of a small debt. ... [p. 119] ...[133]

At Kirtland, Ohio, the Mormons had a successful though brief experience in the outset of their organization which had been imperfectly effected at their starting-place in Manchester, N.Y. The nucleus of their Church and hierarchy may be said to have advanced to maturity at this point in their progress. Their doctrines, at first not at all clearly defined, were yet somewhat vague and contradictory. It is presumed that neither Smith nor Rigdon had at this time determined what should be their precise character. The new religion needed its finishing touch, but the "revelation" capital was ample for this object. Aided as they were by Parley P. Pratt, whose remarkable instantaneous conversion had occurred at Manchester, all confusion and conflict in regard to the fundamental creed were speedily dispelled before the light of the Mormon gospel. [p. 129]

Joseph Smith, Sr., the first "patriarch and president" of the Church,

---

132. Compare I.A.17, ORSON PRATT ACCOUNT, 1840, 13-14.

133. Tucker's continued discussion of the Spaulding theory of the Book of Mormon's origin and other extraneous material (pp. 119-28) have been deleted.

soon removed with his family to Kirtland, and fulfilled the dignity of his office. Harris early made a purchase of property there, and took his place in the Church with the Smiths, Rigdon, Pratt, Cowdery, the Whitmers, and other pioneers—making occasional return visits in looking after his property affairs at Palmyra. ...

9.
PHILETUS B. SPEAR REMINISCENCE, CIRCA 1873

"Joseph Smith and Mormonism Which Started 100 Years Ago. Some Incidents Related About Smith By Professor Philetus B. Spear, D.D., a Man Born in Palmyra in 1811—An Article on Mormonism of Interest to Our Readers—Special Services Were Conducted at Mormon Hill," *Marion Enterprise* (Newark, New York) 43 (28 September 1923): 1.

EDITORIAL NOTE

Philetus Bennett Spear (1811-1901) was born at Palmyra, where he attended high school. He graduated from Madison University (now Colgate University) in Hamilton, New York, in 1836, and from the Madison Theological Seminary in 1838. Upon graduation he became the minister of the Baptist Church in Palmyra. In 1842 he became professor of Latin at Madison University, and in 1850 professor of Hebrew. He married Esther Jackson (d. 1878) of Palmyra in 1848. Retiring from teaching in 1875, he later died at Hamilton, New York (Cathcart 1883, 1089-90; *The Colgate-Rochester Divinity School Bulletin* 3 [October 1930]: xxviii, 12; [Obituary], *Hamilton Examiner,* 31 January 1901; [Obituary], *Hamilton Republican,* 31 January 1901; Spear 1901).

Spear's reminiscence of early Mormonism was written down by the Reverend Jared S. Nasmith (1853-1946) of Marion, New York, then one of Spear's students at Madison University. According to Nasmith, he wrote and published Spear's account "nearly fifty years ago" (c. 1873), although I have been unable to locate the original printing. Regarding the origin of Spear's statement, the *Enterprise* states:

> When Rev. J. S. Nasmith, of Marion, was a student in Hamilton Theological Seminary nearly fifty years ago, he told Dr. Spear one day that he had recently visited Mormon Hill. The professor was interested at once and said that he was born in Palmyra, and knew all about Joe Smith and the beginning of Mormonism. Dr. Spear said that Martin Harris tried to convert his mother to Mormonism. Seeing Nasmith's interest, he gave a number of statements that Mr. Nasmith put in writing, and sent to his home paper in Plattsville, Wisconsin. A copy of the article was preserved and we give it practically in full. ...

The decision of the *Enterprise* to reprint Spear's statement was evidently motivated by the recent Mormon meetings held on the Hill Cumorah, and the belief that "anything that comes from an authentic source regarding Smith and those early days will interest people in this part of the state."

[Joseph] Smith was born in Sharon, Vermont, in 1905 [1805], coming to New York State at an early age.

His father was a fortune-teller, and had a poor reputation among the townsmen. Joe was an ungainly looking lad, clothing poor, with associates of the lower class. He had for a library a copy of the "Arabian Nights," stories of Captain Kidd, and a few novels.

Though of a coarse wit and of some influence, he gave no promise in his youth of the power exercised in his later years.

The attention of the people was first called to him by the claims made that Joe could find anything lost or hidden. Once in a while he would succeed in telling where a thing was to be found, and, forgetting his many failures, the one success was loudly proclaimed.

This prepared the public to believe him when he claimed to know where Captain Kidd had hidden money in Palmyra. A company was organized to dig in a certain hill specified by "Joe." This company was solemnly told that a spell was upon the treasure.

No one could find it unless digging in the night. When they came near the devil would frighten them away. They must never mind him but dig on, or he would drag the treasure down deeper.

The men worked hard and long but saw no signs of gold, when Mr. Ellsworth,[1] growing convinced of his folly, determined to play a joke upon his comrades. Going to the hill before the others, he scattered a train of powder around. About midnight, when the men were thinking of the signs that might come any moment, Ellsworth dropped his pipe on the powder. As it flashed, he shouted: "The Devil is coming! The Devil is coming!" when one and all ran for dear life. Thus ended the work by Company No. 1.

But another company was organized, Smith himself being the leader of this. The entrance to their mine was firmly locked during the day, and guarded at night when they were at work. As no treasure was found, the village began to lose faith. The company kept on when it began to be whispered that they were counterfeiting money, expecting to pass it as the found treasure. It was while digging with this second company that Smith

---

1. Perhaps Philip Ellsworth, in his fifties, listed in the 1830 census of Palmyra, New York.

claimed to find the Gold Bible.

His mother had great faith in him, and every time he returned from the hill she would say: "Well, Joe, what have you found?" Growing tired of answering that nothing had been seen, he put sand into his coat pocket, and when that time she asked the same question, with an air of great mystery, he exclaimed that he had found a Gold Bible. He could not show it to her, as no human eyes but his, could look upon it, without being struck dead.

Going to his room the sand was formed in a box, and kept sacred by him. His mother whispered the story to others, and, to Joe's utmost surprise, the people believed it. Seeing how they were affected he determined to make the most of the matter.

He solemnly told Martin Harris that God had chosen him (Harris) to furnish means for the publication of the Bible, and prevailed upon him to accept the work. Harris' wife had no faith in Smith, and she, seeing their property rapidly diminishing, demanded a sight of the Bible. Smith said no one could see it. She persisted, and he finally, by main force, kept her from opening the box.

The rest is known. Smith found Sidney Rigdon, the cutler, who gave him the manuscript of a novel written by Solomon Spaulding, entitled "Manuscript Found."

Smith altered this same title and gave it to the world as the translation of his "Gold Bible." ...

10.
Palmyra Resident Reminiscence, circa 1876

"The Book of Mormon. The Original Edition Published at Palmyra. Facts About the First Publication of the Bible of the Latter Day Saints—Sketch of Joe Smith," unidentified and undated newspaper clipping, Charles Woodward Scrapbook, New York Public Library, New York, New York (Woodward 1880, 2:210).

EDITORIAL NOTE

This item is evidently reprinted from the *Cincinnati Enquirer,* and the date "1876" is written on the clipping. Internal evidence suggests that the article was written after the publication of the first RLDS edition of the Book of Mormon in 1874. The unnamed author of this item claims that his account is based on the testimony of one of his "personal friends" who was "well acquainted with Joe [Smith]." The informant was evidently Pomeroy Tucker, whose 1867 book is apparent in the wording of the article (compare III.J.8, POMEROY TUCKER ACCOUNT, 1867).

... In 1827-8-9 one of our personal friends was at Palmyra, and being well acquainted with Joe [Smith] had every opportunity to become acquainted with the beginning of the Mormon fraud. Joe was a notorious loafer, spending his time about the saloons or along the creeks, in the woods digging out woodchucks, reading bad novels, joining a Methodist Church occasionally, and in yanking a quarter whenever he could by telling fortunes. At the age of twenty-five he was, according to old man Smith,[1] the *genus* of the family; long, lean, limber and lazy: his face the color of a brick yard, and a conscience that enabled him to achieve a reputation of the most facile liar in Palmyra. After conceiving the plan to account for the American Indians and make a raise by imposing his Golden Bible upon the credulous he succeeded in getting Martin Harris[2] and Oliver Cowdery[3] to help him put

1. On Joseph Smith, Sr. (1771-1840), see "Introduction to Joseph Smith, Sr., Collection."

2. On Martin Harris (1783-1875), see "Introduction to Martin Harris Collection."

3. On Oliver Cowdery (1806-50), see "Introduction to Oliver Cowdery Collection."

the business through. It was while this trio of tricksters were at work that our informant was permitted to hear them read manuscript and talk up the pecuniary gain. In 1829-30 Harris mortgaged his farm and entered into a contract with Grandin,[4] of Palmyra, agreeing to pay $3,000 for an edition of 5,000. Thurlow Weed[5] had refused to do the printing, believing it to be another of the Smith's attempts at swindling, and it was only upon the urgent solicitation of the Smiths that Grandin consented to do the work. Before going to the printer Joe kept the sacred document at home covered up in a box. To keep off some of the credulous and prevent meddling Joe affirmed that instant death would end the days of any one who should dare to look upon the plates from which he was translating. This answered the purpose very well until Hussey[6] and Van Draver[7] offered to run the risk and look at the mysterious book. Joe objected, but before he could prevent, Hussey snatched off the cover, saying, "Egad! I'll see the critter, live or die!" Joe's bible proved to be a large tile! Joe said the joke was on them, and, all taking a drink, the affair passed over with a laugh.[8] In the summer of 1830 the first edition came from the press, and Harris was happy. Smith had a revelation that the bibles should be sold for $1.25 each. Harris had told his wife that if she would only keep still he would make something out of the business. This is the way he ciphered:—Cost of the five thousand bibles, $3,000; five thousand retailed at $1.25 apiece would amount to $6,250—clear of $3,250! The bible speculation fizzled; the book was treated only to contempt and ridicule. Harris endeavored to make sales go "according to revelation" at $1.25 a copy, but buyers were scarce, and Joe had another revelation instructing his father, the old man Smith, to help Harris sell the books. Every sale by old man Smith was just so much dead loss to Harris; but the book wouldn't go—$1.25 a copy was too much for a Joe Smith bible, the author and proprietor being too well known around Palmyra, Manchester and Rochester. One day old Smith went out with a basketful of the books and

4. On Egbert B. Grandin (1806-45), see I.A.15, JOSEPH SMITH HISTORY, 1839, n. 77.

5. On Thurlow Weed (1797-1882), see introduction to III.K.17, THURLOW WEED REMINISCENCES, 1854, 1858, 1880 & 1884.

6. On William T. Huzzy (or Hussy), see I.B.5, LUCY SMITH HISTORY, 1845, n. 222.

7. On Azel Vandruver, see III.J.8, POMEROY TUCKER ACCOUNT, 1867, n. 50.

8. Compare III.J.8, POMEROY TUCKER ACCOUNT, 1867, 31-32.

was arrested for debt. Esquire Tiffany[9] put the old patriarch's obligations—debts, costs, &c.—at $5.63. The old gentleman had no money, but, on condition that his persecutor would keep hush, he agreed, in a private room, to give him seven bibles to effect a clearance! This was something of a fall from the price fixed by revelation, but as there was a second creditor waiting for him outside the office, the old man concluded to cut on the Lord's figures and get away, which he did, escaping through a side door to the infinite enjoyment of the man who had the armful of bibles. The book is the veriest trash, a bungling compound of the Spaulding story, Old Testament and New, Watts' hymns, Shakespeare, Robinson Crusoe and Joe Smith. It is beneath all scholarly criticism, and if the reading of it were not attended by harmless stupefaction of the mental faculties, the sale of it would be an indictable offence—obtaining money under false representations. As a curiosity in the department of human credulity no one can object to the Mormon bible.

9. On A. R. Tiffany, see III.J.8, POMEROY TUCKER ACCOUNT, 1867, n. 120.

11.
PARLEY CHASE TO [JAMES T. COBB?], 3 APRIL 1879

Wilhelm Ritter von Wymetal, *Joseph Smith, the Prophet, His Family and His Friends* (Salt Lake City: Tribune Printing and Publishing Co., 1886), 276.

EDITORIAL NOTE

Besides his interview with Philastus Hurlbut in 1833 (see III.A.10, PARLEY CHASE STATEMENT, 2 DEC 1833), the present item is the only other known source from Parley Chase. Chase's letter, according to Wymetal, is dated Rollin, Michigan, 3 April 1879, and was most likely written to James T. Cobb (1834-?), a Salt Lake City newspaperman who collected many statements about Mormon origins (mostly dated in 1879). Cobb apparently intended to publish his findings in a book (V.D.6, *AMBOY* [IL] *JOURNAL,* 23 APR 1879), but never did so. He shared a great deal of his findings with Wilhelm Wymetal, a German correspondent living in Salt Lake City, and apparently allowed him to publish them (see Wymetal 1886, 75, 79, 207, 211, and 231).[1] Wymetal gives only an excerpt of the original letter, which has not been located.

[Rollin, Michigan]

[April 3, 1879]

When [Joseph] Smith first told of getting the book of plates he said it would tell him how to get hidden treasures in the earth; and his father, soon after they got the plates, came in to my mother's one morning, just after breakfast, and told that Joe had a book and *that it would tell him how to get money that was buried in the ground,*[2] and that he also found a pair of EYE-GLASSES on the book by which he could interpret it, and that the glasses were as big *as a breakfast plate*; and he said that if the angel Gabriel

1. On Wilhelm Ritter von Wymetal (1838-96), see III.H.4, JOHN H. GILBERT TO JAMES T. COBB, 14 OCT 1879, n. 1.

2. The claim that the plates contained the locations of other treasures is also found in III.E.3, *PALMYRA REFLECTOR,* 1828-1831, under 14 February 1831, 102.

should come down and tell him he could not get this hidden treasure, HE WOULD TELL HIM HE WAS A LIAR.

[Parley Chase]

12.
ABEL D. CHASE STATEMENT, 2 MAY 1879

Wilhelm Ritter von Wymetal, *Joseph Smith, the Prophet, His Family and His Friends* (Salt Lake City: Tribune Printing and Publishing Co., 1886), 230-31.

EDITORIAL NOTE

Besides his interview with the Kelleys in 1881 (see III.B.7, ABEL CHASE INTERVIEW, 1881), the present document is the only known statement of Abel D. Chase. Wilhelm Wymetal[1] states that Abel D. Chase's statement was "never published before" (Wymetal 1886, 230). Since the statement is dated 2 May 1879, it was probably taken by John H. Gilbert for James T. Cobb of Salt Lake City, who later shared many of his documents with Wymetal (see discussion in introduction to III.J.11, PARLEY CHASE TO [JAMES T. COBB?], 3 APR 1879).

PALMYRA, Wayne Co., N.Y., May 2, 1879.

I, Abel D. Chase, now living in Palmyra, Wayne Co., N.Y., make the following statement regarding my early acquaintance with Joseph Smith and incidents about the production of the so-called Mormon Bible. I was well acquainted with the Smith family, frequently visiting the Smith boys and they me. I was a youth at the time from twelve to thirteen years old, having been born Jan. 19, 1814, at Palmyra, N.Y. During some of my visits at the Smiths, I saw a STRANGER there WHO THEY SAID WAS MR. RIGDON. He was at Smith's several times, and it was in the year of 1827 when I first saw him there, as near as I can recollect.[2] Some time after that tales were circulated that young [p. 230] Joe had found or dug from the earth a BOOK OF PLATES which the Smiths called the GOLDEN BIBLE. I don't think Smith had any such plates. He was mysterious in his actions. The PEEPSTONE, in which he was accustomed to look, he got of my elder

1. On Wilhelm Ritter von Wymetal (1838-96), see III.H.4, JOHN H. GILBERT TO JAMES T. COBB, 14 OCT 1879, n. 1.

2. Lorenzo Saunders said that "Abel Chase testified that he thought he saw Rigdon before that time [1830], but was not certain" (III.B.12, LORENZO SAUNDERS INTERVIEW, 17 SEP 1884, 4).

brother Willard while at work for us digging a well.[3] It was a singular looking stone and young Joe pretended he could discover hidden things in it.

My brother Willard Chase died at Palmyra, N.Y., March 10, 1871. His affidavit, published in Howe's "History of Mormonism," is genuine.[4] Peter Ingersoll, whose affidavit was published in the same book,[5] is also dead. He moved West years ago and died about two years ago. Ingersoll had the reputation of being a man of his word, and I have no doubt his sworn statement regarding the Smiths and the Mormon Bible is genuine. I was also well acquainted with Thomas P. Baldwin,[6] a lawyer and Notary Public, and Frederick Smith,[7] a lawyer and magistrate, before whom Chase's and Ingersoll's depositions were made, and who were residents of this village at the time and for several years after.

ABEL D. CHASE.

Abel D. Chase signed the above statement in our presence, and he is known to us and the entire community here as a man whose word is always the exact truth and above any possible suspicion.

PLINY T. SEXTON,[8]
J. H. GILBERT.[9]

---

3. See III.A.14, WILLARD CHASE STATEMENT, CIRCA 11 DEC 1833, 247.

4. See III.A.14, WILLARD CHASE STATEMENT, CIRCA 11 DEC 1833.

5. See III.A.9, PETER INGERSOLL STATEMENT, 2 DEC 1833.

6. On Thomas P. Baldwin, see III.A.2, BARTON STAFFORD STATEMENT, 3 NOV 1833, n. 6.

7. On Frederick Smith, see III.A.12, DAVID STAFFORD STATEMENT, 5 DEC 1833, n. 8.

8. Wymetal informs that "Mr. Sexton was at the time of this affidavit the village President of Palmyra and President of the first National Bank there" (Wymetal 1886, 231). Pliny T. Sexton was a successful Palmyra businessman who apparently owned the land on which "Mormon Hill" was located (T. Cook 1930, 77, 80, 101, 246, 253, 265, 277, 285, 289). He was the son of Pliny Sexton, who signed Hurlbut's Palmyra group statement in 1833 (see III.A.11, PALMYRA RESIDENTS GROUP STATEMENT, 4 DEC 1833).

9. John H. Gilbert corresponded with James T. Cobb and helped him obtain statements in the Palmyra/Manchester area (see III.B.12, LORENZO SAUNDERS INTERVIEW, 17 SEP 1884, 4-5). On Gilbert, see "Introduction to John H. Gilbert Collection."

13.
Orlando Saunders, William Van Camp, and John H. Gilbert Interviews with Frederick G. Mather, July 1880

Frederick G. Mather, "The Early Days of Mormonism," *Lippincott's Magazine* (Philadelphia) 26 (August 1880): 198-206, 211.

EDITORIAL NOTE

Frederick Gregory Mather (1844-1925) was born at Cleveland, Ohio. After graduating from Dartmouth in 1867, he studied law at Cleveland until 1870. He served as editor-in-chief of the *Binghamton* (New York) *Republican* (1874-79), as an editorial writer for the *Albany Evening Journal* (1879-80), and thereafter as special Albany correspondent for various newspapers (1880-97). He died at Stamford, Connecticut (*Who Was Who in America,* 1966, 1:177-78).

Mather's account includes interviews with Orlando Saunders, William Van Camp, John H. Gilbert, and unnamed others. In a letter to James T. Cobb, dated 10 September 1880, John H. Gilbert said that he had read an "extract" of Mather's article and that there was "nothing new in it, and some errors" (Theodore A. Schroeder Collection, Wisconsin State Historical Society, Madison, Wisconsin).

... In the year 1815,[1] there came to the town of Palmyra, in Wayne county, a family by the name of Smith. Their former home was Sharon, Vermont.[2] The father's name was Joseph, the mother's maiden name was Lucy Mack, and they were both of Scotch descent. Their son Joseph, afterward "the Prophet," was born on December 23, 1805. Hyrum,[3] another son, helped his father at the trade of a cooper. Joseph, Jr., grew up with the reputation of being an idle and ignorant youth, given to chicken-thieving, and, like his

1. Rather 1816.

2. Rather Norwich, Vermont. Sharon is the birth place of Joseph Smith, Jr.

3. On Hyrum Smith (1800-44), see I.A.15, JOSEPH SMITH HISTORY, 1839, n. 12.

father, extremely superstitious. Both father and sons believed in witchcraft, and they frequently "divined" the presence of water by a forked stick or hazel rod. Orlando Sanders[4] of Palmyra, a well-preserved gentleman of over eighty, tells us that the Smith family worked for his father and for himself. He gives them the credit of being good workers, but declares that they could save no money. He also states that Joseph, Jr., was "a greeny," both large and strong. By nature he was peaceably disposed, but when he had taken too much liquor he was inclined to fight, with or without provocation.[5]

The profession of a water-witch did not bring enough ducats to the Smith family; so the attempt was made to find hidden treasures. Failing in this, the unfolding flower of Mormonism would have been nipped in the bud had not Joe's father and brother been engaged in digging a well upon the premises of Clark Chase in September, 1819.[6] Joseph, Jr., stood idly by with some of the Chase children when a stone resembling a child's foot was thrown from the well. The Chase children claimed the curiosity, as it was considered, but Joe seized and retained it. Afterward, for a series of years, he claimed that by the use of it he was enabled to discover stolen property and to locate the place where treasure was buried.

After living in Palmyra for about ten years,[7] the Smith family moved southward a few miles and settled in Manchester, the northern town of Ontario county. Their residence was a primitive one, even for those days. William Van Camp,[8] the aged editor of the *Democratic Press* at Lyons, recalls

---

4. On Orlando Saunders, see introduction to III.B.6, ORLANDO SAUNDERS INTERVIEW, 1881.

5. Compare III.B.6, ORLANDO SAUNDERS INTERVIEW, 1881.

6. Mather evidently follows Tucker's incorrect date (see III.J.8, POMEROY TUCKER ACCOUNT, 1867, 20, n. 32). Willard Case said the stone was found in the well in 1822 (see III.A.14, WILLARD CHASE STATEMENT, CIRCA 11 DEC 1833, 240).

7. The move from Palmyra to Manchester after "ten years" (1825) is incorrect. Joseph Smith said the move occurred after "about four years," or about 1820 (I.A.15, JOSEPH SMITH HISTORY, 1839, 1). However, the Smiths apparently moved to a small cabin on the northern edge of the township about 1820, purchased their Manchester property in late 1820, and finally moved onto their land when their Manchester cabin was completed about 1822 (see III.L.4, SMITH MANCHESTER [NY] LAND RECORDS, 1820-1830).

8. William Van Camp was born in Madison County, New York, in 1827. He began publication of the *Wayne Democratic Press* at Palmyra in 1855, which was removed to Lyons the same year (French 1860, 689). Camp took over the *Lyons Gazette* from 1852 to 1856, then purchased the *Wayne Democratic Press* from Pomeroy Tucker (McIntosh 1877, 105, 211).

the fact that it was a log house from the following circumstance. Martin Harris, a farmer near Palmyra, visited the Smiths while he was yet in doubt concerning the doctrines of Mormonism. One night, while he was in his room, curtained off from the single large room of the interior, there appeared to him no less a personage than Jesus Christ. Harris was informed that Mormonism was the true faith, and Van [p. 198] Camp knows that it was a log house, although no vestige now remains, because Harris told him that his celestial visitor was lying on the beam overhead!

One mile from the Smith residence was the farm of Alonzo Sanders,[9] now owned by William T. Sampson,[10] commander in the United States Navy. This farm is four miles south of Palmyra, on the road toward Canandaigua. It includes a barren hill which rises abruptly to the height of one hundred and fifty feet. The ridge runs almost due north and south, and from the summit there are beautiful views of the hills surrounding Canandaigua and Seneca Lakes. It is known to the present generation as "Gold Bible Hill:" to Joe Smith it was known as "the Hill Cumorah," where the angel Moroni announced to him the presence of the "golden plates" giving an account of the fate which attended the early inhabitants of America. With these plates would be found the only means by which they could be read, the wonderful spectacles known as the "Urim and Thummim." Joe was not averse to such a revelation, for his hazel rod and his "peek-stone" had already failed him. There had been various religious awakenings in the neighborhood, and when the various sects began to quarrel over the converts Joe arose and announced that his mission was to restore the true priesthood. He appointed a number of meetings, but no one seemed inclined to follow him as the leader of a new religion. In September, 1823, an angel appeared to him, forgave his many lapses from grace and announced the golden plates.

These plates, however, were not found for several years. In the mean time the scene of Smith's operations shifted along the banks of Seneca Lake and down the tributaries of the Susquehanna to the point where that river sweeps southward into Pennsylvania past a borough of its own name, and then northward into New York, before it finally crosses Pennsylvania on its

9. Alonzo Saunders, age twenty-nine, is listed in the 1850 census of Union, Branch County, Michigan, as a farmer (1850:377).

10. At the time the Smiths resided in Manchester, the land on which the Hill Cumorah, or Mormon Hill, was situated was owned by Randall Robinson. After Robinson's death, it fell into the hands of his son Anson Robinson. In the 1870s, William T. Sampson (1840-81) acquired the land (T. Cook 1930, 246, 276).

way to the Chesapeake. ... [p. 199] ...[11]

About these days [1826?], every other means of gaining a living without honest work having been exhausted, the prophet thought it was time to find the golden plates. Returning to the vicinity of Palmyra, Smith and his followers began to dig for the plates on the eastern side of the hill. It was announced that each one of the diggers must be pure in deed, and that no evil thought must cross his mind as he worked. One night a spade struck an iron box at the same moment that an evil thought seized one of the diggers. The box sank to lower depths amid thunder and lightning, while Smith announced that nothing could be done that night but to go home and pray. They were more fortunate, however, in leaving their evil thoughts at home on the night of September 22, 1826 [1827], for then, according to the faithful, the golden plates were taken from "the Hill Cumorah with a mighty display of celestial machinery."[12] It is recorded that after the prize had been delivered to the prophet by angels his eyes were opened and he saw legions of devils struggling with a celestial host to keep the plates concealed. On his return to Susquehanna with a bandaged head, Smith gave out that he had had [p. 200] an encounter with the chief devil, and been severely wounded by a blow "struck from the shoulder."[13]

With the golden plates were also found the Urim and Thummim, the magic spectacles or religious peek-stones, "transparent and clear as crystal," which should translate the hieroglyphics on the plates. There were three witnesses who swore by all that was sacred that the angel of the Lord laid these plates before them, and that "they were translated by the gift and power of God." The three witnesses were Oliver Cowdery, who was finally expelled from the brotherhood in Missouri; David Whitmer, who abandoned the Mormons and settled in Richmond, Missouri, where he still lives; and Martin Harris, who quarrelled with Smith in the same State and returned to New York to live.[14]

---

11. For Mather's account of Smith's activities in Harmony, Susquehanna County, Pennsylvania, see V.C.5, SALLY MCKUNE, MEHETABLE DOOLITTLE, ELIZABETH SQUIRES, JACOB I. SKINNER, AND SAMUEL BRUSH INTERVIEWS WITH FREDERICK G. MATHER, JUL 1880; and V.C.6, SUSQUEHANNA COUNTY RESIDENTS INTERVIEWS WITH FREDERICK G. MATHER, JUL 1880.

12. See III.K.24, HEBER C. KIMBALL AUTOBIOGRAPHY, 1864.

13. This story came from Mather's interviews of Harmony area residents (see V.C.5, SALLY MCKUNE, MEHETABLE DOOLITTLE, ELIZABETH SQUIRES, JACOB I. SKINNER, AND SAMUEL BRUSH INTERVIEWS WITH FREDERICK G. MATHER, JUL 1880).

14. Until his move to Utah in 1870, Harris lived mostly in Kirtland, Ohio.

Such a precious treasure as was now in the hands of Smith was not to be "borne in earthly vessels frail." He applied to Willard Chase, a son of that Clark Chase on whose premises the original peek-stone was discovered, to make him a wooden box for the plates. The compensation was to be a share in the prospective profits from the "Gold Book." Chase's lack of faith in both the man and the book caused him to decline the work.[15] Smith thereupon thrust his gold plates and the rings which connected them into a bag of beans and started for Susquehanna.[16] ... [p. 201] ...[17]

The Saints in the region about the Gold Bible Hill had not been idle while these things were occurring in Susquehanna. William Van Camp relates that he and all the other boys believed Hen Pack Hill, a mile east of Palmyra, would open to allow a giant to step forth and place his foot upon Palmyra to crush it. This would be the end of all disbelievers in Mormonism, and the Saints would at once be gathered together in that vicinity. "I did not know then," says Mr. Van Camp, "how easy it is for men to lie."

Mr. Van Camp is about seventy years old, and Major John H. Gilbert, who still resides in Palmyra, is about seventy-six. Both of these gentlemen were working in the office of the *Wayne Sentinel,* E. B. Grandin proprietor, during the months from September, 1829, to March, 1830, the time during which the Book of Mormon was in process of printing. The office was in the third story of a building now known as "Exchange Row," in the principal street of Palmyra. The foreman was Mr. Pomeroy Tucker,[18] who afterward published a work on Mormonism. Major Gilbert was a compositor and also a dancing-master. His duties in the latter calling took him away from his "case" so frequently that Van Camp "distributed" [the type] in order to give him a chance to work the next day. The "copy" was on ruled paper—an expensive thing in those days—and the letters were so closely crowded together that words like *and* or *the* were divided at the end of the line. The copy was in Cowdery's handwriting, but it was produced from a tightly-buttoned coat every morning by Hyrum Smith. One day's supply only was given at a time, and even this was carefully taken away at night, there being but one occasion when permission was given to Major Gil-

15. See III.A.14, WILLARD CHASE STATEMENT, CIRCA 11 DEC 1833, 245.

16. See III.K.11, EBER D. HOWE ACCOUNT, 1834, 18; and I.A.17, ORSON PRATT ACCOUNT, 1840, 13-14.

17. For Mather's account of Smith's history in the Harmony, Pennsylvania, area, see V.C.6, SUSQUEHANNA COUNTY RESIDENTS INTERVIEWS WITH FREDERICK G. MATHER, JUL 1880.

18. Tucker, however, said Gilbert was foreman (III.J.5, POMEROY TUCKER ACCOUNT, 1858).

bert to take it away from the office. Major Gilbert and others say that David Whitner [Whitmer] of Richmond, Missouri, has this manuscript copy; and it has been stated recently that he has been called upon by officials from Salt Lake City to produce it, and refused.[19]

There were no marks of punctuation in the copy—a sore trial to both Tucker and Gilbert in "reading proof." At such times Cowdery occasionally "held the copy." In the absence of Cowdery the proof-readers often resorted to the orthodox Bible to verify some foggy passage. The "matter" was "paged" so that thirty-two pages could be printed at a time on one of Hoe's "Smith" six-column hand-presses. After the sheets had been run through once and properly dried, they were reversed and printed on the other side. The bookbinder then folded them by hand, and severed them with an ivory paper-cutter. The result was that the [p. 204] twenty-five hundred large sheets made five thousand small sheets, with sixteen pages printed upon each side. Major Gilbert has an unbound copy of the book, which he saved, sheet by sheet, as it came from the press.

Martin Harris furnished the funds for printing the book by a mortgage of three thousand dollars on his farm.[20] He celebrated the completion of the work by inviting all the printers to his house. Mrs. Harris (the same who secreted the manuscript at Susquehanna) had not signed the mortgage. Harris brought his guests within the door—as Van Camp relates it—and introduced them to his wife, who bowed coldly and took no pains to welcome them. At length Harris asked for the cider-pitcher, and went to the spot indicated by his wife. Returning with it in his hand, he showed a large hole in the bottom. "Well," said Mrs. Harris, "it has as much bottom as your old Bible has." There was enough bottom to the Bible, however, to give a comfortable sum of money to "Joseph Smith, Jr., Author and Proprietor." Orlando Sanders, son of Alonzo Sanders before mentioned, says that the Smiths made too much money to walk any longer: he sold them a horse, and he now has a Bible which he took in payment for a bridle. ... [p. 205]

...[21] Major Gilbert testified that [Sidney] Rigdon[22] dogged Smith's

19. Footnote in original reads: "A note of inquiry has elicited from this sole survivor of the original 'three witnesses' the information that he has this manuscript. Perhaps he may yet startle the Mormon world by publishing a *facsimile* edition of the original 'translation.'"

20. See III.L.14, MARTIN HARRIS MORTGAGE, 25 AUG 1829.

21. Mather's discussion of the Spaulding theory (pp. 205-206) is here deleted, except for the following statement from John H. Gilbert.

22. On Sidney Rigdon (1793-1876), see introduction to I.A.13, SIDNEY RIGDON ACCOUNT, CIRCA 1836.

footsteps about Palmyra for nearly two years before the Bible was printed.[23] He is of opinion that Rigdon was among those who listened to Spalding in Conneaut, and took notes on those occasions.[24] The [Mormon] Bible itself is full of the religious questions which stirred the people of Western New York in those days—a most strange thing in a celestial work of such great antiquity.

Immediately after the publication of the Book the Church was duly organized at Manchester.[25] On April 6, 1830, six members were ordained elders—Joseph Smith, Sr., Joseph Smith, Jr., Hyrum Smith, Samuel Smith, Oliver Cowdery and Joseph Knight.[26] The first conference was held at Fayette, Seneca county, in June.[27] A special "revelation" at this time made Smith's wife "the Elect Lady Daughter of God [D&C 25]," with the high-sounding title of "Electa Cyria." In later years this lady became disgusted with her husband's religion, and refused after his death to leave Illinois for Utah. She remained in Nauvoo, and married a Gentile named [Lewis] Bidamon. For a long time she kept the Mansion House in that place, where she died April 30, 1879.

Another revelation was to the effect that Palmyra was not the gathering-place of the Saints, after all, but that they should proceed to Kirtland in Ohio. Consequently, the early part of 1831 saw them colonized in that place, the move being known as "The First Hegira." ... [p. 206] ...

FREDERIC[K] G. MATHER. [p. 211]

---

23. This was Gilbert's opinion based on the testimony of Lorenzo Saunders (see III.B.8, JOHN H. GILBERT INTERVIEW, 1881; and III.H.4, JOHN H. GILBERT TO JAMES T. COBB, 14 OCT 1879).

24. Gilbert's opinion is not based upon fact.

25. Many early sources name Manchester as the location of the church's organization on 6 April 1830 (see I.A.15, JOSEPH SMITH HISTORY, 1839, n. 82).

26. At the organization of the church, Smith and Cowdery were the only two ordained elders. Not until 9 June 1830 were Joseph Sr. and Hyrum ordained priests and Samuel an elder. Joseph Knight was present at the organization but not baptized until 28 June 1830 (see discussion in introduction to IV.A.4, JOSEPH KNIGHT, JR., STATEMENT, 11 AUG 1862).

27. This conference was held 9 June 1830 (see VI.G.2, FAR WEST RECORD, 9 JUN 1830, 26 SEP 1830 & 2 JAN 1831).

14.
ANNA RUTH EATON STATEMENT, 1881

Anna Ruth Eaton, *The Origin of Mormonism* (New York: Woman's Executive Committee of Home Missions, 1881), 4 pp. Also published in *Wayne County Journal,* 28 July 1881; and John McCutchen Coyner, *Hand-Book on Mormonism* (Salt Lake City: Hand-Book Publishing Co., 1882), 1-4.

EDITORIAL NOTE

On 27 May 1881, Anna Ruth (Webster) Eaton (?-1910) of Palmyra, New York, delivered a speech at the Union Home Missionary Meeting held at Buffalo, New York, titled "The Origin of Mormonism." Having moved to Palmyra with her husband, the Reverend Horace Eaton,[1] in 1849—long after the events she attempts to describe—Eaton would have had to rely on the testimony of others, which she unfortunately fails to identify specifically (although she evidently bases much of her statement on the published accounts of Orsamus Turner and Pomeroy Tucker). Compared with her husband, who made only passing references to Mormonism in his published sermons,[2] the following statement by Anna is quite lengthy.

DEAR SISTERS.—A ride of less than three hours on the New York Central, due east, will bring you to the town of Palmyra, in the vicinity of which, the system of Mormonism was initiated. In this town it has been my

1. The Reverend Horace Eaton served as pastor of Palmyra's East Presbyterian Church from February 1849 to at least 1877 (McIntosh 1877, 147). The Eatons moved to Palmyra from New Hampshire (see Eaton Family File, Palmyra King's Daughters and Free Library, Palmyra, New York; T. Cook 1930, 148, 250).

2. The following is an example: "Joseph Smith, the apostle of the Latter Day Saints, came to Palmyra from Sharon, Vermont, when ten years of age. When fifteen years old he began to see visions. On the night of September 21st, 1823, an Angel (?) ordained him to his great work. September 22nd 1827, the Angel placed in his hands the golden plates and the Urim and Thummim by which to translate them. The house where the translation was completed, the old press which struck off the pages are still with us. But if the Mormon Prophet and the Hydesville ghosts did hail from Palmyra, they did not stay here. If we must own the deceivers, the deluded belong elsewhere" (H. Eaton 1876, 33-34; see also H. Eaton 1858, 22).

privilege to reside for the last thirty-two years. I speak to you from credible testimony. Western New York has strong soil and rank weeds are incidental to strong soil. We must own the deceivers. "They went out from us, but they were not of us." The deceived were elsewhere.

As far as Mormonism was connected with its reputed founder, Joseph, always called "Joe Smith," it had its origin *in the brain and heart of an ignorant, deceitful mother.* Joe Smith's mother moved in the lowest walks of life, but she had a kind of mental power, which her son shared. With them both, the imagination was the commanding faculty. It was "vain" but vivid. To it was subsidized reason, conscience, truth. Both mother and son were noted for a habit of extravagant assertion. They would look a listener full in the eye, and without confusion or blanching, would fluently improvise startling statements and exciting stories, the warp and woof of which were alike sheer falsehood. Was an inconsistency alluded to, nothing daunted, a subterfuge was always at hand. As one old man, who knew them well, said to me. "You could'nt face them down. They'd lie and stick to it." Many of the noblest specimens of humanity have arisen from a condition of honest poverty; but few of these from one of dishonest poverty. Agur apprehended the danger when he said, "lest I be poor and steal." Mrs. Smith used to go to the houses of the village, and do family washings. But if the articles were left to dry upon the lines and not secured by their owners before midnight, the washer was often the winner—and in these nocturnal depredations she was assisted by her boys, who favored in like manner poultry yards and grain bins. Her son Joe never worked save at chopping bees and raisings, and then whisky was the impetus and the reward. The mother of the high-priest of Mormonism was superstitious to the last degree. The very air she breathed was inhabited by "familiar spirits that peeped and wizards that muttered." She turned many a penny by tracing in the lines of the open palm the fortunes of the inquirer.[3] All ominous signs were heeded. No work was commenced on Friday. The moon over the left shoulder portended calamity; the breaking of a mirror, death. Even in the old Green Mountain State [of Vermont], before the family immigrated to the Genesee country, the then West, Mrs. Smith's mind was made up that one of her sons should be a prophet.[4] The weak father agreed with her that Joseph was the "genus" of their nine children.[5] So it was established that Joseph should be the prophet. To such

3. See III.D.3, CHRISTOPHER M. STAFFORD STATEMENT, 23 MAR 1885.

4. See III.J.2, ORSAMUS TURNER ACCOUNT, 1851, 213.

5. See III.J.8, POMEROY TUCKER ACCOUNT, 1867, 17.

an extent did the mother impress this idea upon the boy, that all the instincts of childhood were restrained. He rarely smiled or laughed.[6] "His looks and thoughts were always downward bent." He never indulged in demonstrations of fun, since they would not be in keeping with the profound dignity of his allotted vocation. His mother inspired and aided him in every scheme of duplicity and cunning. All acquainted with the facts agree in saying that the evil spirit of Mormonism dwelt first in Joe Smith's mother.

Bad books had much to do with the origin of Mormonism. Joe Smith could read. He could not write. His two standard volumes were "The Life of Stephen Burroughs," the clerical scoundrel, and the autobiography of Capt. Kidd, the pirate.[7] This latter work was eagerly and often perused. There was a fascination to him in the charmed lines:

> "My name was Robert Kidd,
> As I sailed, as I sailed,
> And most wickedly I did,
> And God's laws I did forbid,
> As I sailed, as I sailed."

At the early age of fifteen [1821?], while watching his father digging a well, Joe espied a stone of curious shape.[8] It must have borne resemblance to the stone foot of Buddha, which Mrs. House[9] tells us of at Bankok, Siam. All the difference, this was smaller, like a child's foot. At any rate, it has left footprints on the sands of time. "This little stone was the acorn of the Mormon oak." This was the famous Palmyra "seer" or "peek stone," with which Joseph Smith did most certainly divine. Being before instructed of his mother, he immediately set up a claim to miraculous power. In a kneeling posture, with a bandage on [p. 1] his eyes, so luminous was the sight without it, with the stone in a large white stove-pipe hat, and this hat in front of his face, he saw things unutterably wonderful. He could reveal, full too well, the place where stolen property, or wandering flocks could be found.[10] Caskets of gold stored away by the Spaniards, or by his hero, the redoubtable Captain Kidd, coffers

6. See III.J.15, STEPHEN HARDING TO THOMAS GREGG, FEB 1882, 39.

7. See III.J.8, POMEROY TUCKER ACCOUNT, 1867, 17.

8. According to Willard Chase, the stone was discovered in 1822 while Smith was helping him dig a well on his father's property (III.A.14, WILLARD CHASE STATEMENT, CIRCA 11 DEC 1833, 240-41).

9. This person remains unidentified.

10. See III.I.6, JESSE TOWNSEND TO PHINEAS STILES, 24 DEC 1833, which was published in Tucker 1867, 288-91.

of gems, oriental treasures, the "wealth of Ormus and of Ind," gleamed beneath the ground in adjacent fields and woodlands. Digging became the order of the night, and sleep that of the day. Father and brothers, decayed neighbors, all who could be hired with cider or strong drink, were organized into a digging phalanx. They sallied forth in the darkness. Solemn ceremonies prefaced the work. Not a sod was disturbed by the spades, till Joe's mystic wand, the witch hazel, guided by the sacred stone, pointed out the golden somewhere. Entire silence was one condition of success. When hours had passed, and the answering thud on the priceless chest was about to strike the ear, some one, in a rapture of expectancy, always broke the spell by speaking, the riches were spirited away to another quarter, and the digging must be resumed another night. Thus matters went on for some seven or eight years. Little or no attention was paid to the performances of Smith near his home. Lovers of the marvelous from other towns now and then came in to see and hear some new thing. People from greater distances visited the several excavations and wondered. Newspapers heralded and ridiculed.[11] But so far it amounted to nothing, unless it created a certain atmosphere heavy with myth and mystery, favorable to to future developments.

The perseverance of Joe Smith was equal to his audacity. Both were boundless. But he alone could never have wrought out the institution of Mormonism. Here we have "black spirits, red spirits and gray." Early in the summer of 1827 a "mysterious stranger" seeks admit[t]ance to Joe Smith's cabin.[12] The conferences of the two are most private. This person, whose coming immediately preceded a new departure in the faith, was Sidney Rigdon,[13] a backsliding clergyman, at this time a Campbellite preacher in Mentor, Ohio. Now we have "a literary genius behind the screen." Rigdon was versatile in his gifts, had a taste for theological and scientific discussion, was shrewd, wily, deep and withal utterly unprincipled. Soon after his appearance on the stage, Mormonism begins to assume "a local habitation and a name." Now the angel talks more definitely to Smith, tells him all his sins are pardoned, that none of the sects are accepted of God as his church, but that he shall establish one the Almighty will own; that the North American Indians are a remnant of the Israelites; that hidden beneath the ground are their inspired writings: that these are to be entrusted to him, and to him only, as none other can see them and

11. See III.J.8, POMEROY TUCKER ACCOUNT, 1867, 27.

12. See III.J.8, POMEROY TUCKER ACCOUNT, 1867, 28.

13. On Sidney Rigdon (1793-1876), see introduction to III.A.13, SIDNEY RIGDON ACCOUNT, CIRCA 1836.

live. In the stillness of night Smith seeks alone his hill-top of Cumorah, an eminence four miles south of Palmyra, eight north of Canandaigua. Confronted by the very pyrotechnics of Pluto, he averred that he obtained from that place a series of golden plates, on which were written in hieroglyphics, the records so important in the new dispensation.[14] Accompanying the plates is a pair of huge spectacles, the Urim and Thummim, by the aid of which the tablets are to become available. He soon finds it convenient to visit relatives in Pennsylvania, in which state, Rigdon was then sojourning.[15] After a while he returns with an accurate translation. He appeals to the cupidity of a rich farmer, a semi-monomaniac, and prevails upon him to mortgage his estate to pay for the printing. Here is a copy taken off in sheets from the first edition, kindly loaned me by Major John Gilbert, of Palmyra, the venerable printer, who finished the work in 1830. ... [p. 2] ...[16]

One thought more—and it is a solemn one—*Mormonism may have risen from neglect on the part of Christian workers.* We have no knowledge of the religious influences thrown around the Smith family when living in Vermont. At twelve years of age Joe came to Palmyra,[17] and should have been immediately secured in one of its Sabbath schools. As far [as] we can learn, not any of the family were invited cordially, heartily to the house of God. Some of them strolled in occasionally. But no persistent effort was made to induce them to become regular attendants. The children were not repeatedly visited, clothed or helped to clothe themselves that they might attend the Sabbath school. And this in a community distinguished for the godliness of its early settlers. Had they expressed to the visitor a preference for a denomination other than his own, he should promptly and honorably have given over their names and locality to the pastor of the church of their choice.

Depend upon it, there were redeeming traits somewhere in this family. Joseph Smith's mother was not a malignant woman. She knew the virtues of remedial roots and herbs, and was ever ready to administer and assist when

14. See III.J.8, POMEROY TUCKER ACCOUNT, 1867, 29-30.

15. This historically incorrect statement is taken from III.J.8, POMEROY TUCKER ACCOUNT, 1867, 56.

16. Eaton's rehearsal of the Spaulding theory (pp. 2-3) is here deleted.

17. Smith arrived in Palmyra with his mother during the winter of 1816-17, when he was either ten or eleven (see I.B.5, LUCY SMITH HISTORY, 1845, n. 69).

her lowly neighbors were sick or dying.[18] But ladies of piety and culture never visited Mrs. Smith in her home in a sequestered neighborhood two or three miles from the village, never sat down by her side, and, in a *unpatronizing manner,* sympathized with her in her many cares and labors, wisely dropped a word of friendly advice, supplied the family with reading for the week days and the Sabbath days, and by all possible methods made them feel that *they loved their souls.* No male member of the church halted as he passed the door of the rude, unpainted house on a Sabbath morning, and found room in his capacious family carriage or sleigh for any of the little or big Smiths, that they might go up to the temple of the Lord, and learn to worship there. To the inquiry, "Why was not more done to win them to a better life," I received this reply,—"Oh, they were such an awful family. Nobody wanted to go there. Nobody could. Why, they were the torment and the terror of the neig[h]borhood." Our beloved Master "*came to seek and to save that which was lost.*["] They said of Him, "*He was gone to be guest with a man that is a sinner.*" He was not ashamed or afraid to touch with His hand—mark, with His hand—the demoniac and the leper. Had His dear children in early day reached out theirs to this poor, outcast household, possibly this terrible ulcer of Mormonism might not now be corroding into the very vitals of the nation's purity and life. [p. 3] ...

18. Caroline Rockwell said Lucy Smith "doctored many persons in Palmyra" (III.D.5, CAROLINE ROCKWELL SMITH STATEMENT, 25 MAR 1885; see also III.J.17, WILLIAM H. CUYLER STATEMENT, 1884).

15.
STEPHEN S. HARDING TO THOMAS GREGG, FEBRUARY 1882

Thomas Gregg, *The Prophet of Palmyra* (New York: John B. Alden, 1890), 34-56.

EDITORIAL NOTE

In late 1881 Thomas Gregg (1808-?), a native of Belmont County, Ohio, and a prolific newspaper editor and publisher in northwestern Illinois,[1] wrote to former Utah territorial governor Stephen S. Harding,[2] then a resident of Milan, Indiana, requesting information about Mormon origins in his hometown of Palmyra, New York. On 6 January 1882 a nearly blind Harding dictated a letter to his daughter, which expressed his willingness to make a statement but explained his physical limitations in doing so. He suggested that Gregg either come personally or send a representative to take down his reminiscence. As an inducement for Gregg's added trouble in obtaining his statement, Harding said: "If I were in a condition to write I could give you a detailed statement of the night I spent at Smith's that would be full of interest to your readers ... [or] the night when the book of Mormon was read to me from manuscript ... [or] the willd [wild?] fanaticism especially of Harris and old man Smith and his wife" (Stephen S. Harding to Thomas Gregg, 6 January 1882, Mormon Collection, Chicago Historical Society, Chicago, Illinois).

On 9 February 1882 Gregg sent a letter to Harding explaining the arrangements he had made for obtaining the latter's statement. Subsequently, during the same month, Harding dictated his reminiscences to a "Mr. Wilson," who was evidently paid by Gregg for his services (see Stephen S. Harding to Thomas Gregg, 13 March 1882, Mormon Collection, Chicago Historical Society, Chicago, illinois). For another Harding letter, see III.J.7,

---

1. Gregg's editorial work includes *The Literary Cabinet* (1833, Ohio), *Western Adventurer* (1838, Montrose, Wisconsin), the *Carthagenian* (1836-37), the first paper published in Carthage, Illinois, the *Warsaw Signal* (1847-48), and the *Hamiltonian Representative* (1858-62).

2. On Stephen S. Harding (1808-?), see introduction to III.J.7, STEPHEN S. HARDING TO POMEROY TUCKER, 1 JUN 1867.

STEPHEN S. HARDING TO POMEROY TUCKER, 1 JUN 1867.

MILAN, IND., Feb., 1882.

DEAR SIR:—Yours of the 9th January duly received, and I send you this reply. The incidents [p. 34] I am about to relate would not be worth repeating only as illustrative of the wild fanaticism, superstition, and credulity of persons upon whose veracity mainly depends the authenticity of the *Book of Mormon*. That such a book, replete with self-evident plagiarisms and humbuggery, that sink it below the dignity of criticism, should find tens of thousands of persons of ordinary intelligence throughout Christendom, who have accepted it as a Revelation from God to man, is indeed a moral phenomenon unparalleled in the nineteenth century. In view of these things it is not strange that some daring iconoclast should go forth with his merciless sledge, breaking in fragments the shrines and idols that for thousands of years have struck with reverential awe the hearts of untold millions of men, and leading captive the human will.

In the summer of 1829, I resolved to return to the place of my nativity, in the vicinity of Palmyra, N.Y. It was from this place that my father had emigrated in the spring of 1820, with his large family, to the newly admitted State of Indiana. This was before the days of railroads, and I took stage from Cincinnati for Cleveland, from Cleveland down the lake shore for Buffalo, where I saw, for the first time, the great canal, only recently completed. On this I took passage for Palmyra.

In these nine years of transition from boyhood to manhood, most striking changes had taken place. My old-time playmates were no longer little boys and girls, but grown-up men and women; some of whom had taken their positions in society as husbands and wives, fathers and mothers. Others had gone down to early graves that had

"Hidden from the living
The full-blown promise of life that was." [p. 35]

When I left my home in the West, I had never heard of Mormonism, by that name. When I was a student at Brookville [Indiana], in the fall of 1827, the *Brookville Enquirer* was laid upon my table, when my eye fell upon a paragraph, credited to some Eastern paper, of the finding of a book of metallic plates, called the "Golden Bible."[3] It was found by a young man by the name

3. The only issue of the *Brookville Enquirer* from the year 1827 which I have been able to locate is that of 30 October (vol. 2, no. 48); but this issue does not mention the Book of Mormon. Although the *Enquirer* occasionally

of Joe Smith, who had spent his time for several years in telling fortunes and digging for hidden treasures, and especially for pots and iron chests of money, supposed to have been buried by Captain Kidd. This paragraph interested me more at the time from the fact that all this had happened near the village of Palmyra, N.Y. I had at the time no certain recollection as to who this "Joe Smith" was; but remembered having seen a long-legged, tow-headed boy of that name, who was generally fishing in the mill-pond at Durfee's grist-mill, on Mud Creek, when my elder brother and I went to mill. This boy was about three years older than myself, and it turned out that he was the veritable finder of the "Golden Bible."

Of course the paragraph in the *Enquirer* passed without further notice at the time, and the whole subject was forgotten, until I found myself in the very neighborhood where the thing had happened. At the time the *Book of Mormon* had not been printed, and no Mormon church had been organized. I do not believe that such a thing as the latter had ever been seriously contemplated, and that the publication of the *Book of Mormon* had for its object only the making of money, by publishing and putting on sale a book that could be readily sold as a curiosity at a high profit. Nevertheless, there was something so unusual in the affair, that it excited a good deal of curiosity and comment. The fact that such a man as Martin Harris[4] should mort[p. 36]gage his farm for a large sum, to secure the publisher for printing the book,[5] should abandon the cultivation of one of the best farms in the neighborhood, and change all his habits of life from industry to indolence and general shiftlessness, was truly phenomenal. He, at the same time, was the only man among all the primitive Mormons who was responsible in a pecuniary sense for a single dollar. Nevertheless, he had become absolutely infatuated, and believed that an immense fortune could be made out of the enterprise. The misfortune that attended Harris from that day did not consist in the loss of money merely, and the general breaking up of his business as

---

reprinted items from other papers, it is nevertheless doubtful that an article about the discovery of gold plates in Manchester, New York, appeared as early as the fall of 1827, as Harding claimed; the earliest notices from Smith's own neighborhood date to 26 June 1829 (see III.E.1, *WAYNE SENTINEL,* 1824-1836, under 26 June 1829). Unfortunately, the current files of the *Enquirer* skip from 12 July 1828 to 4 January 1833, so the possibility of Harding seeing an item from 1829 cannot be verified.

4. On Martin Harris (1783-1875), see "Introduction to Martin Harris Collection."

5. This occurred on 25 August 1829 (see III.L.14, MARTIN HARRIS MORTGAGE, 25 AUG 1829).

a farmer; but the blight and ruin fell upon all his domestic relations—causing his separation from his wife and family forever. In early life he had been brought up a Quaker, then took to Methodism as more congenial to his nature. He was noted as one who could quote more Scripture than any man in the neighborhood; and as a general thing could give the chapter and verse where some important passage could be found. If one passage more than another seemed to be in his mind, it was this: "God has chosen the weak things of this world to confound the wise." His eccentricities and idiosyncrasies had been charitably passed over by all who knew him, until his separation from his wife and family, when he was looked upon as utterly infatuated and crazy. I had been acquainted with this man when a little boy, until my father emigrated from that neighborhood in 1820. He was intimately acquainted with my father's family, and on several occasions had visited our house, in company with Mrs. Harris. None in all that neighborhood were more promising in their future prospects than they. [p. 37]

Upon my return to Palmyra, and learning that Martin Harris was the only man of any account, as we say in the West, among all of his near associates, it was but natural that I should seek an early interview with him. I found him at the printing office of the *Wayne Sentinel* in Palmyra, where the *Book of Mormon* was being printed. He had heard several days before of my arrival in the neighborhood, and expressed great pleasure at seeing me. A moment or two after, I was introduced to Oliver Cowdery,[6] Joseph Smith, Sen.,[7] and then to the young "Prophet" himself.

Here was a most remarkable quartette of persons. I soon learned that at least three of them were in daily attendance at the printing-office, and that they came and went as regularly as the rising and setting of the sun. I have the authority of Martin Harris himself, who stated that some one hundred and fifty pages, more or less, of the original manuscript of the *Book of Mormon* had been stolen, lost, or destroyed, by some evil-minded person,[8] and that the angel of the Lord had appeared to young Joseph and informed him that the devil had appeared in the form of a man or woman, and had possessed himself of the sacred MS. [manuscript]; and Joseph had been commanded by the angel to thenceforth always have at least three witnesses to watch over it when in the hands of the printers. This was the reason given me at the

6. On Oliver Cowdery (1806-50), see "Introduction to Oliver Cowdery Collection."

7. On Joseph Smith, Sr. (1771-1840), see "Introduction to Joseph Smith, Sr., Collection."

8. See introduction to III.L.16, BOOK OF MORMON PREFACE, 1829.

time by Harris, why at least three persons should bring the MS. [manuscript] to the office immediately after sunrise, and take it away before sunset in the evening.[9]

After my introduction to Cowdery and the Smiths, I entered into conversation with them—especially with Cowdery and the father of the prophet. But young Joe was hard to be approached. He was very taciturn, and sat most of the time as silent as a Sphynx, seeming to have no [p. 38] recollection of ever having seen me when fishing in Durfee's mill-pond. This young man was by no means of an ordinary type. He had hardly ever been known to laugh in his childhood[10]; and would never work or labor like other boys; and was noted as never having had a fight or quarrel with any other person. But notwithstanding this last redeeming trait, he was hard on birds' nests, and in telling what had happened would exaggerate to such an extent, that it was a common saying in the neighborhood: "That is as big a lie as young Joe ever told."

He was about six feet high, what might be termed long-legged, and with big feet. His hair had turned from tow-color to light auburn, large eyes of a bluish gray, a prominent nose, and a mouth that of itself was a study. His face seemed almost colorless, and with little or no beard.

Indeed (in the language of Martin Harris): "What change a few years will make in everything!" And what a demonstration of this truth was afforded in the life and career of the man before me. At that time his weight was about one hundred and fifty pounds, he had not a dollar in the world, and his character was such that credit was impossible. Let the mind pass over the career of this man to the date of his marriage with Emma Hale; his banking and temple-building at Kirtland; his flight as a fugitive from that place to Independence and Far West, Missouri; his forcible expulsion from that State to Nauvoo; the springing up of a city of 20,000 people as if by magic; and where, beside his divine appointment as "Prophet, Seer, and Revelator," he became Lieut.-General of a Legion that would make a respectable standing army, mounted on a blooded charger in all the military trappings, that filled with awe the thousands of his followers, and even the outside [p. 39] Gentiles. He had now reached the zenith of his glory; and fifteen years from the time I met him at the printing-office, he had become a millionaire, notwithstanding his harem of numerous spiritual wives and concubines.

---

9. See III.H.10, JOHN H. GILBERT MEMORANDUM, 8 SEP 1892.

10. See III.J.14, ANNA RUTH EATON STATEMENT, 1881, 1.

In the neighborhood of Palmyra there lived another prophet, older and wiser than the Mormon prophet. This was old George Crane,[11] who had been born and brought up a Quaker. On one occasion Smith and Cowdery had gone to the house of George, who had manifested some interest in the pretended translation. It was in the evening, and when several chapters had been read, Mr. Crane, who had been an attentive listener, in his straightforward, Quaker soberness said: "Joseph, thy book is blasphemous; and I counsel thee to mend thy ways, or thee will come to some bad end." George Crane lived to see the fulfilment of that prophecy, when this greatest of all modern deceivers fell out of the back window of the Carthage jail riddled with bullets.[12]

I had arrived at the printing-office about nine in the morning, and after my interview with Harris, and introduction, as aforesaid, I spent an hour or two with E. B. Grandin[13] and Pomeroy Tucker,[14] proprietor and foreman of the *Sentinel*. From these gentlemen I learned many particulars that were new to me. I expressed a desire to read the manuscript then in process of being printed; but was informed by them that that was hardly possible, inasmuch as a few sheets only at a time were used as copy in the hands of the printers; and that probably Cowdery and Smith would have no objection to reading it to me, if I would give them an opportunity without interfering with their duties at the office.

It was now noon, and I went home with my cousin (Mr. Tucker) to dinner. On returning to [p. 40] the office, I found Harris, Cowdery, and the Smiths had remained, substituting a lunch for a regular dinner. My intimacy with them was renewed, and Harris talked incessantly to me on the subject of dreams, and the fearful omens and signs he had seen in the heavens. Of course I became greatly interested, and manifested a desire to hear the miraculous MS. [manuscript] read; and it was agreed that I should go out with them to the house of the elder Smith, and remain over night. In the mean time, I remarked that but one at a time left the printing office, even for a short period.

---

11. On George Crane, see III.K.14, JOHN BARBER AND HENRY HOWE ACCOUNT, 1841, n. 4.

12. Compare Harding's version of Crane's prediction with III.K.14, JOHN BARBER AND HENRY HOWE ACCOUNT, 1841; see also III.D.7, JOSEPH ROGERS STATEMENT, 16 MAY 1887.

13. On Egbert B. Grandin (1806-45), see III.A.15, JOSEPH SMITH HISTORY, 1839, n. 77.

14. On Pomeroy Tucker (1802-70), see introduction to III.J.5, POMEROY TUCKER REMINISCENCE, 1858.

The sun had now got down to he roofs of the houses, and the typos had laid by their work. Each page of the MS. [manuscript] that had been used as copy was delivered to Cowdery, and we prepared to return to Smith's. We arrived at our destination a few minutes before sunset. The Smith residence consisted of a log house, not exactly a cabin. Upon our arrival, I was ushered into the best room in company with the others. In a few moments I was left alone, my companions having gone out on private business. An interview with the family was being held by them in the other part of the house. It was not long before they returned, accompanied by Lucy Smith,[15] the prophet's mother. She came close to me, and taking me by the hand, said:

"I've seed you before. You are the same young man that had on the nice clothes, that I seed in my dream. You had on this nice ruffled shirt, with the same gold breast-pin in it that you have now. Yes, jest ezactly sich a one as this!"—suiting the action to the word, taking hold of the ruffle, and scrutinizing the pin closely. It was not long till she left the room, and I, following to the door, saw two stout, bare-footed girls, each with a tin bucket of red raspberries. Soon after, the old [p. 41] man announced that supper was ready. We went into the other part of the house, where supper was waiting, consisting of brown bread, milk, and abundance of fine raspberries before mentioned. There was no lack of these, and if any left the table without a really good supper, it was not the fault of the hostess. She, good soul—full sister to all her sex—began to make excuses, saying:

"If I had only known what a nice visitor I was goin' to have, I would have put on the table flour bread, and not ryn' Injun."

I remarked that it needed no excuses; that the supper was good enough for a king, and that the berries on the table were better than could be bought in any city in America. Beside being true, this had the effect of quieting the feelings of the old lady.

It was now time to begin the reading of the manuscript, and we retired to the room we had occupied. This was before the days of lucifer matches, and there being no fire, it took some time before a light could be brought into the room. This was done by our good hostess, who set upon the table a tin candlestick with a tallow dip in it, remarking: "This is the only candle I can find in the house; I thought I had two, but mabby the rats has eat it up."

Cowdery commenced his task of reading at the table, the others sitting

15. On Lucy Smith (1775-1856), see "Introduction to Lucy Smith Collection."

around. The reading had proceeded for some time, when the candle began to spit and splutter, sometimes almost going out, and flashing up with a red-blue blaze. Here was a phenomenon that could not be mistaken. To say that the blaze had been interrupted by the flax shives that remained in the tow wicking, would not do; but Martin Harris arrived at a conclusion "across lots:" "Do you see that," said he, directing his remark to me and the old lady, who sat beside him. "I know what that means; it is the [p. 42] Devil trying to put out the light, so that we can't read any more." "Yes," replied the old lady; "I seed 'im! I seed 'im! as he tried to put out the burnin' wick, when the blaze turned blue."

The tallow dip shortened at such a fearful rate that the further reading had to be abandoned. It was now past ten, and the other members of the family retired. The MS. [manuscript] was carefully put away, and directions given as to where we were to sleep. In the mean time Mother Smith loaded a clay pipe with tobacco, which she ground up in her hands; a broom splint was lighted in the candle, and the delicious fumes issued in clouds from the old lady's mouth.

She now began to talk incessantly for the little time that remained, and told me at some length the dream that she had, when I appeared before her, "in the nice suit of clothes and ruffled shirt," as she expressed it; and continued: "You'll have visions and dreams, mebby, to-night; but don't git skeered; the angel of the Lord will protect you."

After breakfast, in the morning, Mother Smith followed me as I arose from the table, and plied me with questions as to whether I had had dreams, and whether I had seen a vision that "skeered" me. I told her I had a dream, but so strange that I could not tell it to her or any one else. The fact was communicated to Harris and the rest. All saw that I looked sober, and I determined to leave them in doubt and wonder.

We started back to Palmyra, Cowdery bearing in his hand the sacred scroll. Martin was exceedingly anxious that I should give him at least some glimpse of the strange things I had seen in my dream. I told him that was impossible, and I began to doubt whether I ought to tell it to any human being. They all became interested in my [p. 43] reply; and the prophet himself, forgetting his taciturnity, said: "I can tell you what it was. I have felt just as you do. Wait, and the angel of the Lord will open our eyes." Here we parted, and I returned to the home of my brother. [p. 44]

About two weeks after this I met Martin Harris. He was glad to see me; inquired how I felt since my dream. He told me that since he saw me at Mr. Smith's, he had seen fearful signs in the heavens. That he was standing alone one night, and saw a fiery sword let down out of heaven, and pointing to the east, west, north, and south, then to the hill of Cumorah, where the plates of Nephi were found. At another time, he said, as he was passing with his wagon and horses from town, his horses suddenly stopped and would not budge an inch. When he plied them with his whip, they commenced snorting and pawing the earth as they had never done before. He then commenced smelling brimstone, and knew the Devil was in the road, and saw him plainly as he walked up the hill and disappeared. I said, "What did he look like?"

He replied: "Stephen, I will give you the best description that I can. Imagine a greyhound as big as a horse, without any tail, walking upright on his hind legs."[16]

I looked at him with perfect astonishment. "Now, Stephen," continued he, "do tell me your dream." I dropped my head and answered: "I am almost afraid to undertake it." He encouraged me, and said it was revealed to him that an[p. 45]other vessel was to be chosen, and that Joseph had the gift of interpreting dreams the same as Daniel, who was cast into the lions' den. I said, "Mr. Harris, after considering the matter, I conclude that I ought not to repeat my dream to you, only on one condition: that you will pledge your honor not to tell it to any one." "Oh, do let me tell it to Joseph. He can tell all about what it means." "Well," said I, "What I mean is, you may tell it to whom you please, only you shall not connect my name with it." "I'll do it! I'll do it!" said he, hastily. "Joseph will be able to tell who it was, the same as if I told the name."

[Here the narrator proceeded to relate a wonderful dream that never was dreamed, during the course of which he took occasion to describe some characters that had appeared to him on a scroll—presenting some of them with a pencil, a mixture of stenographic characters and the Greek alphabet, rudely imitated. These were handed to Mr. Harris.][17]

Speechless with amazement, he looked at them for a moment, and then springing to his feet, and turning his eyes toward heaven, with uplifted hands, cried out:

"O Lord, God! the very characters that are upon the plates of Nephi!"

He looked again at the characters, and then at me, with perfect astonishment. His excitement was such that I became positively alarmed, for it seemed to me that he was going crazy. I began to have some compunctions of conscience for the fraud that I had practiced upon him; for I might as well

16. See III.K.28, ALBERT CHANDLER TO WILLIAM LINN, 22 DEC 1898.

17. Brackets in original.

say just here, as well as anywhere, that the dream had been improvised for the occasion. He suggested that we go to the house of old man Smith and there relate my dream. I told him that I would never repeat it again to anybody. He bade me good-bye, saying: "You are a chosen vessel of the Lord." [p. 46]

There is but one excuse for my conduct on this occasion; that was, to fathom the depth of his credulity.

For the next two or three weeks I did not meet Harris or any of the Smiths or Cowdery. About four weeks afterwards I again visited Palmyra, and spent part of the day in the printing-office, where I found the prophet, Cowdery, and Harris again. The latter took me by the hand with a grip and a shake that were full of meaning; even the prophet himself shook hands with me, looking me steadily in the eye as if new ideas possessed him in regard to myself; and it was evident that my dream had been repeated to these people, and that it was a puzzle to them all.

In the meantime the printing of the *Book of Mormon* was proceeding. There was abundant evidence that the proof sheets had been carefully corrected. The printing was done on a lever press of that period; and when a sufficient number of pages for the entire edition of five thousand copies had been completed, the type had to be distributed. This was a slow process in comparison with what is done in a jobbing office of to-day. Mr. Tucker, the foreman, had just received from Albany a font of new type, and had set up with his own hands the title page of the *Book of Mormon,* and preparations were now ready for the first impression. About this time the prophet's father also came in. He, too, had evidently heard of my dream, and shook my hand most cordially. Mr. Grandin and two or three typos were present, as if curious in seeing the first impression of the title page. Tucker took up the ink-balls and made the form ready; then laying the blank sheet upon it, with one pull at the lever the work was done; then taking the impression, looked at it a moment, passed it to Cowdery, who scanned it carefully, and passed it to the [p. 47] prophet himself, who seemed to be examining every letter, and without speaking gave it into the hands of his father and Harris. It was then returned to Tucker. Of course we all looked at it with more or less curiosity, and the work was pronounced excellent. Tucker, who was my cousin, then handed it to me, saying: "Here, Steve, I'll give this to you. You may keep it as a curiosity." I thanked him, and put it carefully in my pocket.

It was not long until rumors of the dream had reached the ears of many persons. Upon hearing this I felt some concerned, for I did not want to be mixed up or identified with this thing in the least. But all of my apprehension soon vanished, when I found my name had no connection with it, and that the dream had been a *real vision of the prophet himself!* Of course this relieved me of all apprehension, and greatly increased my desire to make further experiments in this wild fanaticism.

My next subject was Calvin Stoddard,[18] a very clever man, who had been a kind of exhorter among the Methodists. He was a married man, and lived with his wife [Sophronia Smith][19] in a frame house with unpainted weather-boarding, that had become loose from age and exposure to wind and weather. I had met Mr. Stoddard on several occasions, and his conversation generally turned on the subject of the new revelation. He said that we were living in the latter days spoken of in the Bible, and that wonderful things would come to pass on the earth; that he had seen signs in the heavens that would satisfy any one that a new dispensation was coming. That young Joseph had had a dream that was more wonderful than anything he had ever read in the book of Daniel, and that if the village of Palmyra did not repent it would meet the fate of Sodom and Gomorrah.

Mr. Tucker, in his book, has referred to the [p. 48] *call* that was given to Stoddard on one occasion, to preach the new gospel.[20] In the main, his statement is substantially true; nevertheless, it does great injustice to the dramatic effect of the call that was given. Suffice it to say, that Stoddard and his wife were among the primitive members of the Mormon Church, and in obedience to the call, continued to preach the best that he could to the close of his life. *Requiscat in pace.*[21]

It was now getting about time for me to return West, and in the month of September, 1829, I took passage on a canal packet for Buffalo. In the meantime marvellous stories were being circulated throughout the neighborhood, in regard to the strange dream of the prophet, and the celestial call of Calvin Stoddard to preach the new gospel. I had received from Harris and Cowdery the first and second chapters of the *Book of Mormon.* These, with the title page before mentioned, were carefully put away in my trunk. Three

---

18. On Calvin Stoddard (1801-36), who married Sophronia Smith in 1827, see III.J.7, STEPHEN S. HARDING TO POMEROY TUCKER, 1 JUN 1867, n. 9.

19. On Sophronia Smith (1803-76), Joseph Smith's oldest sister, see I.A.15, JOSEPH SMITH HISTORY, 1839, n. 16.

20. See III.J.7, STEPHEN S. HARDING TO POMEROY TUCKER, 1 JUN 1867, 285-86; and III.J.8, POMEROY TUCKER ACCOUNT, 1867, 80-81.

21. "May he rest in peace." Stoddard's "loud call" was reported in the *Palmyra Reflector* (see III.E.3, PALMYRA REFLECTOR, 1829-31, 14, under 23 September 1829).

or four days before my embarkation, Martin Harris, in company with Cowdery, met me at the village, manifesting a great deal of concern at my intended departure, informing me that young Joseph had been having visions. The day was fixed when I was to leave, and we separated, and the reader may judge of my astonishment when Harris and Cowdery came on board the boat at the first lock below the village, and approached me very much excited, Martin particularly. He wanted to know if I was really starting West. I informed him that I was going directly home to Indiana. He said that the night before the angel of the Lord had visited Joseph, and informed him that I was a [p. 49] chosen vessel of the Lord, and they must pursue me at least as far as Rochester, and inform me of the commands of the angel, and that I must remain in Palmyra until the printing of the *Book of Mormon* was completed; after which I must go to the city of London and there remain until the Lord would inform me what to do. This, I confess, was a new phase in this wild fanaticism, and I felt very much puzzled and confounded. The first I said was: "Where is the money to come from to pay my passage to London?" "Oh," said Martin, "the Lord will find the money. The *Book of Mormon* will sell for thousands and thousands of dollars, and I can furnish the money any day, if necessary."

I confess that for a time I felt very much confused. I had bidden all my friends good-bye, and could not have returned to Palmyra in company with these men without seriously compromising myself. And yet, what a temptation was here presented to me to play the *rôle* of the hypocrite and villain! I had no complications, either of love or business, and was as free as the winds that sweep over the prairies. Many times, since Mormonism has become a most dangerous proselytism throughout all Christendom, have I asked myself: What if I had accepted the apple plucked from the tree of knowledge of good and evil, crucified my own sense of honor and manhood, and sold myself to the devil of ambition! It is hardly probable, notwithstanding all this, that the Dead Sea fruit would have turned to ashes on my lips.

They continued with me until we arrived at Rochester, where we parted. In the mean time it seemed as if these messengers sent to intercept me would hardly take "No" for an answer. Martin, with great earnestness, dwelt upon the danger of disobeying the commands of the Lord, and prophesied that I would soon be removed from the earth, [p. 50] and most probably before I reached my destination, quoting several passages of Scripture fitting my case. On leaving, they shook me by the hand most heartily, Martin warning me of the dangers ahead. The whole scene was worthy of the profoundest study. Here were two men, whose names will go down through the ages as witnesses to the divine authenticity of the *Book of*

Mormon, whose superstition and credulity were such as to unseat all confidence in what are termed miracles; and yet, at that time, the evidence of Martin Harris would have been received in a court of justice against all of the Smiths, Pages, and Whitmers, who have published to the world, in the presence of God, that they had "seen and hefted" the miraculous plates! This, it will be remembered, was before Brigham Young, Heber Kimball, or John Taylor had ever heard of the new dispensation.

In 1847, after the expulsion of the Mormons from Nauvoo, I came home one Saturday night from court, and found a stranger at my house. This was not remarkable, for it was generally understood that my doors had never been shut in the face of any human being in distress, black or white. He was a middle-aged man, an Englishman, named [Robert] Campbell.[22] He told me that he had come from the city of Nauvoo, and was going to some place in Ohio; had heard of me before he left Nauvoo, and hoped I would not consider it an intrusion if he stayed over until Monday morning. He was really an inoffensive-looking person, and was possessed of considerable intelligence. He had emigrated from England a few years before, and was, by trade, a copper-plate engraver. During his stay in my house, I informed him that I had the first title page of the *Book of Mormon,* that was ever printed, and briefly related to him how it came into my possession. I produced it, and as he examined the strange [p. 51] relic it was evident that a feeling of awe and veneration had come over him. "Is it possible! Is it possible!" exclaimed he, his eyes still fixed upon it. "The hand of the Lord is in it." He continued to examine it with so much fascination, I said: "You take so much interest in this that I will give it to you."

"Will you let me take it away?" said he.

"Oh, yes, sir, you may keep it as your own," I said.

"Thank you, sir! God bless you. The angel of the Lord must have directed me to this house." He said it would add greatly to the value of the relic, if I would write something over my own name. I told him I would do so, and wrote the following:

"This is the first title page of the *Book of Mormon* that was ever printed. It was printed in the presence of Joseph Smith, Jr., Joseph Smith, Sr., Oliver Cowdery, Martin Harris, and myself, at the office of the *Wayne Sentinel,* Palmyra, New York, August, 1829,—and which was examined and handled by all the persons above named, and the same is hereby respectfully presented to the Church of Jesus Christ of Latter-Day Saints. STEPHEN S. HARD-

22. On Robert L. Campbell (1825-74), see III.J.7, STEPHEN S. HARDING TO POMEROY TUCKER, 1 JUN 1867, n. 7.

ING, of Milan, Ind."[23]

It will be seen, hereafter, how a little crumb of bread cast upon the waters will be returned. This man was evidently as honest and sincere in his belief as any member of the most orthodox church. When I went to the territory of Utah as Governor, in 1862, Mr. Campbell was almost the first one to meet me. He held a clerkship in Salt Lake City. He was really glad to see me, and shaking my hand, said:

"Governor, the hand of the Lord is in it. This is revelation." .... [p. 52] ...

I soon learned that the first title page had been well preserved in the Historical Society and Museum. It had been placed between two panes of window glass in a stout frame. By this means it could be carefully handled and examined without danger of defacement. It had been examined by thousands and thousands; and after my arrival the number increased. I looked upon it one day myself, in company with a gentleman from San Francisco. ... [p. 53] ...

In your second letter you ask me certain questions, which I will now briefly answer. Oliver Cowdery, the scribe of the prophet, was a young man of about twenty-four or twenty-five, about the age of Smith. I had never known him previous to my return to Palmyra. He had been a school-teacher in country schools, and I am certain had little or no acquaintance with English grammar at that time. If this same Oliver Cowdery studied law and was admitted to practice in Ohio, it must have been after the time that I met him; and if he ever acquired a knowledge of the dead languages, it was certainly afterwards. I never saw, to my knowledge, either Sidney Rigdon,[24] or Parley P. Pratt[25] ...

As for "Joe Smith," the prophet, I have long been satisfied that his intellectual forces as a man have been greatly underrated. In deception and low cunning he has had no peer. Mahomet was a much greater man intellectually; but he never could have played the part of Joe Smith, the Mormon Prophet. Ignorant as he is represented to have been, still he was

---

23. This quote is inaccurate (compare III.J.7, STEPHEN S. HARDING TO POMEROY TUCKER, 1 JUN 1867, n. 8).

24. On Sidney Rigdon (1793-1876), who did not arrive at Fayette, New York, until December 1830, see introduction to I.A.13, SIDNEY RIGDON ACCOUNT, CIRCA 1836.

25. On Parley Parker Pratt (1807-57), who did not come to Manchester, New York, to investigate Mormonism until about August 1830, see introduction to III.K.16, PARLEY P. PRATT AUTOBIOGRAPHY, CIRCA 1854 (PART I).

familiar with the Scriptures, and never tired of reading the miracles in the Old Testament and in the New. The revelations that he pretended to have had, were composed and written by somebody, certainly not Solomon Spaulding. ... [p. 54] ...[26]

When I was in Palmyra in 1829, I heard the particulars of the incident as related by Mr. Tucker, when the Smith family was out of meat, and the manner in which the black wether of William Stafford had been obtained. But I refer the reader to the account given in Mr. Tucker's book.[27] The best part of the story, however, had been forgotten by Mr. T[ucker]., as illustrative of the cunning of the young money-digger. When Stafford was told it required the sacrifice of a black sheep in order to reach the hidden treasure, it was not plain to him why the blood of one sheep was not as good as that of another. His black wether, that had been selected by young Joe, was large and in excellent condition for mutton. Stafford hesitated, and was loth to give him up, offering a white wether of smaller size, yet in good condition. But the coming prophet was not to be foiled in his purpose, and resorted to logic that confounded the objector. "The reason why it must be a *black* sheep," said the young deceiver, "is because I have found the treasure by means of the *black* art." This, of course, was unanswerable, and the *black* wether was given up.

With malice toward none, and charity for all, I subscribe myself,

Respectfully yours,

STEPHEN S. HARDING.

---

26. Harding's discussion of the Spaulding theory has been deleted.

27. See III.J.8, POMEROY TUCKER ACCOUNT, 1867, 24-25; see also III.A.13, WILLIAM STAFFORD STATEMENT, 8 DEC 1833, 239; III.D.4, CORNELIUS R. STAFFORD STATEMENT, [23] MAR 1885; III.J.36, WALLACE MINER STATEMENT, 1930; and III.J.37, WALLACE MINER STATEMENT, 1932.

16.
GORDON T. SMITH REMINISCENCE, CIRCA 1883

"About Days of Long Ago," *Palmyra Courier,* circa 1883. Newspaper clipping from "Wilcox Scrapbook" (plain cover), Palmyra King's Daughters Free Library, Palmyra, New York. Also published with slight variation in Mary Louise Eldredge, comp., *Pioneers of Macedon* (Macedon, New York: Macedon Historical Society, 1912), 98-99.

EDITORIAL NOTE

This clipping from the Wilcox scrapbook contains an interview with Gordon T. Smith (c. 1806-98), the adopted son of Lemuel Durfee, the Smiths' landlord, by a correspondent of the *Palmyra Courier.* The item is undated, but internal evidence indicates that the interview occurred about 1883. The article states that Smith was born about 1806, adopted by Durfee in 1812, and that the interview took place "after the lapse of seventy years." This would date the interview to about 1882. The article also mentions that the "latest" Durfee to die was Mary, daughter of Lemuel, on 9 May 1883. Unfortunately the files of the *Courier* for 1883 are incomplete and exact identification of this item cannot be made. Among other things, Gordon T. Smith related a Durfee family anecdote about Joseph Smith that occurred when the latter occasionally worked for the former's father (see III.L.10, LEMUEL DURFEE ACCOUNT BOOKS, 1827-1829, under August 1827, where it is recorded that Joseph Smith worked for Durfee on at least one occasion).

... Joseph Smith, Sr., was unable to pay for the farm he had taken up on what is now "Mormon Hill."[1] At his request Lemuel Durfee paid for the property and the Smiths continued to occupy it, paying rent considerably in labor.[2] Before harvest it was necessary in the early twenties to get a barrel of whiskey into the cellar. Each morning a square black bottle was brought out

1. The term "Mormon hill" usually referred to the Hill Cumorah, situated about two miles southeast of the Smiths' former residence.

2. Lemuel Durfee purchased the Smith farm on 20 December 1825 (see III.L.4, SMITH MANCHESTER [NY] LAND RECORDS, 1820-1830; and I.B.5, LUCY SMITH HISTORY, 1845, MS:56-58).

and the workmen all had a drink as a ceremony preliminary to breakfast. The bottle stood in a certain place in the pantry. Mr. Durfee thought the bottle was lighter than it ought to be some mornings. A little watching discovered Joseph Smith, the future prophet, getting up early, helping himself, and then after doing chores coming around innocently to drink with the other men. He was not reprimanded but Mrs. Durfee removed the whiskey and put a bottle of pepper-sauce in its place. A sly peep at Joseph the next morning when he was leaving the pantry and crossing the kitchen discovered him with both hands grasping his cheeks and groaning out, "My God, what is that?" ...[3]

---

3. This story is apparently also related in III.J.35, THOMAS L. COOK HISTORY, 1930, 219.

17.
WILLIAM H. CUYLER STATEMENT, 1884

Clark Braden and E. L. Kelley, *Public Discussion of the Issues Between the Reorganized Church of Jesus Christ of Latter Day Saints and the Church of Christ (Disciples) Held in Kirtland, Ohio, Beginning February 12, and Closing March 8, 1884 Between E. L. Kelley, of the Reorganized Church of Jesus Christ of Latter Day Saints and Clark Braden, of the Church of Christ* (St. Louis: Clark Braden, [1884]), 383.

EDITORIAL NOTE

William H. Cuyler, step-son of judge Thomas P. Baldwin (who notarized several of the Hurlbut affidavits), was born about 1812 in Palmyra, New York. He opened a hat and fur store in the 1840s, but retired in the 1860s (T. Cook 1930, 84). While Cuyler's purpose was to substantiate the legal aspects of Hurlbut's gathering of statements in Palmyra and Manchester in 1833, particularly his step-father's participation as notary for three of Hurlbut's statements, he also provides an incidental glimpse into the activities of Lucy, Joseph Jr., Alvin, and William Smith.

STATE OF NEW YORK, | ss
WAYNE COUNTY.

William H. Cuyler of the village of Palmyra, New York, being duly sworn says, I am 72 years old, and have resided in this village all my life. I am the son of Major Wm. Howe Cuyler[1] who was killed in the war of 1812.

After my father's death, my mother married Thomas P. Baldwin[2] and by him had one daughter, Mary, now Mrs. Breck of Greenfield, Mass.

The wife of Joseph Smith [Sr.], the father of the Mormon, nursed my mother at the birth of Mary Baldwin.[3] I attended school with Joseph Smith

1. William Howe Cuyler, credited as "the first lawyer that opened an office in Palmyra," was killed during the War of 1812 at Sacketts' Harbor in October 1812. Cuyler's widow, Eleanor, married Thomas P. Baldwin in 1818 (T. Cook 1930, 16; C. C. Baldwin 1881, 289).

2. On Thomas P. Baldwin (1790-1858), see III.A.2, BARTON STAFFORD STATEMENT, 3 NOV 1833, n. 6.

3. See also III.D.5, CAROLINE ROCKWELL SMITH STATEMENT, 25 MAR 1885; and III.J.14, ANNA RUTH EATON STATE-

the Mormon, and his brothers—particularly Alvin[4] and William.[5]

Thomas P. Baldwin was a lawyer, held the office of Commissioner of deeds for a long time, and was one of the judges of Wayne County Courts from 1830 to 1835, being appointed to the position by Enos T. Throop, the Lieutenant Governor of the State then acting as Governor, as the Governor Martin Van Buren resigned in 1829, on being appointed Secretary of State umder [under] President Jackson.

My step-father always sigmed [signed] his name "Th. P. Baldwin". He died early in the year 1858 at Greene Bay, Wisconsin and was buried there.

(Signed) W. T. CUYLER.

Sworn to before me February 27th, 1884.

(Signed) T. W. COLLINS.[6]
Wayne County Judge.

MENT, 1881, 3.

4. On Alvin Smith (1798-1823), see I.A.15, JOSEPH SMITH HISTORY, 1839, n. 10.

5. On William Smith (1811-93), see "Introduction to William Smith Collection."

6. Thadeus W. Collins, Jr., whose father came to Wayne County in 1813, was a lawyer at Lyons, Wayne County, New York (McIntosh 1877, 156, 207).

18.
ALEXANDER MCINTYRE STATEMENT, CIRCA 1884

1. Clark Braden and E. L. Kelley, *Public Discussion of the Issues Between the Reorganized Church of Jesus Christ of Latter Day Saints and the Church of Christ (Disciples) Held in Kirtland, Ohio, Beginning February 12, and Closing March 8, 1884 Between E. L. Kelley, of the Reorganized Church of Jesus Christ of Latter Day Saints and Clark Braden, of the Church of Christ* (St. Louis: Clark Braden, [1884]), 350.

2. Wilhelm Ritter von Wymetal, *Joseph Smith, the Prophet, His Family and His Friends* (Salt Lake City: Tribune Printing and Publishing Co., 1886), 276.

EDITORIAL NOTE

Alexander McIntyre (1792-1859), son of Alexander and Elizabeth (Robinson) McIntyre, was born at Cummington, Massachusetts. He went to Palmyra in 1800 to live with his uncle, Dr. Gain Robinson. About 1811 he began to study medicine under his uncle. For nearly fifty years McIntyre practiced medicine in Palmyra and vicinity, serving as president of the Wayne County Medical Society several times (1835-38, 1842-43, and 1847-48). In 1818 he married Ann Beckwith. McIntyre was called on during Alvin Smith's last illness, and Lucy Smith described him as "the favorite [physician] of the family [and] a man of Great skill" (I.B.5, LUCY SMITH HISTORY, 1845, MS:46). McIntyre was a member of Palmyra's Mount Moriah Lodge, No. 112, and a high priest of Palmyra's Eagle Chapter, No. 79, of Royal Arch Masons. He was also associated with Palmyra's Western Presbyterian Church, where he purchased a permanent pew for himself and his family in 1847. He died at Palmyra (H. Eaton 1860, 16-17; McIntyre Family File, Palmyra King's Daughters Free Library, Palmyra, New York; see also introduction to III.L.9, PALMYRA [NY] MASONIC RECORDS, 1827-1828).

The original statement of Dr. Alexander McIntyre has not been located. Not even a transcription of the original can be found. The following two excerpts are paraphrases of an unknown source attributed to McIntyre. In 1884 Clark Braden of the Church of Christ made the first reference to this source. Then, in 1886, German correspondent Wilhelm Ritter von Wymetal either referred to the same source or borrowed from the published text of the Braden-Kelley Debate. The context of Braden's reference to McIntyre's statement suggest that it may have been among the statements originally published by the Reverend Chester C. Thorne on 6 April 1880 in the now lost *Cadillac Weekly News* (see III.C.1, *CADILLAC* (MI) *WEEKLY NEWS,* 6 APR 1880).

The harsh assessment of the Smiths attributed to McIntyre in this statement is difficult to reconcile with the seemingly friendly attitude toward the Smiths reported by Lucy Smith (I.B.15, LUCY SMITH HISTORY, 1845, 1853:141), but his attitude may have changed following Hyrum Smith's departure from Manchester in October 1830 without paying a debt owed him (see I.A.5, JOSEPH SMITH TO COLESVILLE SAINTS, 2 DEC 1830; and I.B.5, LUCY SMITH HISTORY, 1845, 1853:162-64).

[*1. Clark Braden Paraphrase, 1884*]

Dr. McIntyre, who was their [the Smiths'] physician, testifies that Joseph Smith, senior, was a drunkard, a liar and a thief, and his house a perfect brothel.[1] That Joe got drunk, stole sugar, got beaten for it, and told the doctor who dressed his bruises that he had a fight with the devil.

[*2. Wilhelm Wymetal Paraphrase, 1886*]

Dr. McIntyre, who was, according to old Lucy, "the family physician" of the Smiths, testifies that Joseph Smith, Senior, was a drunkard, a liar and a thief, and his house a perfect brothel. ...

---

1. This last statement may relate to Katharine Smith's reputation (see III.B.12, LORENZO SAUNDERS INTERVIEW, 17 SEP 1884, 1; III.B.15, LORENZO SAUNDERS INTERVIEW, 12 NOV 1884, 21; III.J.8, POMEROY TUCKER ACCOUNT, 1867, 81-82; and III.D.3, CHRISTOPHER M. STAFFORD STATEMENT, 23 MAR 1885).

19. SAMANTHA PAYNE STATEMENT, CIRCA 1884

Clark Braden and E. L. Kelley, *Public Discussion of the Issues Between the Reorganized Church of Jesus Christ of Latter Day Saints and the Church of Christ (Disciples) Held in Kirtland, Ohio, Beginning February 12, and Closing March 8, 1884 Between E. L. Kelley, of the Reorganized Church of Jesus Christ of Latter Day Saints and Clark Braden, of the Church of Christ* (St. Louis: Clark Braden, [1884]), 350.

EDITORIAL NOTE

During his famous debate with E. L. Kelley, Clark Braden quoted the following statement of Samantha (Stafford) Payne from an unidentified source. Either Braden had someone interview Payne for his own purposes, or, as the context suggests, Braden excerpted from the now lost 6 April 1880 *Cadillac Weekly News* (see III.C.1, *CADILLAC* [MI] *WEEKLY NEWS,* 6 APR 1880; compare III.C.3, SAMANTHA PAYNE AFFIDAVIT, 29 JUN 1881).

She was a schoolmate of Smith. His reputation was bad; he was regarded as a worthless, shiftless fellow, a braggadocio and a blackguard. The mother of Joseph Smith was regarded as a thief by her neighbors. She was exceedingly superstitious and addicted to lying, as were all of the family. She once came to my mother to get a stone the children had found, of curious shape. She wanted to use it as a peepstone.[1] Mother would not trust her to look around the house for it. The Smith's dug for money on nearly every farm for miles around; their excavations can be seen to-day. Some are on the farm on which I now live. The digging was done at night with most absurd superstitious acts. It was done by a gang of men and women of low reputation. They told many absurd stories about it. After Smith came back from Pennsylvania his followers dug a cave in a hillside not far from here.[2] They conducted the

1. See III.B.11, JOHN STAFFORD INTERVIEW, 1881, 167.

2. Joseph Smith returned to Manchester from his first excursion to Pennsylvania about March 1826, but according to Lorenzo Saunders, whose family lived on the land where the cave was dug, the cave had been completed before his father's death on 10 October 1825 (see III.B.12,

work of getting up Mormonism in it. I was in it once. It can be seen to-day. The present owner of the farm, Mr. [Wallace] Miner,[3] dug out the cave, which had fallen in. The cave had a large, heavy plank door and a padlock on it. The neighbors broke it open one night, and found in it a barrel of flour, some mutton, some sheep pelts, and two sides of leather.

LORENZO SAUNDERS INTERVIEW, 17 SEP 1884, 7-8; and III.B.15, LORENZO SAUNDERS INTERVIEW, 12 NOV 1884, 8-9, 12).

3. On Wallace Miner (1843-?), see introduction to III.J.36, WALLACE MINER REMINISCENCE, 1930.

20.
Lorenzo Saunders to Thomas Gregg, 28 January 1885

Charles A. Shook, *The True Origin of the Book of Mormon* (Cincinnati, Ohio: Standard Publishing Co., [1914]), 134-35.

EDITORIAL NOTE

On 19 January 1885, Thomas Gregg[1] of Hamilton, Hancock County, Illinois, wrote to Lorenzo Saunders[2] living near Reading, Michigan, requesting information about Mormon origins. Gregg's letter, as reproduced by Charles A. Shook in 1914, is as follows:

> Mr. Lorenzo Saunders,
>
> Dear Sir: Permit me, a stranger, to "interview" you by letter. Mr. J[ohn]. H. Gilbert, of Palmyra, N.Y., introduces us. He names you among the very few left, who know something about the original of Mormonism, and the life and career of Joe Smith, the pretended prophet. I am engaged on a work—mainly a history of the Mormon Era in Illinois—but with which I wish to incorporate the Rise and Progress of the miserable fraud in and about Palmyra.
>
> The main point I wish to investigate is as to how the Spaulding Manuscript got into Smith's hands previous to 1829 when the B(ook) of M(ormon) was first printed. Some think [Oliver] Cowdery was the medium—some think that it was [Sidney] Rigdon. ... [O]f Rigdon—Gilbert says it is thought you saw him once at Smith's. Can you be sure of that? and whether it was *before* that B[ook] of M[ormon] was printed? ...
>
> your friend and ob[edien]t. Ser[vant].,
>
> Th[omas]. Gregg

Saunders's reply, reproduced below, is comparable to his other statements (see III.B.12, LORENZO SAUNDERS INTERVIEW, 17 SEP 1884; III.B.14, LORENZO SAUNDERS INTERVIEW, 20 SEP 1884; III.B.15, LORENZO SAUNDERS INTERVIEW, 12 NOV 1884; and

1. On Thomas Gregg (1808-?), see introduction to III.J.15, STEPHEN S. HARDING TO THOMAS GREGG, FEB 1882.

2. On Lorenzo Saunders (1811-88), see introduction to III.B.12, LORENZO SAUNDERS INTERVIEW, 17 SEP 1884.

III.D.9, LORENZO SAUNDERS STATEMENT, 21 JUL 1887). The original letter cannot be located, but it was published by Charles A. Shook in 1914. Shook reports that at the time of publication the item was in the R. B. Neal Collection of Thomas Gregg letters in the American Anti-Mormon Association. I have been unable to trace the location of the now defunct association's papers. Shook included the following affidavit attesting to the document's existence:

STATE OF NEBRASKA, }
} ss.
County of Dawson. }

Charles A. Shook, being duly sworn according to law, deposeth and saith that the foregoing letters of Thomas Gregg and Lorenzo Saunders are verbatim copies (except spelling, punctuation and capitalization) of the originals now in the possession of the American Anti-Mormon Association.

CHARLES A. SHOOK.

Subscribed to in my presence and sworn to before me, at Eddyville, Nebraska, this 13th day of February, 1913.

B. R. HEDGLIN, Notary Public.

READING, January 28, 1885.

MISTER GREGG,

Dear Sir. I received your note ready at hand and will try (to) answer the best I can and give all the information I can as respecting Mormonism and the first origin. As respecting Oliver Cowdery,[3] he came from Kirtland in the summer of 1826 and was about there [in Manchester] until fall [1826] and took a school in the district where the Smiths lived and the next summer [1827] he was missing and I didn't see him until fall [1827] and he came back and took our school in the district where we lived and taught about a week and went to the schoolboard and wanted the board to let him off and they did and he went to Smith and went to writing the Book of Mormon and wrote all winter.[4] The Mormons say it want [was not] wrote there but I say

3. On Oliver Cowdery (1806-50), see "Introduction to Oliver Cowdery Collection."

4. Saunders's claim that Cowdery first came to Palmyra and Manchester in the summer of 1826 is not corroborated in any other source. However, it is known that Cowdery's brother Lyman was in the area as early as 1825

it was because I was there. I saw Sidney Rigdon[5] in the Spring of 1827, about the middle of March. I went to Smiths to eat maple sugar, and I saw five or six men standing in a group and there was one among them better dressed than the rest and I asked [Samuel] Harrison Smith[6] who he was (and) he said his name was Sidney Rigdon, a friend of Joseph's from Pennsylvania. I saw him in the Fall of 1827 on the road between where I lived and Palmyra, with Joseph. I was with a man by the name of Jugegsah [Ingersoll] (spelling doubtful, C.A.S.).[7] They talked together and when he went on I asked Jugegsah [Ingersoll] (spelling doubtful, C.A.S.) who he was and he said it was Rigdon. Then in the summer of 1828 I saw him at Samuel Lawrence's[8] just before harvest. I was cutting corn[9] for Lawrence and went to dinner and he took dinner with us and when dinner was over they went into another room and I didn't see him again till he came to Palmyra to preach.[10] You want to know how Smith acted about it. The next morning after he claimed

---

and possibly taught school in Manchester prior to Oliver's arrival for the 1828-29 winter term. This is another example of Saunders's tendency to remember things in conformity with the demands of his interviewers, which should be considered when assessing his statements regarding Rigdon's appearances in the Palmyra/Manchester area (see note 10 below).

5. On Sidney Rigdon (1793-1876), see introduction to I.A.13, SIDNEY RIGDON ACCOUNT, CIRCA 1836.

6. On Samuel Harrison Smith (1808-44), see JOSEPH SMITH HISTORY, 1839, n. 13.

7. Charles A. Shook could not make the name out, but in previous statements Saunders indicated that Peter Ingersoll was the person with him on the occasion described (see III.B.12, LORENZO SAUNDERS INTERVIEW, 17 SEP 1884, 4; III.B.14, LORENZO SAUNDERS INTERVIEW, 20 SEP 1884, 2; and III.B.15, LORENZO SAUNDERS INTERVIEW, 12 NOV 1884, 15).

8. On Samuel Lawrence, see I.B.5, LUCY SMITH HISTORY, 1845, n. 147.

9. Shook notes here: "He probably means plowing corn, as this was too early in the season for the other."

10. This is the last known statement where Saunders claims to have seen Rigdon in Palmyra/Manchester before publication of the Book of Mormon. While these statements of Saunders sound confident and precise, it should be kept in mind that he only arrived at them after a great deal of hesitation and prodding from John H. Gilbert (III.B.15, LORENZO SAUNDERS INTERVIEW, 12 NOV 1884, 13-14). It is worth noting that Saunders was hard-pressed to make any statement in 1879 when Gilbert first approached him, but at the writing of this letter in 1885 he can give not only one but three instances of seeing Rigdon before 1830 (i.e., mid-March 1827, fall 1827, and summer 1828).

to have got (the) plates he came to our house and said he had got the plates and what a struggle he had in getting home with them. Two men tackled him and he fought and knocked them both down and made his escape and secured the plates and had them safe and secure. He showed his thumb where he bruised it in fighting those men.[11] After (he) went from the house, my mother says, "What a liar Joseph Smith is; he lies every word he says; I know he lies because he looks so [p. 134] guilty; he can't see out of his eyes; how dare (he) tell such a lie as that." The time he claimed to have taken the plates from the hill was on the 22 day of September, in 1827, and I went on the next Sunday following[12] with five or six other ones and we hunted the side hill by course and could not find no place where the ground had been broke. There was a large hole where the money diggers had dug a year or two before, but no fresh dirt. There never was such a hole; there never was any plates taken out of that hill nor any other hill in that county, was [or?] in Wayne county. It is all a lie. No, sir, I never saw the plates nor no one else. He had an old glass box with a tile (spelling doubtful, C.A.S.)[13] in it, about 7x8 inches, and that was the gold plates and Martin Harris[14] didn't know a gold plate from a brick at this time. Smith and Rigdon had an intimacy but it was very secret and still and there was a mediator between them and that was Cowdery.[15] The Manuscripts was stolen by Rigdon and modelled over by him and then handed over to Cowdery and he copied them and Smith sat behind the curtain and handed them out to Cowdery and as fast as Cowdery copied them, they was handed over to Martin Harris and he took

11. The event resulting in Smith injuring his thumb occurred a few days after his removing the plates from the hill (see I.B.5, LUCY SMITH HISTORY, 1845, MS:63-66; I.E.3, HERBERT S. SALISBURY REMINISCENCES, 1945 & 1954; and III.F.10, MARTIN HARRIS INTERVIEW WITH JOEL TIFFANY, 1859, 166-67).

12. In another statement, Saunders referred to "the Sunday following" (III.D.9, LORENZO SAUNDERS STATEMENT, 21 JUL 1887; cf. III.J.8, POMEROY TUCKER ACCOUNT, 1867, 35).

13. For the claim that Smith had a "tile-brick" instead of plates, see III.J.8, POMEROY TUCKER ACCOUNT, 1867, 32.

14. On Martin Harris (1783-1875), see "Introduction to Martin Harris Collection."

15. The theory that Cowdery was the medium between Rigdon and Smith was previously expressed in III.F.1, MARTIN HARRIS INTERVIEWS WITH JOHN A. CLARK, 1827 & 1828, 1:94, and Gregg had mentioned in his letter to Saunders that "[s]ome think [Oliver] Cowdery was the medium—some think that it was [Sidney] Rigdon," but Saunders was the first and only so-called "eye witness" to support both theories.

them to Egbert Grandin,[16] the one who printed them, and [John H.] Gilbert[17] set the type. I never knew any of the twelve that claimed to have seen the plates except Martin Harris and the Smiths. I knew all of the Smiths, they had not much learning, they was poor scholars. The older ones did adhere (spelling doubtful, C.A.S.) to Joseph Smith. He had a peep stone he pretended to see in. He could see all the hidden treasures in the ground and all the stolen property. But that was all a lie, he couldn't see nothing. He was an impostor. I now will close. I don't know as you can read this. If you can, please excuse my bad spelling and mistakes.

Yours With Respect,
From LORENZO SAUNDERS.

16. On Egbert B. Grandin (1806-45), see I.A.15, JOSEPH SMITH HISTORY, 1839, n. 77.

17. See John H. Gilbert (1802-95), see "Introduction to John H. Gilbert Collection."

21.
E. E. Baldwin to W. O. Norrell, 3 August 1887

E. E. Baldwin to W. O. Norrell, 3 August 1887, Theodore A. Schroeder Papers, Archives, Wisconsin State Historical Society, Madison, Wisconsin.

EDITORIAL NOTE

Theodore A. Schroeder,[1] an anti-Mormon writer, published a portion of the present letter in his *Lucifer's Lantern* series (No. 9, May 1900, 181-83). In this publication, Schroeder introduced the letter as follows:

> About six years ago there came into my possession a letter dated August 3rd, 1887, which has some additional evidence as to the fraud in the origin of the Book of Mormon. I then asked permission to make its contents public, but the author declined because it was his intention to set forth the facts in a more detailed manner as a magazine article. The author has since died without executing his expressed intention. The original recipient of the letter also declined to consent to its publicity because it might injure business relations. He now consents to its publication if his name shall not, for the present, be made known. The only reason given by the author for not desiring publication no longer existing, I feel at liberty to give this much of the letter to the public.

While Schroeder held back the recipient's name, the following transcription of the original letter indicates that it had been addressed to W. O. Norrell of Salt Lake City, of whom I have been unable to learn anything further. The letter, apparently in Baldwin's hand, is written on six pages that have the following form letter head: "OFFICE OF / E. E. BALDWIN, / ATTORNEY AT LAW." This was perhaps the Edward Eugene Baldwin, son of Joseph D. Baldwin, listed in the *Baldwin Family Genealogy* as a practicing attorney in Bolton, Hinds County, Mississippi, as of 1876 (C. C. Baldwin 1881, 666). The letter is part of the A. T. Schroeder Papers donated to the Wisconsin State Historical Society in 1956.

OFFICE OF
E. E. BALDWIN,

1. On Schroeder's background, see Brudnoy 1971; Embry 1992.

ATTORNEY AT LAW.

Jackson, Miss., Aug. 3rd ***188***7.[2]

W. O. Norrell, Esq.
Salt Lake City, Utah.

Dear Sir.

I have been so busy that I did not find out that you had gone West, until a day or two ago, when Enoch told me where you were. ...

Now that you are where you are, I must tell you a piece of Mormon history, which has never got into the books or papers either. An old uncle of mine, the husband of my father's oldest sister, Mr. James Horton[3]; lived and died at Flint, Mich., dying there just after the war [Civil War]. He was a native of N.Y. State, and was raised in the same town with Joe Smith, and was one of the crowd of boys, with whom Smith used to run, the most of whom became Mormons. Before the war, on several occasions, my uncle told me all about it, how the whole thing was at first gotten up [p. 1] by the crowd of young men under the leader=ship of Smith, as a practical joke, to test the gullibility of the people. My uncle was in it as big as any of them, and helped dig the pit on the side of the hill near town, and fix the stones, &c. in it, where Smith claimed to to have dug up the golden ~~Booh~~ Book of Mormon, under the direction of a revelation.[4] As to the book itself, he told me how they made that, that among them was a young man who was a cab=inet makers apprentice, and they got him to make a box Exactly the shape of a very large Bible, one end of which had a sliding door. That they filled this with sand tightly

2. The portion in bold is Baldwin's printed letter head, which appears on each of the six pages of his letter to Norrell; the filled-in portion of the date appears only on the first page. The remaining five letter heads have been dropped from this transcription.

3. James G. Horton, age forty-seven, is listed in the 1860 census of Flint, Genesee County, Michigan, as a Connecticut-born farmer (1860:109). The 1820 census of Palmyra lists two Hortons, Joseph and Caleb; and the 1820 census of Farmington (later Manchester) lists an Ebenezer Horton. Perhaps James G. Horton belonged to one of these families. However, James would have been fourteen in 1827 when Smith first brought the plates home and was probably too young to be considered "one of the crowd of boys, with whom Smith used to run."

4. Lorenzo Saunders said he visited the hill soon after Smith claimed to have removed the plates, but could find no evidence of the ground being disturbed (e.g., III.J.20, LORENZO SAUNDERS TO THOMAS GREGG, 28 JAN 1885).

packed in, and then sewed a cloth cover over it; and then Smith gave out that it could be felt and handled by common people without harm, but not looked upon by any one except himself, the elect, except with instant death, such was its sacredness.[5] And my uncle often laughed and told me, that if they would undo the Golden Book, ~~the~~ in the Mormon Temple, that is what it will be found to be, a box of sand.[6] He was in the way for some time, until and [at] length Smith [p. 2] commenced to solicit money and material aid, when he and a couple of others went to him and told him that they had gone into it for a joke, and not for a swindle, and that it would not do to carry it any further. Smith told them that he had found there was some money in it, and he proposed to make some some out of it, and that if they did not wish to remain, they could draw out and keep their mouths shut, which they did. I did not know the his=torical value of this when it was told to me, as I was young, but during the war, I grew to know it, and the first time I went North (1867,) I intended to get a full written state=ment from him, of this whole matter, signed and sworn to, but found he had been dead some time. He was one of the most truthful, and reliable men I ever knew, and I put the fullest confidence in his statements about it. He and Smith were good

5. Others from the Palmyra/Manchester area claimed Smith used a box filled with sand to deceive his family and friends (see I.B.5, LUCY SMITH HISTORY, 1845, 1853:133-34; III.A.9, PETER INGERSOLL STATEMENT, 2 DEC 1833, 236; III.K.34, SARA MELISSA INGERSOLL REMINISCENCE, 1899, 7; see also III.J.27, PHILANA A. FOSTER TO E. W. TAYLOR, 16 JUL 1895). A major problem with this claim is that those who felt the plates through the cloth would not have been fooled by a wooden box filled with sand. William Smith testified that he and the other family members could feel the plates through the cloth and "[c]ould raise the leaves" (I.D.5, WILLIAM SMITH TESTIMONY, 1885). Alvah Beman told Harris that he heard the plates make a metallic sound when they were placed in the box (III.F.10, MARTIN HARRIS INTERVIEW WITH JOEL TIFFANY, 1859, 167). Moreover, sand would not have weighed between forty and sixty pounds, as claimed by those who lifted the plates (Ibid., 169; I.D.4, WILLIAM SMITH, *ON MORMONISM,* 1883, 12). As I have previously suggested, Smith perhaps told Peter Ingersoll and others that the box contained sand to discourage those who were attempting to take the plates from him (see III.A.9, PETER INGERSOLL STATEMENT, 2 DEC 1833, n. 14). Possibly Horton or those to whom he related his story transformed these rumors into an actual event.

6. Schroeder explained: "The writer of the letter evidently did not know that Mormons claim to have delivered all plates to the angel after the translation of that part of them which constitutes the Book of Mormon."

friends until the death of the latter. ... [p. 3] ...

Yours Resp[ectfully].
E. E. Baldwin. ... [p. 5]

22.
PALMYRA RESIDENT ACCOUNT, 2 OCTOBER 1888

Andrew Jenson, Edward Stevenson, and Joseph S. Black to *Deseret Evening News,* 2 October 1888, Fayette, Seneca County, New York, *Deseret Evening News,* 11 October 1888.

EDITORIAL NOTE

In late September and early October 1888, Andrew Jenson, Edward Stevenson, and Joseph Smith Black visited the Palmyra/Manchester and Fayette, New York, areas. In a letter, dated 2 October 1888, Fayette, New York, the three men from Utah gave an account of an interview with an unnamed resident of Palmyra, who evidently repeated the well-known story of Joseph Smith's having sacrificed a sheep. According to the journal of Joseph Smith Black, they arrived in Palmyra on 27 September 1888 and departed for Fayette on 2 October ("The Journal of Joseph Smith Black," *Our Pioneer Heritage* 10 [1967]: 294).[1]

FAYETTE, Seneca County,

New York, Oct. 2, 1888.

Editor Deseret News:

... We have heard a great many things about the extraordinary qualities of the Smith family, but nothing that bests the following related to us this morning by a citizen of Palmyra:

"When Joseph Smith," says our informant, "was digging for the Golden Bible, he ran short of provisions, and in order to obtain some mutton from a somewhat simple-minded neighbor, Joseph prevailed on him to furnish a fat sheep, the best he had[,] to be offered as a sacrifice to God. The farmer who at first appeared unwilling, at last consented, and consequently the sheep was brought into a shed back of the Smith family residence. (By the way the identical hill was pointed out to us). But while the Prophet was going through a lengthy ceremony preparatory to offering the sacrifice, one of *his boys,* as

1. Jenson, Stevenson, and Black also interviewed John H. Gilbert (see III.H.9, JOHN H. GILBERT INTERVIEW, SEP 1888).

previously arranged carried off the sheep, weighing 200 pounds which was needed by the family for food."[2]

If one of the Prophet Joseph Smith's boys (his eldest son being born in 1832) could carry off a sheep weighing 200 pounds as early as 1827, five years before birth, it is no wonder that Joseph Smith has made such a great stir in the world. This is a fair specimen of several other stories put in circulation about Joseph Smith and the "Mormons."

In closing this letter we will state however that nothing we have been able to learn through diligent inquiry in this neighborhood about the Smith family has in the least degree shaken us in the confidence we formerly had in their integrity and truthfulness.

ANDREW JENSON,
EDWARD STEVENSON,
JOSEPH S. BLACK.

2. If not an entirely different event, the Palmyra resident probably relates a garbled version of William Stafford's 1833 statement (see III.A.13, WILLIAM STAFFORD STATEMENT, 8 DEC 1833, 239).

23.
William Hyde Interviews, 1888

1. "Birth of Mormonism. The Story of an Old Man Who Was There When the Tables of Stone Were Found," *Chicago Times,* 14 October 1888.

2. "'The Birth of Mormonism,'" *Deseret Evening News,* 10 November 1888, [2].

EDITORIAL NOTE

On 14 October 1888 the *Chicago Times* printed an article titled "Birth of Mormonism," which included statements purportedly made by William Hyde, a former resident of Palmyra, New York. Following publication of the *Times* article, L. E. Odinga, also of Chicago and evidently a member of the LDS church, reinterviewed Hyde concerning his knowledge of Mormon origins. On 23 October 1888 Odinga relayed the substance of this interview to the editors of Salt Lake City's *Deseret Evening News.* Odinga's version substantiated many details of the *Times* interview but challenged others. According to the editors of the *News,* Hyde "was greatly chagrined at being so grossly misrepresented himself by being made to appear as a slanderer of the Smith family, and sought to have appropriate corrections made by that paper, but the opportunity to place himself right was denied him" (10 November 1888). Indeed, I was unable to find any subsequent statement by Hyde in the *Times.* (The item from the *Deseret Evening News* was noted by Stanley S. Ivans; see Stanley S. Ivans Papers, Utah Historical Society, Salt Lake City, Utah.)

William Hyde, according to his own account, was born in 1799 at Portsmouth, New Hampshire, the son of English immigrants. About 1815 he went to Boston to work as a baker's apprentice. He moved to Palmyra, where his uncles Joel and Levi Thayre resided, and opened a grocery store, probably about 1827. The *Wayne Sentinel* for 4 April 1828 lists a William Hyde as receiving mail at the Palmyra Post Office. Although he does not appear in the 1830 census of Palmyra, on 17 April 1833 Hyde, then "in indigent circumstances," was subpoenaed by Wayne County's Grand Jury as a witness in the case of Samuel T. Lawrence of Palmyra, who was indicted for "fraudulently secreting property" (Oyer and Terminer Minutes, 1824-45,

92, Wayne County Courthouse, Lyons, New York). Little is known of Hyde in the intervening years, but in 1881 he apparently purchased the house in Chicago in which he was living in 1888 when he was interviewed by the *Times* reporter.[1]

[*1.* Chicago Times *Interview, 14 October 1888*]

In a cottage at 1845 Frederick street, Lake View, is William Hyde. He knows more about the history of Mormonism than any living man who does not hold a card of the "profesh." Although nearly 90 years of age Mr. Hyde is as active as any "colt" in the Chicago team. He has a remarkable memory, and can recall events that happened when he was 5 years of age with apparently little reflection. His descriptions are very graphic, especially in giving his version of the figureheads of the "Latter-Day Saints." In 1881 he went to Manchester, England, where his parents migrated from in 1797, and inherited a snug legacy, on which he is now living. Mr. Hyde was born at Portsmouth, N.H., in 1799 and was left fatherless when scarcely 2 years old, his widowed mother being then left to depend upon her own resources. At the age of 16 young Hyde left his mother and went to Boston, where he served his time as a baker's apprentice, and after wandering about several years landed at Palmyra, N.Y. A TIMES reporter wended his way to "1845" yesterday and found the old gentleman reading. He said:

"I opened a general store in the village of Palmyra. Joel and Levy Thayer,[2] my uncles, were the principal merchants in the place. They had extensive pork-packing interests and operated a system of twenty-six boats along the canal. In other words they controlled that slice of the earth.

"The Smiths, whom history has chronicled as sheep-thieves[3] and the founders of Mormonism, emigrated from Sharon, Vt. (where Joseph Smith,

---

1. Of the three William Hydes listed in the 1880 census of Chicago (1880:91, 180, 245), none fit the age requirement, which suggests the possibility that Hyde moved to Chicago after the taking of the 1880 census.

2. On Joel and Levi Thayer, see III.A.11, PALMYRA RESIDENTS GROUP STATEMENT, 4 DEC 1833, nn. 9 and 42; see also III.L.11, JOSEPH SMITH RECEIPT TO ABRAHAM FISH ACCOUNT, 10 MAR 1827.

3. See III.A.13, WILLIAM STAFFORD STATEMENT, 8 DEC 1833, 239. Hyde denied making this statement in his interview with L. E. Odinga. That it was interjected by the reporter is supported by Hyde's statement in the same paragraph that he believed the Smiths were innocent of "any misdemeanor."

Jr., was born in 1805), to Palmyra in 1827.[4] They lived in the outskirts of the village, and in the fall of the year the senior Smith[5] was employed by my relatives as a pork-packer, and shortly after his son Joseph was also thus engaged. While visiting the Thayers I became acquainted with the men, who I don't believe were ever guilty of any misdemeanor until they became involved in the religious riffle. One evening in the early part of 1828 Smith senior visited me. He seemed to be such a solemn looking duck that I didn't court his friendship, but he was so entertaining that after conversing with him until after midnight, I told him to call often. He was a slim man about 5 feet 11, and always appeared to be in a deep study. From the time of his first visit until his religious scheme was sprung I don't believe he missed a night without stopping with me for at least three hours. There wasn't a subject he couldn't discuss intelligently, and my opinion of him was high. His memory was something extraordinary. He could repeat several chapters of a book verbatim after it had been read rapidly.

"He was very shrewd and he gradually coached me along until he thought I was in his power and then he rung in his little game. At first he imparted as a great secret that his son 'Joe' had a wonderful 'gift.' That was all I could get him to disclose for over a week, and I guess he lost the confidence he had in me. Rectifying the misunderstanding with Mr. Smith I was again his right bower, and he said the possession consisted of two stones called Urim and Thummin[6] which enabled the boy to seek treasures in the earth and surpass Daniel as a prophet. It might be appropriate to state now that the Smiths were monogamists and not polygamists; their sole object was to obtain riches, which they did, but ultimately it cost the 'modern Daniel' his life.

"The villainous impostors had already became quite popular with about a score of people, but they were without a system to fleece them. Eventually Smith, Sr., the great concocter and originator, enacted a little deal that successfully duped the innocents. It was May 17, 1829.[7] Large banks of black

---

4. The Smiths moved to Palmyra in 1816-17.

5. On Joseph Smith, Sr. (1771-1840), see "Introduction to Joseph Smith, Sr., Collection."

6. The terms "Urim and Thummim" were introduced into Mormon vocabulary after the New York period (see I.A.14, JOSEPH SMITH ANSWERS TO QUESTIONS, 8 MAY 1838, n. 1).

7. One can only speculate how Hyde came up with this date for Joseph Smith's removing the plates from the Manchester hill, which is consistently assigned to 22 September 1827. Perhaps Hyde associated 17 May 1829 (Sunday) with an established event noted in his journal or other records. Hyde may have conflated accounts of Joseph Jr.'s obtaining the plates with

clouds obscured the moon, and the night was hideous. Joseph Smith repaired to some woods about a mile distant from his father's house, and in about an hour returned. During his absence Smith, Sr., had gathered as many of his proposed victims as possible at his house. They were all engaged in conversation when suddenly a rumbling noise was heard, and the boy staggered in and fell on the floor with a large package. A host of people gathered around him. He was unconscious. Being resuscitated he related one of the most thrilling narratives ever heard. While looking through his magnetic arrangement he discovered some peculiar marks on the ground. Scrutinizing them more carefully he was able to discern their meaning, which was instructions for him. He obeyed and unearthed the package, which he carried. As he was about to turn homeward a mounted spirit appeared and demanded he should replace the treasure in the earth. Instead of complying with the mandate he picked up his baggage and ran. By dodging behind trees and in bushes he evaded his pursuer, who never ceased attempting to hit him with his scorpion sword.[8]

"The contents of the parcel were kept secret for a long time and I was the first person Smith, Sr., confided the arrangement to. The mysterious package was alleged to have contained seven gold plates 16 inches long by 10 wide and 1/8 inch thick.[9] Certain marks or hieroglyphics on those plates recorded the history of a highly civilized community that peopled this earth many centuries ago. No one could comprehend the meaning of the characters engraved on the tablets but young Smith, and he had to use his transparent rocks. When translated the golden sheets would be of great value. Hidden treasures would be revealed and everybody who contributed to the grist by way of money would become the possessor of immense wealth. Being the first person to whom the secret was given of course it was only fair that

---

the senior Smith's treasure-seeking activities, described in some detail below, which perhaps did occur in the junior's absence. According to Mormon chronology, Hyde's date of 17 May 1829 falls two days after Joseph Smith and Oliver Cowdery's baptisms in Harmony, Pennsylvania.

8. Hyde's account sounds like a garbled version of the first time Joseph Smith brought the plates home in September 1827 (see I.B.5, LUCY SMITH HISTORY, 1845, MS:63-66; I.E.3, HERBERT S. SALISBURY REMINISCENCES, 1945 & 1954; and III.F.10, MARTIN HARRIS INTERVIEW WITH JOEL TIFFANY, 1859, 166-67).

9. Joseph Smith himself described the plates as being "six inches wide and eight inches long and not quite so thick as common tin. ... The volume was something near six inches in thickness" (I.A.19, JOSEPH SMITH TO JOHN WENTWORTH, 1 MAR 1842, 707).

I should be the first to receive an offer. If I would donate a stipulated sum to the fund Smith, Sr., agreed to install me as treasurer. I had so much faith in the old man that I was inclined to believe his bald-headed assertions, and told him I would go to his house the Sunday following and see the plates.

"He was surprised when I made the payment of my initiation fee conditional. He thought I was so completely in his power that I wouldn't hesitate to subscribe. When I said I would go and see the 'keys' to everlasting riches he was dazed. In fact I paralyzed him. After whipping around the stump with his fire-escape whiskers flapping with the wind he finally said: 'It will mean death for you to attempt to look at the plates. They are sewed in a silk sack and the first person who disbelieves the truth of my assertion will be obliterated.' I began to think now that the man was demented and my belief was strengthened by the fact that Smith senior was a somnambulist. I told him his declaration made me more anxious than ever and if I could die looking at those plates that was just the death I wanted—anything to gratify my appetite for those golden tablets. Finding I wasn't his mark he tried to ensnare others and was successful. Smith's hearers, or proselytes, generally wanted to see the great 'prognosticators,' but Smith's answer would invariably be that the Angel Maroni [Moroni], who had charge of the plates, commanded that no one should see them under penalty of death and confiscation. The generation that existed there were, according to the 'store-keeper,' too corrupt to come in communication with the plates. Slowly the people gained in faith and gradually money poured into the coffers of Smith & Son. Finally the day for the revelation of the hidden treasures came, and after being concealed in a room for several hours with his son, Smith finally emerged and told the leaders of the party to go into a forest, about two and one-half miles from Palmyra, and dig for the treasure. The people rebelled against the prophets and for a few moments Smith & Co. were in very warm water. Joseph Smith, Jr., agreed to go and point out the lucky spot and the people were again appeased. Everybody wanted the young prophet to ride in their vehicle, and it seemed at one time as though a riot was inevitable so eager were the 'gold-seekers' to arrive at the promised land and become rich. The matter was adjusted. Smith was given a horse of his own and there was no preferment.

"Arriving at the designated place each man's territory was apportioned and they went to work on the fool's errand. Such a gang of hustlers you never saw. They beat our Italian street laborers. Toward evening Joe Smith left the diggers and returned to his home. The people continued to dig, not one of them returning that evening for fear of losing their ground. The next day they continued with renewed energy, but no gold or anything else was discovered. Smith would tell them to persevere and they kept on like ground-hogs. This continued for a week and an acre of ground was turned over. In some cases there were excavations twenty feet deep, but for the most part after the miners had gone ten feet they would seek new fields. The people became despondent and clamored for their money. The feeling toward the Smiths was so obnoxious that the brace of scoundrels condescended to go to the scene of their myrmidons' labors, but before this arrangement was made Smith made the plebeians promise they would remain away from the gold-fields for three days.

"At the expiration of the days of grace Smith and his constituents, who had become very wrathy, went to the forest, which looked like the relics of an earthquake or an eruption. It was about 9 o'clock Sunday evening, and after an hour's devotion, in which the junior Smith was very active, the party proceeded to explore the mysterious depths. When they reached the twenty-foot hole Smith commanded all to descend. The mandate was complied with, and while all were engaged in prayer there was a sudden illumination that dazzled the gnome-like occupants. The elder Smith gave one sepulchral grunt and then all was in confusion. The people fled in all directions, leaving their conveyances and implements behind. Several women who were in the party were trampled upon, and the whole fizzle was over. When Smith returned to his home it was surrounded by the disappointed, who were almost wild in denouncing the fiend. He reprimanded them severely and said they were in red-headed luck not to be burned up, as the Lord was very angry, and their dubiousness in believing the word of God caused the whole misunderstanding. So the fools were again satisfied and Smith took care of their donations. Although the first game had caused some dissension in their ranks Smith was not to be baffled by a small thing like a threat of being lynched, and started to unfurl another scheme.

"This is the point where Mormonism got its foothold. It was promulgated that Joseph Smith had a conference with a deputy from Heaven, who authorized him to establish a kingdom on earth and appoint his father high-priest. The ire of the surrounding inhabitants was aroused by this declaration, and the Smiths were threatened with annihilation. But he again restored the people to his confidence and commenced his "bleeding" and work which broke up no less than forty families in the village of Palmyra.[10]

10. This statement was corrected in Hyde's subsequent interview with Odinga, where he reports that to his knowledge "Martin Harris' family was the only one in the town of Palmyra, thus broken up" (see below).

The first one to fall in line was Martin Harris,[11] a farmer estimated to be worth $30,000. Harris' wife objected to his becoming a member of the church, but he was obdurate and wouldn't listen to any suggestions his wife offered. The result was the family split. Mrs. Harris took the farm and stock and her husband $10,000 in cash, which he was to contribute to the Lord. The Smiths got their divvy of this amount and the balance was sucked from the pocket of the unsophisticated farmer. When this racket had got under good headway Smith tried to bring me in again, promising to make an apostle of me. I never consented to join the ranks, but, thinking I was getting there rapidly, Smith unfolded his plans to me.

"The next man to fall in line as a leader was Sidney Rigdon.[12] He came from Ohio and was born in Pennsylvania in February, 1793. He was a fairly educated man and is credited with publishing the first Mormon bible, which was, in fact, composed by old man Smith, although the congregation believed that it was translated from the golden plates by Joseph Smith by means of Urim and Thummim. When the manuscripts were ready they were given to a printer, and Martin Harris paid $3,000 for as many of the handbooks. Services were held openly a short distance from the village, and Smith, Sr., would baptize people by immersion.[13] Generally he would perform four or five ceremonies of this sort every Sunday to the merriment of the citizens, who would be stowed away behind hay-stacks near the pond.

"Having secured as many suckers as possible the prophet proclaimed that they should seek new pastures, and they set out for Kirtland, O. ...

L.F.C.[14]

[2. Deseret Evening News *Interview, 10 November 1888*]

Editor Deseret News:

The foregoing [synopsis of Hyde's interview] appeared in the *Chicago Times* of Sunday, Oct. 14, and is a fair specimen of the generality of articles on the subject of Mormonism, with which the eastern press delights to feed popular prejudice as regards said subject. The ignorance of the great masses

11. On Martin Harris (1783-1875), see "Introduction to Martin Harris Collection."

12. On Sidney Rigdon (1793-1876), see introduction to I.A.13, SIDNEY RIGDON ACCOUNT, CIRCA 1836.

13. Lucy Smith mentioned that her husband baptized two persons following his release from the Canandaigua jail in November-December 1830 (I.B.5, LUCY SMITH HISTORY, 1845, 1853:165).

14. This person remains unidentified.

of the journalists so-called, their unwillingness to properly inform themselves on the subjects on which they pretend to inform the public, their mental imbecility and willful mendacity is proverbial, but the foregoing article beats the record. To anyone who knows the least thing about Mormonism, its doctrines and history, and the character of its founders, the absurdity of the statements made therein is patent, but to make sure of the falsehood of these statements your correspondent went to interview Mr. Hyde, and the following conversation ensued:

"You were a resident of Palmyra, N.Y., at the time the Smith's lived there?"

"Yes, sir, I was a merchant in the town of Palmyra. The Smiths lived at some distance from the town, between Palmyra and Manchester."

"Did you come into frequent contact with them in business transactions?"

"Yes, sir, they came into my store quite often. My uncles, Levi and Joel Thayer, the leading merchants of the town, did a rushing business in pork-packing, and the Smiths were in their employ. Thus I saw a great deal of them."

"Did you see much of the Smiths outside of your business—did you have private intercourse with them?"

"I was well acquainted with the elder Smith; he often came to see me, and we had many long talks together. I did not see much of the younger Smith. He seemed a very quiet, unassuming lad. For the Elder Smith I had the highest regard; he seemed well informed on every imaginable topic, and there was no subject upon which he could not talk intelligently.["]

"Did you make the statement given in the *Times,* that the Smiths were known as sheep-thieves and, in fact, as unscrupulous people, in that community?"

"I did not; the Smiths were respected by everyone in the town and vicinity, and up to the time when the discovery of the plates from which the Book of Mormon was translated, that raised a great excitement in those parts and many people went to digging for hidden treasures, their moral character had never been questioned. If they had not been of such unimpeachable character, they could not have been employed by my uncles who were very facetious [fastidious] in the selection of their employe[e]s. I never as much as thought of doubting Smith's honesty."

"Did you make the statement that Mormonism in those days was a money-making scheme?"

"No, sir; it appeared to me that the elder Smith was desirous of great wealth, and during the gold-digging excitement following the discovery of the mysterious plates, I was at times led to think it possible that the elder Smith might have planned some deep scheme for making money; but when the religious society called the "Chosen People" was formed, and he became active in proselyting and preaching and baptizing, I was nonplussed, for circumstances went to show that Smith could have had no such aim, or if so, had given it up entirely."

"Do you think that his desire for wealth could ever have overcome his honesty?"

"No, no; I never thought that. So far as I knew Smith, I judged that he would not take as much as the value of a pin from anybody."

"What were the sources from which you derived your knowledge of Mormonism?"

"Most of the knowledge that I possess as regards Mormonism, and the plates from which young Joseph translated the Book of Mormon, was derived from conversations with Smith, Sr., and Martin Harris. Smith told me of the stones his son Joseph had found, and by means of which he could see hidden treasures and many wonderful things. They had formed a society at that time—not a religious society, however. He wanted me to identify myself with the understanding and promise to make me treasurer, in that event. Before entering upon it, I required to be shown the plates of which he spoke, but he said if I saw and handled the plates I would be struck dead. I told him, if this was the case, it was just the kind of death I would want to die. But he would not consent, and thus gave me up. I was also well acquainted with Martin Harris. In fact, we were great friends, and I thought often of him in after years. Of late I have often desired to make a journey to California, and on going through Utah, to look for Martin Harris. I know he would have received me with open arms.[15] He often spoke to me of those plates, and I told him that I could not believe that they were what they claimed to be. But he persisted so earnestly in claiming them to be authentic that I was perplexed. I met Martin Harris, several years later, on a steam-boat on Cayuga Lake. He had with him a company of "Saints"—about two hundred of them—bound for Missouri. He preached to the passengers on board, on the "last dispensation" and the Book of Mormon as the word of God, and declared that he often communicated with Christ, as one man with another, and many other statements equally strange. In the course of his sermon, he referred to me, and advised his audience, if they doubted his honesty, to inquire of me concerning his reputation, as I was a townsmen of his and knew him well. The captain of the boat was by my side and enquired of me

15. Martin Harris had died in 1875 at Clarkston, Cache County, Utah.

what sort of a man Harris was. I could not do otherwise than speak well of him; only this I said, that on religious subjects I thought him slightly demented. I was thunderstruck when I heard him speak, and was more perplexed than ever.["]

"What were your religious sentiments at the time—were you connected with a church?"

"I was then a member, and later a warden, of the Episcopal Church, and have been connected with it the greater part of my life."

"Did any of your relatives join the 'Chosen People,' as they were then called?"

"None, save John Hyde,[16] a cousin of mine. I never saw him, but corresponded with him, when I was a boy and lived in Boston, and he was in London. I afterwards learned that he had come to America."

"Did the elder Smith offer any inducements to you—did he promise that you should become possessed of great wealth, if you become a member of that society."

"He said that by means of the Urim and Thummim,[17] which were in the possession of his son Joseph, the secrets of all arts and sciences would be revealed, and that these would be carefully guarded and kept within the society, and that there was no doubt that great wealth would be the result, and if I would join them and contribute some money to the funds of the society, I would be sure to become rich. Well, now I have come to think, if I had done so, I would be better off today than I am, even if the great wealth the senior Smith talked so much about did not materialize."

"Did these conversations between you and Mr. Smith take place before the work of translation from the plates had commenced?"

"Yes, sir; Smith used to tell me then that the writing on the plates was a record of a lost race that once inhabited this continent and was highly civilized; that it had possession of many important secrets in all branches of art and science, and that those secrets were laid open by the writing on the plates, but that the then generation was too wicked to receive them, and therefore the Lord would not grant a translation.

Both Smith and Harris told me that the latter took the plates to Dr. [Samuel L.] Mitchell, of Philadelphia,[18] a reputed linguist, and well versed

16. This person remains unidentified. Perhaps he is John Hyde, a former Mormon and author of *Mormonism: Its Leaders and Designs* (New York: W. P. Fetridge and Co., 1857).

17. See note 6 above.

18. Hyde remembers incorrectly. Samuel L. Mitchell was in New York City, according to Charles Anthon (see V.D.2, CHARLES ANTHON

in heiroglyphics [hieroglyphics], that the professor recognized in the writing on the plates an account of a highly civilized race that once inhabited this continent."

"Are you not mistaken about the plates—was it not an abstract, or a portion of the writing or characters on one of these plates, that was shown to Dr. Mitchell?"

"No, sir; I remember distinctly to have heard both Smith and Harris say that the latter took the plates to Dr. Mitchell."[19]

"Did this take place before the work of translation had commenced?"

"Yes, sir."

"Did you hear of Martin Harris subsequently, that is, after the translation had been entered upon, taking a transcript of some of the writing on the plates to Dr. [Charles] Anthony[20] of New York, and of this linguist having recognized in the transcript the characteers [characters] of some oriental language, but declaring himself unable to read it."[21]

"I never heard of such a translation [transcription?]."

"Did you ever at any time during your acquaintance with the elder Smith, consider him in the light of a schemer?"

"Not exactly in the common sense of the word. The slight suspicion I entertained at one time, that he might be up to some money making scheme, was entirely obliterated by subsequent occurrences, that is, by his taking such a prominent part in religious affairs. I had at all times the highest regard for him. He used to see me night after night and speak to me of former inhabitants of this continent, how a large portion of the earth now covered by the Pacific Ocean was once occupied by land, etc. Many of the things he told me seemed absurd in those days, but have since been proven to be correct, and I have seen with my own eyes in Wisconsin and other parts of this country, at excavations, a verification of the wonderful things he used

---

TO E. D. HOWE, 17 FEB 1834, 270; see also Kimball 1970, 333-34). On Samuel L. Mitchell (1764-1831), see I.A.15, JOSEPH SMITH HISTORY, 1839, n. 45.

19. On this point, Hyde's memory obviously failed him; Harris took a facsimile of the characters said to have been copied from the plates (see V.E.2, BOOK OF MORMON CHARACTERS, DEC 1827-FEB 1828).

20. On Charles Anthon (1797-1867), see introduction to V.D.2, CHARLES ANTHON TO E. D. HOWE, 17 FEB 1834. The first printing of Joseph Smith's History in the *Times and Seasons* in 1842 misspelled Charles Anthon's last name as "Anthony" (2 May 1842, 3:773).

21. For Anthon's account of his encounter with Harris, see V.D.2, CHARLES ANTHON TO E. D. HOWE, 17 FEB 1834; and V.D.3, CHARLES ANTHON TO THOMAS WINTHROP COIT, 3 APR 1841.

to tell me, and while his knowledge of these things seemed marvelous to me at that time, now that this knowledge is proven to be correct, it is incomprehensible to me how he could have obtained it. He was indeed a marvelous man.[”]

“The *Times* makes the statement that you declared that young Joseph Smith endeavored to convert you to the new creed, and promised to make you an apostle, if you accepted the doctrine he promulgated. Is this true?”

“I never spoke to Joseph Smith, Jr., upon the subject, and he never made any such statement to me.”

“Did you ever read the Book of Mormon?”

“I never saw the book. The printer in Palmyra who printed it sent me several proofs, and I read some, but finally grew tired of them and paid no more attention to them.”

“You have no connected idea, then, of the contents of the book in question?”

“No, sir.”

“Martin Harris told me that the plates were sewed in a silk sack, and were never opened at such occasions, but lay on the table while young Joseph Smith placed the Urim and Thummim in his hat, and then “read” the translation of the writing in the stones.”

“Do you know who acted as scribe on these occasions?”

“No, sir.”

“Were you acquainted with the early history of Mormonism—if so, what was their standing in the community?”

“Did you learn any particulars about the work of translation?”

“I did not personally know any one else, save Oliver Cowdery[22]; my acquaintance with him was, however, but slight. He was greatly respected by all, as far as I know, as indeed were all the people in those parts, who accepted the new creed. They were, for the most part substantial farmers. Martin Harris was universally looked up to, and I never heard any one say a word against him.”

“How about that gold-digging affair in the woods, did the Smiths organize it?”

“Young Smith had designated the spot—about an acre of open ground; there were no woods there—and said that by means of the Urim and Thummim he could see ‘treasures’ that were hidden in that ground, and people went to work searching for them. Young Smith was not there then,

22. On Oliver Cowdery (1806-50), see “Introduction to Oliver Cowdery Collection.”

but the elder Smith, and when the sudden flash of light frightened and dispersed the diggers, he declared that the Lord had in this manner shown His displeasure."

"You said a little while ago that no one thought otherwise than well of the Smiths until after the discovery of the plates. How did this ill-feeling originate?"

"The failure of the treasure-seeking expedition and the consequent disappointment of many raised a temporary excitement, but there was nothing very serious said or done, until the religious excitement began—after the translation of the plates and the organization of the 'Church of Jesus Christ'—when the Smiths and their followers, of which there was a great number then, moved away to Ohio. Then families broke up, and the popular feeling against the Smiths became very bitter, their moral character was never attacked even then; they were considered religious fanatics."

"Were there, to your knowledge, many families broken up in this way?"

"I know personally of only one—that of Martin Harris. He perpetrated no wrong against his family. He was a nice, kind, man, and very forbearing.[23] His wife was a quakeress and did not sympathize with his religious views; she could not believe as he did, and his faith was too strong to yield. Thus he left her and the children and her property."

"The *Times* put into your mouth the statement that no less than forty families were broken up, in the village of Palmyra?"

"I repeat Martin Harris' family was the only one in the town of Palmyra, thus broken up."

"Were the Smiths persecuted for speaking and doing as they did? Were they subjected to any kind of annoyance at services and while performing the ceremony of baptism?"

"No sir; their services were orderly and free from annoyance, as I was told, for I never attended any of them. When they went to baptize converts, everything went off quietly and without disturbance of any kind. People went to see, as they would have gone to see a ceremony performed by a Christian minister, and both believers and unbelievers behaved properly."

"Is the account the *Times* gives of the subsequent history of Mormonism from your pen, or in any way authorized by you?"

"No sir; I know nothing of what transpired after the Smiths and their followers left the parts where I then lived, for Ohio—save what I could glean

23. However, see III.A.7, LUCY HARRIS STATEMENT, 29 NOV 1833.

from current rumors."

"Did you authorize or encourage the scathing language used in the *Times* article."

"No sir; I would not speak ill of the Smiths, or Martin Harris, or Oliver Cowdery under any consideration, I wrote an article on the 'Birth of Mormonism,' but it was entirely different from the *Times* article. The most important items of my article were omitted by the reporter who took charge of my manuscript.["]

Mr. Hyde, though nearly 90 years old, is as yet of a bright intellect, and displays a marvelous memory. He is of a liberal mind and greatly surprised your correspondent with his views on polygamy and the action of certain politicians on the Mormon question, wondering how many of those who are so active in "extirpating polygamy," or trying to do so, would dare to submit their private life to the scrutiny of the public who applaud their action. Mr. Hyde is about to become an author, being now engaged in writing an autobiography, which promises to be an interesting work, as he is well-read, and an acute observer, and has traveled considerably both in Europe and in America. He desired to know more about the doctrines advocated by the Latter-day Saints, and about the history of the Church, especially the circumstances that led to the tragic death of the Smiths, since, as he said, he could not believe that Joseph Smith could have been guilty of any misdeed deserving of the death penalty.

L. E. ODINGA,

Chicago, Ill., Oct. 23d, 1888.

24.
Orson Saunders Account, 1893

"Mormon Leaders at Their Mecca. ... Joe Smith's Life at Palmyra," *New York Herald,* 25 June 1893, 12.

EDITORIAL NOTE

In this interview Orson Saunders (c. 1838-189?), youngest son of Orlando and Belinda Saunders and nephew of Lorenzo and Benjamin Saunders, relates what he heard his uncle Benjamin say about 1891 regarding Joseph Smith's obtaining the gold plates. Orson worked his father's farm, never married, and died in the 1890s (U.S. Census, Palmyra, Wayne County, New York, 1860:844; 1880:340B; T. Cook 1930, 236-37). On 23 June 1893 he was interviewed by a correspondent of the *New York Herald,* who at the same time interviewed John H. Gilbert and others in Palmyra and Manchester (see III.H.11, JOHN H. GILBERT INTERVIEW, 1893; III.J.25, PALMYRA-MANCHESTER RESIDENTS ACCOUNT, 1893). The *Herald* introduces Orson's statement with the following:

> While on the hill [Cumorah] Orson Saunders, the frisky bachelor farmer of Palmyra, gave the story that Smith had told his uncle of how he found the golden tablets. It is no doubt authentic, because the Saunders boys are trustworthy and their uncle was well acquainted with the Smith family. Their farms adjoined. The uncle's name is Benjamin Saunders. He is eighty years old and lives at Banker's Station, near Hillsdale, Mich. He repeated the narrative only a year or two ago to Orson. This is the story: ...

Besides his interview with William H. Kelley in 1884 (see III.B.13, BENJAMIN SAUNDERS INTERVIEW, CIRCA SEP 1884), the present account is the only other source that purports to record Benjamin Saunders's reminiscence. However, because the *Herald*'s reporting is third-hand (a newspaperman's reporting of Orson Saunders's two-year-old memory of his uncle Benjamin's more than sixty-year-old memory of what Joseph Smith told him) and uncorroborated, caution is in order. Although Orson's account contains elements similar to Benjamin's interview with Kelley, for the most part Orson's statement is unique. That Orson was reported accurately is supported by the correspondent's interview with John H. Gilbert in the same publication, which compares favorably with other Gilbert interviews. Since most of Orson's account cannot be corroborated elsewhere and it is unlike Benjamin's previous statement, which is similar to Willard Chase's account (III.A.14, WILLARD CHASE STATEMENT, CIRCA 11 DEC 1833, 242), one might conclude Orson embellished his uncle's account. However, it is also possible that Benjamin Saunders felt restrained with the critical, believing Kelley, but spoke more freely with his nephew.

HOW JOE SMITH FOUGHT DEVILS.

... [Joseph] Smith had received several communications from the archangel, and was told on a certain day to repair that night to the holy mountain and dig in a certain place, which he would recognize. It was shown him in the vision. Accordingly he went there at midnight with a shovel and crowbar. He recognized the spot and dug until he came to a large, flat stone. To use Smith's own words:—

"I forced the crowbar under the stone and raised it without difficulty. There I beheld a casket of golden plates, on which were inscribed the new gospels. The glory of heaven shone around them and upon them. The place seemed on fire. I was about to remove the plates when an enormous toad appeared, squatting upon the pages.[1]

"Instantly it was revealed to me that I had forgotten to carry out some request made by the angel in digging for the plates. I had forgotten to give thanks to God, and I knew what was passing in the toad's mind. Instantly the beast arose and expanded as large as a dog, then as a bullock, then it rose far above me, a flaming monster with glittering eyes, until it seemed to fill the heavens, and with a blow like lightning it swept me from the mountain into the valley beneath.[2]

---

1. In 1884 Benjamin told William H. Kelley that the creature "looked some like a toad" (III.B.13, BENJAMIN SAUNDERS INTERVIEW, CIRCA SEP 1884, 23). Pomeroy Tucker reported in 1867 that "Smith told a frightful story of the display of celestial pyrotechnics on the exposure to his view of the sacred book," adding that "this story was repeated and magnified by the believers" (III.J.8, POMEROY TUCKER ACCOUNT, 1867, 30-31; see also III.K.24, HEBER C. KIMBALL AUTOBIOGRAPHY, 1864).

2. In 1884 Benjamin Saunders simply said the creature "rose up into a man which forbid him to take the plates" (III.B.13, BENJAMIN SAUNDERS INTERVIEW, CIRCA SEP 1884, 23). Willard Chase similarly stated that Smith saw in the box "something like a toad, which soon assumed the appearance of a man, and struck him on the side of his head ... and knocked him three or four rods, and hurt him prodigiously" (III.A.14, WILLARD CHASE STATEMENT, CIRCA 11 DEC 1833, 242).

ANOTHER VISITATION.

"The sun was shining high in the heavens when I came to my senses. Again the angel of the Lord appeared and instructed me how I should further proceed. I acknowledged the mistake I had made and on that night I again repaired to the holy mountain. But the stone was not there, nor was there any sign that it had ever been there or that I had dug for it. But a revelation came to me on the spot. A new place to dig was pointed out and in a few moments I reached a big flat stone, and offering up thanks I removed it with the crowbar. The golden plates were flaming again in celestial splendor. The toad was not there. Then I knew it was all right.

"Again thanking the Almighty I removed the plates, but was so agitated I could hardly move. The moment I touched them a thousand devils sprang into light. They were all around the hill; the mountain seemed alive with them; they were in the air; they perched on my shoulders. They could do nothing, however. I was protected by the angel of God. But I had to fight for it. It was a struggle to get down from the mountain. Many a time I thought the holy plates would be taken from me, but I never let go of them until I found a place to hide, that I might rest and recover my strength. The country was heavily timbered in those days, but I was not afraid to go through the woods. On the following day I had the plates safely clasped to my breast and I carried them home and afterward hid them in a cave, where I began the first translation of the inspired pages." ...

25.
Palmyra-Manchester Residents Account, 1893

"Mormon Leaders at Their Mecca. ... Joe Smith's Life at Palmyra," *New York Herald,* 25 June 1893, 12.

EDITORIAL NOTE

This reporter's account of statements collected from persons living in the Palmyra-Manchester area in 1893 must be read with caution since his sources are not identified, although he evidently relied on Pomeroy Tucker's published account (III.J.8, POMEROY TUCKER ACCOUNT, 1867). The reporter also interviewed John H. Gilbert and Orson Saunders, nephew of Benjamin Saunders (see III.H.11, JOHN H. GILBERT INTERVIEW, 1893; and III.J.24, ORSON SAUNDERS ACCOUNT, 1893). What follows is the unidentified portion of the report.

SMITH'S LIFE AT HOME.

The brief story of Joe Smith's career, as told in this town, is as follows:—He was of a family of nine children, who came to Palmyra from Royalton, Vt., in 1816.[1]

At first the Smiths opened a cake and ale stand in the village of Palmyra. The boys "worked round," dug wells and chopped wood now and then, but Joseph, Jr., was opposed to manual labor except in great emergencies. According to people who knew him best he was a silent, lazy boy—often called stupid. But he was a well built fellow, with blue eyes and light hair, sometimes spoken of as a full faced, chuckle headed lad who took life easy and dreamed and schemed while others toiled.[2]

At that time there was a craze for treasure hunting, and many things of value had been discovered in Indian mounds. Smith took advantage of the mania, and when digging for gold he superintended the job and showed an unusual amount of energy in making people believe in his strange fancies. It was his custom to go out with a party and dig for money or relics on the hills

1. Rather Norwich, Vermont. The reporter evidently follows III.J.8, POMEROY TUCKER ACCOUNT, 1867, 12.

2. See III.J.8, POMEROY TUCKER ACCOUNT, 1867, 12.

at midnight. Usually he was half asleep and idle, but on special days, at general musters, elections and political meetings, he turned out with the whole Smith family. They put their cheap merchandise on sale, with cakes, beer, hard cider and boiled eggs. Joseph is described as a silent boy who never smiled, and he kept himself in the background while developing his schemes for creating a sensation; then he came to the front and appeared as a leader. Incessant and tireless, he pursued his game. As young Smith grew older, he became the master of the family—father and brothers followed him to the end. Joe was the chief vagabond of this New England gypsy family. Horses, whiskey, craft and story telling characterized his worldly career.

Three years after the family had opened their little shop of gingerbread and ale in Palmyra the Smiths "squatted" on a piece of timber land of one hundred and fifty or two hundred acres, about two miles south of the village certre. First they had a log house, which was never completely finished; then they built a frame house which was not finished until long afterward.[3] All survivors agree that the Smiths were a shiftless lot, particularly Joseph, Jr.

MORMON FARMING.

Their fields were half cleared, half ploughed, half cultivated and half harvested. At times they made brooms and baskets, peddled vegetables and were hucksters rather than farmers. When other boys were hoeing corn Joe was hunting or fishing or getting up a party to dig for money. He claimed to have a clairvoyant insight into things that other people could not see. He always had two or three pots of money or chests of valuables on tap in his mind's eye, and this explains why the hills of Palmyra to-day are covered with holes which Apostle Joe Smith, Jr., had inveigled his fellow citizens into digging. The money mania was the talk of the country for miles around. When Joe and his followers visited Pennsylvania and began turning up the clay of that State many people thought Joe Smith a great man if not an honest one.

In the autumn of 1819[4] an incident occurred which put young Joe Smith into a wider field of operations. It was the beginning of a series of fake discoveries, which culminated in his claim that with the assistance of a beautiful angel he had discovered the golden plates of a new Gospel.

The elder Smith was digging a well for Clark Chase,[5] two miles south of Palmyra. The Chase children were playing about the well, when one of

3. See III.J.8, POMEROY TUCKER ACCOUNT, 1867, 13.

4. Should be 1822; the reporter follows the error in III.J.8, POMEROY TUCKER ACCOUNT, 1867, 19 (see Ibid., n. 32).

5. See III.J.8, POMEROY TUCKER ACCOUNT, 1867, n. 33.

the Smith boys shovelled out a clear white stone shaped like a human foot. It was quite transparent, something like a "peep" stone which the Chase children had used as a plaything. One of the girls said that when she peeped into the stone she saw things that had been lost. She was quite joyous over the treasure until young Joe, who was idling about the well, seized the agate and carried it away.[6] Joe was quiet for several days. Presently it was whispered that he had discovered a charm in which he could see wonders. With an air of mystery he would look at the stone shaded in his hat and see visions and any amount of lost property. Each day he had new revelations for his open mouthed followers.

In a few weeks people were paying money for his oracles. Many a man was sent over the hills in search of lost cattle, on a fool's errand, of course, but Joe made money and the public apparently fancied humbugging, and that made him a great success.

SMITH'S SPIRITUAL VISIONS.

It was not long before he had heavenly visions. Men paid to join his search for treasures. His conditions were that no person should speak during the digging. A whisper would cause the box of gold to vanish forever. A confederate generally broke the charm at the proper moment and thus prevented exposure.

Next, young Joe must have a sacrifice and soak the ground with blood, to enable him to discover the hidden treasure. A fat sheep was given, its throat cut, but somebody extinguished the torches, and amid Smith's protests and cries of indignation the sheep disappeared. On the following day there was a grand feast under the prophet's roof.[7] The mutton was tender and Joe a power in the family. He kept the pots filled with mutton, and the Smith family waxed notorious.

These gypsy feats and impostures continued until Joe Smith and his gold diggers were visited by people from other States. Nearly all of young Smith's followers were without money or character. The exception was Martin Harris,[8] an honest farmer, who lived near the village. He was a business man by nature, had a good farm, but his weakness was in his belief

6. See III.A.14, WILLARD CHASE STATEMENT, CIRCA 11 DEC 1833, 240.

7. See III.A.13, WILLIAM STAFFORD STATEMENT, 8 DEC 1833, 239.

8. On Martin Harris (1783-1875), see "Introduction to Martin Harris Collection."

in Joe Smith's spiritual powers. He affirmed that he had every proof of Joe Smith's divine nature.

ORIGIN OF THE MORMON BIBLE.

At this point in the Smith narrative the Mormon Bible hoax enters. Volumes have been written about it and strenuously denied by the Mormons. The best informed people of Palmyra, however, believe the story of the stealing of what was known as the Spalding manuscript, which Joe Smith had copied and interpolated with passages from the Bible and palmed off as a revelation from God. ...[9]

Not long after this [about 1827] a mysterious stranger appeared closeted with Joe Smith. It was [Sidney] Rigdon.[10] He had frequent interviews with the young apostle, and there was evidently something important brewing. Smith's revelations grew more frequent. He had a new dispensation to relate every time he visited the village. Farmer Harris, the only follower of Smith who had more money than he knew what to do with, mentioned Smith's name with new reverence. Smith told him that he had met an angel and would have a new gospel for the public very soon. Later he came into town pale and exhausted, but his eyes were radiant. He said he had been on a mountain by direction of the angel, had had a fight with the devil, and after a long conflict had secured the golden pages of the new gospel. He would translate it by means of spiritual spectacles which accompanied the metal pages.[11]

In a few days[12] Martin Harris, the honest farmer, was ready to sacrifice his life for the only true revelation. He went to Mr. Grandin,[13] the village editor, who listened to his proposition to put the Bible in print. Mr. Grandin refused to do the work. Harris visited Thurlow Weed's[14] printing

---

9. Then follows a discussion of the Spaulding theory.

10. See III.J.8, POMEROY TUCKER ACCOUNT, 1867, 28. On Sidney Rigdon (1793-1876), see introduction to I.A.13, SIDNEY RIGDON ACCOUNT, CIRCA 1836.

11. This is incorrect since Harris did not learn of Smith's discovery of gold plates until the month after Smith had taken them from the hill (see III.F.10, MARTIN HARRIS INTERVIEW WITH JOEL TIFFANY, 1859, 167-68).

12. The events described in this paragraph occurred in June 1829, not "a few days" after the discovery of the plates in September 1827.

13. On Egbert B. Grandin (1806-45), see I.A.15, JOSEPH SMITH HISTORY, 1839, n. 77.

14. On Thurlow Weed (1792-1882), see introduction to III.K.17, THURLOW WEED REMINISCENCES, 1854, 1858, 1880 & 1884.

office in Rochester and received a similar answer.[15]

Then Mr. Harris returned, went to Mr. Grandin and put his offer in business form; said he would give bonds to pay for the work if necessary. Mr. Grandin finally consented to print an edition of 5,000 copies, as stated at the beginning of this article, for 3,000 cash. It was a large sum in those days and ultimately Martin Harris, the honest man, had to mortgage his farm to pay the bill.[16] ...

15. See III.J.8, POMEROY TUCKER ACCOUNT, 1867, 51-52.
16. See III.L.14, MARTIN HARRIS MORTGAGE, 25 AUG 1829.

26.
Daniel Hendrix Reminiscence, 1893

"Origin of Mormonism. Joe Smith and His Early Habits. How He Found the Golden Plates. A Contemporary of the Prophet Relates Some Interesting Facts," *San Francisco Chronicle,* 14 May 1893, 12. Reprinted in *New York Times,* 15 July 1895, 5; *St. Louis Daily Globe-Democrat,* 21 February 1897, 34; *New York Sun,* 21 March 1897; and *New York Advertiser,* 28 May 1897; unidentified newspaper clipping, 16 April 1897, William H. Samson Scrapbooks, 78:2-3, Rochester Public Library, Local History Room, Rochester, New York; unidentified newspaper clipping, April 24 [1897?], Arthur B. Deming Collection, Chicago Historical Society, Chicago, Illinois; unidentified newspaper clipping, undated [1897?], "Journal History," 1930 section, LDS Church Archives, Salt Lake City, Utah; and *Buffalo Courier,* 6 August 1899.

EDITORIAL NOTE

The reliability of Daniel Hendrix's statement has been challenged by Richard L. Anderson, who writes: "The lateness of the 'recollection' demands verification. ... To date rather diligent investigation has failed to verify the existence of Daniel Hendrix (whose other rambling descriptions are not notably accurate)" (R. L. Anderson 1970, 310, n. 53). I also have failed to verify the existence of Daniel Hendrix in civil records, although I have located a purported photograph of Hendrix and additional biographical information.

Various dates have been given for Hendrix's birth, 1806,[1] September 1809,[2] and 1811.[3] Prior to his removal to Palmyra in 1822, where he worked in a store, he lived in Rochester, New York. Following his move from Palmyra about 1830, nothing is known of his life until the late 1880s when he relocated from Ohio to southern California to be near his children and

1. *Buffalo Courier,* 6 August 1899, states: "He was born in 1806, and was therefore almost 94 years of age when he died."

2. *New York Times,* 15 July 1895, states: "Daniel Hendrix will be eighty-six years old next September"; and *St. Louis Daily Globe-Democrat,* 21 February 1897, says: "He is 87 years of age ..."

3. *San Francisco Chronicle,* 14 May 1893, says: "He is 82 years of age ..."

Daniel Hendrix, as published in the *Buffalo Courier*, 6 August 1899.

grandchildren.[4] The interview was conducted in May 1893 by Henry G. Tinsley, formerly of Lyons, Wayne County, New York,[5] a correspondent of the *San Francisco Chronicle,* who refers to Hendrix as "a visitor in Rincon, in San Bernardino county [California]." Tinsley also reports that the elderly Hendrix "is now confined to his granddaughter's home by severe physical ailments." When Hendrix's reminiscence was reprinted with a new introduction in the *New York Times,* 15 July 1895, the report originated from Ontario, San Bernardino, California, and stated that Hendrix "has made his home with his daughter and grandchildren on a little alfalfa ranch several miles southwest from this place in the Pomona Valley."[6]

Subsequent reprintings suggest that Hendrix moved to the adjacent Riverside County. In 1887 the *St. Louis Daily Globe-Democrat* said Hendrix "lives at the home of his son in this vicinity," referring to San Jacinto, Riverside County, California. And an unidentified newspaper clipping in the LDS church's "Journal History," mistakenly attributed to the year 1930, introduces Hendrix's reminiscence with the statement that "[he] lives at the

4. The *Buffalo Courier,* 6 August 1899, states that Hendrix "came to live with his children in Ontario, Cal., ten years ago."

5. A notice in the *Arcadian Weekly Gazette* (Newark, New York) for 31 May 1893 reads: "We have a copy of the San Francisco Chronicle containing an interesting article on Mormonism and its origin, from the pen of Henry G. Tinsley, of Pomona, Cal., formerly of Lyons [New York]. It contains the story of Daniel Hendrix, who told the story to Mr. Tinsley in Rincon, Cal. Mr. Hendrix was formerly of Palmyra, and claims to be one of the four men now living who were actual witnesses of the earliets [earliest] days of Mormonism in Palmyra."

6. Diedrich Willers, Jr., of Fayette, New York, who was conducting research for his *Centennial Historical Sketch of the Town of Fayette, Seneca County, New-York, 1800-1900,* which included information on Mormon origins (see VI.E.3, DIEDRICH WILLERS, JR., HISTORICAL SKETCH, 1900), saw the *New York Times* article and attempted to contact Hendrix. In a letter addressed to Daniel Hendrix, Ontario, California, dated 27 July 1895, Willers wrote: "I saw an article in the New York *Times,* contain=ing some of your recollections of Joseph Smith the founder of the Mormon Church—which I read with great interest" (Diedrich Willers, Jr., Collection, Seneca Falls Historical Society, Seneca Falls, New York). In the letter Willers criticized Hendrix for ignoring Smith's activities in Fayette and questioned the claim that Smith translated in a cave in Manchester. According to a notation on the envelope, the letter was "Unclaimed" and "Advertised," presumably in a southern California newspaper (the normal procedure for unclaimed letters in nineteenth-century post offices). However, the letter remained unclaimed and was therefore returned to Willers.

home of his son in San Jacinto, California."

Finally, the *Buffalo Courier* for 6 August 1899, which included a photograph of Hendrix and reprinted Hendrix's statement with new opening material, reported that Hendrix, "a lifelong, devout Presbyterian," had "died in Santa Monica, Cal., the other day" (see also William H. Samson Scrapbook, 79:56, Local History Room, Rochester Public Library, Rochester, New York). However, a search of death records for 1899 for Los Angeles County, California, failed to turn up a death certificate for Daniel Hendrix.[7]

... "I was a lad, or a very young man, in a store in Palmyra, N.Y., from 1822 until 1830," said Mr. Hendrix, "and among the daily visitors at the establishment was Joseph Smith, Jr. Every one knew him as Joe Smith. He had lived in Palmyra a few years previous to my going there from Rochester. Joe was the most ragged, lazy fellow in the place, and that is saying a good deal. He was about 25 years old.[8] I can see him now, in my mind's eye, with his torn and patched trousers, held to his form by a pair of suspenders made out of sheeting, with his calico shirt as dirty and black as the earth, and his uncombed hair sticking through the holes in his old battered hat. In winter I used to pity him, for his shoes were so old and worn out that he must have suffered in the snow and slush, yet Joe had a jovial, easy, don't-care way about him that made him a lot of warm friends. He was a good talker and would have made a fine stump-speaker if he had had the training. He was known among the young men I associated with as a romancer of the first water. I never knew so ignorant a man as Joe was to have such a fertile imagination. He never could tell a common occurrence in his daily life without embellishing the story with his imagination, yet, I remember that he was terribly grieved one day when old Parson Reed[9] told Joe that he was going to hell for his lying habits.

"Mrs. Smith, Joe's mother, was a staunch Presbyterian,[10] and was a great

7. Since this source also claims Hendrix's children were located in Ontario, California, I also searched for a death record in San Bernardino County with the same result (Anne L. Brandt, Research Assistant at the San Bernardino County Archives, San Bernardino, California, to Dan Vogel, 12 October 1993).

8. Joseph Smith was twenty-five on 23 December 1830.

9. Richard L. Anderson has complained that he was unable to verify the existence of "Parson Reed" (R. L. Anderson 1970, 310 n. 53), but Parson might refer to his position as a clergyman rather than his name.

10. See III.L.20, PALMYRA (NY) PRESBYTERIAN CHURCH RECORDS, MAR 1830.

admirer of her son, despite his shiftless and provoking ways. She always declared that he was born with a genius, and did not have to work. 'Never mind about my son Joseph,' said she one day when my employer had rallied her upon her heir's useless ways, 'for the boy will be able some of these fine days to buy the whole of Palmyra and all the folks in it. You don't know what a brain my boy has under that old hat.'[11]

"For over two years Joe Smith's chief occupation was digging for gold at night and sleeping in the daytime. He was close-mouthed on the subject of his gold-seeking operations around on the farms of Wayne county, where not a speck of gold was ever mined, and when people joked him too severely concerning his progress in getting the precious metal, he would turn his back upon the jokers and bystanders and go home as fast as possible. With some of us young men, however, who were always serious with him and affected an interest in his work, he was more confidential.

"Joe, in his excursions after gold, carried a divining rod to tell him where there was hidden treasure, and he left many holes in the ground about that region, which testified that he could work if the spirit moved. He had all the superstitions of the money-diggers of the day, one of which was that the digging must be done at night and not a word must be spoken, for at the first utterance the gold would fly away to some other locality; in fact, Joe claimed that he had more than once been on the point of reaching some great treasure, when, in his eagerness, some unlucky exclamation would escape him and, presto! the treasure would vanish from under his feet.

"Finally in the fall—in September, I believe—of 1823 Joe went about the village of Palmyra telling people of the great bonanza he at last found. I remember distinctly his sitting on some boxes in the store and telling a knot of men, who did not believe a word they heard, all about his vision and his find. But Joe went into such minute and careful details about the size, weight and beauty of the carvings [engravings] on the golden tablets, the strange characters and the ancient adornments, that I confess he made some of the smartest men in Palmyra rub their eyes in wonder. The women were not so skeptical as the men and several of the leading ones in the place began to feel at once that Joe was a remarkable man after all.

"Joe declared with tears in his eyes and the most earnest expression you can imagine that he had found the gold plates on a hill six miles south of Palmyra, on the main road between that place and Canandaigua. Joe had dug and dug there for gold for four years, and from that time hill has been known as Gold [Bible] hill.

---

11. Compare III.J.8, POMEROY TUCKER ACCOUNT, 1867, 17.

"For the first month or two at least Joe Smith did not say himself that the plates were any new revelation or that they had any religious significance, but simply said that he had found a valuable treasure in the shape of a record of some ancient peoples, which had been inscribed on imperishable gold for preservation. The pretended gold plates were never allowed to be seen, though I have heard Joe's mother say that she had lifted them when covered with cloth, and they were very heavy, so heavy, in fact, that she could scarcely raise them, though she was a very robust woman.[12] What Joe at that time expected to accomplish seems difficult to understand, but he soon began to exhibit what he claimed to be copies of the characters engraved on the plates, though the irreverent were disposed to think that he was more indebted to the characters found on China tea chests and in histories of the Egyptians and Babylonians than to any plates he had dug up near Palmyra.[13] Before long, however, a new party appeared on the scene in the person of one Sidney Rigdon,[14] and thenceforward a new aspect was put upon the whole matter.[15]

"I remember Rigdon as a man of about 40 years,[16] smooth, sleek and with some means. He had a wonderful quantity of assurance, and in these days would be a good broker or speculator. He was a man of energy of contrivance, and would make a good living anywhere and in any business. He was distrusted by a large part of the people in Palmyra and Canandaigua, but had some sincere friends. He and Joe Smith fell in with each other and were cronies for several months. It was after Rigdon and Smith were so intimate that the divine part of the finding of the golden plates began to be spread abroad. It was given out that the plates were a new revelation and were a part of the original Bible, while Joe Smith was a true prophet of the Lord, to whom it was given to publish among men.

"Rigdon, who, from his first appearance, was regarded as the 'brains' of the movement, seemed satisfied to be the power behind the throne. Not only were pretended copies of the engraved plates exhibited, but whole chapters of what were called translations were shown; meetings were held at the Smith

12. See I.B.2, SALLY PARKER TO JOHN KEMPTON, 26 AUG 1838.

13. See V.E.2, BOOK OF MORMON CHARACTERS, DEC 1827-FEB 1828.

14. On Sidney Rigdon (1793-1876), see introduction to I.A.13, SIDNEY RIGDON ACCOUNT, CIRCA 1836.

15. Hendrix may have followed Tucker in assuming Rigdon was responsible for the Book of Mormon (see III.J.8, POMEROY TUCKER ACCOUNT, 1867, 28).

16. Sidney Rigdon was forty in 1833.

house and in the barns on the adjoining farms,[17] which were addressed by Smith and Rigdon, and an active canvass for converts was inaugurated. Strange as it may appear from the absurdity of the claims set forth, and the well-known character of Joe Smith, these efforts were to quite a degree successful, particularly among the unsophisticated farmers of the vicinity, and a number of them, who were regarded as equal in intelligence to the average rural population became enthusiastic proselytes of the new faith.

"One feature of the claim in relation to the translation from the plates was quite in character with the claims that have been from time to time set up by the Mormon church down to the present day. Joe Smith was, of course, an illiterate man and some way must be provided for the translation of his record. But Joe, or Rigdon, was equal to the emergency, for he claimed to have found with the "Gold Bible," as they then always called it, a wonderful pair of spectacles, which he described as having very large round glasses, larger than a silver dollar, and he asserted that by placing the plates in the bottom of a hat or other deep receptacle, like a wooden grain measure, he could put on those spectacles, and, looking down upon the plates, the engraved characters were all translated into good, plain English and he had only to read it off and have it recorded by a copyist.

"This claim with all its absurdity was not more absurd than one that was made to me personally by Martin Harris,[18] who was one of the early and most faithful proselytes. Harris was a farmer of good property, residing about a mile from the village, with whom I was well acquainted as a customer of a firm where I was employed. On one occasion I had been out on horseback on a collecting trip, and, returning in the early evening as I passed the house of Mr. Harris, he came out, and joining me we rode together toward the village. It was a beautiful evening in October, and as we were on elevated ground sloping eastward toward the village in the same direction in which we were going, the full moon, which was just rising, made everything before us look most charming.

"As I made some remark on the beauty of the moon, he replied to the effect that if I could only see it as he had done I might well call it beautiful. I was at once anxious to know what he meant, and plied him with questions; but beyond the assertion that he had actually visited the moon in his own

17. Ezra Thayre mentions Smith and Rigdon preaching in his barn in Canandaigua (see III.J.6, EZRA THAYRE REMINISCENCE, 1862); however, this occurred in December 1830 after the Smiths had moved to Fayette.

18. On Martin Harris (1783-1875), see "Introduction to Martin Harris Collection."

proper person and seen its glories face to face, he was not disposed to be communicative, remarking that it was only "the faithful that were permitted to visit the celestial regions," and with that he turned the conversation in less ethereal channels.[19]

"For three or four years Smith, Rigdon and Harris worked for converts to the new faith. They all became from constant practice and study good speakers, and Smith was at that time as diligent and earnest as he had previously been lazy and careless. The three men traveled all over New York State, particularly up and down the Erie canal. They were rotten-egged in some places, hooted and howled into silence in others, and had some attention in a few communities. Their meetings were generally poorly attended, and people regarded the men as fools whose cause would soon die out. I attended several of the meetings in Wayne and Ontario counties. Smith would always tell with some effect how the angel had appeared to him, how he felt an irresistible desire to dig where he did, and how he heard celestial music and the chanting of a heavenly host as he drew the golden plates from the earth and bore them to his home.

"He became so proficient in his description of the ecstatic joy in heaven when he found the plates that I have known a large audience to hold its breath as the sentences rolled from Smith's mouth. I have seen some farmer's wives become powerless and almost unconscious in the spell of religious enthusiasm that Smith and Rigdon had created. The latter told in scores of meetings, and to everyone with whom he came in contact, how he was frequently transported to celestial spheres at night, while his body lay on his bed at home; how he had listened to counsels from Moses and Elisha, how he actually walked in flowery fields and down golden streets on some far off planet, and he would repeat instructions that he pretended he had from Bible characters in the other world.[20]

"Of the printing of the 'Book of Mormon,' I have a particularly keen recollection. Smith and Rigdon had hard work to get funds together for the new Bible. Smith told me himself that the world was so wicked and perverse that it was hard to win converts; that he had a vision to print the Bible and that as soon as that was done the work would be prospered wonderfully. A new convert named Andrews,[21] a plain old farmer, in Auburn, New York,

19. See Dan Vogel and Brent Metcalfe, "Joseph Smith's Scriptural Cosmology," in Vogel 1990, 187-219.

20. Regarding Rigdon's visions during his visit to New York in December 1830-January 1831, see VI.F.3, EZRA BOOTH ACCOUNTS, 1831. See also note 19 above.

21. A reminiscence by Thomas Davies Burrall mentions that "two credulous men in Palmyra" applied for mortgages to print the Book of Mor-

mortgaged his property for $3000 to start the printing. The Wayne *Sentinel,* published at Palmyra, did the work, on a contract for 5000 copies for $5000.[22] The printing office was on an upper floor, near the store where I worked, and I was one of the few persons who was allowed about the office while the publishing was going on.

"I helped to read proof on many pages of the book, and at odd times set some type. The copy was about half ready for the printer when there came a halt in the proceedings, for Mrs. Harris,[23] wife of Martin Harris, had become so disgusted with her husband's conversion to the new religion and his abandonment of his fine farm for preaching Mormonism, that she one morning threw in the fire all the Bible manuscript that had been brought to him for review by Smith. It was weeks before Joe Smith and Rigdon recovered from their dismay at this act. Harris went down into his pockets for $300 to repay the loss caused by his wife's destruction of the manuscript.[24]

"The copy for the 'Book of Mormon' was prepared in a cave that Smith and others dug near the scene of the finding of the golden plates on Gold [Bible] hill. I went out there frequently for a Sunday walk during the process of the translation of the plates, and the printing of the book. Some one of the converts was constantly about the entrance to the cave, and no one but Smith and Alvin [Oliver] Cowdry,[25] a school teacher there, who had proselyted that season, was allowed to go through the door to the cave. Rigdon had some hopes of converting me, and I was permitted to go near the door, but not so much as to peep inside. Smith told me later that no one had ever seen the golden plates but himself, and that he wore the glasses found with the plates, and was thus able to translate the new message from heaven to the people. He read aloud, and Cowdry, who was seated on the other side of a screen or partition in the cave, wrote down the words as pronounced by Joe.[26]

"The penmanship of the copy furnished was good, but the grammar,

---

mon (III.K.27, THOMAS DAVIES BURRALL REMINISCENCE, 1876). However, this claim is highly unlikely since Martin Harris's mortgage adequately covered the cost of printing.

22. Actually $3,000 (see I.L.14, MARTIN HARRIS MORTGAGE, 25 AUG 1829).

23. On Lucy Harris (1792-1837), see introduction to III.A.7, LUCY HARRIS STATEMENT, 29 NOV 1833.

24. This is an extremely garbled account of the loss of the manuscript in June/July 1828, which Hendrix mistakenly dates to 1829/30.

25. On Oliver Cowdery (1806-50), see "Introduction to Oliver Cowdery Collection."

26. Compare III.J.8, POMEROY TUCKER ACCOUNT, 1867, 48-50.

spelling and punctuation were done by John H. Gilbert, who was chief compositor in the office. I have heard him swear many a time at the syntax and orthography of Cowdry and declare that he would not set another line of type. The copy came in one conglomerate mass and there were no paragraphs, no punctuation and no capitals. All that was done in the printing office, and what a time there used to be in straightening sentences out, too![27]

"During the work of printing the book I remember that Joe Smith kept in the background. He was wanted several times at the printing office to explain some obscure sentence and apparent blunders in composition, but he never came near the printers. He sent word by his brother Hyram[28] that the work of translating absorbed his mind and functions so that he could not attend to mundane business. Every morning Hyram Smith appeared at the office with installments of copy of twenty-four pages buttoned up in his vest, and came regularly and punctually for them at night.

"The publication of the book of 538 [588] pages was pushed with spirit, but until it was completed not a copy was allowed to leave the office, but every volume was packed in an upper room, and the pile they made struck me at the time, and has since been vividly in my mind, as comparing in size and shape with a cord of wood, and I called it a cord of Mormon Bibles. The work was finished in the spring of 1830. Not long after the publication was completed Smith and his followers began their preparations for a removal, and ere long the parties, with their converts, packed up all their belongings and left for Kirtland, O[hio].

"This removal was not 'on compulsion' from any complaints of their neighbors, like those they were subsequently compelled to make from Kirtland and Nauvoo, but all seemed to enter into it readily and with the utmost cheerfulness, though many abandoned homes of great comfort and comparative wealth. In the exodus there were farmers who were customers of the firm where I was employed, that sold their farms to the amount of $15,000, all of which was committed to the care and tender mercy of Joe Smith, and the votaries committed themselves to his care and guidance."

HENRY G. TINSLEY.

POMONA, May 3, 1893.

---

27. See III.H.10, JOHN H. GILBERT MEMORANDUM, 8 SEP 1892.

28. On Hyrum Smith (1800-44), see I.A.15, JOSEPH SMITH HISTORY, 1839, n. 12.

27.
PHILANA A. FOSTER TO E. W. TAYLOR, 16 JULY 1895

Philana A. Foster to E. W. Taylor, 16 July 1895, Theodore A. Schroeder Papers, Archives, Wisconsin State Historical Society, Madison, Wisconsin.

EDITORIAL NOTE

Writing on behalf of anti-Mormon writer Theodore A. Schroeder, lawyer and notary public Edward W. Taylor[1] of Salt Lake City addressed a letter to Philana A. Foster of Albion, New York, dated 26 June 1895, requesting information from her father about Mormon origins. The following is Taylor's letter:

> Dear madam:—
>
> Your favor of June 4th 1895 with reference to the letter of my friend, Mr. Schroeder, concerning Mormonism is at hand.
>
> In the first place Mr. Schroeder would like to get as many as possible of the early papers and magazines referring to Mormonism, especially those published between 1825 and 1835. You, probably, will have none of them, but can give him information by which he may be able to obtain some.
>
> In Mr. [Pomeroy] Tucker's book on Mormonism it is reported that [Joseph] Smith told many inconsistent stories with reference to the finding of the plates. Mr. S[chroeder]. desires to get as many of those stories as possible from the persons to whom they were told and especially any published record of them which may have been made at that time. Of course the greatest detail is desirable because it is upon the details that the contradictions will most likely appear.
>
> Mr. S[chroeder]. also desires a statement from your father of his connection with the making of the golden plates. It seems to be that your father several times stated to me that he knew about their manufacture and was connected with it. Kindly write me the facts about this, giving as much as possible of Smith's conversation and story concerning the plates. I trust your father will give us a full and frank statement of this affair. ... (E. W. Taylor to Philana A. Foster, Theodore A. Schroeder Collection, Archives,

---

1. Edward W. Taylor appears in the *Salt Lake City Directory* as a "lawyer & notary public" (e.g., 1897 and 1898) and "special agent and collector [for] F. A. Timby" (1903).

Wisconsin State Historical Society, Madison, Wisconsin).

The letter which follows, dated 16 July 1895, is Foster's handwritten response. Philana Foster, age forty-one, is listed with her husband Thomas L. Foster (age sixty-three), in the 1870 census of Albion, Orleans County, New York, as a "School Teacher" (1870:70A). She served as a preceptress under Theodore T. Chapin, the principal of Albion Academy from 1870 to 1874 (Signor et al. 1894, 191). I have been unable to learn Philana's maiden name, so the identity of her father remains unknown at present.

Albion[,] July 16th [18]95

Mr. E. W. Taylor

Dear Sir

I am very sorry to have been so long in replying to your letter. 1st In regard to the stories Father knew of only the one, that the golden plates <and a stone> through which ~~he~~ <Smith> had to look to read them were found in the side of a hill near Palmyra while he was diggin[g] for buried treasure. Father had nothing to do with making of the plates,[2] ~~they~~ and never saw them; as a great favor he was allowed to "heft" them and to [p. 1] feel them in the bag in which they were kept and which was made like a pillow case. He does not think that any one besides "Joe Smith" ever saw the plates; at least Cowdrey[3] who wrote the Book of Mormon from Smiths dictation did not, nor did Harris,[4] who mortgaged his <farm> to Egbert Grandin[5] the proprietor of The Wayne Co[unty]. Sentinel, to pay for the printing nor <did> Major Gilbert[6] who set the type ~~and~~ He died last winter I think. He was one of Father's most intimate friends. Father says that he never knew of

2. Foster's statement that her father "had nothing to do with making of the plates" may indicate Schroeder's continued search for the "young man who was a cab=inet makers apprentice" who E. E. Baldwin had claimed in a previous letter had made a box which was filled with sand and then placed in a sack and used by Joseph Smith to deceive people into thinking he possessed gold plates (see III.J.21, E. E. BALDWIN TO W. O. NORRELL, 3 AUG 1887).

3. On Oliver Cowdery (1806-50), see "Introduction to Oliver Cowdery Collection."

4. On Martin Harris (1783-1875), see "Introduction to Martin Harris Collection."

5. On Egbert B. Grandin (1806-45), see JOSEPH SMITH HISTORY, 1839, n. 77.

6. On John H. Gilbert (1802-95), see "Introduction to John H. Gilbert Collection."

their being dishonest accordin[g] to the common acceptation of the word. They were a good natured, ignorant, shif<t>less family, disliking hard work, spending their time in selling gingerbread, telling [p. 2] fortunes, locating water for wells, and digging for ~~hid~~ <buried> treasures; it was the ridicule, ~~which~~ people thought, which ~~made him into~~ he received for dig=ging ~~whi~~ that made <him> invent the story of the golden plates. In the troubles the Mormons had at Nauvo[o], Hiram Smith[7] was killed, and Oliver Cowdrey left them and went to ~~Na~~ Wisconsin, studied law and practiced there, till he died. The Wayne Co<unty> Sentinel pub=lished at Palmyra and the Ontario Messenger or Repository I forget which Published at Canandaigua <Ontario County> are all the paper~~p~~s that I know about. Remember me kindly to Mrs Taylor and And Mar=guerite and tell her that I am very much pleased to hear how nicely she is progressing

Yours respectfully

[s] Philana A Foster

[*Note written sideways on page*]

Father says that as far as he knows he is the only one living who resided in Palmyra at that time.

7. On Hyrum Smith (1800-44), see JOSEPH SMITH HISTORY, 1839, n. 12.

28.
ALBERT CHANDLER TO WILLIAM LINN, 22 DECEMBER 1898

Albert Chandler to William Linn, 22 December 1898, William Linn, *The Story of the Mormons* (New York: Macmillan Co., 1902), 48-49.

EDITORIAL NOTE

In 1898 William Linn[1] obtained the present recollection of Albert Chandler (c. 1813-?), who worked with Luther Howard in 1830 binding the first edition of the Book of Mormon. Subsequently Chandler worked briefly for Egbert B. Grandin as an apprentice printer. In 1835 Chandler moved to Michigan, where, according to Linn, he was "connected with several newspapers in that state, editing the *Kalamazoo Gazette,* and founding and publishing the *Coldwater Sentinel.* He was elected the first mayor of Coldwater, serving several terms" (p. 49). In the 1850 census of Coldwater, Branch County, Michigan, the thirty-six-year-old Chandler is listed as a farmer from New York (1850:350). This information coincides with that provided by Linn, who states that Chandler "was in his eighty-fifth year when the above letter was written" (p. 49).

COLDWATER, MICH., Dec. 22, 1898.

My recollection of Joseph Smith Jr. and of the first steps taken in regard to his Bible have never been printed. At the time of the printing of the Mormon Bible by Egbert B. Grandin[2] of the *Sentinel* I was an apprentice in the book-bindery connected with the *Sentinel* office. I helped to collate and

---

1. William Alexander Linn (1846-1917), journalist, was born at Deckertown (now Sussex), New Jersey. After graduating from Yale in 1868, he became a reporter for the *New York Tribune.* In 1871 he became editor of the *New York Evening Post.* After retiring from the *Post* in 1900, he published several works, including *Story of the Mormons* (1902), *Rob and His Gun* (1902), and *Horace Greeley* (1903) (*National Cyclopaedia of American Biography,* 1891-1980, 26:218-19).

2. On Egbert B. Grandin (1806-45), see I.A.15, JOSEPH SMITH HISTORY, 1839, n. 77.

stitch the Gold Bible,[3] and soon after this was completed, I changed from book-binding to printing. I learned my trade in the *Sentinel* office.

My recollections of the early history of the Mormon Bible are vivid to-day. I knew personally Oliver Cowdery,[4] who translated [transcribed?] the Bible, Martin Harris,[5] who mortgaged his farm to procure the printing, and Joseph Smith Jr., but slightly. What I knew of him was from hearsay, principally from Martin Harris, who believed fully in him. Mr. Tucker's "Origin, Rise, and Progress of Mormonism"[6] is the fullest account I have ever seen. I doubt if I can add anything to that history.

The whole history is shrouded in the deepest mystery. Joseph Smith Jr., who read through the wonderful spectacles, pretended to give the scribe the exact reading of the plates, even to spelling, in which Smith was wofully deficient.[7] Martin Harris was permitted to be in the room with the scribe, and would try the knowledge of Smith, as he told me, saying that Smith could not spell the word February, when his eyes were off the spectacles through which he pretended to work. This ignorance of Smith was proof positive to him that Smith was dependent on the spectacles for the contents of the Bible. Smith and the plates containing the original of the Mormon Bible were hid from view of the scribe and Martin Harris by a screen.

I should think that Martin Harris, after becoming a convert, gave up his entire time to advertising the Bible to his neighbors and the public generally in the vicinity of Palmyra. He would call public meetings and address them himself. He was enthusiastic, and went so far as to say that God, through the Latter Day Saints, was to rule the world. I heard him make this statement, that there would never be another President of the United States elected[8]; that soon all temporal and spiritual power would be given over to

---

3. According to E. R. Crandall, Chandler told him that he also worked in Grandin's shop as a printer's "devil," meaning an apprentice or errand boy, at the time the Book of Mormon was being printed ("Former Palmyra Man Writes of Residents Past and Present," *Wayne County Journal,* 21 November 1918).

4. On Oliver Cowdery (1806-50), see "introduction to Oliver Cowdery Collection."

5. On Martin Harris (1783-1875), see "Introduction to Martin Harris Collection."

6. See III.J.8, POMEROY TUCKER ACCOUNT, 1867.

7. See III.G.18, OLIVER COWDERY INTERVIEW WITH SAMUEL W. RICHARDS, JAN 1849.

8. See III.H.10, JOHN H. GILBERT MEMORANDUM, 8 SEP 1892, 5; III.F.6, EBER D. HOWE ON MARTIN HARRIS, 1834, 14; see also Vogel 1989, 26.

the prophet Joseph Smith and the Latter Day Saints. His extravagant statements were the laughing stock of the people of Palmyra. His stories were hissed at, universally. To give you an idea of Mr. Harris's superstitions, he told me that he saw the devil, in all his hideousness, on the road, just before dark, near his farm, a little north of Palmyra.[9] You can see that Harris was a fit subject to carry out the scheme of organizing a new religion.

The absolute secrecy of the whole inception and publication of the Mormon Bible estopped positive knowledge. We only knew what Joseph Smith would permit Martin Harris to publish, in reference to the whole thing.

The issuing of the Book of Mormon scarcely made a ripple of excitement in Palmyra.

ALBERT CHANDLER.

9. See III.J.15, STEPHEN S. HARDING TO THOMAS GREGG, FEB 1882, 45.

29.
A. C. Buck Reminiscence, 1899

"Rambling Recollections about Mormonism and Other Matters," *Shortsville Enterprise,* 11 February 1899, 3.

EDITORIAL NOTE

This item is attributed to "B.C.A.," but a typed copy by an unidentified Manchester Village historian identifies the author as "A. C. Buck" (Ontario County Historical Society, Canandaigua, New York).[1] Buck wrote the present item in response to Elizabeth Cummings's article "Two Strange Men," which appeared in the *Shortsville Enterprise,* 4 February 1899 (p. 3), wherein she recounted Joseph Smith's story of obtaining the plates and outlined the Spaulding theory of the Book of Mormon's origin.

Editor of the Enterprise:

I have read with much interest, as doubtless many of your readers have, the excellent article on Mormonism contained in the ENTERPRISE of last week. It is concise, right to the point, and is worth preserving by the residents of this town as a well told bit of Mormon history. Few persons now living remember much about Mormonism in its early days. I am more particularly interested in this matter because I was in my boyhood somewhat familiar with the rise and early history of this celebrated sect in the town of Manchester. Oliver Cowdery,[2] the person referred to, once lived in the village of Manchester. He was a man of some education, a sort of pettifogging half-fledged lawyer and often attended suits before Squire Mitchell,[3] Squire

---

1. There is an Arin C. Buck, age forty-six, listed in the 1900 census of Shortsville, Ontario County, New York. But this Buck is too young to be the author of the present item, who describes himself as being born about 1818.

2. This part of A. C. Buck's reminiscence is not about Oliver Cowdery as claimed, but rather apparently about Lyman Cowdery, Oliver's brother, who became a lawyer about 1825 and later served as an Ontario County probate judge as well as two terms in the state legislature (Mehling 1911, 172; see also III.B.3, DANFORD BOOTH INTERVIEW, 1881).

3. Perhaps Peter Mitchell, in his forties, listed in the 1830 census of Manchester, Ontario County, New York (1830:168).

[Nathan] Pierce[4] and other Magistrates in this part of the country. Like most lawyers he had a most wonderful gift of gab.

My father belonged to the same persuasion as pettifogger Cowdery; often attended suits before a Justice of the Peace at the same time in opposition to his friend. As was quite natural they became intimate and he often visited at our house. I remember quite distinctly when I was a boy about 12 years old, taking a trip in a one horse wagon (buggies like those we use now were then unknown) with my father and this man Oliver Cowdery to Palmyra. This was after Cowdery had joined the Mormons, and during this ride I recollect how he used all the powers of his persuasive eloquence to induce father to cast in his fortune with him in the new sect then much talked about, telling him what wonderful honors and promotions were waiting the acceptance of his invitation; but credulity was not one of my father's characteristics and all Cowdery's promises of promotion in the church failed in making a proselyte. Though nearly seventy years have passed since then the writer remembers distinctly little bits of the conversation referred to. Cowdery told my father that not long before, the Lord, in a mysterious manner had appeared to him in the form of a young deer, who crossed the road before him one day when he was driving to Palmyra and disappeared instantly as if by magic.[5] Whether Cowdery was a credulous fanatic or a designing knave this deponent saith not. He was not a fool; whatever else he may have been.

In this connection let me say how well I recollect going with the two pettifoggers before referred to, (Cowdery and father) my father as a witness and Cowdery as attorney for plaintiff or defendant, I forget which, to attend a lawsuit at the "poplar tavern" (Harmon's.) A Canandaigua lawyer was there to oppose Cowdery and in his final summing up address for his client he made some disparaging remarks with reference to my father's testimony which made me so angry that I could scarcely contain myself. Indeed I was so indignant that I wrote to this Canandaigua lawyer, I have forgotten his name, a letter which I suppose now was a very impertinent one, to which very properly he paid no attention whatever. I was a young, simple, sensitive boy then, and years afterwards when I had gained more knowledge of the world and its ways, I learned that this lawyer had no personal ill feeling against my father but was simply discharging his duty to his employer and working

4. On Nathan Pierce, see introduction to III.L.19, NATHAN PIERCE DOCKET BOOK, 1830.

5. Compare III.F.1, MARTIN HARRIS INTERVIEWS WITH JOHN A. CLARK, 1827 & 1828.

along the line of his profession and according to his knowledge in the interests of his client. The case was not decided until late in the evening, after which we drove home by way of Manchester where we left Cowdery and went on to our own home in Shortsville. Just after we passed Henry's tannery near the old Jed Dewey place we were overtaken by a terrific thunder storm which I shall never forget as long as I live. The night was as dark as black ink and I never heard such thunder or saw such lightning before or since. I was a timid boy and I was dreadfully frightened. I remember how I wondered that Cowdery and father could possibly carry on their conversation in the ordinary indifferent manner. I thought it was extremely irreverent in the face of what seemed to me most imminent danger.

I never knew or heard anything about Joseph Smith in those early days but I have often heard the late Mrs. Walker[6] say that while she did not recollect ever having seen Joseph Smith herself she knew and had heard a great deal about him when she was a girl. She said he was considered by the community generally as a simple-minded though shrewd fortune-teller whose moral character was not first class. Mrs. Walker said he used to travel around the country telling the fortunes of people who were possessed of more credulity than sense, by means of a magic stone that he looked at concealed in an old hat which he carried around with him.

The first Mormon church, or rather the first church of Jesus Christ of the latter day saints, was organized in the town of Manchester[7] on the 6th day of April, 1830, but where this organization took place, whether in the village of Manchester, at some school house, church or private residence we have no record to show. The next year (1831) "the saints" removed to Kirtland, Ohio. ...

In the article you quote it is stated that "There is no reliable record that any one save Smith ever saw the 'golden plates.'" This may be true, still there is evidence (perhaps not reliable) that other persons than Joe Smith saw and handled those plates, which had the appearance of being gold. Just read the following solemn declaration: ...[8] A similar declaration is made by Oliver Cowdery and Martin Harris.[9]

---

6. While there are a number of Walkers in Manchester, I have been unable to specifically identify this Mrs. Walker.

7. A number of early sources designate Manchester as the location of the church's organization (see I.A.15, JOSEPH SMITH HISTORY, 1839, n. 82).

8. The Testimony of Eight Witnesses has been deleted (see III.L.13, TESTIMONY OF EIGHT WITNESSES, JUN 1829).

9. See VI.G.1, TESTIMONY OF THREE WITNESSES, JUN 1829.

These declarations are found in the Mormon bible. What are we to think of all this? These men were said to have been respectable citizens, intelligent men. Were they designing knaves and impostors, or deceived, credulous fanatics? Who can tell?

B.C.A.

30.
CHARLES W. BROWN ACCOUNT, 1904

[Charles W. Brown], "Manchester in the Early Days," *Shortsville Enterprise,* 11 March 1904 and 18 March 1904. Undated clippings of Charles W. Brown's series in the *Shortsville Enterprise* are located in the Shortsville Free Press file, Special Collections, Harold B. Lee Library, Brigham Young University, Provo, Utah.

EDITORIAL NOTE

Charles W. Brown published a series of articles on early Manchester history. Articles dealing with Mormon origins are numbered XXXIII-XXXVI (each article was published in two installments). Only article XXXIV is published here, since articles XXXIII and XXXV are largely reworkings of III.J.2, ORSAMUS TURNER ACCOUNT, 1851, and XXXVI relies heavily on III.J.8, POMEROY TUCKER ACCOUNT, 1867. Charles W. Brown, age thirty-one, is listed in the 1880 Manchester, Ontario County, New York, census as a book keeper (1800:292). He was also the census taker for the 1880 Manchester enumeration.

[*Article XXXIV, Part 1, 11 March 1904*]

As was stated in the preceding article, the Smith family were firm believers in the truth of various legends which designated Mormon Hill as the depository of large deposits of untold treasure. Night after night had the father and sons, Alvah [Alvin][1] and Joseph, delved and dug in different spots, but so far as the outer world knew their search was never rewarded with success. Occasionally they would tell of important discoveries, but these stories were always related to some person whose pecuniary or other substantial assistance they desired, and so their marvelous tales soon came to be received with many grains of allowance, and finally were greeted with the cold stare of unbelief. They claimed to have in their possession a miraculous stone which although it was densely opaque to ordinary eyes, was still luminous and transparent to the orbs of Joseph, Jr. This stone was one of the common horn blende variety; some of which may be picked up any day on the shores of lake Ontario. It was kept in a mysterious box, carefully

1. On Alvin Smith (1798-1823), see I.A.15, JOSEPH SMITH HISTORY, 1839, n. 10.

wrapped in cotton.[2] As an illustration of the ludicrous manner in which this stone was made to innure [inure] to the physical prosperity of its owners, the following well authenticated anecdote is related: It was claimed that Joseph, Jr., by placing it in a hat could discover by looking into the hat the precise spot where the hidden treasure was buried. Among the many dupes which were victimized by this story, was one William Stafford.[3] They repeated the tale to him time and time again, with such solemn asseverations of its truth, that at last he began to believe that there might be something in it, and so consented to join them in one of their midnight expeditions. When the evening which had been agreed upon came around, he hied him to the Smith domicile, and there awaited developments. Soon Joseph joined the circle before the hearth, bearing with him the stone carefully concealed in a well worn and antiquated beaver [hat]. Seating himself, he placed his face where his pate ought to have been, and after peering intently into the recesses thereof, made the encouraging announcement that he saw a pot full to overflowing with glittering shiners, and that he could lead the assembled coterie to the precise spot and by a little dilligent digging combined with a strict observations of all the conditions imposed, they could speedily exhume the same, and make a pro rata division of the contents thereof. No time was now lost in getting under way, and arming themselves with shovels, pick axes and implements of a like nature, they started forth with Joseph and the magic stone at the head of the column. "Tramp, tramp, tramp" they went "marching on," through the forests and across the fields, until after a long and weary march their leader commanded a halt. Joseph, Sr.[4] now came to the front and produced a piece of twine with a sharp pointed stake attached to each of its ends. A solemn injunction to preserve the strictest silence was now laid upon every one of the party, as it was said that the Evil One was around listening, that if he heard them, he too would then know where the buried gold was, and before they could dig down to it, would spirit it away to some other locality, and thus deprive them of the fruits of their nocturnal travels and labors. Joseph now advanced on tip toe to the spot he had selected, and taking one of the stakes from his father, forced the same into the soil, while his worthy sire unwound the string, and firmly grasping the other stake in his hand proceeded to strike out, and "swing around," the magic circle

2. This introductory material is a reworking of III.J.2, ORSAMUS TURNER ACCOUNT, 1851.

3. On William Stafford (c. 1786-1863), see introduction to III.A.13, WILLIAM STAFFORD STATEMENT, 8 DEC 1833.

4. On Joseph Smith, Sr. (1771-1840), see "Introduction to Joseph Smith, Sr., Collection."

within which the treasure was to be found. Work was now commenced in earnest. Silently and mysteriously the delvers delved. Not a word was uttered, not even a whisper disturbed the profound and unearthly silence; the laborers hardly dared to breathe, and the only sound which was heard was that which was made by the instruments of excavation as they went deeper and deeper into the bowels of the earth. Time rolled on, the minutes lengthened into hours, the pile of disturbed earth grew larger and larger, the hole grew deeper and deeper, the laborers grew wearier and wearier, until they began to be doubtful of success. The advent of the coming morn was near at hand when the puendo [pseudo?] prophet with drew himself into a thicket, and after looking into the cavernous depths of the superannuated chapeau, dolorously announced to his followers, that some of the prescribed conditions had been violated, and that Satan had carried off the concentrated riches to some other locality. They dug no longer but went to their homes, where it is suspected that they did ample justice to the matutinal meals. Before separating however, Joseph took another look into the hat, and made the encouraging announcement that his precious pebble had revealed to him the precise spot where [Le Diablo?] had secreted his ill gotten and recently acquired wealth. He told them that inasmuch as the prophet of lies had now got the lucre into his possession, it would be necessary when they dug again to use some extraordinary means of enchantment to drive him away; that he had a mortal aversion to blood drawn from any bleeding animal, and that the stone had revealed to him the important fact, that if a black bell wether should be led around the circle with its throat cut and bleeding, Satan would be completely outwitted, and their recovery of the treasure would be the certain result. Now it so happened that Mr. [William] Stafford was the owner of an animal which fully answered to all the prescribed conditions, but of course Jo did not know this fact! Oh no, he was a prophet and a seer, and therefore could not burden his mind with such small matters, as to which particular one of all his neighbors was the owner of a lusty, black bell wether. But some of the party remembered the fact, and brought it to the attention of Joseph. Immediately Mr. Stafford was importuned by one and all to consent to the sacrifice of his sheep, which he finally did. What was one sheep in comparison to the untold wealth which had haunted his dreams, and which when acquired, was to bring to him comfort and ease luxury for the balance of his life? This little matter having been satisfactorily adjusted, and having agreed upon the time when the performance should take place, the party separated.

[*Article XXXIV, Part 2, 18 March 1904*]

The appointed night again came on and the same party was again assembled in the best room of the Smith mansion, but outside the door might have been heard the occasional jingling of a bell, which told that the black bell wether was on hand, prepared and ready for the sacrifice. The same performance of hat gazing was again gone thro[ugh] with, and once again they started forth. At length they arrived at the designated spot, far removed from the former one. Again the same cautions as to silence were uttered, again the stakes were planted and once again the magic circle was drawn. The wether led by the hand of his master was brought to the circle, and as his mild eyes rested confidently upon the group, he received the death dealing stroke. His throat was severed, as per directions of the horn blende pebble, and as his life blood welled forth, he was led around the ring pouring it on the ground as he staggered and stumbled along. The single revolution was at length completed and poor bell wether was left to expire as best he might, while his cruel and avaricious executioners seizing their implements commenced eagerly to throw out the earth. Will you believe it, dear reader? They didn't find a dollar; there was no money there, nor no pot to put money in. How long they worked is unknown, but it was until the prophet in embryo had again consulted the stone, and so gave to his dupes some reason for their failure, which undoubtedly was as simple and foolish as the whole proceeding had been. But now a singular circumstance occurred; Mr. Stafford on looking for the carcass of his black bell wether, undoubtedly having in view a broiled leg of mutton, was somewhat nonplussed to find that it had disappeared as mysteriously as the coveted riches; he also made the farther discovery, and a singular coincidence it was, that the seer's paternal progenitor was also missing. The fact was that while Stafford had dug, Smith had dressed the carcass, and when its absence was discovered was far advanced on his homeward route. When Mr. Stafford learned, as learn he did, that for a few days the Smiths had regaled themselves on mutton chops, &c., he lost all faith in human nature, the scales fell from his eyes and he saw that he had been victimized. It may be that the investment of the black bell wether in the course of time proved to be a profitable one, as it assuredly did, if thereby he was saved from a belief in the Bible hoax. They might have made a Martin Harris[5] of him, but knowing that a hooked fish is not apt to bite the second time, they never attempted to hoodwink him again.[6] Many instances of a similar nature occurred, always resulting in some substantial gain to the

5. On Martin Harris (1783-1875), see "Introduction to Martin Harris Collection."

6. Concerning the sacrifice of William Stafford's sheep, see III.A.13, WILLIAM STAFFORD STATEMENT, 8 DEC 1833, 239.

exchequer or the cellar of the Smiths, but this one must suffice as an illustration of them all. Soon other stories of a more mysterious and uncanny nature still began to be put in circulation, the most notable of which was the following: They pretended that "while digging for money at Mormon Hill they came across a chest, three by two feet in size, covered with a dark colored stone. In the center of the stone was a white spot about the size of a six pence. Enlarging, the spot increased to the size of a twenty-four pound shot, and then exploded with a terrible noise. The chest vanished and all was utter darkness."[7] This palpable fraud was whispered in the ears of the credulous, with what design cannot be told, but that they had some sinister object in view cannot be reasonably doubted. Among the other methods which the Smith family employed to "keep the wolf from the door," was that of manufacturing and selling oil cloths. This work was principally performed by Mrs. Smith. She wove the threads and painted the cloths herself, and when a sufficient stock was found to be on hand, it was her custom to start out herself and hawk her wares from door to door. This afforded a good opportunity for the dissemination of her doctrines and she improved it. It was while she was thus engaged that she commenced to prophesy the advent of a new religion of which her son was to be the prophet. By this means, a sense of expectation for the coming of some great event, was diffused thro[ugh] the community, and so when it was announced that Joseph had actually found the massive golden tablets, there were some whose credulity led them to believe that the story was a truthful one, because it had been predicted, while still another class who had doubted the prophecy, began to have faith in it because of the seeming confirmation of it which was made by the discovery of the tablets. But by far the major portion of the community had sense enough to see that neither the prophecy nor the event had any proof of their verity, except what came from the Smiths, and to see that if their statements were to be unquestionably accepted as the truth, it was easy enough to manufacture any pretended event, to confirm the prophecies which had fell from their lips. While these mysterious hints were being circulated thro[ugh] the community, the conspirators had excavated for their own use a hole in the ground. This was nothing more nor less than an artificial cave which they had dug in a side hill now owned by the Chauncey Miner heirs.[8] This hill may be found at any time on lot 77 of the

---

7. This quote, as well as the preceding two sentences, are from III.J.2, ORSAMUS TURNER ACCOUNT, 1851, 216.

8. See III.B.12, LORENZO SAUNDERS INTERVIEW, 17 SEP 1884, 7-8; and III.B.15, LORENZO SAUNDERS INTERVIEW, 12 NOV

original survey,[9] to the south of the highway running from the Palmyra Plank road [Canandaigua Road] to the residence of Mark Jefferson.[10] It is situated about equi-distance between the terminii of the road and faces to the north. The entrance to this cave was guarded by an iron-plated door.[11] The cave itself was about sixty feet in length and ten feet high. From the door for a distance of forty feet, there was a hall fifteen feet wide which led to the chamber beyond. This chamber or audience room was twenty feet square, and was furnished with one rude table and half a dozen uncouth stools.[12] It was here that the secret meetings of the plotters were held up to the time they commenced holding public meetings for the purpose of making converts. In this small recess, secure from any interference by skeptical persons, by the flaring light of a tallow candle, was the plan of operations fully discussed and decided upon. It is stated that Darius Pierce,[13] one of the sons of Nathan, at the head of a party of his associates surprised the parties when they were assembled together in one of their noctur[n]al consultations and that a lively time ensued. And now the fulness of time had come, "all things had conspired together for good," and the incipient fraud was on the eve of its consummation. One morning as the settlers went to their daily work a strange rumor was passed from mouth to mouth that the night before, the Smiths in one of their midnight expeditions had commenced digging on the north-western spur of Mormon Hill, and had been rewarded by the discovery of several golden tablets, which were covered with hieroglyphics. The rumor spread from house to house, but dilligent inquiry failed to discover any evidence beyond that of the Smiths themselves, which would serve in the least to verify the statement. But the seed had been implanted in the minds of the credulous, and for a brief time was left to grow of its own

---

1884, 8.

9. The major portion of the hill is situated on Manchester Lot 2 with a small portion on Lot 77.

10. The present name of this "highway" is Miner Road.

11. According to Pomeroy Tucker, the door was made of wood (III.J.8, POMEROY TUCKER ACCOUNT, 1867, 49).

12. This description of the cave is incorrect. When it was reopened in 1974 by then owner Andrew H. Kommer, the cave was "about six feet high at the largest point in the middle and 10-12 feet long" ("Palmyra Farmer Claims Cave Dug by Mormon Prophet, Church Founder," *Palmyra Courier Journal,* 1 May 1974).

13. Darius Pierce, son of Justice Nathan Pierce, is also mentioned in III.B.1, KELLEY NOTES, 6 MAR 1881, 3, back; see also III.J.38, CARLOS OSGOOD STATEMENT, 1932; and III.D.2, SYLVIA WALKER STATEMENT, 20 MAR 1885.

volition. Other rumors soon began to circulate, to the effect that Joseph, the prophet, was engaged in a translation of his discovered record of antiquity, which was soon to be printed in common English and submitted to the inspection of an unregenerated world.

31.
W. C. ACCOUNT, 1904

Wayne County Journal, 24 March 1904.

EDITORIAL NOTE

This late account is attributed to "W. C.," evidently a longtime resident in the vicinity of Palmyra, perhaps William Chapman, then owner of the Smiths' former Manchester property (see n. 2 below).

... That Joseph Smith has gone to a better land is not believed by those of the old inhabitants who knew him as a neighbor. They say he was idle and shiftless; a dreamer, a treasure seeker and addicted to chicken raising.

The place where this splendid fraud was planned was an artificial cave which the conspirators had dug in a side hill to the south of the highway running from the old Palmyra plank road [Canandaigua Road] to the residence of Mark Jefferson. The entrance of the cave was guarded by an iron-plated door, and the cave was fully sixty feet in length and ten feet high. At the end was a broad chamber furnished with a rude table and stools. Here it was that the treasure seekers were want to meet and consult the "peek stone," and in the latter days the first converts to the new faith made their rendezvous before they began to hold public meetings for the purpose of making converts. It is stated that Darius Pierce, at the head of a party of neighbors surprised one of the nocturnal assemblies and that a lively time ensued.[1]

Another meeting place was the log cabin in the woods where dwelt the Smith family. Sometimes these meetings were interrupted by thunderings overhead, as if the Lord were answering their prayers from heaven. In later years when the building was torn down several cannon balls were found concealed under a false roof over the rafters. They could be moved by a string so as to give forth a rolling sound as of thunder. This is the method employed in modern theatres for the same purpose.[2] ...

---

1. Compare III.J.30, CHARLES W. BROWN ACCOUNT, 1904, and accompanying notes.

2. This account is similar to William Chapman's statement to a reporter of the *New York Herald* in 1893. Chapman, who then owned the Smiths' former property, recalled that while "making repairs in the roof" of

... He [Smith] often attempted to prove his semi-divine nature by various devices. He twice attempted to walk upon the water but in each case the planking gave way and he was ingloriously dunked.[3]

The writer's grandfather, a Walworth [Wayne County] farmer, was approached by Smith one day while he was at work beside the fire in the cooper shop, which he maintained on his farm. He became impatient of Smith's extravagant claims and at length offered to put Smith in hot coals as a test, whereupon the prophet desisted and withdrew, never to return. ...

W.C.

---

the Smiths' old frame house "he had found two old cannon balls battered and rusted lying upon the heavy plate timber on which the rafters rest. For the life of him he could not explain why the cannon balls were there. The only reason he could give was that the Smiths had placed them there to bring them good luck or to keep away evil spirits" (*New York Herald,* 25 June 1893).

3. Concerning Smith's walking on water, which is usually assigned to Colesville, see IV.D.5, GEORGE COLLINGTON, SMITH BAKER, HARRIET MARSH, AND REBECCA NURSE INTERVIEWS WITH FREDERICK G. MATHER, JUL 1880.

32.
CARLOS OSGOOD STATEMENT, CIRCA 1907

"Some Early Mormon History," *Wayne County Journal,* 11 July 1907.

EDITORIAL NOTE

Carlos P. Osgood, age forty-three, with his wife, Daisy (b. 1868), of eleven years, is listed in the 1900 census of Manchester, Ontario County, New York, as an "Insurance Agent" (1900:632). He was the grandson of Ezra Pierce, who was interviewed by the Kelleys in 1881 (see III.B.4, EZRA PIERCE INTERVIEW, 1881). See also III.J.38, CARLOS OSGOOD STATEMENT, 1932.

MANCHESTER, July 5.—Since the recent pilgrimage of the Mormons to "Gold Bible Hill," two miles north of this village to view the place where Joseph Smith claimed to have discovered the golden plates upon which Mormonism was founded, the oldest residents of Manchester have been recalling incidents connected with the founding of this religious sect, many of which are of an interesting nature and to the outside world generally unknown. ...

An amusing incident connected with the digging for those plates was recently related by C[arlos]. P. Osgood, to whom it was told by his grandfather, Ezra Pierce, and who is known to be one of the young men of the early days who had an abundance of courage and was always ready to play a joke on friends or foe. As the digging for those supposed plates was usually carried on at night and at that time had been in progress for several evenings, a huge cave had been made on the side of the hill not far from the top.

As they were unsuccessful, Smith explained to the men who were doing the digging that there were evil influences which were keeping them from finding the plates. As he made those remarks Mr. Pierce and a companion who had quietly crept up to the side of the cave, dropped a huge black sheep on the working Mormons, which caused consternation in the party, all supposing that it was his satanic majesty, and no more searching was done that night.

Smith told his followers that the blood of a lamb would keep the devil away, and it is said that a neighboring farmer lost his bell wether that night, and a circle was found around the cave in the morning made with the sheep's blood. ...[1]

1. The same story is told in III.J.30, CHARLES W. BROWN ACCOUNT, 1904, with Darius Pierce as the primary instigator of the prank.

33.
ELISHA W. VANDERHOOF ACCOUNT, 1907

E[lisha]. W[oodward]. Vanderhoof (1832-?), *Historical Sketches of Western New York* (Buffalo, New York: Printed for private distribution by the Matthews-Northrop Works, 1907), 138-39.

... In September, 1819,[1] a trifling and apparently unimportant event occurred which, however, had much to do in establishing the Mormon Church. This was the discovery of the celebrated Peek Stone. It was unearthed by the Prophet's father and elder sons while engaged in digging a well near Palmyra for Mr. Clark Chase. It first attracted the attention of Mr. Chase's children by the peculiarity of its shape, which nearly resembled the foot of a young child. When washed it was whitish, glossy, and opaque in appearance. Joseph, Jr., who was an idle looker-on at the labors of his father and brethren, at once possessed himself of this geological oddity, but not without strenuous protest on the part of the children, who claimed it by right of discovery, and because it was found upon their father's premises. Joseph, however, kept it, and though frequent demands were made, after it became famous, for its restoration, it was never returned to the claimants. Very soon it became noised abroad that by means of this stone the inchoate Prophet could locate buried treasure and discover the whereabouts of stolen property. In the latter case he might not have had to look a great way. People from far and near who had lost valuables consulted Joseph. With his eyes bandaged and his Peek Stone at the bottom of a tall white hat, he satisfied all inquirers for a fee of seventy-five cents. My grandfather[2] paid that sum to learn what had become of a valuable mare stolen from his stable, and he was a tolerably shrewd and prosperous Dutchman for those days. He recovered his beast, which Joe said was somewhere on

---

1. The first portion of Vanderhoof's account apparently follows III.J.8, POMEROY TUCKER ACCOUNT, 1867, 19-20. According to Willard Chase, the stone was found in 1822 (III.A.14, WILLARD CHASE STATEMENT, CIRCA 11 DEC 1833, 240).

2. If Vanderhoof refers to his paternal grandfather, this is perhaps Jacob or John Vanderhoof listed in the 1820 census of Farmington, Ontario County, New York (1820:311).

the lake shore, and about to be run over to Canada. Anybody could have told him that, as it was invariably the [p. 138] way a horsethief would take to dispose of a stolen animal in those days. ...

34.
CHARLES F. MILLIKEN HISTORY, 1911

Charles F. Milliken (1854-?), *History of Ontario County, New York, and Its People* (New York: Lewis Historical Publishing Co., 1911), 415-19.

THE BIRTH OF MORMONISM.

Mormonism, which has become one of our greatest national evils, originated in this town [Manchester], and in turn, it has given to Manchester a national renown. Joseph Smith, Jr., the first Mormon prophet and founder of Mormonism and the Church of Latter Day Saints, was born in Sharon, Windsor county, Vermont, December 13th [23rd], 1805. He came at an early age with his father to Palmyra, where they ran a small "cake and beer" shop. In 1818 they squatted on a piece of land on Stafford street in the northwestern corner of this town [Manchester], but they vacated this land in 1830 and the property for many years has been in the possession of the Chapman family, and was sold by William Chapman in 1907 to Apostle George A. Smith, of Salt Lake City, a grandson of the prophet Smith.[1]

By their neighbors the Smiths were regarded as a shiftless and most untrustworthy family. They were visionary and superstitious and were always digging for hidden treasures. So that Oliver Cowdery,[2] a schoolmaster on Stafford street, had little trouble in enthusing them into the mysteries that could be unearthed.

Their favorite digging place came to be on the hill since known as the "Hill of Camorah," which being interpreted signifies "Mormon Hill," often called Gold Bible hill. This hill is located two and one-half miles north of Manchester village, on the old stage road [Canandaigua Road] between Canandaigua and Palmyra.

Joe Smith, Jr., possessed even less than ordinary intellect, and among the boys he was always a butt for their jokes, which have become local history. ... [p. 415] ...[3]

---

1. Taken from III.J.8, POMEROY TUCKER ACCOUNT, 1867, 12.

2. On Oliver Cowdery (1806-50), see "Introduction to Oliver Cowdery Collection."

3. Milliken then reproduces III.A.1, MANCHESTER RESIDENTS GROUP STATEMENT, 3 NOV 1833; and III.A.10, PARLEY CHASE

It was the mother who exercised the larger influence on her son's life, and the Smith's interest and belief in a hidden treasure seems to have been part of their early training.[4]

In 1819,[5] while the Smiths were digging a well near Palmyra, on the farm of Mr. Clark Chase,[6] a stone of peculiar shape was unearthed. It resembled in form a child's foot, and was white, glossy, and opaque in appearance. Joe kept the stone and by its aid he claimed to see wonderful things. In a short time his reputation grew and with the stone to his eyes he claimed to be able to reveal "both things existing and things to come." This stone came to be known as the famous Peek stone and is truly called the "Acorn of the Mormon oak."[7] [p. 416] ...

About the year 1830, Joe Smith and his followers left the town of Manchester with their unsold bibles and removed to Kirtland, Ohio. ... [p. 418]

STATEMENT, 2 DEC 1833.

4. See III.J.2, ORSAMUS TURNER ACCOUNT, 1851, 213.

5. The date should be 1822 (see III.J.8, POMEROY TUCKER ACCOUNT, 1867, n. 32).

6. On Clark Chase, see III.J.8, POMEROY TUCKER ACCOUNT, 1867, n. 33.

7. See III.J.8, POMEROY TUCKER ACCOUNT, 1867, 19.

35.
THOMAS L. COOK HISTORY, 1930

Thomas L. Cook, *Palmyra and Vicinity* (Palmyra, New York: Press of the Palmyra Courier-Journal, 1930), 219-21, 237-38, 246.

EDITORIAL NOTE

Thomas L. Cook (1838-?) was born in Lyme, Grafton County, New Hampshire. He moved to Palmyra with his parents in 1844. Keenly interested in the history of the region, he published a history of *Palmyra and Vicinity* in 1930. In his introduction, Cook explained his objective: "I have lived in and round Palmyra for over 85 years, thus giving me an opportunity to become familiar with both village and country, and when the light of memory is flashed upon the screen of time, how vividly the scenes of other days are brought to remembrance. ... Although I have quoted some early history, my aim has been to write something we do not find in history, something I heard old people say when I was a boy, what happened when they were young. The most of this history is from memory and observation. ... In this history there will be a good deal the historian will not care about, but it may interest some others who might be a friend or relative. Then my aim and object will be accomplished" (T. Cook 1930, 10).

... Adjoining this farm [of William Dixon] on the south is the Joseph Smith farm, where Mormonism first originated. In the Autumn of 1816, Joseph Smith, sr.,[1] came from Royalton, Vermont,[2] to Palmyra. In this family were nine children, six boys and three girls. Soon after arriving in Palmyra he opened a "cake and beer shop." He continued in this business until 1818, when they moved to this tract of wild land to occupy it as squatters, as there was no one who seemed to be looking after it,[3] and on the west side of the road and north of where the barn stands, he built a log cabin that contained two rooms on the ground floor, with two divisions in the garret. Later an

1. On Joseph Smith, Sr. (1771-1840), see "Introduction to Joseph Smith, Sr., Collection."

2. Actually Norwich, Vermont.

3. This follows III.J.8, POMEROY TUCKER ACCOUNT, 1867, 12-13. Cook, however, differs from Tucker in that he states the family moved to Palmyra in the autumn rather than the summer of 1816.

addition was put up that was made of slabs and used for a sleeping room.[4] In this cabin they made their home for a dozen years.[5] Finally Mr. Smith contracted for the land from Lemuel Durfee,[6] who owned the property and to him made a small payment on the same, paying the interest on the balance each year by letting his son, Joseph, work for Mr. Durfee, through harvest.[7] In those days it was customary to have whiskey, especially through harvest. When the country was new, fever and ague was quite prevalent among the new settlers, and to ward off this malady, nearly every family had a preparation they called No. 6, that was made of red peppers and other things that were powerful.

Early one morning, while yet in bed, Joseph contemplated the coming day was going to be hot, and was fearful they might have fish for dinner as he had always heard that fish would make a man dry. With all this flittering before his imagination, and to ward off the coming danger of a sun stroke, he got out of bed, crept softly down stairs and across the old kitchen into the pantry, but unfortunately he tapped the wrong bottle and instead of getting whiskey, he took a good big swig out of No. 6, which nearly strangled

---

4. Cook evidently refers to the Jennings cabin first occupied by the Smiths about 1819 (see III.L.2, PALMYRA [NY] HIGHWAY SURVEY, 13 JUN 1820). Since the cabin no longer stood in 1930, Cook apparently borrowed his description from III.J.8, POMEROY TUCKER ACCOUNT, 1867, 13. However, because the Jennings cabin is located in Palmyra and the cabin Tucker described was located in Manchester, there is a possibility that Cook's description does not apply to the Jennings cabin (see III.L.2, PALMYRA [NY] HIGHWAY SURVEY, 13 JUN 1820).

5. From about 1825 to 1829, the Smiths lived in their frame house, while newly married Hyrum and family occupied the cabin. In April 1829 the Smiths were forced to vacate their home and join Hyrum's family in the cabin (see III.L.4, SMITH MANCHESTER [NY] LAND RECORDS, 1820-1830).

6. On Lemuel Durfee (1759-1829), see introduction to III.L.10, LEMUEL DURFEE ACCOUNT BOOKS, 1827-1829.

7. This statement contains a number of inaccuracies. The Smiths did not contract for the land with Lemuel Durfee, but rather with the heirs of Nicholas Evertson, probably in 1820. When the Smiths faced financial difficulties in December 1825, Lemuel Durfee purchased their land and allowed the Smiths to remain as renters (see III.L.4, MANCHESTER [NY] LAND RECORDS, 1820-1830). Samuel Smith is known to have worked for Durfee as a means of paying rent on the Manchester property (see III.L.10, LEMUEL DURFEE ACCOUNT BOOKS, 1827-1829, under 16 April 1827; see also under August 1827, where it is recorded that Joseph Smith worked for Durfee on at least one occasion).

him, and upon finding out his mistake, he rushed outdoors to the well and down went the bucket for water. Mr. Durfee, hearing the rumpus, got out of bed to find out the cause of this tumult, and upon looking out of the window, saw the sainted Joseph strangling and black in the face, trying to drink water out of the old "oaken bucket that hung in the well."[8]

The Smiths occupied this tract until 1829, when the new religion was ushered into existence. Up to this time, but very little had been done to clear up the land. A short time before leaving the farm, they erected a small frame for a house on the same site of the present farm house, using the old house for a barn.[9] The new house was never finished by the Smiths. They got their living by making baskets, birch brooms, maple sugar, maple syrup and hunting, fishing and trapping.

The Smiths took their departure in 1831. ...

When the Smith family left the farm, it passed into other hands that were more progressive and prosperous. The forest was cleared away, fields were fenced off, where nature heretofore had its unmolested sway and in its season, golden grain nodded in the wind. The unfinished house [p. 219] was soon made into a substantial farm house. A new and convenient barn was erected, an orchard was planted and the trail of the squatter was soon lost.[10]

In the early [18]50's the late Morgan Robinson came into possession of the farm by purchase. In the [18]60's the late Avery Chapman, a native of Massachusetts, bought the farm. At his death, his son, William, came into possession of the farm, and through early training he became one of the best farmers in Ontario County. While in the Civil War he contracted rheumatism from which after a time he became unable to carry on the farm any longer and sold out to W. W. Bean, a Mormon elder, who came from Salt Lake City. Mr. Chapman moved into the village where he died a few years later.[11] ...

---

8. This story is also related in III.J.16, GORDON T. SMITH REMINISCENCE, CIRCA 1883.

9. Cook relies on III.J.8, POMEROY TUCKER ACCOUNT, 1867, 13. However, Tucker's statement is probably inaccurate.

10. If the Smiths were ever squatters, it was only briefly since they contracted for the land shortly after July 1820.

11. Morgan Robinson acquired the property from Judson R. Hill on 30 March 1855. Robinson sold the farm to Absalom Weeks on 2 May 1859, who then sold it to Seth T. Chapman on 4 April 1860. Chapman deeded the farm to William Avery Chapman on 14 July 1881, and on the same day William leased the farm to Seth. On 10 June 1907 William Avery Chapman sold the farm to George Albert Smith (these transactions are traced in Porter 1971, 356-59). Willard W. Bean lived on the farm after it was purchased by the

Returning to Stafford Street: A short distance from the corner, as we go south, we cross a little stream where in early day near the road, a dam was built across by the late Russell Stoddard,[12] an early settler, for the purpose of operating a sawmill. After the mill was completed a neighbor told Mr. Stoddard that there would not be power enough to run the mill, and he would furnish the first log and give him the lumber if he would saw it. But for want of power the mill was never started.

But, however, in all probability, although unconscious of the fact, at the time the pond was built, yet the Mormons might claim the building of the pond was directed by a higher power, and for a nobler cause than sawing logs, for in this little pond the first Mormon was baptized.[13] ... [p. 220] ...

Passing on a little further [continuing south on Stafford Road], at our

---

LDS church.

12. Russell Stoddard lived on the east side of Stafford Road, three farms south of the Smiths, and attempted to open a sawmill situated on Hathaway Brook (T. Cook 1930, 220). In 1867 he was listed as a "retired farmer" of Manchester (Child 1867, 168). It has been suggested that Russell Stoddard was the carpenter who attempted to swindle the Smiths out of their land in 1825 (see Enders 1985, 19; I.B.5, LUCY SMITH HISTORY, 1845, 51).

13. Several accounts locate the organization of the church in Manchester (see I.A.15, JOSEPH SMITH HISTORY, 1839, n. 82). Tucker locates the first baptisms in Manchester (III.J.8, POMEROY TUCKER ACCOUNT, 1867, 59). Joseph Knight said he saw Joseph Smith, Sr., and Martin Harris baptized in Manchester on 6 April 1830 (IV.A.1, JOSEPH KNIGHT, SR., REMINISCENCE, CIRCA 1835-1847). While the exact location of these baptisms is unknown, the residents of Manchester remembered baptisms being performed near the Stoddard mill. In 1932 Brigham Young University professor M. Wilford Poulson interviewed Dr. John R. Pratt of Manchester, who said "his memory include[d] a story of the place where the first Mormon baptisms took place. It was near the John Stafford home about one-fourth mile farther south from where the road turns east off from Stafford St. to go to Cumorah. It was at a pond near where a turn in the road is now & where I remember once was a set of posts for a flume[.] It is at a creek about a mile from the Smith place. This was related by Dr. [John] Stafford to Dr. Pratt himself" (M. Wilford Poulson, Notebook, Special Collections, Harold B. Lee Library, Brigham Young University, Provo, Utah). John Stafford elsewhere reported that he "was present at the first baptism, when old Granny Smith and Sally Rockwell were 'dipped' and came up 'white as snow'" (*Shortsville Enterprise,* 18 March 1904). Ezra Thayre said that he and Northrop Sweet were baptized in October 1830 "just below the mill" south of the Smith farm (III.J.6, EZRA THAYRE REMINISCENCE, 1862).

left, back from the road on a little knoll, was the old William Stafford[14] homestead, until a few years ago when it was destroyed by fire. ...

He [William Stafford] was also a neighbor of the Smiths and had a good opportunity to know something of the wonderful power Joseph possessed, and he was at one time personally interested in one of Joseph's prophetic visions. While passing, mention might be made of a little circumstance that transpired between him and Joseph. But before doing this we will go back to a time a little previous to this transaction with Joseph.

In September, 1819,[15] the older Smith and his sons, Alvin[16] and Hiram,[17] in digging a well (of which the location will be pointed out as we advance in our journey) threw up a stone of vitreous though opaque appearance and in form like an infant's foot. This stone was secured by Joseph and turned to account as a revelator of present and future in the role of fortune telling. Small amounts were received from the credulous, and thus the imposter was encouraged to enlarge his field by asserting a vision of gold and silver, buried in iron chests in the vicinity. The stone was finally placed in his hat to shade its marvelous brightness when its services were required. Persisting in his apparitions, there were those who in the Spring of 1820 contributed to defray the expense of digging for the buried treasure.[18]

At midnight dupe's laborers and himself, with lanterns, repaired to the hillside east of the Smith house, where following mystic ceremony, digging began in enjoined silence. Two hours elapsed when just as the money box was about to be unearthed someone spoke and the treasure vanished. This was the explanation of the failure, and to this they all agreed.

But Joseph had another vision, assuming to see where vast treasures lay entombed. Joseph asserted that a "black sheep" was necessary as an offering upon the ground before the work of digging could begin. ...

---

14. On William Stafford (c. 1786-1863), see introduction to III.A.13, WILLIAM STAFFORD STATEMENT, 8 DEC 1833.

15. Cook follows III.J.8, POMEROY TUCKER ACCOUNT, 1867, 19. However, Willard Chase dated the discovery of the stone to 1822 (see III.A.14, WILLARD CHASE STATEMENT, CIRCA 11 DEC 1833, 240-41).

16. On Alvin Smith (1798-1823), see I.A.15, JOSEPH SMITH HISTORY, 1839, n. 10.

17. On Hyrum Smith (1800-44), see I.A.15, JOSEPH SMITH HISTORY, 1839, n. 12.

18. This follows III.J.8, POMEROY TUCKER REMINISCENCE, 1867, 21, where Tucker possibly intends the spring after Smith's procurement of the Chase stone, that is, the spring of 1823.

[p. 221] ...[19]

As we pass on south [on the Canandaigua Road] we come to the concrete post that marks the line between the towns of Palmyra and Manchester; also the county line of Wayne and Ontario counties. [p. 237]

Looking to the southwest we can plainly see "Old Sharp," the hill on which Joseph Smith sacrificed the sheep, as before mentioned.

After Joseph had found the golden plates on Mormon Hill, Thum Moroni, his guardian angel, told him to go east of the house and dig a cave. There he would meet him and reveal to him the hieroglyphics on the golden plates, and following the command he commenced digging on the east side of "Old Sharp." After digging about twenty feet Thum Moroni informed him it was not holy ground. From here he went to the next hill east, on the west side of Canandaigua Road, where he again commenced digging. After he had dug about twenty feet he was again told he was not yet on holy ground.

He then repaired to the east side of Miner's Hill, which was at that time covered with forest, and after digging twenty feet it was made known to him that this was the accepted spot and to dig twenty feet more, making nearly forty feet.

After the cave had been dug a door was put at the opening and fastened, and every evening, just at twilight, for the next three months he visited the cave, always accompanied by two or more, but always entering the cave alone.[20]

For several years this cave remained practically intact. After it had commenced to fall in, Wallace W. Miner, a grandson of Amos Miner, the owner of the hill at that time, partly restored the old cave.[21] The grandson,

19. Then follows (pp. 221-22) Wallace Miner's account of William Stafford's story of Joseph Smith sacrificing a sheep, which is treated separately (see III.J.36, WALLACE MINER REMINISCENCE, 1930).

20. Concerning this cave see III.B.12, LORENZO SAUNDERS INTERVIEW, 17 SEP 1884, 7-8; and III.B.15, LORENZO SAUNDERS INTERVIEW, 12 NOV 1884, 8.

21. In 1867 Pomeroy Tucker reported that "[f]rom the lapse of time and natural causes the cave has been closed for years, very little mark of its former existence remaining to be seen" (III.J.8, POMEROY TUCKER ACCOUNT, 1867, 49). Manchester resident Ezra Pierce told the Kelleys in 1881 that the cave was still closed (III.B.4, EZRA PIERCE INTERVIEW, 1881). Then, in 1884, Samantha Payne said that the cave "can be seen today. The present owner of the farm, Mr. [Wallace] Miner, dug out the cave, which had fallen in" (III.J.19, SAMANTHA PAYNE STATEMENT, CIRCA 1884).

who is now over eighty six years of age, owns and occupies the farm, but no trace of the old Joe Smith cave can be found.[22]

"Old Sharp" was just across the town line going south, located on the Chase farm. Mr. [Clark] Chase was one of the early settlers. As mentioned before,[23] his log house was about thirty rods south of the town and county line and on the east side of the [Canandaigua] road or new highway.

The well that supplied the family with water was dug by the Smiths shortly after they came here. This was the well from which the peep-stone came, as mentioned before.

This well was kept open until the [18]80's when it was filled up.[24] ...

---

22. A reporter from the *New York Herald,* who visited the cave with John H. Gilbert and Orson Saunders in 1893, gave the following account and description of the site: "It is situated on the eastern brow of Cave Hill. ... The door jambs leading into the cave are still sound and partly visible, but the earth has been washed down by storms and the opening to the cave nearly filled, so that it cannot be entered at present. A few years ago it was dug out, the earth removed from the door and Orson Saunders, who went in, said that he found quite a large chamber many feet in extent, with the marks of the pick plainly visible in the light of his candles. The passageway within the chamber was eight feet wide and seven feet high. ... The door jamb is heavy plank of beech or maple, and the inscriptions, which had evidently been cut deeply by a sharp knife, were partially worn away. ... It is quite a severe climb to reach the mouth of the cave" (*New York Herald,* 25 June 1893). The cave remained closed until April 1974, when Andrew H. Kommer, then the owner of the property, cleared the cave's opening with a bulldozer. At that time the cave was described as "about six feet high at the largest point in the middle and 10-12 feet long," and "carved into a rock-hard clay hillside. ... The walls and ceiling of the cave appear to have been dug or picked by hand" (*Palmyra Courier-Journal,* 1 May 1974; and *Rochester Times-Union,* 25 April 1974). Today the entrance of the cave is again closed and overgrown with foliage.

23. See L. Cook 1930, 226.

24. The well was apparently still open when visited by a reporter from the *New York Herald* in 1893, who gave the following description: "The well was dug about sixty-five years ago near the Chase farm house. The homestead has disappeared. The garden and the yard in front of the house have been plowed up. ... But the well remains and it was found nearby full of water in a field of corn. ... A cover of ancient, weatherbeaten boards fastened with cleats and rusty nails covered the well and was held in place by a fence rail the Major [John H. Gilbert] and his friend Orson Saunders estimated was at least sixty years old. We uncovered the well and found it heavily walled with large boulders which had remained undisturbed since the days they were laid in place by Joe Smith's father and brothers. There seems to be more mois-

[p. 238] ...

Our next farm on the south [on the Canandaigua Road] is the Randall Robinson homestead, more familiarly known as the Mormon Hill farm. This old homestead standing back from the road, almost beneath the shadow of Mormon Hill that almost hides it from view, is where Mr. Robinson came and settled in early days and was an old pioneer.

Mormon Hill of Joseph Smith fame is so well known all over the United States and parts of Europe that it needs no comment.

At Mr. Robinson's death the farm went to his son, Anson Robinson. In the [18]70's the late Admiral William T. Sampson acquired the property by purchase and it was carried on by his brother George Sampson for several years. After the Admiral's death the farm came into the hands of Pliny T. Sexton. ... [p. 246]

---

ture in the soil now than in Smith's day, for it is only five or six feet down to the water. It looked dark and brackish and no doubt many a reptile has taken a bath in its depths" (*New York Herald,* 25 June 1893).

36.
WALLACE MINER REMINISCENCE, 1930

Thomas L. Cook, *Palmyra and Vicinity* (Palmyra, New York: Press of the Palmyra Courier-Journal, 1930), 222.

EDITORIAL NOTE

The following is a secondhand account of a conversation between William Stafford and Wallace Miner sometime before Stafford's death on 9 January 1863, wherein Stafford reiterated the portion of his 1833 statement to Hurlbut dealing with the Smiths surreptitiously procuring one of his sheep (see III.A.13, WILLIAM STAFFORD STATEMENT, 8 DEC 1833, 239). Wallace W. Miner (1843-?), son of Chauncey Miner and grandson of Amos Miner, was born in Palmyra, New York. In the 1870s, he married Beal Hammond. After her death, he married Margaret Cavanough, who died a short time later. Miner spent his last years alone, living on the land on which was located the cave that had been dug under Joseph Smith's direction in the early 1820s (T. Cook 1930, 46, 221, 238, 241-42).

Wallace Miner's visit to Salt Lake City in 1915 was noticed by the editors of the *Deseret Evening News*: "W. W. Miner of Palmyra, N.Y., and Mr. and Mrs. A. M. Miner of Rochester, N.Y. are visitors in the city. This morning they called at the office of the First Presidency. They are being shown about the city by Elder George Albert Smith of the Council of the Twelve, who has known the family for many years, back in their eastern home. ... 'As a boy,' said Mr. [Wallace] Miner, 'I heard all these stories about Joseph Smith. In our neighborhood he was considered an eccentric character because he did different things from other people. At the same time I never heard anything bad of his character, but much of interest. He was said never to have been known to smile, but always wore a most serious expression. Stories are told in the town of the manuscript of the Book of Mormon being taken by the prophet to John Gilbert, head printer of [Egbert B.] Grandin" (*Deseret Evening News,* 10 November 1915).

After meeting Miner in 1927, RLDS president Frederick M. Smith wrote of him: "[He] seems to think he is 'authority' on early Palmyra history. He regaled us right then and there with a run of years of the sheep stealing treasure digging, holy-cave making activities of 'Joe' Smith, which are amusing though *ad nauseam*! Bah! how long will these old women's yarns pass for 'history'" (*Saints' Herald* 74 [27 July 1927]: 858).

Still, Miner's testimony was sought out on at least two occasions. The Kelleys wrote Wallace Miner's name down in their notebook in March 1881, probably in relation to the sheep story, but apparently did not have an opportunity to visit him. In 1930 Miner related William Stafford's story to Palmyra historian Thomas L. Cook, who stated that since "I have been personally and intimately acquainted with Mr. Miner for over eighty years, I believe this [Miner's account] to be true" (T. Cook 1930, 221). Two years later Miner related the same story to Brigham Young University professor M. Wilford Poulson (see III.J.37, WALLACE MINER STATEMENT, 1932).

"The location for this sacrifice was on the second hill east of the Smith house, at that time on the Chase farm. This hill was called by the neighbors, 'Old Sharp'[1] and by divine command he was to go to the barnyard of William Stafford[2] and take from the fold a black sheep without leave or license, and lead it to the place where it was to be sacrificed. That night the parties met at the appointed hour, at the chosen spot with lanterns. Joseph traced a circle within which the wether was placed and his throat cut; the blood saturated the ground. Silently and solemnly, but with vigor, excavation began.

"Three hours of futile labor had passed, when it was discovered that the older Smith, assisted by one of his boys, had taken the sheep quietly away, thus giving the Smith family a stock of fat mutton for family use.

"The next day Joseph went to Mr. Stafford and said to him: 'I suppose you have missed your black wether. God owns all the cattle and sheep on the hills and commanded me to come and take that wether. I am willing to pay for the sheep. I have no money, but I will work for you until you are satisfied you are paid.'

"Joseph could make good sap buckets and Mr. Stafford needed a few more so he told Joseph he could make him sap buckets enough to pay for the sheep, which he did to the satisfaction of Mr. Stafford.[3]

---

1. Cook locates the hill on the west side of the Canandaigua Road, just southwest of the Palmyra/Manchester township line (see III.J.35, THOMAS L. COOK HISTORY, 1930, 222, 237-38).

2. On William Stafford (c. 1786-1863), see introduction to III.A.13, WILLIAM STAFFORD STATEMENT, 8 DEC 1833.

3. Following his 1907 interview with Manchester, New York, resident Jason Estey, George Edward Anderson recorded in his diary: "Has cedar tub said to have been made by Joseph Smith Jr. before he was twenty-one years or when he was a big boy or minor. Made for Mrs. Balinda White Sa[u]nders, wife of Orlando Sa[u]nders, one of Mr. Smith's near neighbors;

"In regard to the sheep, who knows but what there was an understanding between Joseph and his father, that he was to come for the carcass after Joseph had sacrificed the blood of the sheep, and if Joseph paid for the sheep, why was not the sheep his, and who had a better right than he and his family? This matter we will leave for philosophers to decide upon."

---

and Mr. Estey took it after the death of [the] old people. Lived with them nine and one-half years and knew them well for about thirty years" (Diary, 171, Daughters of Utah Pioneers Museum, Salt Lake City, Utah, cited in Holzapfel, Cottle, and Stoddard 1995, 181).

37.
Wallace Miner Statement, 1932

M. Wilford Poulson, "Notebook containing statements made by residents of Palmyra, N.Y., Manchester, N.Y., and other areas ...," 1932, [21-22], M. Wilford Poulson Collection, Brigham Young University, Provo, Utah.

EDITORIAL NOTE

Brigham Young University professor M. Wilford Poulson (1884-1969), a collector and avid student of Mormon history, traveled to the Palmyra/Manchester area in 1932 and interviewed Wallace Miner,[1] keeping notes of his interview with Miner in his notebook. Although undated, Miner's statement is preceded in Poulson's notebook by Poulson's notes "From Willard Bean's Scrap Book / Copied at Palmyra, N.Y. Aug. 25, 1932." Poulson recorded Miner's statement in his notebook and had the aged Miner sign his name.

Wallace Miner 93 yrs. [years] of age born about a mile south of here.[2]

Knew a great many who knew J[oseph]. S[mith]. Staffords, Stoddards, Parkers, Dur=feys, Andersons etc. I used to go over swimming over near where the Smith's lives—I once asked asked [William] Stafford[3] if Smith did steal a Smith [sheep] from him. He said no not exactly. He said he did miss a black sheep but soon Joseph came & admitted he took it for sacrifice but he was willing to work for it. He made wooden sap buckets to fully pay for it. In the early days we didn't here [hear] so much that was disreputable about the Smiths.

I was in S[alt]. L[ake]. C[ity]. in 1815 [1915][4] and J[oseph]. F. S[mith].[5]

---

1. On Wallace W. Miner (1843-?), see introduction to III.J.36, WALLACE MINER REMINISCENCE, 1930.

2. At the time of the interview, Miner lived on Manchester Lot 2, near the corner of Canandaigua Road and Miner Road.

3. On William Stafford (c. 1786-1863), see introduction to III.A.13, WILLIAM STAFFORD STATEMENT, 8 DEC 1833.

4. Miner's visit to Salt Lake City was noted in the *Deseret Evening News,* 10 November 1915 (see introduction to III.J.36, WALLACE MINER REMINISCENCE, 1930).

5. On Joseph F. Smith (1838-1918), see introduction to VI.A.7, DAVID WHITMER INTERVIEW WITH ORSON PRATT AND

said he couldn't believe J[oseph]. S[mith]. went around digging in the earth. But I [p. 21] know that he did but this isn't against Smith. He dug a 40 ft. [foot] cave right on this vary farm.[6] He used [to] live near the village. He dug in about 20 ft. [feet] and the angel told him this was not holy ground, but to move south.

Martin Harris[7] stayed at this home when I was about 13 yrs. [years] of age [c. 1856] and I used to go over to the diggings about 100 rods or a little less S[outh]. E[ast]. of this house. It is near a clump of bushes. Martin Harris regarded it as fully as sacred as the Mormon Hill diggings.[8]

They used to say mean things about Smith but I think they were a good family. Mrs. [Lucy] Smith[9] was told in a dream she would give birth to a son who would be a great leader.[10]

I once made a map for George Albert Smith[11] showing the location of houses and farms around here. This he has framed & is in the church archives. I did this about 1910 or 1912, I worked on it about two months.

The early baptisms of the church were just west of the Smith barn where they damed of[f] the creek.[12]

JOSEPH F. SMITH, 7-8 SEP 1878.

6. This cave is mentioned in several sources (see, e.g., III.B.12, LORENZO SAUNDERS INTERVIEW, 17 SEP 1884, 7-8).

7. On Martin Harris (1783-1875), see "Introduction to Martin Harris Collection."

8. Miner had similarly told George Edward Anderson in 1907: "Martin Harris visited here when Mr. Miner was a boy about twelve or thirteen years. 'Went on the hill (cave) a number of times with Martin Harris. He always removed his hat on the hill. Said it was 'this is holy ground, my boy.' God came here. This is like Mt. Sinai and Mt. Zion. At one time, he prayed on the hill, earnestly, for the welfare of the Mormon people ...'" (Diary, 172, Daughters of Utah Pioneers Museum, Salt Lake City, Utah, Holzapfel, Cottle, and Stoddard 1995, 183, 186).

9. On Lucy Smith (1775-1856), see "Introduction to Lucy Smith Collection."

10. Speaking of Lucy Smith, Orsamus Turner said in 1851 that "the incipient hints, the first givings out that a Prophet was to spring from her humble household, came from her" (III.J.2, ORSAMUS TURNER ACCOUNT, 1851, 213).

11. George Albert Smith (1870-1951), son of John Henry Smith, was born in Salt Lake City, Utah. He became an apostle in 1903, then eighth president of the LDS church in 1945 (Jenson 1971, 3:776-778; Van Wagoner and Walker 1982, 276-81).

12. Baptisms may have also been performed in the same creek a few miles south (see III.J.35, THOMAS L. COOK HISTORY, 1930, 220).

Smith only had only a common school education but I suppose [Sidney] Rigdon[13] was more academic.

Mr. [Thomas L.] Cook[14] who wrote a Palmyra Hist[ory]. was a very dear friend of mine. I helped him with his history. He had a wonderful memory and was about five years older than I was.

When I first remember Palmyra it was practically as big a place as it is to-day.

[s] W Miner[15]

---

13. On Sidney Rigdon (1793-1876), see introduction to I.A.13, SIDNEY RIGDON ACCOUNT, CIRCA 1836.

14. On Thomas L. Cook (1838-?), see introduction to III.J.35, THOMAS L. COOK HISTORY, 1930.

15. Miner's almost illegible signature appears at the top of page 22.

38.
CARLOS OSGOOD STATEMENT, 1932

M. Wilford Poulson, "Notebook containing statements made by residents of Palmyra, N.Y., Manchester, N.Y., and other areas ...," 1932, [17-19], M. Wilford Poulson Collection, Brigham Young University, Provo, Utah.

EDITORIAL NOTE

Carlos Osgood[1] of Manchester, New York, was interviewed in 1932 by M. Wilford Poulson (1884-1969), a Brigham Young University professor of psychology. The statement, which is found in Poulson's notebook, was written by Poulson and signed by Osgood. Although undated, the Osgood item is preceded by Poulson's notes "From Willard Bean's Scrap Book / Copied at Palmyra, N.Y. Aug. 25, 1932." Poulson was led to interview Osgood perhaps because Dr. John R. Pratt of Manchester had told him that "Carlos Osgood who lives at the telephone office is much in=terested in Manchester history" (p. [16]). Prior to his interview with Poulson, Osgood had made statements about Joseph Smith's treasure searching that were published in the *Wayne County Journal* in 1907 (see III.J.32, CARLOS OSGOOD STATEMENT, CIRCA 1907).

Carlos Osgood, Manchester, N.Y.

Says his father was slightly younger than the prophet Joseph Smith

Says he has lived long enough so he wouldn't say anything was impossible. Strange things have happened.

Says his father says there was nothing esp[ecially]. startling about the Prophet—He worked occassional[y] at digging wells & used to carry a stone in his hat.

My Uncle Derious Pierce[2] who lived here while they were digging for the plates. He says they used to sacrifice a black sheep at mid=night & he says the Smith family lived on mutton for a no. [number] of days after. This may just be a sheep story I don't know.[3]

---

1. On Carlos Osgood, see introduction to III.J.32, CARLOS OSGOOD STATEMENT, CIRCA 1907.

2. On Darius Pierce, see III.D.2, SYLVIA WALKER STATEMENT, 20 MAR 1885, n. 12.

3. Compare III.J.30, CHARLES W. BROWN ACCOUNT, 1904.

No doubt many exaggerated and colored stories have come down and it is hard to pick out the gen=uine from the other.

I have known many who have known the Prophet but they're all gone.

I wrote an article once about Dict. [district] no. [number] 11 of Manchester[4] & I said then that I didn't know whether or not Joseph Smith went to school there but I found out later that he did [p. 17] attend school there. I found this thru [through] Ezra G. Smith[5] of El Paso, Tex[as]. His uncle Moses C. Smith[6] attended with the Prophet & once they had an altercation. It ended in a fight. It was probably just a boy's scrap. Ezra lives at 3030 Memphis St. in El. Paso.

The Prophet was very well known here abouts. Father once says Joseph was once working in a harvest field for one Russell Stoddard.[7] It was a very hot day & Joseph had on an overcoat all buttoned up. They asked him why. He said to keep the heat out. I've heard Father till [tell] that a good many times.

My grandfather Pierce[8] said they were putting up the frame of a barn and my grandfather[,] Ezra Smith & Joseph Smith were there—my grandfather was a young giant—about 16 or 18 yrs [years] old. The Prophet was some years older. Like most pioneer gatherings of that nature while the crowd were gathering they endulged in wrestling & feats of strength and my grandfather & the Prophet pulled the stick so they sat on the ground & put their feet together[,] took hold of the stick & tried to find out which one could pull the other up. and grandfather told me. Says Joe was quite a good solid boy [p. 18] but I just gave him one good twitch and Joe went clean over my head. My grandfather was tremendously strong. He was a powerful man.

[s] Carlos P. Osgood

---

4. According to early maps of Manchester, the Smiths' former residence was included in school district 11 (Ontario County Historical Society, Canandaigua, New York).

5. This person remains unidentified.

6. On Moses C. Smith, see III.A.1, MANCHESTER RESIDENTS GROUP STATEMENT, 3 NOV 1833, n. 9.

7. On Russell Stoddard, see I.B.5, LUCY SMITH HISTORY, 1845, n. 107; III.L.4, SMITH MANCHESTER (NY) LAND RECORDS, 1820-1830, n. 4.

8. Ezra Pierce, who mentioned pulling sticks with Smith when interviewed by the Kelleys in 1881 (see III.B.4, EZRA PIERCE INTERVIEW, 1881).

39.
MITCHELL BRONK ACCOUNT, 1948

Mitchell Bronk, "The Baptist Church at Manchester," *The Chronicle: A Baptist Historical Quarterly* 11 (January 1948): 23-24.

EDITORIAL NOTE

Mitchell Bronk (1862-1950), son of Abraham Bronk, was born in Manchester, New York. His mother, Cynthia Brewster, was a granddaughter of Nathan Pierce, Sr. After graduating from the University of Rochester in 1886, Bronk attended New York City's Union Theological Seminary. He was the author of several books and numerous articles on the early history of Manchester. According to one source, "Rev. Mitchell Bronk has contributed more history and facts about old Manchester than any other one person" (Dubler 1954, 61-62). In the following account, which is partly based on his memory of conversations with his grandfather and other old Manchester townsmen, Bronk describes some of the Smiths' associations in Manchester.

... The Antimasonry disturbance was not yet over when the church had to stand by and witness the birth of a new religion, or pseudo-religion. Writers on Mormonism have paid too much at[p. 23]tention to Palmyra and not enough to Manchester in connection with Joe Smith—my old townsmen never dignified him with "Joseph!" But Gold Bible Hill (Cumorah, forsooth!) is in Manchester, not Palmyra, and the Smith family lived in our town. They traded at Manchester and Shortsville. Joe's amanuensis, Oliver Cowdery, had taught the Manchester school. What more concerns us here, however, is the fact that Joe occasionally attended the stone church[1]; especially the revivals, sitting with the crowd—the "sinners"—up in the gallery. Not a little of Mormon theology accords with the preaching of Elder [Anson] Shay.[2] It is significant that immersion became the form of baptism practiced by the Saints. It should be pointed out that in the eighteen twenties the Manchester area was experiencing an unusual amount of religious

1. The First Baptist Church of Manchester was founded on 13 February 1797 (Manchester Baptist Church File, Ontario County Historical Society, Canandaigua, New York).

2. Anson Shay was minister of the First Baptist Church of Manchester from 1804 to 1828 (Dubler 1954, 47).

excitement—*excitable religion.*

The newfangled religion created little disturbance in the church. In fact the people of the town didn't take Joe seriously; or didn't know what to make of his revelations. It did, however, cause religious confusion and unsettlement among the religious ignorant and erratic. There was a feeling of Good Riddance when the hegira took place, and some of us natives of Manchester have always been ashamed that Manchester gave Mormonism to the world. ...

40.
PARSHALL TERRY FAMILY HISTORY, 1956

Mr. and Mrs. Terry Lund, comp., *Parshall Terry Family History* (N.p.: N.p., 1956), 31.

EDITORIAL NOTE

Parshall and Hannah Terry were among the early settlers of Palmyra, New York. Seven of their thirteen children were born at Palmyra (spanning 1803-17). The Lunds report the following family tradition: "The story goes that when the Parshall Terry family were living in East Palmyra, New York, their son Jacob was a school associate and friend of young Joseph Smith, they being the same age" (p. 31).

Jacob E., the Terrys' second child, was born in Palmyra on 4 July 1805. The event described occurred prior to the family's removal from Palmyra, which, according to the Lunds, happened "about the year 1818" (ibid.). It certainly occurred before the birth of Jane Terry on 21 May 1819 at St. Louis, Lincoln County, Canada. Thus it is possible for Jacob E. Terry to have attended school with Joseph Smith either in the winter of 1816-17 or 1817-18.

In their compilation, the Lunds also include the statement of Elizabeth Terry Heward, Jacob's sister, who was born on 17 November 1814: "My parents moved from Palmyra to the town of Sheldon, Genesee County, New York, when I was two years old [c. 1817], and when I was four years old [c. 1819] they moved to Upper Canada. We lived in several different places near little York, (since called T[o]ronto) till the 2nd day of July, 1822, we moved to the Township of Albion, Home District Upper Canada" (p. 66; date of this statement unknown). If Elizabeth's recollection is to be accepted, the Terry family moved some time after the birth of her brother David in Palmyra on 17 August 1817 and before her third birthday on 17 November 1817. This would indicate that Joseph Smith attended school immediately after his arrival at Palmyra sometime during the winter of 1816-17.[1]

... the story goes that when the Parshall Terry family were living in East

1. There is a Parshall Terry listed in the Palmyra Highway Tax records for Road District 27 for the years 1817, 1819, 1820 and 1822. However, this would conflict with an 1817 removal to Canada.

Palmyra, New York, their son Jacob was a school associate and friend of young Joseph Smith, they being the same age. ...

41. PALMYRA RESIDENT REMINISCENCE, NO DATE

"Concerning Joseph Smith," no date, typed copy, Palmyra King's Daughters Free Library, Palmyra, New York.

EDITORIAL NOTE

Internal evidence indicates that this statement was probably written in the early twentieth century, following the elections of LDS general church authorities Brigham H. Roberts to the U.S. House of Representatives in 1898 and Reed Smoot to the U.S. Senate in 1903 and after the death of Hiram Scutt, a resident of Port Gibson, Wayne County, New York, in 1907.

Nearly fifty years ago[1] it was my fortune to reside in the village of Port Gibson [Wayne County, New York] in the extreme northern part of the county. about a mile southwest of the village there were the crumbling foundations of what had once been a dwelling. I was informed on inquiry, that it had been the home of a man named Smith,[2] who had resided there with his family and that he and his boys had worked among the farmers in the vicinity for a livliehood [livelihood], but they had removed years before to Palmyra. While living there his son, Joseph claimed to dig up the plates on what has since been known as Mormon Hill, a few miles north of the village of Manchester, from which he he pretended to translate and compile his Book of Mormon. I knew personally many older people who remembered Joseph Smith as a boy working among the farmers and also later when he went among them trying to obtain subscriptions to his book. I have this on the authority of the late Capt. Hiram Scutt[3] who remembered the

1. This would have been in the 1850s or later.

2. The claim that the Smiths lived in Port Gibson prior to locating in Palmyra is extremely doubtful. Perhaps some residents confused Joseph Smith, Sr., with another Smith.

3. Hiram Scutt (1823/25-1907) was born at Port Gibson, Ontario County, in 1823 or 1825. He was a captain in the Civil War, and was wounded in 1864. He was a delegate to the first National convention at Philadelphia, and served two terms as state assemblyman (Sanford D. Van Alstine genealogical card files, Palmyra King's Daughters Free Library, Palmyra, New

circum=stances perfectly. The Mormon society was formed in Palmyra and the late John Stacy[4] and his wife Joined them and on their removal to Kirtland, Ohio they accompanied them and remained until the Mormons were forced to move further west, when they returned to their old home where they ended their days. I received this information from Mr. Stacy himself. Today, the Mormon church dominates almost the entire western country and its influence is felt even in the Congress and Senate.

York).

4. Perhaps John B. Stacy, a member of the Free Methodist Church of Alton, mentioned in McIntosh 1877, 173.

42.
Mrs. Palmer Reminiscence, No Date

"Stories from the Notebook of Martha Cox, Grandmother of Fern Cox Anderson," LDS Church Archives, Salt Lake City, Utah.

EDITORIAL NOTE

Martha Cragun Cox (1852-1932) recounts the statement of a Mrs. Palmer, who grew up on a farm near the Smiths in Manchester, New York. Cox was born in Salt Lake City, married LDS bishop Isaiah Cox in 1869, and taught school in Overton and Panaca, Nevada. After the death of her husband, she lived in Mexico. Returning to Utah in the 1920s, Cox was probably interviewed by her granddaughter Fern Cox Anderson (Bitton 1977, 77; Jenson 1971, 3:55; Martha Cragun Cox, "Biographical Record," St. George Public Library, St. George, Utah).

The notebook of Martha Cox introduces the reminiscence of Mrs. Palmer, whose personal history remains largely unknown, as follows: "The spirit of the Lord remained with Joseph Smith from the time at which he received his first vision. Mrs. Palmer, a lady advanced in years, came to Utah with her daughter who was a teacher in the Presbyterian schools of our State. The daughter taught in Monroe, Sevier Co[unty], died there and is buried in the Monroe Cemetery."

Martha Cox noted in her biographical record under 18 September 1929: "I separated the little stories of the prophet I have gathered from early years and wrote them in a mem[o] book and gave them to Donnetta Smith Kesler, dau[ghter]. of Pres[ident]. Joseph F. Smith. She seemed very pleased to get the little book. They are little incidents that have never been published. Stories told by Jesse W. Crosby, Allen J. Stout, Joseph I Earl, Aunt Esther Pulsipher, Margaret Burgess, Mrs. Palmer, a Presbyterian lady whose family lived near the Smiths' in New York" (typescript, 216, Utah Historical Society, Salt Lake City, Utah). A nearly identical copy can be found in LaFayette C. Lee, Notebook (n.d.), photocopies located at LDS Church Archives, Salt Lake City, Utah; and Special Collections, Harold B. Lee Library, Brigham Young University, Provo, Utah.

Mrs. Palmer's father, according to a story told by her, owned a farm near to that of the Smith family in New York. Her parents were friends of the Smith family, which, she testified was one of the best in that locality—honest, religious and industrious, but poor. The father of the family, she said, was above average in intelligence. She had heard her parents say he bore the appearance of having descended from royalty. Mrs. Smith was called "Mother Smith" by many. Children loved to go to her home.

Mrs. Palmer said her father loved young Joseph Smith and often hired him to work with his boys. She was about six years old, she said, when he first came to their home. She remembered going into the field on an afternoon to play in the corn rows while her brother worked. When evening came she was too tired to walk home and cried because her brothers refused to carry her. Joseph lifted her to his shoulder and, with his arm thrown across her feet to steady her and her arm about his neck, he carried her to their home.

She remembered the excitement stirred up among the people over the boy's first vision,[1] and of hearing her father content [contend] that it was only the sweet dream of a pure minded boy.

She stated that one of their church leaders came to her father to remonstrate against his allowing such close friendship between his family and the "Smith boy", as he called him. Her father, she said, defended his own position by saying that the boy was the best help he had ever found. He told the churchman that he always fixed the time of hoeing his large field to that when he could secure the services of Joseph Smith, because of the influence that boy had over the wild boys of the neighborhood, and explained that when these boys worked by themselves, much time would be spent in arguing and quarreling, which often ended in a ring fight.

But when Joseph Smith worked with them, the work went steadily forward and he got the full worth of the wages he paid.

She remembered the churchman saying in a very solemn and impressive tone, that the very influence the boy carried was the danger they feared for the coming generation; that not only the young men, but all who came in contact with him would follow him, and he must be put down.

---

1. It is unclear if this is a reference to what has come to be known as Joseph Smith's "first vision" of 1820, absent from early and contemporary accounts, or to the first appearance of the angelic messenger on 21/22 September 1823, subsequently identified as "Moroni." The latter is most likely. It must also be remembered that Palmer's account is thirdhand and filtered through a traditional Mormon mind.

Not until Joseph had a second vision[2] and began to write a book which drew many of the best and brightest people of the churches away from them, did her parents come to a realization of the fact that their friend, the churchman, had told them the truth. Then her family cut off their friendship for all the Smiths, for all the family followed Joseph. Even the father, intelligent man that he was, could not discern the evil he was helping to promote.

Her parents then lent all the aid they could in helping to crush Joseph Smith; but it was too late. He had run his course too long. He could not be put down.

Mrs. Palmer recognized the picture of Joseph Smith placed among other pictures as a test, and said of him that there was never a truer, purer, nobler boy than he before he was led away by superstition.

2. This "second vision" apparently refers to Joseph Smith's obtaining the plates on 22 September 1827.

K.
Miscellaneous Non-resident Sources

1.
ROCHESTER (NY) *GEM*, 15 MAY 1830

"Imposition and Blasphemy!!—Money Diggers, &c.," *Rochester* (NY) *Gem* 2 (15 May 1830): 15.

EDITORIAL NOTE

This early report compares the coming forth of the Book of Mormon with the Rochester money diggers.

Some months ago a noise was made among the credulous of the earth, respecting a wonderful production said to have been found as follows. An ignoramus near Palmyra, Wayne county, pretended he had found some "Gold Plates," as he is pleased to call them, upon which is said to be engraved characters of marvellous and misunderstandable import, which he, but no other mortal could divine. These characters he has translated into the English language, and lo! they appear to be no other than the mysticisms of an unrevealed Bible! A person [Martin Harris] more credulous or more cunning, than him who found the plates, ordered the translation thereof, mortgaged his farm, sold all he had, and appropriated it to the printing and binding of several thousand copies of this pearl, which is emphatically of *great price!* The book comes before the public under the general title of the "Book of Mormon," arranged under different heads, something as follows. The book of Mormon—containing the books of Nephi, Nimshi,[1] Pukei,[2] and Buckeye[3]—and contains some four of five hundred pages. It comes out under the 'testimony of three witnesses,' and of 'six witnesses,'[4] who say they 'have seen and hefted the plates,' that 'they have the appearance of gold,' and that divers and strange characters are 'imprinted on them.'—The author, who

---

1. Nimshi, an early American term, means "a fool, a silly person, a nitwit" (M. Mathews 1951, 2:1133). Cf. 1 Kings 19:16.

2. Puke, an early American term, means "a poor puny, unhealthy-looking person" (M. Mathews 1951, 2:1326). See also III.E.3, *PALMYRA REFLECTOR,* 1829-1831, under 12 June 1830.

3. Buckeye is an early American nickname for a "backwoodsman" and carries a connotation of "inferiority" (M. Mathews 1951, 1:202).

4. See III.L.13, TESTIMONY OF EIGHT WITNESSES, JUN 1829.

has the "copy-right secured according to law,"[5] says, 'that he was commanded of the Lord in a dream,' to go and find, and that he went and found. At one time it was said that he was commanded of the Lord not to show the plates, on pain of instant death—but it seems he has shown them to the said witnesses, and yet is alive! At another time it is said that none could see them but he who was commanded;—that though they should lie in the middle of the street beneath the broad glare of a meridian sun, in the presence of hundreds, yet no eye but his could see them! The translator, if we take his word for it, has been directed by an angel in this business, for the salvation and edification of the world! It partakes largely of Salem Witchcraft-ism, and Jemima Wilkinson-ism, and is in point of blasphemy and imposition, the very summit. But it is before the public, and can be had for money, at various places.

This story brings to our mind one of similar nature once played off upon the inhabitants of Rochester and its vicinity, near the close of the last war [of 1812]. During the war, we were subject to many inconveniences at this place, and were in constant danger of attack from the enemy. Those who lived here at that time, can well remember the frequent attempts made by the enemy to land at the mouth of the Genesee, at which point our army had deposited heavy stores [stones?]. Our village was then young, and the abodes of men were 'few, and far between.' If we remember aright, it was in the year 1815, that a family of Smiths moved into these parts, and took up their abode in a miserable hut on the east bank of the river, now near the late David K. Carter's tavern. They had a wonderful son, of about 18 years of age, who, on a certain day, as they said, while in the road, discovered a round stone of the size of a man's fist, the which when he first saw it, presented to him on the one side, all the dazzling splendor of the sun in full blaze—and on the other, the clearness of the moon. He fell down insensible at the sight, and while in the trance produced by the sudden and awful discovery, it was communicated to him that he was to become an oracle—and the keys of mystery were put into his hands, and he saw the unsealing of the book of fate. He told his tale for *money*. Numbers flocked to him to test his skill, and the first question among a certain class was, if there was any of [Captain William] Kidd's money hid in these parts in the earth. The oracle, after adjusting the stone in his hat, and looking in upon it sometime, pronounced that there was. The question of where, being decided upon, there forthwith emerged a set, armed with "pick-axe, hoe and spade," out

---

5. See III.L.12, BOOK OF MORMON COPYRIGHT, 11 JUN 1829.

into the mountains, to dislodge the treasure. We shall mention but one man of the money-diggers. His name was Northrop. He was a man so unlike anything of refined human kind, that he might well be called a demi-devil sent forth upon the world to baffle the elements of despair, and wrestle with fate. As you will suppose, he was an enemy to all fear. Northrop and his men sallied out upon the hills east of the river, and commenced digging—the night was chosen for operation—already had two nights been spent in digging, and the third commenced upon, when Northrop with his pick-axe struck the chest! The effect was powerful, and contrary to an explicit rule laid down by himself he exclaimed, "d—n me, I've found it!"

The charm was broken!—the scream of demons,—the chattering of spirits—and hissing of serpents rent the air, and the treasure moved! The oracle was again consulted, who said that it had removed to the Deep Hollow. There, a similar accident happened—and again it was removed to a hill near the village of Penfield, where, it was pretended the undertakers obtained the treasure.

About this time the enemy's fleet appeared off the mouth of the Genesee, and an attack at that point, was expected—this produced a general alarm.—There are in all communities, a certain class, who do not take the trouble, or are not capable of thinking for themselves, and who, in cases of alarm, are ready to construe every thing mysterious or uncommon into omens of awful purport. This class flocked to the oracle. He predicted that the enemy would make an attack; and that blood must flow.—The story flew, and seemed to carry with it a desolating influence—some moved away into other parts, and others were trembling under a full belief of the prediction. At this time a justice of the peace of the place visited the oracle, and warned him to leave the country. He gravely told the magistrate that any one who opposed him would receive judgements upon his head, and that he who should take away the inspired stone from him, would suffer immediate death! The magistrate, indignant at the fellow's impudence, demanded the stone, and ground it to powder on a rock nearby—he then departed promising the family further notice.

The result was the Smiths were missing—the enemy did not land—the money-diggers joined in the general execration, and declared that they had had their labor for their pains—and all turned out to be a hoax! Now in reference to the two stories, "put that to that, and they are noble pair of brothers."

2.
WAYNE COUNTY (PA) *INQUIRER*, CIRCA MAY 1830

Wayne County (PA) *Inquirer,* circa May 1830, as reprinted in *Cincinnati Advertiser and Ohio Phoenix* 8 (2 June 1830): 1.

EDITORIAL NOTE

The *Wayne County Inquirer* was published in Bethany, Pennsylvania, in the next county east of Susquehanna County. Because of the incomplete files of the *Inquirer,* I have been unable to locate an original printing of this item. The following reprint in the *Cincinnati Advertiser and Ohio Phoenix* was first located by Dale Morgan (see J. P. Walker 1986, 342).

A fellow by the name of Joseph Smith, who resides in the upper part of Susquehanna county, has been, for the last two years we are told, employed in dedicating [dictating?] as he says, by inspiration, a new bible. He pretended that he had been entrusted by God with a golden bible which had been always hidden from the world. Smith would put his face into a hat in which he had a *white stone,*[1] and pretend to read from it, while his coadjutor transcribed. The book purports to give an account of the "Ten Tribes," and strange as it may seem, there are some who have full faith in his Divine commission. The book it seems is now published. We extract the following from the Rochester Republican. ...[2]

---

1. Smith primarily used a brown-colored stone in translating, but he also possessed a white stone (see IV.F.1, BAINBRIDGE [NY] COURT RECORD, 20 MAR 1826).

2. For what follows, see *Rochester Republican,* 6 April 1830, in III.K.31, HENRY O'REILLY REMINISCENCE, 1879.

3.
GEAUGA (OH) GAZETTE, CIRCA 23 NOVEMBER 1830

"Delusion," *Geauga* (OH) *Gazette,* circa 23 November 1830, as reprinted in *Morning Courier and New-York Enquirer,* 7 December 1830.

EDITORIAL NOTE

In the latter part of October 1830, Oliver Cowdery, Parley P. Pratt, Peter Whitmer, Jr., and Ziba Peterson left Manchester, New York, for Missouri. En route they preached in Kirtland, Geauga County, Ohio, and vicinity. By 12 November fifty-five persons had been baptized, including Sidney Rigdon, a former Campbellite preacher in nearby Mentor.[1] Shortly after, the *Geauga Gazette* published the following account of the origin of the missionaries' religion. I have been unable to locate an original printing in the incomplete files of the *Geauga Gazette,* but Dale Morgan found the following reprint in the *Morning Courier and New-York Enquirer* (J. P. Walker 1986, 345-46).

About a couple of weeks since, three men, calling themselves Oliver Cowdry, David Whitmer and Martin Harris,[2] appeared in our village, laden with a new revelation, which they claim to be a codicil to the New Testament. ...

The account which they give is substantially as follows:—at a recent period an angel appeared to a poor ignorant man residing in or near Palmyra in Ontario County in the State of New York, directed him to open the earth at a place designated, where he would find the new revelation engraved on plates of metal. In obedience to the celestial messenger, Smith repaired to

1. Newel Knight, Journal [C] (c. 1846), in private possession. While 14 or 15 November 1830 is usually cited as the date on which Rigdon was baptized, Cowdery's letter dates his baptism sometime between 5 and 12 November 1830. If the *Painesville Telegraph* is correct in assigning Rigdon's baptism to a Monday, then 8 November is likely the correct date (*Painesville Telegraph,* 15 February 1831).

2. Rather Oliver Cowdery, Parley P. Pratt, Peter Whitmer, Jr., and Ziba Peterson. The writer apparently assumed the men were the three witnesses.

the spot, and on opening the ground discovered an oblong stone box tightly closed with cement. He opened the sacred depository and found enclosed a bundle of plates resembling gold, carefully united at one edge with three silver wires so that they opened like a book. The plates were about 7 inches long and 6 broad, and the whole pile was about 6 inches deep, each plate about the thickness of tin. They were engraved in a character unintelligible to the learned men of the United States, to many of whom it is said they have been presented. The angel afterwards appeared to the three individuals, and showed them the plates. To Smith was given to translate the character[s] which he was enabled to do by looking through two semi-transparent stones, but as he was ignorant of the art of writing, Cowdry and the others wrote as Smith interpreted. They say that part of the plates escaped from them in a supernatural manner and are to be again revealed when the events of the time shall require them. ...

4.
ROCHESTER (NY) *GEM*, 25 DECEMBER 1830

"Book of Mormon," *Rochester* (NY) *Gem,* 2 (25 December 1830): 135.

In the 2d number of the GEM,[1] we gave a full length portrait of this bantling of wickedness and credulity. By a late Painsville, Ohio paper, we perceive that this pretended revelation from heaven has found some believers, and that there are preachers travelling about in those parts who pretend that it is the only revelation which men can safely live and die by. In Canandaigua, it is also said, that there is a book of Mormon preacher, who is attempting to push his way forward, in spite of all opposition.[2] The reason for these efforts is obvious. When the work spoken of came before the world, it proved to be such a spawn of wickedness, that the press aimed a blow at it, and it fell, ere it had scarce seen the light. The getters-up therefore, seeing their hopes all blasted, and their names coupled with infamy, have determined to 'make a raise' on the public by *some* means, and thus they are going about "like roaring lions, seeking whom they may devour." We do not anticipate a very great turning to this heresy. The public are too much enlightened.

---

1. See III.K.1, *ROCHESTER* (NY) *GEM,* 15 MAY 1830.

2. Perhaps a reference to W. W. Phelps, who the day previous to the publication of this account met Joseph Smith for the first time. Although Phelps was not baptized until 16 June 1831, according to his own account, he believed in the Book of Mormon as early as April 1830 (see III.I.9, W. W. PHELPS TO OLIVER COWDERY, 21 FEB 1835). It is also possible that this report refers to Sidney Rigdon, who preached in the Canandaigua Courthouse about this time (see III.J.6, EZRA THAYRE REMINISCENCE, 1862, 83-84).

5.
DAVID S. BURNETT ACCOUNT, 1831

David S. Burnett, "Something New—'The Golden Bible,'" *Evangelical Inquirer* (Dayton, Ohio), 7 March 1831, 217-19, 220.

EDITORIAL NOTE

David S. Burnett became pastor of the First Baptist Church of Dayton, Ohio, in 1827, where he "met with such success that the church grew rapidly under his ministry" (C. Conover 1932, 1:399). He developed an interest in the teachings of Alexander Campbell and carried a majority of his congregation over into the Campbellite organization in 1829 (*History of Dayton, Ohio,* 1889, 602). In 1830 Burnett became publisher and editor of the Dayton, Ohio, monthly *Evangelical Inquirer,* which occasionally included information about Mormonism. In March 1831 Burnett published an article about Joseph Smith and the coming forth of the Book of Mormon, which introduced lengthy extracts from the *Painesville Telegraph.*

... Notwithstanding all [p. 217] this, some hundreds of the rabble and a few intelligent citizens of the western part of New York and the eastern part of Ohio, have, with the wildest enthusiasm, embraced a feigned revelation purporting to be literally new. From the advocates of this new religion called *Mormonism,* from a letter received from the intelligent Post Master at Palmyra,[1] extracts from Mr. Thomas Campbell's letters[2] and other sources, embracing the subjoined pieces taken from the Telegraph of Painesville, O.: from these different quarters I learn the following particulars. For a long time in the vicinity of Palmyra, there has existed an impression, especially among certain loose classes of society, that treasures of great amount were concealed near the surface of the earth, probably by the Indians, whom they were taught to consider the descendants of the ten lost Israelitish tribes, by the celebrated Jew who a few years since promised to gather

1. Martin Wilcox was postmaster of Palmyra from 16 August 1829 to 17 February 1839, when Pomeroy Tucker took over (T. Cook 1930, 283).

2. Thomas Campbell's letters were published in the *Painesville Telegraph* (see Howe 1834, 116-23; also *Evangelical Inquirer,* 7 March 1833, 229-37).

Abraham's sons on Grand Island, thus to be made a Paradise.[3] The ignorance and superstition of these fanatics soon conjured up a ghost, who they said was often seen and to whom was committed the care of the precious deposit. This tradition made money diggers of many who had neither intelligence nor industry sufficient to obtain a more reputable livelihood. But they did not succeed and as the money was not dug up, something must be dug up to make money. The plan was laid, doubtless, by some person behind the curtain, who selected suitable tools. One Joseph Smith, a perfect ignoramus, is to be a great prophet of the Lord, the fabled ghost the angel of his presence, a few of the accomplices the apostles or witnesses of the imposition, and, to fill up the measure of their wickedness and the absurdity of their proceedings, the hidden golden treasure, is to be a golden bible and a new revelation. This golden bible consisted of metallic plates six or seven inches square, of the thickness of tin and resembling gold, the surface of which was covered with hieroglyphic characters, unintelligible to Smith, the finder, who could [p. 218] not read English. However the angel (ghost!) that discovered the plates to him, likewise informed him that he would be inspired to translate the inscriptions without looking at the plates, while an amanuensis would record his infallible reading; all which was accordingly done. But now the book must be published, the translation of the inscriptions which Smith was authorized to show to no man save a few accomplices, who subscribe a certificate of these pretended facts at the end of the volume. Truly a wise arrangement! Among the gang none had real estate save one, who mortgaged his property to secure the printer and binder in Palmyra, but who was so unfortunate as not to be able to convert his wife to the new faith, though he flogged her roundly for that purpose several times.[4] The book, an octavo of from 500 to 1000 pages (for when I saw it I did not notice the number) did not meet ready sale and consequently about 500 copies were sent to the eastern part of this state, which was considered a better market. Though at

---

3. Mordecai M. Noah, a prominent New York Jew who purchased Grand Island in the Niagara River and there dedicated the city of Ararat as a refuge for oppressed Jews around the world. In a dedicatory speech, Noah proclaimed that the Indians were "in all probability the descendants of the lost tribes of Israel," and invited them to join their brother Jews on the Island. Noah's speech was published in the *Wayne Sentinel,* 4 October 1825 (see Vogel 1986, 43, 56, 90 n. 45).

4. Martin Harris mortgaged his farm to print the Book of Mormon (III.L.14, MARTIN HARRIS MORTGAGE, 25 AUG 1829). He was also accused of beating his wife (see III.A.7, LUCY HARRIS STATEMENT, 29 NOV 1833).

home it had but little success, the subjoined pieces will show that in the Western Reserve it found better. ... [p. 219] ...

EDITOR. [p. 220]

6.
James Gordon Bennett Account, 1831

1. James Gordon Bennett, Diary, 7-8 August 1831, Rare Books and Manuscripts Division, New York Public Library, New York, New York.

2. [James Gordon Bennett], "Mormonism—Religious Fanaticism—Church and State Party," Part I, *Morning Courier and Enquirer,* 31 August 1831. Reprinted in *Christian Register* (Boston), 24 September 1831.

3. [James Gordon Bennett], "Mormon Religion—Clerical Ambition—Western New York—The Mormonites Gone to Ohio," Part II, *Morning Courier and Enquirer,* 1 September 1831. Reprinted in *Christian Register* (Boston), 24 September 1831.

EDITORIAL NOTE

James Gordon Bennett (1795-1872) was born near Keith, Scotland. He migrated to Nova Scotia in 1819, and later to New York City where he worked briefly for the *Courier.* He first received national recognition when, in 1827, he became the Washington, D.C., correspondent for the *New York Enquirer.* In 1829 he received financial backing from the supporters of Andrew Jackson to purchase the *Enquirer.* He then combined that paper with the *Courier* to publish the *Morning Courier and New York Enquirer.* Under Bennett's four-year associate editorship (1829-32), the *Courier and Enquirer* became one of the leading eastern newspapers. In 1835 he founded the *New York Herald,* which became under Bennett's editorship one of the most influential newspapers in America. Bennett died in New York City (Wilson and Fiske 1887, 1:238; *National Cyclopaedia of American Biography,* 1891-1980, 7:241; Arrington 1970, 353-54).

From 12 June to 18 August 1831, Bennett went on an interviewing tour of upstate New York with Martin Van Buren and Nathaniel S. Benton. Bennett's personal diary of this trip is in the Manuscripts Division of the New York Public Library. He recorded in his diary various topics of interest, but of importance to early Mormon studies are the two entries (7 and 8 August 1831) he made at Geneva, a town about sixteen miles southeast of the Smith farm in Manchester. While in Canandaigua on 15 August, Bennett wrote an account of early Mormonism that drew on his diary entries, which was printed in the *Morning Courier and Enquirer* on 31 August and 1 September 1831. While Bennett's report contains obvious inaccuracies, partly due to his desire to rush into print, they also "reflect myths about the coming forth of the Book of Mormon which were already in the process of formation in 1831" (Arrington 1970, 356).

[*1. Diary, 7-8 August 1831*]

Geneva Aug[us]t 7—1831—

Mormonism—Old [Joseph] Smith[1] was a healer—a great story teller—very glib—was a [vender?]—made gingerbread and buttermints &c &c—Young [Joseph] Smith was careless, idle, indolent fellow—22 years old—brought up to live by his wits—which means a broker of small wants—[Martin] Harris[2] was a hardy industrious farmer of Palmyra—with some money—could speak off the Bible by heart—Henry ~~Rign~~ Ringdon [Sidney Rigdon][3] a parson in general—smart fellow—he is the author of the Bible—they dig first for money—a great many hills—the Golden Bible Hill where there is a hole 30 or forty feet into the side—6 feet diameter[4]—dug [among?] and the chest fled his approach—turned it into a religious plot and gave out the golden plates—the Hill a long <narrow> hill which spreads out broad to the South—covered with Beach[,] Maple, Basswood and White Wood—the north end quite naked—the trees cut off in the road from Canandaigua to Palmyra between Manchester & Palmyra—several fine orchards on the east—~~the~~ and fine farms on the west—here the ground is hilly—but small hills—very uneven—the outlet [of Lake Canandaigua] runs past part of it—Mormonites went to Ohio because the people here would not pay any attention to them—Smith's wife [Emma] looked into a hole and

1. On Joseph Smith, Sr. (1771-1840), see "Introduction to Joseph Smith, Sr., Collection."

2. On Martin Harris (1783-1875), see "Introduction to Martin Harris Collection."

3. On Sidney Rigdon (1793-1876), see introduction to I.A.13, SIDNEY RIGDON ACCOUNT, CIRCA 1836.

4. Regarding evidence of considerable digging on the eastern slope of the Hill Cumorah, see III.J.20, LORENZO SAUNDERS TO THOMAS GREGG, 28 JAN 1885, 135; III.K.32, EDWARD STEVENSON REMINISCENCE, 1893.

the chest fled into a trunk and he lost several of them[.] [William W.] Phelps[5] of the [Ontario] Phoenix was converted to Mormonism and is now a teacher or elder— ...

—Aug[us]t 8 [1831]—

Mormonism—C[harles]. Butler[6] saw [Martin] Harris [they?] wanted to borrow money to print the Book—he told him he carried the engravings from the plates to New York—showed them to professor Anthon who said that he did not know what language they were—told him to carry them to Doc[tor] [Samuel L.] Mitchell[7]—Doct[o]r Mitchell examined them—and compared them with other hieroglyphics—thought them very curious—and they were the characters of a nation now ex=tinct which he named—Harris returned to Anthon who put some questions to him and got angry with Harris[.]

[*2. Article, 31 August 1831*]

CANANDAIGUA, Aug. 15th, 1831.

New York has been celebrated for her parties—her sects—her explosions—her curiosities of human character—her fanaticism political and religious. The strangest parties and wildest opinions originate among us. The human mind in our rich vales—on our sunny hills—in our crowded cities or thousand villages—or along the shores of our translucent lakes bursts beyond all ordinary trammels; throws aside with equal fastidiousness the maxims of ages and the discipline of generations, and strikes out new paths for itself. In politics—in religion—in all the great concerns of man, New York has a character peculiarly her own; strikingly original, purely American—energetic and wild to the very farthest boundaries of imagination. The centre of the state is quiet comparatively, and grave to a degree; but its two extremities, Eastern and Western; the city of the Atlantic, and the continuous villages of the Lakes, contain all that is curious in human character—daring in conception—wild in invention, and singular in practical good sense as well as in solemn foolery.

---

5. On W. W. Phelps (1792-1872), see introduction to III.G.6, OLIVER COWDERY TO W. W. PHELPS, 7 SEP 1834.

6. On Charles Butler (1802-97), see introduction to III.F.3, MARTIN HARRIS INTERVIEW WITH CHARLES BUTLER, CIRCA 1830-1831.

7. On Samuel L. Mitchell (1764-1831), see I.A.15, JOSEPH SMITH HISTORY, 1839, n. 45.

You have heard of MORMONISM—who has not? Paragraph has followed paragraph in the newspapers, recounting the movements, detailing their opinions and surprising distant readers with the traits of a singularly new religious sect which had its origin in this state. Mormonism is the latest device of roguery, ingenuity, ignorance and religious excitement combined, and acting on materials prepared by those who ought to know better. It is one of the mental exhalations of Western New York.

The individuals who gave birth to this species of fanaticism are very simple personages, and not known until this thrust them into notice. They are the old and young Joe Smith's, Harris a farmer, Ringdon [Rigdon] a sort of preacher on general religion from Ohio, together with several other persons equally infatuated, cunning, and hypocritic. The first of these persons, Smith, resided on the borders of Wayne and Ontario counties on the road leading from Canandaigua to Palmyra.[8] Old Joe Smith had been a country pedlar in his younger days, and possessed all the shrewdness, cunning, and small intrigue which are generally and justly attributed to that description of persons. He was a great story teller, full of anecdotes picked up in his peregrinations—and possessed a tongue as smooth as oil and as quick as lightning. He had been quite a speculator in a small way in his younger days, but had been more fortunate in picking up materials for his tongue than stuff for the purse. Of late years he picked up his living somewhere in the town of Manchester by following a branch of the "American System"—the manufacture of gingerbread and such like domestic wares.[9] In this article he was a considerable speculator, having on hand during a fall of price no less than two baskets full, and I believe his son, Joe, Junior, was at times a partner in the concern. What their dividends were I could not learn, but they used considerable molasses, and were against the duty on that article.[10] Young Joe, who afterwards figured so largely in the Mormon religion, was at that period a careless, indolent, idle, and shiftless fellow. He hung round the villages and strolled round the taverns without any end or aim—without any positive

8. The Smiths lived on Stafford Road, not on the Canandaigua Road.

9. Compare III.J.8, POMEROY TUCKER ACCOUNT, 1867, 12, 14.

10. To avoid paying duty on sugar, refiners began importing molasses. From May 1828 to May 1830, a duty of 10 cents per gallon was imposed on molasses. But in May 1830, following public outrage, the duty was reduced to 5 cents per gallon (Vogt 1908, 21; V. S. Clark 1949, 279). The Smiths are known to have made their own molasses (see I.D.7, WILLIAM SMITH INTERVIEW WITH E. C. BRIGGS, 1893; and III.J.8, POMEROY TUCKER ACCOUNT, 1867, 14).

defect or as little merit in his character. He was rather a stout able bodied fellow, and might have made a good living in such a country as this where any one who is willing to work, can soon get on in the world. He was however, the son of a speculative Yankee pedlar, and was brought up to live by his wits. Harris also one of the fathers of Mormonism was a substantial farmer near Palmyra—full of passages of the scriptures—rather wild and flighty in his talk occasionally—but holding a very respectable character in his neighborhood for sobriety, sense and hard working.

A few years ago the Smith's and others who were influenced by their notions, caught an idea that money was hid in several of the hills which give variety to the country between the Canandaigua Lake and Palmyra on the Erie Canal. Old Smith had in his pedling excursions picked up many stories of men getting rich in New England by digging in certain places and stumbling upon chests of money. The fellow excited the imagination of his few auditors, and made them all anxious to lay hold of the bilk axe and the shovel. As yet no fanatical or religious character had been assumed by the Smith's. They exhibited the simple and ordinary desire of getting rich by some short cut if possible. With this view the Smith's and their associates commenced digging, in the numerous hills which diversify the face of the country in the town of Manchester. The sensible country people paid slight attention to them at first. They knew them to be a thriftless set, more addicted to exerting their wits than their industry, readier at inventing stories and tales than attending church or engaging in any industrious trade. On the sides & in the slopes of several of these hills, these excavations are still to be seen. They would occasionally conceal their purposes, and at other times reveal them by such snatches as might excite curiosity. They dug these holes by day, and at night talked and dreamed over the counties' riches they should enjoy, if they could only hit upon an iron chest full of dollars. In excavating the grounds, they began by taking up the green sod in the form of a circle of six feet diameter—then would continue to dig to the depth of ten, twenty, and sometimes thirty feet. At last some person who joined them spoke of a person in Ohio near Painesville, who had a particular felicity in finding out the spots of ground where money is hid and riches obtained. He related long stories how this person had been along shore in the east—how he had much experience in money digging—how he dreamt of the very spots where it could be found. "Can we get that man here?" asked the enthusiastic Smiths. "Why," said the other, "I guess as how we could by going for him." "How far off?" "I guess some two hundred miles—I would go for him myself but I want a little change to bear my expenses." To work the whole money-digging crew went to get some money to pay the expenses of bringing on a man who could dream out the exact and particular spots where money in iron chests was hid under ground. Old Smith returned to his gingerbread factory—young Smith to his financing faculties, and after some time, by hook or by crook, they contrived to scrape together a little "change" sufficient to fetch on the money dreamer from Ohio.

After the lapse of some weeks the expedition was completed, and the famous Ohio man made his appearance among them. This recruit was the most cunning, intelligent, and odd of the whole. He had been a preacher of almost every religion—a teacher of all sorts of morals.—He was perfectly *au fait* with every species of prejudice, folly or fanaticism, which governs the mass of enthusiasts. In the course of his experience, he had attended all sorts of camp-meetings, prayer meetings, anxious meetings, and revival meetings. He knew every turn of the human mind in relation to these matters. He had a superior knowledge of human nature, considerable talent, great plausibility, and knew how to work the passions as exactly as a Cape Cod sailor knows how to work a whale ship. His name I believe is Henry Rangdon or Ringdon [Sidney Rigdon], or some such word.[11] About the time that this person appeared among them, a splendid excavation was begun in a long narrow hill, between Manchester and Palmyra. This hill has since been called by some, the *Golden Bible Hill*. The road from Canandaigua to Palmyra, runs along its western base. At the northern extremity the hill is quite abrupt and narrow. It runs to the south for a half mile and then spreads out into a piece of broad table land, covered with beautiful orchards and wheat fields. On the east, the Canandaigua outlet runs past it on its way to the beautiful village of Vienna in Phelps. It is profusely covered to the top with Beech, Maple, Bass, and White-wood—the northern extremity is quite bare of trees. In the face of this hill, the money diggers renewed their work with fresh ardour, Ringdon partly uniting with them in their operations.

---

11. Bennett apparently conflated separate stories then circulating in the Palmyra/Manchester area about two individuals. The first, Luman Walters the Magician, probably appeared in the area in the early or mid-1820s. The *Palmyra Reflector* had published accounts describing Walters as Smith's occult mentor. The second, Sidney Rigdon, came to Fayette, New York, in December 1830. Believing Smith ignorant, Palmyra residents speculated that Rigdon had authored the Book of Mormon, although at the time they had no direct evidence connecting Rigdon with the Smiths prior to the book's publication. It is unclear whether the conflation of the two men originated with Bennett or his sources.

[*3. Article, 1 September 1831*]

About this time a very considerable religious excitement came over New York in the shape of a revival. It was also about the same period, that a powerful and concerted effort was made by a class of religionists, to stop the mails on Sunday[12]—to give a sectarian character to Temperance and other societies—to keep up the Pioneer lines of stages and canal boats, and to organize generally a religious party, that would act altogether in every public and private concern of life. The greatest efforts were making by the ambition, tact, skill and influence of certain of the celery, and other lay persons, to regulate and control the public mind—to check all its natural and buoyant impulses—to repress effectually freedom of opinion—and to turn the tide of public sentiment entirely in favor of blending religious and worldly concerns together. Western New York has for years, had a most powerful and ambitious religious party of zealots, and their dupes. They have endeavored ever since the first settlement of Rochester, to organize a religious hierarchy, which would regulate the pursuits, the pleasures, and the very thoughts of social life. This organization was kept up by banding churches and congregations together—by instituting laws similar to those of excommunication—by a species of *espionage,* as powerful and as terrible as that of a Spanish Inquisition. Every occupation in life—every custom of the people—every feeling and every thought, from the running of a stage or of a lady's tongue up to the legislation of the state, or of Congress, was to be regularly marked and numbered like so many boxes of contraband or lawful merchandise, by these self-created religious censorships and divines. Rochester is, and was the great headquarters of the religious empire. The late Mr. [Josiah] Bissell,[13] one

12. On the Sunday Mail Movement, see Schlesinger 1945, 350-60; and Holms 1939.

13. Josiah Bissell, a merchant and land speculator, was an early settler in Rochester. An elder in Rochester's Third Presbyterian Church and president of Monroe County's Bible Society, Bissell headed a nationwide campaign to abolish the transportation of mail and the opening of post offices on Sundays. In Rochester Bissell attempted to replace moderate politicians with evangelicals who would support his Sabbatarian movement. He invested his fortune in a line of stagecoaches and packet boats that did not run on Sundays, and called for a boycott of post offices and stage lines which refused to honor the sabbath. Jacksonians, like Bennett, resisted Bissell's efforts as a violation of the principle of the separation of church and state. Bissell died bankrupt in 1831 (Wilson and Fiske 1887, 1:271; P. E. Johnson 1978, 16, 27, 85, 92-94).

of the most original and talented men in matters of business, was equally so in religious enthusiasm, and all measures calculated to spread it among the people.—The singular character of the people of western New York—their originality, activity, and proneness to excitement furnished admirable materials for enthusiasts in religion or roguery to work upon. Pure religion—the religion of the heart and conduct—the religion that makes men better and wiser—that makes woman more amiable and benevolent—that purifies the soul—that represses ambition—that seeks the private oratory and not the highway to pour forth its aspirations: such a religion was not that of the party of which I speak. Theirs is the religion of the pomp and circumstance of glorious controversy—the artificial religion of tracts. Magdalen Reports,[14] lines of stages—the religion of collecting money from those who should first pay their debts—of sending out missionaries to spend it, and of letting the poor and ignorant at home starve and die. Such mistaken principles and erroneous views must when attempted to be carried into effect, breed strange results. Men's minds in this age will not submit to the control of hypocrisy or superstition or clerical ambition. They may be shackled for a day through their wives and daughters—for a month—a year, but it cannot be lasting; when the first die or the last get husbands, independence will be asserted.

This general impulse given to religious fanaticism by a set of men in Western New York, has been productive among other strange results of the infatuation of Mormonism. This piece of roguery, folly and frenzy (for it partakes of all) is the genuine fruit of the same seeds which produced the Sunday Mail movement—the Pioneer line of stages—the Magdalen Reports &c. &c. It is religion run into madness by zealots and hypocrites.

It was during this state of public feeling in which the money diggers of Ontario county, by the suggestions of the Ex-Preacher from Ohio, thought of turning their digging concern into a religious plot, and thereby have a better chance of working upon the credulity and ignorance of the[i]r associates and the neighborhood. Money and a good living might be got in this way. It was given out that visions had appeared to Joe Smith—that a set of golden plates on which was engraved the "Book of Mormon," enclosed in an iron chest, was deposited somewhere in the hill I have mentioned.

14. The "Magdalen Report" was issued in 1830 by Presbyterian minister John R. McDowall. It was aimed at reforming prostitutes in New York City. But its lurid, clinically detailed account of prostitution was decried even by McDowall's fellow reformers. The "Magdalen Report" was reprinted in 1833 in *McDowall's Journal,* which was declared a nuisance by a New York grand jury. McDowall died in 1833 (Coles 1977, 126-27).

People laughed at the first intimation of the story, but the Smiths and Rangdon persisted in its truth. They began also to talk very seriously, to quote scripture, to read the bible, to be contemplative, and to assume that grave studied character, which so easily imposes on ignorant and superstitious people. Hints were given out that young Joe Smith was the chosen one of God to reveal this new mystery to the world; and Joe from being an idle young fellow, lounging about the villages, jumped up into a very grave parsonlike man, who felt he had on his shoulders the salvation of the world, besides a respectable looking sort of a blackcoat. Old Joe, the ex-preacher, and several others, were the believers of the new faith, which they admitted was an improvement in christianity, foretold word for word in the bible. They treated their own invention with the utmost religious respect. By the special interposition of God, the golden plates, on which was engraved the Book of Mormon, and other works, had been buried for ages in the hill by a wandering tribe of the children of Israel, who had found their way to western New York, before the birth of christianity itself. Joe Smith is discovered to be the second Messiah who was to reveal this word to the world and to reform it anew.

In relation to the finding of the plates and the taking the engraving, a number of ridiculous stories are told.—Some unsanctified fellow looked out the other side of the hill. They had to follow it with humility and found it embedded beneath a beautiful grove of maples. Smith's wife, who had a little of the curiosity of her sex, peeped into the large chest in which he kept the engravings taken from the golden plates, and straightway one half the new Bible vanished, and has not been recovered to this day.[15] Such were the effects of the unbelievers on the sacred treasure. There is no doubt but the ex-parson from Ohio is the author of the book which was recently printed and published in Palmyra, and passes for the new Bible.[16] It is full of strange narratives—in the style of the scriptures, and bearing on its face the marks of some ingenuity, and familiar acquaintance with the Bible. It is probable that Joe Smith is well acquainted with the trick, but Harris the farmer and the recent converts, are true believers.—Harris was the first man who gave credit to the story of Smith and the ex-preacher. He was their maiden convert—the Ali of the Ontario Mahomet, who believed without a reason and without a murmur. They attempted to get the Book printed, but could not raise the

---

15. Apparently a distorted account of Martin Harris's loss of a portion of the translation manuscript in June 1828.

16. Bennett's is probably the first published account that attempts to credit Sidney Rigdon with authoring the Book of Mormon.

means till Harris stept [stepped] forward, and raised money on his farm for that purpose.[17] Harris with several manuscripts in his pocket, went to the city of New York, and called upon one of the Professors of Columbia College for the purpose of shewing them to him. Harris says that the Professor thought them very curious, but admitted that he could not decypher them.[18] Said he to Harris, "Mr. Harris you had better go to the celebrated Doct. Mitchell and shew them to him. He is very learned in these ancient languages, and I have no doubt will be able to give you some satisfaction." "Where does he live," asked Harris. He was told, and off he posted with the engravings from the Golden Plates to submit to Doc. Mitchell—Harris says[19] that the Doctor received him very "purlitely," looked at his engravings—made a learned dissertation on them—compared them with the hieroglyphics discovered by Champollion in Egypt—and set them down as the language of a people formerly in existence in the East, but now no more.

The object of his going to the city to get the "Book of Mormon" printed, was not however accomplished. He returned with his manuscript or engravings to Palmyra—tried to raise money by mortgage on his farm from the New York Trust Company—did raise the money, but from what source—whether the Trust Company or not I am uncertain.[20] At last a printer in Palmyra undertook to print the manuscript of Joe Smith, Harris becoming responsible for the expense. They were called translations, but in fact and in truth they are believed to be the work of the Ex-Preacher from Ohio, who stood in the background and put forward Joe to father the new bible and the new faith. After the publication of the golden bible, they began to make converts rapidly. The revivals and other religious excitements had thrown up materials for the foundation of a new sect, they soon found they had not dug for money in vain—they began to preach—to pray—to see more visions—to prophesy and perform the most fantastic tricks—there was now no difficulty in getting a living and the gingerbread factory was abandoned. They created considerable talk over all this section of the country. Another revelation came upon them, and through Joe and some other of these prophets, they were directed to take up their march and go out to the promised land—to a place near Painesville, Ohio [D&C 37]. Money was raised in a twinkling from the new converts. Their principles—their ten-

17. See III.L.14, MARTIN HARRIS MORTGAGE, 25 AUG 1829.

18. See discussion in "Introduction to Martin Harris Collection."

19. Bennett is reporting hearsay since Harris had left for Ohio in March 1831.

20. See III.F.3, MARTIN HARRIS INTERVIEW WITH CHARLES BUTLER, CIRCA 1830-1831.

ets—their organization—their discipline were as yet unformed and unfashioned, and probably are so to this day. Since they went to Ohio they have adopted some of the worldly views of the Shakers and have formed a sort of community system where everything is in common.[21] Joe Smith, Harris, the Ex-pedlar and the Ex-parson are among their elders and preachers—so also now is [William W.] Phelps one of Mr. Granger's[22] leading anti-masonic editors in this village.

Such is a brief view of the rise and progress of the *Mormon Religion* one of the strangest pieces of fanaticism to which the ill-advised and the worst regulated ambition and folly of certain portions of the clergy in Western New York ever gave birth. What a lesson it ought to teach us!

---

21. Communitarianism was alluded to in 4 Nephi 1:24-26. On early Mormon communitarianism, see Arrington 1953; and L. Cook 1985.

22. Francis Granger (1792-1868), American political leader, was born in Suffield, Connecticut. After graduating from Yale College, he settled in Canandaigua, New York, in 1816 and practiced law. In 1825 Granger was elected to the State Assembly. After the disappearance of William Morgan in 1826, he became a leader of the anti-Masonic movement in western New York. He was chosen by anti-Masons and National Republicans for governor in 1830 and 1832, but both times was defeated. In 1834 he was elected to Congress as a Whig, where he served until 1843. From 1861 until his death, he lived in retirement at Canandaigua (Malone 1962, 7:482-83).

7.
ILLINOIS PATRIOT, 16 SEPTEMBER 1831

Illinois Patriot (Jacksonville), 16 September 1831, as reprinted in *New Hampshire Miscellany,* 11 October 1831. Also reprinted in *New Hampshire Gazette,* 25 October 1831 (Quinn 1987, 146), and *Independent Volunteer* (Montrose, Pennsylvania), 11 November 1831.

EDITORIAL NOTE

This item was originally published in the *Illinois Patriot* (Jacksonville), 16 September 1831, but original copies of the *Patriot* are extremely rare and I have been unable to locate an original printing. I have therefore reproduced a portion of the item below from a reprint in the *New Hampshire Miscellany,* 11 October 1831 (Kirkham 1951, 2:405-6). This source is a report of an unknown Mormon preacher's account of the coming forth of the Book of Mormon.

The Mormonites.—A Preacher of this sect visited us last Saturday. We heard a part of his lecture, which occupied more than two hours. From his account, this sect came into existence a little more than a year since in the following manner:—A young man about 23 years of age, somewhere in Ontario county, N.Y. was visited by an *angel!* (here the preacher looked around him apparently to see if the credulity of the people in this enlightened age, could be thus imposed on) who informed him three times in one night by visiting a certain place in that town he would have revealed to him something of importance. The young man was disturbed, but did not obey the summons until the following day, when the angel again visited him. At the place appointed he found in the earth a box which contained a set of thin plates resembling gold, with Arabic characters inscribed on them. The plates were minutely described as being connected with rings in the shape of the letter D, which facilitated the opening and shutting of the book. The preacher said he found in the same place two stones with which he was enabled by placing them over his eyes and putting his head in a dark corner to decypher the hieroglyphics on the plates!—This we were told was performed to admiration, and now, as the result, we have a book which the speaker informed us was the Mormon Bible—a book second to no other—without [which] the holy Bible, he seemed to think, would be of little use. ...

8.
BROOME COUNTY (NY) *COURIER*, 29 DECEMBER 1831

"Mormonism," *Broome County Courier* (Binghamton, New York) 1 (29 December 1831): 2, reprinted from the *United States Gazette*. Reprinted in *The Herald of Truth* (Philadelphia), 17 December 1831.

EDITORIAL NOTE

This item is apparently influenced by James Gordon Bennett's article in the *Morning Courier and Enquirer,* 31 August and 1 September 1831 (see III.K.6, JAMES GORDON BENNETT ACCOUNT, 1831). However, it is different enough to justify its inclusion here. The item includes the following note of introduction: "From a correspondent of the Salem Gazette, dated Marietta, (Ohio,) Nov. 16, 1831."

You are sensible how celebrated has become western New York and the adjacent counties of Ohio, for their sects—their parties—their fanaticism, religious, political and anti-masonic. Their conceits are wild to the very farthest bounds of imagination. Wild in invention, and singularly successful in carrying into effect their solemn fooleries. You have heard of the Mormonites; the newspapers have given detailed accounts of those fanatics, but perhaps their origin is not so well known. Mormonism is the fruit of religious excitement in this quarter, combined with roguery, ingenuity and ignorance frequently operating successfully on those who ought to know better.

The inventors of this species of fanaticism are very simple personages, and were unknown till thus brought into notice. They are old and young, Joe Smith, one [Martin] Harris,[1] a farmer, all of New York, and one Ringdon [Sidney Rigdon],[2] a sort of preacher, from Ohio, with several other infatuated, cunning hypocrites. Old Joe Smith was once a pedlar, and possessed all that cunning shrewdness and small intrigue characteristic of that description

---

1. On Martin Harris (1783-1875), see "Introduction to Martin Harris Collection."

2. On Sidney Rigdon (1793-1876), see introduction to I.A.13, SIDNEY RIGDON ACCOUNT, CIRCA 1836.

of persons. He had a smooth tongue, was a ready story-teller, full of anecdotes he had picked up his peregrinations, and had been more fortunate in picking up materials for his tongue thus for supplying his purse. He at one time set up the manufacture of gingerbread, but on the fall of the article, failed in business.—Young Joe was an idle, strolling, worthless fellow, although he afterwards flourished so largely in the Mormon religion. He was, however, the son of a Yankee pedlar, and brought up to live by his wits. Harris, whom I have mentioned, was considered as a substantial farmer near Palmyra, of a wild imagination, full of passages of scripture, had heard and seen much of the extravagance of the day produced by modern revival meetings, and believed fully in the wonders and miracles wrought on these occasions.

The Smiths had conceived of the idea of getting rich by some short cut: the usual expedient of digging for hidden treasures was hit upon. Having heard many wonderful stories of men getting rich by digging and stumbling upon chests of money on the shores of New-England, the fellow succeeded by his oratorical powers, in exciting the imagination of a few auditors, and made them so anxious to possess themselves of those hidden treasures, that at it they went with shovel and spade, excavating the ground in many places between Canandaigua Lake and Palmyra. These excavations are still to be seen in many places. They continued their labors until, at length one of the party, tired of a laborious and unsuccessful search, spoke of a person in Ohio near Painesville, on Lake Erie, who had a wonderful facility in finding the spots where money was hid, and how he could dream of the very spots where it was to be found; "Can we get that man here?" asked the infatuated Smiths. "Why," replied the other, "I guess as how we might by going after him; and if I had a little change to pay the expenses, I would go myself." Away they went; some to his farm, and some to his merchandise, to gain money to pay the expense of bringing the money dreamer from Ohio. The desired object was at length accomplished, and Ringdon, the famous Ohio man, made his appearance.[3] He had been a preacher of various religions, and a teacher of almost all kinds of morals. He was experienced in all sorts of camp meetings, anxious meetings, and revivals, or four days meetings. He knew every turn of the human mind relative to these matters. He had considerable talent and great plausibility.—He partly united with the money diggers in making an excavation in what has since been called the "*Golden Bible Hill.*"

These were times and these are a people admirably suited to the

---

3. Concerning the suggestion that Sidney Rigdon was connected with Smith's money-digging activities before publication of the Book of Mormon, see III.K.6, JAMES GORDON BENNETT ACCOUNT, 1831, n. 11.

promulgation of a new Bible and a new religion. Such fanatics as these, were the murderers of [William] Morgan.[4] In such times and under such circumstances, was bred the Mormon religion.

In this age of wonders, the cunning expreacher from Ohio suggested to the money diggers to turn their digging concern into a religious plot. It was therefore given out that a vision had appeared to Joe Smith, that there was deposited in the hill I have mentioned an iron chest containing golden plates on which was engraved the "*Book of Mormon.*" These engravings were said to be in unknown characters, to all but the translator, and were deposited there by a wandering tribe of the children of Israel before the Christian era. It was now given out that young Joe Smith was the chosen one of God to reveal this new ministry to the world—to be the second Messiah to reveal to the world this word of life, and to reform it anew. So Joe, from being an idle, lounging fellow, became a grave, parson-like man, with a respectable looking sort of a black coat, and with the salvation of the whole world upon his shoulders. Old Joe, the ex-preacher, and several others were the converts to the new faith, which they asserted was foretold in the Bible. But Harris was undoubtedly a true convert, and the first man who gave credit to the whole story. He was the Ali of the New York Mahomet. Ringdon the preacher knew well how to work upon the credulity of a people already excited to religious enthusiasm. His aspect was grave and contemplative, and he could quote abundance of scripture to prove his assertions. This exparson is no doubt the author of the book.—It is full of strange narrative, in the style of the scriptures, and evinces some ingenuity.

A fac-simile of the characters on the golden plates was carried to Dr. [Samuel L.] Mitchell,[5] by Harris. The Doctor gave some learned observations on them, but wiser heads than he were employed in the translation. Harris raised money on a mortgage of his farm, and got the translation printed at Palmyra. The book came out to the world, and the diggers soon found they had not dug for money in vain, for by its precepts money could be raised in a twinkling from the new converts, who were daily flocking to the new

4. William Morgan, a stonemason from Batavia, New York, disappeared in September 1826. A disaffected Freemason, Morgan had just finished writing an exposé of the secret rituals of the fraternity and was believed to have been murdered by Masons. Morgan's book was published posthumously in 1826 under the title *Illustrations of Masonry: By One of the Fraternity Who Has Devoted Thirty Years to the Subject* (Batavia, New York: David C. Miller, 1826).

5. On Samuel L. Mitchell (1764-1831), see I.A.15, JOSEPH SMITH HISTORY, 1839, n. 45.

standard. Another revelation now came upon them.—The prophets were directed to lead the way to the promised land, a place near Painesville, Ohio, and subsequently to some place on the Mississippi river, where they have adopted some of the worldly views of the Shakers, having formed a sort of community system. The roads in Trumbull county [Ohio] were at times crowded with these deluded wretches, with their wagons and effects, on their way to the promised land.

The infatuation of these people is astonishing beyond measure. Husbands tearing themselves from their wives and such of their families as refuse to go, and wives deserting their husbands, to join the infatuated clan.—A respectable physician of Trumbull county [Ohio], who informed me of the latter proceedings, also informed me of several instances where the sick have died, refusing medical aid, persisting in the belief that faith in the Mormon religion would save their lives. That he actually had been called in cases of the last extremity, where their faith had finally failed them.

9.
LOCKPORT (NY) *BALANCE*, 1832

Lockport (New York) *Balance,* 1832, as quoted in *New York Evangelist,* 1832, as published in "Mormonism," *Boston Recorder,* 10 October 1832, 1.

EDITORIAL NOTE

The present item originally appeared in the *Lockport* (New York) *Balance* in 1832, sometime before October. Because this paper is extremely rare for the year 1832, this item is only known through reprints in two sources. On 10 October 1832, the *Boston Recorder* reprinted an item from the *New York Evangelist,* a Presbyterian periodical published in New York City, which included a lengthy quotation from the *Balance.* The *Evangelist* introduced the quote from the *Balance* as follows:

> We have not heretofore thought in [it] necessary to occupy our columns with the rise and progress of this singular delusion. But we understand its abettors are sending out their agents, and actually making proselytes in different parts of the country. And therefore we have concluded to give a brief account of the matter. The leaders of the affair claim to have been selected as the medium of a new revelation from heaven. The Lockport, N.Y. Balance, published in the vicinity where it first began, has given a brief account of its origin from which we learn that ...

The principal personage in this farce, is a certain *Jo Smith,* an ignorant, and nearly unlettered young man, living at, or near the village of Palmyra; the second, an itinerant pamphlet pedlar, and occasionally, a journeyman printer, named *Oliver Cowdry*[1]; the third, *Martin Harris,*[2] a respectable farmer at Palmyra. Others less important actors, have been brought in, as the exigencies of the case required. About two years since, Smith pretended to have been directed, in a dream, or vision, to a certain spot located between the village of Palmyra and Manchester. A slight excavation of the earth, enabled him to arrive at this new revelation, written in mysterious characters,

---

1. On Oliver Cowdery (1806-50) and his brief experience as a printer, see "Introduction to Oliver Cowdery Collection."

2. On Martin Harris (1783-1875), see "Introduction to Martin Harris Collection."

upon gold plates. A pair of spectacles, of strange and peculiar construction were found with the plates, to aid the optics of the prophet. Soon after another very fortunate circumstance occurred. This was the introduction of Oliver Cowdry, to whom, and whom only, was given the ability—with the aid of the spectacles—to translate the mysterious characters[3]; all this arranged, but one thing was wanting to promulgate the new revelation—*money*. Martin Harris was possessed of a valuable farm, acquired by industry and economy; in religion he was a credulous zealot. His credulity and his money, were too conspicuous to be overlooked by the modern apostles. In due time, a *divine* command came to Harris, through Jo, to devote his property, and all that was his, to the project. Harris' farm was mortgaged, and the printing of the Bible executed.[4] It is a book of over 500 pages, and is entitled "Book of Mormon." Of the book, it is only necessary to say that it is a ridiculous imitation of the manner of the Holy Scriptures; and in many instances, a plagiarism upon their language. With all its glaring inconsistencies, it can hardly claim the poor merit of common ingenuity. The projectors of the scheme have attempted to connect a story, historically consistent. The surmise connected with the destruction of Babylon, is brought to their aid, that a portion of the Jews, wandered to this continent, and by Divine command, deposited the "Book of Mormon," in the obscure spot, where the lucky stars of Jo Smith directed him.

It is supposed that there are already more than a thousand persons carried away with this strange delusion. Their prophet selected a place in the town of Kirtland, Geneva [Geauga] county, which he called "the promised land."

Hither the deluded followers of the false prophet, repaired by boat loads along the canal, principally from the counties of Ontario and Wayne. Such as have property, convert it to a common stock, and thus create an induction which is not overlooked by the idle and vicious. Families, in some instances, have been divided, and in others, mothers have been obliged to follow their deluded husbands, or adopt the disagreeable alternative, of parting with them and their children. ...

---

3. The writer errs since Smith was the "only" person to use the spectacles.

4. See III.L.14, MARTIN HARRIS MORTGAGE, 25 AUG 1829.

10.
William E. McLellin to Samuel McLellin, 4 August 1832

William E. McLellin to Samuel McLellin, 4 August 1832, McLellin Papers, RLDS Church Library-Archives, Independence, Missouri.

EDITORIAL NOTE

William E. McLellin (1806-83) was born in Smith County, Tennessee. He first heard the Mormon gospel preached while living in Paris, Illinois, and was subsequently baptized in August 1831 at Independence, Missouri. He was ordained an elder on 24 August 1831, and an apostle on 15 February 1835. Following the death of his first wife, Cynthia, he married Emeline Miller (1819-?) on 26 April 1832. After several years of difficulty with church leaders, McLellin was excommunicated in 1838. After practicing medicine a short time in Hampton, Illinois, he attempted to organize a new church in Kirtland, Ohio, in 1847. Following his wife's baptism into the RLDS church in 1870, McLellin moved to Independence, Missouri, where he subsequently died (L. Cook 1981, 106-7; Jenson 1971, 1:82-83).

Writing from Independence, Missouri, to his brother, Samuel, and other relatives in Tennessee on 4 August 1832, McLellin announced his conversion to Mormonism and included a brief account of the coming forth of the Book of Mormon. The letter's cover reads: "Mr. Samuel McLelin / Carthage / Smith County / Tennessee."

Jackson County, Missouri, Independence, 4th August 1832.

Beloved Relatives. Long! Long has it been since I've heard from you. And no doubt, you have thought the time long since you have heard from me. Probably you have thought that I was no more! Distracted, Cast away or that I had for=gotten <you> forever—But I can assure you that I yet remember you with the warmest feelings of heart. I wrote a letter to you the last of last November [1831][1] but I think it uncertain whether you read it; at least, I will now give a short account of my peregrinations and the scenes that I have experienced for one year past.

1. This letter has not been recovered.

Some time in July 1831, Two men[2] came to Paris [Illinois] & held an evening meeting, only a few at=tended, but among the others, I was there. They delivered some ideas which appeared very strange to me at that time. They said that in September 1827 an Angel appeared to Joseph Smith (in Ontario Co. New York) and showed to him the confusion on the earth respecting true religion. It also told him to go a few miles distant to a certain hill and there he should find some plates with engravings, which (if he was faith=ful) he should be enabled to translate. He went as directed and found plates (which had the appearance of fine gold) about 8 inches long 5 or 6 inches wide and alltogether about 6 inches thick; each one about as thick as thin paste board fastened together and opened in the form of a book containing engravings of reformed Egyptian Hiero=glyphical characters: which he was inspired to translate and the record was pub=lished in 1830 and is called the book of Mormon. It is a record which was kept on this continent by the ancient inhabitants. Those men had this book with them and they told us about it, and also of the rise of the church (which is now called Mormonites from their faith in this book &c.) They left Paris very early next morning and pursued their journey westward. But in a few days two others came into the neighbourhood proclaiming that these were the last days, and that God had sent forth the book of Mormon to show the times of the fulfillment of the ancient prophecies when the Saviour shall come to destroy iniquity off the face of the earth, and reign with his saints in Mellennial Rest. One of these was a witness to the book and had seen an angel which declared its truth (his name was David Whitmer).[3] They were in the neighbourhood about a week. I talked with them by way of enquiry and argument, They believed Joseph Smith to be an inspired prophet. They told me that he and between 20 and thirty [of] their preachers were on their way to Independence. My curiosity was roused <up> and my anxiety also to know the truth—And though I had between 30 & 40 students and the people generally satisfied with me as teacher—yet I closed my school on the 29th July [1831] and on the 30th I mounted Tom[4] and left for Independence. ... [p. 1] ... Thence August the 18th I took breakfast in Independence (after

2. Samuel H. Smith and Reynolds Cahoon (Jenson 1971, 1:82).

3. Under the date 18 July 1831, McLellin wrote in his journal: "D[avid]. Whitmer then arose and bore testimony to having seen an Holy Angel who had made known the truth of this record to him" (William E. McLellin, Journal, 18 July 1831, LDS Church Archives, Salt Lake City, Utah). On David Whitmer (1805-88), see "Introduction to David Whitmer Collection."

4. Tom was the name of his horse.

having made about 450 miles from Paris). But to my sorrow I learned that Jos. S[mith]. and 12 or 15 others had done their business and started to the east again a few days before. But there had a church come on of about 60 from [New] York State and there were about a dozen Elders who had not gone back. I examined the book, the people, the preachers, and the old scriptures [Bible], and from the evidences which I had before me I was bound to believe the book of Mormon to be a divine Revelation; and the people to be Christians, consequently I joined them. And on the 24th I was ordained an Elder in the church of Christ and on the 25th I started to the east with brother Hiram Smith[5] a brother to Joseph. ...

[s] Wm. E. & Emiline McLelin

5. On Hyrum Smith (1800-44), see I.A.15, JOSEPH SMITH HISTORY, 1839, n. 12.

11.
EBER D. HOWE ACCOUNT, 1834

E. D. Howe, *Mormonism Unvailed: or, A Faithful Account of That Singular Imposition and Delusion, from Its Rise to the Present Time* (Painesville, Ohio: E. D. Howe, 1834), 11-13, 17-18, 19, 275-76.

EDITORIAL NOTE

In his 1834 book, *Mormonism Unvailed,* Eber D. Howe[1] of Painesville, Ohio, summarized what he had learned about Joseph Smith's history in New York and Vermont. His sources were Hurlbut's affidavits, "various verbal accounts," and his own correspondence with readers of Abner Cole's *Palmyra Reflector,* if not Cole himself. Howe's account of the plates being hid in a barrel of beans, supported in later Mormon accounts, is perhaps an indication of the reliability of some, if not all, of his personal investigations. Chapter headings have been omitted.

With the exception of their natural and peculiar habits of life, there is nothing in the character of the Smith family worthy of being recorded, previous to the time of their plot to impose upon the world by a pretended discovery of a new Bible, in the bowels of the earth. They emigrated from the town of Royalton, in the State of Vermont, about the year 1820, when Joseph, Jun. was, it is supposed, about 16 years of age.[2] We find them in the town of Manchester, Ontario county, N.Y. which was the principal scene

1. On Eber D. Howe (1798-?), see "Introduction to Philastus Hurlbut Collection."

2. This statement is inaccurate. The Smiths emigrated from Norwich, Vermont, probably in 1816-17, when Joseph Jr. was about ten or eleven years old. Howe probably followed the statements of several Manchester residents who said they had first become acquainted with the Smiths in 1820 (see III.A.13, WILLIAM STAFFORD STATEMENT, 8 DEC 1833, 237; III.A.14, WILLARD CHASE STATEMENT, CIRCA 11 DEC 1833, 240; III.A.2, BARTON STAFFORD STATEMENT, 3 NOV 1833, 250; III.A.15, HENRY HARRIS STATEMENT, CIRCA 1833; and III.A.4, JOSHUA STAFFORD STATEMENT, 25 NOV 1833, 258). Howe evidently assumed 1820 was the date of the Smiths' arrival in New York unaware that they had lived about four years in the Village of Palmyra previous to their move to Stafford Road.

of their operations, till the year 1830. All who became intimate with them during this period, unite in representing the general character of old Joseph and wife, the parents of the pretended Prophet, as lazy, indolent, ignorant and superstitious—having a firm belief in ghosts and witches; the telling of fortunes; pretending to believe that the earth was filled with hidden treasures, buried there by [Captain] Kid or the Spaniards. Being miserably poor, and not much disposed to obtain an honest livelihood by labor, the energies of their minds seemed to be mostly directed towards finding where these treasures were concealed, and the best mode of acquiring their posses[p. 11]sion. Joseph, Jun. in the mean time, had become very expert in the arts of necromancy, jugling, the use of the *divining rod,* and looking into what they termed a "peep-stone," by which means he soon collected about him a gang of idle, credulous young men, to perform the labor of digging into the hills and mountains, and other lonely places, in that vicinity, in search of gold. In process of time many pits were dug in the neighborhood, which were afterwards pointed out as the place from whence the plates were excavated. But we do not learn that the young impostor ever entered these excavations for the purpose of assisting his sturdy dupes in their labors. His business was to point out the locations of the treasures, which he did by looking at a stone placed in a hat. Whenever the diggers became dissatisfied at not finding the object of their desires, his inventive and fertile genius would generally contrive a story to satisfy them. For instance, he would tell them that the treasure was removed by a spirit just before they came to it, or that it sunk down deeper into the earth.

The extreme ignorance and apparent stupidity of this modern prophet, were, by his early followers, looked upon as his greatest merit, and as furnishing the most incontestible proof of his divine mission. These have ever been the ward-robe of impostors. They were even thrown upon the shoulders of the great prince of deceivers, Mohammed, in order to carry in his train the host of ignorant and superstitious of his time; although he afterwards became a ruler of Nations. That the common advantages of education were denied to our prophet, or that they were much neglected, we believe to be a fact. His followers have told us, that he could not at the time he was "chosen of the Lord," even write his own name. But it is obvious that all those deficiencies are fully supplied by a natural genius, strong inventive powers of mind, a deep study, and an unusually correct esti[p. 12]mate of the human passions and feelings. In short, he is now endowed with all the requisite traits of character to pursue most successfully the humbug which he has introduced. His address is easy, rather fascinating and winning, of a mild and sober deportment, when not irritated. But he frequently becomes boisterous by the impertinence or curiosity of the skeptical, and assumes the bravado, instead of adhering to the meekness which he professes. His followers, of course, can discover in his very countenance all the certain indications of a divine mission.

For further illustrations of the character of the Smith family, the reader is referred to the numerous depositions and certificates attached to this work.[3] ... [p. 13] ...[4]

The various verbal accounts, all contradictory, vague, and inconsistent, which were given out by the Smith family respecting the finding of certain Gold or brazen plates,[5] will be hereafter presented in numerous depositions

---

3. This refers to the statements collected by Philastus Hurlbut (see "Philastus Hurlbut Collection").

4. Then follows brief sketches of the three witnesses (pp. 13-16; see III.F.6, EBER D. HOWE ON MARTIN HARRIS, 1834; VI.A.1, EBER D. HOWE ON DAVID WHITMER, 1834).

5. Certainly Howe was aware that several of Hurlbut's witnesses mention Joseph Smith's claim to have found "gold plates" (e.g., III.A.7, LUCY HARRIS STATEMENT, 29 NOV 1833, 254, 255; III.A.9, PETER INGERSOLL STATEMENT, 2 DEC 1833, 234, 236; III.A.13, WILLIAM STAFFORD STATEMENT, 8 DEC 1833, 239; III.A.14, WILLARD CHASE STATEMENT, CIRCA 11 DEC 1833, 242, 245, 246, 247), as well as the *Palmyra Reflector*'s repeated references to the "Gold Bible" (see III.E.3, *PALMYRA REFLECTOR,* 1829-1831, especially under 19 March 1831, 126, from which Howe borrowed his description of the plates [VI.A.1, EBER D. HOWE ON DAVID WHITMER, 1834]; see also Howe's use of the term on pages 37, 39, 100, 103). So why does Howe equivocate on the metallic composition of the plates and later make reference to Nephi's "plates of brass" (e.g., 23)? Perhaps he is simply following Alexander Campbell's lead, who in his 1831 review of the Book of Mormon said, "Nephi made brazen plates soon after his arrival in America." Then, in discussing the Testimony of Eight Witnesses, he says, "these 'men handled as many of the brazen or golden leaves as the said Smith translated'" ("The Mormonites," *Millennial Harbinger* 2 [Feb. 1831]: 87, 95). This statement is apparently a play on the Testimony's statement that the plates have the "appearance of gold" and "as many of the leaves as the said Smith has translated, we did handle with our hands." I would suggest that Campbell and Howe were reflecting an early Mormon apologetic that attempted to reconcile Smith's statements that the plates were made of gold and estimates that they only weighed between forty and sixty pounds (e.g., I.D.4, WILLIAM SMITH, *ON MORMONISM,* 1883, 12; III.F.10, MARTIN HARRIS INTERVIEW WITH JOEL TIFFANY, 1859). From the beginning, this was a problem for the skeptical (III.E.3, *PALMYRA REFLECTOR,* 1829-1831, under 19 Mar. 1831, 126). A block of solid tin measuring 6 x 8 x 6 inches (the measurements Smith

which have been taken in the neighborhood of the plot.—Since the publication of the book they have been generally more uniform in their relations respecting it. They say that some two years previous to the event taking place, Joseph, Jun. began his interviews with Angels, or spirits, who informed him of the wonderful plates, and the manner and time of obtaining them. This was to be done in the presence of his wife and first child, which was to be a son.[6] In the month of September, 1827, Joseph got possession of the plates, after a considerable struggle with a spirit. The remarkable event was soon noised abroad, and the Smith family commenced making proselytes among the credulous, and lovers of the marvellous, to the belief that Joseph had found a record of the first settlers of America. Many profound calculations were made about the amount of their profits on the sale of such a book. A religious speculation does not seem to have seriously entered into their heads at that time. The plates in the mean time were concealed from human view, the prophet declaring that no man could look upon them and live. They at the same time gave out that, along with the plates, was found a huge pair of silver spectacles, altogether too large for the present race of men, but which were to be used, nevertheless, in translating the plates. [p 17]

The translation finally commenced. They were found to contain a language not now known upon the earth, which they termed "reformed Egyptian characters." The plates, therefore, which had been so much talked of, were found to be of no manner of use. After all, the Lord showed and communicated to him every word and letter of the Book. Instead of looking at the characters inscribed upon the plates, the prophet was obliged to resort

---

gave for the plates), or 288 cubic inches, would weigh 74.67 pounds. If one allows for a 30 percent reduction due to the unevenness and space between the plates, the package would then weigh 52.27 pounds. Using the same calculations, plates of gold would weigh 140.5 pounds. The obvious disparity between the weight of the plates and gold may have prompted some early Mormons to equivocate on the plates' material makeup. Much as the Testimony of Eight Witnesses had emphasized "appearance of gold," Cole, in the same article cited above, reports David Whitmer describing the plates as being constructed of "metal of a *whitish yellow* color." Possibly Smith was aware of the discrepancy much earlier and opened the way for equivocation by not having the Book of Mormon commit itself on the material used to make the plates, only that Nephi "did make plates of ore" (1 Ne. 19:1). This is in contradistinction to the book's specific mention of "brass plates" brought by Nephi to the New World (e.g., 1 Ne. 5:10, 18) and "plates of pure gold" discovered by Limhi's people (Mos. 8:9).

6. Apparently a distortion of V.B.1, JOSHUA MCKUNE STATEMENT, 1834; and V.A.5, SOPHIA LEWIS STATEMENT, 1834.

to the old "peep stone," which he formerly used in money-digging. This he placed in a hat, or box, into which he also thrust his face. Through the stone he could then discover a single word at a time, which he repeated aloud to his amanuensis, who committed it to paper, when another word would immediately appear, and thus the performance continued to the end of the book.

Another account they give of the transaction, is, that it was performed with the big spectacles before mentioned, and which were in fact, the identical *Urim and Thumim* mentioned in Exodus 28-30, and were brought away from Jerusalem by the heroes of the book, handed down from one generation to another, and finally buried up in Ontario county, some fifteen centuries since, to enable Smith to translate the plates *without looking at them!*[7]

Before the work was completed, under the pretence that some persons were endeavoring to destroy the plates and the prophet, they relate that the Lord commanded them to depart into Pennsylvania, where they could proceed unmolested. Smith, accordingly, removed his family thither; but it appears that it was at the request of his father-in-law, instead of the command of the Lord. A box, which he said contained the plates, was conveyed in a barrel of beans, while on the journey.[8] ... [p. 18] ...

The Golden Bible was finally got ready for the press, and issued in the summer of 1830, nearly three years from the time of its being dug up. ... [p. 19] ...

The reader will already have observed, that a great variety of contradictory stories were related by the Smith family, before they had any fixed plan of operation, respecting the finding of the plates, from which their book was translated. One is, that after the plates were taken from [p. 275] their hiding place by Jo, he again laid them down, looked into the hole, where he saw a *toad,* which immediately transformed itself into a spirit, and gave him a tremendous blow.[9] Another is, that after he had got the plates, a spirit assaulted him with the intention of getting them from his possession, and

---

7. This is incorrect. Smith claimed to have possessed the "Urim and Thummim, which were given to the brother of Jared upon the mount, when he talked with the Lord face to face" (D&C 17:1; Ether 3:23-28, 4:5). The introduction of the term Urim and Thummim about 1832, and the intentional comparison with the Old Testament instrument mentioned in Exodus 28:30, have caused some understandable confusion (see I.A.14, JOSEPH SMITH ANSWERS TO QUESTIONS, 8 MAY 1838, n. 1).

8. See, e.g., I.A.17, ORSON PRATT ACCOUNT, 1840, 13-14.

9. Compare III.A.14, WILLARD CHASE STATEMENT, CIRCA 11 DEC 1833, 242.

actually jerked them out of his hands—Jo, nothing daunted, in return seized them again, and started to run, when his Satanic Majesty, (or the spirit) applied his foot to the prophet's seat of honor, which raised him three or four feet from the ground. ... That the prophet has related a story of this kind, to some of his "weak saints," we have no manner of doubt.[10] ... [p. 276]

10. See "Joseph Smith Addendum," under "7. James A. Briggs Account, late March 1834 (Painesville, Ohio)."

12.
MARY A. NOBLE AUTOBIOGRAPHY, CIRCA 1834-1836

"A Journal of Mary A. Noble," 2-3, 4, 6, LDS Church Archives, Salt Lake City, Utah.

EDITORIAL NOTE

Mary Adeline Noble (1810-51), daughter of Alvah Be(a)man and wife of Joseph B. Noble, was born in Livonia, Livingston County, New York. She began teaching school in 1828. The Beman family was early acquainted with Joseph Smith, Sr., who occasionally visited them on their farm in Livonia, and Mary's father Alvah, a rodsman, participated in treasure searching near the Smiths' Manchester home. In late June 1830 Samuel Smith visited Livonia to preach the Book of Mormon (I.B.5, LUCY SMITH HISTORY, 1845, 1853:152-53). In 1834 Mary married Joseph B. Noble, and soon after they moved to Kirtland, Ohio. She died in Salt Lake City (see Black 1987; Bitton 1977, 260).

The journal of Mary A. Noble is bound with her husband's journal (see III.K.13, JOSEPH B. NOBLE AUTOBIOGRAPHY, CIRCA 1834-1836). This item is apparently in the hand of Mary A. Noble. Internal evidence suggests that her autobiography was written probably about 1834-36.

Father [Alvah Beman][1] sold his place in Levonia and removed with his family to Avon[,] Livingston County[.] some years previous to this my Father became acquainted with Father Joseph Smith the Father of the Prophet[.] he frequently would go to Palmira to see Father Smiths and his family during this time Brother Joseph Smith came in possession of the plates which contained the Book of Mormon[.] [p. 2] as soon as it was noised around that there was a golden Bible found (for that was what it was called at that time) the minds of the people became so excited and it arose at such a pitch that a mob collected together to search the house of Father Smith to find the records[.] my father was there at the time and assisted in concealing the plates in a box in a secluded place where no one could find them although

---

1. On Alvah Be(a)man (1775-1837), see I.B.5, LUCY SMITH HISTORY, 1845, n. 151.

he did not see them[.][2] my Father soon returned. ... [p. 3]

... Father Smith & Samuel had been to Fathers before this on business. ... [p. 4]

... in the spring of 1834 Brother Joseph Smith came from Kirtland[,] Ohio to my Fathers in [New] York State[,] Avon[,] Livingston Co: this was the first time I ever beheld a Prophet of the Lord and I can truly say at the first sight [p. 5] that I had a testimony within my own bosom that he was a man chosen to God to bring forth a great work in the last days. ... [p. 6] ...

2. A few days after removing the plates from the hill, Joseph Smith brought the plates home and hid them under the hearth. Alvah Beman was present and helped (see I.B.5, LUCY SMITH HISTORY, 1845, MS:67-68; I.B.2, SALLY PARKER TO JOHN KEMPTON, 26 AUG 1838; III.D.5, CAROLINE ROCKWELL SMITH STATEMENT, 25 MAR 1885; III.F.10, MARTIN HARRIS INTERVIEW WITH JOEL TIFFANY, 1859, 166-67; IV.A.1, JOSEPH KNIGHT, SR., REMINISCENCE, CIRCA 1835-1847; III.K.13, JOSEPH B. NOBLE AUTOBIOGRAPHY, CIRCA 1834-1836; and V.D.7, RHAMANTHUS M. STOCKER ACCOUNT, 1887, 554-55; see also III.K.37, ELIZABETH KANE INTERVIEW WITH BRIGHAM YOUNG, ARTEMISIA [BEAMAN] SNOW, AND ORRIN ROCKWELL, 1872-1873).

13.
Joseph B. Noble Autobiography, circa 1834-1836

"Journal of Joseph B. Noble," 11, LDS Church Archives, Salt Lake City, Utah.

EDITORIAL NOTE

Joseph Bates Noble (1810-1900) was born in New York. He was converted to Mormonism by Brigham Young and Heber C. Kimball. Concerning his conversion, Noble recalled: "I was baptized in the fall of 1832, as also some four or five others, who bore out testimony in favor of the work of God, that he had commenced in these last days by revealing to his servant, Joseph Smith, the keys of the Holy Priesthood, authorizing him to build up his kingdom on the earth." He married Mary A. Be(a)man in 1834, and soon after moved to Kirtland, Ohio. In 1835 he was called to the First Quorum of Seventy. He moved to Missouri in 1838, then to Nauvoo, Illinois, and finally to Utah. He died at Wardboro, Bear Lake County, Idaho (Cook and Backman 1985, 96).

In his Autobiography, Noble recorded family tradition about his father-in-law, Alvah Be(a)man, being present in Manchester (probably in late September 1827) when Joseph Smith brought the plates home for the first time and hid them under the hearth. Internal evidence suggests that Noble wrote this autobiographical sketch about 1834-36. Compare III.K.12, MARY A. NOBLE AUTOBIOGRAPHY, CIRCA 1834-1836.

... My first introduction to this young woman [Mary A. Beman] was at McMillins my place of bording. She was teaching School in the neighborhood. her ~~parents~~ <Father> Alvah Beman[1] lived about two 1/2 miles distance[.] a man well off as to houses and land and goods of this world and very highly esteemed among men for his word[.] this man [Alvah Beman] was well acquainted with the Smith family before the coming forth of the Book of Mormon, and was with Joseph at one time, assisting him in hiding

1. On Alvah Be(a)man (1775-1837), see I.B.5, LUCY SMITH HISTORY, 1845, n. 151.

the plates from the mob.[2] He was permitted to handle the plates with a cloth coming over them. ... [p. 11]

2. See III.K.12, MARY A. NOBLE AUTOBIOGRAPHY, CIRCA 1834-1836, n. 2.

14.
JOHN BARBER AND HENRY HOWE ACCOUNT, 1841

John W. Barber and Henry Howe, *Historical Collection of the State of New York* (New York: S. Tuttle, 1841), 580-81.

EDITORIAL NOTE

Barber and Howe introduce their account of early Mormonism with the following claim: "The following account of [Joseph] Smith, and his operations, is derived from authentic sources of information" (p. 580). That Barber and Howe were the first to publish an account of George Crane's interview with Joseph Smith suggests that they had interviewed the Palmyra/Manchester residents themselves.

Joseph Smith, the founder of Mormonism, was born in Royalton, Vt.,[1] and removed to Manchester, Ontario county, N.Y., about the year 1820,[2] at an early age, with his parents, who were in quite humble circumstances. He was occasionally employed in Palmyra as a laborer, and bore the reputation of a lazy and ignorant young man. According to the testimony of respectable individuals in that place, Smith and his father were persons of doubtful moral character, addicted to disreputable habits, and moreover extremely superstitious, believing in the existence of witchcraft. They at one time procured a mineral rod, and dug in various places for money. Smith testified that when digging he had seen the pot or chest containing the treasure, but never was fortunate enough to get it into his hands. He placed a singular looking stone in his hat, and pretended by the light of it to make [p. 580] many wonderful discoveries of gold, silver, and other treasures, deposited in the earth. He commenced his career as the founder of the new sect when about the age of 18 or 19,[3] and appointed a number of meetings

---

1. Joseph Smith was born in Sharon, Windsor County, Vermont. Concerning the confusion about Smith's birthplace, consult II.A.3, DANIEL WOODWARD ACCOUNT, 1870.

2. This statement is inaccurate (see III.K.11, EBER D. HOWE ACCOUNT, 1834, n. 2).

3. Smith was seventeen when he announced his discovery of the plates in 1823, but he was twenty-four in 1830 when he published the Book of

in Palmyra, for the purpose of declaring the divine revelations which he said were made to him. He was, however, unable to produce any excitement in the village; but very few had curiosity sufficient to listen to him. Not having the means to print his revelations, he applied to Mr. [George] Crane,[4] of the society of Friends, declaring that he was moved by the spirit to call upon him for assistance. This gentleman bid him to go to work, or the state prison would end his career.[5] Smith had better success with Martin Harris,[6] an industrious and thrifty farmer of Palmyra, who was worth about $10,000, and who became one of his leading disciples. By his assistance, 5,000 copies of the Mormon Bible, (so called,) were published at an expense of about $3,000. It is possible that Harris might have made the advances with the expectation of a profitable speculation, as a great sale was anticipated. This work is a duodecimo volume, containing 590 pages, and is perhaps one of the weakest productions ever attempted to be palmed off as a divine revelation. It is mostly a blind mass of words, interwoven with scriptural language and quotations, without much of a leading plan or design. It is in fact such a production as might be expected from a person of Smith's abilities and turn of mind. ...[7]

Mormon and founded his church.

4. George Crane, in his seventies, is listed in the 1830 census of Macedon, Wayne County, New York (1830:101). He does not appear in the 1840 census and may have died before the publication of the Barber and Howe account. See also III.J.8, POMEROY TUCKER ACCOUNT, 1867; III.J.15, STEPHEN S. HARDING TO THOMAS GREGG, FEB 1882, 40.

5. Recorded before Smith's murder in 1844, Barber and Howe's account of Quaker George Crane's prediction—that "state prison would end [Smith's] career"—is probably more authentic than some later versions which attempt to amend the prediction to fit historical reality. Pomeroy Tucker, for instance, reported Crane as predicting Smith's religious career "would be certain to end in his death upon the gallows, or in some equally ignominious manner" (III.J.8, POMEROY TUCKER ACCOUNT, 1867, 37). Joseph Rogers's 1887 statement to Arthur Deming claimed that "Farmers said he [Smith] was a terror to the neighborhood and that he would either have to go to State prison, be hung, or leave the country, or he would be killed" (see III.D.7, JOSEPH ROGERS STATEMENT, 16 MAY 1887). However, Stephen S. Harding's version was more vague, writing to Thomas Gregg in 1882 that Crane had said Smith's career would have "some bad end" (see III.J.15, STEPHEN S. HARDING TO THOMAS GREGG, FEB 1882, 40).

6. On Martin Harris (1783-1875), see "Introduction to Martin Harris Collection."

7. At this point, Barber and Howe quote the Title Page of the Book of Mormon and Testimony of Eight Witnesses (see III.L.12, BOOK OF

It is stated by persons in Palmyra, that when he exhibited these plates to his followers, they were done up in a canvas bag, and Smith made the declaration, that if they uncovered them, the Almighty would strike them dead. It is said that no one but Smith could read what was engraved upon them; which he was enabled to do by looking through a peculiar kind of spectacles found buried with the plates. ...

MORMON COPYRIGHT, 11 JUN 1829; and III.L.13, TESTIMONY OF EIGHT WITNESSES, JUN 1829).

15.
JAMES COLIN BREWSTER ACCOUNT, 1843

James Colin Brewster, *Very Important! To the Mormon Money Diggers. Why do the Mormons rage, and the People imagine a vain thing?* ([Springfield, Illinois]: N.p., [20 March 1843]), 2-3, 5.

EDITORIAL NOTE

James Colin Brewster (1826-?) was born in Black Rock, Erie County, New York. His parents, Zephaniah and Jane, joined the LDS church in Westfield, Chautaugua County, New York, in the early 1830s and soon after removed to Kirtland, Ohio. During the conflict which followed the failure of the Kirtland Bank in 1837, James began receiving spiritual manifestations that culminated in the publication of *The Words of Righteousness to All Men, Written from One of the Books of Esaras [Esdras]* in 1842. This purported revelation criticized LDS church leaders and called the church to repentance. Consequently Brewster and his followers were cut off from the church. In 1850 Brewster attempted to lead a small colony of believers to the promised land of California to establish the revealed city of refuge for the saints. The company traveled as far as New Mexico and disbanded. The last that is known of him is a note in Stephen Post's journal that he had baptized Brewster and his wife Elizabeth in July 1867 into the organization headed by Sidney Rigdon (Stephen Post, Journal, July 1867, LDS Church Archives, Salt Lake City, Utah; see also Vogel 1994).

On 1 December 1842 the *Times and Seasons* noted that Brewster's Book of Esdras was "assiduously circulated, in several branches of the church," and denounced it as "a perfect humbug." The editor, Apostle John Taylor, concluded by affirming institutional imperatives, quoting the revelation Joseph Smith had produced in September 1830 to discredit revelations Hiram Page had received through a stone. This revelation declared that Smith was the only person appointed to receive revelation for the church (D&C 28:2). Taylor instructed church members not to fellowship Brewster. According to the editorial, Brewster "has professed for several years to have the gift of seeing and looking through or into a stone; and has thought that he has discovered money hid in the ground in Kirtland, Ohio. His father and some of our weak brethren, who perhaps have had some confidence in the ridiculous stories that are propagated concerning Joseph Smith, about money digging, have assisted him in his foolish plans, for which they were dealt with by the church" (*Times and Seasons* 4 [1 December 1842]:32).

In March 1843 Brewster responded to Taylor's charges by publishing a pamphlet addressed "To the Mormon Money Diggers." While his denials are not always convincing, Brewster's account of Alvah Beman and Joseph Smith, Sr., participating in treasure seeking in Kirtland and the latter's confessed involvement in the practice in New York is probably accurate. Brewster's account is followed by his father's statement, which among other things certified "that the above account of the money digging business is true" and that "[i]n the year 1837, in the month of May or June, we commenced the money digging under the kind care and protection of Joseph Smith sen'r, then first President of the church of Latter Day Saints" (p. 5).

... The fact is that my father ever regarded money diggers with the utmost contempt, but believing in the Gospel as preached by the Mormons, and, becoming a member of that church, removed to Kirtland, Ohio. While residing at that place Joseph Smith Senr, the Prophet's father, with others of high standing in the church, came to see us, and stated that they knew there was money hid in the earth, that it was our duty to assist in obtaining it, and if we did not the curse of God would rest upon us. We were foolish enough to believe them, not knowing at that time the weakness and folly of those men. They also told us concerning their digging for money in the state of N.Y., and [p. 2] that the places where the treasures were deposited were discovered by means of the mineral rods and a seeing stone; likewise to prevent the Devil deceiving them they anointed the mineral rods and seeing stones with consecrated oil, and prayed over them in the house of the Lord in Kirtland, and then sent a man into the state of N.Y. to obtain the money that was supposed the mineral rods pointed out, but they found no treasure and returned empty. Soon after this interview, I and my father were requested by J[oseph]. Smith, Sen'r[1] and Eld[er]. [Alvah] Beaman[2] to come to the house of the Lord. We went in and the door was locked;—after some conversation with J[oseph]. Smith sen'r, Beaman and [Joshua] Holeman,[3]

---

1. On Joseph Smith, Sr. (1771-1840), see "Introduction to Joseph Smith, Sr., Collection."

2. On Alvah Be(a)man (1775-1837), see I.B.5, LUCY SMITH HISTORY, 1845, n. 151.

3. Joshua Sawyer Holman (1794-1846) was born at Templetown, Worchester County, Massachusetts. He lived in New York in the 1820s and early 1830s, resided in Kirtland, Ohio, from 1836-38, and moved to northern Missouri in 1838. He died at Winter Quarters, Douglas County, Nebraska (Cook and Backman 1985, 88).

Eld[er]. Beaman called upon the Lord—they then proceeded to lay their hands upon my head and pronounced a blessing upon me, in the name of the Father, Son, and Holy Spirit, and sealed it up on me by the power of the Holy Priesthood, which they held, J[oseph]. Smith sen'r then acting as first President of the Church in Kirtland. The prophetic blessing was that I should be a Prophet, a Seer, a Revealer, and Translator, and that I should have power given me of God to discover and obtain the treasures which are hid in the earth. The men above mentioned, went with me and my father several times in pursuit of the money, but it was not obtained. Joseph Smith sen'r and Beaman, being old and feeble, thought best to remain in the Temple, while the remainder of the party went to dig. John[4] and Asel Smith[5] joined with those who remained in the Temple to pray and continue their supplications until a very late hour; this was repeated several times, and at length afraid of being discovered in the Temple they retired to a barn in a remote part of the town, and continued there the most part of the night, still no treasure was obtained. By this time my father was convinced that we should not succeed, and they gave up the business entirely. All this was carried on privately, being understood only by those concerned. ... [p. 3] ... In Kirtland, Joseph Smith sen'r, the Prophet's father, said in Council: "I know more about money digging, than any man in this generation, for I have been in the business more than thirty years." Father Smith, in private conversation with my father, told many particulars, which happened in N.Y. where the money digging business was carried on to a great extent by the Smith family. The writer of the article in the "Times and Seasons" calls it a ridiculous and pernicious practice. I would ask him who was the author of this practice among the Mormons? If he has a good memory, he will remember the house that was rented in the city of Boston [Salem], with the expectation of finding a large sum of money buried in or near the cellar.[6] If he has forgotten these things, I have not. And, if he is not satisfied with what I have written, he can have the remainder shortly. ... [p. 4] ...

4. On John Smith (1781-1854), see introduction to I.G.2, JOHN SMITH AUTOBIOGRAPHY, 20 JUL 1839.

5. On Asael Smith, Jr. (1773-1848), see I.B.5, LUCY SMITH HISTORY, 1845, n. 17.

6. A number of independent sources implicate Joseph Smith and other church leaders in a treasure-seeking excursion to Salem, Massachusetts, in August 1836, presumably as a means of relieving economic pressure on the church. See *The Return* (Davis City, Iowa), 1:1:105-6; Joseph Smith to Emma Smith, 19 August 1836, in *Saints' Herald* 26 (1 December 1879): 357; Proper 1964; R. L. Anderson 1984, 499-506; Godfrey 1984; and Cannon 1984.

I have written the above that the people may know who the "weak brethren" are that assisted us in the money digging business. The Mormons may deny it, but every word it contains is true; and I might have written much more, but I think it unnecessary. But if the Mormons publish another line of falsehood concerning us, they shall have the history of the money diggers from the beginning. ...

JAMES COLIN BREWSTER.

16.
Parley P. Pratt Autobiography (Part I), circa 1854

Parley P. Pratt, *The Autobiography of Parley P. Pratt,* ed. Parley P. Pratt, Jr. (New York: Russell Brothers, 1874), 36-42, 46-47, 49.

EDITORIAL NOTE

Parley P. Pratt (1807-57) was born in Burlington, Otsego County, New York. He married Thankful Halsey in 1827 in Canaan, Columbia County, New York. Prior to his conversion, he was a Campbellite minister in northern Ohio. He was baptized and ordained an elder about 1 September 1830 in Fayette, New York. The following month Pratt, with Oliver Cowdery, Peter Whitmer, Jr., and Ziba Peterson, left on a mission to the Indian tribes in Missouri. On the way Pratt and the others stopped and preached in the Kirtland, Ohio, area, converting Sidney Rigdon and most of his congregation. Following his ordination as an apostle in February 1835, Pratt became a prolific writer and pamphleteer. A decade after his immigration to the Great Salt Lake Valley in 1847, Pratt was murdered by an enraged and jealous husband at Van Buren, Crawford County, Arkansas (L. Cook 1981, 45-47; Jessee 1989, 507).

In May 1854 Pratt started his second mission in California, during which time he apparently began writing his *Autobiography*. Regarding work on his life's story, Pratt wrote: "I devoted the time I could spare from the ministry to writing my history. ... Some time in August [1854], Elders George Q. Cannon, J. Howkins, Bigler and Farran, of the Island Mission, landed, and Brother Cannon assisted me some forty days in copying my autobiography" (Pratt 1874, 409). After his return to Salt Lake City on 27 June 1856, he mentions that he spent time "writing my history, assisted by my wife Kenzia, as copyist" (ibid., 432). Following Pratt's death in 1857, John Taylor assisted Pratt's son, Parley P. Pratt, Jr., in editing the manuscript for publication. The following excerpt tells of Parley Sr.'s conversion.

... In August, 1830, I had closed my business, completed my arrangements, and we bid adieu to our wilderness home and never saw it afterwards.

On settling up, at a great sacrifice of property, we had about ten dollars left in cash. With this small sum, we launched forth into the world, determining first to visit our native place, on our mission, and then such other places as I might be led to by the Holy Spirit.

We made our way to Cleveland [Ohio], 30 miles. We then took passage on a schooner for Buffalo [New York], a distance of 200 miles. We had a fair wind, and the captain, being short of hands, gave me the helm, the sails being all set, and turned in. I steered the vessel the most of the day, with no other person on deck. Of course, our passage cost us little besides my labor. Landing in Buffalo, we engaged our passage for Albany [New York] on a canal boat, distance 360 miles. This, including board, cost all our money and some articles of clothing.

Arriving at Rochester [New York], I informed my wife that, notwithstanding our passage being paid through the whole distance, yet I must leave the boat and her to pursue her passage to our friends; while I would stop awhile in this region. Why, I did not know; but so it was plainly manifest by the Spirit to me. I said to her, "we part [p. 36] for a season; go and visit our friends in our native place; I will come soon, but how soon I know not; for I have a work to do in this region of country, and what it is, or how long it will take to perform it, I know not; but I will come when it is performed."

My wife would have objected to this; but she had seen the hand of God so plainly manifest in His dealings with me many times, that she dare not oppose the things manifest to me by His spirit.

She, therefore, consented; and I accompanied her as far as Newark [New York], a small town upwards of 100 miles from Buffalo, and then took leave of her, and of the boat.

It was early in the morning, just at the dawn of day, I walked ten miles into the country, and stopped to breakfast with a Mr. Wells.[1] I proposed to preach in the evening. Mr. Wells readily accompanied me through the neighborhood to visit the people, and circulate the appointment.

We visited an old Baptist deacon by the name of Hamlin.[2] After hearing of our appointment for evening, he began to tell of a *book,* a STRANGE BOOK, a VERY STRANGE BOOK! in his possession, which had been just published. This book, he said, purported to have been originally written on plates either of gold or brass, by a branch of the tribes of Israel; and to have been discovered and translated by a young man near Palmyra, in the State of New York, by the aid of visions, or the ministry of angels. I inquired of him how or where the book was to be obtained. He promised me the perusal of it, at his house the next day, if I would call. I felt a strange interest

1. This person remains unidentified.
2. This person remains unidentified.

in the book. I preached that evening to a small audience, who appeared to be interested in the truths which I endeavored to unfold to them in a clear and lucid manner from the Scriptures. Next morning I called at his house, where, for the first time, my eyes beheld the "BOOK OF MORMON,"—that book [p. 37] of books—that record which reveals the antiquities of the "*New World*" back to the remotest ages, and which unfolds the destiny of its people and the world for all time to come;—that Book which contains the fulness of the gospel of a crucified and risen Redeemer;—that Book which reveals a lost remnant of Joseph, and which was the principal means, in the hands of God, of directing the entire course of my future life.

I opened it with eagerness, and read its title page. I then read the testimony of several witnesses in relation to the manner of its being found and translated. After this I commenced its contents by course. I read all day; eating was a burden, I had no desire for food; sleep was a burden when the night came, for I preferred reading to sleep.

As I read, the spirit of the Lord was upon me, and I knew and comprehended that the book was true, as plainly and manifestly as a man comprehends and knows that he exists. My joy was now full, as it was, and I rejoiced sufficiently to more than pay me for all the sorrows, sacrifices and toils of my life. I soon determined to see the young man who had been the instrument of its discovery and translation.

I accordingly visited the village of Palmyra, and inquired for the residence of Mr. Joseph Smith. I found it some two or three miles from the village. As I approached the house at the close of the day I overtook a man who was driving some cows, and inquired of him for Mr. Joseph Smith, the translator of the "*Book of Mormon*." He informed me that he now resided in Pennsylvania; some one hundred miles distant. I inquired for his father, or for any of the family. He told me that his father had gone a journey[3]; but that his residence was a small house just before me; and, said he, I am his brother. It was Mr. Hyrum Smith.[4] I informed him of the interest I felt in the Book, and of my desire to learn more about it. He welcomed me [p. 38] to his house, and we spent the night together; for neither of us felt disposed to sleep. We conversed most of the night, during which I unfolded to him

3. Joseph Smith, Sr., and Don Carlos were in St. Lawrence County, New York, visiting relatives (see I.G.4, GEORGE A. SMITH REMINISCENCES, 1846, 1857 & CIRCA 1858; and I.B.5, LUCY SMITH HISTORY, 1845, 1853:154, 157).

4. On Hyrum Smith (1800-44), see I.A.15, JOSEPH SMITH HISTORY, 1839, n. 12.

much of my experience in my search after truth, and my success so far; together with that which I felt was lacking, viz: a commissioned priesthood, or apostleship to minister in the ordinances of God.

He also unfolded to me the particulars of the discovery of the Book; its translation; the rise of the Church of Latter-Day Saints, and the commission of his brother Joseph, and others, by revelation and the ministering of angels, by which the apostleship and authority had been again restored to the earth. After duly weighing the whole matter in my mind I saw clearly that these things were true; and that myself and the whole world were without baptism, and without the ministry and ordinances of God; and that the whole world had been in this condition since the days that inspiration and revelation had ceased—in short, that this was a *new dispensation* or *commission,* in fulfilment of prophecy, and for the restoration of Israel, and to prepare the way before the second coming of the Lord.

In the morning I was compelled to take leave of this worthy man and his family—as I had to hasten back a distance of thirty miles, on foot, to fulfill an appointment in the evening. As we parted he kindly presented me with a copy of the Book of Mormon. I had not yet completed its perusal, and was glad indeed to possess a copy of my own. I travelled on a few miles, and, stopping to rest, I commenced again to read the book. To my great joy I found that Jesus Christ, in his glorified resurrected body, had appeared to the remnant of Joseph on the continent of America, soon after his resurrection and ascension into heaven; and that he also administered, in person, to the ten lost tribes; and that through his personal ministry in these countries his gospel was revealed and written in countries and among nations entirely unknown to the Jewish apostles. [p. 39]

Thus revealed, written, handed down and preserved, till revealed in this age by the angels of God, it had, of course, escaped the corruptions of the great and abominable church; and been preserved in purity.

This discovery greatly enlarged my heart, and filled my soul with joy and gladness. I esteemed the Book, or the information contained in it, more than all the riches of the world. Yes; I verily believe that I would not at that time have exchanged the knowledge I then possessed, for a legal title to all the beautiful farms, houses, villages and property which passed in review before me, on my journey through one of the most flourishing settlements of western New York.

Surely, thought I, Jesus had *other sheep,* as he said to his Apostles of old [John 10:16]; and here they were, in the wilderness of the world called new. And they heard the voice of the Good Shepherd of Israel; and he brought them to his fold. Truly, thought I, he was not sent (in person) save to the lost sheep of the house of Israel, as he told the woman of Canaan [Matthew 15:24]; and here were a portion of them. Truly, thought I, the angels sung with the spirit and with the understanding when they declared: "*We bring you glad tidings of great joy, which shall be to* ALL PEOPLE [Luke 2:10]."

In his mortal tabernacle he confined his ministry and that of his Apostles to the land of Judea; but afterwards, released from the bonds of mortal life, or rather death, and clothed with an immortal body, and with organs strong and lasting as the immortal mind, he possessed all power in heaven and on earth; he was then enabled to extend his ministry to heaven, earth or hell. He could take the wings of the morning, and, with the speed of light, make his way to the Heaven of Heavens; and converse and counsel among the sons of God; or receive counsel from his Father in Heaven; or, leaving again the starry worlds, he could descend to the dark and gloomy abodes of the [p. 40] spirits in prison and preach to them the gospel—bursting off their shackles and unlocking their prison doors; while these once dark abodes were now brilliant with light, and, instead of prison groans, were heard joyful acclamations of deliverance to the captive, and the opening of the prison to them that are bound; or coming again to visit the earth, he could soar away beyond the waves and tempests, which had before set bounds to the geographical knowledge of man, and stood up as an impregnable barrier to the intercourse of nations; and there, in other tribes and tongues, make known the riches of his grace, and his *triumph* over death.

And when ages had passed, and nations slumbered in the dust—when cruelty and bloodshed had blotted almost every trace of priesthood and apostleship from the earth; when saints had been worn out and overcome; times, laws and ordinances changed; the Bible itself robbed of its plainness; and all things darkened and corrupted; a pure and faithful record of his ministry to other nations is forthcoming from among the archives of the dead, to reveal the "*mystery of iniquity*;" to speak, as with a voice of thunder, in rebuking the evil and revealing the fulness of the gospel. Such was the Book of Mormon—such its effect upon the startling nations. [p. 41]

Having rested awhile and perused this sacred book by the roadside, I again walked on.

In the evening I arrived in time to fill my appointment. I met a crowded house, and laid before them many interesting truths, which were listened to with deep interest.

The next evening I had another appointment, and the people came out in great numbers, and were filled with the spirit of interest and inquiry.

They urged me very much to continue my discourses among them; but I felt to minister no more till I had attended to some important duties for myself. I had now found men on earth commissioned to preach, baptize, ordain to the ministry, etc., and I determined to obey the fulness of the gospel without delay. I should have done so at the first interview with Elder Hyrum Smith; but these two appointments were already out, and thirty miles' travel required all the time I had.

I now returned immediately to Hyrum Smith's residence, and demanded baptism at his hands. I tarried with him one night, and the next day we walked some twenty-five miles to the residence of Mr. [Peter] Whitmer,[5] in Seneca County. Here we arrived in the evening, and found a most welcome reception. [p. 42] ...[6]

Renewed in spirit and filled with joy I now pursued my way, and arrived at my aunt [Lovina] Van Cott's,[7] not weary, but refreshed with a long walk, and deep communion with myself and God.

Having lifted a warning voice to multitudes in all this region of country, I now took leave, and repaired again to the western part of New York, and to the body of the Church.

On our arrival, we found that brother Joseph Smith, the translator of the Book of Mormon, had returned from Pennsylvania to his father's residence in Manchester, near Palmyra, and here I had the pleasure of seeing him for the first time.[8]

He received me with a hearty welcome, and with that frank and kind manner so universal with him in after years.

On Sunday we held meeting at his house; the two [p. 46] large rooms were filled with attentive listeners, and he invited me to preach. I did so, and afterwards listened with interest to a discourse from his own mouth, filled with intelligence and wisdom. We repaired from the meeting to the water's edge, and, at his request, I baptized several persons.[9]

---

5. On Peter Whitmer, Sr. (1773-1854), see I.A.15, JOSEPH SMITH HISTORY, 1839, n. 59.

6. For Pratt's experience in Fayette, New York, see VI.F.6, PARLEY P. PRATT AUTOBIOGRAPHY (PART II), CIRCA 1854.

7. Lovina Van Cott, sister of Parley's father, Jared Pratt, was born on 6 August 1787 at Canaan, Columbia County, New York (E. Watson 1975, 3).

8. Joseph and Emma Smith apparently arrived at Manchester in early October 1830 (see I.B.5, LUCY SMITH HISTORY, 1845, 1853:159, 166-67). In 1858 Pratt recalled: "Returning to western New York the same autumn, I saw for the first time Joseph Smith, the Prophet, at his father's house, in Manchester" (Parley P. Pratt, "History of Parley P. Pratt," *Deseret News* 8 [19 May 1858]: 53).

9. Probably Ezra Thayre, Northrop Sweet, and Oliver Cowdery's stepmother Keziah Pearce Cowdery (III.J.6, EZRA THAYRE REMINIS-

President Joseph Smith was in person tall and well built, strong and active; of a light complexion, light hair, blue eyes, very little beard, and of an expression peculiar to himself, on which the eye naturally rested with interest, and was never weary of beholding. His countenance was ever mild, affable, beaming with intelligence and benevolence; mingled with a look of interest and an uncon[s]cious smile, or cheerfulness, and entirely free from all restraint or affectation of gravity; and there was something connected with the serene and steady penetrating glance of his eye, as if he would penetrate the deepest abyss of the human heart, gaze into eternity, penetrate the heavens, and comprehend all worlds.

He possessed a noble boldness and independence of character; his manner was easy and familiar; his rebuke terrible as the lion; his benevolence unbounded as the ocean; his intelligence universal, and his language abounding in original eloquence peculiar to himself—not polished—not studied—not smoothed and softened by education and refined by art; but flowing forth in its own native simplicity, and profusely abounding in variety of subject and manner. He interested and edified, while, at the same time, he amused and entertained his audience; and none listened to him that were ever weary with his discourse. ... [p. 47]

It was now October, 1830. A revelation had been given through the mouth of this Prophet, Seer and Translator, in which Elders Oliver Cowdery,[10] Peter Whitmer,[11] Ziba Peterson[12] and myself were appointed to go into the wilderness, through the western States, and to the Indian territory. Making arrangements for my wife in the family of the Whitmers, we took

---

CENCE, 1862, 82-83). These baptisms may have occurred on Sunday, 10 October 1830, as Thayre says he was baptized by Pratt on the Sunday following Smith's arrival in Manchester (see note 8 above). In 1858 Pratt recalled that he "heard him [Joseph Smith] preach, and preached in his [father's] house, at the close of which meeting we baptized seven persons" (Parley P. Pratt, "History of Parley P. Pratt," *Deseret News* 8 [19 May 1858]: 53). Dolly Proper and perhaps her husband George may have been among the four unidentified persons baptized, probably by Oliver Cowdery (see III.B.12, LORENZO SAUNDERS INTERVIEW, 17 SEP 1884, 13 [back]; III.B.15, LORENZO SAUNDERS INTERVIEW, 12 NOV 1884, 7; III.J.8, POMEROY TUCKER ACCOUNT, 1867, 38).

10. On Oliver Cowdery (1806-50), see "Introduction to Oliver Cowdery Collection."

11. On Peter Whitmer, Jr. (1809-36), see I.A.15, JOSEPH SMITH HISTORY, 1839, n. 63.

12. On Richard Ziba Peterson (?-1849), see I.A.15, JOSEPH SMITH HISTORY, 1839, n. 105.

leave of our friends and the church late in October,[13] and started on foot.

After travelling for some days we called on an Indian nation at or near Buffalo; and spent part of a day with them, instructing them in the knowledge of the record of their forefathers. We were kindly received, and much interest was manifested by them on hearing this news. We made a present of two copies of the Book of Mormon to certain of them who could read, and repaired to Buffalo. Thence we continued our journey, for about two hundred miles, and at length called on Mr. [Sidney] Rigdon,[14] my former friend and instructor, in the Reformed Baptist Society. ... [p. 49] ...

---

13. Because the four men signed a document known as the "Missionaries Covenant," dated 17 October 1830, in Manchester, New York, it is generally assumed that they left for the west from that location (III.L.22, MISSIONARIES COVENANT, 17 OCT 1830); however, Pratt stated elsewhere: "We started this mission in October, 1830. From Father Whitmer's, in western New York, we travelled nearly fifteen hundred miles ..." (Parley P. Pratt, "History of Parley P. Pratt," *Deseret News* 8 [19 May 1858]: 53). Actually the Lamanite Mission was organized during the 26-28 September 1830 conference held at the Whitmer home in Fayette, New York, and Pratt may have therefore had this event as a reference point rather than imply the missionaries had returned to Fayette before leaving for the west. Pratt had previously said his journey to Ohio began on 15 October 1830 (P. Pratt 1838, 41), although the "Missionaries Covenant" was signed two days later.

14. On Sidney Rigdon (1793-1876), see introduction to I.A.13, SIDNEY RIGDON ACCOUNT, CIRCA 1836.

17.
THURLOW WEED REMINISCENCES, 1854, 1858, 1880 & 1884

1. [Thurlow Weed], "The Beginning of Mormonism," *Albany Evening Journal* (31 July 1854). Reprinted in *New York Times* 3 (3 August 1854).

2. [Thurlow Weed], "Prospect of Peace with Utah," *Albany Evening Journal* 29 (19 May 1858): 2.

3. [Thurlow Weed], "From the Troy Times," *Albany Evening Journal* 29 (21 May 1858): 2.

4. Thurlow Weed to Ellen E. Dickinson, 12 April 1880, in Ellen E. Dickinson, *New Light on Mormonism ... With Introduction by Thurlow Weed* (New York: Funk and Wagnalls, 1885), 260-61.

5. Thurlow Weed, *Autobiography of Thurlow Weed,* ed. Harriet A. Weed (Boston: Houghton, Mifflin and Co., 1884), 358-59.

EDITORIAL NOTE

Thurlow Weed (1797-1882) was born in Green County, New York. After editing various papers between 1817 and 1821, he became editor of the *Rochester Telegraph* in 1821 and owner in 1825. Following the murder of William Morgan in 1826, Weed became a leading anti-Mason and in 1828 began editing the *Anti-Masonic Enquirer,* which supported John Quincy Adams for president. In 1829 he was elected to the New York State Assembly in Albany, where for three decades he edited the *Albany Evening Journal* (1830-60). In 1867 he became editor of the *New York Commercial Advertiser.* He died at New York City (*Who Was Who in America,* 1967, 640).

In June 1829 Joseph Smith approached Egbert B. Grandin to publish the Book of Mormon, but Grandin declined. Smith next appealed to Thurlow Weed of Rochester, who also rejected the offer. When Elihu F. Marshall of Rochester apparently expressed a willingness to publish the book, Martin Harris visited Grandin a second time and assured him that the Book of Mormon would be printed in Rochester if he again declined to do the work. Through the encouragement of friends, and Harris's willingness to mortgage his farm, Grandin finally agreed to print the Book of Mormon in Palmyra (see III.H.8, JOHN H. GILBERT STATEMENT, 23 OCT 1887; III.H.10, JOHN H. GILBERT MEMORANDUM, 8 SEP 1892; III.J.5, POMEROY TUCKER REMINISCENCE, 1858; and III.J.8, POMEROY TUCKER ACCOUNT, 1867, 52). The following sources report Weed's brief encounter with Joseph Smith and Martin Harris.

[*1. Article, 1854*]

Twenty-eight years ago JOE SMITH, the founder of this sect, and [Martin] HARRIS, his first convert, applied to the senior editor of the *Journal,* then residing in Rochester, to print his "Book of Mormon," then just transcribed from the "Golden Bible" which JOE had found in the cleft of a rock to which he had been guided by a vision.

We attempted to read the first chapter, but it seemed such unintelligible jargon that it was thrown aside. JOE was a tavern idler in the village of Palmyra. HARRIS, who offered to pay for the printing, was a substantial farmer. Disgusted with what we considered a "weak invention" of an imposter, and not caring to strip HARRIS of his hard earnings, the proposition was declined.[1]

The manuscript was then taken to another printing office across the street, from whence, in due time, the original "Mormon Bible" made its advent.

"Tall trees from little acorns grow,"

But who would have anticipated from such a bald, shallow, senseless imposition, such world wide consequences? To remember and contrast JOE SMITH, with his loafer-look, pretending to read from a miraculous slate-stone placed in his hat, with the Mormonism of the present day, awakens thoughts alike painful and mortifying. There is no limit, even in this most enlightened of all the ages of knowledge, to the influence of imposture and credulity. If knaves, or even fools, invent creeds, nothing is too monstrous

---

1. In a subsequent statement, Weed explained another reason for rejecting Smith's offer to print the Book of Mormon: "But as we were only in the newspaper line, we contented ourself with reading a chapter of what seemed such wretched and incoherent stupidity, that we wondered how 'Joe' had contrived to make the first fool with it" (*Oxford* [New York] *Times* 8 [18 December 1875]: 2, reprinting from the *Albany Evening Journal*).

for belief. Nor does the fact—a fact not denied or disguised—that all the Mormon leaders are rascals as well as imposters, either open the eyes of their dupes or arrest the progress of delusion.

[*2. Article, 1858a*]

... Within our recollection, Mormonism was "a speck, not bigger than a man's hand." The original Imposter, JOE SMITH, came to the writer of this article, only thirty-two years ago, with the manuscript of his Mormon Bible, to be Printed. He then had but one follower, (a respectable and wealthy Farmer of the Town of Macedon) who offered himself as security for the Printing. But after reading a few Chapters, it seemed such a jumble of unintelligible absurdities, that we refused the work, advising HARRIS not to mortgage his Farm and beggar his Family. But JOE crossed over the way to our neighbor ELIHU F. MARSHALL,[2] and got his "Mormon Bible" printed.[3] ...

[*3. Article, 1858b*]

From the Troy Times.

Mr. Elihu F. Marshall did *not* print the Mormon Bible. It was printed by Mr. Egbert Grandin, (now deceased,) at the office of the Wayne *Sentinel,* Palmyra. We happen to *know* this fact. Mr. John Gilbert,[4] now residing at Palmyra, did all the press-work, and a portion of the type-setting on the Bible. If Mr. Weed doubts this, we can show him a copy of the Mormon Bible with the imprint.[5]

We have no right to "doubt" the correctness of this statement, though we were strongly impressed with the belief that our Quaker neighbor, MARSHALL, printed the *first* edition of the Mormon Bible. Was not the Book referred to by the Editor of the Times, a portion only of what became

---

2. On Elihu F. Marshall, see III.J.5, POMEROY TUCKER REMINISCENCE, 1858, n. 6.

3. Weed's mistaken claim that Elihu F. Marshall published the Book of Mormon was corrected by the *Troy* (New York) *Times,* 20 May 1858, quoted in Weed's article below, as well as Pomeroy Tucker (see III.J.5, POMEROY TUCKER REMINISCENCE, 1858).

4. On John H. Gilbert (1802-95), see "Introduction to John H. Gilbert Collection."

5. This paragraph was taken from the *Troy Times,* 20 May 1858, which begins: "*All* this is not within your 'recollection,' Mr. Weed. ..." The following paragraph is Weed's statement.

the Mormon Bible? When JOE SMITH called on us he professed to read fresh revelations from a miraculous Tablet deposited in his Hat. Will the Editor of the Troy Times oblige us with the copy of the Book it refers to? It can be sent and will be carefully returned, by Express?[6]

[*4. Letter, 1880*]

NEW YORK, April 12, 1880.

In 1825,[7] when I was publishing the Rochester *Telegraph,* a man introduced himself to me as Joseph Smith, of Palmyra, N.Y., whose object, he said, was to get a book published. He then stated he had been guided by a vision to a spot he described, where, in a cavern, he found what he called a golden Bible. It consisted of a tablet, which he placed in his hat, and from which he proceeded to read the first chapter of the "Book of Mormon."

I listened until I became weary of what seemed to me an incomprehensible jargon. I then told him I was only publishing a newspaper, and that he would have to go to a book publisher, suggesting a friend who was in that business. A few days afterward Smith called again, bringing a substantial farmer with him, named Harris. [p. 260] Smith renewed his request that I should print his book, adding that it was a divine revelation, and would be accepted, and that he would be accepted by the world as a prophet. Supposing that I had doubts as to his being able to pay for the publishing, Mr. Harris, who was a convert, offered to be his security for payment. Meantime I had discovered that Smith was a shrewd, scheming fellow, who passed his time at taverns and stores in Palmyra, without business, and apparently without visible means of support. He seemed about thirty years of age, was compactly built, about five feet eight inches in height, had regular features, and would impress one favorably in conversation. His book was afterward published in Palmyra. I knew the publisher, but cannot at this moment remember his name.[8] The first Mormon newspaper was published at Canandaigua, New York, by a man named Phelps,[9] who accompanied Smith as an apostle to

---

6. See III.J.5, POMEROY TUCKER REMINISCENCE, 1858, for Tucker's comments about Weed's exchange with the *Troy Times.*

7. Dickinson reports that Weed later said "that he was mistaken as to the year 1825; that it must have been two or three years later" (Dickinson 1885, 41).

8. Egbert B. Grandin (1806-45) (see I.A.15, JOSEPH SMITH HISTORY, 1839, n. 77).

9. On William W. Phelps (1792-1872), see introduction to III.G.6, OLIVER COWDERY TO W. W. PHELPS, 7 SEP 1834. Prior to his conversion in 1831, Phelps edited the *Ontario Phoenix,* an anti-Masonic paper

Illinois, where the first Mormon city, Nauvoo, was started.

(Signed) THURLOW WEED.

[*5. Autobiography, 1884*]

... About 1829 a stout, round, smooth-faced young man, between twenty-five and thirty, with the air and manners of a person [p. 358] without occupation, came into the "Rochester Telegraph" office and said he wanted a book printed, and added that he had been directed in a vision to a place in the woods near Palmyra, where he resided, and that he found a "golden Bible," from which he was directed to copy the book which he wanted published. He then placed what he called a "tablet" in his hat, from which he read a chapter of the "Book of Mormon," a chapter which seemed so senseless that I thought the man either crazed or a very shallow impostor, and therefore declined to become a publisher, thus depriving myself of whatever notoriety might have been achieved by having my name imprinted upon the title-page of the first Mormon Bible.

It is scarcely necessary to add that this individual was Joseph Smith, the founder of the Mormon creed. On the day but one following he came again, accompanied by Martin Harris, a substantial farmer residing near Palmyra, who had adopted the Mormon faith, and who offered to become security for the expense of printing. But I again declined, and he subsequently found a publisher in E. B. Grandin, of Palmyra, in 1830.

---

published at Canandaigua, New York. This paper was not a Mormon publication. Phelps, however, did publish the first Mormon paper, *The Evening and The Morning Star* (1832-33) at Independence, Missouri.

18.
THOMAS FORD ACCOUNT, 1854

Thomas Ford, *A History of Illinois, from Its Commencement As a State in 1818 to 1847* (Chicago: S. C. Griggs and Co., 1854), 256-58.

EDITORIAL NOTE

Thomas Ford (1800-50) was born at Uniontown, Fayette County, Pennsylvania. After passing the Illinois state bar in 1823 and practicing law for several years, he served as judge of the circuit court in northern Illinois (1835-37), and then in the Galena district (1839). In 1841 he was appointed to the supreme court of Illinois, and the following year elected governor. He died in Peoria, Illinois (Jessee 1992, 545).

In 1854 Ford published *A History of Illinois,* which included a brief sketch of the rise of Mormonism in New York. The major portion of Ford's account of Mormonism came from previously published sources and is therefore excluded from the present excerpt. Unique to Ford's account, however, is his version of the eight witnesses seeing the Book of Mormon plates in Manchester, New York, which Ford claimed came from "men who were once in the confidence of the prophet." Unfortunately, Ford did not name his sources,[1] but his account is strangely similar to the claims of dissident Mormons in Ohio and Missouri in 1838, one of whom quoted Martin Harris as saying that the three witnesses saw the plates with "spiritual eyes" and that the eight witnesses "never saw them" with their physical eyes (see III.F.7, STEPHEN BURNETT TO LYMAN E. JOHNSON, 15 APR 1838; see also introduction to III.L.13, TESTIMONY OF EIGHT WITNESSES, JUN 1829).

... And the prophet was not without his witnesses. Oliver Cowdney [Cowdery],[2] Martin Harris,[3] and Daniel Whiteman [David Whit-

---

1. For this reason Fawn Brodie was perhaps mistaken to place so much weight on Ford's account (Brodie 1945, 79-80; see also R. L. Anderson 1981, 159-61).

2. On Oliver Cowdery (1806-50), see "Introduction to Oliver Cowdery Collection."

3. On Martin Harris (1783-1875), see "Introduction to Martin Harris Collection."

mer],[4] solemnly certify "that we have seen the plates which contain the records; that they were translated by the gift and power of God, for his voice hath declared it unto us, wherefore we know of a surety that the work is true; and we declare with words of soberness that an angel of God came down from heaven and brought and laid before our eyes, that we beheld and saw the plates and the engravings thereon."[5] Eight other witnesses certify that "Joseph Smith, the translator, had shown them the plates spoken [p. 256] of, which had the appearance of gold; and as many of the plates as the said Smith had translated, they did handle with their hands, and they also saw the engravings thereon, all of which had the appearance of ancient work and curious workmanship."[6]

The most probable account of these certificates is, that the witnesses were in the conspiracy, aiding the imposture; but I have been informed by men who were once in the confidence of the prophet, that he privately gave a different account of the matter. It is related that the prophet's early followers were anxious to see the plates; the prophet had always given out that they could not be seen by the carnal eye, but must be spiritually discerned; that the power to see them depended upon faith, and was the gift of God, to be obtained by fasting, prayer, mortification of the flesh, and exercises of the spirit; that so soon as he could see the evidences of a strong and lively faith in any of his followers, they should be gratified in their holy curiosity. He set them to continual prayer, and other spiritual exercises, to acquire this lively faith by means of which the hidden things of God could be spiritually discerned; and at last, when he could delay them no longer, he assembled them in a room, and produced a box, which he said contained the precious treasure. The lid was opened; the witnesses peeped into it, but making no discovery, for the box was empty, they said, "Brother Joseph, we do not see the plates." The prophet answered them, "O ye of little faith! how long will God bear with this wicked and perverse generation? Down on your knees, brethren, every one of you, and pray God for the forgiveness of your sins, and for a holy and living faith which cometh down from heaven." The disciples dropped to their knees, and began to pray in the fervency of their

4. On David Whitmer (1805-88), see "Introduction to David Whitmer Collection."

5. Compare VI.G.1, TESTIMONY OF THREE WITNESSES, JUN 1829.

6. Compare III.L.13, TESTIMONY OF EIGHT WITNESSES, JUN 1829.

spirit, supplicating God for more than two hours with fanatical earnestness; at the end of which time, looking again into the box, they were now persuaded that they saw the plates. I leave it to philosophers to determine whether the fumes of an enthusiastic and fanatical [p. 257] imagination are thus capable of blinding the mind and deceiving the senses by so absurd a delusion. ...

19.
BRIGHAM YOUNG ACCOUNTS, 1855 & 1857

1. "A discourse by President Brigham Young, Delivered in the Tabernacle, Great Salt Lake City, Feb. 18, 1855," *Journal of Discourses of the Church of Jesus Christ of Latter-day Saints,* 26 vols. (Liverpool: Albert Carrington [and others], 1853-1886), 2:180-81.

2. "Remarks by President Brigham Young, made in the Bowery, Great Salt Lake City, July 19, 1857," *Journal of Discourses of the Church of Jesus Christ of Latter-day Saints,* 26 vols. (Liverpool: Albert Carrington [and others], 1853-1886), 5:55.

EDITORIAL NOTE

Brigham Young (1801-77) was born at Wittingham, Windham County, Vermont. He joined the Methodist church about 1822. On 8 October 1824 he married Miriam Works in Aurilius, New York. In 1829 he moved to Mendon, New York, where he worked as a carpenter, joiner, painter, and glazier. He first heard about Mormonism through Solomon Chamberlain in 1830 (see III.J.1, SOLOMON CHAMBERLAIN ACCOUNTS, 1845 & CIRCA 1858, 1:53), but was not baptized until April 1832. He was ordained an apostle in February 1835. As president of the Twelve Apostles, he became the leader of the largest group of Mormons after Joseph Smith's death, establishing its headquarters at Salt Lake City, Utah. Young died at Salt Lake City (L. Cook 1981, 279-81; Arrington 1985).

In the following two accounts, Young relates events that occurred in the Palmyra/Manchester, New York, area in 1827, particularly the attempt of an unnamed "fortune-teller" to locate Smith's gold plates. While Young could not recall the man's name in either 1855 or 1857, in 1986 D. Michael Quinn suggested Luman Walters, a necromanic treasure seeker from nearby Pultneyville whom Abner Cole named as Smith's occult mentor (Quinn 1987, 83; III.E.3, *PALMYRA REFLECTOR,* 1829-1831, n. 21). Another source seems to confirm Quinn's suspicions (see III.K.37, ELIZABETH KANE INTERVIEW WITH BRIGHAM YOUNG, ARTEMISIA [BEAMAN] SNOW, AND ORRIN ROCKWELL, 1872-1873). While Young claims "personal knowledge" about the coming forth of the Book of Mormon and related events, his information is secondhand since he learned of the Mormon scripture only after its publication in 1830 and was introduced to Smith for the first time in 1832. Later, Young met the "fortune-teller," who may have briefly converted to Mormonism,[1] and from him learned the details of the story he here relates.

[*1. Discourse, 1855*]

... It was priests who first persecuted Joseph Smith. I will here relate a few of the circumstances which I personally knew concerning the coming forth of the plates, from a part of which the Book of Mormon was translated. This fact may be new to several, but I had a personal knowledge with regard to many of those circumstances.

I well knew a man who, to get the plates, rode over sixty miles[2] three times the same season they were obtained by Joseph Smith. About the time of their being delivered to Joseph by the angel, the friends of this man sent for him, and informed him that they were going to lose that treasure, though they did not know what it was. The man I refer to was a fortune-teller, a necromancer, an astrologer, a soothsayer, and possessed as much talent as any man that walked on the American soil, and was one of the wickedest men I ever saw. The last time he went to obtain the treasure he knew where it was, and told where it was, but did not know its value. Allow me to tell you that a Baptist deacon[3] and others of Joseph's [p. 180] neighbors were the very

---

1. In an 1850 sermon, Young evidently alluded to the same person: "I remember once at the commencement of this church, a necromancer embraced it, but he could not be satisfied; he came and said he had fingered and handled the perverted priesthood so much, the course I have taken is downwards, the devil has too fast hold of me, I cannot go with you; but the rest slide off" (*Millennial Star* 12 [15 September 1850]: 275).

2. Lucy Smith also mentioned that enemies in Palmyra "sent for a conjuror to come 60 miles to divine the place where the record was deposited by magic art" (I.B.5, LUCY SMITH HISTORY, 1845, MS:63). D. Michael Quinn has suggested that this person might have been Luman Walters, who resided in Pultneyville, about twenty-five miles north of the Smith home in Manchester, and believes that this "proximity could be the geographic reference for Young's later reminiscences" (1987, 83). Young, however, evidently believed, probably mistakenly, that Walters had lived "on the Hudson [River] South of Albany" (see III.K. 37, ELIZABETH KANE INTERVIEW WITH BRIGHAM YOUNG, ARTEMISIA (BEAMAN) SNOW, AND ORRIN ROCKWELL, 1872-1873).

3. In 1987 Quinn suggested that the "Baptist deacon" referred to by Young was Alvah Be(a)man of Livonia, New York. Despite the tradition that Beman helped the Smiths conceal the plates under their hearth (see I.B.5,

men who sent for this necromancer the last time he went for the treasure. I never heard a man who could swear like that astrologer; he swore scientifically, by rule, by note. To those who love swearing, it was musical to hear him, but not so to me, for I would leave his presence. He would call Joseph everything that was bad, and say, "I believe he will get the treasure after all." He did get it, and the war commenced directly.

When Joseph obtained the treasure, the priests, the deacons, and religionists of every grade, went hand in hand with the fortune-teller, and with every wicked person, to get it out of his hands, and, to accomplish this, a part of them came out and persecuted him. ...

[*2. Remarks, 1857*]

... Do you not think that those [evil] spirits knew when Joseph Smith got the plates? Yes, just as well as you know that I am talking to you now. They were there at the time, and millions and millions of them opposed Joseph in getting the plates; and not only they opposed him, but also men in the flesh. I never heard such oaths fall from the lips of any man as I heard uttered by a man who was called a fortune-teller, and who knew where those plates were hid. He went three times in one summer to get them,—the same summer in which Joseph did get them. Baptist, Presbyterian, and Methodist

---

LUCY SMITH HISTORY, 1845, MS:67-68; III.K.12, MARY A. NOBLE AUTOBIOGRAPHY, CIRCA 1834-1836; and III.K.13, JOSEPH B. NOBLE AUTOBIOGRAPHY, CIRCA 1834-1836), Joseph Knight reported that Beman came to the Smiths' home with Samuel Lawrence and used his rod to discover the location of the plates under the hearth (IV.A.1, JOSEPH KNIGHT, SR., REMINISCENCE, CIRCA 1835-1847, 3). Quinn suggested that "Beman became disaffected from Joseph Smith, when the latter obtained the Book of Mormon plates in September 1827, and briefly joined with Palmyra neighbors Willard Chase and Samuel F. Lawrence who turned against the Smiths and tried to steal the gold plates" (1987, 35). Quinn also noted: "In the manuscript of his *Journal of Discourses* address, Brigham Young remarked that one of Joseph Smith's neighbors was a Baptist deacon who sent for the necromancer [Luman Walters] in 1827 to take the gold plates from Joseph Smith, but that this neighbor became converted to Joseph Smith's claims and remained a faithful elder in the LDS Church until his death" (1987, 35, n. 3). The recent publication of Elizabeth Kane's journal has confirmed Quinn's previous supposition. In this source Young is quoted as saying, "Beman was one of those who sent for him [the fortune teller]" (see III.K. 37, ELIZABETH KANE INTERVIEW WITH BRIGHAM YOUNG, ARTEMISIA [BEAMAN] SNOW, AND ORRIN ROCKWELL, 1872-1873).

priests and deacons sent for him to tell where those plates were, and to get them out of the hill where they were deposited; and he had not returned to his home from the last trip he made for them more than a week or ten days before Joseph got them. Joseph was what we call an ignorant boy; but this fortune-teller, whose name I do not remember, was a man of profound learning.

He had put himself in possession of all the learning in the States,—had been to France, Germany, Italy, and through the world,—had been educated for a priest, and turned out to be a devil.[4] I do not know but that he would have been a devil if he had followed the profession of a priest among what are termed the Christian denominations. He could preach as well as the best of them, and I never heard a man swear as he did. He could tell that those plates were there, and that they were a treasure whose value to the people could not be told; for that I myself heard him say. Those spirits driven from heaven were with him and with others who tried to prevent Joseph's getting the plates; but he did get and secrete them, though he had to knock down two or three men, as he was going home, who were waylaying him to kill him.[5] From that day to this, a part of the host of heaven made mention of in the Bible, with the cursed corrupt priests and the cursed scoundrelly Gentiles with them, have been trying to put down this work. ...

---

4. Quinn sees this description as pointing to Luman Walters, citing Clark Braden who said Walters "had been a physician in Europe. This person had learned in Europe the secret of Mesmerism or animal magnetism" (Braden and Kelley [1884], 367; see also Quinn 1987, 83, 96). However, Braden failed to state the authority upon which his assertion rested.

5. See I.B.5, LUCY SMITH HISTORY, 1845, MS:63-66; and III.F.10, MARTIN HARRIS INTERVIEW WITH JOEL TIFFANY, 1859, 166-67.

20.
EMER HARRIS ACCOUNT, 1856

Utah Stake General Minutes (1855-1860), L.R. 9629, Series 11, 10:268-70, entry of 6 April 1856, LDS Church Archives, Salt Lake City, Utah.

EDITORIAL NOTE

Emer Harris (1781-1869), elder brother of Martin Harris, was born at Cambridge, Washington County, New York. He married Roxana Peas in 1802, and together they parented six children, all born at Cambridge, New York (1803-13). Following the death of his first wife, he married Deborah Lott in January 1819 in Pennsylvania. Their five children were all born at Windham, Luzerne County, Pennsylvania (1819-25), where he probably married his third wife, Parna Chapel (1792-1857), in 1826. This union produced four children: two born at Windham, Luzerne County, Pennsylvania (1827, 1830), and two at Brownhelm, Lorain County, Ohio (1832, 1834). He was therefore living at or near Windham when he converted to Mormonism through the missionary efforts of Newel Knight and Hyrum Smith (see IV.A.2, NEWEL KNIGHT JOURNAL, CIRCA 1846, 23; IV.A.3, NEWEL KNIGHT AUTOBIOGRAPHY, CIRCA 1846, 65). He was baptized by Newel Knight on 10 February 1831. By June 1831, Emer had moved to Kirtland, Ohio, where he was ordained an elder. In 1852 he migrated to Utah, where he was called as a patriarch the following year. He died at Logan, Cache County, Utah (Jessee 1989, 489; L. Cook 1981, 154-55; Porter 1971, 207; Family Group Record, Family History Library, Salt Lake City, Utah).

At a Provo, Utah, stake conference, on 6 April 1856, Emer Harris gave a brief account of the coming forth of the Book of Mormon, loss of the translation manuscript, and organization of the church. Emer states that he learned of the events connected with the Book of Mormon "as they transpired," presumably from his brother Martin Harris.

Provo [Utah] Sunday Ap[ri]l 6/[18]56[.] Meeting op[e]ned at 1/2 past 10 AM[.] Father [Emer] Harris said Brethren I am glad to see so Many here this Morning[.] it seems to be to Me an Omen of better Days[.] I am not in habit of preaching often to the Saints so that I am not so used to it as i was when i preached to the World[.] Br Brigham [Young] says there [are] Many preachers but not Many fathers, he often says he hears Many of the Elder[s] preach [things?] wich astonished him[.] Brethren it is more [than] 26 years since this Chirch was Organized with but Six Members[.] there are Many here who are not long in [the] church therefore I will give you a History of the Church according to My own Knowledge as they transpired[.] My Br Martin Harris[1] wrote near 200 pages and as he had wrote and advanced Money for the printing the same he thought he had some right to the writings consequently he desired to show them to some one[.][2] Joseph Enquired of the Lord [and] the answer was no[.] notwithstanding [this] he still persisted in doing the same[.] but on his way to Exebit the writings, he lost them[.] After I heard this i spoke of it to Many of My Nei=ghbours[.] the[y] thought i was some[one] singular and said i was intended to become somebody by the operation of this Book[.] As soon as i heard of this book i mad[e] all Enquiry to Obtain this Book, During this time Joseph hid the plates in the woods. the people hired an astrologer to finde the plates. he kept Track of them But could not finde them[.][3] Josephs friends send his Wife Emmy[4] on a stray horse to tell Joseph to come home for the plates were in Danger[.] he came and hid the plates under the House but as the house was built a little above the ground he removed them in a cooper shop [and] hid them in some flags[.] the same Night the floor in the house was took up[.] Next day he took them from the Shop from the flags and hid them in a Barrel of Beens and whil[e] he was Moveing a Mob gathered around him [p. 268][5] And would have got them but they could not finde them[.] so you see the Trouble Br joseph had to Bring the Book of Mormon forward[.] ~~Nel~~ Well I made all Enquiry respecting it[.] I saw from the Countinance of Joseph an[d] his Brothers that the thing was true[.] yes the[y] told me with all the Sincerity and simplicity of honest Men I Commenced to investigate and to be more particu=lar[.] Made a Concordance to it and i compared it with the Bible an[d] the Apockaphy [Apocrypha]. I ~~a~~ was at that time a Mec<h>anick and

1. On Martin Harris (1783-1875), see "Introduction to Martin Harris Collection."

2. The event Emer describes occurred in June 1828, more than a year before Martin mortgaged his land to print the Book of Mormon (see III.L.14, MARTIN HARRIS MORTGAGE, 25 AUG 1829). Martin had given $50 to help relocate Smith in Harmony, Pennsylvania.

3. Compare III.K.19, BRIGHAM YOUNG ACCOUNTS, 1855 & 1857.

4. On Emma Hale Smith (1804-79), see "Introduction to Emma Smith Collection."

5. At the top of page 269 is added in the same hand: "116 p[ages] lost not to be translated and the thing is hid from the Saints to this Day."

i tried the things by the Square[.] the Bible was My Square and i laid My Square on it [and] if it fit i concluded it was true. ... this the birth day of our Church let us Keep it Sacred as it this is the 26 year of the Church[.] now I will give way for some of my Bretheren[.] [p. 269] May the Lord Bless you amen ...

21.
PARLEY P. PRATT REMINISCENCE (PART I), 1856

Parley P. Pratt, "Discourse By Elder Parley P. Pratt, Bowery, Sunday, September 7th, 1856. Reported by J. V. Long," *Deseret News* 6 (24 December 1856): 332.

EDITORIAL NOTE

The following is an excerpt from a discourse delivered by Parley P. Pratt[1] in the bowery in Salt Lake City, Utah, on 7 September 1856, in which he recounted the events surrounding his early conversion to Mormonism.

... The first thing that attracted my attention towards this work was the Book of Mormon, I happened to see a copy of it. Some man, nearly a stranger to it, and not particularly a believer in it, happened to get hold of a copy; he made mention of it to me, and gave me the privilege of coming to his house and reading it. This was at a place about a day's journey from the residence of Joseph Smith, the Prophet, and his father,[2] and while I was returning to the work of my ministry; for I was then traveling and preaching, being connected with a society of people sometimes called Campbellites, or reformed Baptists.

I had diligently searched the scriptures, and prayed to God to open my mind that I might understand them; and he had poured his Spirit and understanding into my heart, so that I did understand the scriptures in a good degree, the letter of the gospel, its forms and first principles in their truth, as they are written in the Bible. These things were opened to my mind, but the power, the gifts and the authority of the gospel I knew were lacking, and did really expect that they would be restored, because I knew that the things that were predicted could never be fulfilled, until that power and that authority were restored. I also had an understanding of the literal fulfilment

1. On Parley P. Pratt (1807-57), see introduction to III.K.16, PARLEY P. PRATT AUTOBIOGRAPHY, CIRCA 1854.

2. Actually the residence of Hyrum Smith and his father; at this time (August 1830) Joseph Smith lived in Harmony, Pennsylvania.

of the prophecies in the Bible, so that I really did believe in and hope for the literal restoration of Israel, the cutting off of wickedness, the second coming of the Lord Jesus Christ and the triumph of his kingdom on the earth. All this I was looking for, and the Spirit seemed to whisper to my mind that I should see it in my day.

Under these circumstances I was traveling to impart the light which I had to others, and while doing this I found, as I before stated, the Book of Mormon. I read it carefully and diligently, a great share of it, without knowing that the priesthood had been restored, without ever having heard of anything called "Mormonism," or having any idea of such Church and people.

There were the witnesses and their testimony to the book, to its translation and to the ministration of angels, and there was the testimony of the translator, but I had not seen them, I had not heard of them, and hence I had no idea of their organization, or of their priesthood. All I knew about the matter was what, as a stranger, I could gather from the book; but as I read I was convinced that it was true, and the Spirit of the Lord came upon me while I read and enlightened my mind, convinced my judgment and reveted [riveted] the truth upon my understanding, so that I knew that the book was true, just as well as a man knows the daylight from the dark night, or any other thing that can be implanted in his understanding. I did not know it by any audible voice from heaven, by any ministration of an angel, by any open vision; but I knew it by the spirit of understanding in my heart, by the light that was in me. I knew it was true, because it was light and had come in fulfilment of the scriptures, and I bore testimony of its truth to the neighbors that came in during the first day that I sat reading it, at the house of an old Baptist deacon named Hamblin.[3]

This same Spirit led me to enquire after and search out the translator, Joseph Smith; and I traveled on foot during the whole of a very hot day in August [1830], blistering my feet, in order to go where I heard he lived; and at night I arrived in the neighborhood of the little village of Manchester, then in Ontario County, New York. On the way I overtook a man driving some cows, and enquired for Joseph Smith, the finder and translator of the Book of Mormon. He told me that he lived away off, something more than a hundred miles from there, in the State of Pennsylvania. I then enquired for the father of the Prophet, and he pointed to the house, but said that the old gentleman had gone a journey to some distant place. After a while, in

3. This person remains unidentified.

conversation, the man told me that his name was Hyrum Smith,[4] and that he was a brother to the Prophet Joseph. This was the first Latter Day Saint that I had ever seen.

He invited me to his home, where I saw mother [Lucy] Smith,[5] and Hyrum Smith's wife [Jerusha][6] and sister [Sarah] Rockwell,[7] the mother of Orin Porter Rockwell.[8] We sat up talking nearly all night, for I had not much spare time, having two appointments out and a long day's journey for a man to walk. I had to return the next morning, and we conversed during most of the night, without being either sleepy or weary.

During that conversation I learned something of the rights of the Church, its organization, the restoration of the priesthood and many important truths. I felt to go back and fill the two appointments given out, and that closed my ministry, as I felt that I had no authority and that I would go back and obey the priesthood which was again on the earth.

I attended to my appointments, and was back again the next morning to br. Hyrum's. He made me a present of the Book of Mormon, and I felt richer in the possession of that book, or the knowledge contained it, than I would could I have had a warrantee deed of all the farms and buildings in that country, and it was one of the finest regions in the world. I walked a while, and then sat down and read awhile, for it was not my mind to read the book through at once. I would read, and then read the same portion over again, and then walk on. I was filled with joy and gladness, my spirit was made rich, and it was made to rejoice, almost as vividly as if I had seen it myself, that the Lord Jesus Christ did appear in his own proper person, in his resurrected body, and minister to that people in America in ancient times. ...

As before stated, I fulfilled my two appointments; crowds heard me and were interested, and solicited me to make more appointments. I told them that I would not, that I had a duty to perform for myself. I bid them farewell,

---

4. On Hyrum Smith (1800-44), see I.A.15, JOSEPH SMITH HISTORY, 1839, n. 12.

5. On Lucy Smith (1775-1856), see "Introduction to Lucy Smith Collection."

6. On Jerusha Barden Smith (1805-37), see I.A.15, JOSEPH SMITH HISTORY, 1839, n. 120.

7. On Sarah Witt Rockwell (1785-?), see I.A.15, JOSEPH SMITH HISTORY, 1839, n. 90.

8. On Orrin Porter Rockwell (1813-78), see I.A.15, JOSEPH SMITH HISTORY, 1839, n. 121.

and returned to Hyrum Smith, who took me to a place, about twenty-five miles off, in Seneca county, New York. ...[9]

9. For Pratt's account of events in Fayette, New York, see VI.F.7, PARLEY P. PRATT REMINISCENCE (PART II), 1856.

22.
THOMAS B. MARSH AUTOBIOGRAPHY, 1857

Thomas B. Marsh, "History of Thomas Baldwin Marsh. (Written by himself in Great Salt Lake City, November 1857)," Manuscript History of Brigham Young, vol. G, 107-112, LDS Church Archives, Salt Lake City, Utah. Published in Thomas B. Marsh, "History of Tho[ma]s. Baldwin Marsh," *Deseret News* 8 (24 March 1858): 18; and reprinted in *Millennial Star* 26 (11 June 1864): 375.

EDITORIAL NOTE

Thomas B. Marsh (1799-1866) was born at Action, Middlesex County, Massachusetts. He married Elizabeth Godkin of Long Island, New York, in 1820, and soon set up a type foundry business in Boston, Massachusetts. Marsh appears in the 1830 census of Charleston, Middlesex County, Massachusetts, with his wife and three children (1830:42). In the present history, Marsh reports that he was travelling through western New York when he heard about Joseph Smith and the Book of Mormon. When curiosity led him to visit Palmyra, Marsh "found Martin Harris at the printing office ... where the first sixteen pages of the Book of Mormon had just been struck off, the proof sheet of which I obtained from the printer and took with me." He also visited the Smith residence and met Oliver Cowdery, "who gave me all the information concerning the book I desired." He was baptized by David Whitmer in Fayette, New York, on 3 September 1830, and soon after ordained an elder. The following year he moved from his home in Massachusetts and relocated at Kirtland, Ohio. An early revelation declared Marsh a "physician unto the church" (D&C 31:10). He was ordained a high priest in June 1831, and president of the Quorum of Twelve Apostles in April 1835. Following his excommunication for apostasy in 1839, Marsh remained in Missouri for eighteen years. After his rebaptism on 16 July 1857 at Florence, Nebraska, he immigrated to Utah, settling in Spanish Fork, Utah, where he taught school. He died at Ogden, Utah (Jenson 1971, 1:74-76; L. Cook 1981, 42-43; Jessee 1989, 499).

Marsh began writing his history the month following his arrival in Utah. The editor of the *Deseret News* informs readers that Marsh's history was "Written by himself in Great Salt Lake City, November 1857." Marsh's history is reproduced below from the Manuscript History of Brigham Young, written apparently in Thomas Bullock's hand.

... Immediately after marrying [in November 1820] I commenced in the grocery business, in New York, in which business I remained one and a half years, but did not succeed. I then engaged in a type foundry in Boston, where I continued seven years.

While engaged in this business I joined the Methodist church and tried for two years to be a genuine Methodist, but did not succeed any better in getting Methodist religion than I did in the grocery business. I compared Methodism with the Bible, but could not make it correspond.

I withdrew from all sects, and being about to leave Boston my old class leader wished me to take a good certificate, but I informed him I did not want it. I had a measure of the spirit of prophecy and told him that I expected a new church would arise, which would have the truth in its purity. He said to me, "You no doubt mean to be a leader in that new sect." I told him I had no such intentions. He said, he prayed that the Lord would make me a firebrand in the midst of that new religious body, as reformation was necessary. [p. 107]

My wife, unknown to me, however, got a certificate for herself and me on one paper. I informed her that I <never> would attend, but I would find a suitable class for her if she wanted to join.

I remained in Boston several years, engaged in the type foundry. During this period I became acquainted with several friends whose opinions concerning religion were like my own. We kept aloof from sectarians, and were called by them Quietists, because we resembled so much a sect in France known by that name professing to be led by the Spirit.

I believed the Spirit of God dictated me to make a journey west. I started in company with one Benjamin Hall,[1] who was also led by the Spirit. I went to Lima, Livingston county, New York, where I stayed some three months, and then left for home. I called on my return at Lyonstown, on a family, whose names I do not recollect. On leaving there next morning the lady enquired if I had heard of the Golden Book found by a youth named Joseph Smith. I informed her I never heard anything about it, and became very anxious to know con=cerning the matter. On enquiring, she told me I could learn more about it from Martin Harris,[2] in Palmyra.

---

1. This person remains unidentified.
2. On Martin Harris (1783-1875), see "Introduction to Martin Harris Collection."

I returned back westward and found Martin Harris at the printing office, in Palmyra, where the first sixteen pages of the Book of Mormon had just been struck off, the proof sheet of which I obtained from the printer and took with me.[3] As soon as Martin Harris found out my intentions he took me to the house of Joseph Smith Sen.,[4] where Joseph Smith Jun., resided,[5] who could give me any information I might wish. Here I found Oliver Cowdery,[6] who gave me all the information concerning the book I desired. After staying there two days I started for Charleston, Mass., highly pleased with the information I had obtained concerning the new found book.

After arriving home and finding my family all well, I showed my wife the sixteen pages of the Book of Mormon which I had obtained, with which she was well pleased, believing it to be the word of God. From this time for about one year I corresponded with Oliver Cowdery[7] and Joseph Smith Jun., and prepared myself to move west.

Learning by letter that the Church of Jesus Christ had been organized on the 6th day of April 1830, I moved to Palmyra, Ontario co., in September following, and landed at the house of Joseph Smith, sen., with my whole family. During this month I was baptized by David Whitmer, in Cayuga lake,[8] and in a few days I was ordained an Elder by Oliver Cowdery with six Elders, at Father Whitmer's house.[9]

Joseph received a revelation appointing me a physician to the church [D&C 31].

---

3. This occurred after printing began in late August 1829, probably after Joseph Smith's departure from the area in late September, and before 25 October 1829 when Oliver Cowdery mentioned receiving a letter from Marsh, who had returned to his home in Massachusetts (see III.F.3, OLIVER COWDERY TO JOSEPH SMITH, 6 NOV 1829, 8).

4. On Joseph Smith, Sr. (1771-1840), see "Introduction to Joseph Smith, Sr., Collection."

5. At this time (October 1829), Joseph Smith was living in Harmony, Pennsylvania.

6. On Oliver Cowdery (1806-50), see "Introduction to Oliver Cowdery Collection."

7. See III.F.2, OLIVER COWDERY TO JOSEPH SMITH, 6 NOV 1829, 8.

8. Marsh was baptized on 3 September 1830 (Porter 1971, 263).

9. Probably at the 26 September 1830 church conference (see VI.G.2, FAR WEST RECORD, 9 JUN 1830, 26 SEP 1830 & 2 JAN 1831). Smith mentions receiving a revelation "in the presence of six elders" (I.A.15, JOSEPH SMITH HISTORY, 1839, 56).

After remaining in that State, during the fall and winter the church moved to Ohio. In the spring of 1831 I journeyed with the main body to Kirtland. [p. 108] ...

23.
PHINEAS HOWE YOUNG AUTOBIOGRAPHY, 1863

[Phineas Howe Young], "History of Brigham Young," [History of Phineas Howe Young], *Millennial Star* 25 (6 June 1863): 360-61; and 25 (13 June 1863): 374-75.[1]

EDITORIAL NOTE

Phineas Howe Young (1799-1879), brother of Brigham Young, was born at Hopkinton, Massachusetts. He married Clarissa Hamilton in 1818, and later Lucy Cowdery, Oliver Cowdery's half sister. He was a Methodist preacher at the time he received a copy of the Book of Mormon from Samuel Smith in 1830. He was baptized in April 1832, and soon after moved to Kirtland, Ohio. In 1847 he emigrated to Utah. He died at Salt Lake City (Cannon and Cook 1983, 297; Cook and Backman 1985, 109; Jessee 1989, 525).

[*6 June 1863*]

In April, 1830, having received the Book of Mormon, as I was on my way home from the town of Lima [Livingston County, New York], where I had been to preach, I stopped at the house of a man by the name of Tomlinson,[2] to get some dinner. While engaged in conversation with the family, a young man came in, and walking across the room to where I was sitting, held a book towards me, saying,—"There is a book, sir, I wish you to read." The thing appeared so novel to me that for a moment I hesitated, saying,—"Pray, sir, what book have you?" "The Book of Mormon, or, as it is called by some, the Golden Bible." "Ah, sir, then it purports to be a revelation." "Yes," said he, "it is a revelation from God." I took the book, and by his request looked at the testimony of the witnesses. Said he—"If you will read this book with a prayerful heart, and ask God to give you a witness, you will know of the truth of this work." I told him I would do so, and then asked him his name. He said his name was Samuel H. Smith.[3] "Ah," said I,

---

1. Phineas Howe Young's history was published serially in the *Star* under the title "History of Brigham Young" and should not be confused with Brigham Young's history published under the same title, also in the *Star*.

2. This person remains unidentified.

3. On Samuel Harrison Smith (1808-44), see I.A.15, JOSEPH SMITH HISTORY, 1839, n. 13.

["]you are one of the witnesses." [p. 360] "Yes," said he, "I know the book to be a revelation from God, translated by the gift and power of the Holy Ghost, and that my brother Joseph Smith, jun., is a Prophet, Seer and Revelator."

This language seemed to me very strange, and, I thought, rather ridiculous; still I said but little more to him, but thought he must be deceived, and that the book was a production got up to lead people astray; however, I thought it my duty to read it, as I had promised, and search out the errors, and, as a teacher in Israel, expose such errors and save the people from the delusion.

I bought the book and went home, and told my wife I had got a week's work laid out, and I hoped that nothing would occur to prevent my accomplishing my task. She said, "Have you anything new to attend to?" I replied, "I have got a book here, called the Book of Mormon, and it is said to be a revelation, and I wish to read it and make myself acquainted with its errors, so that I can expose them to the world."

I commenced and read every word in the book the same week. The week following I did the same, but to my surprise I could not find the errors I anticipated, but felt a conviction that the book was true.

On the next Sabbath I was requested to give my views on the subject, which I commenced to do. I had not spoken ten minutes in defence of the book when the Spirit of God came upon me in a marvellous manner, and I spoke at great length on the importance of such a work, quoting from the Bible to support my position, and finally closed by telling the people that I believed the book. The greater part of the people agreed with my views, and some of them said they had never heard me speak so well and with such power. My father[4] then took the book home with him, and read it through. I asked him his opinion of it. He said it was the greatest work and the clearest of error of anything he had ever seen, the Bible not excepted.

I then lent the book to my sister Fanny Murray.[5] She read it and declared it a revelation. Many others did the same. [p. 361]

---

4. John Young (1763-1839) (see III.K.24, HEBER C. KIMBALL AUTOBIOGRAPHY, 1864, n. 4).

5. Fanny Young (1787-1859), daughter of John Young, was born at Hopkinton, Massachusetts. She married Robert Carr in 1803. She also married Roswell Murray in 1832, and Joseph Smith in 1843. She died at Salt Lake City (Arrington 1985, 418; L. Cook 1981, 120 n. 4).

[*13 June 1863*]

In August [1830] following, my brother Joseph Young[6] came from Canada to see me. He had been there preaching, and having a desire to have me in this field of labor for a season, he came over to the States with the intention of getting me to go back with him.

We accordingly left for Kingston, in Upper Canada, about the 20th of August [1830]; and passing through the town of Lyons [Wayne County, New York], we called on an old acquaintance by the name of Solomon Chamberlain.[7] We had no sooner got seated than he began to preach Mormonism to us. He told us there was a Church organized, and ten or more were baptized, and every body must believe the Book of Mormon or be lost.

I told him to hold on, when he had talked about two hours setting forth the wonders of Mormonism—that it was not good to give a colt a bushel of oats at a time. I knew that my brother had but little idea of what he was talking, and I wanted he should have time to reflect; but it made little difference to him, he still talked of Mormonism.

We tarried a short time with him and then went on our way, pondering upon the things we had heard. This was the first I had heard of the necessity of another church, or of the importance of re-baptism; but after hearing the old gentleman's arguments on the importance of the power of the holy Priesthood, and the necessity of its restoration in order that the power of the Gospel might be made manifest, I began to inquire seriously into the matter, and soon became convinced that such an order of things was necessary for the salvation of the world.

We soon reached the place of our destination, it being but 18 miles from Kingston, in Earnest Town, where we commenced our labor. I tarried some time with my brother, trying to preach, but could think of but little except the Book of Mormon and what I had heard of Mormonism.

One day after I had been preaching in Loborough, I said to my brother, "What did you think of my preaching to-day?" "O," said he, "if you had just come from the priest factory in the States, I should have thought you did very well, but I don't think there was much God in it." I then told him

6. On Joseph Young (1797-1881), see I.B.5, LUCY SMITH HISTORY, 1845, n. 286.

7. On Solomon Chamberlain (1788-1862), see introduction to III.J.1, SOLOMON CHAMBERLAIN ACCOUNTS, 1845 & CIRCA 1858.

I could not preach, and that I should return home. I accordingly started in a few days.

On my way I attended a quarterly meeting, held by the Episcopal Methodists in Kingston, at the close of their Annual Conference. At the close of the meeting an Indian gave an appointment to preach in the British Chapel [p. 374] at early candle-light. I determined to go, for the Book of Mormon and the Lamanites were before me continually. As soon as the candles were lit, I was in my seat near the desk. The preacher was there and soon commenced. I listened with great interest while he set forth the traditions of his fathers in a masterly way, and made many statements corroborating the truth of the Book of Mormon.

After meeting I went to my hotel, where the most of the members of the conference assembled for the night. I think Bishops Heading and George were present. After all were seated in two large rooms, I took my place at the door between the two rooms, and, calling the attention of the people, I asked them if any one present had ever read the Book of Mormon? I paused for an answer, and after a short pause a gentleman said that he had never seen or heard of such a work. I then said the book was called by some the Golden Bible.

This seemed to take the attention of the whole assembly, consisting of more than one hundred. A gentleman requested me, in behalf of the people present, to give them some account of the book. I commenced by telling them that it was a revelation from God, translated from the Reformed Egyptian language by Joseph Smith, jun., by the gift and power of God, and gave a full account of the aborigines of our country, and agreed with many of their traditions, of which we had been hearing this evening, and that it was destined to overthrow all false religions, and finally to bring in the peaceful reign of the Messiah.

I had forgotten everything but my subject, until I had talked a long time and told many things I had never thought of before. I bore a powerful testimony to the work, and thus closed my remarks and went to bed, not to sleep, but to ponder with astonishment at what I had said, and to wonder with amazement at the power that seemed to compel me thus to speak.

The next morning I took passage on a packet for the States, landed at Old Oswego, took passage on a canal-packet for Manlius Square [Onondaga County, New York], where I met a great number of my friends who had assembled for our Annual Conference; among the number was my old friend Solomon Chamberlain. He told me he had come to offer the conference the Book of Mormon, saying that if they rejected it they would all go to destruction. He soon filled his mission, and was driven from the place by the voice of the conference.

One man whose name was Buckley,[8] and an elder in the Methodist Reformed Church, railed on brother Chamberlain and abused him shamefully. He immediately went crazy, and was carried home to the town of Smyrnia, a distance of 20 or 30 miles, and died in a few days raving mad.

I attended the conference, bore my testimony, and left for home in company with my brother-in-law, John P. Greene.[9]

On our arrival we found our families all well. I still continued to preach, trying to tie Mormonism to Methodism, for more than a year, when I found that they had no connection and could not be united, and that I must leave the one and cleave to the other.

About this time my brother Brigham[10] came to see me, and very soon told me that he was convinced that there was something in Mormonism. I told him I had long been satisfied of that. ...[11]

---

8. This person, also named by Chamberlain, remains unidentified (III.J.1, SOLOMON CHAMBERLAIN ACCOUNTS, 1854 & CIRCA 1858, 2:11-12).

9. John Portineus Greene (1793-1844) was born at Herkimer, New York. He married Rhoda Young, sister of Brigham Young. He was baptized in 1832 and soon after moved to Kirtland, Ohio. He died in Illinois (Cannon and Cook 1983, 264).

10. On Brigham Young (1801-77), see introduction to III.K.19, BRIGHAM YOUNG ACCOUNTS, 1855 & 1857.

11. Phineas then recounts the events leading up to his baptism on 5 April 1832, beginning with his introduction in January 1832 to the Saints living in Bradford County, Pennsylvania.

24.
HEBER C. KIMBALL AUTOBIOGRAPHY, 1864

Heber C. Kimball, "History of Brigham Young," [History of Heber C. Kimball], *Millennial Star* 26 (23 July 1864): 472; and 26 (30 July 1864): 487.

EDITORIAL NOTE

Heber C. Kimball (1801-68) was born at Sheldon, Franklin County, Vermont. His family moved to West Bloomfield, New York, where he apprenticed as a blacksmith and a potter. He married Vilate Murray in November 1822 at Mendon, New York. In April 1832 he was baptized and soon after ordained an elder. The following year he moved to Kirtland, Ohio, where he worked as a potter. He was ordained an apostle in February 1835. In 1847 he emigrated to Salt Lake City, and soon after was sustained as a counselor to Brigham Young. He died at Salt Lake City (L. Cook 1981, 263-64).

A significant feature of Kimball's autobiography is his description of seeing unusual phenomena in the earth's atmosphere, which he later believed had occurred the night Joseph Smith had removed the plates from the hill. Kimball's account is only the most elaborate version of a modern religious myth that developed among early Mormon converts. Pomeroy Tucker reported in 1867 that "Smith told a frightful story of the display of celestial pyrotechnics on the exposure to his view of the sacred book" on 22 September 1827, adding that "this story was repeated and magnified by the believers" (III.J.8, POMEROY TUCKER ACCOUNT, 1867, 30-31). Frederick G. Mather reported in 1880 that "according to the faithful," Smith's removal of the plates from the hill was accompanied by "a mighty display of celestial machinery" (III.J.13, ORLANDO SAUNDERS, WILLIAM VAN CAMP, AND JOHN H. GILBERT INTERVIEWS WITH FREDERICK G. MATHER, JUL 1880, 200).

Among the "faithful" who joined Kimball in reporting the appearance of unusual atmospheric phenomena the night Joseph Smith obtained the plates was Aaron M. Baldwin, a resident of western New York who, according to an 1882 reminiscence of his son Nathan B. Baldwin, saw the signs in the heavens, including visions of armies and other scenes, in 1827; like Kimball, Baldwin later learned that it was on the night that Smith received the plates (Nathan B. Baldwin, Journal, LDS Church Archives, Salt Lake City, Utah). Jonathan H. Hale reported that his father, Solomon Hale, also a resident of western New York, had seen on the night of 22 September 1827 the same phenomena in the sky (see Jonathan H. Hale, Journal, typescript, 5-6, LDS Church Archives, Salt Lake City, Utah). Benjamin F. Johnson, who lived in Pomfret, Chataqua County, New York, with his parents, remembered in an autobiography he began writing in 1885:

> In the year 1829, in our village paper, was published an account of some young man professing to have seen an angel, who had shown and delivered to him golden plates, engraved in a strange language and hid up in the earth, from which he had translated a new Bible, and I could hardly refrain from wishing or hoping it might be so. I think it was the year previous [1828?] that there was seen at night in the heavens a large ball of light, like fire, which passed from the east to the western horizon. My older brothers who were out hunting coons, saw it and came home to tell of the wonder they had seen. When I asked mother what its cause or meaning was, she said it was one of the signs of the near approach of the coming of Christ, or the day of judgment. This remained upon my mind a subject of deep thought, and I afterwards learned from those who should know, that this sign was given the night following the day on which the plates were taken from the earth by the Prophet Joseph (B. F. Johnson 1947, 9-10).

Atmospheric phenomena such as the northern lights and meteor showers were occasional events in that time. Parley P. Pratt, for instance, saw similar phenomena in September 1830 (see VI.F.6, PARLEY P. PRATT AUTOBIOGRAPHY, CIRCA 1854 [PART II], 45-46), and Joseph Smith recorded a similar sighting in his journal under the date 13 November 1833 (Faulring 1987, 14). Presently there is no corroborative evidence to support the early Mormon reminiscences linking atmospheric phenomena and Smith's obtaining the plates. Stanley B. Kimball, Heber C. Kimball's biographer, has reported: "The Director of the Local History Division of the Rochester Public Library and the Monroe County Historian were unable to locate any contemporary account of this event" (Kimball 1981, 22 n. 10). I also failed in the attempt. Moreover, if such signs were displayed on the night of 22 September 1827, both Joseph Smith and his mother Lucy failed to mention it in their histories. Other observers close to the Mormon advent—such as Joseph Knight and Martin Harris—are similarly silent. It is not improbable that atmospheric phenomena occurred in 1827 or 1828, which at the time were interpreted as a sign of Jesus' coming but later reinterpreted and associated with the coming forth of the Book of Mormon. Johnson admitted that he could not remember when the phenomenon occurred, but was persuaded by others that it was on 22 September 1827. Likewise, Kimball did not put the two events together in his mind for at least three years, sometime after he first heard Mormonism preached in 1830. Because it is the most detailed and elaborate version of the early Mormon myth, perhaps triggering in Kimball a simultaneous visionary experience, Kimball's account is included in this collection.

[*23 July 1864*]

... Sept. 22, 1827, while living in the town of Mendon, I having retired to bed, John P. Greene,[1] a travelling reformed Methodist preacher, waked me up calling upon me to behold the scenery in the heavens. I called my wife[2] and sister Fanny Young[3] (sister of Brigham Young) who was living with me; it was so clear that you could see to pick up a pin, we looked to the eastern horizon and beheld a white smoke arise towards the heavens, and as it ascended it formed itself into a belt, and made a noise like the rushing of a mighty wind, and continned [continued] southwest, forming a regular bow dipping in the western horizon. After the bow had formed it began to widen out and grow clear and transparent of a blueish cast, it grew wide enough to contain twelve men abreast.

In this bow an army moved, commencing from the east and marching to the west. They moved in platoons, and walked so close, the rear ranks trod in the steps of their file leaders, until the whole bow was literally crowded with soldiers. We could see distinctly the muskets, bayonets, and knapsacks of the men, who wore caps and feathers like those used by the American soldiers in the last war [of 1812] with Britain; also their officers with their swords and equipage, and heard the clashing and jingling of their instruments of war and could discover the form and features of the men. The most profound order existed throughout the entire army, when the foremost man stepped, every man stepped at the same time: I could hear the step. When the front rank reached the Western horizon a battle ensued, as we could distinctly hear the report of the arms and the rush. [p. 472]

[*30 July 1864*]

No man could judge of my feelings when I beheld that army of men,

---

1. On John Portineus Greene (1793-1844), see III.K.23, PHINEAS HOWE YOUNG AUTOBIOGRAPHY, 1863, n. 9.

2. Vilate Murray Kimball, daughter of Roswell and Susannah Murray, was born in 1806 at Florida, New York. She married Heber C. Kimball in November 1822 (Jenson 1971, 1:34).

3. On Fanny Young (1787-1859), see III.K.23, PHINEAS HOWE YOUNG AUTOBIOGRAPHY, 1863, n. 5.

as plainly as I ever saw armies of men in the flesh; it seemed as though every hair of my head was alive. This scenery we gazed upon for hours, until it began to disappear.

Subsequently I learned this took place the same evening that Joseph Smith received the records of the Book of Mormon from the Angel Moroni. John Young, sen.,[4] and John P. Green's wife, Rhoda,[5] were also witnesses of this scenery. My wife, Vilate, being frightened at what she saw, said 'Father Young, what does all this mean?' He replied in a lively, pleased manner, 'why, its one of the signs of the coming of the Son of Man.' The next night similar scenery was beheld in the west, by the neighbors, representing armies of men who were engaged in battle. ... [p. 487]

---

4. John Young (1763-1839), father of Brigham Young, was born at Hopkinton, Massachusetts. He married Abigail (Nabby) Howe in 1785. He is listed in the 1830 census of Mendon, Monroe County, New York (1830:116). He was baptized in 1832 and died at Quincy, Illinois (Arrington 1985, 418).

5. Rhoda Young Greene, daughter of John Young, was born in 1789 in Plataua district, New York. She married John Portineus Greene on 11 February 1813 (Jenson 1971, 2:633).

25.
Silas Hillman Reminiscence, 1866

Silas Hillman, Autobiography (1838-1875), January 1866, Special Collections, Herald B. Lee Library, Brigham Young University, Provo, Utah.

EDITORIAL NOTE

Silas Hillman (1820-?) was born in New York. His parents, Mayhew (1793-1839) and Sarah (King) Hillman (1797-1870), were converted through the preaching of Solomon Chamberlain at Spafford, Onondaga County, New York, in early 1831 (see III.J.1, SOLOMON CHAMBERLAIN ACCOUNTS, 1845 & CIRCA 1858). In the fall of 1833 the Hillmans moved to Kirtland, Ohio. Afterwards Silas lived in Missouri, then Nauvoo, Illinois, where in 1843 he married his first wife. After the death of his wife, he married Emily Ann Cox in 1850. He immigrated to Utah in 1852 and soon after became a counselor to Bishop Stephen Markham in the Palmyra, Utah, ward. In 1857 he moved to Spanish Fork, where he was elected justice of the peace two years later. In 1871 he moved to Faust Station, Rush Valley, Utah, where his autobiography ends (see Bitton 1977, 157; Backman 1983, 35; Cook and Backman 1985, 87). The portion of Hillman's autobiography that follows is his account of his early conversion to Mormonism and is dated January 1866.

My Father & Mother emigrated when I was three years old from Washington County[,] St[ate] of N.Y., to the west about 160 miles in the Same St[ate] the county being new and opened up a new farm we lived there in a town by the name of Spafford, County of ~~Gea~~ Onon=dagua. In the year 1831, a man by the name of Chamberlain came there bringing the book of Mormon: he gave a history of its origin, how it was obtained, and its translation. A young man by the name of Joseph Smith: was visited by an Angel of the Lord: who informed him that a record of an Ancient people that once inherited this land was hid up unto the Lord in a cirtain hill in Palmyra[,] N.Y. He was informed that if he would obey the instruction of the Angel: that in the due time of the Lord. He shoul[d] have power to obtain the record and have power given him to translate them, which was fulfilled: and the man spoken of had the said translation printed and bound. And it was called the book of Mormon. I believed it when I first became acquainted with it. I was then only 11 years old: My mother was baptized Soon after and father Soon after Mother. Father Sold his farm and in the faul [fall] of 1833 Started for Kirtland[,] Ohio. ...

26.
HAMILTON CHILD ACCOUNT, 1867

Hamilton Child (1836-?), *Gazetteer and Business Directory of Wayne County, N.Y. for 1867-8* (Syracuse, New York: Journal Office, 1867), 52-54.

... Here [Palmyra, Wayne County, New York] the insidious monster, Mormonism, was nursed and cradled; which, like the "serpent in Eden," has chosen for its victims the fairest of God's creatures. For 37 years it has dragged its slimy footsteps through the annals of American history. Its progenitor, [p. 52] Joseph Smith Jr., was born in Sharon, Windson [Windsor] county, Vt., Dec. 23, 1805. He removed to Palmyra, with his father, Joseph Sr.,[1] and family, in 1815 or '16.[2] They soon after moved just over the town line into Manchester, some two miles south-west of Palmyra village. Joseph Smith, the father of the "Prophet," previous to the Mormon dispensation, supported himself and family by digging and peddling "rutes and yarbs," selling cake, beer, &c.[3] In 1819 or '20, they commenced digging for money for a subsistence.[4] The vocation was noised around among the community, and not a few were credulous enough to believe that they were within reach of a "chest of gold," ("which had repeatedly eluded their grasp,") and contributed money to the Smiths to enable them to continue their excavations. They, however, used the money thus obtained for the support of the family, and in the meantime kept their friends in a fever of excitement while treasure hunting. ...[5] Joseph Smith would repair at night to a cave in the hillside, and dictate to his amanuensis, (Oliver Cowdery,)[6] what he "mysteriously translated from golden plates," which he pretended to have found while digging

1. On Joseph Smith, Sr. (1771-1840), see "Introduction to Joseph Smith, Sr., Collection."

2. Joseph Smith, Sr., probably arrived in the summer or fall of 1816, and Lucy and the children in the winter of 1816-17 (see I.B.5, LUCY SMITH HISTORY, 1845, n. 69).

3. Compare III.J.5, POMEROY TUCKER REMINISCENCE, 1858.

4. Perhaps following Pomeroy Tucker's dating (see III.J.8, POMEROY TUCKER ACCOUNT, 1867, 19).

5. Child's brief discussion of the Spaulding theory has been deleted.

6. On Oliver Cowdery (1806-50), see "Introduction to Oliver Cowdery Collection."

for money in Sept. 1823, by spirit of revelation, but was not permitted to take them from the earth until 1827, about the time the Bible was commenced. The greatest secrecy was observed during the pretended revelations, which were only given in the cave at night, without any light, no one else being able to read the inscription on the plates but he.[7] When it was completed, they were in a great dilemma to know [p. 53] how they were to get it printed. This difficulty was soon obviated by Martin Harris,[8] a convert, mortgaging his farm to defray the expenses, ruining himself in doing so.[9] Application was made about June 1829, to Mr. Egbert B. Grandin,[10] the publisher of the *Wayne Sentinel* at Palmyra, for the printing of the book.[11] Grandin at once advised them against the supposed folly of the enterprise. All importunity, however, was resisted by Harris, and resented with assumed pious indignation by Smith. Upon the refusal of Grandin, they applied the same year to Mr. Weed, of the *Anti-Masonic Inquirer,* at Rochester [New York], and there met with a similar refusal.[12] They again applied to Mr. Grandin, who, upon seeing their determination, consented to print it, stipulating to print 5,000 copies of the book for a compensation of $3,000. ...

---

7. The assertion that Smith translated the plates in a cave is repeated in several sources (e.g., III.J.8, POMEROY TUCKER ACCOUNT, 1867, 48-49).

8. On Martin Harris (1783-1875), see "Introduction to Martin Harris Collection."

9. See III.L.14, MARTIN HARRIS MORTGAGE, 25 AUG 1829.

10. On Egbert B. Grandin (1806-45), see I.A.15, JOSEPH SMITH HISTORY, 1839, n. 77.

11. Compare III.J.8, POMEROY TUCKER ACCOUNT, 1867, 50.

12. See III.K.17, THURLOW WEED REMINISCENCES, 1854, 1858, 1880 & 1884.

27.
THOMAS DAVIES BURRALL REMINISCENCE, 1867

"Joe Smith, the Mormon Prophet," *Rochester Daily Union and Advertiser* 40 (1 October 1867): 3. Reprinted in *Louisville* (Kentucky) *Daily Courier* 36 (5 October 1867): 1.

EDITORIAL NOTE

Thomas Davies Burrall (1786-1872) settled in Geneva, New York, in 1812. He purchased a large tract of land in 1814. Most of the 370-acre lot was timbered, so he employed a large number of wood cutters to clear the land. For convenience Burrall divided the men into groups of ten to fifteen, each group headed by a foreman who paid the men under him. The foreman of one of the groups was a "Joe Smith," whom Burrall mistook for the Joseph Smith he later heard had become the Mormon prophet. The history of Geneva published in 1912 evidently relates the same story:

> Joe Smith from about 1812, was a laborer on the farm in what is now the northern section of Geneva. It was said of him at this time that he was in every way unworthy of confidence, in fact, an unprincipled scalawag. But this Smith, a little after being discharged for dishonesty, "discovered" in the western part of Ontario County the gold plates of the book of Mormon, upon which later the Mormon Church was founded. ... (Monroe 1912, 40-41).

The claim that Joseph Smith was a laborer on a Geneva farm from 1812 to 1820 has obvious difficulties since Smith was only seven to twelve years of age and his family did not arrive in the area from Vermont until 1816-17. Burrall obviously employed a much older man named "Joe Smith" and confused him with the Mormon prophet.

Burrall also includes an account of Martin Harris's application for a loan with the New York Life Insurance and Trust Company of Geneva, which Charles Butler verified had occurred (see III.F.3, MARTIN HARRIS INTERVIEW WITH CHARLES BUTLER, CIRCA 1830-1831).

MESSRS. EDITORS:—In your last evening's paper (Saturday) in speaking of Mr. Tucker's forthcoming book on Mormonism, you ask who and what was Joe Smith, and you speak of men in Western New York who can intelligently answer these and more questions from personal knowledge.

I knew him well before his book was published. He was then a woodcutter on my farm, more willing to live by his wits than his axe, and worked through the winter in company with some twenty or thirty others, rough back-woodsmen. He and his two associates built a rude cabin of poles and brush, covered with leaves and earth, in the woods open to the south, with a camp-kettle in front for cooking; and here, at night, around a huge fire, he and his companions would gather, ten or a dozen at a time, to tell hard stories, and sing songs and drink cheap whisky, (two shillings per gallons[)], and although there were some hard cases among them, Joe could beat them all for tough stories and impracticable adventures, and it was in this school, I believe, that he first conceived his wonderful invention of the golden plates and marvelous revelations. And as these exercises were rehearsed nightly to his hearers, and as their ears grew longer to receive them, so his tales grew the more marvelous to please them, until some of them supposed that *he also* believed his own stories. But of this fact there is no proof. He was impudent and assuming among his fellows, but ignorant and dishonest, plausible and obsequious to others, with sufficient low cunning to conceal his ignorance, but in my estimation, utterly unqualified to compose even such a jumble of truth and fiction as his book contained.

The most probable theory of its origin that I remember to have heard, is that it was the strange work of an eccentric Vermont clergyman, written to while away the tedious hours of long confinement by nervous debility, and that this idle production, after his decease, fell into Joe's hands, and that having learned something of the gullibility of his cronies, this incidental matter incited in him the first idea of turning his foolish stories to account, and thus enable him to make the surreptitious manuscript the text-book of his gross imposition. I speak understandingly in saying he was shameless as well as dishonest, and I relate a small matter to prove it. During the winter he was chopping for me, I was in the habit of riding through the clearing daily to see that the brush was piled as agreed, the wood fairly corded and no scattering trees left uncut, and in this way became well acquainted with the conduct of every man; and on each Saturday took an account and paid the hands. My mode was to ride around while each party measured their ranks and turned a few sticks on the top to show they had been counted. In this way I one day took Joe's account, he accompanying me and removing the sticks on the top of each rank. After thus going the rounds and returning to the shanty, he said he had another rank or two that I had not seen, and led me in a different direction in a roundabout way, to wood that I had already measured, but the sticks on top had all been laid back to their places. I saw the trick at once, and could only make him confess his attempt to cheat by re-measuring the whole lot; and all this he thought would have been a fair trick if I had not found it out. So much for the man in small things.

After he left in the spring I lost sight of him until my friend Judge Whiting[1] (long since deceased) of the very respectable firm of Whiting & Butler, attorneys, who was then loaning money on mortgages for a trust company, asked me if I knew anything about Joe Smith. I told him that I knew him for a great rogue in a small way, when he informed me that he pretended to be a prophet, and was about publishing a Book of Revelations; and had induced two credulous men in Palmyra to apply to him (Judge W[hiting].) for money on mortgage to publish it.[2]

I learned afterward that Joe and an associate had prevailed on a worthy citizen of Waterloo (Col. C.)[3] who was then in a state of great depression from the recent loss of his wife, to join their fraternity and cast in his lot among them; and that while they were at his house taking an inventory of his effects for the purpose, his son, a spirited young man, came in, and on finding what they were about threatened them so strongly with a prosecution as swindlers, that they left for the time until his father had recovered from his delusion, and thus escaped them.

I know nothing further of his doings here, but after his removal to Ohio, when he established a bank that failed, I was shown one of his bills, and I recollect that on examining it I thought the device on the face of it was most admirably appropriate, viz: *A sturdy fellow shearing a sheep.*

T.D.B.

---

1. Bowen Whiting was state senator, district attorney of Ontario County, and partner with Charles Butler in the New York Life Insurance and Trust Company of Geneva (see III.F.3, MARTIN HARRIS INTERVIEW WITH CHARLES BUTLER, CIRCA 1830-1831). Whiting, in his thirties, is listed in the 1830 census of Seneca, Ontario County, New York (1830:84; also 1840:125).

2. Martin Harris applied for a second mortgage on his farm with Charles Butler, perhaps in 1830 or early 1831 (see III.F.3, MARTIN HARRIS INTERVIEW WITH CHARLES BUTLER, CIRCA 1830-1831). On the claim that there were "two credulous men" who mortgaged their farms to pay for the Book of Mormon's printing, see also III.J.26, DANIEL HENDRIX REMINISCENCE, 1879, where it is stated that in addition to Harris a Mr. "Andrews" of Auburn, New York, mortgaged property in order to raise publication funds. However, since Harris's mortgage was sufficient to cover the entire cost of printing, there was no need for an additional mortgager.

3. This person remains unidentified.

28.
W. H. McIntosh, *History of Ontario County* (NY), 1876

[W. H. McIntosh], *History of Ontario Co., New York* (Philadelphia: Everts, Ensign and Everts, 1876), 42-43.

EDITORIAL NOTE

W. H. McIntosh[1] based his account of early Mormonism on those of Orsamus Turner and Pomeroy Tucker (see III.J.2, ORSAMUS TURNER ACCOUNT, 1851; and III.J.8, POMEROY TUCKER ACCOUNT, 1867). See also III.K.29, W. H. MCINTOSH, *HISTORY OF WAYNE COUNTY* (NY), 1877.

... Mormonism had its origin in Ontario County. The natural credulity of the ignorant has ever made them the dupes of design, and there has never been a creed promulgated so fallacious or so monstrous but that it has found followers. Indignant citizens have ejected the contaminating influence from their midst, and, glorified by persecution, the evil has grown and perpetuated itself. Time hallows the past, custom sanctions usage, and the usurper in the course of events becomes authority. The society of Jemima Wilkinson soon dissolved, but the new religion with active workers drew proselytes from every quarter, and numbers thousands of firm believers. It is of interest, then, to place on record here a brief outline of its founder. The father of Joseph Smith[2] was from near the Merrimac river, New Hampshire. His first settlement was in or near Palmyra village, but in 1819 he became the occupant of new land on Stafford street, Manchester, near the Palmyra line. His cabin was of the rudest, and a small tract about it was underbrushed as a clearing. He had been a Universalist, but had changed to Methodism. His character was that of a weak, credulous, litigious man.[3]

---

1. I have been unable to specifically identify W. H. McIntosh. The Family History Library of the LDS church, Salt Lake City, identifies him as Walter H. McIntosh, but I have been unable to verify this identification.

2. On Joseph Smith, Sr. (1771-1840), see "Introduction to Joseph Smith, Sr., Collection."

3. Compare this paragraph with III.J.2, ORSAMUS TURNER ACCOUNT, 1851; and III.J.8, POMEROY TUCKER ACCOUNT, 1867, 212-13.

Mrs. Smith,[4] originally designing profit and notoriety, was the source from which the religion of the Latter-Day Saints was to originate. The Smiths had two sons. The elder, Alvah [Alvin],[5] sickened and died, and Joseph was designated as the coming prophet,—a subject the most unpromising in appearance and ability. Legends of hidden treasure had pointed to Mormon Hill as the depository. Father and son had visited the place and dug for buried wealth by midnight, and it seemed natural that the Smiths should in time connect themselves with the plan of a new creed, with Joseph Smith as the founder. As the scheme developed, Oliver Cowdery[6] and Martin Harris[7] gave it their support, and Sydney Rigdon[8] joined the movement later. Cowdery was a school-teacher in the district, and intimate with the Smiths. Harris was owner of a good farm two miles north of Palmyra village. The farm went to pay for the publication of the Mormon Bible. Harris was an honest, worthy man, but a religious enthusiast. Rigdon came from Ohio, and attached himself to the scheme of imposture. He had been a Baptist preacher, but had forfeited his standing by disreputable action. His character was that of a designing, dishonest, disreputable man. In him the Smiths found an able manager, and he found them fit agents of his schemes. Joseph Smith, Jr., had in his possession a miraculous stone, opaque to others, luminous and transparent to himself. It was of the common hornblende variety, and was kept in a box, carefully wrapped in cotton. Placed in a hat, and looked upon, Smith alleged ability to locate hidden treasure. Mrs. Smith made and sold oil-cloths, and, while so engaged, prophesied a new religion, of which her son should be the prophet. One morning as the settlers went to their work a rumor circulated that the Smiths, in a midnight expedition, had commenced digging on the northwest spur of Mormon Hill, and had unearthed several heavy golden tablets covered with hieroglyphics. It was stated that Joseph was able to translate this record, and was engaged upon the work. To make money and indulge a love of notoriety was the first plan, and to found a new religion a later thought. The mysterious symbols were to be translated

---

4. On Lucy Smith (1775-1856), see "Introduction to Lucy Smith Collection."

5. On Alvin Smith (1798-1823), see I.A.15, JOSEPH SMITH HISTORY, 1839, n. 10.

6. On Oliver Cowdery (1806-50), see "Introduction to Oliver Cowdery Collection."

7. On Martin Harris (1783-1875), see "Introduction to Martin Harris Collection."

8. On Sidney Rigdon (1793-1876), see introduction to I.A.13, SIDNEY RIGDON ACCOUNT, CIRCA 1836.

and published in book-form. Money was wanted, and Harris mortgaged his farm for two thousand five hundred dollars, which was to secure him half the proceeds of the sales of the Gold Bible. Joseph Smith told Harris that an angel had directed where on Mormon Hill the golden plates lay buried, and he himself unwillingly must interpret and publish the sacred writing, which was alleged to contain a record of the ancients of America, engraved by Mormon, the son of Neephi [Nephi]. Upon the box in which were the plates had been found large spectacles, whose glasses were transparent only to the prophet. None save Smith were to see the plates, on pain of death. Harris and Cowdery were the amanuenses, who wrote as Smith, screened from their view, dictated. Days passed, and the work proceeded. Harris took his copy home, to place in the hands of the type-setters. His wife a woman of sense and energy. She seized one hundred pages of the new revelation, and they were burned or concealed. This portion was not again written, lest the first being found, the versions should not agree. The author of the manuscript pages from which the book was published is unknown. One theory gives them as the work of a Mr. Spaulding, of Ohio, who wrote it as a religious novel, left the manuscript with a printer, and, being appropriated by Rigdon, was brought to Manchester and turned to account.[9] The general and most probable opinion is that Smith and Cowdery were the authors, from these reasons: it is a poor attempt at counterfeiting the Scriptures; modern language is inconsistently blended, and chronology and geography are at variance. It is a strange medley of Scripture, to which is appended a "Book of Commandments," the work of Rigdon, perhaps assisted by Spaulding's papers. The date of the Gold Bible is fixed as the fall of 1827. The first edition of the Book of Mormon was printed by E. B. Grandin,[10] of Palmyra, New York, and consisted of five thousand copies. The work of printing began June [18]29. It was completed in 1830, and offered for sale at [p. 42] one dollar and twenty-five cents per copy, but it would not sell. Smith went to Pennsylvania, clad in a new suit from funds provided by Harris; here he married a daughter of Isaac Hale,[11] and both were baptized by Rigdon after the Mormon ritual.[12] This wife is living near Nau-

---

9. On the Spaulding theory of the Book of Mormon's origin, see Bush 1977.

10. On Egbert B. Grandin (1806-45), see I.A.15, JOSEPH SMITH HISTORY, 1839, n. 77.

11. On Emma Hale Smith (1804-79), see "Introduction to Emma Smith Collection."

12. This error was probably based on III.J.8, POMEROY TUCKER ACCOUNT, 1867, 56. Joseph Smith was baptized by Oliver Cowdery on 15 May 1829, and Emma Smith by Cowdery on 28 June 1830. This occurred

voo, Illinois, in comfortable circumstances. The original edition of the book has this preface: "The *Book of Mormon*; an account, written by the hand of Mormon upon plates taken from the plates of Nephi," and concludes with "By Joseph Smith, Jr., *Author* and *Proprietor*." Later editions designate Smith "translator." The contents give fifteen "Books," and the edition contains five hundred and eighty-eight pages, common duodecimo, small pica letter. A formal organization was desirable. A meeting was held at the house of Joseph Smith, Sr., in June [April?], 1830. The exercises consisted of readings and interpretations of the new Bible. Smith, Sr., was installed "Patriarch and President of Latter-Day Saints."[13] Cowdery and Harris were given limited and conditional offices. From the house the party adjourned to a brook near by, where a pool had been made by the construction of a small dam. Harris and Cowdery were first baptized at their own request.[14] The latter, now qualified, administered the same rite to Joseph Smith, Sr., Mrs. Smith, his wife, Hiram Page, Mrs. Rockwell, Dolly Proper, and some of the Whitemer brothers.[15] Calvin Stoddard,[16] a neighbor, early believed in Mormonism, and was possessed with the notion that he should go out and preach the gospel. While in a state of doubt, two men, Stephen S. Harding[17] and Abner Tucker,[18] played a practical joke, which confirmed his faith. At midnight they repaired to his house, struck three heavy blows with a stone upon his door, awaking him; then one solemnly spoke, "Calvin Stoddard! the angel of the Lord commands that before another going down of the sun thou shalt go forth among the people and preach the gospel of Nephi, or thy wife shall be a widow, thy children orphans, and thy ashes scattered to the four winds of heaven."[19]

---

prior to Rigdon's arrival in December 1830.

13. This did not occur until 1833 (see "Introduction to Joseph Smith, Sr., Collection"). Compare III.J.8, POMEROY TUCKER ACCOUNT, 1867, 58.

14. Cowdery had been baptized by Joseph Smith on 15 May 1829, and Cowdery baptized Martin Harris on 6 April 1830.

15. See III.J.8, POMEROY TUCKER ACCOUNT, 1867, 59, and n. 115 for correction.

16. On Calvin Stoddard (1801-36), see III.J.7, STEPHEN S. HARDING TO POMEROY TUCKER, 1 JUN 1867, n. 9.

17. On Stephen S. Harding (1808-?), see introduction to III.J.7, STEPHEN S. HARDING TO POMEROY TUCKER, 1 JUN 1867.

18. On Abner Tucker, see III.J.8, POMEROY TUCKER ACCOUNT, 1867, n. 127.

19. This story is told in III.J.7, STEPHEN S. HARDING TO POMEROY TUCKER, 1 JUN 1867, 285-86; and III.J.8, POMEROY TUCKER ACCOUNT, 1867, 79-81.

Next day the first Mormon missionary, in full faith, began to preach from house to house, and so began that missionary system so successful and so potential to this new sect. Soon after organizing, the Mormons migrated to Kirtland, Ohio. ...[20]

20. In addition to his account of early Mormonism, McIntosh incorrectly claimed (on p. 59) that the paper on which the first edition of the Book of Mormon was printed came from a mill at Canandaigua. But this claim was challenged by Stephen Brewster, one of the proprietors of the Shortsville paper mill who said Grandin's paper came from Shortsville (*Shortsville Enterprise,* 17 April 1903; Backman 1980, 33). An earlier account also stated that the Book of Mormon was printed "on paper manufactured at Shortsville, by Case & Brown—size 22 x 32" (*Wayne County Journal,* 19 April 1877; see also Glen M. Leonard, *Church News,* 31 March 1990). See also III.K.34, *WAYNE COUNTY* (NY) *JOURNAL,* 23 APR 1908, which incorrectly asserted that the Book of Mormon was printed on paper from the firm of Alling & Cary of Rochester.

29.
W. H. MCINTOSH, *HISTORY OF WAYNE COUNTY* (NY), 1877

[W. H. McIntosh], *History of Wayne County, New York* (Philadelphia: Everts, Ensign & Everts, 1877), 149-51.

EDITORIAL NOTE

Under the subheading "Mormonism and Its Founder," W. H. McIntosh gives an account of Mormon origins in Wayne and Ontario Counties. His account is largely based on Pomeroy Tucker's 1867 history (see III.J.8, POMEROY TUCKER ACCOUNT, 1867).

Mormonism had its origin with the family of Joseph Smith, Sr.,[1] who came in the summer of 1816, from Royalton, Vermont, and settled in the village of Palmyra.[2] The family consisted of nine children, viz.: Alvin, Hiram, Sophronia, Joseph, Samuel H., William, Catharine, Carlos, and Lucy.[3] Arrived at Palmyra the elder Smith opened a "cake and beer shop," as his sign indicated, and the profits of the shop, combined with occasional earnings by himself and eldest sons at harvesting, well-digging, and other common employments, enabled him to provide an honest living for the family. The shop, with its confectionery, ginger-bread, root-beer, and such articles, was well patronized by the village and country youth, and on public occasions did a lively business. A hand-cart, fashioned by Joseph Smith, Sr., was employed to peddle his wares through the streets. For two and a half years the family resided in the village, and in 1818 settled upon a wild tract of land located about two miles south of Palmyra. Anticipating a removal hither, a

1. On Joseph Smith, Sr. (1771-1840), see "Introduction to Joseph Smith, Sr., Collection."

2. Although they had twice lived in Royalton, the Smiths immigrated to New York from Norwich, Vermont.

3. On Alvin, Hyrum, Sophronia, Samuel Harrison, Don Carlos, and Lucy Smith, see I.A.15, JOSEPH SMITH HISTORY, 1839, nn. 10, 12, 13, 15, 16, 18. On William Smith, see "Introduction to William Smith Collection"; and on Katharine Smith, see "Introduction to Katharine Smith Collection." However, Lucy Smith (1821-82) did not arrive with the Smith family from Vermont, but was born in Palmyra, New York.

small log house had been built, and in this they made their home for a dozen years.[4] The cabin contained two rooms on the ground floor, and [p. 149] a garret had two divisions. Some time after occupation a wing was built of slabs for a sleeping-apartment.

The land thus settled was owned by non-resident minor heirs, who had no local agent to look after it; hence the squatters were not disturbed. Mr. Smith finally contracted for the land, made a small payment, and occupied the tract till 1829, when the new religion was ushered into existence. The family were an exception to Vermonters, and did little to improve their state or clear the land. A short time before leaving the farm they erected the frame of a small house and partially inclosed it, and here they lived in the unfinished building till they took their departure. The old cabin was put to use as a barn. The Smiths left in 1831, and that once wild tract, the abode of the squatter family, is now a well-organized farm located on Stafford street, running south of the village. The Smiths obtained a livelihood from this lot by the sale of cordwood, baskets, birch-brooms, maple-sugar, and syrup, and on public days resumed the cake and beer business in Palmyra. Much the larger portion of the time of the Smiths was employed in hunting, trapping muskrats, fishing, and lounging at the village. Joseph, Jr., was active in catching woodchucks, but practically ignored work.

Nocturnal depredations occurred among neighbors, and suspicion rested upon the family, but no proof of their being implicated has been adduced. "A shiftless set" was an appropriate designation to the Smiths, and Joseph, Jr., was the worst of the lot. During his minority he is recalled as indolent and mendacious. In appearance dull-eyed, tow-haired, and of shiftless manner. Taciturn unless addressed, he was not believed when he did speak. He was given to mischief and mysterious pretense, was good-natured, and was never known to laugh. Having learned to read, the lives of criminals engrossed his attention, till from study of the Bible he became familiar with portions of the Scripture, and especially found interest in revelation and prophecy. Revivals occurred, and Smith joined a class of probationers in the Methodist church of Palmyra, but soon withdrew.

In September, 1819,[5] the elder Smith and his sons Alvin and Hiram, in digging a well near Palmyra, threw up a stone of vitreous though opaque appearance, and in form like an infant's foot. This stone was secured by

4. The Smiths also constructed a frame house, which was completed in the fall of 1825.

5. The stone was found while digging a well on the Chase property in 1822 (see III.J.8, POMEROY TUCKER ACCOUNT, 1867, n. 32).

Joseph, and turned to account as a revelator of present and future. In the rôle of fortune-teller, small amounts were received from the credulous, and the impostor was encouraged to enlarge his field by asserting a vision of gold and silver buried in iron chests in the vicinity. The stone was finally placed in his hat to shade its marvelous brightness when its services were required. Persisting in his assertions, there were those who in the spring of 1820[6] contributed to defray the expenses of digging for the buried treasure. At midnight, dupes, laborers, and himself, with lanterns, repaired to the hill-side near the house of Smith, where, following mystic ceremony, digging began by signal in enjoined silence. Two hours elapsed, when, just as the money-box was about to be unearthed, some one spoke and the treasure vanished. This was the explanation of the failure, and it was sufficient for the party. The deception was repeated from time to time in the interval between 1820 and 1827, and, despite the illusory searches for money, he obtained contributions which went towards the maintenance of the family.

A single instance illustrates the mode of procedure at a search for money. Assuming to see where treasure lay entombed, Smith asserted that a "black sheep" was necessary, as an offering upon the ground, before the work of digging could begin. William Stafford,[7] a farmer, had a fat black wether, and agreed to furnish the sacrifice in consideration of an equitable division of the results of the venture. The party repaired with lanterns at the appointed hour of the night to the chosen spot; Smith traced a circle, within which the wether was placed and his throat cut; the blood saturated the ground, and silently and solemnly, but with vigor, excavation began. Three hours of futile labor ensued, when it was discovered that the elder Smith, assisted by a son, had taken away the sheep and laid in a stock of mutton for family use. Such were the foolish and worse than puerile acts which served as a prelude to the crowning act in the life of Joseph Smith,—the inauguration of Mormonism.[8]

In the summer of 1827 a stranger appeared, and made frequent visits at the Smith cabin.[9] Smith announced a vision wherein an angel had appeared and promised the revelation of a true and full gospel, which should supersede all others. Again the angel appeared to Smith, and revealed "That the

---

6. See III.J.8, POMEROY TUCKER ACCOUNT, 1867, n. 35.

7. On William Stafford (c. 1786-1863), see introduction to III.A.13, WILLIAM STAFFORD STATEMENT, 8 DEC 1833.

8. Regarding the sacrifice of Stafford's sheep, consult III.A.13, WILLIAM STAFFORD STATEMENT, 8 DEC 1833, 239; and II.J.8, POMEROY TUCKER ACCOUNT, 1867, 23-24.

9. Concerning the appearance of this stranger, see III.J.8, POMEROY TUCKER ACCOUNT, 1867, n. 42.

American Indians were a remnant of the Israelites, who, after coming to this country, had their prophets and inspired writings; that such of their writings as had not been destroyed were safely deposited in a certain place made known to him, and to him only; that they contained revelations in regard to the last days; and that, if he remained faithful, he would be the chosen prophet to translate them to the world."

Fall came, and Smith assumed the rôle of a prophet. He told his family, friends, and believers, that upon a fixed day he was to proceed alone to a spot designated by an angel, and there withdraw from the earth a metallic book of great antiquity,—in short, a hieroglyphic record of the lost tribes and original inhabitants of America. This mystic volume Smith alone could translate, and power was given him as the Divine agent. The expectant revelation was duly advertised, when the prophet, with spade and napkin, repaired to the forest, and at the end of some three hours returned with some object encased in the napkin. The first depositary of the sacred plates was under the heavy hearthstone of the Smith cabin. Willard Chase,[10] a carpenter and joiner, was solicited to make a strong chest wherein to keep the golden book in security, but no payment being anticipated, the interview was fruitless. Later a chest was procured, and kept in the garret. Here Smith consulted the volume upon which no other could look and live. William T. Hussy[11] and Ashley Vanduzer,[12] intimates of Smith, resolved to see the book, and were permitted to observe its shape and size under a piece of canvas. Smith refused to uncover it, and Hussy, seizing it, stripped off the cover, and found—a tile-brick. Smith claimed to have sold his visitors by a trick, and treating them to liquor, the matter ended amicably.[13] A huge pair of spectacles were asserted to have been found with the book, and these were the agency by which translation was to be effected. A revelation of a Golden Bible, or Book of Mormon, was announced, and the locality whence the book was claimed to have been taken has since been known as "Mormon Hill," and is located in the town of Manchester. Smith described the book "as consisting of metallic leaves or plates resembling gold, bound together in

10. On Willard Chase (1798-1871), see introduction to III.A.14, WILLARD CHASE STATEMENT, CIRCA 11 DEC 1834.

11. On William T. Hussy, see I.B.5, LUCY SMITH HISTORY, 1845, n. 222.

12. On Azel Vanduver, see III.J.8, POMEROY TUCKER ACCOUNT, 1867, n. 50; and introduction to III.L.9, PALMYRA [NY] MASONIC RECORDS, 1827-1828.

13. Compare III.J.8, POMEROY TUCKER ACCOUNT, 1867, 31-32.

a volume by three rings running through one edge of them, the leaves opening like an ordinary paper book." Translation began, and the result was shown to ministers and men of education. The "Nephites" and "Lamanites" were outlined as the progenitors of the American aborigines. The Bible was evidently the basis of the work, and portions of Isaiah, Jeremiah, and Matthew were almost bodily employed. Smith, being unable to write, sat behind a blanket and evidently read to his scribe, whose name was Oliver Cowdery, who had been a schoolmaster, and wrote at dictation. It was desirable to get this manuscript into print. George Crane,[14] of Macedon, a Quaker, and a man of intelligence, was shown several quires of the "translations." His opinion was asked and his aid solicited. Mr. Crane advised Smith to give up his scheme, or ruin would result to him, and, as is well known, the Friend spoke prophetically.[15]

Followers may be obtained for any creed. He formed an organization denominated "Latter-Day Saints." They are enumerated as Oliver Cowdery, Samuel Lawrence, Martin Harris, Preserved Harris, Peter Ingersoll, Charles Ford, George and Dolly Proper, of Palmyra, Ziba Peterson, Calvin Stoddard and wife Sophronia, of Macedon, Ezra Thayer, of Brighton, Leeman Walters, of Pultneyville, Hiram Page, of Fayette, David Whitmer, Jacob Whitmer, as well as Christian, John, and Peter, Jr., of Phelps, Simeon Nichols, of Farmington, William, Joshua, and Gad Stafford, David and Abram Fish, Robert Orr, K. H. Quance, John Morgan, Orrin and Caroline Rockwell, Mrs. S[ally]. Risley, and the Smith family.[16] A man named Parley P. Pratt,[17] from Ohio, stepped off a canal-boat at Palmyra, and joined the organization. Martin Harris desired the new book printed, and avowed to his wife his intention of incurring the expense. She knew that the result would be a loss of the farm, and while her husband slept secured and burnt the manuscript. The burning she kept secret, and Smith and Harris, fearing that they might be produced, dared not rewrite the manuscript. Again translation was effected, this time within a cave dug in the east side of the forest hill, and guarded by one or more disciples. In June, 1829, Smith, accompanied by his brother Hiram, Cowdery, and Harris, called on Eg-

---

14. On George Crane, see III.J.8, POMEROY TUCKER ACCOUNT, 1867, n. 55.

15. Compare III.J.8, POMEROY TUCKER ACCOUNT, 1867, 37.

16. Compare this list of persons with III.J.8, POMEROY TUCKER ACCOUNT, 1867, 39.

17. On Parley Parker Pratt (1807-57), see introduction to PARLEY P. PRATT AUTOBIOGRAPHY (PART I), CIRCA 1854.

bert B. Grandin,[18] publisher of the *Wayne Sentinel,* at Palmyra, and inquired the cost of an edition of three thousand copies. An estimate was furnished, but publication refused. An application to Thurlow Weed,[19] of the *Anti-Masonic Inquirer,* at Rochester, met a like rebuff, and Harris was advised "not to beggar his family." Elihu F. Marshall,[20] a book publisher of Rochester, gave terms. Mr. Grandin was again visited, and a contract was made whereby for three thousand dollars five thousand copies of the Book of Mormon were printed, bound, and delivered in the summer of 1830. Harris gave bond and mortgage in security for payment. John H. Gilbert[21] did the type-setting and press-work, and retained a copy of the book in the original sheets. Harris and his wife separated. She received eighty acres of land, and occupied her property in comfort till her death. The mortgaged farm was sold in 1831. It is land located a mile and a half north of Palmyra. Anticipating profits from the sale of the work, Smith obtained cloth for a suit of clothing from the store of David S. Aldrich,[22] of Palmyra, and in November, 1829, went to northern Pennsylvania, where he was married by Sidney Rigdon,[23] after the Mormon ritual, to a daughter of Isaac Hale.[24]

In June [April], 1830, the organization took place. Smith read and expounded some passages of the new bible, and then installed his father as "Patriarch and President of the Church of Latter-Day Saints," while Harris and Cowdery were invested with limited authority. Baptism was administered by Smith to Cowdery, and Harris' and other baptisms were conducted by Cowdery. The pool where the rite was celebrated was formed by

---

18. On Egbert B. Grandin (1806-45), see I.A.15, JOSEPH SMITH HISTORY, 1839, n. 77.

19. On Thurlow Weed (1797-1882), see introduction to III.K.17, THURLOW WEED REMINISCENCES, 1854, 1858, 1880 & 1884.

20. On Elihu F. Marshall, see III.J.5, POMEROY TUCKER REMINISCENCE, 1858, n. 6.

21. On John H. Gilbert (1802-95), see "Introduction to John H. Gilbert Collection."

22. On David S. Aldrich, see III.J.8, POMEROY TUCKER ACCOUNT, 1867, n. 108.

23. On Sidney Rigdon (1793-1876), see introduction to I.A.13, SIDNEY RIGDON ACCOUNT, CIRCA 1836.

24. Compare III.J.8, POMEROY TUCKER REMINISCENCE, 1867, 56. Emma Smith specifically denied this accusation (see I.F.3, EMMA SMITH BIDAMON INTERVIEW WITH JOSEPH SMITH III, FEB 1879, 289). Joseph Smith and Emma Hale were married on 18 January 1827 by Justice Tarbell of South Bainbridge, New York.

obstructing a brook near the place of assembly. Smith was not baptized, he averring that brother Rigdon had performed the ceremony in Pennsylvania.[25] [p. 150]

A few days elapsed, and a party of about a dozen went to Fayette, and similar observances, in the presence of a congregation of about thirty persons, followed. Sidney Rigdon, a renegade Baptist clergyman, resident in Ohio, had so far kept in the background. He now came to Palmyra as the first regular Mormon preacher. All the churches were closed to him, but the hall of the Palmyra Young Men's Association was opened, and a small audience assembled to hear the first discourse. The attempt was never repeated by Rigdon or any other of his creed in Palmyra. In the summer of 1830, the Mormon founders removed to Kirtland, Ohio, and from Rigdon's former congregation increased their number, till over one hundred persons had embraced Mormonism. The imposture was now under headway, and the "prophet" and his followers had departed from western New York, and with them we have done. ...

---

25. This is incorrect as Joseph Smith had been baptized by Oliver Cowdery on 15 May 1829.

30.
BRIGHAM YOUNG ACCOUNT, 1877

1. "Discourse by President Brigham Young, Delivered at a Special Conference Held at Farmington [Utah], for the Purpose of Organizing a Stake of Zion for the County of Davis, on Sunday Afternoon, June 17, 1877," *Journal of Discourses of the Church of Jesus Christ of Latter-day Saints,* 26 vols. (Liverpool: Albert Carrington [and others], 1853-1886), 19:37-38.

2. "A Life Sketch of William Blood," 64-65, LDS Church Archives, Salt Lake City, Utah.

EDITORIAL NOTE

In a sermon delivered about two months prior to his death, Brigham Young (1801-77) related a story told to him by Orrin Porter Rockwell (1813-78) of digging for an enchanted treasure chest in Manchester, New York, and another story related by Oliver Cowdery (1806-50) of returning the gold plates to a cave in the Hill Cumorah.

[*1. Official Version*]

... Orin P. Rockwell[1] is an eye-witness to some powers of removing the treasures of the earth. He was with certain parties that lived near by where the plates were found that contain the records of the Book of Mormon. There were a great many treasures hid up by the Nephites. Porter was with them one night where there were treasures, and they could find them easy enough, but they could not obtain them.

I will tell you a story which will be marvelous to most of you. It was told me by Porter, whom I would believe just as quickly as any man that lives. When he tells a thing he understands, he will tell it just as he knows it; he is a man that does not lie. He said that on this night, when they were engaged hunting for this old treasure, they dug around the end of a chest for some twenty inches. The chest was about three feet square. One man who was determined to have the contents of that chest, took his pick and struck

1. On Orrin Porter Rockwell (1813-78), see I.A.15, JOSEPH SMITH HISTORY, 1839, n. 121.

into the lid of it, and split through into the chest. The blow took off a piece of the lid, which a certain lady kept in her possession until she died.[2] That chest of money went into the bank. Porter describes it so [making a rumbling sound][3]; he says this is just as true as the heavens are. I have heard others tell the same story. I relate this because it is [p. 37] marvelous to you. But to those who understand these things, it is not marvelous.

... I could relate many very singular circumstances. I lived right in the country where the plates were found from which the Book of Mormon was translated, and I know a great many things pertaining to that country. I believe I will take the liberty to tell you of another circumstance that will be as marvelous as anything can be. This is an incident in the life of Oliver Cowdery,[4] but he did not take the liberty of telling such things in meeting as I take. I tell these things to you, and I have a motive for doing so. I want to carry them to the ears of my brethren and sisters, and to the children also, that they may grow to an understanding of some things that seem to be entirely hidden from the human family. Oliver Cowdery went with the Prophet Joseph when he deposited these plates. Joseph did not translate all of the plates; there was a portion of them sealed, which you can learn from the Book of Doctrine and Covenants. When Joseph got the plates, the angel instructed him to carry them back to the hill Cumorah, which he did. Oliver [Cowdery] says that when Joseph and Oliver went there, the hill opened, and they walked into a cave,[5] in which there was a large and spacious room.

---

2. Sixteen years earlier, Brigham Young privately identified the woman as Lucy Smith (Brigham Young, Office Journal, 21 November 1861; cited in Quinn 1987, 49). William Blood's version of Young's statement significantly varies from the official version by assigning the event to Kirtland, Ohio (see below). Compare Joshua Stafford's statement that "Joseph once showed me a piece of wood which he said he took from a box of money, and the reason he gave for not obtaining the box was, that it *moved*" (III.A.4, JOSHUA STAFFORD STATEMENT, 15 NOV 1833, 258).

3. Bracketed material in original.

4. On Oliver Cowdery (1806-50), see "Introduction to Oliver Cowdery Collection."

5. Earlier, on 11 December 1869, Young had told the School of the Prophets: "... in relation to Joseph Smith return=ing the Plates of the Book of Mormon that He did not return them to the Box from wh[ence?] He had Received [them][.] But He went [into?] a Cave in the Hill Comora with Oliver Cowdry & deposited those plates upon a table or shelf & in that room were deposited a large amount of gold plates Containing sacred records, & when they first visited that Room the sword of Laban was Hanging upon the wall & when they last visited it the sword was drawn from the scabbard &

He says he did not think, at the time, whether they had the light of the sun or artificial light; but that it was just as light as day. They laid the plates on a table; it was a large table that stood in the room. Under this table there was a pile of plates as much as two feet high, and there were altogether in this room more plates than probably many wagon loads; they were piled up in the corners and along the walls. The first time they went there the sword of Laban hung upon the wall; but when they went again it had been take down

---

lain upon the table & a Messenger who was the keeper of the room informed them that that sword would never be returned to its scabbard untill the Kingdom of God was established upon the Earth & untill it reigned triumphant over Evry Enemy[.] Joseph Smith said that Cave Contained tons of Choice Treasures & records" (Journal of Wilford Woodruff, LDS Church Archives; also cited in Kenney 1983-84, 6:508-9). The earliest known account of the cave story was given by William W. Phelps in 1855, who said he heard it from Hyrum Smith. According to this account, "Joseph, Hyrum, Cowdery & Whitmere went to the hill Cormorah. As they were walking up the hill, a door opened and they walked into a room about 16 ft square. In that room was an angel and a trunk. On that trunk lay a book of Mormon & gold plates, Laban's sword, Aaron's breastplate" (William H. Dame, Journal, 14 January 1855, typescript, Special Collections, Harold B. Lee Library, Brigham Young University, Provo, Utah). The following year Heber C. Kimball spoke of "the vision that Joseph and others had, when they went into a cave in the hill Cumorah, and saw more records than ten men could carry? There were books piled up on tables, book upon book" (Young et al. 1853-86, 4:105). In a private meeting in 1867 Kimball expanded upon this "vision," telling some missionaries "about Father Smith, Oliver Cowdery and others walking into the Hill Cumorah and seeing records upon records piled upon tables, they walked from cell to cell and saw the records that were piled up" (Brigham Young, Manuscript History, 5 May 1867, LDS Church Archives). In 1893 Edward Stevenson recalled that in his December 1877 interview with David Whitmer that the aged witness said that "Oliver Cowdery told him that the prophet Joseph and himself had seen this room and that it was filled with treasure, and on a table therein were the breastplate and the sword of Laban, as well as the portion of gold plates not yet translated, and that these plates were bound by three small gold rings. ..." (Stevenson 1893, 14). Although there may be some basis to the story that folk-memory has distorted and expanded, the historical setting—of Smith and Cowdery's returning the plates to the hill—is questionable in light of the translation's completion in June-July 1829 and Cowdery's statement that he had not visited the hill until 1830, long after Smith's need for the plates had elapsed (*Messenger and Advocate* 2 [October 1835]: 196). See also III.K.37, ELIZABETH KANE INTERVIEW WITH BRIGHAM YOUNG, ARTEMISIA (BEAMAN) SNOW, AND ORRIN ROCKWELL, 1872-1873.

and laid upon the table across the gold plates; it was unsheathed, and on it was written these words: "This sword will never be sheathed again until the kingdoms of this world become the kingdom of our God and his Christ." I tell you this as coming not only from Oliver Cowdery, but others who were familiar with it, and who understood it just as well as we understand coming to this meeting, enjoying the day, and by and by we separate and go away forgetting most of what is said, but remembering some things. So is it with other circumstances in life. I relate this to you, and I want you to understand it. I take this liberty of referring to those things so that they will not be forgotten and lost. Carlos Smith[6] was a young man of as much veracity as any young man we had, and he was a witness to these things. Samuel Smith[7] saw some things, Hyrum[8] saw a good many things, but Joseph was the leader. ... [p. 38]

[*2. William Blood Version*][9]

June 17 & 18 [1877] Jane[10] and I attended Stake Conference at Farmington where Brigham Young spoke on a num=ber of subjects that interested me. 1st In speaking of the plates from which the Book of Mormon was trans=lated he said: Oliver Cowdery to[ld] me [Young] that when the Prophet Joseph & he returned the plates to the hill Comorah, the hill opened & they entered a large room that was brilliantly lighted but he did not notice the source of the light. The room had shelves around it and up=on & under these were plates more than fifty horses could draw. There was also a table

6. On Don Carlos Smith (1816-41), see I.A.15, JOSEPH SMITH HISTORY, 1839, n. 15.

7. On Samuel Harrison Smith (1808-44), see I.A.15, JOSEPH SMITH HISTORY, 1839, n. 13.

8. On Hyrum Smith (1800-44), see I.A.15, JOSEPH SMITH HISTORY, 1839, n. 12.

9. William Blood's autobiography appears mostly in his own hand, with a small portion at the end in his daughter's hand. William Blood (1839-?), son of William and Mary Blood, was born at Barton, Staffordshire, England. He joined the Mormons and immigrated to Nauvoo, Illinois, in 1844. He moved to Council Bluffs, Iowa, in 1846, then to Utah in 1849. The following year he settled on a farm in Kaysville, where he spent the remainder of his life. In 1857 he was ordained a seventy. He also served as justice of the peace in 1874. He married Jane Wilkie Hooper in November 1872, then took Sarah Jane Colemere as his plural wife (see Jenson 1971, 1:465-66; I. Hill 1962).

10. Jane Wilkie Hooper, Blood's first wife.

and Oliver told me: "We laid the plates on the table." The sword of Laban hung on the wall. When we returned to the room, [p. 64] this sword was taken from the wall & unsheathed and laid on the table. It was there written: "This sword shall neve[r] be sheathed again until the kingdoms of this world become the kingdoms of our God & his Christ."

2nd Soon after we came to Utah, Porter Rockwell came to me [Young] one day and said he had found a gold mine and he gave me a nugget—which I have in my office now. He asked me what he should do about his mine. I told him to leave it alone. Later, when prospectors came to Utah[,] Porter came to me in a hurry and said they were now within one hundred yards of his claim and asked again what he should do. I told him to get a surveyor and stake out his claim. Now comes the funny part. When he went to look for it he could not find the place or the gold. I told him that the Lord had moved it. The Lord has a means of moving things under the ground as we have of moving things on the ground. To substantiate this he [Young] related the following: Some of the brethren in Kirtland[11] were hauling gravel from a gravel bank. While they were working[,] the gravel fell from the hill uncovering the corner of a stone box. One of the men climbed up the hill to it and struck it with his pick breaking off a piece from the corner. The box went through the gravel bank with a rush and they saw it no more. The piece that was chipped from the corner of the box was picked up & given to Mother Smith.

11. If Blood's version accurately places the stone-box event in Kirtland, Ohio, then the story's relevance to Mormon origins in New York is greatly diminished.

31.
Henry O'Reilly Reminiscence, 1879

1. "Blasphemy—'Book of Mormon,' alias 'The Golden Bible,'" *Rochester Republican,* 6 April 1830, 3.

2. Henry O'Reilly, "Origin of Mormonism[:] First Commentaries on the 'Golden Bible,' so called—otherwise, the 'Book of Mormon'—The foundation of the new Sect now wide spread throughout the World," 1879, Rochester Historical Society Library, Rochester, New York.

EDITORIAL NOTE

Henry O'Reilly (1806-86), leader of the Irish Catholics in Rochester, New York, was editor of Rochester's *Republican* and *Daily Advertiser,* and author of the highly regarded *Sketches of Rochester* (1838). He was also associated with the development of the magnetic telegraph (O'Reilly 1838, 325; W. F. Peck 1884, 133, 349; P. E. Johnson 1978, 20; U.S. Census, Rochester, Monroe County, New York, 1830:230).

The first item presented below is O'Reilly's editorial on the publication of the Book of Mormon, dated 6 April 1830. The second item, apparently written by O'Reilly in 1879 and amended in 1883, was intended as an introduction to a reprint of his *Rochester Republican* editorial.

[*1. Article, 6 April 1830*][1]

The "Book of Mormon" has been placed in our hands. A viler imposition was never practised. It is an evidence of fraud, blasphemy and credulity, shocking to the Christian and moralist. The "author and proprietor" is one "Joseph Smith, jr."—a fellow who, by some hocus pocus, acquired such an influence over a wealthy farmer of Wayne county, that the latter mortgaged

1. This item was also published in the *Rochester Daily Advertiser and Telegraph* 4 (2 April 1830): 2. Both the *Advertiser and Telegraph* and the *Republican* were printed and published by Luther Tucker, which explains the identical typesetting used in both printings of O'Reilly's article. I have used the *Republican* printing because O'Reilly's reference to it in his subsequent writing indicates that he considered it the primary printing (see below).

his farm for $3000, which he paid for printing and binding 5000 copies of the blasphemous work. The volume consists of about 600 pages, and is divided into the books of Nephi, of Jacob, of Mosiah, of Alma, of Mormon, of Ether, and of Helaman.—"Copy-right secured!" The *style* of the work may be conjectured from the "preface" and "testimonials" which we subjoin. ...[2]

[*2. Reminiscence, 1879*]

In the "Rochester Republican" of the 30th April, 1830,[3] in the N.Y. Historical Library, is an article in which I (then the Editor of that print as well as of the "Roch=ester Daily Advertiser") alluded to, and published extracts from, the Book Just then printed but not yet published, by the "Prophet," Joe Smith.

Mr. [Abner] Cole,[4] an old Citizen of Palmyra, told me, that, when that "Prophet's" attention was called to my comments as they were republished in some neighboring Journal, he swore, with more than commical vigor, that he would "go to Rochester & thrash that damned O'Rielly, for writing in that way about his book.["]*

A copy of the [w]ork had been bro't [brought] to Rochester by a Journeyman printer named Macaully,[5] then employed in our office. And he, supposed it would interest me, loaned it to me. Hense I learnt first about the contents, & mentioned it in my paper, giving some extracts as indicia [indicative?] of the contents.—The article, as published by me in April 1830, is contained in one of the newspaper volumes of my Contri=butions at the Rochester Historical Library: and is as follows:—(viz. in the "Rochester Republican")+

(Henry O'Rielly—1879.) 1883.

* A threat which, happily for the writer, (probably,) the "Prophet" never realized.

---

2. Then follows the Book of Mormon's Preface, Testimony of Three Witnesses, and Testimony of Eight Witnesses (see III.L.16, BOOK OF MORMON PREFACE, 1829; VI.G.1, TESTIMONY OF THREE WITNESSES, JUN 1829; and III.L.13, TESTIMONY OF EIGHT WITNESSES, JUN 1829).

3. Rather 6 April 1830; there was no issue for 30 April 1830.

4. On Abner Cole (?-1835), see introduction to III.E.3, *PALMYRA REFLECTOR,* 1829-1831.

5. John H. Gilbert mentioned that Egbert B. Grandin and Thomas McAuley did the actual work of printing the Book of Mormon (III.H.10, JOHN H. GILBERT MEMORANDUM, 8 SEP 1892, 4).

+ Note—I learnt, after I wrote the above critique, that the Mormon church was organized on the 6th of April 1830

32.
EDWARD STEVENSON REMINISCENCE, 1893

Edward Stevenson, *Reminiscences of Joseph, the Prophet and the Coming Forth of the Book of Mormon* (Salt Lake City: Edward Stevenson, 1893), 10-13.

EDITORIAL NOTE

Edward Stevenson[1] visited the Palmyra/Manchester, New York, area in 1870 and 1871. In the following selection from his 1893 *Reminiscences,* he describes his visit to the Hill Cumorah.

... Early on a summer's morning in the year 1870, after a gentle shower during the night, with just sufficient rainfall to lay the dust, I set out to walk to the hill. Never can I forget the lovely scenery of that lonely but interesting walk down that most excellent Canandaigua turnpike. Among the objects passed on the way was the former home of Joseph Smith, and the very old and comely schoolhouse where he learned some of his early lessons.

Arriving near the object of my morning's walk, I set about inquiring for the Hill Cumorah. But not one could I find in all the country round who could give me the desired information; until one, and the right one too, who was made to comprehend my mind and wish, said, "Is it Mormon Hill that you want, or what is more familiarly known among us in this country as 'Bible Hill,' where old Joe Smith found the Mormon Bible? Is it this place you wish to find?"

Having answered affirmatively the question, I was not only enabled, by my friend's direction, to learn the third and last name given to this hill, but to find myself standing upon the summit of one of the most interesting objects of my 100,000 miles' travel. ... [p. 10] ...

At the period of the discovery of the gold plates, there stood upon the side of the hill, about fifteen feet above where the stone box had so long reposed, a lone, solitary, sugar maple tree, and there continued to grow until twenty-two years ago; just as described by Brother Holt,[2] who was so highly

---

1. On Edward Stevenson (1820-97), see introduction to I.A.9, JOSEPH SMITH RECITAL TO PONTIAC (MI) SAINTS, OCT 1834.

2. Edward Holt of the South Jordan Ward had a vision of the Hill Cumorah, which as described by Stevenson (p. 11) included a single tree near its northern summit.

favored of God as to see the whole scene in a vision or dream.

What made Brother Holt's vision all the more deeply interesting to me was that in 1871 I had enjoyed the great privilege and pleasure of visiting the hill in person, and of seeing the very identical spot of ground where Mormon concealed the stone box and its precious records and where Moroni, his son, finished the writing and sealed up these records. But there was no tree standing there as was described in the vision, for it had been cut down shortly before and was lying on the ground, not having as yet been removed. ... [p. 11]

... My guide who accompanied me on my visit in 1871, pointed out to me many places of interest, and also entertained me hospitably at his table. ... Cordially bidding good-day to my very hospitable host, I proceeded on my [p. 12] way and found an old gentleman who lived west of the hill and who was quite agreeable and conversational on the subject of my visit to Cumorah. He was well acquainted with some of the history of the coming forth of the book which was to "speak out of the ground," although spiritually, he did not seem to have greatly benefited by this "marvelous work and a wonder." Still, from him I gleaned some useful information. He pointed out the spot of ground where the stone box was placed, near the summit, and on the west side of the point of the hill. He likewise stated that soon after the rumor so widely spread regarding "Joe" Smith finding a gold bible, that there was great excitement throughout the whole country, and that it was about this time the Rochester Company located and searched for hidden treasure.

Questioning him closely he stated that he had seen some good sized flat stones that had rolled down and lay near the bottom of the hill. This had occurred after the contents of the box had been removed and these stones were doubtless the ones that formerly composed the box. I felt a strong desire to see these ancient relics and told him I would be much pleased to have him inform me where they were to be found. He stated that they had long since been taken away.[3] He further said that he knew "Joe" Smith as a "money

3. Earlier the same year, Andrew Galloway had visited the Hill Cumorah and later reported: "I spent one day on the Hill, and saw the Box that had contained the plates from which the Book of Mormon was translated. The Box as far as I remember was something like three feet long a little over two feet wide and two feet in depth. The Box and lid showed no marks of any tools having been used. The Box was made of lightish gray rock, of what I think geologists would say of the Carboniferous Period" (Andrew Galloway Collection, LDS Church Archives, cited in Holzapfel 1995, 45). The impression that Galloway saw the stone box intact at the top of the hill is contra-

digger" and a "visionary man" and Martin Harris[4] as an honest reliable farmer. Joseph in his history says that he worked in a mine for Mr. [Josiah] Stowel,[5] hunting for hidden treasures, at fourteen dollars per month, hence his name as a money-digger. I then inquired if he ever knew Joseph Smith to be convicted of crime. He replied that he had not known him as having been convicted. ... My loquacious guide showed me another and much deeper cavity made on the east side of the hill by the above named Rochester treasure seekers, a company of prospectors.[6] They said that science aided by mineral rods did not lie and that most assuredly there were rich treasures concealed in the hill, and they were determined to have them. But with all their science and laborious excavations they failed to get a glimpse of the coveted treasures and returned to their homes if not richer, at least it is to be hoped wiser men, for the only results of their efforts were the holes they left on the hillside. Notwithstanding this, there are strong and feasible reasons for believing that there is abundance of treasure hid up in Cumorah, but it is guarded by the hand of the Lord and none shall ever pos[s]ess it until made known in the due time of the Lord. ...[7] [p. 13]

---

dicted by Stevenson and others. Galloway likely saw the rocks at the bottom of the hill and mentally reconstructed the box (see Vogel 1995).

4. On Martin Harris (1783-1875), see "Introduction to Martin Harris Collection."

5. On Josiah Stowell (1770-184?), see introduction to IV.B.2, MARTHA CAMPBELL TO JOSEPH SMITH, 19 DEC 1843.

6. The Rochester money-digging company was well-known (see III.K.1, *ROCHESTER GEM,* 15 MAY 1830), but it is unlikely that they were responsible for the excavation on the eastern slope of the Hill Cumorah. The hole was probably the work of Joseph Smith and his former money-digging associates. Lorenzo Saunders said the hole was dug one or two years previous to Joseph Smith's removal of the plates in September 1827 (III.J.20, LORENZO SAUNDERS TO THOMAS GREGG, 28 JAN 1885).

7. Stevenson then quotes Brigham Young's 1877 sermon giving an account of Joseph Smith and Oliver Cowdery entering into a cave in the Hill Cumorah (see III.K.30, BRIGHAM YOUNG ACCOUNT, 1877). Stevenson adds: "It was likewise stated to me by David Whitmer in the year 1877 that Oliver Cowdery told him that the Prophet Joseph and himself had seen this room and that it was filled with treasure, and on a table therein were the breastplate and the sword of Laban, as well as the portion of gold plates not yet translated, and that these plates were bound by three small gold rings, and would also be translated, as was the first portion in the days of Joseph" (p. 14).

33.
Perry Benjamin Pierce Statement, 1899

Perry Benjamin Pierce, "The Origin of the 'Book of Mormon,'" *American Anthropologist* 1 (October 1899): 680.

... In 1861 I visited the site of the hill out of which the alleged "plates" were allegedly taken. Over thirty years had then passed since the new religion had been launched and the *Book of Mormon* given to the world. But the country neighborhood still had, at that time, many living people who, while they cared very little for "Mormonism," had a very definite remembrance of the Smith family,—father, mother, and sons. I talked with men who were contemporaries of the boys,—"went to school" with them, as they phrased it, always qualifying the statement by the additional one, as one old farmer put it: "None of them Smith boys ever went to school when they could get out of it."[1] Indeed, I found no person willing to say a complimentary word of any member of the Smith family. ...

1. William Smith confirmed this allegation, at least as it pertained to himself (see I.D.4, WILLIAM SMITH, *ON MORMONISM,* 1883, 6).

34.
SARA MELISSA INGERSOLL REMINISCENCE, 1899

Sara Melissa Ingersoll, "Mormonism Unveiled," copy in letter to Hellen Miller Gould, 27 November 1899, Manuscripts and Archives, New York Public Library, New York, New York.

EDITORIAL NOTE

In a cover letter to her friend Hellen Miller Gould, dated 27 November 1899, Sara Melissa (Barber) Ingersoll (b. 1850) of Sioux City, Iowa, wrote: "Pardon my tardiness in answering your letter for I had many interruptions in copying the M.S. [manuscript] I send you to day a copy of the paper of which I wrote about to you on Mormonism hoping it may be of use and also come up to your expectations[.] I do not see as it will be of any particular use to you now, only to show how mormonism first started ..."

In her paper, titled "Mormonism Unveiled," Sara included Peter Ingersoll's testimony about Joseph Smith as related to her by her husband Byron Ingersoll (1824-1904), Peter's nephew.[1] She claimed the information resulted from her husband's many conversations with his uncle when the two lived near one another in Flint, Michigan, prior to Peter's death in 1867. There are many inaccuracies in Sara's account, but there are similarities to Peter Ingersoll's statement published in Eber D. Howe's 1834 book *Mormonism Unvailed* (see III.A.9, PETER INGERSOLL STATEMENT, 2 DEC 1833).

The real author of the "Book of Mormon" was one Solomon Spalding. Having failed as a clergyman and having a smattering of biblical knowledge he was very fond of writing and wrote a manuscript as an addition to the Bible sometime between the years 1761-1816.[2] The work was so flat and stupid that no publisher could be induced to print it or bring it before the world. Spalding at length went to his grave and the manuscript remained in

1. Byron, son of Samuel (b. 1785) and Mary (Nelson) Ingersoll, was born 20 December 1824 in Genesee County, New York. Following the deaths of his first two wives in 1857 and 1861, Ingersoll married Sara Melissa Barber, age twenty-five, in 1870. Byron died at Sioux City, Iowa (Avery 1926, 58, 84).

2. On the Spaulding theory, see Bush 1977.

the possession of his widow[.]

This manuscript fell into the hands of one "Joseph Smith" the real founder of "Mormonism" who pretended to be a prophet and claimed they were a direct revelation to himself from heaven[.]

Joseph Smith of Palmyra, Ontario Co.[,] N.Y. was a tall well built young man with a keen eye and a manner that was at once pleasing and winning. He was one of those illiterate, lazy, shiftless fellows [p. 1] of whom one may not approve, but is strongly inclined to like, seemingly of a rather pious and imaginative turn of mind[.] He seems to have possessed the magnetic power of controlling the minds of others to a great extent[.]

In a book written by one Sidney Rigdon [Pomeroy Tucker] of or near Palmyra, N.Y. Rigdon claimed one Peter Ingersoll <of the same place> (Uncle of Byron Ingersoll of Sioux City, Iowa,) as one of the first believers in Mormonism[.][3]

Peter Ingersoll and Joseph Smith were intimate friends and Joseph proposed to him that he "Joseph" should preach and have revelations. Ingersoll being very fond of fun and excitement encouraged Smith in his undertaking[.] Ingersoll being married Smith staid there a good deal of the time, and sometimes worked for him—although it was never revealed to Smith that he should work— [p. 2]

In the year 1822 or 23 Smith began preaching[.] He would hold meetings in the district school-house and draw large crowds to hear him. He would preach for a while and then go into a trance and seem to be perfectly unconscious during this trance, and he would repeat some Jargon in an unknown tongue, then he would interpret the unknown sounds and assure those present they were the pure "Adamic language[,] the language in which Adam courted Eve in the garden of Eden[.]"

Strange as it may seem he began to have believers as at first it was done in a spirit of mischief and fun[.]

After holding these meetings "Joe" as he was called would come to uncle Peter's house—if uncle Peter was not with him—and tell him of the success he had had, how many converts he made, and laugh till he would drop on the floor with mirth[.] [p. 3]

---

3. She evidently refers to Pomeroy Tucker's *Origin, Rise, and Progress of Mormonism* published in 1867, which on page 38 states that Peter Ingersoll was among Joseph Smith's "pioneer Mormon disciples." See pages 14-15 of Sara Ingersoll's manuscript for her further comments about this matter. On Sidney Rigdon (1793-1876), see introduction to I.A.13, SIDNEY RIGDON ACCOUNT, CIRCA 1836.

After meeting with so much encouragement Joe thought he might make a success of it and commenced in real earnest. He would perform miracles such as walking on water, which he did by placing a board under the water out of sight. But it was not a grand success as sometimes he got a wetting. Then he would tell his followers it was because his faith was not strong enough.[4]

One time he told his followers it was revealed to him that he would find the "Golden Plates[.]" His followers were to dig in a certain spot on uncle Peter's farm—these diggings were always done in the night—but if during the process of digging any one spoke a word the treasure would vanish. He did a great deal of digging but some how the treasure always vanished; somebody would speak, or their faith was not strong enough, and they must have more "Faith" if they expected any reward[.] [p. 4]

Another time he conceived the idea of making it pay. One of his followers had a nice black, fat, pet sheep. He told them it was revealed to him that they should dig a trench around a certain spot on uncle Peters farm—cut the artery in the sheep's neck, walk him around the trench and form a circle of blood—to keep the evil spirit outside of the circle.—then commence digging; but if any one spoke a word the treasure would surely vanish. They dug quietly for a while, then one of the diggers struck his spade on a stone and instantly exclaim=ed "I have found it!" "No use digging any more!" said Joe, "you have spoken and it has vanished." So it had, and so had the dead sheep. Joe's brothers had taken it home and dressed it, and no doubt Joe feasted for awhile, as his parents were always "landless and shiftless[.]"[5]

After these diggings Joe's followers did not always fill [p. 5] up the holes again—and there were many of them—and aunt Kate (uncle Peters wife) complained about it and said they must fill up the holes or stop digging on their farm.

Then Joe's fertile brain conceived the idea of making a "Bible"[.] One day as he was in a field hoeing, he went into the timber lot to rest—as he had many tried [tired?] spells—There had been a wind storm recently and it

4. Regarding Smith's walking on water, which is usually assigned to Colesville, New York, see IV.D.5, GEORGE COLLINGTON, SMITH BAKER, HARRIET MARSH, AND REBECCA NURSE INTERVIEWS WITH FREDERICK G. MATHER, JUL 1880.

5. If not an entirely different event, the sacrifice of William Stafford's sheep according to tradition was performed on a hill located on Chase property (see III.J.35, THOMAS L. COOK HISTORY, 1930, 238; and III.A.13, WILLIAM STAFFORD STATEMENT, 8 DEC 1833, 239).

had uprooted a large tree and revealed a bed of pure white sand. As Joe sat resting and playing with the sand, Satan who is never idle, whispered to him—why not make a bible of this? Joe having on an apron made of ticking, something like a carpenter's apron, filled it with sand, patted it in shape, and it seemed heavy like gold. At once the idea struck him, why not make a "Golden Bible" of this.

He went to uncle Peter showed him the beautiful sand, told him he thought they could <make> a box in [p. 6] the form of a book, and wanted his assistance. Uncle Peter nothing loath, told him if he would get some thin boards and tools, and come down in a back lot—out of sight of passers by—where he was at work harrowing, he would help him.

Joe got the tools and material and went to where uncle Peter was at work, and uncle Peter hitched his team and they went into the timber lot and made a box, letting the edge come over like the cover of a book, filled it with sand covered it with cloth, fastened it tight, took it home, and put it in a chest.[6]

Then Joe told his followers he had found the "Golden Plates[.]" They wanted to see them. He told them it was revealed to him that no person could look on them with the natural eye and live, until they had been translated, but they might put their hand on them and feel of them.

He would raise the lid of the chest just enough for them to put [p. 7] their hand in and the chest being wide and the box being at arms length it seemed heavy as gold, and they were satisfied[.]

All this time Joe held meetings at every opportunity and as his followers increased his troubles increased also.

---

6. In 1833 Peter Ingersoll testified that Smith had privately confessed to him that he had deceived his family with some sand wrapped in his frock (III.A.9, PETER INGERSOLL STATEMENT, 2 DEC 1833, 235-36); however, by failing to mention the construction of a box one was left to wonder how a mere bundle of sand could be taken for plates. Sara Ingersoll's account is not only a more plausible version but suggests that Peter Ingersoll withheld information that would have implicated him in Smith's fraud. As previously suggested (III.A.9, PETER INGERSOLL STATEMENT, 2 DEC 1833, n. 14), Smith may have led Ingersoll and others to believe he had deceived his family with a box of sand in an effort to discourage his former treasure-seeking friends from attempting to take the plates from him. Perhaps Smith involved Ingersoll in the construction of a box as a means of making his subterfuge more convincing. See also III.J.21, E. E. BALDWIN TO W. O. NORRELL, 3 AUG 1887, n. 5.

How to get the "bible" printed he knew not but trusted to time and luck[.]

His followers consisted mostly of the poor and illiterate class of people, but among them was a man by the name of Martin Harris[7] who was a firm believer in Mormonism. His wife, though inclined that way, was not so firm in the faith. This man Harris tho[ugh]' an illiterate man was quite wealthy, owning a nice farm and other property[.]

By this time Joe was getting quite uneasy about getting his "Bible" printed—but as the devil always helps his own he helped him out this time[.] [p. 8] As Joe was walking out one morning he saw this man Harris coming toward him. Now thought Joe is my time, here is the man. He saluted him in a slow drawling tone of voice and said: "Good morning brother Harris." "Good morning" said Harris. "I had a great revelation last night["] said Joe. It was revealed to me that the first man that I met this morning was to furnish the means to print the "Golden Bible" and you are the first man."[8]

Harris began to hem and haw, but could not see quite clearly how he could do it[.] but Joe reiterated "you must! you are the man and must do it!" Harris said he would see his wife and see what she said about it. Now Harris' ~~wfie~~ wife having worked and helped accumulate the property and not being so firm in the mormon faith as her husband flew the track at once, and would not consent to the revelation.

Now to show the power of one [p. 9] mind over another, and the firm belief Harris had in Joseph Smith and his religion Harris and his wife agreed to divide the property, separate and each go their way which they did.

Then Joseph Smith took the Spalding manuscript—which he had kept unknown to all but uncle Peter—and had it printed somewhere in N.Y. City, made into a book and called it the "Mormon Bible" claimed he had it translated from the plates of the Golden Bible which he claimed were written in hieroglyphics and had to be translated by revelation by himself.

He had a pair of great big eye glasses made from the glass they used to use in the back of carriages. he put two of them together in the form of spectacles and called them "God's spectacles." When he wished to translate he would put them on and look and act as wise and sedate as a Judge claiming to translate by the "Urim and Thummim[.]" [p. 10] After the separation of

---

7. On Martin Harris (1783-1875), see "Introduction to Martin Harris Collection."

8. Compare I.A.5, JOSEPH SMITH HISTORY, 1839, 9; I.B.5, LUCY SMITH HISTORY, 1845, MS:73; and III.A.14, WILLARD CHASE STATEMENT, CIRCA 11 DEC 1833, 246.

~~Lu~~ Harris and his wife, that and some other trouble caused quite a commotion in the community and people began to take sides and look seriously on the matter. Uncle Peter Ingersoll never dreaming that it would terminate so seriously went before the court and testified to all that he knew about mormonism.[9] but such being the power of Joseph Smith, and the ignorance of his followers, and there [their] firm belief in mormonism—that his testimony could not stay the result[.] I think it was in the year 1827 when Smith claimed to have found the Golden plates and the translation was not finished until 1829 when it was published.

By this time it had become pretty warm for Smith and his converts. They broke up his meetings in Palmyra, so he gathered all his followers that would go, including his father, mother, brothers and some of his other near relatives and they removed to Kirtland, Ohio. There he was Joined by Brigham Young[10] in the year 1832 and Brigham was so "lifted up" on beholding the "Prophet Joseph"—for so he was now called by his followers— [p. 11] that he "spake in tongues" that no one could understand but Joe Smith. Smith interpreted the sounds and assured them it was the pure Adamic language[.]

After Smith left Palmyra uncle Peter did not know so much of his proceedings only such reports as would come to him. But up to the time he left Palmyra what I have written were such things as uncle Peter knew to be true[.] He told many things of Smith after he left Palmyra but of course they were the current reports that he had heard. ... [p. 12] ...[11]

During the years 1865 to 1867 or 8 Uncle Peter Ingersoll lived and died in the city of Flint, Mich[igan].,[12] and Byron Ingersoll then being a resident of the same place, had many conversations with him on the subject

---

9. Ingersoll may have been among the witnesses who testified against Smith at Lyons in March 1829. According to Lucy Smith, a witness testified falsely that "Joseph Smith told him that the box which he had, contained nothing but sand; and he, Joseph Smith, said it was gold, to deceive the people" (I.B.5, LUCY SMITH HISTORY, 1845, 1853:133-34).

10. On Brigham Young (1801-77), see introduction to III.K.19, BRIGHAM YOUNG ACCOUNTS, 1855 & 1857.

11. Sara Ingersoll's account of the Mormon occupation of Kirtland, Ohio, their persecutions in Missouri, the establishment of Nauvoo, and Joseph Smith's death, which appears on pages 12-14, has been deleted.

12. Peter Ingersoll is listed in the 1860 census of Flint, Genesee County, Michigan, in the household of Ira Wright, who had married Ingersoll's daughter Marietta in 1842 (1860:988; *History of Genesee County, Michigan,* 1879, 184). Ingersoll died at Flint, Michigan, on 22 April 1867 (Avery 1926, 58).

of Mormonism[.] He Byron Ingersoll read the book Sidney Rigdon [Pomeroy Tucker] had written on Mormonism to uncle Peter,[13] and uncle [p. 14] Peter would deny or affirm what of it was true, but on the whole said it was pretty correct, with the exception of some of the original points, and one point in particular that Rigdon [Tucker] knew was false, was, that he Peter Ingersoll was or ever was a believer in Mormonism; He and Rigdon [Tucker] being well acquainted and that Rigdon knew better.[14] ... [p. 15] ...[15]

In writing this brief sketch of the origin of mormonism I have simply related the facts as they were given me, and on which I have not enlarged, though they may sound rather ridicul=ous. ...[16] [p. 17] ...

[s] Sara Melissa Ingersoll

Mrs. Byron Ingersoll
619 Virginia St.
Sioux City, Iowa.
Nov 27th 1899. [p. 18]

---

13. This perhaps confirms Richard L. Anderson's suspicion that some of Hurlbut's witnesses were illiterate and that their affidavits were written by someone else, perhaps by Hurlbut himself (R. L. Anderson 1970). However, the implication that Hurlbut therefore misrepresented his witnesses or that the witnesses did not have control over the content of their affidavits is unfounded.

14. Peter Ingersoll's supposed denial is questionable since Ingersoll died in April 1867 and Tucker's book was not published until after June of that year.

15. Discussion of the three and eight witnesses to the Book of Mormon, which appears on pages 15-17, has been deleted.

16. Discussion of the Book of Mormon's contents on page 17 has been deleted.

35.
WAYNE COUNTY (NY) *JOURNAL*, 23 APRIL 1908

"Rochester Furnished Paper. Book of Mormon Printed on Stock From Founder of Wellknown Paper Firm," *Wayne County* (NY) *Journal*, 23 April 1908.

EDITORIAL NOTE

The claim in the title of the present source—that the Book of Mormon was printed on paper provided by the Alling & Cory Paper Firm of Rochester, New York—is false. The Book of Mormon was printed on paper evidently obtained from Case & Brown of Shortsville, New York (see introduction to III.K.28, W. H. MCINTOSH, *HISTORY OF ONTARIO COUNTY* [NY], 1876). However, the title perhaps misrepresents its source since the article itself claims that Joseph Smith obtained from their store, located on Rochester's Exchange Street, some writing paper and theological books prior to the Book of Mormon's publication. This claim presumably originated with William Alling (d. 1890), who was a clerk in the store until Elihu F. Marshall sold the business to him in 1834. David Cory (d. 1897) became Alling's business partner in 1859. Eventually the business passed into the hands of their sons, Joseph T. Alling and David W. Cory, the former of whom probably transmitted his father's statement into published form in 1908.[1]

Alling & Cory, Rochester's wellknown paper firm, gave a reception to Western New York publishers and printers at their new warehouse on Jones and Dean streets Saturday last and the occasion was made most pleasant. Luncheon was served by Teall and during the forenoon the publishers' association held a business meeting.

An historical item of interest to Palmyra is contained in a little booklet issued by Alling & Cory and the paragraph in question reads as follows:

It may be of interest in this connection to know that one of the early customers of Mr. Alling was a man who became famous as the founder of

1. For a brief history of the Alling & Cory Paper Firm, see *One Hundred Years in the Paper Business, 1819-1919*, 1919.

Mormonism, Joseph Smith. He used to come in on Mondays from his home in Palmyra and spend hours reading and selecting books and talking theology. It was at this time that he was engaged in writing his "Book of Mormon," but the present firm disclaims all responsibility for Mr. Smith's religious conclusions, even if he did buy his books and writing paper from their store.

36.
Lockwood R. Doty History, 1925

Lockwood R. Doty, *History of the Genesee Country,* 4 vols. (Chicago: S. J. Clarke Publishing Co., 1925), 1:561-63.

EDITORIAL NOTE

Lockwood R. Doty (1858-?), county judge and surrogate of Livingston County, New York, was recognized as "one of the foremost authorities upon Livingston county and the Genesee country" (Doty 1925, 4:865-66). Doty mostly relies on previously published material for his account, and he is inaccurate in some of his statements.

... The town of Manchester was the birthplace of Mormonism, or Church of the Latter Day Saints. Many volumes relating to the merits or demerits of this peculiar sect have been written, but it is fitting that a brief account of its beginning should be included in this sketch of the town where it originated. Joseph Smith, the first prophet and founder of the church, was born in Windsor County, Vermont, December 13 [23], 1805. While still in early boyhood his parents came to Palmyra, New York, where his father opened a small tavern.[1] The father was a man of little worth, but the mother was of stronger character, and both parents were ignorantly imbued with religious fanaticism. Mrs. Smith firmly believed that her son was destined to be a prophet, even during his early boyhood.[2] In 1819 the family moved to a small farm on the road known as Stafford Street, in the northern part of Manchester. Soon after locating here the Smiths, father and son, were employed by Clark Chase[3] to dig a well. While engaged in this work, a white, glossy pebble, resembling a human foot in shape, was found. The future prophet kept the pebble and soon pretended to have discovered that it possessed supernatural powers. In the pebble he claimed to discern happenings in distant places and to read the course of future events. This pebble became known as the "peek stone," al-

1. Compare III.J.8, POMEROY TUCKER ACCOUNT, 1867, 12.
2. Compare III.J.2, ORSAMUS TURNER ACCOUNT, 1851, 213.
3. On Clark Chase, see III.J.8, POMEROY TUCKER ACCOUNT, 1867, n. 33.

though Smith was the only one who could make it do tricks, which was evidence enough to him that he was the destined prophet.[4]

Near the Smith home was a hill and, according to rumor, hidden treasure was buried therein. This rumor was told to the credulous Smiths by Oliver Cowdery,[5] a school teacher residing on Stafford Street.[6] Young Joseph immediately consulted his peek stone in order to locate the treasure. How many times the father and son spent the midnight hours spading up the hillside is not known, but no treasure was found. Loath to acknowledge defeat, the Smiths maintained that they found a chest, three feet long, covered with a dark stone, in the center of which was a white spot. Upon being exposed to the air, the white spot began to spread and finally exploded loudly, and then the chest vanished.[7]

When Joseph, Jr., was about nineteen years old he attended a Methodist camp meeting and was converted.[8] Having no further use for his remarkable stone, he now communed directly [p. 561] with the angels. One of these accommodating spirits directed him to dig in the "Hill of Camorah" for some gold plates containing "a record of the ancient inhabitants of this country, engraved by Mormon, the son of Nephi." Smith "obeyed" and "found" the plates September 21 [22], 1827. With them was a pair of spectacles, the lenses of which were opaque to all except the prophet, and only by wearing these spectacles could the record be translated. Apparently with great reluctance, Smith undertook the task, at the same time announcing that anyone else who gazed upon the plates would be stricken with death. As a business man, Smith was without a superior in his day. Seated behind a curtain, he donned the spectacles and read from the plates, while his words were written down by Martin Harris and Oliver Cowdery.

Various stories of the finding and translation of the gold plates have been told. One of these, apparently authentic, is that Smith did not claim for

---

4. Compare III.J.8, POMEROY TUCKER ACCOUNT, 1867, 19.

5. On Oliver Cowdery (1806-50), see "Introduction to Oliver Cowdery Collection."

6. The claim that Oliver Cowdery told the Smiths about treasures in the Hill Cumorah is incorrect. Cowdery did not come to Palmyra until at least a year after the plates had been removed from the hill.

7. Compare III.J.2, ORSAMUS TURNER ACCOUNT, 1851, 216.

8. This could have been during the Palmyra revival of 1824-25, which Smith describes but places in 1820. Doty likely follows Tucker's account of Smith's joining the "probationary class of the Methodist church in Palmyra" (see III.J.8, POMEROY TUCKER ACCOUNT, 1867, 18), but Tucker did not assign a date to the event.

the plates any religious significance, but that they were simply a historical record of the ancient inhabitants of America.[9] About the time the translation commenced, Sidney Rigdon,[10] of Ohio, attracted to Smith by the news of the great discovery, appeared on the scene. Rigdon had been a Baptist minister, but had fallen into disrepute with that denomination. There seems to be little doubt that it was Rigdon who gave the Book of Mormon, or Gold Bible, its religious color. It has been intimated that the greater part of the "translation" was prepared by Rigdon, then read behind the curtain by the prophet to his secretaries.[11]

Martin Harris[12] mortgaged a good farm in Palmyra to raise the necessary $2,500 to pay for the printing of the first edition of the Book of Mormon.[13] It was printed at Palmyra by E. B. Grandin in 1830. Mrs. Harris, with a woman's intuition, had no faith in the book which had so captivated her husband, and she got hold of about a hundred pages of the manuscript, which she either hid or destroyed. Smith, Cowdery and Harris agreed not to make another translation, because "the evil spirit might get up a story that the second translation differed from the first."[14]

The Mormon Church was founded on the Gold Bible. About 1832 all those who had joined the church gathered at Kirtland, Ohio. ... [p. 562]

---

9. This claim is also made in III.A.3, JOSEPH CAPRON STATEMENT, 8 NOV 1833.

10. On Sidney Rigdon (1793-1876), see introduction to I.A.13, SIDNEY RIGDON ACCOUNT, CIRCA 1836.

11. See III.J.8, POMEROY TUCKER ACCOUNT, 1867, 28, 48, 75-76.

12. On Martin Harris (1783-1875), see "Introduction to Martin Harris Collection."

13. See III.L.14, MARTIN HARRIS MORTGAGE, 25 AUG 1829.

14. See III.L.16, BOOK OF MORMON PREFACE, 1829.

37.
Elizabeth Kane Interview with Brigham Young, Artemisia (Beaman) Snow, and Orrin Rockwell, 1872-1873

Norman R. Bowen and Mary Karen Bowen Solomon, eds., *A Gentile Account of Life in Utah's Dixie, 1872-73: Elizabeth Kane's St. George Journal* (Salt Lake City: University of Utah Tanner Trust Fund, 1995), 69-77.

EDITORIAL NOTE

Elizabeth Dennistoun (Wood) Kane (1836-1909), wife of Major General Thomas L. Kane (d. 1883), was born near Liverpool, England. She married Kane in 1853. In 1857 the Kanes were briefly separated when Thomas left Philadelphia to mediate difficulties between the Mormons and the U.S. government in Utah. Over the years a friendship developed between Kane and Brigham Young, who in 1872 invited the Kanes and their two little boys, Evan and William, to spend the winter with him in newly settled St. George, Utah. In 1874 she published *Twelve Mormon Homes Visited in Succession on a Journey through Utah to Arizona* (Philadelphia), which highlighted her experience with polygamous Mormon families. This publication, however, did not include an account of her two-month stay in St. George. With the help of E. Kent Kane (d. 1978), Elizabeth's grandson and Kane family historian, Norman R. Bowen edited and published Elizabeth Kane's St. George journal in 1995.

In St. George the Kanes stayed with Erastus Snow, then president of the LDS church's Southern Mission. On the evening of 15 January 1873, the Kanes were invited to dine at the home of Artemisia (Beaman) Snow, the first of Erastus Snow's three wives (married 1838). Several of the "leading people" were present, including Brigham Young. After dinner, some of the party retired to the parlor where Artemisia Snow, Brigham Young, and Elijah F. Sheets began reminiscing about Joseph Smith. Also included is a reminiscence of Orrin Porter Rockwell, whom Kane must have interviewed in Salt Lake City in late November 1872 prior to her trip to St. George. The Elizabeth Kane Collection in the Archives of the Harold B. Lee Library, Brigham Young University, Provo, Utah, is presently unavailable to researchers—hence my reliance on the published version.

After dinner most of the female guests withdrew, to the kitchen I suppose, for I could see them flitting in to the dinning room now and then to put away pieces of the dinner service. Mrs. Artemisia Snow[1] and I were accompanied to the parlour by the gentlemen. The lamp on the mantlepiece shed but a faint light compared to the vivid changeful glow of the blazing pine logs on the hearth, and some allusion to the solidity with which the fireplace was built, led to the remark that it was under the hearth at the Beman farm [in Livonia, New York] that the "Plates" of the Book of Mormon were hidden.[2] Mrs. Snow [p. 69] was a daughter of Mr. Beman,[3] a wealthy farmer of Livingston[,] Livonia County, New York.[4] She was only a girl when the plates were brought there, but remembered perfectly the anxiety they all felt after the plates were buried, and a fire kindled on the hearth above them, round which the family sat as usual. I asked "Who were searching for the plates?"

She answered "The people of the neighborhood. They did not know what Joseph Smith had found, but that it was treasure, and they wanted to get it away. This was long before there was any dream of religious persecution."

Mrs. Snow sate [sat] knitting a stocking as she talked, like any other homely elderly woman. She certainly seemed to *think* she had actually gone through the scene she narrated. I know so little of the history of the Mormons

---

1. Artemisia (Beaman) Snow (1819-82), daughter of Alvah Beaman, was born in Livonia, Livingston County, New York. She married Erastus Snow in 1838, the first of his three plural wives and mother of eleven children. She died at St. George, Utah (Black 1987, s.v. "Artemisia Snow").

2. Actually the plates were hidden under the Smiths' hearth in Manchester, New York, while Alvah Beman was visiting in late September 1827. The mistake was not Kane's, but Artemisia's as indicated by Erastus Snow's comment that his father-in-law "was an early associate of the Smith family in the State of New York, and assisted the Prophet Joseph in hiding the plates under the hearth in his own home, at times when his enemies were searching for them" ("Autobiography of Erastus Snow, Dictated to his son Franklin R. Snow in the year 1875," *Utah Genealogical and Historical Magazine* 14 [July 1923]: 106). Artemisia was eight in 1827; older sister Mary, however, got the story right (see III.K.12, MARY A. NOBLE AUTOBIOGRAPHY, CIRCA 1834-1836, 3, and n. 2).

3. On Alvah Beaman (1775-1837), see I.B.5, LUCY SMITH HISTORY, 1845, n. 151.

4. Actually Livonia, Livingston County, New York.

that the stories that now followed by the flickering firelight were full of interest to me. I shall write down as much as I can remember, though there must be gaps where allusions were made to things I had never heard of and did not understand enough to remember accurately. The most curious thing was the air of perfect sincerity of all the speakers. I cannot feel doubtful that they believed what they said.

A blue eyed Pennsylvanian with rosy cheeks and snow white hair, a man who has a thoroughly good benevolent face, Bishop Sheetz,[5] of Montgomery County [Pennsylvania], said, speaking of his [p. 70] first interview with Joseph Smith—they oftenest speak of him as "Joseph" or "Brother Joseph" "I thought him the image of everything prepossessing and noble. I felt to be thankful that I had lived to a wonderful day when God was again communicating with man."

Brigham Young[6] described his first visit to him [Joseph Smith]. "I had received the testimony before," he said, "but I wanted to see him. I felt I would know him to be the man. I went with by brother Phineas[7] and Heber C. Kimball[8] to old man Smith's [Joseph Smith, Sr.'s][9] and found neither of the sons at home, but he said the boys were in the woods. Accordingly we went about a quarter of a mile to where Jos. & Hyrum[10] were, following the tracks of their woodsled through a light snow that was melting. They had just felled a tree, and Joseph greeted us pleasantly, and asked us if we could handle an axe. We then took hold one after another, and got the branches off and the tree cut up into logs very soon, and work being over for the day he invited us home to talk. We attended a meeting in the evening too, and

---

5. Elijah F. Sheets (1821-1904) was born in Charlestown, Chester County, Pennsylvania. He was baptized by Erastus Snow in 1840 and met Joseph Smith shortly after his arrival at Nauvoo, Illinois, in September 1841. Following his ordination as an elder in April 1842, he served a mission to Pennsylvania (1842-44) and England (1844-46). In 1856 he was set apart as bishop of Salt Lake City's Eighth Ward, where he served for more than forty-five years (Jenson 1971, 1:614-16; Black 1987, s.v. "Sheets, Elijah Funk").

6. On Brigham Young (1801-77), see introduction to III.K.19, BRIGHAM YOUNG ACCOUNTS, 1855 & 1857.

7. On Phineas Howe Young (1799-1879), see introduction to III.K.23, PHINEAS HOWE YOUNG AUTOBIOGRAPHY, 1863.

8. On Heber C. Kimball (1801-68), see introduction to III.K.24, HEBER C. KIMBALL AUTOBIOGRAPHY, 1864.

9. On Joseph Smith, Sr., (1771-1840), see "Introduction to Joseph Smith, Sr., Collection."

10. On Hyrum Smith (1800-44), see I.A.15, JOSEPH SMITH HISTORY, 1839, n. 12.

I was fully satisfied."[11] ...

I forget what came next, but after Mrs. Snow had been mentioned as being Beaman's daughter, I asked some question [p. 71] respecting the original discovery of the plates which was answered as nearly as I can remember.

A man named Walters[12] son of a rich man living on the Hudson [River] South of Albany,[13] received a scientific education, was even sent to Paris.[14] After he came home he lived like a misanthrope, he had come back an infidel, believing neither in man nor God. He used to dress in a fine broadcloth overcoat, but no other coat nor vest, his trousers all slitted up and patched, and sunburnt boots—filthy! He was a sort of fortune teller, though he never stirred off the old place. For instance, a man I [Brigham Young][15] knew rode up, and before he spoke, the fortune teller said, "You needn't get off your horse, I know what you want. Your mare ain't stolen."

Says the man "How do you know what I want?"

---

11. Reflecting on his November 1832 introduction to Joseph Smith in Kirtland, Ohio, Young elsewhere said: "We went to his [Joseph Smith's] father's house, and learned that he [Joseph] was in the woods, chopping. We immediately repaired to the woods, where we found the Prophet, and two of his brothers, chopping and hauling wood. Here my joy was full at the privilege of shaking the hand of the Prophet of God, and received the sure testimony, by the Spirit of prophecy, that he was all that any man could believe him to be, as a true Prophet. He was happy to see us, and bid us welcome. We soon returned to his house, he accompanying us" (*Millennial Star* 25 [1863]: 439).

12. Apparently a reference to Luman Walters (c. 1788-1860) of Pultneyville, Wayne County, New York (see III.E.3, *PALMYRA REFLECTOR,* 1829-1831, n. 21). In 1857 Brigham Young could not remember the astrologer's name but may have subsequently remembered it himself or learned it from other pioneer Mormons such as Orrin Porter Rockwell or Heber C. Kimball (see III.K.19, BRIGHAM YOUNG ACCOUNTS, 1855 & 1857).

13. Presently there is no evidence to connect Luman Walters with this area of New York.

14. See III.K.19, BRIGHAM YOUNG ACCOUNTS, 1855 & 1857, n. 4.

15. Since Brigham Young was last quoted in reference to his first meeting Joseph Smith, Kane evidently attributed the following statement about Walters to Young, not Artemisia Snow as D. Michael Quinn has interpreted (1998, 117, 120, 131). Kane's wording is very similar to known statements of Young (compare III.K.19, BRIGHAM YOUNG ACCOUNTS, 1855 & 1857), and she later attributes a portion of the statement to him (see note 16 below).

Says he, "I'll give you a sign. You've got a respectable wife, and so many children. At this minute your wife has just drawn a bucket of water at the well to wash her dishes. Look at your watch and find out if it ain't so when you get home. As to your mare, she's not a dozen miles from home. She strayed into such neighborhood, and as they didn't know whose she was they put her up till she should be claimed. My fee's a dollar. Be off!"

This man was sent for three times to go to the hill Cumorah to dig for treasure. People knew there was treasure there.[16] Beman was one of those who sent for him. He came. Each time he said there was treasure there, but that *he* couldn't get it; though there was one that could. The last time he came he pointed out Joseph Smith, who was sitting quietly among a group of men in the tavern, and said *There* was the young man that could find it, and cursed and swore about him in a scientific manner: awful!"[17] [p. 72]

I asked where Cumorah was. "In Manchester Township[,] Ontario County[,] New York." I think this is near Rochester. I have heard Porter Rockwell,[18] a bronzed seafaring looking man, with long hair tucked behind his ears, in which he wears little gold rings, tell of Joseph Smith's failures and final success in finding the plates. Rockwell was a schoolmate and friend of Smith's, and in spite of his intimate knowledge of the humble Yankee settler's life, the log-house, lit up at night by pine chips because they were too poor to burn candles, the daily trudge to the rude school house and the association with him when they were "hired men" together, evidently believes in his Prophet and hero, falsifying the proverb about "No man being a hero to his valet de chambre [manservant]." His story about the discovery of the plates sounded like the German legends of the demons of the Herz Mountains [Harz Mountains, East and West Germany], but his description of the life of his neighborhood made me understand what Brigham Young meant by saying the people knew there was treasure in the Hill Cumorah. It seems that the time was one of great mental disturbance in that region. There was much religious excitement; chiefly among the Methodists. People felt free to do very queer things in the new country, which the lapse of a single generation has made us consider Old New England. . . . [p. 73] . . .

Not only was there religious excitement, but the phantom treasure of

---

16. This statement is directly attributed to Brigham Young (see below, p. 73).

17. This paragraph is very similar to Young's previous statements (see III.K.19, BRIGHAM YOUNG ACCOUNTS, 1855 & 1857).

18. On Orrin Porter Rockwell (1813-78), see I.A.15, JOSEPH SMITH HISTORY, 1839, n. 121.

Captain Kidd[19] were sought for far and near, and even in places like Cumorah where the primeval forest still grew undisturbed the gold finders sought for treasure without any traditionary rumor even to guide them. Rockwell said his mother[20] and Mrs. Smith[21] used to spend their Saturday evenings together telling their dreams, and that he was always glad to spend his afternoon holiday gathering pine knots for the evening blaze on the chance that his mother would forget to send him to bed, and that he might listen unnoticed to their talk. The most sober settlers of the district he said were "gropers" though they were ashamed to own [up to] it; and stole out to dig of [on] moonlight nights, carefully effacing the traces of their ineffectual work before creeping home to bed. He often heard his mother and Mrs. Smith comparing notes, and telling how Such an one's dream, and Such another's pointed to the same lucky spot: how the spades often truck the iron sides of the treasure chest, and how it was charmed away, now six inches this side, now four feet deeper, and again completely out of reach. Joseph Smith was no gold seeker by trade; he only did openly what all were doing privately; but he was considered to be "lucky."

How he found the plates, saw them plainly, and lost sight of them again, I have read in some Mormon book since I came here. Brigham Young said that the night Joseph found the plates "there was a wonderful light in the heavens. I was about [p. 74] 70 miles from there and stood for hours watching it. There were lances darting and the sound of cannon and armies just at hand, and flashes of light, though there were no clouds.[22] Joseph's discovery was in the papers directly,[23] and everywhere people remarked the coincidence, because for hundreds of miles they had been out watching like myself."

I asked where the plates were now, and saw in a moment from the expression of the countenances around that I had blundered. But I was answered that they were in a cave; that Oliver Cowdery[24] though now an

---

19. On Robert Kidd (1645-1701), see III.J.8, POMEROY TUCKER ACCOUNT, 1867, n. 30.

20. On Sarah Witt Rockwell (1785-?), see I.A.15, JOSEPH SMITH HISTORY, 1839, n. 90.

21. On Lucy Smith (1775-1856), see "Introduction to Lucy Mack Smith Collection."

22. See III.K.24, HEBER C. KIMBALL AUTOBIOGRAPHY, 1864.

23. The earliest known newspaper account of Joseph Smith's gold plates was in the *Wayne Sentinel,* 26 June 1829 (see III.E.1, *WAYNE SENTINEL,* 1824-1836).

24. On Oliver Cowdery (1805-50), see "Introduction to Oliver Cowdery Collection."

apostate would not deny that he had seen them.[25] He had been to the cave, I did not understand exactly whether Oliver Cowdery was there three times, or whether he accompanied Joseph the third time *he* went there, and Brigham Young's tone was so solemn that I listened bewildered like a child to the evening witch stories of its nurse. Nor do I understand whether the plates were all transcribed by this time or not. The plates are the thin leaves of gold shaped like thin sections of a cow-bell, to speak profanely, and threaded on golden rings which the Mormons believe Joseph to have found in the hill Cumorah. The curious characters inscribed upon them he was enabled to translate by means of a magic, or hallowed, pair of immense eye-glasses, to speak profanely [p. 75] again of what the Mormons reverence, called the Urim & Thummim found in the same small chest in which the plates were. This translation is the Book of Mormon.

Brigham Young said that when Oliver Cowdery and Joseph Smith were in the cave this third time, they could see its contents more distinctly than before, just as your eyes get used to the light of a dim candle, and objects in the room become plain to you. It was about fifteen feet high and round its sides were hanged boxes of treasure. In the centre was a large stone table empty before, but now piled with similar gold plates, some of which also lay scattered on the floor beneath. Formerly the sword of Laban hung on the walls sheathed, but it was now unsheathed and lying across the plates on the table; and One that was with them said it was never to be sheathed until the reign of Righteousness upon the earth."[26]

I would have liked to hear more, half expecting the apparition of some Frederick Barbarossa,[27] but Brigham Young ceased speaking and Bishop Snow related a long dream which had recently been vouchsafed to him. By this time my poor little boys[28] were so tired after their long ride that they were nodding [p. 76] as they stood beside my chair. ...

---

25. At this time Cowdery had been dead for twenty-three years, prior to which he had rejoined the church.

26. At the bottom of this journal page, Elizabeth Kane wrote: "I found a long account of the 'sword of Laban' in a copy of the Book of Mormon on the table this morning in the 1st Chapter of the Book of Nephi." Brigham Young subsequently related the story about the cave in the Hill Cumorah in a public sermon (see III.K.30, BRIGHAM YOUNG ACCOUNT, 1877).

27. Frederick I ("Frederick Barbarossa") (1123?-90), king of Germany and the Holy Roman Empire, 1152-90.

28. Evan and William.

L.
Miscellaneous Documents

1.
PALMYRA (NY) ROAD LISTS, 1817-1822

"A Copy of the Several Lists of the Mens Names Liable to Work on the Highways in the Town of Palmyra in the Year 1804 ...," typescript by Doris Nesbitt, microfilm in LDS Family History Library, Salt Lake City, Utah.

EDITORIAL NOTE

Although a microfilming crew for the LDS church filmed the Nesbitt transcription at Palmyra's King's Daughters Free Library in 1970, neither the original nor the typescript can be located at present. Richard Palmer of the Palmyra Historical Society told one reesearcher that the original book containing the road lists may have been accidentally destroyed about 1976 when someone took the wrong boxes to the town dump (Walters 1987).

New York law required all land owners ("free holders") and all free males of twenty-one years of age or older to work at least one day during the year maintaining public roads. This work usually consisted of filling ruts and removing vegetation from the road's surface, clearing ditches and culverts, and repairing bridges. The road system was divided into districts, of which Palmyra had (for the years of the Smiths' residence in the township) thirty-one in 1817, thirty-four in 1818 and 1819, thirty-five in 1820, thirty-seven in 1821, and forty in 1822. The law stipulated that town meetings were to be held on the first Tuesday in April, at which time three Commissioners of Highways were to be elected, along with an overseer for each road district in the township. Overseers were to submit a list of all those in their district who were required by law to work on the roads to the commissioners within sixteen days of their elections. After approval by the commissioners, these lists were turned over to the town clerk in the latter part of April and recorded by him (see *Laws of the State of New York, Revised,* 1813, 2:125, 271-75, 309).

The present record lists Joseph Smith, Sr., on Palmyra road district 26 from 1817 through 1822. During the Smiths' residence in Palmyra, district 26 began on the east end of Main Street near its intersection with the road from Canandaigua, ran west into what is now Macedon township, and included Stafford Road, which ran south to the boundary of Palmyra township (see Record of Roads of the Town of Palmyra, 1793-1901, 94-95, 104, microfilm copies in State Library, Albany, New York, and Family History Library, Salt Lake City, Utah).

The Palmyra Road list of 1817 is the earliest known record of Joseph Smith, Sr., in Palmyra. He is not listed on any road district prior to 1817, indicating that he probably arrived in Palmyra sometime after April 1816 and before April 1817. This fits with Lucy Smith's claim that Joseph Sr. left Norwich, Vermont, after the failure of their third harvest, either in late summer or early fall of 1816 (I.B.5, LUCY SMITH HISTORY, 1845, MS:33; see also II.B.16, SMITH FAMILY WARNING OUT OF NORWICH [VT], 27 MAR 1816).

The names on the road lists are generally arranged in the order in which their residences and businesses appear moving west along Main Street, then south on Stafford Road. In 1817 Joseph Smith, Sr., appeared as fifteenth on a list of thirty-eight names, indicating that the Smiths were probably living somewhere toward the west end of Main Street in 1817. While this location conflicts with a later tradition that the Smiths "rented a small frame building on the eastern outskirts of the village near where Johnson Street takes off Vienna" (Bean 1938, 12), it is consistent with earlier information imparted by Palmyra Presbyterian minister Horace Eaton in 1857 and 1863. In an 1857 sermon Eaton said the Smiths resided "on lower Main street" (H. Eaton 1858, 28-29). In an 1863 sermon, which remains unpublished, Eaton expanded on this subject: "Where Asa Chase now resides there once stood a house built by Sam[uel] Jennings. This house was occupied by ~~Jos~~ the father of Joseph Smith, the founder of Mormonism, who came from Sharon Vt. [in] 1817. ~~Levi~~ Afterwards Levi Daggett resided there & here occurred the wedding of Henry Wells & Sarah Daggett" ("Continuation of the History of Palmyra. A Sermon preached on the Annual day of Thanksgiving. Nov. 26, 1863. H. Eaton. Palmyra N.," Palmyra King's Daughters Free Library, Palmyra, New York).[1] According to a 1907 history of Palmyra, "Henry Wells married his first wife—Sally Daggett—in the little weather beaten house that stands opposite Stafford street on the north side of Main Street" (*Palmyra[,] Wayne County[,] New York,* 1907, 27). An early map of Palmyra, dating from the late 1860s or 1870s, identifies at this location the building and lot of "[Asa] Chase & [Zebulon] Williams" (Palmyra King's Daughters Free Library, Palmyra, New York).

At this first residence, according to Pomeroy Tucker, Joseph Smith, Sr., opened a "cake and beer shop" (III.J.8, POMEROY TUCKER ACCOUNT, 1867, 12). Wesley P. Walters speculated that Joseph Sr. may

1. Sarah Daggett (1803-59) married Henry Wells on 5 September 1827, their four children being born in Palmyra before moving to Aurora, New York (Doggett 1973, 149-50, 199).

have also worked nearby at Joseph D. Hayward's cooper shop (Walters 1987).

The Smiths apparently remained at this location for at least two years, Joseph Sr. being listed fifteenth on a list of thirty-two names in 1818, and twentieth on a list of forty names in 1819. Then, in 1820, Alvin Smith appears as fifteenth and Joseph Sr. as forty-second on a list of forty-four names. This undoubtedly indicates that sometime between April 1819 and April 1820 part of the Smith family moved to the southern end of Stafford Road. Two months later, on 13 June 1820, the record of a road survey mentions "Joseph Smith's dwelling house" as being located about fifty-nine feet north and west of where the road meets the township line dividing Palmyra and Farmington (later Manchester) (see III.L.2, PALMYRA [NY] HIGHWAY SURVEY, 13 JUN 1820). This is consistent with the statements of neighbors who said they first became acquainted with the Smiths about 1820 (III.A.13, WILLIAM STAFFORD STATEMENT, 8 DEC 1833, 237; III.A.14, WILLARD CHASE STATEMENT, CIRCA 11 DEC 1833, 240; III.A.2, BARTON STAFFORD STATEMENT, 3 NOV 1833, 250; III.A.15, HENRY HARRIS STATEMENT, CIRCA 1833, 251; and III.A.4, JOSHUA STAFFORD STATEMENT, 15 NOV 1833, 258).

Alvin's name appearing on the 1820 road list separate from his father's probably indicates that he continued to maintain the family store on Main Street. By law, Alvin should have been listed in 1819 since he turned twenty-one on 11 February 1819. Alvin may not have been present in April 1819, perhaps boarding and working in a neighboring township.

In 1821 Joseph Sr., Alvin, and Hyrum (who turned twenty-one on 9 February 1821) were listed as fifty-eighth, fifty-ninth, and sixtieth respectively on a list of sixty-one names. In 1822 Joseph Sr. and Alvin were listed as thirty-first and thirty-second respectively on a list of fifty-four names. The absence of Hyrum's name in 1822 suggests two possibilities: he either was hired out to work in a neighboring town or was living on the family's Manchester land (for which they had contracted over a year previously), perhaps dwelling in the partially constructed cabin (see III.L.4, SMITH MANCHESTER [NY] LAND RECORDS, 1820-1830).

Unfortunately there are no road lists for 1823-25 for Palmyra, but it is unlikely that the Smiths would have been listed for 1823, since their Manchester cabin had been completed, and it is likely that they had moved into it sometime between April 1822 and April 1823 (see III.L.4, SMITH MANCHESTER [NY] LAND RECORDS, 1820-1830). Below is the information taken from the Palmyra road lists pertaining to the Smiths.

PALMYRA ROAD DISTRICT 26 (1817-1822)			
Year	*Name*	*Position on List*	*Total Names*
1817	Joseph Sr.	15	38
1818	Joseph Sr.	15	32
1819	Joseph Sr.	20	40
	[Alvin absent]		
1820	Alvin	15	44
	Joseph Sr.	42	
1821	Alvin	58	61
	Joseph Sr.	59	
	Hyrum	60	
1822	Joseph Sr.	31	54
	Alvin	32	
	[Hyrum absent]		

2.
PALMYRA (NY) HIGHWAY SURVEY, 13 JUNE 1820

"Old Town Record, 1793-1870," 221, Township Office, Palmyra, New York.

EDITORIAL NOTE

On 13 June 1820, a survey crew laid out the extension of Stafford Street, which ran from the extreme southern end of Palmyra township northward to intersect Main Street. The survey began at the southern line which divided Palmyra from Farmington (later Manchester) township "three rods fourteen links [58.74 feet] southeast of Joseph Smith's dwelling house." The Smith cabin was therefore situated about fifty-nine feet northwest of the center of Stafford Road at the southern border of Palmyra township.

In 1982 an excavation team from Brigham Young University confirmed that a dwelling had existed at this location (Berge 1985; Enders 1985). Dale L. Berge, a professor of archaeology at Brigham Young University, summarized the physical remains at the site:

> When we began work, the site was in the middle of a cornfield. ... The land had been plowed regularly, as deeply as ten inches, year after year since the Smiths first worked it. ... Consequently, all artifacts to the ten-inch level had been disturbed.
>
> The foundation of the Smith cabin was probably like that of the Peter Whitmer log house—shallow, possibly two cobbles wide and deep. Plowing would have disturbed these stones, and over the years farmers would have removed them from the plowed field. ...
>
> Three disturbances below the plow zone were identified: a well, a shallow cellar, and an unknown feature of rocks.
>
> The well measured ten feet across at its opening, narrowing to five feet. ... A number of large rocks in the well appear to have been thrown in, and not laid as a casing. Most of the rocks were burned on one side, indicating that they were probably once part of the cabin fireplace. The few burnt-brick fragments we found suggest that the fireplace was made of cobblestones with a brick fire-box and possibly a hearth. ...
>
> The small cellar measured ten feet by six feet, with a depth of two and one-half feet. Inside we found many artifacts: ceramics, straight pins, buck-

> les, knives, forks, spoons, burnt wheat and beans, and a lid for a cast-iron pot. The small objects suggest that the cellar was under the floor of the kitchen, because these types of objects could fall through cracks in the floorboards. The larger objects, which were stratigraphically higher, may have fallen into the cellar when the cabin was torn down or abandoned. We also found construction debris in the cellar, including brickbats and nails.
>
> The unknown feature of rocks measured eight feet by six feet and two feet deep. The center of this shallow pit contained a row of laid cobbles, perhaps two or three feet deep. This feature may have been a footing, possibly to the bedroom addition.
>
> We are in the process of analyzing the artifacts—several thousand pieces of ceramics (which date from 1790 to 1830, within the time range of the occupation of the cabin), bottle glass, flat window glass, metal, and construction materials. ... The artifacts suggest that the Smith family was middle-class American, using daily objects that were popular throughout the country at the time (Berge 1985, 24-26).

Orsamus Turner undoubtedly described this cabin in his 1851 history. According to Turner, Joseph Smith, Sr., "first settled in or near Palmyra village, but as early as 1819 was the occupant of some new land on 'Stafford street' in the town of Manchester, near the line of Palmyra." In a footnote, Turner added: "Here the author remembers to have first seen the family, in the winter of [18]19, [18]20, in a rude long house, with but a small spot underbrushed around it" (III.J.2, ORSAMUS TURNER ACCOUNT, 1851, 212-13; see also III.J.35, THOMAS L. COOK HISTORY, 1930, 219). Turner's account is consistent with information derived from the Palmyra road lists indicating that sometime between April 1819 and April 1820 part of the Smith family moved to the south end of Stafford Road (see III.L.1, PALMYRA [NY] ROAD LISTS, 1817-1822).

Because the cabin mentioned in the 1820 survey is located in Palmyra on land then owned by Samuel Jennings,[1] one researcher has suggested that "the Smiths inadvertently built their cabin on the Palmyra side" (Enders 1985, 16). However, the evidence suggests the construction of a second cabin located on the Smith property in Manchester.[2] The reasons for the existence

---

1. Jennings owned 145 acres in the southwest corner of Palmyra Lot 43 (see Manchester Assessment Records, 1817-21, Ontario County Records Center and Archives, Canandaigua, New York).

2. This possibility was first advanced by Wesley P. Walters in 1987 (see Walters 1987). Most of the arguments given below were outlined by Walters.

of a Manchester cabin are as follows:

1. Lucy Smith reported that her husband and two oldest sons "set themselves about raising the means of paying for 100 Acres of land for which Mr. Smith contracted and which was then in the hands of a land agent. ... In one years time we made nearly all of the first pay=ment[.] The Agent advised us to build a log house on the land and commenced clearing it[.] we did" (I.B.5, LUCY SMITH HISTORY, 1845, MS:37; cf. I.D.2, WILLIAM SMITH NOTES, 1875, 17). The Smiths' land agent was Zachariah Seymour, who received the power of attorney for the land on 14 July 1820 (Miscellaneous Records, Ontario County Records Center and Archives, Canandaigua, New York, Book C, 342-44, 347-48). So the Smiths did not start building their cabin until after July 1820—the Jennings cabin being already in existence. Moreover, a cabin built on the Palmyra side of the line would not have been an improvement on land that they did not yet own.

2. On 7 July 1821 and 29 June 1822, the Smiths' Manchester land was assessed at $700, a typical price for unimproved land. But in the following year's assessment, taken on 24 July 1823, the same property was assessed at $1000, a significant increase from the previous year (see III.L.6, SMITH MANCHESTER [NY] LAND ASSESSMENT RECORDS, 1821-1823 & 1830). Since, according to Lucy Smith, the Smiths' frame house was not begun until November 1823 (I.B.5, LUCY SMITH HISTORY, 1845, MS:46), the increase in the 1823 assessment would indicate completion of the cabin after June 1822 and before July 1823.[3]

3. Lucy Smith said that in April 1829 her family was forced to vacate their frame house and move "back to the log house we had formerly lived in ... which was now occupied by Hyrum" (LUCY SMITH HISTORY, 1845,

3. Donald L. Enders puts too much weight on Lucy Smith's statement that "in 2 years from the time we entered Pal=myra strangers destitute of friends . . . home or emp=loyment. We were able to settle ourselves upon our own land in a snug comfortable though humble habitation built and neatly furnished by our own industry" (I.B.5, LUCY SMITH HISTORY, 1845, MS:38). Accordingly, Enders dates the construction of the Smiths' cabin (i.e., the Jennings cabin) to 1818 (Enders 1985, 16). However, Lucy makes it clear that the cabin had been completed about 1822, since she describes the events of 1823 as "the spring after we moved onto the farm" and the "3rd harvest time . . . since we opened our new farm" (I.B.5, LUCY SMITH HISTORY, 1845, MS:39, 40).

MS:92). Yet this cabin is consistently described as being located in Manchester.

a. Although Hyrum had occupied the cabin since his marriage to Jerusha Barden in November 1826, his name does not appear on the 1827 or 1828 road lists for Palmyra.

b. Hyrum's daughter Lovina was born on 16 September 1827, during his residence in the cabin, and according to Smith family genealogy the event occurred "in Manchester, Ontario Co. New York" (Joseph F. Smith, Genealogical Notes, Book 1, 105, George A. Smith Papers, Special Collections, Marriott Library, University of Utah, Salt Lake City, Utah).

c. Law suits against both Joseph Smith, Sr., and Hyrum Smith were brought before Manchester justice of the peace Nathan Pierce; Levi Daggett's case against Hyrum, initiated in June 1830, is most telling since Daggett was a resident of Palmyra; had both Daggett and Hyrum been residents of Palmyra, Pierce would have had no authority in the matter (III.L.19, NATHAN PIERCE DOCKET BOOK, 1830).

d. The 1830 U.S. census lists the Joseph Smith, Sr., family in Manchester (III.L.21, MANCHESTER [NY] CENSUS, 1830).

e. In 1830 Hyrum Smith was taxed for fifteen acres on Manchester Lot 1 (III.L.6, SMITH MANCHESTER [NY] LAND ASSESSMENT RECORDS, 1821-1823 & 1830).

f. In narrating events occurring in her home in 1830, Lucy repeatedly refers to her residence in Manchester (I.B.5, LUCY SMITH HISTORY, 1845, MS:frag. 9 [front]; 1853:151, 157, 158, 168, 170).

g. Those who visited the Smith residence during this 1829-30 period—Joseph Knight and Parley P. Pratt—said it was in Manchester (IV.A.1, JOSEPH KNIGHT, SR., REMINISCENCE, CIRCA 1835-1847, 5, 6, 8; III.K.16, PARLEY P. PRATT AUTOBIOGRAPHY, CIRCA 1854 [PART I], 46; III.K.21, PARLEY P. PRATT REMINISCENCE, 1856 [PART I]).

h. Various documents written during 1829-30 are dated and attributed to Manchester, including the following: several of Joseph Smith's revelations (D&C 19, 21, 23; as per headings in Book of Commandments, chaps. XVI-XXII); two letters of Oliver Cowdery (III.G.2, OLIVER COWDERY TO JOSEPH SMITH, 6 NOV 1829; III.G.3, OLIVER COWDERY TO

JOSEPH SMITH, 28 DEC 1829); Joseph Smith, Sr., and Martin Harris agreement regarding the sale of copies of the Book of Mormon, witnessed by Oliver Cowdery (III.L.17, JOSEPH SMITH, SR., AND MARTIN HARRIS AGREEMENT, 16 JAN 1830); and the "Missionaries Covenant," signed by Oliver Cowdery, Parley P. Pratt, Peter Whitmer, Jr., and Ziba Peterson, and witnessed by Joseph Smith and David Whitmer (III.L.22, MISSIONARIES COVENANT, 17 OCT 1830).

4. In his 1867 history, Pomeroy Tucker described the Smith cabin as "a small, one-story, smoky log-house, which they had built prior to removing there. This house was divided into two rooms, on the ground-floor, and had a low garret, in two apartments. A bedroom wing, built of sawed slabs, was afterward added" (III.J.8, POMEROY TUCKER ACCOUNT, 1867, 12-13).[4] Tucker said the cabin was on the Smiths' former property located "on the north border of the town of Manchester," and that the property was then owned by Seth T. Chapman. Since land records indicate that Chapman owned the Smiths' former property in Manchester since 1860 and that he did not own property in Palmyra Township,[5] the cabin described by Tucker must have been in Manchester.

Thus it is with some justification that some researchers postulate the existence of a Manchester cabin prior to the Smiths' building their frame home. To argue for the existence of only the Jennings cabin, which the Smiths inadvertently built on the Palmyra side of the township line, one must assume that the error was perpetuated not only by the Smiths but also by authorities in both counties. However, the existence of the names of Joseph Sr., Alvin, and Hyrum on the Palmyra road lists for 1820-22 strongly argues that both the Smiths and village authorities understood that the cabin was in Palmyra township. The surveyors of June 1820 certainly knew the location of the township line. When the Smiths' youngest child, Lucy, was born on

---

4. Tucker's description of the Smiths' cabin is typical of most cabins in the area.

5. Absalom Weeks, Deed to Seth T. Chapman, 2 April 1860, Liber 119, 262, Ontario County Records Center and Archives, Canandaigua, New York; cf. Porter 1971, 358. Both the Grantor and Grantee Indexes for 1823-69 fail to list any land transactions for Seth T. Chapman in Wayne County, New York. In fact, at the time of Tucker's writing in 1867, the cabin on Jennings's former land was then owned by Cornelius Drake and Harmon M. Chapman, who purchased the land from Absalom Weeks on 6 June 1864 (Liber 85, 528-29, Wayne County Clerk's Office, Lyons, New York; see also T. Cook 1930, 218-29).

18 July 1821, probably in the Jennings cabin, it was understood to have occurred in Palmyra (I.H.1, SMITH FAMILY GENEALOGY, 1834). William Stafford, who lived farther south on Stafford Road, apparently understood in 1833 that the cabin was situated in Palmyra when he said: "I first became acquainted with Joseph Smith, Sen. and his family in the year 1820. They lived, at that time, in Palmyra, about one mile and a half from my residence" (III.A.13, WILLIAM STAFFORD STATEMENT, 8 DEC 1833, 237). It is therefore unlikely that had the Jennings cabin been the residence of Hyrum and his family (and later Lucy and Joseph Sr.) that Manchester authorities as well as the Smiths would have mistakenly believed it was in Manchester. The existence of a second cabin on the Smiths' Manchester land harmonizes an otherwise inexplicable group of historical sources.

Despite the probability of the existence of a second cabin in Manchester, the Smiths did occupy the Jennings cabin on 13 June 1820 when the following survey of Stafford Road was executed.

Minutes of the survey of a public Highway beginning on the south line of Township No. 12[,] 2d range of townships in the town of Palmyra, three rods fourteen links southeast of Joseph Smith's dwelling house, thence N[orth]. 3 [degrees] West 192 rods thence N[orth] 2 deg[rees] east 24 rods thence North 3 deg[rees] west 76 rods, thence N[orth] 2 [degrees] W[est] 58 rods thence North 7 [degrees] east 26 rods thence N[orth]. 11 [degrees] E[ast] 47 rods to the line of lots owned by Zebulun Williams[6] and the heirs of John Hurlbut[7] thence N[orth] 1 1/2 [degrees] E[ast] on said line 68 rods thence N[orth]. 4 deg[rees] West 42 rods to the south line of main Street two rods west of the north west corner of a Lot of land formerly owned by Joseph D Hayward[.][8] the above minutes are calculated to be the center of the road and were taken by the poor old town compass, actually explored and surveyed by us this 13th day of June 1820

6. Zebulon Williams came from Seneca County, New York, settled in Palmyra about 1805, and became "Palmyra's first merchant." He also owned a large tract of land (T. Cook 1930, 117, 122, 183).

7. On John Hurlbut, see III.A.11, PALMYRA RESIDENTS GROUP STATEMENT, 4 DEC 1833, n. 15.

8. Joseph D. Hayward owned the land on Stafford Road just south of Jackson Street. Hayward, between twenty-six and forty-five years of age, is listed in the 1820 census of Palmyra, Ontario County, New York (1820:331).

Isaac Durfee[9]	Coms' of
Lumon Harrison[10]	Highways

I certify that the above is a true copy of the original minutes of which a copy was posted on the door of the town house on the 13th day of June 1820 by me

James White T[ow]n Cl[er]k[11]

9. Isaac Durfee (1785-1855) was the son of Lemuel Durfee (T. Cook 1930, 210; Reed 1902, 1:318).

10. Luman Harrison, in his fifties, is listed in the 1830 census of Palmyra, Wayne County, New York (1830:51).

11. James White opened a store at the east end of Main Street in Palmyra in 1817. He was the founder of Palmyra's Old Academy, a stock organization, incorporated about 1821 (McIntosh 1877, 140; T. Cook 1930, 101, 226, 274).

3.
Farmington (NY) Census Record, 1820

Federal Census Records, Farmington, Ontario County, New York, 1820:318. Family No. 524. Original in National Archives, Washington, D.C.

EDITORIAL NOTE

Census taking by law was to begin on the first Monday in August (7 August 1820) and was completed by 5 February 1821 (Wright 1900, 134, 137). According to the *Ontario Repository* of August 1820, the 1820 enumeration began on time. Since the Smiths appear as family No. 524 on a 661-name list, they were counted toward the end of the census in Farmington (later Manchester), but not necessarily as late as February 1821.

FARMINGTON CENSUS DATA		ANALYSIS TO SMITH FAMILY	
number	*sex*	*age*	
2	male	0-10	consistent for William (age 9) and Don Carlos (age 4)
2	male	16-26	consistent for Alvin (age 22), Hyrum (age 20)
1	male	45-	consistent for Joseph Sr.(age 49)
1	female	0-10	consistent for Katharine(age 8)
1	female	16-26	consistent for Sophronia (age 17)
1	female	26-45	consistent for Lucy (age 44)

Note that both Joseph Jr. (age 14) and Samuel Harrison (age 12) are missing. The 1820 enumerators were instructed not to include family members whose "usual place of abode was, on the first Monday of August, in another family" (Wright 1900, 135-36). Richard L. Anderson's suggestion that the two Smith boys "were likely boarded temporarily at another farm for some type of harvest labor" is probably correct (R. L. Anderson 1969b, 22). Both William and Joseph Smith mentioned that the Smith boys were sometimes hired out and temporarily away from home (I.D.7, WILLIAM SMITH INTERVIEW WITH E. C. BRIGGS, 1893; I.A.15, JOSEPH SMITH HISTORY, 1839, 7).[1]

The 1820 census also indicates the occupations of the three adult males listed in the Smith family: two in "agriculture," and one under "manufactures." Concerning the enumeration of manufacturers, census takers were instructed: "[I]n the column of manufactures will be included not only all the persons employed in what the act more specifically denominates manufacturing *establishments,* but all those artificers, handicrafts men, and mechanics, whose labor is preeminently of the hand, and not upon the field" (Wright 1900, 135). Richard L. Anderson is likely correct when he states, "This probably means that Joseph Smith, Sr. plied his trade of coopering and similar production, whereas Alvin and Hyrum, then twenty-one and twenty, were engaged mainly in the heavy work of farming" (R. L. Anderson 1969b, 22).

In June 1820, the Smiths were still in the Jennings cabin on the Palmyra side of the township line (III.L.2, PALMYRA [NY] HIGHWAY SURVEY, 13 JUN 1820), where they apparently remained until sometime after April 1822 (see III.L.1, PALMYRA [NY] ROAD LISTS, 1817-1822). The listing in the Farmington census rolls for 1820 only seems possible on the basis that the Smiths had already contracted for their Manchester land (perhaps working a portion of it) and were planning to move onto the property (see Walters 1989). It is also possible that the census takers, like Orsamus Turner, were mistaken about the location of the cabin. While the surveyors of Stafford Road knew the location of the township line, its exact location at this early period may not have been known by the general public.

---

1. Quinn's suggestion that the fourteen-year-old Joseph Jr. was either in Windsor, New York, or Harmony, Pennsylvania, working as a treasure seer in 1820 is erroneous (1998, 51-52). See Vogel 1994, 213-27 and various annotations in vol. 4 forthcoming.

4.
Smith Manchester (NY) Land Records, 1820-1830

Heirs of Nicholas Evertson, Land Transfer to Lemuel Durfee, 20 December 1825, Deeds, Liber 44, 232, Ontario County Records Center and Archives, Canandaigua, New York.

EDITORIAL NOTE

The Smiths' occupation of their Manchester land, or a portion of it, spanned from shortly after July 1820 to October 1830 and constitutes the longest residence of the Smith family at any one location. The following is a chronologically arranged summary of important events and documents dealing with the Smiths' Farmington/Manchester land[1]:

1. *16 December 1795*: Thomas Morris and James Wadsworth sell lands to Nicholas Evertson and Benjamin Kissam of New York City, which includes the Smiths' Manchester property (Deeds, Liber 20, 39).

2. *12 July 1805*: Cornelia Kissam, widow of Benjamin Kissam, releases land to Nicholas Evertson of New York City (Deeds, Liber 20, 39).

3. *1807*: Nicholas Evertson dies.

4. *21 June 1820*: The executors of Nicholas Evertson's estate convey to Casper W. Eddy, a New York City physician, power of attorney to sell Nicholas Evertson's land holdings (Wills, Book 47, 7-11, Surrogate's Court, Manhattan Borough, New York County, New York).

5. *22 June 1820*: The entire 300 acres of Farmington Lot 1 is taxed to the heirs of Nicholas Evertson, indicating that the Smiths had not yet contracted for the land (Farmington Assessment Roll, 1820, Ontario County Records Center and Archives, Canandaigua, New York).

6. *14 July 1820*: In Canandaigua, New York, Casper W. Eddy transfers his power of attorney for Evertson lands to Zachariah Seymour (Miscellaneous Records, Book C, 342-44, 347-48, Canandaigua Records Center and

---

1. Farmington became Burt on 31 March 1821, and Burt became Manchester on 16 April 1822.

Archives, Canandaigua, New York).

7. *14 July 1820-5 February 1821 (probably summer of 1820)*[2]: Joseph Smith, Sr., and Alvin Smith contract with Zachariah Seymour for 100 acres of Farmington Lot 1. The original "Articles of Agreement" have not been located and would not have been copied into county records until final payment, which the Smiths failed to do. That such an "article" existed is proven by the record of Squire Stoddard's purchase of lands to the south of the Smith property in November 1825. The record states that Stoddard's new land was situated immediately south of "lands heretofore articled to Joseph and Alvin Smith" (Deeds, Liber 44, 220). The Smiths' "Articles of Agreement" apparently broke the payments down into three installments, each due on the anniversary of the original contract, the first consisting of a down-payment and an unspecified number of payments due in the course of the first year. Lucy Smith said that the family had "made nearly all of the first payment" in one year, but that "the second payment was now coming due and no means as yet of meeting it." Alvin therefore left home to find work and raise "the second payment and the remainder of the first," and returned with "the necessary amount of money for all except the last payment" (I.B.5, LUCY SMITH HISTORY, 1845, MS:37-40). In absence of the original purchase agreement, the amount of down-payment and terms of agreement are unknown.[3]

8. *7 August 1820-5 February 1821*: Smiths enumerated in the Farmington census, indicating that they had contracted for their property before that time (III.L.3, FARMINGTON [NY] CENSUS, 1820).

9. *7 July 1821*: Smiths taxed for 100 acres on Manchester Lot 1 for the first time. Smith land assessed at $700, typical value of unimproved land (III.L.6, SMITH MANCHESTER [NY] LAND ASSESSMENT RECORDS, 1821-1823 & 1830).

---

2. Dates derived from III.L.6, SMITH MANCHESTER (NY) LAND ASSESSMENT RECORDS, 1821-1823 & 1830; and III.L.3, FARMINGTON (NY) CENSUS RECORD, 1820.

3. Richard L. Bushman has pointed out that 5 percent of the total purchase price was common (Bushman 1984, 202 n. 14; cf. J. P. Walker 1986, 223). Bushman, following the traditional purchase date of 1818, has also suggested that the Smiths contracted for their land "a year too soon" since land prices in the Genesee Valley dropped in 1819 (ibid., 210 n. 75). Now that the date can be narrowed to 1820, Bushman may have inadvertently explained the Smiths' sudden ability to purchase land.

10. *14 July 1821-5 February 1822 (probably summer of 1821)*: Second payment due on Smith property (see 7 above).

11. *April 1822*: Peter Ingersoll moves onto Jennings's property (see introduction to III.A.9, PETER INGERSOLL STATEMENT, 2 DEC 1833).

12. *29 June 1822*: Smiths' land assessed at $700, indicating that no significant improvements had been made (SMITH MANCHESTER [NY] LAND ASSESSMENT RECORDS, 1821-1823 & 1830).

13. *2 July 1822*: Smiths' land agent, Zachariah Seymour, dies.

14. *14 July 1822-5 February 1823 (probably summer of 1822)*: Third and final payment due on Smith property (see 7 above). Smiths unable to make this last payment due to the death of land agent Zachariah Seymour (see I.B.5, LUCY SMITH HISTORY, 1845, MS:39-40).

15. *24 July 1823*: Smiths' Manchester land assessed at $1,000, suggesting completion of their log cabin (III.L.6, SMITH MANCHESTER [NY] LAND ASSESSMENT RECORDS, 1821-1823 & 1830).

16. *November 1823*: Smiths raise frame of house on their Manchester property. On 19 November 1823, Alvin dies; on his death bed he instructs his brothers to finish the house (I.B.5, LUCY SMITH HISTORY, 1845, MS:45-46).

17. *17 May 1824*: John Greenwood, a lawyer in New York City, receives power of attorney over Evertson lands (Miscellaneous Records, Book C, 458-59, Ontario County Records Center and Archives, Canandaigua, New York). Greenwood gives Smiths until 25 December 1825 to make the last payment on their land (I.B.5, LUCY SMITH HISTORY, 1845, MS:51).

18. *October 1825*: Josiah Stowell comes to the Smith residence "a short time before the house was completed." Joseph Sr. and Jr. accompany Stowell to Harmony, Pennsylvania, in search of buried treasure (I.B.5, LUCY SMITH HISTORY, 1845, 1853:91).

19. *November/December 1825*: In Joseph Sr.'s absence, a Mr. Stoddard attempts to swindle the Smiths out of their land (I.B.5, LUCY SMITH HISTORY, 1845, MS:53-58).[4]

---

4. By 1 November Joseph Sr. and Joseph Jr. were in Harmony, Pennsylvania, searching for buried treasure with Josiah Stowell (V.E.1, ARTICLES OF AGREEMENT, 1 NOV 1825). According to Lucy Smith, the

20. *20 December 1825*: Lemuel Durfee purchases the Smith property for $1,135 and allows them to remain in their home as "renters" (Deeds, Liber 44, 232; I.B.5, LUCY SMITH HISTORY, 1845, MS:56-58; see also I.D.4, WILLIAM SMITH, *ON MORMONISM,* 1883, 13-14). Lucy Smith said, "Mr Durfy gave us the priviledge of the place [for] one year with this provision that samuel our 4th son was to labor for him 6 months. ... These things were all settled upon and The con=clusion was that if after we had kept the place in this way one year we still chose to remain we could have the priviledge" (I.B.5, LUCY SMITH HISTORY, 1845, MS:57-58).

21. *12 June 1826*: Lemuel Durfee's will is drafted containing a provision for the Smith property: "I hereby authorize empower my executors hereinafter named to sell and con=vey the lot of land called the Evertson lot situate[d] in the north West corner of the town of Manchester in the county of Ontario being the lot on which Joseph Smith now lives containing about one hundred acres of land and the avails of such sales to be distributed as follows amongst my heirs (viz) two thirds thereof to be equally distributed amongst my four sons Isaac, Oliver, Samuel and Bailey and the remaining third to be distributed amongst my four daughters Phebe, Prudence, Mary and Irena in equal proportions" (Wills, Book A, 225, Wayne County Clerk's Office, Lyons, New York).

22. *16 April 1827*: Lemuel Durfee records in his account book: "S[amuel]. Harrison Smith Son of Joseph Smith began to Work for me by the Month. is to Work 7 Months for the use of the place Where Said Joseph Smith Lives" (see III.L.10, LEMUEL DURFEE ACCOUNT BOOKS, 1827-1829). This evidently represents a continuation of the agreement Durfee offered the Smiths in 1825 (see 20 above). According to Lucy Smith, "we had agreed

---

two Josephs returned to Manchester on Thursday, 15 December (I.B.5, LUCY SMITH HISTORY, 1845, MS:55). While uncertainty surrounds the identity of the "Mr. Stoddard" who attempted to acquire the Smith farm through fraudulent means (see Ibid., n. 107), a recently discovered entry in an Ontario County judgment docket strongly favors Russell Stoddard, who sued Joseph Smith, Sr., on 19 February 1825 for $66.59 (Joseph Smith vs. Russell Stoddard, 19 February 1825, Judgment Docket, Ontario County Records Center and Archives, Canandaigua, New York). Stoddard, who lived about a mile south of the Smiths, ran a lumber mill and may have supplied materials for the construction of the Smiths' frame house. The unpaid debt may have provided Stoddard with leverage when negotiating with the land agent for the Smiths' property.

for the place <2> years" (I.B.5, LUCY SMITH HISTORY, 1845, MS:92-93).

23. *April 1829*: Smiths vacate their frame house and move back into their former cabin with Hyrum and his family (I.B.5, LUCY SMITH HISTORY, 1845, MS:92-93). Apparently Roswell Nichols and his wife Mary Durfee, daughter of Lemuel, moved into the Smiths' former home (see III.A.8, ROSWELL NICHOLS STATEMENT, 1 DEC 1833).

24. *8 August 1829*: Lemuel Durfee dies (*Wayne Sentinel,* 14 August 1829; Reed 1902, 1:318).

25. *31 August 1829*: Isaac Hussee and Peter Harris take oath to appraise Lemuel Durfee's estate. Their inventory of Durfee's estate lists an unpaid note of Joseph Smith, Sr., and Abraham Fish for $37.50, plus $1.42 in interest, a total of $38.92 (see III.L.18, LEMUEL DURFEE PROBATE PAPERS, 1830; and III.L.19, NATHAN PIERCE DOCKET BOOK, 1830).

26. *5 July 1830*: Fifteen acres on Manchester Lot 1, valued at $157.00, taxed to Hyrum Smith (III.L.6, SMITH MANCHESTER [NY] LAND ASSESSMENT RECORDS, 1821-1823 & 1830). This may have been the land on which the Smiths' Manchester cabin was situated, but this cannot be proven from the assessment record; other records, especially Nathan Pierce's docket book, argue strongly for the Smiths' cabin being located on this land (see discussion in introduction to III.L.2, PALMYRA [NY] HIGHWAY SURVEY, 13 JUN 1820).

27. *Early October 1830*[5]: Hyrum Smith and his family move to Colesville, Broome County, and reside with Newel Knight (IV.A.3, NEWEL KNIGHT AUTOBIOGRAPHY, CIRCA 1846, 65; Porter 1971, 109).

28. *Late October/Early November 1830*: Before Joseph Sr.'s release from the Canandaigua jail, Samuel Smith moves his mother and sister Lucy to their new residence near Waterloo, Seneca County, New York (I.B.5, LUCY SMITH HISTORY, 1845, 1853:167).

29. *9 April 1834*: The Smiths' former Manchester property is sold by Durfee's executors, Oliver and Lemuel Durfee, Jr., to Mary (Durfee) Nichols for $2,000 (Deeds, Liber 55, 558).

---

5. On the date of Hyrum's move to Colesville, see I.B.5, LUCY SMITH HISTORY, 1845, n. 266.

The document below is the record of the purchase of the Smith farm by Lemuel Durfee on 20 December 1825 (see 20 above).

This Indenture Made the twentieth day of December in the year of our Lord one thousand eight hundred and twenty five between Eliza Evertson[6] and David B. Ogden[7] the majority of the surviving executors and trustees appointed in and by the last will and testament of Nicholus Evertson deceased bearing date the twelfth day of April in the year of our Lord one thousand eight hundred and seven of the first part and Lemuel Durfee of Palmyra in Wayne County in the state of New York of the second part witnesseth that the said parties of the first part by virtue of the power and authority of them given in and by the said last will and testament and for and in consideration of the sum of one thousand one hundred and thirty five dollars lawful money of the United States of America to the said parties of the first part in hand paid by the said party of the second part at and before the presenting and delivery of these presents the receipt whereof whereby acknowledged and the said party of the second part his heirs, executors and [p. 232] administrators thereof and therefrom forever hereby acquitted and discharged have granted bargained sold unliened released and confirmed and by these presents do grant bargain sell alien release and confirm unto the said party of the second part his heirs and assigns forever All that certain piece or parcel of land situated in the town of Manchester county of Ontario and state of New York viz Lot No one of the subdivision of original lot No one north of the centre line in township of No 11 number eleven in the second range of townships in said county of Ontario and bounded as follows viz beginning at the northwest corner of said original lot No 1 number one thence running easterly on the north line of said lot forty one chains and fifty links thence southerly twenty four chains and nine links thence westerly forty one chains and sixty three links to the west line of said original lot No 1 and from thence northerly on the said west line twenty four chains and eight links to the place of beginning containing ninety nine and an half acres inclusive of all highways on the same agreeable to the survey of James Smedley Esquire[8] together with all and singular the edifices buildings rights members priv=ileges advantages

---

6. Eliza Evertson, in her fifties, is listed in the 1830 census of New York City (1830:240).

7. David B. Ogden, in his fifties, is listed in the 1830 census of New York City (1830:322).

8. See III.L.2, PALMYRA (NY) HIGHWAY SURVEY, 13 JUN 1830.

hereditaments and appurtenances to the Same belonging or in any wise appertaining and the reversion and remainder and remainders rents issues and profits thereof and every part and parcel thereon with the appurtenances And also all the estate right title interest claim and demand whatsoever both in law and equality which the said testator had in his life time and at the time of his decease and which the said parties of the first part or either of them have or hath by virtue of the said last will and ~~testament~~ <testament> or otherwise of in and to the same and of in and to every part and parcel there=of with the appurtenances to have and to hold the said premises above mentioned and described and hereby granted and conveyed or intended so to be with the appurtenances unto the said party of the second part his heirs and assigns to the only proper use benefit and behoof of the second part his heirs and assigns forever And the said parties of the first part for themselves severally and respectively and for their several and respective heirs executors and admin=istrators do severally and not jointly nor the one for the other or others of them nor for the heirs executors or administrators or acts or deeds of the other or others of them but each and every [one] of them for himself and herself only and for his her and their heirs executors and administrators and his her and their several and separate acts and deeds only do covenant promise grant and agree to and with the said party of the second part his heirs and assigns that the said party of the second part his heirs and assigns shall and lawfully may from time to time and at all times forever hereafter peaceably and quietly have hold use occupy possess and enjoy all and singular the said heredita=ments and premises hereby granted and conveyed or intended so to be with their and every of their appurtenances and receive and take the rents issues and profits thereof to and for his and their own use and benefit without any lawful let suit hindrance molestation interruption or denial whatsoever of from or by them the said parties of the first part their heirs or assigns or of from or by any other person or persons whomsoever lawfully claiming or who shall or may lawfully claim hereafter by from or under them or either of them by from or under the said testator or by from or under them or either of their [p. 233] right title interest or estate and that free and clear and freely and clearly discharged acquitted and exonerated or otherwise well and rightly be saved defended kept harmless and indemnified by them the said parties of the first part their heirs and assigns of from and against all and all manner of former and other gifts grants bargains sales mortgages and judgments and all other charges and incumbrances whatsoever had made committed executed suffered or done by them the said parties of the first part or by through or with their or either of their acts deeds means consent procurement or [-] In witness whereof the said parties to these presents have hereunto interchangeably set their hands and seals the day and year first above written

Sealed and delivered in the presence
of F. Fairlie

Eliza Evertson Executr. &c
of N Evertson deceased
David B. Ogden

City and County of New York ss

On the twentieth day of December in the year of our Lord one thousand eight hundred and twenty five appeared before me Eliza Evertson and David B. Ogden known to me to be the same persons described in the foregoing deed who acknowledged before me that they executed the same for the uses and purposes therein mentioned I <do> allow the same to be recorded.

Frederick Fairlie Commissioner
to take acknowledgements of deeds &c

5.
Gain C. and Cains C. Robinson Account Books, 1820-1830

1. Gain C. and Cains C. Robinson Invoice Book, 1819-1831 (entries of 13 July 1820, 30 October 1823, 17 November 1823, 9 June 1828, 8 May 1829), Palmyra King's Daughters Free Library, Palmyra, New York.

2. Cains C. Robinson & Co. Account Book, 1819-1831 (entries of 17 November 1823, 1 January 1829), Palmyra King's Daughters Free Library, Palmyra, New York.

3. Gain C. Robinson Day Book, 21 July 1823-2 June 1826 (entry of 20 November 1823), Palmyra King's Daughters Free Library, Palmyra, New York.

4. Gain C. Robinson Store Book, 1825-1829 (entries of 2 May 1825, 1 February 1828, 26 March 1829), Palmyra King's Daughters Free Library, Palmyra, New York.

5. Cains C. Robinson Journal Book, 11 February 1826-1 September 1828 (entries of 16 July 1827, 18 September 1827, 12 July 1828, 22 July 1828, 20 August 1828), Palmyra King's Daughters Free Library, Palmyra, New York.

6. Cains C. Robinson Day Book, 2 June 1827-3 January 1829 (entry of 18 September 1827), Palmyra King's Daughters Free Library, Palmyra, New York.

7. Gain C. Robinson Day Book, 20 June 1826-30 August 1827 (entries of 16 April 1827, 23 April 1827), Palmyra King's Daughters Free Library, Palmyra, New York.

8. Gain C. Robinson Day Book, 1 September 1827-12 February 1830 (entries of 29 January 1828, 9 June 1828, 11 September 1828, 1 January 1829, 11 March 1829, 25 March 1829, 16 January 1830), Palmyra King's Daughters Free Library, Palmyra, New York.

9. Gain C. Robinson Index, undated, Palmyra King's Daughters Free Library, Palmyra, New York.

EDITORIAL NOTE

Gain C. Robinson (c. 1769-1831), a physician who had an office and drug store at the west end of Main Street (T. Cook 1930, 125), was probably one of the doctors who attended Alvin on the day of his death (I.B.5, LUCY SMITH HISTORY, 1845, MS:46). As a member of Palmyra's Presbyterian church, he was disciplined on 16 March 1828 for "immoderate and in=temporate use of Spiritous liquors to the great injury of his christian character and usefulness" ("Records of the Session of the Presbyterian Church in Palmyra," 2:1, microfilm copy, Harold B. Lee Library, Brigham Young University, Provo, Utah). Robinson, in his sixties, is listed in the 1830 census of Palmyra, New York (1830:36). Robinson died at Palmyra on 21 June 1831 (*Wayne Sentinel,* 24 June 1831; McIntosh 1877, 142).

Robinson was apparently in business with Cains C. Robinson, perhaps his son, who, in his twenties, also appears in the 1830 census of Palmyra (1830:36).

A note accompanying Gain C. Robinson's Day Book (20 June 1826-30 August 1827), dated 1 December 1923, indicates that descendant Edwin H. Robinson turned the books over to Sanford D. Van Alstine, who evidently placed them in the Palmyra King's Daughters Free Library. Caution is advised since it is not always clear if the Smiths referred to in the Robinson account books are members of the Joseph Smith, Sr., family. The 1820 and 1830 federal censuses list several Smith families in the area.

[*1. Gain C. and Cains C. Robinson Invoice Book, 1819-1831*][1]

date	*name*	*debt*	*amount*	*page*
1820 July 13	Smith Alvin	[GR Bad]	.63	32

1. The following accounts, which have been extracted from the Gain C. and Cains C. Invoice Book, appear in ledger form with the customer's name entered on the left side of the page and the amounts entered in one of four columns to the right. At the top of each column appears the following designations: "GR good" (= Gain Robinson good debt, or credit), "GR bad" (= Gain Robinson bad debt), "CCR good" (= Cains C. Robinson good debt, or credit), and "CCR bad" (= Cains C. Robinson bad debt). Evidently the two men ran separate businesses but kept their records in the same book.

1823 Nov 17[2]	Smith Joseph	[GR Bad]	6.63	34
		[CCR Bad]	6.13	34
[1828] June 9	Smith Hiram "One Cow" [?]	[CCR Bad]	16.75	36
[1829] May 8	Smith William[3]	[GR Good]	1.00	36
1823 Oct 30	Smith Joseph "Note"	[GR Bad]	4.25	37
1823 Oct. 30	Smith Hiram	[GR Bad]	11.75	37

[2. *Cains C. Robinson & Co. Account Book, 1819-1831*][4]

Joseph Smith Dr[5]
1823, November 17th[6]

P.B.[7] 36,300,,48,100,,

---

2. Among the purchases made on this date, which was two days following Alvin's taking a lethal dose of Calomel and two days before his death, might be the medicine prescribed by Dr. Alexander McIntyre in an attempt to dislodge the Calomel (I.B.5, LUCY SMITH HISTORY, 1845, MS:45-46). Compare entry of 17 November 1823 in "Cains C. Robinson & Co. Account Book, 1819-1831" (item 2 below).

3. The three references to William Smith included in this collection may not refer to William Smith, the son of Joseph Smith, Sr. The 1820 census of Farmington (now Manchester) lists two other William Smiths (family Nos. 552 and 607). In the 1830 census of Manchester, there are listed in succession a "William F. Smith" and a "Shubel Smith" (family Nos. 104 and 105), as well as two other William Smiths (family Nos. 363 and 387). The medical entries in the Gain Robinson Day Book, 1826-1827 (item 7 below), are especially suspect since a third entry for 7 May 1827 reads: "Wm Smith by Shubal Smith <Visit med> .50."

4. This account book is arranged with names written on opposing pages: first names on the left and last on the right. On the right side of each page are columns: side A for debts, and side B for credits.

5. "Dr" signifies "debtor" or "debt record."

6. This entry ties in with one under the same date in the Robinson invoice book (see item 1 above).

7. Meaning of the initials "P.B." and "B.C." are unknown, perhaps the initials of clerks. The numerical entries apparently represent: 36 at \$3.00 + 48 at \$1.00 + 208 at 50¢ + 117 at 50¢ + 151 at 50¢ = \$5.50; and 39 at 13¢ + 170 at 25¢ + 344 at 75¢ = \$1.13; for a total of \$6.63. The numbers might be codes for specific items for sale in the Robinson store.

	208,50,,117,50,,151,,50	5.50	
	39,13,, B.C. 170,25,,344,75,,	1.13	6.63
			[p. 144a]

[Joseph Smith] Cr[8]
1829 Jany 1st

B.C. 232,37,, [p. 144b]

[*3. Gain C. Robinson Day Book, 1823-1826*]

[20 Nov 1823][9]	Joseph Smith	visit attend	3.00	[p. 36]

[*4. Gain C. Robinson Store Book, 1825-1829*][10]

Dr Joseph Smith

1825 May 2nd, B.A.[11] 29,6,,	. 6
270,75,,301,2,44,,040.	3.19
413,75,,416,175,,200,,422,100,,	5.50
434,50,,62,13,,	.63
	9.38

[Joseph Smith] Cr.

---

8. "Cr" signifies "credit" or "credit record."

9. Larry C. Porter incorrectly dated this entry to 19 November 1823, the date of Alvin's death (Porter 1971, 74). But this entry is clearly under 20 November 1823, the possible date of Alvin's autopsy. Robinson was evidently one of the four doctors described by Lucy Smith as accompanying Dr. Alexander McIntyre during his treatment of Alvin and subsequent autopsy (I.B.5, LUCY SMITH HISTORY, 1845, MS:46; Porter 1971, 71-76). Robinson was Dr. McIntyre's uncle and medical mentor.

10. In this record entries appear on a single page, with debts recorded on the left side and credits on the right. For convenience, credits and debts have been separated.

11. Meaning of the initials "B.A." remains a puzzle, but the numerical entries apparently represent: 29 at 6¢ = 6¢ + 270 at 75¢ + 301 at \$2.44 = \$3.19 (040 unexplained; added in different ink); and 413 at 75¢ + 416 at \$1.75 + \$2.00 + 422 at \$1.00 = \$5.50; and 434 at 50¢ + 62 at 13¢ = 63¢; for a total of \$9.38.

1828 Feby 1 D.B.[12] 346,2.00,,412,87,422,38,, 3.25
[p. 38]

Dr Hiram Smith

1829 March 26 J.C. 105,25,, [p. 224]

[*5. Cains C. Robinson Journal Book, 1826-1828*]

[*A. 16 July 1827*]

38[13]	Joseph Smith for Wife	Dr		
	To 1/4th Vermillion[14]	@ 16/—	[-]	
	2 oz chrome yellow[15]	@ 1/—	[-]	
				[p. 270]

[*B. 18 September 1827*]

Tuesday Sept. 18th 1827 ...

Joseph Smith for Son			Dr
To	9 Papers L[amp]. Bl[ac]k[16]	1/—	1.13
	Red Lead[17]	6 @	06

---

12. Meaning of the initials "D.B." remains unknown, but the numbered entries apparently represent: 346 at $2.00 + 412 at 87¢ + 422 at 38¢ = $3.25.

13. The number "38" that frequently appears next of Joseph Sr.'s name is evidently an account number.

14. A bright red or scarlet pigment, probably used in paint. Lucy Smith is known to have worked at "painting oil cloth coverings for tables[,] stands &c" (I.B.5, LUCY SMITH HISTORY, 1845, MS:37, 1835:70).

15. A pigment made from chromium compound, probably used in paint (see note 14 above).

16. Quinn has speculated that the purchase of "lampblack" only days before Joseph Smith's final visit to the hill was for occult-magical purposes (Quinn 1987, 141). But this is unlikely not only because the entry could pertain to any of Joseph Sr.'s sons, but also because lampblack was commonly used to finish furniture, which is the more probable use judging by the other items purchased at the same time (see III.B.12, LORENZO SAUNDERS INTERVIEW, 17 SEP 1884, 2, who mentions Lucy Smith's painting chairs with lampblack). Lampblack (soot) was also used to make ink. Compare entry of 18 September 1827, under item 6 below.

17. Probably used as a pigment in paint (see note 14 above).

G[u]m Shlack [shellac][18]	6 @	06
Litharge[19]	6 @	06
1 Gal. L[inseed]. oil[20]	9/—	1.13
		2.44

[p. 301]

[*C. 12 July 1828*]

Saturday July 12th 1828

38	Joseph Smith	Cr	
	By Cash—	7/—	.87 [p. 412]

[*D. 19 July 1828*]

Saturday July 19th 1828 ...

38	Joseph Smith		Dr	
	To 1/2th	Gum Shellac	@3/—	.19
	" 1/2 "	White Lead[21]	@1/4—	.08
	" 1/2 "	Vermillion	@14/—	.44
	" 1/4 "	Prussian Blue[22]	@22/—	.69
	" 1/4 "	Crome Yellow	@10/—	.31
	" 1/4 "	Sal. Glauber[23]	@1/4	.14
				$1.75

[p. 416]

[*E. 22 July 1828*]

Tuesday July 22nd 1828 ...

38 Joseph Smith Dr /to Son

18. Probably used to finish furniture (see note 16 above).

19. Perhaps "Litharge Plaster," used externally for medicinal purposes (see Seaman 1811, 32).

20. Probably used in finishing furniture and making oil-based paint from pigment.

21. Probably used as a pigment in paint (see note 14 above).

22. Probably used as a pigment in paint (see note 14 above).

23. "Sal glauberi," called "Glauber's salt" or "sulphate of soda," made from burnt bones and other additives, was sometimes used for medicinal purposes (see *Pharmacopaeia of the Massachusetts Medical Society,* 1808, 51-52, 206, 225, 267; *Pharmacopaeia Nosocomii Neo-Eboracensis,* 1816, 82, 88, 135, 137).

To 1	Gallon Linseed Oil	@ 8/	1.00	
" 4th	Lamp Black	@ 2/	1.00	
			$2.00	[p. 416]

[F. 20 August 1828]

Wednesday August 20th 1828

38	Joseph Smith			[Dr]	
	To 1th	Lamp Black	2/	.25	
	" 1	Gl [gallon] Terpentine[24]	2/	.25	.50
					[p. 434]

[6. Cains C. Robinson Day Book, 1827-1829]

Tuesday Sept 18th 1827 ...

Joseph Smith for Son			Dr
To	9 papers Lamp Black	@ 1/	1.13
	1 Red Lead	6¢	06
	1 Gam Shelac	6¢	06
	Litherage	6¢	06
	1 gallon Linseed Oil	@ 9/	1.13
			2.44

[p. 73]

[7. Gain C. Robinson Day Book, 1826-1827]

[A. 16 April 1827]

144[25]	Joseph Smith	visit med[icine]	.50
	Wm Smith, Manchester, visit <Mother> med[icine]		2.00

[B. 23 April 1827]

Wm Smith, Manchester, Visit <mother> med[icine] 1.00

---

24. Probably used as a thinner or solvent in paint, especially in staining wood, although it was also used medicinally (see *Pharmacopaeia Nosocomii Neo-Eboracensis,* 1816, 24, 151).

25. The number "144" that appears before Joseph Sr.'s name several times is apparently an account number.

[*8. Gain C. Robinson Day Book, 1827-1830*]

[*A. 29 January 1828*]

144 Joseph Smith Sen To Calomel[26] <for wife> .13 [p. 39]

[*B. 9 June 1828*]

Hiram Smith Extract Dent[est?] .25 [p. 94]

[*C. 11 September 1828*]

144 Joseph Smith Med[icine] & cons [?]
<for Boy Harrison>[27] .15 [p. 170]

[*D. 1 January 1829*]

144 Joseph Smith Cr
By balance on M [Porter?] Order .37 [p. 232]

[*E. 11 March 1829*]

LC 63 Hiram Smith visit & med[icine] .50 [p. 258]

[*F. 25 March 1829*]

LC 133 Hiram Smith visit Med[icine]
& [-] Sick <for wife> .75 [p. 266]

[*G. 16 January 1830*]

144 Joseph Smith To 1/3 of [Michael] Eggleston[28]
Charges .75 [p. 344]

---

26. Calomel, a white, tasteless power sometimes used as a laxative (see *Pharmacopaeia Nosocomii Neo-Eboracensis,* 1816, 79, 149).

27. This may have been when Lucy and Joseph Sr. returned to Manchester from visiting Joseph and Emma at Harmony, Pennsylvania, and found Samuel Harrison and Sophronia "very sick" (see I.B.5, LUCY SMITH HISTORY, 1845, MS:86-87).

28. An entry for Eggleston reads: "28 D.B. Michael Eggleston 1/3 of Dr [debt] J[oseph?]. S[mith?]. [-] .58" (p. 348). Eggleston, over forty years of age, is listed in the 1820 census of Palmyra.

[*9. Index, undated*][29]

Smith & Fish[30] — C P Stout [page] 11
Smith Wm — C Finly [page] 30

29. Although catalogued and filmed by Utah Genealogical Society with "Gain C. Robinson Store Book, 1815-1829," this unpaginated item is an alphabetical listing and index to a record not presently found among the Robinson papers.

30. Perhaps Abraham Fish (see III.L.11, JOSEPH SMITH RECEIPT TO ABRAHAM FISH ACCOUNT, 10 MAR 1827; III.L.18, LEMUEL DURFEE PROBATE PAPERS, 1830; and III.L.19, NATHAN PIERCE DOCKET BOOK, 1830). On Abraham Fish (c. 1773-1845), see III.I.4, NATHANIEL W. HOWELL AND OTHERS TO ANCIL BEACH, JAN 1832, n. 3.

6.
SMITH MANCHESTER (NY) LAND ASSESSMENT RECORDS, 1821-1823 & 1830

1. Farmington Assessment Roll, 7 July 1821, 25, Ontario County Records Center and Archives, Canandaigua, New York.

2. Manchester Assessment Roll, 29 June 1822, 16, Ontario County Records Center and Archives, Canandaigua, New York.

3. Manchester Assessment Roll, 24 July 1823, 17, Ontario County Records Center and Archives, Canandaigua, New York.

4. Manchester Assessment Roll, 5 July 1830, 23, Ontario County Historical Society, Canandaigua, New York.

EDITORIAL NOTE

The Farmington/Manchester land assessment records that pertain to the Smiths' property were recovered from the basement of the Ontario County Courthouse in 1985. Except for the years 1830, 1833, and 1835 (which are housed in the Ontario County Historical Society), the original assessment records are now located in the Ontario County Records Center and Archives, Canandaigua, New York. Unfortunately, the assessment records for the years 1824 through 1829 are presently missing.

Joseph Smith, Sr., appears on the Farmington assessment roll for 1821, and on the Manchester assessment rolls for 1822 and 1823, while Hyrum appears on the Manchester assessment rolls for 1830. The assessments were recorded on a printed form arranged in seven columns, each designated as follows: Names of Possessors; Remarks by Assessors; Description of Real Estate; Amount of Real Estate; Amount of Personal Estate; Total, Real and Personal Estate; and Tax to be paid thereon. The assessment records yield the following information about the Smiths:

1. Farmington Assessment Roll, 7 July 1821:

Names of Possessors.	Smith Joseph
Remarks by Assessors.	p[ar]t Lot No 1 2d [Range]
Description of Real Estate.	100 [acres]
Amount of Real Estate.	[$]700
Amount of Personal Estate.	

Names of Possessors.	Remarks by Assessors.	Description of Real Estate.		Amount of Real Estate.		Amount of Personal Estate.		Total, Real and Personal Estate.		Tax to be paid thereon.	
			acres	Dollars.	Cents.	Dollars.	Cents.	Dollars.	Cents.	Dollars.	Cents.
Smith James F.	2 Quality of land	Vil[illegible] lot 15.	44/100	150							57
Smith Silas	2 — —	part of lot 57.	25	200							77
[illegible] Erastus	2 — —	— — 110.	50	450						1	72
Stoddard Russell	2 — —	— — 22.5.	77	1225						4	69
Smith Joseph	2 — —	— — 1.	100	1000						3	83
Stacy Erastus	2 — —	— — 52.	50	400						1	53
[illegible] Sarah	2 — —	— — 52.	19	190							72
Stimpson John B.	2 — —	— — 74.86.	20	240							92
Stafford Joshua	2 — —	— — 67.	123	1476						5	64
Stafford Abraham	2 — —	— — 11.3.	137	3000						11	48
[illegible]	2 — —	— — 65.	154	3500						13	39
Throop Axel	2 — —	— — 111.112.84.	117	1600						6	12
Throop [illegible]	2 — —	— — 84.121.	91	1092		64		1156		4	42
[illegible] James	2 — —	— — 52.	30	300						1	15
Teachout John	2 — —	— — 84.121.	3[illegible]	32[illegible]						1	23
				15,143		64		15.207		58	18

Manchester Assessment, 24 July 1823. Showing Smith property assessed at $1,000 and taxed for $3.83. Courtesy Ontario County Records Center and Archives, Canandaigua, New York.

Total, Real and Personal Estate.	[$]700
Tax to be paid thereon.	[$]1.58

In the above assessment, Joseph Sr. is taxed for 100 acres of land on Manchester Lot 1 for the first time. The previous assessment of 1820 indicates that the entire 300 acres of Lot 1 was taxed to the heirs of Nicholas Evertson (see Farmington Assessment Roll, 22 June 1820, Ontario County Records Center and Archives, Canandaigua, New York); and the 1821 assessment shows the remaining 200 acres of Lot 1 were taxed to Evertson's heirs. The value of $700 for the land, or $7 an acre, is what uncleared land sold for in the area at that time (Walters 1987; Enders 1993, 218; see also Brodie 1945, 10).

2. Manchester Assessment Roll, 29 June 1822:

Names of Possessors.	Smith Joseph
Remarks by Assessors.	[part of Lot No] 1
Description of Real Estate.	100 [acres]
Amount of Real Estate.	[$]700
Amount of Personal Estate.	
Total, Real and Personal.	[$]700
Tax to be paid thereon.	[$]2.01

In this assessment, the Smiths' 100-acre farm is valued at $700, the same as the previous year's assessment, indicating that no significant improvement had been made by 29 June 1822.

3. Manchester Assessment Roll, 24 July 1823:

Names of Possessors.	Smith Joseph
Remarks by Assessors.	2 [Quality of Land] [part of lot] 1
Description of Real Estate.	100 [acres]
Amount of Real Estate.	[$]1000
Amount of Personal Estate.	
Total, Real and Personal Estate.	[$]1000
Total to be paid thereon.	[$]3.83

In this assessment, the Smiths' 100-acre farm is valued at $1,000, a $300 increase from the previous year's assessment. The Smiths' increase of over 40 percent, when compared with the average 4 percent increase for the township, indicates that the Smiths had completed construction of their cabin and cleared and cultivated a significant portion of their land (Walters 1987).[1]

4. Manchester Assessment Roll, 5 July 1830:

Names of Possessors.	Smith Hiram
Remarks by Assessors.	[Part Lot No] 1
Description of Real Estate.	15 [acres] [2nd Quality]
Amount of Real Estate.	[$]157
Amount of Personal Estate.	
Total—Real and Personal Estate.	[$]157
Tax to be paid thereon.	.39

In this assessment, Hyrum is taxed 39 cents for fifteen acres on Lot 1. That this "Hiram Smith" is the son of Joseph Sr., and not the other "Hiram Smith" also living in Manchester at the time, is supported both by his location on Lot 1 and the absence of this "Hiram Smith" from subsequent assessments. It is probable that the Smiths' Manchester cabin stood on this fifteen-acre farm, but this cannot be proven from the assessment itself. Instead numerous historical and legal sources place Hyrum's cabin in Manchester (see discussion in introduction to III.L.2, PALMYRA [NY] HIGHWAY SURVEY, 13 JUN 1820). That Hyrum did not own this property is made clear from the fact that on 26 October 1830 Constable Harrington tried to collect the remainder of a debt that Hyrum owed but returned the warrant to Justice Pierce with the notation, "no property nor body to be found." Hyrum had suddenly moved to Colesville, New York, earlier that month, leaving the debt unpaid and no real estate that could be seized for its recovery (see III.L.19, NATHAN PIERCE DOCKET BOOK, 1830). Wesley P. Walters argued that "the tax probably represents an arrangement with the Durfees in

---

1. Donald L. Enders, who argues that Samuel Jennings's Palmyra cabin was the only cabin in the area in which the Smiths lived, suggested to me (July 1993) that the $300 increase in value in 1823 could have been due to the construction of the frame house, rather than to an additional cabin and clearing of the land. This suggestion is contradicted not only by Lucy Smith, who said the frame house was begun in November 1823 immediately preceding Alvin's death, but a host of other evidences as well (see discussion in introduction to III.L.2, PALMYRA [NY] HIGHWAY SURVEY, 13 JUN 1820). Unfortunately, the Manchester assessments from 1824 through 1829 are missing, but Lemuel Durfee purchased the Smiths' property on 20 December 1825 for $1,135, a $135 increase from 1823 (see III.L.4, SMITH MANCHESTER [NY] LAND RECORDS, 1820-1830). Larry C. Porter has suggested at least two locations where the Manchester log cabin could have stood (Porter 1971, 43-44).

which Hiram [Hyrum] was to pay the annual assessment as a part of the agreement" (Walters 1987).

The table below compares the significant information taken from the four assessments discussed above.

ITEMS TAXED	1821	1822	1823	1830
Names of Possessors	Joseph	Joseph	Joseph	Hiram
Acres	100	100	100	15
Value of Real Estate	$700	$700	$1,000	$157
Value of Personal Property	000	000	000	000
Taxes paid	$1.58	$2.01	$3.83	.39

7.
Samuel Jennings Estate Papers, 1822

"An inventory of the property of Samuel Jennings Deceased," 5 June 1822, 10, 12, Samuel Jennings Estate Papers, Ontario County Records Center and Archives, Canandaigua, New York.

EDITORIAL NOTE

Samuel Jennings (?-1821) owned a store at the east end of Main Street since at least 1812 (T. Cook 1930, 66; Backman 1980, 36). Sometime between April 1819 and April 1820, the Smiths apparently moved from the west end of Main Street to a small cabin on Jennings's property located south of Palmyra village on Stafford Road,[1] where they evidently remained until they moved onto their Manchester property sometime between June 1822 and July 1823 (see III.L.4, SMITH MANCHESTER [NY] LAND RECORDS, 1820-1830).[2] The Smiths were evidently still living in the Jennings cabin when its owner died on 1 September 1821. When an inventory of Jennings's estate was made on 5 January 1822 by administrators Margaret Jennings and Isaac Howell, Joseph Smith, Sr., was listed twice showing a debt of $11.50 (p. 10, line 23)[3] and, under an inventory of Jennings's store, $1.00 (p. 12, line 10). The inventory ends with the following certification: "The forgoing Inventory Sworn to by the Administrators before me Ira Selby Sarrogate[.] June 5th 1822." On 13 February 1822, the following notice appeared in the *Western Farmer*:

NOTICE.

> All persons having unsettled accounts with the estate of *Samuel Jennings,* deceased, are requested to call on the subscribers and settle the same on as before the first day of April next [1822].

---

1. Jennings owned 145 acres on the southwest portion of Palmyra Lot 43 (Farmington Assessment, 1820, Ontario County Records Center and Archives, Canandaigua, New York).

2. Peter Ingersoll moved onto the Jennings property about April 1822 (see introduction to III.A.9, PETER INGERSOLL STATEMENT, 2 DEC 1833).

3. It cannot be proven, but possibly this debt includes rent on the Jennings cabin.

All notes contracted to be paid in gain to said estate, which become due in January and February next will be received accordingly, if delivered when due.

MARGARET Jennings, | *Adm[inistrator]'s*
Isaac Howell |

Palmyra, Dec. 25, 1[8]21

[See accompanying photographic reproduction.]

George Culver	2	69
Samuel Rufsel		40
Stephen Rogers	6	75
David S Jackways	2	42
Philip Elsworth	2	65
Jonathan M Adams	27	04
Robert Curtis	2	89
Isaac Springer	4	64
Durfee Chace	2	43
Aaron Drake	2	13
Elisha Turner	1	42
Mumford Kenyon	2	18
Justin Phelps	5	35
Benjamin Hoag jun		14
Benjamin L Hoag	3	81
Hudson Merrill	2	05
Micah Rogers	1	10
Esq Malling		38
Bela Tinker		72
	2	[illegible]
Luke phelps	3	91
Fradrick Loper		88
Mary Goldsmith	11	50
Joseph Smith	5	13
Abram Botts	1	04
Isaac Crandle		50
Jabez Aldridge	2	28
Thomas Cooper	2	[illegible]
Peter Cooper	1	26
Wilson Osland	11	44
Joseph D Hayward	15	78
Rufsel Cole	5	75
Thomas Stafford	2	82
John Castler		71
Daniel Hende		59
Ebenezer H Champlain	7	10
John H Crandle	3	88
Elihu Warner ontario		99
Seth Harnes		
amount Carried out	4061	40

Samuel Jennings Estate Papers, 5 June 1822, p. 10. Showing a debt of $11.50 for Joseph Smith, Sr. Courtesy Ontario County Records Center and Archives, Canandaigua, New York.

8.
ALVIN SMITH GRAVESTONE, 19 NOVEMBER 1823

Alvin Smith Gravestone, 19 November 1823, General John Swift Memorial Cemetery, Palmyra, New York.

EDITORIAL NOTE

One of the pivotal events in the lives of Smith family members was the death of Alvin Smith.[1] Both Joseph Smith and Lucy Smith perpetuated an incorrect date for Alvin's death, believing that it had occurred in 1824 (see I.A.15, JOSEPH SMITH HISTORY, 1839, 7; and L. Smith 1853, 40, 87). Alvin Smith's gravestone at Palmyra's General John Swift Memorial Cemetery confirms his death date as 19 November 1823. Alvin's gravestone reads:

In memory of
Alvin, Son of Joseph
& Lucy Smith, who
died Nov. 19, 1823,
in the 25, year of
his age.

The General John Swift Memorial Cemetery is located on the west side of Church Street one-half block north of Main Street. John Swift, who died in 1814, donated the land for Palmyra's first cemetery (T. Cook 1930, 262). Alvin's gravestone, which is now preserved in a granite casing and stands upright, is located in the southwest corner of the cemetery. At the top of the original gravestone appears a "weeping willow" tree. Concerning the prevalence of this gravestone image, Allen I. Ludwig has written: "Trees abound on the carved stone markers of New England and during the late years of the 18th century they were taken over by the newer neoclassical stones when they were transformed into the still popular weeping willow seen so often on 19th century mourning pictures" (Ludwig 1966, 121). Alvin's marker may have been carved by Mason Sherman, who advertised

---

1. For an account of the events related to Alvin's death, see I.B.5, LUCY SMITH HISTORY, 1845, MS:45-49.

Alvin Smith Gravestone, General John Swift Memorial Cemetery, Palmyra, New York. Photograph by Rick Grunder, 1992.

his stone cutting business in the *Wayne Sentinel* (e.g, 1 October 1823).

[See accompanying photograph.]

9. PALMYRA (NY) MASONIC RECORDS, 1827-1828

"Return of the Mount Moriah Lodge No. 112 held in the Town of Palmyra in the County of Wayne and State of New York from June 4th AL 5827 [1827] to June 4th AL 5828 [1828]," Grand Lodge of Free and Accepted Masons of the State of New York, Chancellor Livingston Library, New York, New York.

EDITORIAL NOTE

This record lists a "Hiram Smith" as one of the members of the Mount Moriah Masonic Lodge No. 112 of Palmyra, New York, for the years 1827-28. Concerning this source, Richard L. Anderson has written: "Hyrum indeed appears on the Palmyra report covering the period to June 4, 1828, just a year before he became a Book of Mormon witness. He is one of fifty-nine members, and is not named as newly initiated that year. This means that normal Masonic procedures of unanimity had admitted him on grounds that his character would honor that organization" (R. L. Anderson 1981, 145). Although it is not altogether certain that the "Hiram Smith" listed in this record is Hyrum Smith, the son of Joseph Smith, Sr., Anderson is probably correct.

The presence of another Hiram Smith in Manchester at the same time brings Anderson's assumption into question. A Hiram Smith is listed as the overseer of Manchester road district 30 for the years 1829, 1834, and 1837 (Manchester Town Records, Manchester Town Hall, Manchester, New York). This same Hiram Smith signed Philastus Hurlbut's general Manchester affidavit (I.A.11, MANCHESTER RESIDENTS GROUP STATEMENT, 3 NOV 1833), and was most likely the person whom Theophilus Short sued on 22 February 1830 (see III.L.19, NATHAN PIERCE DOCKET BOOK, 1830). This other Hiram Smith does not appear in the 1830 census of Manchester, which probably indicates that he was not the head of a household and was perhaps enumerated with his father.[1]

Despite these reservations, several sources confirm the fact that Hyrum

---

1. Of the nine other Smiths listed in the 1830 Manchester census, Shubel Smith (with three sons in their twenties) is the only one who qualifies as the possible father of Hiram Smith.

did belong to Palmyra's Mount Moriah Lodge, No. 112. The Nauvoo (Illinois) Masonic records state that Hyrum Smith's membership was transferred into that lodge from Palmyra's Mount Moriah Lodge (see Hogan 1971). Heber C. Kimball also mentioned that "Hyrum Smith received the first three degrees of masonry in Ontario County, New York" (Whitney 1945, 11). Because Palmyra became part of Wayne County in 1823, Kimball's statement may point to a pre-1823 initiation date for Hyrum.

Presently, there is no reliable record for Hyrum's initiation and membership in the Palmyra lodge. Indeed, no other Hiram Smith is listed in any of the extant Mount Moriah Lodge returns between 1821, the earliest Hyrum could have joined (one had to be at least twenty-one), and 1827. Mervin Hogan has suggested that Hyrum joined in 1823, but gives no evidence for this assertion (Hogan 1971, 8). Perhaps Hogan was led to this conclusion because the records of the Palmyra lodge are missing for June 1820-June 1821 and December 1822-December 1823; if so, 1821 would be another possibility. If Hyrum was initiated during one of these gaps in the records, his absence from the remaining records suggests that he failed to attend meetings on a regular basis.

Records which perhaps contain the date of Hyrum's initiation may yet be discovered. While at Rochester, New York, in 1932, M. Wilford Poulson interviewed Sanford H. Van Alstine (1872-1933), a Palmyra historian who had moved to Rochester about 1906, and Poulson recorded in his notebook that Van Alstine "has a complete copy of the minutes of the Masonik lodge at Palmyra from about 1804 to 1827" (M. Wilford Poulson Collection, Special Collections, Harold B. Lee Library, Brigham Young University, Provo, Utah; see also T. Cook 1930, 110, 112). To date, I have been unable to locate these records.

According to William H. McIntosh, "A lodge of Masons known as the *Mount Moriah Lodge, No. 112,* was early instituted at Palmyra, and prospered till the Morgan excitement, when their charter was surrendered to the Grand Lodge" (McIntosh 1877, 143). In August 1827 Palmyra Baptists took measures forbidding members to join any Masonic lodge ("Book of Records for the first Baptist Church in Palmyra 1813," 1813-28, Baptist Historical Society, Rochester, New York). The record of the return for the year 1827 indicates that the Palmyra lodge was struggling financially, perhaps from the gradual withdrawal of support, and could not pay its dues to the Grand Lodge: "And we further State that our Dues have not been remitted, and in consequence of the embarased situation of the Lodge we are not able to pay them, and pray that the Grand Lodge might remit them." However, that the Mount Moriah Lodge continued to issue returns to the Grand Lodge,

Return of Mount Moriah Lodge No. 112 held in the town of Palmyra in the County of Wayne and State of New York from June 4th A L 5827 to June 4th A L 5828

Names of Members	Admission	Initiation	Amount of Quarterage	Register fees	Total
Amos C Foote Master			33		
Sutton Birdsall S. W.			50		
John Hoogland J W			50		
Cornelius C Coleman Secretary			50		
Robert W Smith Treasurer			50		
David White Past Master			50		
William Winslow Past Master			50		
Pelatiah West Past Master			50		
Arnold Isaac			50		
Benson James			50		
Baker Joseph M			50		
Bates Nathaniel			50		
Bingham Jeremiah			50		
Baldwin Thomas P			50		
Billings Sandford M			50		
Bingham George S			50		
Baker Morton			50		
Baker Norman C			50		
Capron William P			50		
Cadwell Horace			50		
Carus Thomas			50		
Cook William B			37		
Curtis John J			50		
Daggett Levi			50		
Durfee Barzilla			50		
Eddy Harvey			46		
Furgerson Alanson			46		
Flint Asher Jr			42		
Hemingway Truman			50		
Hufsey William T			50		
Hurd Lovell			50		
Hunt William			50		

Palmyra Masonic Record, 1827-28, p. 1. Courtesy Grand Lodge of Free and Accepted Masons of the State of New York, Chancellor Livingston Library, New York, NY.

Hoston Caleb			50		
Jarvis William			50		
Kellogg Erastus			50		
Lilly Asa			50		
McIntyre Alexander			50		
Miller Kingsley			50		
Moore James			25		
Robinson Andrew			50		
Smith David 1st			50		
Sherman Stephen			50		
Smith Asa			50		
Smith Silas			50		
Spear Erastus			50		
Stimpson Thomas J			50		
Smith David 2nd			50		
Sprague Michael P			50		
Sherman Jacob			50		
Smith Hiram			50		
Spear Samuel			50		
Turner Avery W			50		
Thomas Benjamin			50		
Tucker Luther			50		
Tucker Pomeroy			50		
Willcox Martin W			50		
Whipple Mason			50		
Van Duren Azel			50		
Van Ostrand Rufus B			33		28.62
Adjoining Members					
Foot Amos C	1 00			12½	1.12½
Van Ostrand Rufus B	1 00			12½	1.12½
Jarvis William	1 00			12½	1.12½
Furgerson Alanson	1 00			12½	1.12½
Moore James	1 00			12½	1.12½
Candidates Newly initiated					

Palmyra Masonic Record, 1827-28, p. 2. Showing a "Hiram Smith" as a member who was charged 50 cents for quarterly dues. Courtesy Grand Lodge of Free and Accepted Masons of the State of New York, Chancellor Livingston Library, New York, NY.

apparently without the same financial difficulty (1830-31), is an indication of the lodge's continuance or that it had surrendered its charter only briefly.

While the Morgan excitement directly affected Hyrum's lodge, it remains uncertain about Hyrum's position on the matter. It is also unknown how Hyrum might have responded to the anti-Masonic politics during the U.S. presidential election of 1828, or how he may have personally interpreted the Book of Mormon's warning against "secret combinations" (Vogel 1989). In December 1830 Joseph warned his brother to "beware of the freemasons, [Alexander?] McIntyre heard that you were in Manchester and he got a warrant and went to your father's to distress the family but Harrison [Samuel Harrison Smith] overheard their talk and they said that they cared not for the debt, if they could obtain your body. They were there with carriages. Therefore beware of the Freemasons" (I.A.5, JOSEPH SMITH TO COLESVILLE SAINTS, 2 DEC 1830). In this regard, several names in the Palmyra return of 1827-28 are of interest, particularly the Smiths' physician, Alexander McIntyre; Judge Thomas P. Baldwin, before whom many of Hurlbut's witnesses appeared; William T. Hussy and Azel Vandruver, the men who claimed to be friends of Smith who tried to look at the plates (see III.J.8, POMEROY TUCKER ACCOUNT, 1867, 31); Levi Daggett, who sued Hyrum Smith in June 1830 and tried to have him arrested for an unpaid debt (see III.L.19, NATHAN PIERCE DOCKET BOOK, 1830); and Pomeroy Tucker.

Presently, there is no evidence for Masonic membership for anyone in the Smith family besides Hyrum prior to the Nauvoo period. Some have wondered if a "Joseph Smith" listed in the record of the Ontario Lodge, No. 23, which met in Canandaigua, was Joseph Smith, Sr. However, this is unlikely since this record, which covers the year 1818, indicates that this "Joseph Smith" was initiated on 26 December 1817 and that he lived in Canandaigua (see Membership Record of Ontario Lodge, No. 23, 27 December 1817-27 December 1818, Library and Museum of the Grand Lodge of the State of New York, New York, New York),[2] while Joseph Sr. lived in Palmyra Village at this time and would have more likely attended the Palmyra lodge.

[See accompanying two-page photographic reproduction.]

2. Although the 1820 census does not list a Joseph Smith living in Canandaigua, it does list nine other Joseph Smiths in Ontario County. Evidently the Joseph Smith living in Canandaigua in 1818 moved before the 1820 enumeration and is perhaps one of these nine Joseph Smiths.

10.
LEMUEL DURFEE ACCOUNT BOOKS, 1827-1829

1. Lemuel Durfee Account Book, May 1813-July 1829 (entry of 16 April 1827), Ontario County Historical Society, Canandaigua, New York.

2. Lemuel Durfee Account Book, 1 September 1817-10 July 1829 (entries of 31 May 1827, 26 June 1827, August 1827, 1 September 1827, 13 May 1828, 18 June 1828, 20 June 1828, 7 July 1828, 20 July 1828, 7 August 1828, June 1829), Palmyra's King's Daughters Free Library, Palmyra, New York.

EDITORIAL NOTE

Lemuel Durfee (1759-1829), son of Gideon and Anne Durfee, was born at Tiverton, Rhode Island. He was a Quaker with extensive property holdings in Palmyra and Manchester, New York. He had arrived at Palmyra sometime before 23 April 1808, when he signed an indenture for land (original in Palmyra King's Daughters Free Library, Palmyra, New York). When a Mr. Stoddard sought to take the Smiths' land from them, they solicited the aid of Lemuel Durfee, who purchased the farm on 20 December 1825 and allowed the Smiths to remain as "renters" (I.B.5, LUCY SMITH HISTORY, 1845, MS:56-58; III.L.4, SMITH MANCHESTER [NY] LAND RECORDS, 1820-1830). Durfee died on 8 August 1829 at Palmyra (*Wayne Sentinel,* 14 August 1829; Reed 1902, 1:318; "Record of the Family of Job Durfee," *Palmyra Courier,* c. 1883, undated newspaper clipping in Wilcox Scrapbook, Palmyra King's Daughters Free Library, Palmyra, New York). Below are entries from Durfee's account books that pertain to the Smiths.

[*1. Account Book, 1813-1829*]

[*16 April 1827*]

April the 16 day the year 1827 S[amuel]. Harrison Smith Son of Joseph Smith began to Work for me by the Month. is to Work 7 Months for the use of the place Where Said Joseph Smith Lives[1]

[*2. Account Book, 1817-1829*]

[*A. 31 May 1827*]
Joseph [Sr./Jr.?][2] and Hiram Smith Dr. [debit] to three barrels of Cider at 9 [shillings] per barrel May the Last 1827 [p. 41]

[*B. 26 June 1827*]
June the 26 day Joseph Smith [Sr./Jr.?] Dr [debit] to Veal hind Quarter 23 pound <$0.69> also one fore Quarter Wt. [weight] 22 pounds $.55 .55 [p. 42]

[*C. August 1827*]
august Credit by Joseph Smith [Sr.] by Mo[w]ing three days & Joseph Smith, Ju Jnr. two days Mowing & Hiram Smith one day Mowing even [p. 42]

[*D. 1 September 1827*]
Sept. first to two barrels of Cider racked of[f] to Joseph [Sr./Jr.?] & Hiram Smith at 9 [shillings] / per barrel $2.25 [p. 42]

[*E. 13 May 1828*]
May the 13th Joseph [Sr.][3] & Harrison Smith Dr [debit] to three barrels of Cider the Liqure at $3.38 [p. 43]

[*F. 18 June 1828*]
June the 18 day the year 1828 Credit By Hiram & Har[r]ison Smiths a hoeing

1. Lucy Smith commented that when Durfee purchased their farm on 20 December 1825, "Mr Durfy gave us the priviledge of the place [for] one year with this provision that samuel our 4th son was to labor for him 6 months. ... These things were all settled upon and The conc=lusion was that if after we had kept the place in this way one year we still chose to remain we could have the priviledge" (I.B.5, LUCY SMITH HISTORY, 1845, MS:57-58). Since there is a lapse of more than a year, it is likely that this entry in Durfee's account book represents a similar arrangement worked out with the Smiths at the end of the first year.

2. Since Joseph Jr. was in Manchester from January to December 1827, except for a brief trip to Harmony, Pennsylvania, it is uncertain if this refers to Joseph Sr. or Joseph Jr. This is also true for the entries of 31 May, 26 June, and 1 September 1827.

3. Since Joseph Jr. moved to Harmony, Pennsylvania, in December 1827, this refers to Joseph Sr. This is also true for entries of 20 June, 7 July, 20 July 1828, and June 1829.

one Day a piece [p. 44]

[*G. 20 June 1828*]
June the 20 day Joseph [Sr.] & Harrison Smiths Dr. [debit] to the Liqure of three barrels of Cider at 9/0 [shillings] per barrel $3.38 [p. 44]

[*H. 7 July 1828*]
July 7 day Credit by J[oseph]. Smith [Sr.] & Rockwell[4] by hoeing three days [p. 44]

[*I. 20 July 1828*]
July 20 Jos. Smith [Sr.] & Harrison Cr. [credit] by Work binding Wheat[.] one day of william and three days of Harrison Work [p. 44]

[*J. 7 August 1828*]
august 7 Credit <by> Rockwell to two days Mowing for me by Harrison Smith by three days a Mowing for me [p. 44]

[*K. June 1829*][5]
Smith [Sr.] & Rockwell Dr. [debit] to the Liqure of two barrels of Cider $2.50 [p. 46]

---

4. It is uncertain whether this refers to Orin Rockwell (1784-?) or to his son Orrin Porter Rockwell (1813-29). Probably the senior Rockwell since, according to his daughter Caroline Rockwell, Orrin Porter "[w]hen ten years old he broke his leg and a young doctor in Palmyra set it so one leg was shorter than the other and it always troubled him so he could not work at farming" (III.D.5, CAROLINE ROCKWELL SMITH STATEMENT, 25 MAR 1885). This is also true for entries of 7 August 1828 and June 1829.

5. Entries before and after this entry indicate that it was recorded between 4 and 17 June 1829.

11.
JOSEPH SMITH RECEIPT TO ABRAHAM FISH ACCOUNT, 10 MARCH 1827

Joseph Smith, Receipt to Abraham Fish Account, 10 March 1827, Joseph Smith Papers, LDS Church Archives, Salt Lake City, Utah.

EDITORIAL NOTE

Abraham Fish (c. 1773-1845)[1] was a neighbor of the Smiths who, according to Pomeroy Tucker, believed in Joseph Smith's treasure seeing abilities (III.J.8, POMEROY TUCKER ACCOUNT, 1867, 39). On 10 March 1827, six months before obtaining the plates and his separation from the money digging company, Joseph Smith, Jr., paid four dollars to Abraham Fish's account at Joel and Levi Thayre's store in Palmyra.[2] The Thayres were twin brothers who among other things ran a grocery store on Main Street, advertisements of which appeared frequently in the *Wayne Sentinel*. According to Thomas L. Cook, the Thayre brothers had "an extensive business. They bought produce, dealt heavily in the purchase of cattle and were of material benefit to the village" (T. Cook 1930, 76). Besides the present note, Abraham Fish had other financial connections with the Smiths (see III.L.19, NATHAN PIERCE DOCKET BOOK, 1830; and III.I.4, NATHANIEL W. HOWELL AND OTHERS TO ANCIL BEACH, JAN 1832, 1-2).

Palmyra 10th March 1827

Rec[eive]d of Joseph Smith Jr Four dollars which is credited to the account of A[braham]. Fish

J & L Thayer
[for?] C E Thayer

---

1. On Abraham Fish (c. 1773-1845), see III.I.4, NATHANIEL W. HOWELL AND OTHERS TO ANCIL BEACH, JAN 1832, n. 3.

2. On Levi and Joel Thayre, see III.A.11, PALMYRA RESIDENTS GROUP STATEMENT, 4 DEC 1833, nn. 9 and 42.

12.
Book of Mormon Copyright, 11 June 1829

Book of Mormon Copyright, 11 June 1829, LDS Church Archives, Salt Lake City, Utah.

EDITORIAL NOTE

On 11 June 1829, Joseph Smith obtained a copyright for the Book of Mormon. The original copyright is found in the LDS Church Archives, Salt Lake City, Utah (photographically reproduced in *Church History in the Fulness of Times,* 1989, 62). A second nearly identical copy of the Book of Mormon's copyright is found in the Library of Congress (Copyright Records, vol. 116 [September 1826-May 1831], entry 107, Library of Congress, Washington, D.C.; photographically reproduced in *Ensign* 13 [December 1983]: 40). A third copy of the copyright is found on the first page of the printer's manuscript in the handwriting of Oliver Cowdery (RLDS Church Archives, Independence, Missouri).

The Book of Mormon's copyright was obtained from the "Office" of Richard R. Lansing of Utica, New York. Richard Ray Lansing (1789-1855) settled in Utica about 1810. He became the law partner of Judge Morris S. Miller in 1815, and shortly after was appointed Clerk of the District Court of the United States for the Northern District of New York. An 1817 city directory for Utica lists Lansing as follows: "Lansing, Richard R., Attorney & Counsellor at Law; dwelling, Broadway; office, 2 Catherine St." (*Reprint of the First Utica Directory, For the Year 1817,* 1920, 10). Lansing apparently lived at Utica until late 1829, but moved to New York City before the taking of the 1830 census. In New York City, he was a partner in the wine and liquor business of "Lansing, Munroe & King." When the business burned to the ground in the great fire of 1835, Lansing moved to Michigan and, although Lansing was named after him, he lived mostly in Detroit, where he died (Bagg 1877, 332-34).

The particulars of Smith's obtaining the copyright are vague. Perhaps Smith filed the copyright in person shortly after his return to Fayette from Palmyra where he had just concluded his negotiations with Egbert B. Grandin to print the Book of Mormon. Smith's History perhaps too closely associates his Palmyra negotiations with obtaining a copyright: "Mean time our translation drawing to a close, we went to Palmyra, Wayne County, N.Y: Secured the Copyright; and agreed with Mr Egbert Grandin to print five thousand Copies for the sum of three thousand dollars." The draft, however, reverses the order and separates the events: "Mean time our translation drawing to a close, we went to Palmyra, and agreed there <with Mr> Egbert Grandin to print ~~and publish~~ five thousand <copies> for three thousand Dollars, and about this time secured the copy right" (I.A.15, JOSEPH SMITH HISTORY, 1839, 34, DRAFT:9).

The copyright is a printed form (represented in this transcription in bold type), which was completed by hand, presumably by Lansing.

Northern **District of**
New York | **To Wit:**

Be it remembered, That on the eleventh **day of** June **in the** fifty third **year of the Independence of the United States of America, A.D. 18**29 Joseph Smith Junior **of the said District, ha**th **deposited in this Office the title of a** book **the right whereof** he **claim**s **as** author **in the words following, to wit:**

The Book of Mormon; an account written by the hand of Mormon upon plates taken from the plates of Nephi. Wherefore it is an abridgement of the record of the people of Nephi; and also of the Lamanites, written to the Lamanites, which are a remnant of the House of Israel; and also to Jew & Gentile, written by way of commandment; and also by the spirit of prophesy & revelation, written & sealed & hid up unto the Lord that they might not be destroyed, to come forth by the gift & power of God unto the interpretation thereof, sealed up by the hand of Moroni & hid up unto the Lord, to come forth in due time by the way of Gentile, the interpretation thereof by the gift of God; an abridgement taken from the book of Ether, also, which is a record of the people of Jared, which were scattered at the time the Lord confounded the language of the people, when they were building a tower to get to Heaven; which is to shew unto the [remnant] of the House of Israel how great things the Lord hath done for their fathers; & that they may know the covenants of the Lord, that they are not cast off forever; and also to the convincing of the Jew & Gentile that Jesus is the

Christ, the eternal God, manifesting himself unto all nations. And now if there be ~~a~~ fault, it be the mistake of men; wherefore con=demn not the things of God, that ye may be found spotless at the judgment seat of christ.[1] By Joseph Smith Junior, author & proprietor.[2]

In conformity to the act of the Congress of the United States, entitled "An act for the encouragement of learning, by securing the copies of Maps, Charts, and Books, to the authors and proprietors of such copies, during the times therein mentioned;" and also, to the act entitled "An act supplement=ary to an act entitled 'An act for the encouragement of learning, by securing the copies of Maps, Charts, and Books, to the authors and proprietors of such copies during the times therein mentioned,' and extending the benefits there=of to the arts of Designing, Engraving and Etching historical and other prints."

R. R. Lansing[,] Clerk of
the United States Dist[rict]. Court for the
Northern Dist[rict]. of New York

1. For Smith's explanation for the source of the Book of Mormon's title page, see I.A.15, JOSEPH SMITH HISTORY, 1839, 34.

2. Much has been made of the first edition's use of "author and proprietor," but the wording obviously reflects the language of the copyright rather than a supposed oversight by Joseph Smith.

13.
TESTIMONY OF EIGHT WITNESSES, JUNE 1829

"Testimony of Eight Witnesses," June 1829, Printer's Manuscript of the Book of Mormon, 464, Restoration Scriptures, RLDS Church Library-Archives, Independence, Missouri.

EDITORIAL NOTE

The printer's manuscript of the Book of Mormon, prepared by Oliver Cowdery and others between July 1829 and about February 1830, includes the earliest known copy of the Testimony of Eight Witnesses; the original apparently has not survived. The Testimony, including the names of the witnesses, is in Oliver Cowdery's handwriting.

As a historical document, the Testimony of Eight Witnesses is disappointing. It fails to give historical details such as time, place, and date. Neither does it describe the historical event or events, but simply states that the eight signatories, collectively, have seen and handled the plates. Joseph Smith's History is vague about events behind the Testimony of Eight Witnesses, dating the vision of the three witnesses to June 1829, with the experience of the eight witnesses occurring "soon after" (I.A.15, JOSEPH SMITH HISTORY, 1839, 24, 26). David Whitmer was more precise, stating that the three witnesses saw the plates in the "latter part" of June 1829 and the eight witnesses one or two days later (VI.A.7, DAVID WHITMER INTERVIEW WITH ORSON PRATT AND JOSEPH F. SMITH, 7-8 SEP 1878). Lucy Smith, whose husband and two sons were among the Eight Witnesses, said the event occurred in Manchester, New York, a "few days" after the experience of the Three Witnesses in Fayette, on a Thursday (I.B.5, LUCY SMITH HISTORY, 1845, MS:102). Combining the observations of Whitmer and Lucy Smith, the last Thursday of June, 25 June 1829, emerges as a possible date for the experience of the eight witnesses, although 2 July should not be ruled out.

Nor does Smith's History describe the historical setting in which the eight men saw the plates. Lucy Smith said a "few days" after the experience of the three witnesses in Fayette, New York, Joseph Jr., Oliver Cowdery, Hiram Page, and the Whitmers arrived at Palmyra in order to arrange for the printing of the Book of Mormon. It was during this visit, according to

Lucy, that the "male part of the company repaired to a little grove where it was custom=ary for the family to offer up their secret prayers," and there saw the plates (I.B.5, LUCY SMITH HISTORY, 1845, MS:102). Lucy further stated that "Joseph had been instructed that the plates would be carried" to the grove "by one of the ancient Nephites," and that "after the witnesses returned to the house the Angel again made his appearance to Joseph and received the plates from his hands" (I.B.5, LUCY SMITH HISTORY, 1845, MS:102, 104). While Lucy's account provides details otherwise unavailable,[1] she did not describe the actual viewing of the plates.

Details of what transpired in the Smith grove are unknown, and the nature of the experience of the eight witnesses is a matter of controversy. Unlike the Testimony of Three Witnesses (VI.G.1, TESTIMONY OF THREE WITNESSES, JUN 1829), subsequent statements by the eight witnesses shed very little light on the historical event behind their Testimony. Individual statements by the eight witnesses are rare due to largely to their early deaths. Below is a compilation of their individual testimonies arranged according to the order of their deaths:[2]

---

1. John Whitmer, one of the eight witnesses, reportedly gave an account that significantly differs from Lucy Smith's version. According to P. Wilhelm Poulson, Whitmer said in an 1878 interview that the witnesses saw the plates "in Joseph Smith's house. ... At that time Joseph showed the plates to us, we were four persons, present in the room, and at another time he showed them to four persons more" (VI.B.7, JOHN WHITMER INTERVIEW WITH P. WILHELM POULSON, APR 1878). Poulson's version of the interview, however, is perhaps suspect since John Whitmer was dead at the time of publication and David Whitmer complained about the accuracy of Poulson's interview with him (see introduction to VI.A.6, DAVID WHITMER INTERVIEW WITH P. WILHELM POULSON, CIRCA APR 1878).

2. In addition to the individual statements presented here, the eight witnesses sometimes bore public testimony as a group. On the evening following the experience of the eight witnesses, Lucy Smith reported, "all the witnesses bore testimony to the facts" as later stated in their printed testimony (I.B.5, LUCY SMITH HISTORY, 1845, 1853:141; MS:104). Luke Johnson reported that at a church conference in Orange, Cuyahoga County, Ohio, on 25 October 1831, "the eleven witnesses to the Book of Mormon, with uplifted hands, bore their solemn testimony to the truth of that book, as did also the Prophet Joseph" (*Deseret News,* 26 May 1858; rept. *Millennial Star,* 17 December 1864, 835). Unfortunately those who reported hearing the eight men testify neglected to give details.

1. Christian Whitmer (1798-1835).

No known statements.

2. Peter Whitmer, Jr. (1809-36).

No known statements.

3. Joseph Smith, Sr. (1771-1840).

No known statements.[3]

4. Hyrum Smith (1800-44).

Apparently against the claim that the eight witnesses only saw the plates with their "spiritual eyes" (see III.F.7, STEPHEN BURNETT TO LYMAN E. JOHNSON, 15 APR 1838), Hyrum reportedly said during a visit to Sunbury, Ohio, in 1838:

> he had but too [two] hands and too [two] eyes[.] he said he had seene the plates with his eyes and handeled them with his hands and he saw a brest plate and he told how it wass maid[.] it wass fixed for the brest of a man with a holer [hollow or concave] stomak and too [two] pieces upon eatch side with a hole throu them to put in a string to tye <it> on but that wass not so good gold as the plates for that was pure[.] why i write this is because thay dis=put[e] [the] Book so much (Sally Parker to John Kempton, 26 August 1838, microfilm, Family History Library, Salt Lake City, Utah; a portion cited in R. L. Anderson 1981, 159).

In December 1839, Hyrum evidently referred to his testimony when he said "I felt a determination to die, rather than deny the things which my eyes had seen, which my hands had handled, and which I had borne testimony to" (*Times and Seasons* 1 [December 1839]: 23). Joseph Fielding, Hyrum's brother-in-law by his second marriage, said in 1841: "My sister [Mary Fielding Smith] bears testimony that her husband has seen and handled the plates, &c." (Joseph Fielding to Parley P. Pratt, 20 June 1841, in *Millennial Star* 2 [1841]: 52). Recalling a sermon Hyrum delivered in 1844, Angus Cannon said: "When I was but ten years of age, I heard the testimony of the Patriarch Hyrum Smith ... to the divinity of the Book of Mormon and the

---

3. William Stafford claimed that the "elder Joseph would say that he had seen the plates and that he knew them to be gold; at other times he would say that they looked like gold; and other times he would say he had not seen the plates at all" (III.A.13, WILLIAM STAFFORD STATEMENT, 8 DEC 1833, 240). But it is uncertain if this statement has direct bearing on Joseph Sr.'s testimony, or if his alleged denial of having seen the plates was given before or after his experience as one of the eight witnesses.

appearance of the plates from which it was translated" (Salt Lake Stake Historical Record, 25 January 1888, cited in R. L. Anderson 1981, 146).

5. Samuel Harrison Smith (1808-44).

In a late reminiscence, Daniel Tyler reported that in the spring of 1832 Samuel Smith said "he knew his brother Joseph had the plates, for the prophet had shown them to him, and he had handled them and seen the engravings thereon" (Tyler 1883, 23).

6. Hiram Page (1800-52).

In an 1847 statement, Page rejected the idea that he "could know a thing to be true in 1830, and know the same thing to be false in 1847." He also denied that his mind had become "so treacherous that I had forgotten what I saw" (VI.C.1, HIRAM PAGE TO WILLIAM MCLELLIN, 30 MAY 1847). One of Page's sons told Andrew Jenson in 1888: "I knew my father to be true and faithful to his testimony of the divinity of the Book of Mormon until the very last. Whenever he had an opportunity to bear his testimony to this effect, he would always do so, and seemed to rejoice exceedingly in having been privileged to see the plates" (*Historical Record* 7 [1888]: 614). Philander Page, son of Hiram Page, told George Edward Anderson in 1907 that his father "Never faltered in his testimony about the plates and the characters. Often related to Philander what they had seen and passed through" (Diary, 29, Daughters of Utah Pioneers Museum, Salt Lake City, Utah, cited in Holzapfel, Cottle, and Stoddard 1995, 70). John C. Whitmer, son of Jacob Whitmer, said in 1888: "I knew [Hiram Page] at all times and under all circumstances to be true to his testimony concerning the divinity of the Book of Mormon" (*Deseret News,* 17 September 1888, 2; rept. *Saints' Herald* 35 [13 October 1888]: 651).

7. Jacob Whitmer (1800-56).

Andrew Jenson, Edward Stevenson, and Joseph S. Black quoted John C. Whitmer, son of Jacob Whitmer, as stating: "My father, Jacob Whitmer, was always faithful and true to his testimony to the Book of Mormon, and confirmed it on his deathbed" (*Deseret News,* 17 September 1888, 2; rept. *Saints' Herald* 35 [13 October 1888]: 651).

8. John Whitmer (1802-87).

Of the eight witnesses, John Whitmer lived the longest and left the most on record. In 1836 Whitmer said that he had "no hesitancy" about his testimony in the Book of Mormon "but with confidence have signed my name to it. ... I have most assuredly seen the plates from whence the book of Mormon is translated, and that I have handled these plates" (VI.B.2,

JOHN WHITMER TESTIMONY, 1836). Whitmer reportedly said to Theodore Turley in April 1839: "I handled those plates; there was fine engravings on both sides. I handled them. ... [T]hey were shown to me by a supernatural power" (VI.B.3, JOHN WHITMER TESTIMONY, 1839). According to E. C. Brand of the RLDS church, in 1875 Whitmer "declared that his testimony, as found in ... the Book of Mormon, is strictly true" (see "John Whitmer Addendum"). On 5 March 1876, Whitmer wrote Mark H. Forscutt of the RLDS church: "I have never heard that any one of the three, or eight witnesses ever denied the testimony that they have borne to the Book [of Mormon]" (VI.B.4, JOHN WHITMER TO MARK H. FORSCUTT, 5 MAR 1876). On 11 December 1876, Whitmer wrote to Heman C. Smith of the RLDS church concerning his testimony in the Book of Mormon: "*That testimony was, is, and will be true, henceforth and forever*" (VI.B.5, JOHN WHITMER TO HEMAN C. SMITH, 11 DEC 1876). Whitmer told Myron Bond in 1878 that he "saw and handled" the plates (*Saints' Herald* 25 [1878]: 253). In a not too reliable interview of April 1878, P. Wilhelm Poulson said Whitmer affirmed his testimony, stating that he handled the plates, that they were handed over "uncovered into our hands, and we turned the leaves sufficient to satisfy us," and that they were "as material as anything can be" and "very heavy" (VI.B.7, JOHN WHITMER INTERVIEW WITH P. WILHELM POULSON, APR 1878; see note 1 above).

As can be seen, except for Poulson's late interview with John Whitmer, specific declarations by the witnesses about handling the plates are few and vague. Published twenty days after John Whitmer's death, Poulson's version of the interview is questionable, not only because it conflicts with Turley's 1839 report that Whitmer claimed to have seen and handled the plates "by a supernatural power," but because of the historical setting in which Poulson places the event, in the Smiths' Manchester cabin with Smith showing the plates in two shifts of four witnesses (see note 1 above). A similar situation subsequently occurred when Poulson published his interview with David Whitmer in August 1878 (see VI.A.6, DAVID WHITMER INTERVIEW WITH P. WILHELM POULSON, CIRCA APR 1878). In a letter to S. T. Mouch, dated 18 November 1882, David Whitmer accused Poulson of inventing dialogue (see introduction to ibid.). Among the possible statements Whitmer found objectionable are: that all three witnesses were together at the time of their vision of the angel and the plates; and that Whitmer had seen the stone box from which the plates were taken (see Vogel 1995). One can easily detect from this brief examination that Poulson's errors are not random but consistently result from his attempt to strengthen the testimony of the witnesses.

Poulson's interview aside, there remains no reliable description of the manner in which the eight witnesses saw and handled the plates. Nevertheless, despite the naturalistic tone of the published Testimony of Eight Witnesses, there is reason to believe that their experience was at least partly visionary.

Stephen Burnett, who rejected the Book of Mormon based partly on statements Martin Harris made in a public meeting in Kirtland, Ohio, reported in April 1838 that Harris had announced that he "never saw the plates with his natural eyes," and that "the eight witnesses never saw them [plates] & hesitated to sign that instrument for that reason, but were persuaded to do it" (see III.F.7, STEPHEN BURNETT TO LYMAN E. JOHNSON, 25 APR 1838). It is unlikely that either man meant to say that the eight witnesses never saw the plates or that their written Testimony was a fabrication. Harris was apparently simply claiming that the Testimony of Eight Witnesses misrepresented the actual experience of the eight men, whom he knew well. It was for this reason, according to Harris, that they "hesitated to sign" the written Testimony.

Warren Parrish's reporting of Harris's statement tends to support this interpretation. Parrish, also a Kirtland dissenter, reported in August 1838 that "Martin Harris, one of the subscribing witnesses, has come out at last, and says he never saw the plates, from which the book [of Mormon] purports to have been translated, except in vision, and he further says that any man who says he has seen them in any other way is a liar, Joseph [Smith] not excepted" (*Evangelist* [Carthage, Ohio] 6 [1 October 1838]: 226). Parrish then referred to a revelation dictated by Joseph Smith in June 1829, which promised the three hopeful witnesses a view of the plates, on condition of faith, and included the instruction that "ye shall testify that you have seen them, even as my servant Joseph Smith, Jun., has seen them; for it is by my power that he has seen them, and it is because he had faith" (D&C 17:5). Thus, rather than report that Harris claimed the eight witnesses never saw the plates, Parrish said that Harris denied that anyone had seen the plates except in vision.

Although Harris had rejected Joseph Smith's leadership, he continued to believe in the Book of Mormon and had little desire to impart any information that could damage the book. According to Burnett, Harris later remarked that "he never should have told that the testimony of the eight [witnesses] was false, if it had not been picked out of [h]im but should have let it passed as it was." Regardless, Harris's statements provided justification for some dissenters to reject the Book of Mormon.

Hyrum Smith's apparent response to the Kirtland dissenters, as reported by Sally Parker in August 1838, is an indirect confirmation that the dissenters were spiritualizing the experience of the eight witnesses. Parker wrote to "comfort" her relatives in Maine who were evidently troubled about the developments in Kirtland.[4] She offered two evidences that the plates were real. First, she heard Hyrum Smith, who had recently visited her central Ohio town of Sunbury, declare that "he had but [two] hands and [two] eyes," and that "he had seene the plates with his eyes and handeled them with his hands." Next, she had lived near Lucy Smith and had heard her describe hiding the plates under the hearth and claim to have "hefted and handled" the plates while covered (Sally Parker to John Kempton, 26 August 1838, microfilm, Family History Library, Salt Lake City, Utah; cf. I.B.2, SALLY PARKER TO JOHN KEMPTON, 26 AUG 1838).

Hyrum's remark that "he had but ... [two] eyes" seems especially designed to counter dissenter claims that the eight witnesses saw the plates with their "spiritual eyes." His statement is not unlike the response of David Whitmer, who evidently became weary by questions about the nature of his visionary experience. Nathan Tanner, who interviewed Whitmer in 1886, reported that Whitmer said, "I have been asked if we saw those things with our natural eyes. Of course they were our natural eyes. There is no doubt that our eyes were prepared for the sight, but they were our natural eyes nevertheless" (Nathan Tanner, Jr., to Nathan A. Tanner, 17 February 1909, typed copy, LDS Church Archives, Salt Lake City, Utah). Thus Hyrum was not necessarily denying dissenter claims that he and the other witnesses had seen the plates in vision, only denouncing the implication that a vision was inferior to a purely physical experience.

Similar events in Missouri presented another of the eight witnesses with an opportunity to clarify his testimony. On 5 April 1839, Theodore Turley, who was then the church's business agent in Far West, publicly questioned John Whitmer concerning his Book of Mormon testimony. Whitmer had joined the dissenters in Missouri and, unlike Harris, not only rejected Joseph Smith but also the Book of Mormon. Turley wanted to know how Whitmer's testimony about the plates could be true and yet the Book of Mormon be false. Before his anti-Mormon friends, Whitmer reaffirmed his testimony of the Book of Mormon, that he had both seen and handled the plates, but concluded by stating that the plates had been "shown to me by a supernatural power" (see above). Given his experience with the plates—even

4. Parker also states that she was responding to the dissenters because "they disput[e] [the] Book [of Mormon] so much."

if supernatural—Turley wondered how Whitmer could reject the Book of Mormon. Whitmer responded that he could not read the original and therefore he had no guarantee that Smith had translated it correctly.

If the visual experience of the eight witnesses was visionary, then their handling of the plates was possibly a separate experience. Meaning that the plates were present in a box or cloth covering and the eight witnesses saw through the box or cloth; thus each man could claim that he had both seen and handled the plates. This possibility is very much like what Harris suggested was his experience with the plates prior to his June 1829 vision with Smith. Harris told John A. Clark in 1828 that he saw the plates "with the eye of faith ... just as distinctly as I see any thing around me,—though at the time they were covered over with a cloth" (III.F.1, MARTIN HARRIS INTERVIEWS WITH JOHN A. CLARK, 1827 & 1828, 2:99). He also told Stephen Burnett and others in 1838 that "he had hefted the plates repeatedly in a box [or] with only a tablecloth or a handkerchief over them, but he never saw them only as he saw a city through a mountain" (III.F.7, STEPHEN BURNETT TO LYMAN E. JOHNSON, 25 APR 1838).[5]

With such limited historical sources, the exact nature of the experience of the eight witnesses may never be entirely known. However, the preceding discussion is an indication that their experience was probably more complex than their group statement implies. Indeed, the Testimony of Eight Witnesses is a collective document, unifying what might have been varying and diverse experiences of the eight men.

And also the testimony of eight witnesses

Be it known unto all Nations[,] kindreds[,] tongues & people unto whom this work shall come that Joseph Smith Jun. the author & proprietor of this work has shewn unto us the plate[s] of which hath been spoken which have the appearance of gold & as many of the leaves as the said Smith has translated we did handle with our hands & we also saw the engravings thereon all of which has the appearance of ancient work & of curious workmanship & this we bear record with words of soberness that the said Smith has got the plates of which we have spoken & we give our names unto the world to wit=ness unto the world that which we have seen & we lie not God bearing witness of it

Christian Whitmer
Jacob Whitmer

5. See also III.K.18, THOMAS FORD ACCOUNT, 1854.

Peter Whitmer Jun.
John Whitmer
Hiram Page
Joseph Smith sen.
Hyrum Smith
Samuel H Smith

14. MARTIN HARRIS MORTGAGE, 25 AUGUST 1829

Martin Harris, Mortgage to Egbert B. Grandin, 25 August 1829, Mortgages, Liber 3, 325, Wayne County Clerk's Office, Lyons, New York.

EDITORIAL NOTE

Martin Harris (1783-1875)[1] settled in Palmyra in 1792, eventually owning about 320 acres of land (Jessee 1989, 489-90; L. Cook 1981, 9; Gunnell 1955; 38-39; James 1983, 163 n. 264). In early June 1829 he accompanied Joseph Smith to Egbert B. Grandin's printing establishment in Palmyra to discuss the possibility of publishing the Book of Mormon. Grandin declined. In a few days Harris returned to Grandin's office informing him of the possibility of printing the book in Rochester. When Harris offered his farm as collateral, Grandin finally agreed to print 5,000 books for $3,000 (III.H.8, JOHN H. GILBERT STATEMENT, 23 OCT 1887; III.H.10, JOHN H. GILBERT MEMORANDUM, 8 SEP 1892). On 25 August 1829, Harris mortgaged about 151 acres of land to Grandin for $3,000. The mortgage stipulated that Harris was to pay "the sum of three thousand dollars at or before the expiration of eighteen months from the date thereof"—that is, by 25 February 1831—or Grandin would be at liberty to sell the property. Printing of the Book of Mormon commenced in late August 1829, and on 26 March 1830 the *Wayne Sentinel* announced that books were for sale in the Palmyra Book Store (III.E.1, *WAYNE SENTINEL,* 1824-1836, under 26 March 1830).

The Book of Mormon, however, did not sell as well as anticipated, and it quickly became apparent that Harris would have to sell his land. In late March 1830, as the first books were coming from the binder, Harris complained to Smith that "The Books will not sell for no Body wants them." According to Joseph Knight, Harris resisted the idea that he should at that time sell his land and demanded a "commandment" from Smith (IV.A.1, JOSEPH KNIGHT, SR., REMINISCENCE, CIRCA 1835-1847, 6-7). The next day Smith dictated a revelation which declared, "I command thee

1. On Martin Harris (1783-1875), see "Introduction to Martin Harris Collection."

[Harris] that thou shalt not covet thine own property, but impart it freely to the printing of the Book of Mormon" (D&C 19:26). David Whitmer said that Harris's attitude about selling his farm led Hyrum Smith to suggest the possibility of selling the Book of Mormon's copyright in Canada in order to pay off the mortgage and free themselves from any obligation to Harris (see VI.A.33, DAVID WHITMER, *ADDRESS,* 1887, 31). Harris is also known to have approached Charles Butler, agent for the New York Life Insurance and Trust Company in Geneva, for a second mortgage. The timing of Harris's visit is not clear, but it may have been shortly after Smith's March 1830 revelation (see introduction to III.F.3, MARTIN HARRIS INTERVIEW WITH CHARLES BUTLER, CIRCA 1830-1831).

Finally, on 1 April 1831, Martin Harris agreed to sell about 151 acres of his farm to Thomas Lakey, an early settler and extensive property holder in Palmyra who ran a wagon and sleigh business (T. Cook 1930, 21, 37), for $3,000. Grandin may have allowed Harris a grace period before sale of the farm since the printing of the Book of Mormon took longer than anticipated (III.G.2, OLIVER COWDERY TO JOSEPH SMITH, 6 NOV 1829, 8). The terms of the purchase agreement, dated 1 April 1831, were as follows:

> Articles of agreement made and concluded this first day of April, in the year 1831, between Martin Harris of the first part, and Thomas Lakey of the second part, both of Palmyra in the County of Wayne, and the State of New York, in the manner and form following:
>
> The said Martin Harris, for the consideration hereinafter mentioned, agrees to sell to the said Thomas Lakey the farm on which he now resides, containing by estimation, one hundred and fifty acres, for the sum of twenty dollars for each acre, and, forthwith to obtain a correct survey of said premises, and give a good warranty deed of same, and give immediate possession of everything. Always excepting and reserving the privilege of living in the house till the first of May next. The said Thomas Lakey is to have all the wheat on the ground except the acres sown by Mr. [Flanders] Dyke, and the one-half of the said ten acres shall belong to the said Thomas Lakey after the said Dyke shall harvest the same and shock it up in the field.
>
> In consideration whereof, the said Thomas Lakey agrees to pay to the said Martin Harris, one third of the purchase money on the first day of next May, and one third in the month of October next, and the remaining one third in the month of October in the year eighteen hundred and thirty-two. In consideration whereof the parties bind themselves in the penal sum of five hundred dollars, being damages assessed and agreed upon by the parties. In witness whereof, the parties have hereunto interchangeably set their hands and seals, the day and year first above written.

(Signed) MARTIN HARRIS, L.S.
THOMAS LAKEY, L.S.[2]

On 7 April 1831, six days after signing the agreement, Harris deeded the land to Lakey (deed reproduced in Gunnell 1955, 99-100). Pomeroy Tucker said that "the farm mortgaged was sold by Harris in 1831 at private sale, not by foreclosure, and a sufficiency of the avails went to pay Grandin—though it is presumed Harris might have paid the $3,000 without the sale of the farm" (III.J.8, POMEROY TUCKER ACCOUNT, 1867, 54-55). Tucker's presumption about Harris's financial situation, however, is likely mistaken.

The terms of Harris's 1 April 1831 agreement with Lakey indicate that Grandin would not receive full payment for another eighteen months (October 1832). However, James Reeves claimed Harris was paid by Lakey three weeks later, evidently just before Harris departed for Ohio (III.F.19, JAMES H. REEVES ACCOUNT, 1872). The agreement also stipulated that Harris vacate his residence on 1 May 1831. The *Wayne Sentinel* reported on 27 May 1831 that Martin Harris and several other families "took up their line of march from this town [Palmyra] last week for the 'promised land.'" According to Thomas L. Cook, Lakey later sold the farm to John Graves, an English emigrant who paid $3,000 in gold (T. Cook 1930, 205).[3]

This Indenture, Made the twenty fifth day of August in the year of our Lord one thousand eight hundred and twenty nine between Martin Harris of the town of Palmyra in the county of Wayne & State of New York, of the first part, and Egbert B. Grandin of the same place of the second part

2. As published in Gunnell 1955, 38-39; also in *Wayne County Journal,* 28 May 1874. Gunnell reports: "A copy of the terms of agreement was originally obtained from Carl Lakey, son of Thomas Lakey. Willard Bean sent this and other data to William Pilkington, Jr. sometime after July twenty-fourth in the year 1935" (Gunnell 1955, 39). A copy of the Harris/Lakey agreement is in Wayne County Book of Deeds, Liber 10, 515-16, Wayne County Clerk's Office, Lyons, New York (Gunnell 1955, 99-100). "L.S." apparently represents "legal seal."

3. Harris later sold the remaining portions of his land: Martin Harris to Flanders Dike (Dyke) (son-in-law), 17 May 1837; Martin Harris to George B. Harris (son), 1 November 1842; Martin Harris to Amos Adams (son-in-law), 1 November 1842; and Martin Harris to Job Booth, 9 July 1859 (see James 1983, 163 n. 266). Harris had also deeded eighty acres to his wife on 29 November 1825.

Witnesseth, that the said party of the first for and in consideration of the sum of three thousand dollars to him in hand, paid by the said party of the second part, the receipt whereof is hereby confessed and acknowledged; hath granted, bargained, sold, remised, released; enfeoffed and confirmed; and by these presents doth grant, bargain, sell, remise, release, enfeoff and confirm, unto the said party of the second part; and to his heirs and assigns forever. All that certain tract or parcel of land situate in the said town of Palmyra aforesaid bounded on <the> south by lands belonging to Preservid Harris[4] on the east by Red Creek, on the north by lands belonging to Emer Harris[5] & the high=way & on the west by the east line of the town of Macedon, being the same tract of land or farm upon which the said Martin Harris now resides. To have and to hold the above bargained premises to the said party of the second part, his heirs, and assigns, to the sole and only proper use benefit and behoof of the said part of the second part, his heirs and assigns forever Provid<ed> always, and these presents are upon this express condition that if the said Martin Harris his heirs execut[ors] or adminis=trators shall pay or cause to be paid unto the said party of the second part his heirs executors administrators or assigns the sum of three thousand dollars at or before the expiration of eighteen months from the date hereof, then these presents shall cease and be null and void but in case of the non-payment of the said sum of Money, or any part thereof, at the time above limited for the payment thereof, then and in such case it shall and may be lawful for the said party of the second part, his heirs executors administrators or assigns and the said party of the first part doth hereby empower and authorize the said party of the second part his heirs executors, administrators or assigns to grant, bargain, sell, release and convey the said premises, or any part or portion thereof with the appurtenances at public auction or vendue and on such sale to make and execute to the purchaser or purchasers his or their heirs and assigns forever good ample or sufficient deed or deeds of conveyance in the law pursuant to the statute in that case made and provided. Rendering the surplus moneys (if any there should be) to the said party of the first part his heirs, executors or administra=tors ~~or assigns~~ after deducting the costs and charges of such vendue and sale aforesaid. In witness whereof the party of the first part hath hereunto set his hand and seal the day and year first above written. The nineteenth and a part of the twentieth and twentyfirst lines

4. On Preserved Harris (1785-1867), see I.A.15, JOSEPH SMITH HISTORY, 1839, n. 48.

5. On Emer Harris (1781-1869), see introduction to III.K.20, EMER HARRIS ACCOUNT, 1856.

obliterated before ex=ecution.

Martin Harris. [seal]

Signed Sealed and delivered in
in presence of Fred'k Smith

State of New York[,] Wayne County SS.

On the 26th day of August 1829, per=sonally appeared before me Frederick Smith a Judge of Wayne County the within grantor to me known to be the person described in and who executed the within deed & acknowledged that he executed the same as his voluntary act and deed for the purposes therein contained.

Fred'k Smith.[6]

6. On Frederick Smith, see III.A.12, DAVID STAFFORD STATEMENT, 5 DEC 1833, n. 7.

15.
JOSEPH SMITH AND OLIVER COWDERY BIBLE INSCRIPTION, 8 OCTOBER 1829

The Holy Bible (Cooperstown, New York: H. and E. Phinney Co., 1828). Inscription on front flyleaf indicates ownership by Joseph Smith and Oliver Cowdery, 8 October 1829, RLDS Church Library-Archives, Independence, Missouri.

EDITORIAL NOTE

The inscribed Bible, a large pulpit-style edition containing the King James Version of the Old and New Testaments as well as the Apocrypha and printed at Cooperstown, New York, by H. and E. Phinney Company in 1828, was subsequently used by Joseph Smith in producing his Inspired Version or New Translation of the Bible. The notation is written on the front flyleaf in the large handwriting of Joseph Smith and occupies the top quarter and lower eighth of the page. The Bible was purchased by Oliver Cowdery on 8 October 1829 at E. B. Grandin's bookstore on Palmyra's Main Street. Since Smith had left the area, arriving at Harmony, Pennsylvania, by 4 October 1829 (see I.A.1, JOSEPH SMITH TO OLIVER COWDERY, 22 OCT 1829), it follows that Cowdery purchased the Bible in Smith's absence and that Smith later penned the inscription.

The Book of the Jews And the property of
Joseph Smith Junior and Oliver Cowdery
Bought October the 8th 1829 at Egbert B Grandins
Book Store Palmyra[,] Wayne County[,] New York

Price $3.75

Holiness to the Lord

16.
Book of Mormon Preface, 1829

Joseph Smith, "Preface" to the Book of Mormon, Printer's Manuscript, Restoration Scriptures, RLDS Church Library-Archives, Independence, Missouri.

EDITORIAL NOTE

The printer's manuscript includes the earliest known copy of Joseph Smith's "Preface" to the first edition of the Book of Mormon. The wording of Smith's "Preface" largely draws on a revelation of May 1829 dealing with the lost first portion of the translation manuscript (D&C 10; date as per Book of Commandments). However, there are two items in the Preface which are not taken from the revelation. First, Smith calls the lost manuscript "the Book of Lehi ... an account abridged from the plates of Lehi, by the hand of Mormon" (cf. 1 Ne. 10:15, where Nephi refers to his father's book). Second, this is the earliest source to mention the number of pages lost as 116.

Smith's mention of the loss of 116 pages has possible implications for the dating of the Preface as well as for the early progress of Cowdery's work on the printers manuscript. Where did Smith get this number? It is unlikely that he could remember exactly how many pages were lost. Did he guess? Or did he simply look at the original manuscript's opening portion of the book of Mosiah to find the next page number, assuming the previous numbering system was preserved? Unfortunately, this portion of Mosiah has not survived and subsequent portions from Alma, Helaman, and 3 Nephi are not well preserved. However, an interesting coincidence occurs in the printer's manuscript. In the printer's manuscript, the first portion of the present Book of Mormon (First Nephi through The Words of Mormon)—the portion Smith dictated last to replace the lost manuscript—is half a sentence more than 116 pages. It seems improbable, assuming the lost manuscript was really 116 pages, that Cowdery's copy of the original manuscript would coincidentally fall on the same page.[1] For whatever reason,

1. Royal Skousen has reported that the recently restored fragments of the dictated or original manuscript from the Wilford Wood collection were found to include two leaves from Jacob 6 through Enos 1 and that they are numbered 111 through 114 (Skousen 1992, 22). Since the corresponding pages from the printer's manuscript are numbered 107 through 111, Oliver

Smith probably referred to the printer's manuscript when writing his Preface (see also Metcalfe 1993, 395 n. 1).

When did Joseph Smith write the Preface to the first edition of the Book of Mormon? It was evidently written during his stay in Manchester, New York, which lasted from late June to early October 1829. The Preface must have been written before the printer began setting type in mid-August since it was included in the first signature (see III.H.10, JOHN H. GILBERT MEMORANDUM, 8 SEP 1892).

If the above analysis is correct, Cowdery must have at least reached page 116 in his copying before Smith wrote his Preface. Cowdery probably began copying the manuscript near the beginning of July 1829, since arrangements had already been made to publish the Book of Mormon in Palmyra, and had reached Alma 36 about 6 November 1829 (see III.G.2, OLIVER COWDERY TO JOSEPH SMITH, 6 NOV 1829). Averaging the number of pages per day, Cowdery would have copied the first 116 pages by about the beginning of August. It therefore seems probable that the Preface was written shortly before printing began in mid-August.

Two traditions have come down regarding the fate of the stolen pages. The tradition among Lucy Harris's relatives is that she burned them (Sillitoe and Roberts 1988, 155; III.F.19, JAMES H. REEVES ACCOUNT, 1872). E. D. Howe reported in 1834 that the Mormons "sometimes charged the wife of Harris with having burnt it; but this is denied by her" (V.D.1, EBER D. HOWE ACCOUNT, 1834, 22). Lucy Harris's denial was probably passed on to him by Philastus Hurlbut, who had interviewed her in November 1833. Lorenzo Saunders, however, said Lucy Harris told him that she had burned the manuscript (III.B.15, LORENZO SAUNDERS INTERVIEW, 12 NOV 1884, 4).

A second tradition claims that the manuscript has survived. This tradition, although doubtful, was encouraged by Joseph Smith when he explained in the Book of Mormon's Preface that "some person or persons have stolen & kept from me" 116 pages of original manuscript "notwithstanding my utmost exer=sion to recover it again." At the time of writing the Preface, Smith still seemed concerned about the existence of the stolen manuscript and its possible comparison with the first portion of the published

---

Cowdery being able to condense the text in copying, it is unlikely that the Words of Mormon in the original manuscript also concluded on page 116. Five more pages were required for Cowdery to condense the original text for the printer's copy of Jarom to the Words of Mormon, which would have brought the original manuscript to page 119 or 120.

Book of Mormon, so that Smith found it necessary to explain that he had not retranslated the lost portion.

William R. Hine of Colesville, Broome County, New York, claimed that Lucy Harris stole the manuscript and gave it to a "Dr. Seymour." Hine reported, "Dr. Seymour lived one and a half miles from me. He read most of it to me when my daughter Rene was born, he read them to his patients about the country. It was a description of the mounds about the country and similar to the 'Book of Mormon'" (IV.D.10, WILLIAM R. HINE STATEMENT, CIRCA MAR 1885). Hine might have had reference to Ezra Seymour (b. 1784) of Colesville, who is listed in the 1850 census as a physician.

Yet another claim for the manuscript's survival comes from the Franklin D. Richards family. Charles Comstock Richards, son of Apostle Franklin D. Richards, accompanied his father and other family members on a genealogical tour of New England in 1880. In 1947 Charles recalled that he and his father visited Palmyra, New York, and "we called upon Dr. J. R. Pratt, M.D. who told my father that he could put his hand on the manuscript which Martin Harris lost, in an hour, if it was needed" (see C. Richards 1947, 2; Bitton 1977, 290). This was probably John R. Pratt (b. 1826) of Manchester, who is listed in the 1880 and 1900 censuses as a physician (see also McIntosh 1876, 181).

At the time of the manuscript's disappearance, Martin Harris believed his wife had taken the manuscript and had given it to others (III.F.1, MARTIN HARRIS INTERVIEW WITH JOHN A. CLARK, 1827 & 1828, 247-48). In later years Harris evidently came to believe that his wife had burned the manuscript (III.F.21, MARTIN HARRIS INTERVIEWS WITH WILLIAM PILKINGTON, 1874-1875). This conclusion is probably correct since Lucy Harris was less interested in exposing Smith than with putting a stop to the production of the Book of Mormon as well as to her husband's financial involvement with the project.

PREFACE

To the Reader—

As many fals[e] reports have been sirculated respecting ~~this~~ <the following> work & also many unla=wful measures taken by evil desineing persons to destroy me & also the work I would inform you that I translated by the gift & power of God & caused to be written one hundred & sixteen pages the which I took from the Book of Lehi which was an acc=ount abridged from the plates of Lehi by the hand of Mormon which said account some person or persons have stolen & kept from me notwithstanding my utmost exer=sion to recover it again & being commanded of the Lord that I should not translate the same over again for Satan had put it into their hearts to tempt the Lord their God by altering the words that they did read conterary from that which I translated & caused to be written & if I should bring forth the same words again or in other words if I should translate the same over again they would publish that which they had stolen & Satan would stir up the hearts of this generation that they might not receive this work but behold the Lord said unto me I will not suffer that Satan shall accomplish his evil design in this thing therefore thou shalt translate from the plates of Nephi until ~~you~~ ye come to that which ye have translated which ye have retained & behold ye shall publish it as the record of Nephi & thus I will confound those who have altered my words I will not suffer that they shall destroy my work yea I will shew unto them that my wisdom is greater then [than] the cunning of the Devil wherefore to be obediant unto the commandments of God I have through his grace & mercy accomplished that which he hath commanded me respecting this thing I would also inform you that the plates of which hath been spoken ~~was~~ <were> found in the township of Manchester[,] Ontario County[,] New-York[.]

The Author

17.
JOSEPH SMITH, SR., AND MARTIN HARRIS AGREEMENT, 16 JANUARY 1830

Joseph Smith, Sr., and Martin Harris, Agreement Regarding Sale of Book of Mormon, 16 January 1830, Simon Gratz Collection, Historical Society of Pennsylvania, Philadelphia, Pennsylvania.

EDITORIAL NOTE

Orsamus Turner probably referred to this document when he remarked that "the only business contract—veritable instrument in writing, that was ever executed by spiritual agents, has been preserved, and should be among the archives of the new state of Utah. It is signed by the Prophet Joseph himself, and witnessed by Oliver Cowdery, and secures to Martin Harris one half of the proceeds of the sale of the Gold Bible until he was fully reimbursed in the sum of $2,500, the cost of printing" (III.J.2, ORSAMUS TURNER ACCOUNT, 1851, 216). As to the parties and sum involved in the agreement, Turner was mistaken since the original is signed by Joseph Smith, Sr., not Jr.,[1] and Harris owed Grandin $3,000, rather than $2,500 (III.L.14, MARTIN HARRIS MORTGAGE, 25 AUG 1829).

The agreement points to Joseph Sr.'s role in the Book of Mormon

1. I do not agree with Scott Faulring's recent assertion that the signature on the present Agreement is that of Joseph Smith, Jr. (Faulring 1995, 206, n. 2). The "S" in "Sr" is very clearly an "S," not a "J" as Faulring reads. Also, despite Faulring's assertion, Joseph Sr. did sometimes include the designations "Sen." or "Sr." with his name as the following documents attest: Articles of Agreement, 1825 (V.E.1, ARTICLES OF AGREEMENT, 1 NOV 1825); Testimony of Eight Witnesses, June 1829 (III.L.13, TESTIMONY OF EIGHT WITNESSES, JUNE 1829); several entries in the deed records of Geauga County, Ohio, 1837-38, including land purchases and a power of attorney (Deeds, 24:363-64, 25:150-51, 266-67, 322-23, 27:122, Geauga County Courthouse, Chardon, Ohio); and William Swartzell's deacon's license, March 1838 (Swartzell 1840, iv). Because the Joseph Sr. signature in the Nathan Pierce docket book varies only slightly from that of his son's, and the sample of Joseph Sr. holograph signatures is extremely small, certainly one cannot exclude Joseph Sr. with the finality that Faulring does.

project, although it is not clear in what capacity he served. Pomeroy Tucker possibly gave a hint: "The book, as a money-making enterprise, fell dead before the public. ... It found no buyers, or but very few. ... Hence another 'command' became necessary in regard to the sale of the book, after a few week's faithful but unsuccessful trial of the market by Harris as a monopolist salesman. This was easily called down by Smith in favor of his patriarch father. ... The patriarch having been permitted by this changed revelation, with the consent of Harris, to appropriate a portion of the avails of sales toward his family necessities, he effected some sales, chiefly in barter trades, on accommodating terms for the purchasers of the books, always maintaining the revealed price of ten shillings" (III.J.8, POMEROY TUCKER ACCOUNT, 1867, 61-62). Tucker's account is garbled since the terms of agreement are the reverse of what he describes. It is the senior Smith who agrees to give Harris "an equal privilege with me & my friends." Moreover, the date of the agreement is 16 January 1830, two months before the Book of Mormon was released for sale.

The wording of the agreement indicates that as of 16 January 1830 Harris anticipated that the sale of the books would fully pay off his $3,000 mortgage to Grandin, and that the surplus would go to Joseph Sr. and friends. However, the lack of sales would eventually force Harris to sell about 151 acres of land to Thomas Lakey (deed dated 7 April 1831; see introduction to III.L.14, MARTIN HARRIS MORTGAGE, 25 AUG 1829).

The terms of the agreement may not have pleased Harris, who seems to have hoped to make a profit from his investment in the Book of Mormon. According to Tucker, "Harris was led to believe that the book would be a profitable speculation for him, and very likely in this may be traced his leading motive for taking the venture. He was vouchsafed the security of a 'special revelation' commanding that the new Bible should in no instance be sold at a less price than 'ten shillings,' and that he himself should have the exclusive right of sale, with all the avails. ... Indeed, he figured up the profits ... thus: 5,000 books at $1.25 per book, $6,250. First cost, $3,000. Showing a clear speculation of over one hundred per sent upon the investment" (III.J.8, POMEROY TUCKER ACCOUNT, 1867, 55; see also III.A.7, LUCY HARRIS STATEMENT, 29 NOV 1833; III.A.6, ABIGAIL HARRIS STATEMENT, 28 NOV 1833, 254). If Harris held any speculative notions about profiting from his financing the book before 16 January 1830, his limited interest in the Book of Mormon was clearly defined in this agreement.

Moreover, not only was Harris excluded from profiting from the Book of Mormon, the agreement also stipulated that he was only entitled to half of the proceeds from sales until his debt to Grandin was paid off. This meant that all 5,000 copies of the first edition had to be sold by 25 February 1831 to prevent the sale of Harris's farm. Little wonder Harris expressed concern about the slow sale of the books (see introduction to III.L.14, MARTIN HARRIS MORTGAGE, 25 AUG 1829).

The pedigree of the agreement and the particulars of Simon Gratz's procurement of it are unknown. It was acquired by the Historical Society of Pennsylvania, along with Gratz's enormous autograph collection, in the 1920s. It is apparently in Oliver Cowdery's handwriting and signed by Joseph Smith, Sr.

I hereby agree that Martin Harris shall have an equal privilege with me & my friends of selling the Book of Mormon of the Edition now printing by Egbert B Grandin until enough of them shall be sold to pay for the printing of the same or until such times as the said Grandin shall be paid for the printing the aforesaid Books or copies[.]

[s] Joseph Smith Sr

Manchester January the 16th 1830—

Witness [s] Oliver H P Cowdery[2]

2. Cowdery's use of middle initials is consistent with other documents dating from this period (see I.A.1, JOSEPH SMITH TO OLIVER COWDERY, 22 OCT 1829; III.G.3, OLIVER COWDERY TO JOSEPH SMITH, 28 DEC 1829; and III.G.1, OLIVER COWDERY TO HYRUM SMITH, 14 JUN 1829; V.E.5, JOSEPH SMITH HARMONY [PA] LAND RECORDS, 1828-1833).

18.
LEMUEL DURFEE PROBATE PAPERS, 1830

Lemuel Durfee, Probate Papers, filed 22 January 1830, Wayne County Clerk's Office, Lyons, New York.

EDITORIAL NOTE

Lemuel Durfee, the Smiths' landlord, died on 8 August 1829. On 31 August, Isaac Hussee and Peter Harris were appointed to appraise Durfee's personal property. Among his papers was evidently found a promissory note from Joseph Smith, Sr., and Abraham Fish to Durfee for $37.50. The inventory of Durfee's estate, which was filed on 22 January 1830 by Durfee's executors Oliver Durfee and Lemuel Durfee, Jr., lists the Smith/Fish note. This document, a portion of which is reproduced below, lists the $37.50 note as well as $1.42 in interest, for a total of $38.92.

On 19 January 1830, three days before the filing of Durfee's probate papers, Lemuel Durfee, Jr., entered a plea before Justice of the Peace Nathan Pierce for judgement against Joseph Smith, Sr., and Abraham Fish for $39.92, both of whom signed a consent for the judge to enter a judgement against them for damages for that amount. It was evidently some time before Durfee recovered his damages as the docket book indicates that on 13 September 1830 Durfee received $41.44, which included $1.52 in additional interest (see III.L.19, NATHAN PIERCE DOCKET BOOK, 1830). Judging from the interest paid for the nearly eight months (from 19 January to 13 September 1830), nineteen cents per month, the $1.42 interest perhaps points to a January/February 1829 date (or seven and a half months previous) for the creation of the Smith/Fish note. Unfortunately, the record fails to indicate the reason for the Smith/Fish debt.

One note Signed by Joseph Smith and Abra=
ham Fish thirty Seven dollars and fifty cents 37.50
interest 1.42

19.
NATHAN PIERCE DOCKET BOOK, 1830

Nathan Pierce Docket Book, 1827-1830, 25, 32, 76b (entries of 19 January 1830, 22 February 1830, 28 June 1830, and "execution" order of 14 August 1830), Manchester Township Office, Clifton Springs, New York.

EDITORIAL NOTE

Nathan Pierce was a justice of the peace in Manchester, New York. He also served as town assessor and collector (Milliken 1911, 410). Pierce, in his thirties, is listed in the 1830 census of Manchester (1830:169).

Pierce's docket book contains a number of entries for a "Joseph Smith" and a "Hiram Smith" (and/or "Hyram Smith"). Although Richard L. Anderson has expressed some caution about these entries (1970, 292), in every instance but one (item 2 below), it is fairly certain that the cases involve either Joseph Smith, Sr., or his son Hyrum. Transcriptions are provided for the following four items:

1. Lemuel Durfee vs. Joseph Smith and Abraham Fish.

On 19 January 1830, Lemuel Durfee, Jr., entered a plea before Justice of the Peace Nathan Pierce for a judgment against Joseph Smith, Sr., and Abraham Fish for $39.92, both of whom signed a consent for the justice to enter a judgment against them for that amount. Durfee sought the judgment because an inventory of his recently deceased father's estate had found an unpaid promissory note of Joseph Smith, Sr., and Abraham Fish to Lemuel Durfee for $37.50 (the inventory occurred on 31 August 1829; see III.L.18, LEMUEL DURFEE PROBATE PAPERS, 1830). However, Durfee Jr. entered his plea three days before Lemuel Durfee Sr.'s probate papers were filed, at a time of year when many farmers would find it difficult to pay off debts. On 7 May 1830, Pierce issued an "execution" to Constable Sylvester Southworth to collect damages from Fish and Smith. In an entry of 28 August 1830, Pierce noted his success in collecting both damages and legal fees from Smith and Fish (who were undoubtedly able to pay their debt with the proceeds from selling wheat). In a final entry of 13 September 1830, Lemuel Durfee acknowledges payment of $41.44.

A summary of the charges in this case are as follows: At the time of the inventory, Durfee was entitled to $1.42 in interest, for a total of $38.92. The 19 January 1830 judgment, however, is for $39.92, and the additional $1.00

is unexplained. To this was added justice's costs of 31 cents, bringing the judgment to a total of $40.23. On 7 May 1830, Constable Southworth was issued an execution order against Smith and Fish at a cost of 19 cents. Adding 82 cents for interest, the total would have come to $41.24. On 28 August 1830, Pierce noted that he received payment for the damages, his costs, and execution fee. He then rewrote the amounts due: Durfee's damages $39.92, interest $1.52, costs 60 cents, and total $42.04. In September, Durfee signed Pierce's docket book, stating that he had received his damages of $41.44: that is, $39.92 plus $1.52 in interest. Judging from the interest paid for the nearly eight months from 19 January to 13 September, or 19 cents per month, the $1.42 interest indicated in the Durfee inventory perhaps points to a January/February 1829 date (or seven and a half months previous) for the original Smith/Fish note.

2. Theophilus Short vs. Hiram Smith.

On 22 February 1830, Theophilus Short sued a "Hiram Smith" for $50.00 for not fulfilling his contract to provide "barrel headings." Pierce issued his "summons" on 22 February 1830, and the parties appeared on 5 March 1830. The case was evidently deferred to justice Holet, but settled before the hearing date of 17 March. This person is probably the Hiram Smith who signed Hurlbut's 1833 affidavit and served as overseer of Manchester Road District 30 for the years 1829, 1834, and 1837 (see III.A.1, MANCHESTER RESIDENTS GROUP STATEMENT, 3 NOV 1833; introduction to III.L.9, PALMYRA [NY] MASONIC RECORDS, 1827-1828; and R. L. Anderson 1970, 292). Note also the spelling of "Hiram" in this case and that of "Hyram" of the other cases (see below).

3. Levi Daggett vs. Hyrum Smith.

On 8 June 1830, Justice Nathan Pierce issued a "summons" for Hyrum Smith to appear, which was returned on 18 June without Hyrum, who was attending conference in Fayette. A second "summons" was therefore issued on 18 June, which was served on 21 June but also returned on 28 June without Hyrum. On this day Levi Daggett sued Hyrum Smith for an outstanding debt, which evidently consisted of a note dated 7 April 1830 (amount not specified in docket), interest, and 69 cents for shoeing horses, totaling $20.07. On the same day Joseph Smith, Sr., appeared before Pierce representing Hyrum, who had directed his father to allow Pierce to enter a judgment against him for $20.07.

In the left hand margin, Pierce noted the events of the case. On 14 August 1830, Pierce issued an "execution," which permitted the sheriff either to collect on the judgment (of 28 June 1830) or to take Hyrum to the "common Jail." On 13 September, Pierce noted that the execution had been returned, that Constable Harrington collected from Hyrum $12.81, and that Daggett was paid $9.94. Pierce reissued the execution on 27 September, which was returned on 26 October with Constable Harrington reporting that "no property nor body to be found" (item 4 below). Hyrum and his family had evidently moved to Colesville, Broome County, New York, in early October (I.B.5, LUCY SMITH HISTORY, 1845, 1853:159, and note 266).

New York law allowed a suit to be filed either in the township where the plaintiff lived or (as in this case) in the township where the defendant lived (*Revised Statutes,* 1829, 2:226, sec. 8). A summons could only be issued in the county where the person summoned resided (ibid., 2:228, sec. 13). Since Daggett was a resident of Palmyra, this would tend to support Wesley P. Walters's contention that Hyrum's residence, the original Smith cabin, was located in Manchester, not Palmyra as some have suggested (Walters 1987 and 1989; see also introduction to III.L.4, SMITH MANCHESTER [NY] LAND RECORDS, 1820-1830).

4. Execution Order.

Having found in favor of Levi Daggett (item 3 above), Justice Pierce issued an "execution" on 14 August 1830 authorizing Constable Southworth to collect from Hyrum Smith damages amounting to $21.07, plus $1.79 for legal costs, and 18 cents interest (a total of $23.04), to be paid by 13 September 1830, or to confine Hyrum in the "common Jail." The execution being returned on 13 September without satisfaction, Pierce reissued and extended it to 27 September 1830. On the reverse side of the execution, A. K. Daggett signed on behalf of Levi Daggett acknowledging the receipt of $9.94 from Constable Harrington on 13 September 1830. This is followed by the signed statement by Constable Harrington that on 13 September he had received from the Smiths a total of $12.81. The execution was evidently reissued on 27 September 1830. A note on the back signed by Constable Harrington and dated 26 October 1830 reports that "No property to be found Nor Boddy and I return the Execution." This execution is a printed form and was found inserted amoung the pages of Pierce's docket book.

Richard L. Anderson's statement that the Pierce docket book "shows the attempt of the Smiths to be honest in their financial obligations" is true in the case of Lemuel Durfee vs. Joseph Smith and Abraham Fish but not for Levi Daggett vs. Hyrum Smith. The latter case tends to support the accusations of former neighbors that the Smiths had skipped town without paying their debts (e.g., III.A.8, ROSWELL NICHOLS STATEMENT, 1 DEC 1833). Following his sudden removal to Colesville in early October

1830, Hyrum was not only sought by Levi Daggett for an unpaid debt but also by Alexander McIntyre, who, according to Joseph Smith, had taken out a warrant against Hyrum (see I.A.5, JOSEPH SMITH TO COLESVILLE SAINTS, 2 DEC 1830). Joseph Smith, Sr., was also wanted in Palmyra for an unpaid debt. From Kirtland, Ohio, Joseph Smith wrote Hyrum at Colesville on 3 March 1831, warning him that "David Jackways has threatened to take father with a sup=reme writ[.] In the spring you had <better> Come to fayette and take father along with you[.] Come in a one horse wagon ~~if~~ if you Can[.] do not Come threw Bufalo for th[e]y will lie in wait for you" (Jessee 1984, 231-32).

With the possible exception of one entry for 19 February 1825 involving a Russell Stoddard vs. Joseph Smith, in an Ontario County Judgment Docket, the Nathan Pierce Docket Book is the only known legal record of the Smiths' financial difficulties in the Palmyra/Manchester area.[1] Dale Morgan has cited two judgments and two execution orders against a "Joseph Smith" in late 1822 as evidence of "how desperately poor the Smiths were at this time" (J. P. Walker 1986, 364 n. 17). However, the Joseph Smith of these Ontario County records was one of the other nine Joseph Smiths enumerated in the 1820 census of Ontario County.[2]

1. In light of the Smiths' difficulties with a "Mr. Stoddard" in December 1825, the entry of Russell Stoddard vs. Joseph Smith, 19 February 1825, Ontario County Judgment Docket, is intriguing. The Joseph Smith of this record was ordered by Justice Peter Mitchell to pay the plaintif $66.59 and the court 25 cents (Ontario County Records Center, Canandaigua, New York; see also I.B.5, LUCY SMITH HISTORY, 1845, n. 107; and III.L.4, SMITH MANCHESTER [NY] LAND RECORDS, 1820-1830, n. 4).

2. Actually, these cases began during the August 1820 term of the Ontario County Court of Common Pleas, which issued two judgements against a "Joseph Smith": Abner Woodworth vs. Joseph Smith (for $98.25) and Job F. Brooks vs. Joseph Smith (for $61.73). In late 1822, interest having swelled Smith's debts to $115.61 and $79.09, Woodworth and Brooks obtained additional judgements, as well as two execution orders. In response to the first order, the sheriff reported back on 27 November 1822 that Smith had "no goods or chattels lands or tenements whereon to levy." The second execution of 20 December 1822 resulted in satisfying the Brooks judgement, but the sheriff's report remained the same for the Woodworth judgement (Court of Common Pleas, August 1820 Term, and Book of "Executions," under "S", Ontario County Records Center and Archives, Canandaigua, New York). The statement in the executions that there were no lands to levy does

[*1. Lemuel Durfee vs. Joseph Smith, Sr., and Abraham Fish, 19 January 1830*]

In Justice Court before Nathan Pierce justice

Lemuel Durfee
vs
Joseph Smith
Abraham Fish

The hereby [defendants] confess Judgement in this cause at the suit of the above named plaintiff for thirty nine dollars and ninety two cents damages this 19th day of January 1830 and consent that the Said Justice inter Judg=ment against us accordingly

[s] Joseph Smith

his
Abraham + Fish
mark

Judgement Rendered on the above confession for the said sum of thirty nine dollars and ninety two cents Damages against the Said Joseph Smith and Abraham Fish in favor of the Said Lemuel Durfee

January 19th 1830	Damages		$39.92
	Costs		.31
Nathan Pierce Justice of the peace		Judgement	$40.23
7th May 1830 Execution Issued to		Execution	.19
S. Southworth[3]	Interest		82
			[$41.2]4

28th August 1830 received the damage and my costs of S. Southworth

---

not fit the Smiths since they were taxed for their Manchester property in 1821 (see III.L.6, SMITH MANCHESTER [NY] LAND ASSESSMENT RECORDS, 1821-1823 & 1830; and III.L.4, SMITH MANCHESTER [NY] LAND RECORDS, 1820-1830). Job F. Brooks is difficult to trace, but Abner Woodworth was a town supervisor and justice of the peace in Benton, Ontario County (now Yates County), New York (Aldrich 1892, 364; U.S. Census, Benton, Ontario County, New York, 1820:254). The "Joseph Smith" (between twenty-six and forty-five years of age), also listed in the 1820 census of Benton, is most probably the person Woodworth sued in 1820 and 1822 (1820:262).

3. Sylvester Southworth, in his twenties, is listed in the 1830 census of Manchester, New York (1830:80).

Damages	$39.92
Interest	1.52
Costs	.60
	$42.04

13th Sept 1830 received my damage $41.44

[s] Lemuel Durfee[p. 25]

[2. *Theophilus Short vs. Hiram Smith, 22 February 1830*]

Theophilus Short[4]
ads [adversus]
Hiram Smith

Summons Issued 22d February 1830 Ret[urned] 5th March one oclock my house court called parties present plaintiff declares for cash and for damage in not delivering barrel heading according to contract <to—his damage fifty dollars—> Plea the general Issue and set off of Barrel heading and [bushing?] the same parties agree to adjourn this cause to J. [Daneve?] Holet on 17th March at one oclock after noon[.]

Parties Setled cost taxed to plaintiff

S. Southworth court fees	$0.40	
Justice fees Paid by plaintiff	.43	[p. 32]

[3. *Levi Daggett vs. Hyrum Smith, 28 June 1830*]

Levi Daggett[5]
vs
Hyram Smith

---

4. Theophilus Short moved to Manchester in 1804 and opened the first flour and saw mill. In 1822 he built a second flour mill north of the first (McIntosh 1876, 59, 178, 179; Milliken 1911, 414).

5. Levi Daggett, Sr. (1768-1835), a manufacturer and machinist, was born at Needham, Massachusetts. He moved to Saratoga, New York, then to Palmyra, New York. He married Lydia Patterson in 1795; they had nine children (Doggett 1973, 149-50). He was also a member of Palmyra's Mount Moriah Lodge of Freemasons in 1827 (see introduction to III.L.9, PALMYRA [NY] MASONIC RECORDS, 1827-1828). Daggett was a witness in the case of Hyrum, Samuel, and Lucy Smith's "Neglect of public worship" at Palmyra's Western Presbyterian Church in March 1830 (see III.L.20, PALMYRA [NY] PRESBYTERIAN CHURCH RECORDS, MAR 1830).

8th June 1830 Sum[mons] plea trespass on the Case Ret[urned] 18th June my house 3 oclock after noon and returned served by copy by S. Southworth

18th June 1830 another Summons issued Ret[urned] 28th day of June 1830 at one oclock after noon to S. Southworth and returned served by Copy 21st of June 1830

28th June 1830 Joseph <Smith> father of the Defendant appeared and the Case was called and the plaintif declared for a note and account[.] Note dated 7th April 1830 for $20.07 on Interest and on account for Shoeing horses of ballance due on account $0.69[.] Joseph Smith sworn and saith that his Son the Defendant engaged him to Come down at the return of the sum=mons and direct the Justice to enter Judgment against the defendant for the amount of the note & account[.] Judgment for the plaintif for twenty one dollars seven cents[.]

	Costs S. Southworth Court fees	$0.80
	Witness fees	.12½
	Lamar [Pick?] served Sub[poena]	.12½
	Justice costs	.55
		1.60
Paid by Justice		$21.07
4th April 1831		1.60
		22.67

[*remainder written in left margin*]

14th August 1830 Execution issued to Erastus Cole[6]

13th September 1830 this Execution returned in [hand?] by N. Harrington[7] that he had collected $12.81 and paid plaintif 9.94 by receipt on Execution and I received of said constable $1.79 court costs

The above Execution received and returned to plaintif this 27th Sept 1830 for to collect this amount due—

---

6. Perhaps Erastus Cole, over forty-five years of age, listed in the 1820 census of Jerusalem, Ontario County, New York (1820:207).

7. Nathan Harrington, between twenty-six and forty-five years of age, is listed in the 1820 census of Farmington, Ontario County, New York (1820:310).

26th October 1830 Execution returned no property nor body to be found by N. Harrington Constable [p. 76b]

[*4. Execution Order, 14 August 1830*][8]

Execution

County, ss.—The People of the State of New York, by the Grace of God Free and Independent:

To any Constable of the said County, Greeting:

WHEREAS Judgment was rendered before me Nathan Pierce **Esq. one of the Justices of the Peace of the said county, on the** 28th **day of** June 1830 **against** Hyrum Smith **in favor of** Levi Daggett **for** twenty one **Dollars** Seven **Cents, the damages, and** one **Dollars** Seventy nine **Cents, the costs:—THESE are therefore to command you to levy on the goods and chattels of the said defendant (except such as are by law exempted from execution) the amount of the said judgment, and bring the money before me, on the** 13th **day of** September **183**0 **at my office in the town of** Manchester **in the said county, to render to the said plaintiff. And if no goods or chattels can be found, or not sufficient to satisfy this execution, then you are hereby commanded to take the body of the said defendant and convey** him **to the common Jail of the county aforesaid, there to remain until this execution shall be satisfied and paid. Hereof fail not at your peril. Given under my hand, at** Manchester **this** 14th **day of** August **in the year of our Lord, 183**0

Damages	$21.07
Costs	1.79
Interest	18
	$23.04

This Execution renewed for to Collect this amount due thereon this 27th September 1830

fees 19 cents

[s] Nathan Pierce **Justice of the Peace.**

---

8. The printed part of the document is reproduced in bold.

Sold by Bemis & Ward, Canandaigua.

[*reverse of execution*]

Received of Nathan Harrington $9.94 Cents for Levi dgget [Daggett] Septtember the 13th 1830

Levi Daggett
By
[s] A K Daggett

Received on this execution $12.81 this 13th day of September 1830

[s] Nathan Harrington
Constable

No property to be found Nor Boddy and I return this Execution October the 26—1830

[s] N Harrington
Constable

$23.04
1.59

$24.63
12

$24.75

20.
PALMYRA (NY) PRESBYTERIAN RECORDS, MARCH 1830

"Records of the Sessions of the Presbyterian Church in Palmyra," 2:11-13, located at the Western Presbyterian Church of Palmyra, New York (microfilm copy, Harold B. Lee Library, Brigham Young University, Provo, Utah).

EDITORIAL NOTE

During the residency of the Joseph Smith, Sr., family in the Palmyra/Manchester area (1816-30), Palmyra's Western Presbyterian Church possessed the only meeting house in Palmyra Village. It was a frame building located a half-block north of Main Street on the west side of Church Street. When an 1816 revival swelled membership, fifty-six members separated from the parent church, formed the Western Presbyterian Church of Palmyra, and installed Jesse Townsend (1817-20) as pastor (Backman 1980, 67; T. Cook 1930, 261). Lucy Smith and three of her older children (Hyrum, Samuel Harrison, and Sophronia) were members of this church.

The exact date when Lucy and the others joined the Presbyterian church is presently unknown. Volume one of the session records, which probably contained this information, "has been missing since at least 1932" (Walters 1969a, 76 n. 37). However, judging from the available historical sources, it is most probable that Lucy and her children joined Palmyra's Western Presbyterian Church during the revival of 1824-25, at which time the Reverend Benjamin B. Stockton was pastor (1824-28) (Walters 1969a; Walters 1969b; M. Hill 1982). Although Lucy dates her membership to after Alvin's death (19 November 1823), she apparently contradicts this chronology when she states that she was free from all churches until Alvin became twenty-two (on 11 February 1820) (I.B.5, LUCY SMITH HISTORY, 1845, MS:24). The apparent contradiction may result from Martha Coray's editing, or perhaps Lucy alludes to her attendance at the church prior to her seeking membership there (R. L. Anderson 1969a, 390-91 n. 55). Indeed, that Alvin's funeral service was conducted by the Reverend Stockton may indicate the Smith family's previous connection with this church.

According to the sessions record herein transcribed, a Presbyterian committee was appointed on 3 March 1830 to visit Lucy, Hyrum, and Samuel Harrison Smith, to inquire about their absence from church, and to report their responses at the next meeting. Sophronia, who is not mentioned in the sessions record, might have withdrawn earlier, perhaps resulting from her marriage on 2 December 1827 to Calvin Stoddard, a former Baptist with Methodist leanings (Backman 1980, 69 n. 25; Bushman 1984, 205 n. 32; Walters 1969b, 98). On 10 March the committee reported that they had visited the Smiths and "received no satisfaction," and that the Smiths "acknowledged that they had en=tirely neglected the ordinances of the church for the last eighteen months and that they did not wish to united with us any more." This indicates that Lucy and the others had ceased attending services for at least eighteen months, or since about September 1828. The session then resolved to order the appearance of the three Smiths at the next meeting (24 March) to answer the charges of the committee's six witnesses. The Smiths did not appear before the Presbyterian council on 24 March, nor on 29 March, and the session appointed George Beckwith in their defense. The trial resulted in the Smiths' suspension from church worship.

Lucy Smith misdates her meeting with the Presbyterian committee (although she may be describing an entirely different event) to about October/November 1829, stating that the Presbyterian council sent "three delegates" to persuade her and her two sons to denounce the Book of Mormon (I.B.5, LUCY SMITH HISTORY, 1845, MS:105-110; R. L. Anderson 1969a, 390-91). The sessions record mentions only the Reverend Alfred E. Campbell and Henry Jessup being sent, but Lucy said George Beckwith acted as spokesman for the committee of three.

The following transcription from the sessions record includes notes of the four meetings pertinent to the Smiths' case: 3, 10, 24, and 29 March 1830.

[*3 March 1839*]

March 3d 1830 Session met pursuant to notice—opened with prayer
Present Revd Alfred E Campbell[1] Moderr [moderator]

1. Alfred E. Campbell was commissioned by the Home Missionary Society, installed as pastor on 18 November 1828, and remained over two years (McIntosh 1877, 71, 147; T. Cook 1930, 261).

Henry Jessup[2] Geo Beckwith[3] David White[4] Pelatiah West[5] Newton Foster[6]	Elders

A letter was recieved from the Presbyterian Church in South hampton informing us of the unchristian conduct of John White 3d a member of this church in the following particulars

First—A total neglect of the worship of God.

Second—Intemperate to an allarming degree.

Whereup<on> resolved that a commission be made out by the mod=erator to the Session of the church in South hampton empower=ing and requesting them to take the testimony in the above case and transmit it to us.

Resolved that the Revd A. E. Campbell and H Jessup be a com=mittee to visit Hiram Smith[,] Lucy Smith[,] and Samuel Harrison Smith and report at the meeting of Session

Closed with prayer—

Recorded from the Moderators minutes[7]

Geo. N. Williams Cl[er]k[8]

[*10 March 1830*]

March 10th 1830 Session met pursuant to notice—

---

2. On Henry Jessup, see I.B.5, LUCY SMITH HISTORY, 1845, n. 106. Jessup also signed Hurlbut's Palmyra group affidavit (see III.A.11, PALMYRA RESIDENTS GROUP STATEMENT, 4 DEC 1833).

3. On George Beckwith (1790-1867), see III.A.11, PALMYRA RESIDENTS GROUP STATEMENT, 4 DEC 1833, n. 37.

4. David White was one of the earliest settlers in Palmyra (McIntosh 1877, 140; T. Cook 1930, 13).

5. On Pelatiah West, see III.A.11, PALMYRA RESIDENTS GROUP STATEMENT, 4 DEC 1833, n. 29.

6. Newton Foster, in his twenties, is listed in the 1830 census of Palmyra, New York (1830:51).

7. These minutes have not been located.

8. On George N. Williams (1797-1867), see III.A.11, PALMYRA RESIDENTS GROUP STATEMENT, 4 DEC 1833, n. 4.

Opened with prayer—

Present Revd Alfred E. Campbell Modr [moderator]

Geo Beckwith Henry Jessup Pelatiah West Newton Foster	Elders

The committee appointed to visit Hiram Smith[,] Lucy Smith and Samuel Harrison Smith reported that they had visited them and recieved no satisfaction. They acknowledged that they had en=tirely neglected the ordinances of the church for the last eighteen months and that they did not wish to unite with us any more—

Whereupon Resolved that they be cited to appear before the Ses[p. 11]sion on the 24th day of March inst at 2 Oclk P.M. at this Meeting House to answer to the following charge to wit Neglect of public worship and the Sacriment of the Lords Supper for the last eighteen months—

Witnesses	Henry Jessup	James Robinson[9]
	Harvey Shel	Rob[er]t W Smith[10]
	Levi Dagget[11]	Fred[erick] U. Sheffield[12]

Closed with prayer—Adjourned to 24 inst 2 Oc[loc]k P.M.

Recorded from the minutes of the Moderator

Geo. N. Williams cl[er]k

[*24 March 1830*]

March 24th 1830 Session met pursuant to adjournment—

Opened with prayer

9. James Robinson, in his twenties, is listed in the 1830 census of Palmyra, New York (1830:43).

10. On Robert W. Smith, see III.A.11, PALMYRA [NY] RESIDENTS GROUP STATEMENT, 4 DEC 1833, n. 28.

11. On Levi Daggett (1768-1835), who subsequently sued Hyrum for not paying a debt, see III.L.19, NATHAN PIERCE DOCKET BOOK, 1830, 5.

12. Frederick U. Sheffield was elected to the New York State Assembly in 1841 (McIntosh 1877, 43).

Present the Revd Alfred E. Campbell Modr [moderator]

Henry Jessup Geo. Beckwith Peletiah West Newton Foster David White	Elders

Hiram Smith[,] Lucy Smith and Samuel Harrison Smith not appearing pursuant to the citation served upon them by P[elatiah]. West—Resolved that they be again cited to appear before this Session on Monday the 29th inst at this place at 2 oc[loc]k P.M.—and that P[elatiah]. West served said citation—

Closed with prayer—adjourned to 29th 2 Oc[loc]k P.M.

Recorded from the minutes of the Moderator

Geo. N. Williams cl[er]k ... [p. 12] ...

[*29 March 1830*]

March 29th 1830 Session met pursuant to adjournment—

Opened with prayer—

Present Revd Alfred E. Campbell Modr [moderator]

Geo Beckwith Newton Foster Peletiah West Henry Jessup	Elders

The persons before cited to wit. Hiram Smith[,] Lucy Smith and Samuel Harrison Smith not appearing and the Sess=ion having satisfactory evidence that the citations were duly served Resolved that they be censured for their contumacy Resolved that George Beckwith manage their defense—The charge in the above case being fully sustained by the tes=timony of Henry Jesup[,] Harvey Shel[,] Rob[er]t W Smith and Frederick U Sheffield—(see minutes of testimony on file with the clerk)[13] the Session after duly consid-ering the matter were unanimously of opinion that Hiram Smith[,] Lucy Smith and Samuel Harison Smith ought to be Suspended—

13. These minutes have not been recovered.

Resolved that Hiram Smith[,] Lucy Smith and Samuel Harrison Smith be and they hereby are suspended from the Sacrament of the Lords Supper—

Closed with prayer—adjourned—

Recorded from the minutes of the Moderator

Geo. N. Williams cl[er]k ... [p. 13]

21.
Manchester (NY) Census Record, 1830

Federal Census Records, Manchester, Ontario County, New York, 1830:170. Family No. 124. Original in National Archives, Washington, D.C.

EDITORIAL NOTE

Following the death of their landlord, Lemuel Durfee, the Smiths were ordered to vacate their frame house. Consequently, about 1 April 1829, the Smiths returned to their log cabin, which had been occupied by Hyrum following his marriage in November 1826 (I.B.5, LUCY SMITH HISTORY 1845, MS:92). Sometime between 2 August and 20 November 1820, the Smiths were enumerated in the 1830 Federal Census for Manchester, Ontario County, New York.[1] This event suggests that the Smiths' cabin was situated in Manchester, not in Palmyra as some have assumed.[2] Below is an analysis of census data as it relates to the Smith family.

MANCHESTER CENSUS DATA		ANALYSIS TO SMITH FAMILY	
number	*sex*	*age*	
1	male	0–15	consistent for Don Carlos (age 14)
1	male	15-20	consistent for William (age 19)

1. The 1830 census by law was to begin on the first Monday in August (2 August 1830) and be completed by February 1831. A notation at the end of the Ontario County census suggests completion by 20 November 1830. It is unknown if the 1830 enumeration was taken before or after Hyrum's move to Colesville in early October (I.B.5, LUCY SMITH HISTORY, 1845, 1853:159, note 266); the appearance of Hyrum and his family in the Manchester census does not indicate their actual presence in the township since enumerators were instructed to list all those residing in the area on 1 June 1830 (Wright 1900, 140).

2. For a discussion of the location of the Smiths' cabin, see III.L.2, PALMYRA [NY] HIGHWAY SURVEY, 13 JUN 1820; III.L.4, SMITH MANCHESTER [NY] LAND RECORDS; and III.L.6, SMITH MANCHESTER [NY] ASSESSMENT RECORDS, 1821-1823 & 1830.

2	male	20-30	consistent for Hyrum(age 30), Samuel (age 22)
1	male	50-60	consistent for Joseph, Sr. (age 59)
2	female	0-5	corresponds to Hyrum's children: Lovina (age 2), and Mary (age 1)
1	female	5-10	consistent for Lucy (age 9)
1	female	20-30	consistent for Hyrum's wife Jerusha (age 25)
1	female	30-40	unknown person
1	female	50-60	consistent for Lucy (age 54)

Missing from the list is Katharine (age 17), who may have been hired out to neighbors. Reflecting on the events of October 1830, Lucy Smith mentioned that both Katharine and Don Carlos were "away from home" (I.B.5, LUCY SMITH HISTORY, 1845, 1853:159), although she did not state the reason for their absence. The 1830 enumerators were instructed "not to include any person whose usual abode was not in the family they are enumerating on the said 1st day of June [1830]" (Wright 1900, 140), suggesting that Katharine had been away from home for some time.[3]

3. An entry in the judgement docket for Victor, New York, provides possible evidence for Katharine's teaching school in neighboring towns. The entry, dated February to June 1829, reports that a "Catharine Smith" sued the trustees of Farmington school district No. 5 for unpaid wages. If this entry pertains to the daughter of Joseph and Lucy Smith, it suggests that Katharine Smith may have left home as early as the winter of 1828-29 to teach school (Catharine Smith v. Trustees of Farmington School District No. 5, February-June 1829, Judgment Docket, Victor, Ontario County Historical Society, Canandaigua, New York).

22.
MISSIONARIES COVENANT, 17 OCTOBER 1830

Ezra Booth to Ira Eddy, 24 November 1831, *Ohio Star* (Ravenna, Ohio), 8 December 1831. Reprinted in E. D. Howe, *Mormonism Unvailed* (Painesville, Ohio: E. D. Howe, 1834), 213-14.

EDITORIAL NOTE

At the commencement of a three-day church conference, held 26-28 September 1830 at the home of Peter Whitmer, Sr., in Fayette, New York, Joseph Smith dictated a revelation which commanded Oliver Cowdery to "go unto the Lamanites and preach my gospel" (D&C 28:8). Later the same day, another revelation instructed Peter Whitmer, Jr., to "journey with your brother Oliver ... [and] build up my church among the Lamanites" (D&C 30:5, 6). As the two missionaries prepared for their journey, the Mormon prophet received another revelation (D&C 32) in Manchester, New York, on or just before 17 October, which instructed Parley P. Pratt and Ziba Peterson to accompany Cowdery and Whitmer (L. Cook 1981, 128 n. 1). According to Smith, the four missionaries left Manchester "immediately" after the revelation was received, taking a copy of it with them (I.A.15, JOSEPH SMITH HISTORY, 1839, 60-61). Also, prior to their departure, the four missionaries signed their names to a missionaries covenant, dated 17 October 1830, which outlined the two objectives of their mission: to preach to the Indians and to locate the site of the New Jerusalem temple.

While the four men fulfilled their mission by preaching to the Indian tribes located near Buffalo, New York, and on the Missouri frontier in the fall and winter of 1830-31, and were instrumental in locating the temple lot in Independence, Missouri, their most important contribution to the fledgling church was made during a side trip to the vicinity of Mentor, Ohio, where they converted Sidney Rigdon and others in November 1830 (see Jennings 1971; R. L. Anderson 1971a).

The original missionaries covenant evidently has not survived, but it was included in Ezra Booth's letter to the Reverend Ira Eddy, dated 24 November 1831, Nelson, Ohio, and first published in the *Ohio Star* on 8 December 1831 (see also Howe 1834, 212-13). Richard L. Anderson has observed, "[T]he Booth letters are the first printed source for the revelations of Joseph Smith, mostly reproduced in short extracts. ... His quotations are generally accurate, particularly the fairly long revelation calling Oliver Cowdery on the Lamanite [Indian] mission [D&C 28]. ... Since Booth responsibly copied the Oliver Cowdery revelation, an associated document [i.e., the missionaries covenant] very probably originated from a manuscript source" (R. L. Anderson 1971a, 476-77).

MANCHESTER, Oct. 17, 1830.

I, Oliver [Cowdery], being commanded of the Lord God, to go forth unto the Lamanites, to proclaim glad tidings of great joy unto them, by presenting unto them the fullness of the Gospel, of the only begotten son of God; and also, to rear up a pillar as a witness where the Temple of God shall be built, in the glorious New-Jerusalem[1]; and having certain brothers with me, who are called of God to assist me, whose names are Parley, Peter and Ziba, do therefore most solemnly covenant with God, that I will walk humbly before him, and do this business, and this glorious work according as he shall direct me by the Holy Ghost; ever praying for mine and their prosperity, and deliverance from bonds, and from imprisonment, and whatsoever may befal us, with all patience and faith.—Amen.

OLIVER COWDERY.[2]

We, the undersigned, being called and commanded of the Lord God, to accompany our Brother Oliver Cowdery, to go to the Lamanites, and to assist in the above mentioned glorious work and business. We do, therefore, most solemnly covenant before God, that we will assist him faithfully in this thing, by giving heed unto all his words and advice, which is, or shall be given him by the spirit of truth, ever praying with all prayer and supplication, for our and his prosperity, and our deliverance from bonds, and imprison-

---

1. The Book of Mormon predicted the establishment of a New Jerusalem in America (3 Ne. 20-21; Eth. 13). On 26 September 1830, it was revealed that the New Jerusalem would be located "on the borders by the Lamanites" (28:9), but the exact place remained undisclosed. In July 1831 Smith dictated a revelation that designated Independence, Missouri, as the site for the New Jerusalem, and specifically revealed that "a spot for the temple is lying westward, upon a lot which is not far from the court-house" (D&C 57:3). See also Vogel 1988, 190-95.

2. On Oliver Cowdery (1806-50), see "Introduction to Oliver Cowdery Collection."

ments, and whatsoever may come upon us, with all patience and faith.—Amen.

Signed in presence of[3]
JOSEPH SMITH, Jun.
DAVID WHITMER,[4]
P. P. PRATT,[5]
ZIBA PETERSON,[6]
PETER WHITMER.[7]

---

3. The typesetting for this document, as it appears in the *Ohio Star,* probably incorrectly represents the original. Thus when E. D. Howe published Ezra Booth's letters (1834, 213-14), he arranged the names as follows:

P. P. PRATT,
ZIBA PETERSON,
PETER WHITMER.

signed in presence of
JOSEPH SMITH, JUN.
DAVID WHITMER

4. On David Whitmer (1805-88), see "Introduction to David Whitmer Collection."

5. On Parley Parker Pratt (1807-57), see introduction to III.K.16, PARLEY P. PRATT AUTOBIOGRAPHY (PART I), CIRCA 1854.

6. On Richard Ziba Peterson (?-1849), see I.A.15, JOSEPH SMITH HISTORY, 1839, n. 105.

7. On Peter Whitmer, Jr. (1809-36), see I.A.15, JOSEPH SMITH HISTORY, 1839, n. 63.

BIBLIOGRAPHY

Aldrich, Lewis Cass. *History of Yates County, N.Y.* Syracuse, NY: D. Mason and Co., 1892.

Anderson, Richard Lloyd. "Circumstantial Confirmation of the First Vision Through Reminiscences." *Brigham Young University Studies* 9 (Spring 1969): 373-404.

——. "The Reliability of the Early History of Lucy and Joseph Smith." *Dialogue: A Journal of Mormon Thought* 4 (Summer 1969): 13-28.

——. "Joseph Smith's New York Reputation Reappraised." *Brigham Young University Studies* 10 (Spring 1970): 283-314.

——. "The Impact of the First Preaching in Ohio." *Brigham Young University Studies* 11 (Summer 1971a): 474-96.

——. *Joseph Smith's New England Heritage: Influences of Grandfathers Solomon Mack and Asael Smith.* Salt Lake City: Deseret Book, 1971b.

——. *Investigating the Book of Mormon Witnesses.* Salt Lake City: Deseret Book Co., 1981.

——. "The Mature Joseph Smith and Treasure Searching." *Brigham Young University Studies* 24 (Fall 1984): 489-560.

Arrington, Leonard J. "Early Mormon Communitarianism: The Law of Consecration and Stewardship." *Western Humanities Review* 7 (Autumn 1953).

——. "James Gordon Bennett's 1831 Report on 'The Mormonites.'" *Brigham Young University Studies* 10 (Spring 1970): 353-64.

——. *Brigham Young: American Moses.* New York: Alfred A. Knopf, 1985.

Avery, Lillian Drake. *A Genealogy of the Ingersoll Family in America, 1629-1925.* New York: Grafton Press, 1926.

Backman, Milton V., Jr. *Joseph Smith's First Vision: Confirming Evidence and Contemporary Accounts.* 2nd ed. Revised and enlarged. Salt Lake City: Bookcraft, 1980.

——. *A Profile of Latter-day Saints of Kirtland, Ohio, and Members of Zion's Camp, 1830-1839: Vital Statistics and Sources.* Provo, UT: Brigham Young University, 1983.

Bagg, M. M. *The Pioneers of Utica.* Utica, NY: Curtiss and Childs, 1877.

Baldwin, Charles Candee. *The Baldwin Genealogy, from 1500 to 1881.* Cleveland, OH: Lender Printing Co., 1881.

Bean, Willard. *A.B.C. History of Palmyra and the Beginning of "Mormonism."* Palmyra, NY: Palmyra Courier Co., 1938.

Berge, Dale L. "Archaeological Work at the Smith Log House." *Ensign* (August 1985): 24-26.

Bitton, Davis. *Guide to Mormon Diaries and Autobiographies*. Provo, UT: Brigham Young University, 1977.

Black, Susan Easton. *Membership of the Church of Jesus Christ of Latter-day Saints, 1830-1848*. 50 vols. Provo, UT: Religious Studies Center, Brigham Young University, 1987.

Blair, Frederick B., comp. *The Memoirs of President W. W. Blair*. Lamoni, IA: Herald Publishing House, 1908.

Boase, Frederick. *Modern English Biography*. 9 vols. Truro, England: Netherton and Worth, 1892-1921.

Braden, Clark, and Kelley, E. L. *Public Discussion of the Issues Between the Reorganized Church of Jesus Christ of Latter Day Saints and the Church of Christ (Disciples) Held in Kirtland, Ohio, Beginning February 12, and Closing March 8, 1884 Between E. L. Kelley, of the Reorganized Church of Jesus Christ of Latter Day Saints and Clark Braden, of the Church of Christ*. St. Louis: Clark Braden, [1884].

Brodie, Fawn M. *No Man Knows My History: The Life of Joseph Smith the Mormon Prophet*. New York: Alfred A. Knopf, 1945.

Brudnoy, David Barry. "Liberty's Bugler: The Seven Ages of Theodore Schroeder." Ph.D. dissertation, Brandies University, 1971.

Bush, Lester E., Jr. "The Spalding Theory Then and Now." *Dialogue: A Journal of Mormon Thought* 10 (Autumn 1977): 40-69.

Bushman, Richard L. *Joseph Smith and the Beginnings of Mormonism*. Urbana and Chicago: University of Illinois Press, 1984.

Cannon, Donald Q. "Joseph Smith in Salem (D&C 111)." In Robert L. Millet and Kent P. Jackson., eds. *Studies in Scripture, Volume 1: The Doctrine and Covenants*. Sandy, UT: Randall Book Co., 1984. Pp. 432-37.

Cannon, Donald Q., and Cook, Lyndon W. *Far West Record: Minutes of the Church of Jesus Christ of Latter-day Saints, 1830-1844*. Salt Lake City: Deseret Book Co., 1983.

Cathcart, William. *The Baptist Encyclopaedia*. Philadelphia: Louis H. Everts, 1883.

Child, Hamilton. *Gazetteer and Business Directory of Ontario County*. Syracuse, NY: Journal Office, 1867.

Church History in the Fulness of Times. Salt Lake City: The Church of Jesus Christ of Latter-day Saints, 1989.

Clark, Victor S. *History of Manufactures in the United States*. 3 vols. New York: Peter Smith, 1949.

Coles, Charles C., Jr. *The Social Ideas of the Northern Evangelists, 1826-1860*. New York: Octagon Books, 1977.

Conover, Charlotte Reeve, ed. *Dayton and Montgomery County: Resources and People*. 3 vols. New York: Lewis Historical Publishing Co., 1932.

Conover, George S., ed. *History of Ontario County, New York*. Syracuse, NY: D. Mason and Co., 1888.

Cook, Lyndon W. *The Revelations of the Prophet Joseph Smith: A Historical and Biographical Commentary of the Doctrine and Covenants*. Provo, UT: Seventy's Mission Book Store, 1981.

——. *Joseph Smith and the Law of Consecration*. Provo, UT: Grandin Book Co., 1985.

Cook, Lyndon W., and Backman, Milton V., Jr. *Kirtland Elders' Quorum Record, 1836-1841*. Provo, UT: Grandin Book Co., 1985.

Cook, Thomas L. *Palmyra and Vicinity*. Palmyra, NY: Press of the Palmyra Courier-Journal, 1930.

Dickenson, Ellen E. *New Light on Mormonism*. New York: Funk and Wagnalls, 1885.

Doggett, Samuel Bradlee. *A History of the Doggett-Daggett Family*. Baltimore: Gateway Press, 1973.

Doty, Lockwood R. *History of the Genesee Country*. 4 Vols. Chicago: S. J. Clarke Publishing Co., 1925.

Dubler, Allice M. *Manchester Through the Years*. Houghton, NY: Houghton College Press, 1954.

Eaton, Horace. *The Early History of Palmyra: A Thanksgiving Sermon, Delivered at Palmyra, N.Y., November 26, 1857, By Horace Eaton, Pastor of the Presbyterian Church, Palmyra, New York*. Rochester, NY: Press of A. Strong and Co., 1858.

——. *The Great Physician: A Sermon on Occasion of the Death of Alexander McIntyre, M.D., Delivered in the Presbyterian Church, Palmyra, N.Y., July 24, 1859*. New York: Printed by John F. Trow, 1860.

——. *A Memorial of the Celebration at Palmyra, N.Y., of the Centennial Fourth of July, 1876*. Rochester, New York: E. R. Andrews, 1876.

Embry, Jessie L. "Ultimate Taboos: Incest and Mormon Polygamy." *Journal of Mormon History* 18 (Spring 1992): 93-113.

Emerson, Edgar C., ed. *Our County and Its People: A Descriptive Work on Jefferson County, New York*. Boston, MA: The Boston History Co., 1898.

Enders, Donald L. "'A Snug Log House': A Historical Look at the Joseph Smith, Sr., Family Home in Palmyra, New York." *Ensign* (August 1985): 14-23.

——. "The Joseph Smith, Sr., Family: Farmers of the Genesee." In *Joseph Smith: The Prophet, the Man*. eds. Susan Easton Black and Charles D. Tate, Jr. Religious Studies Center Monograph Series, vol. 7. Provo, UT: Brigham Young University, 1993. Pp. 213-25.

Faulring, Scott H., ed. *An American Prophet's Record: The Diaries and Journals of Joseph Smith*. Salt Lake City: Signature Books, 1987.

——. [Book Review]. H. Michael Marquardt and Wesley P. Walters. *Inventing Mormonism: Tradition and the Historical Record*. Salt Lake City: Signature Books, 1994. In *Dialogue: A Journal of Mormon Thought* 21 (Fall 1995): 203-8.

French, John H. *Historical and Statistical Gazetteer of New York State*. Syracuse, NY: R. P. Smith, 1860.

Godfrey, Kenneth W. "More Treasures Than One: Section 111." In *"Hearken, O Ye People": Discourses on the Doctrine and Covenants.* Sperry Symposium, 1984. Sandy, UT: Randall Book Co., 1984.

Griffin, Edward D. *A Letter to the Rev. Ansel D. Eddy, of Canandaigua, N.Y. on the Narrative of the Late Revivals of Religion, in the Presbytery of Geneva.* Williamstown, [MA]: Printed by Ridley Bannister, 1832.

Gunnell, Wayne C. "Martin Harris: Witness and Benefactor to the Book of Mormon." MA thesis, Brigham Young University, 1955.

Hill, Ivy Hooper Blood, comp. and ed. *William Blood his Posterity and Biographies of their Progenitors.* Logan, UT: J. P. Smith and Son, 1962.

Hill, Marvin S. "The First Vision Controversy: A Critique and Reconciliation." *Dialogue: A Journal of Mormon Thought* 15 (Summer 1982): 31-46.

History of Dayton, Ohio. Dayton, OH: United Brethren Publishing Co., 1889.

History of Genesee County, Michigan. Philadelphia: Everts and Abbott, 1879.

Hogan, Mervin B. "The Founding Minutes of Nauvoo Lodge." In *Further Light in Masonry.* Des Moines: Research Lodge No. 2, [February 1971].

Holms, Oliver W. "Sunday Travel and Sunday Mails: A Question Which Troubled Our Forefathers." *New York History* 20 (October 1939): 413-24.

Holzapfel, Richard Neitzel, Cottle, T. Jeffery, and Stoddard, Ted D. *Church History in Black and White: George Edward Anderson's Photographic Mission to Latter-day Saint Historical Sites, 1907 Diary, 1907-8 Photographs.* Provo, UT: Religious Studies Center, Brigham Young University, 1995.

Hotchkin, James H. *A History of the Purchase and Settlement of Western New York, and the Rise, Progress, and Present State of the Presbyterian Church in That Section.* New York: M. W. Dodd, 1848.

Howe, E. D. *Mormonism Unvailed: or, A Faithful Account of That Singular Imposition and Delusion, from Its Rise to the Present Time.* Painesville, OH: E. D. Howe, 1834.

James, Rhett. *The Man Who Knew: The Early Years. A Play About Martin Harris, 1824-1830.* Cache Valley, UT: Martin Harris Pageant Committee, 1983. ["Dramatic Biography Annotations," 95-169.]

Jennings, Warren A. "The First Mormon Mission to the Indians." *Kansas Historical Quarterly* 38 (Autumn 1971): 288-99.

——. *Latter-Day Saint Biographical Encyclopedia.* 4 vols. Salt Lake City: Andrew Historical Co., 1901-1936; rept. Salt Lake City: Western Epics, 1971.

Jessee, Dean C. "The Writing of Joseph Smith's History." *Brigham Young University Studies* 11 (Spring 1971): 439-73.

——. "The John Taylor Nauvoo Journal: January 1845-September 1845." *Brigham Young University Studies* 23 (Summer 1983): 1-96.

——, comp. and ed. *The Personal Writings of Joseph Smith.* Salt Lake City: Deseret Book, 1984.

——, ed. *The Papers of Joseph Smith: Autobiographical and Historical Writings. Vol. 1.* Salt Lake City: Deseret Book, 1989.

——, ed. *The Papers of Joseph Smith: Journal, 1832-1842. Vol 2.* Salt Lake City: Deseret Book, 1992.

Johnson, Benjamin F. *My Life's Review.* Independence, MO: Zion's Printing and Publishing Co., 1947.

Johnson, Paul E. *A Shopkeeper's Millennium: Society and Revivals in Rochester, New York, 1815-1837.* New York: Hill and Wang, 1978.

Kenney, Scott G., ed. *Wilford Woodruff's Journal.* 9 vols. Midvale, UT: Signature Books, 1983-84.

Kimball, Stanley B. "The Anthon Transcript: People, Primary Sources and Problems." *Brigham Young University Studies* 10 (Spring 1970): 325-64.

——. *Heber C. Kimball: Mormon Patriarch and Pioneer.* Urbana, IL: University of Illinois Press, 1981.

Kirkham, Francis W. *A New Witness for Christ in America: The Book of Mormon.* 2 vols. Independence, MO: Zion's Printing and Publishing Co., 1951.

Laws of the State of New-York, Revised and Passed at Thirty-Sixth Session of the Legislature. 2 vols. Albany, NY: H. C. Southwick and Co., 1813.

Ludwig, Allen I. *Graven Images: New England Stonecarving and Its Symbols, 1650-1815.* Middletown, CT: Wesleyan University Press, 1966.

Malone, Dumas. *Dictionary of American Biography.* 20 vols. New York: Charles Scribner's Sons, 1936.

Mathews, Mitford M., ed. *A Dictionary of Americanisms on Historical Principles.* 2 vols. Chicago: University of Chicago Press, 1951.

[McIntosh, W. H.] *History of Ontario Co., New York.* Philadelphia: Everts, Ensign and Everts, 1876.

McIntosh, W. H. *History of Wayne County, New York.* Philadelphia: Everts, Ensign and Everts, 1877.

Mehling, Mary Bryant Alverson. *Cowdrey-Cowdery-Cowdray Genealogy.* N.p.: Frank Allaben Genealogical Co., 1911.

Metcalfe, Brent Lee, ed. *New Approaches to the Book of Mormon: Explorations in Critical Methodology.* Salt Lake City: Signature Books, 1993.

Milliken, Charles F. *A History of Ontario County, New York and Its People.* New York: Lewis Historical Publishing Co., 1911.

Monroe, Joel H. *A Century and a Quarter of History—Geneva.* Geneva, NY: W. F. Humphrey, 1912.

Morris, Robert. *William Morgan; Political Anti-Masonry, Its Rise, Growth and Decadence.* New York: Robert Macoy, 1883.

The National Cyclopaedia of American Biography. 59 vols. New York: James T. White and Co., 1891-1980.

One Hundred Years in the Paper Business, 1819-1919: Being a Brief History of the Founding of the Paper Business of The Alling & Cory Company, together with an Account of its Growth During the Centenary Period of its Existence. Rochester, NY: The Alling & Cory Company, 1919.

O'Reilly, Henry. *Sketches of Rochester; With Incidental Notices of Western New-York.* Rochester, NY: William Alling, 1838.

Pattengill, C. N. *Light in the Valley. Memorial Sermon Delivered at the Funeral of Pomeroy Tucker, Palmyra, Wayne County, N.Y., July 3d, 1870.* Troy, NY: Times Steam Printing House, 1870.

Peck, William F. *Semi-Centennial History of the City of Rochester.* Syracuse, NY: D. Mason and Co., 1884.

Perciaccante, Marrianne. "Backlash Against Formalism: Early Mormonism's Appeal in Jefferson County." *Journal of Mormon History* 19 (Fall 1993): 35-63.

Pharmacopaeia of the Massachusetts Medical Society. Boston: E. and J. Larkin, 1808.

Pharmacopaeia Nosocomii Neo-Eboracensis; or, The Phamacopaeia of the New-York Hospital. New York: Collins and Co., 1816.

Porter, Larry C. "A Study of the Origins of the Church of Jesus Christ of Latter-day Saints in the States of New York and Pennsylvania, 1816-1831." Ph.D. dissertation. Provo, UT: Brigham Young University, 1971.

——. "Solomon Chamberlain—Early Missionary." *Brigham Young University Studies* 12 (Spring 1972): 314-18.

——. "Solomon Chamberlain's Missing Pamphlet: Dreams, Visions, and Angelic Ministrants." *Brigham Young University Studies* 37 (1997-98): 113-40.

Pratt, Parley P. *Mormonism Unveiled: Zion's Watchman Unmasked.* New York: O. Pratt and E. Fordham, 1838.

——. *Autobiography of Parley P. Pratt,* ed. Parley P. Pratt, Jr. New York: Russell Brothers, 1874.

Proper, David R. "Joseph Smith and Salem." *Essex Institute Historical Collections* 100 (April 1964): 93-97.

Quinn, D. Michael. *Early Mormonism and the Magic World View.* Salt Lake City: Signature Books, 1987.

——. *Early Mormonism and the Magic World View.* 2nd ed. rev. and enl. Salt Lake City: Signature Books, 1998.

Reed, William F. *The Descendants of Thomas Durfee of Portsmouth, R.I.* 2 vols. Washington, D.C.: Gibson Brothers, 1902.

Reprint of the First Utica Directory, For the Year 1817. Utica, NY: William Williams, 1920.

The Revised Statutes of the State of New-York. 3 vols. Albany: Printed by Packard and Van Benthuysen, 1829.

Richards, Charles C. "An address delivered by Charles C. Richards at the Sacrament

Meeting, held in . . . Salt Lake City, Utah, Sunday Evening, April 20, 1947." Signed typescript. LDS Church Archives, Salt Lake City, Utah.

Schlesinger, Arthur M., Jr. *The Age of Jackson*. Boston and Toronto: Little, Brown and Co., 1945.

Seaman, Valentine. *Pharmacoepia Chirurgica*. New York: Wood, 1811.

Signor, Isaac S., et al. *Landmarks of Orleans County, New York*. Syracuse, NY: D. Mason and Co., 1894.

Sillitoe, Linda, and Roberts, Allen. *Salamander: The Story of the Mormon Forgery Murders*. Salt Lake City: Signature Books, 1988. Includes an appendix with a forensic analysis of the Hofmann documents by George J. Throckmorton.

Skousen, Royal. "Piecing Together the Original Manuscript." *BYU Today* (May 1992): 18-24.

——. "New Evidence about Book of Mormon Scribes." *Insights* (January 1993): 1.

Smith, Joseph, Jr. *History of the Church of Jesus Christ of Latter-day Saints,* ed. B. H. Roberts. 7 vols. 2nd ed. rev. Salt Lake City: Deseret Book, 1948 printing.

Smith, Lucy Mack. *Biographical Sketches of Joseph Smith the Prophet, and His Progenitors for many Generations*. Liverpool: S. W. Richards, 1853.

Spear, F. B. *In Memoriam: Philetus Bennett Spear, D.D.* Marquette, MI: Mining Journal Co., 1901.

Stevenson, Edward. *Reminiscences of Joseph, the Prophet and the Coming Forth of the Book of Mormon*. Salt Lake City: Edward Stevenson, 1893.

Swartzell, William. *Mormonism Exposed, Being a Journal of a Residence in Missouri from the 28th of May to the 20th of August, 1838*. Pekin, OH: Published by the Author, 1840.

Taylor, Alan. "Rediscovering the Context of Joseph Smith's Treasure Seeking." *Dialogue: A Journal of Mormon Thought* 19 (Winter 1986): 18-28.

Tucker, Pomeroy. *Origin, Rise, and Progress of Mormonism*. New York: D. Appleton and Co., 1867.

Turner, O[rsamus]. *Pioneer History of the Holland Purchase of Western New York*. Buffalo, NY: George H. Derby and Co., 1850.

——. *History of the Pioneer Settlement of Phelps and Gorham's Purchase*. Rochester, NY: W. Alling, 1851.

Tyler, Daniel. "Incidents of Experience." In *Scraps of Biography*. Tenth Book of the Faith-promoting Series. Salt Lake City: Juvenile Instructor Office, 1883.

Van Wagoner, Richard, and Walker, Steven. *A Book of Mormons*. Salt Lake City: Signature Books, 1982.

Vogel, Dan. *Indian Origins and the Book of Mormon: Religious Solutions from Columbus to Joseph Smith*. Salt Lake City: Signature Books, 1986.

——. *Religious Seekers and the Advent of Mormonism*. Salt Lake City: Signature Books, 1988.

——. "Mormonism's 'Anti-Masonick Bible.'" *John Whitmer Historical Association Journal* 9 (1989): 17-30.

——. *The Word of God: Essays on Mormon Scripture.* Salt Lake City: Signature Books, 1990.

——. "James Colin Brewster: The Boy Prophet Who Challenged Mormon Authority." In Roger D. Launius and Linda Thatcher, eds. *Differing Visions: Dissenters in Mormon History.* Urbana and Chicago: University of Illinois Press, 1994. Pp. 120-39.

——. "The Locations of Joseph Smith's Early Treasure Quests." *Dialogue: A Journal of Mormon Thought* 27 (Fall 1994): 197-231.

——. "More on Treasure Seeking." Letter to John H. Wittorf. *Dialogue: A Journal of Mormon Thought* 28 (Winter 1995): viii-x.

Vogt, Paul L. *The Sugar Refining Industry in the United States.* Philadelphia: John C. Winston Co., 1908.

Walker, John Philip, ed. *Dale Morgan on Early Mormonism: Correspondence and a New History.* Salt Lake City: Signature Books, 1986.

Walker, Ronald W. "The Persistent Idea of American Treasure Hunting." *Brigham Young University Studies* 24 (Fall 1984): 429-59.

——. "Martin Harris: Mormonism's Early Convert." *Dialogue: A Journal of Mormon Thought* 19 (Winter 1986): 29-43.

Walters, Wesley P. "New Light on Mormon Origins from the Palmyra Revival." *Dialogue: A Journal of Mormon Thought* 4 (Spring 1969): 60-81.

——. "A Reply to Dr. Bushman." *Dialogue: A Journal of Mormon Thought* 4 (Spring 1969): 94-100.

——. "Joseph Smith's Move to Palmyra and Manchester, N.Y." Unpublished paper, 1987.

——. "The Joseph Smith Family's Move to Palmyra and Manchester, N.Y." Paper read at Sunstone Theological Symposium, Salt Lake City, 1989.

Watson, Elden J., comp. *The Orson Pratt Journals.* Salt Lake City: Elden J. Watson, 1975.

Whitney, Orson F. *Life of Heber C. Kimball.* Salt Lake City: Bookcraft, 1945.

Who Was Who, 1897-1916. London: A & C Black, 1920.

Who Was Who in America: A Compact Volume of Who's Who in American History. 5 vols. Chicago: Marquis Publications, 1966.

Who Was Who in America: Historical Volume, 1607-1896. Chicago: Marquis Publications, 1967.

Wiley, Allen. "Introduction and Progress of Methodism in Southeastern Indiana." *Indiana Magazine of History* 23 (December 1927). Originally published in *Western Christian Advocate* (Cincinnati), 2 October 1846.

Wilson, James Grant, and Fiske, John, eds. *Appletons' Cyclopaedia of American Biography*. 7 vols. New York: D. Appleton and Co., 1887.

Woodward, Charles. *The First Half Century of Mormonism*. 2 vols. New York, 1880. Scrapbooks of newspaper clippings in the New York Public Library.

Wright, Carroll D. *History and Growth of the United States Census*. Washington, D.C.: Government Printing Office, 1900.

Wymetal, Wilhelm Ritter von. *Joseph Smith, the Prophet, His Family and His Friends*. Salt Lake City: Tribune Printing and Publishing Co., 1986.

Young, Brigham, et al., *Journal of Discourses of the Church of Jesus Christ of Latter-day Saints*. 26 vols. Liverpool: [Albert Carrington and others], 1853-1886.

INDEX